PEARSON CUSTOM LIBRARY PHILOSOPHY

CRITICAL THINKING AND CREATIVE PROBLEM SOLVING
IN ORGANIZATIONS AND SOCIETIES

CRT 100

Jones International University

Pearson Learning Solutions

New York Boston San Francisco
London Toronto Sydney Tokyo Singapore Madrid
Mexico City Munich Paris Cape Town Hong Kong Montreal

Senior Vice President, Editorial and Marketing: Patrick F. Boles
Senior Sponsoring Editor: Natalie Danner
Development Editor: Mary Kate Paris
Editorial Assistant: Jill Johnson
Operations Manager: Eric M. Kenney
Database Product Manager: Jennifer Berry
Art Director: Renée Sartell
Cover Designer: Tess Mattern

Cover Art: Courtesy of Photodisc/Getty Images.

Printed in the United States of America.

Please visit our websites at *www.pearsoncustom.com.*

Attention bookstores: For permission to return any unsold stock, contact us at *pe-uscustomreturns@pearson.com.*

Pearson
Custom Publishing
is a division of

www.pearsonhighered.com

ISBN 10: 0-558-28042-0
ISBN 13: 978-0-558-28042-0

Contents

Developing Your Thinking: An Overview

Is thinking an activity that is done automatically, without conscious effort, or one that we can direct? Is daydreaming a kind of thinking? Are feelings an effective substitute for thinking? Do exceptional thinkers experience mental blocks, lapses in concentration, and confusion the same way average thinkers do? Can thinking skill be acquired, or does one have to be born with it?

In this chapter you will find answers to these questions and other basic facts that will enable you to use this book confidently.

Claude is a high school student. His English teacher has just asked the class to identify the theme of the short story they read for homework. When no one answers, she admonishes them, "Class, you're just not thinking. Get busy and *think*."

Claude wrinkles up his nose, furrows his brow, scratches his chin, and stares up at the ceiling. "Think, think, I've got to think. What's the theme of that story? The theme, the theme, what could be the theme?" He shifts his gaze to the right and to the left, purses his lips, then reaches down purposefully, opens his book, and begins flipping pages as if looking for something. All the while his mind is repeating, "Think . . . think . . . theme. . . ."

Is Claude thinking? No. He's trying to, hoping to, but not really doing so. His mental motor is racing, but his transmission is in neutral. He's ready to go, but not going.

Let's consider another case. Agatha, a college student, is sitting in the campus cafeteria, drinking her morning coffee. To all outward appearances she is not only thinking but totally lost in thought. Here is what is taking place in her mind:

> So much work to do today . . . must remember to meet Jim at 6 p.m. . . . I'll have to begin my term paper soon . . . That Bertha is such a slob—I wish she'd clean her part of the room sometime this semester . . . my hair looks so awful—if only I could fix it like Martha's, it would look neat, yet demand little attention . . . If winter would only end, I wouldn't be so depressed—why is my mood so dominated by the weather? . . . This coffee is bitter—you'd think the staff here could at least make a decent cup of coffee . . . I can't wait to get home to have a real meal again . . . wonder how much weight I've gained; perhaps jogging is the solution. . . .

Agatha's mental behavior is much closer to thinking than Claude's. Ideas, images, and notions are drifting through her mind, and she is dutifully watching them float by. But her role is passive; she is a spectator to the activity of her mind. Thinking, as we will view it in this chapter (and as most authorities view it), is something more than aimless daydreaming.

WHAT IS THINKING?

What, then, is thinking? To begin with, it is purposeful mental activity over which we exercise some control. *Control* is the key word. Just as sitting in the driver's seat of a car becomes driving only when we take the steering wheel in hand and control the car's movement, so our mind's movements become thinking only when we direct them.

There are, of course, as many different purposes in thinking as there are in traveling. We may be on a business trip or a pleasant drive through the countryside with no particular destination. Similarly, we may drive in varying conditions and with varying degrees of success or efficiency. We may travel in darkness or in light, proceed slowly or quickly, take the correct turn or the wrong one, arrive at our intended destination or a different one, or find that we are hopelessly lost en route. Nevertheless, as long as we are steering our mind, we are thinking.

This does not mean that thinking must always be conscious. The evidence that the unconscious mind can join in purposeful mental activity is overwhelming. The most dramatic example is the fact that insights often come to us when we are no longer working on a problem but have turned away from it to other activities. (We will see a number of examples of this phenomenon in Chapter 9.)

With these important considerations in mind, we can attempt a more formal definition of thinking: *Thinking is any mental activity that helps formulate or solve a problem, make a decision, or fulfill a desire to understand. It is a searching for answers, a reaching for meaning.* Numerous mental activities are included in the thinking process. Careful observation, remembering, wondering, imagining, inquiring, interpreting, evaluating, and judging are among the most important ones. Often, several of these activities work in combination, as when we solve a problem or make a decision. We may, for example, identify an idea or dilemma, then deal with it—say, by questioning, interpreting, and analyzing—and finally reach a conclusion or decision.

There have been many attempts to explain the nature of thinking. One of the most popular notions, now largely discredited, is that thinking is entirely verbal. According to this theory, we arrange words in our minds or silently whisper to ourselves when we think. Yet if this were the case, Albert Einstein would not be considered a thinker. His thinking consisted more of images than of words.[1] Contemporary authorities agree that the form a thought takes in our minds is usually verbal, but not necessarily so. Just as we may *express* an idea in mathematical symbols or pictures, in addition to words, we may also *conceive* of it in that way.

THE IMPORTANCE OF THINKING

Successful problem solving and issue analysis require factual knowledge—that is, familiarity with the historical context of the problem or issue and an understanding of the relevant principles and concepts. But factual knowledge is something already known, whereas in the great majority of cases, solutions are unknown, brand new, and specifically formulated to fit particular problems or issues. For this reason, the possession of factual knowledge does not by itself guarantee success in problem solving. You may, in fact, be the proverbial "walking encyclopedia" and perform quite dismally. To be a successful problem solver, you will need both factual knowledge and proficiency in thinking.

To appreciate the importance of thinking proficiency, consider the various situations in which you are or will be called upon to solve problems, analyze issues, and make decisions. The choice of a major in college and the decision of whom to marry, where to live, what religion (if any) to embrace, and what political party to join are but a few of the most obvious situations. Every day brings new and difficult challenges: how to deal with difficult people, what to do when your parents can no longer care for themselves, how to be a good parent, how to sort through hyperbole and false claims in advertisements, how to manage your investments wisely, how to determine which political candidate will do the most good (or least harm) for the country.

Skill in problem solving, issue analysis, and decision making is increasingly expected of employees. Only a generation or so ago, "scientific management" was still in vogue. In that system, executives did the thinking and other employees merely carried out their assigned tasks. Since the advent of "quality management," employers have learned to value employees who are willing and able to contribute ideas for the improvement of the company. In recent years, this perspective has been reinforced by three developments: the knowledge explosion, the communications technology revolution, and the rise of the global economy.

Improvements in research capability have dramatically increased the information base in virtually every field, making it difficult for anyone to master even a single discipline's knowledge in its entirety. In addition, because new knowledge is not merely being added each year but *multiplied*, before long such mastery will be impossible. More important, the information base acquired in high school and college, which used to be sufficient for an entire career, will in the future become obsolete within a decade or less.

The communications technology revolution has been even more remarkable. Within less than 20 years, the personal computer was developed and hundreds of hardware and software manufacturers sprang into existence, marketing products no one could have imagined a generation earlier. Hundreds of billions of dollars flowed into upstart companies like Microsoft, Intel, Dell, and a host of "dot.coms," ending the seeming omnipotence (and complacency) of such corporate giants as IBM. For individual companies and entire industries, the result has been a loss of stability. Even successful, well-run organizations can experience a rapid change of fortune and be forced to downsize their operations and lay off workers. Individuals who possess problem-solving and decision-making skills are more flexible than others and are therefore (1) less likely to become victims of downsizing and (2) more likely to find satisfactory employment if they are laid off.

The development of a global economy has resulted from the satellite transmission of television programming; the opening of former Soviet bloc countries to trade; the increase in business *competition* from other countries, notably Japan; and the signing of a new generation of trade agreements such as the North American Free Trade Agreement (NAFTA) and the General Agreement on Tariffs and Trade (GATT). Meeting the challenges and seizing the opportunities presented by the global economy require skill in creative and critical thinking. Employees who possess that skill will enjoy a significant advantage over those who do not.

BRAIN AND MIND AT WORK

Throughout this century, researchers have deepened our understanding of human thought. We now know that thinking is not a mystical activity, unknowable and unlearnable. Thinking occurs in patterns that we can study and compare to determine their relative objectivity, validity, and effectiveness. This knowledge can be used to reinforce good thinking habits and to overcome bad ones. As James Mursell has observed, "Any notion that better thinking is intrinsically unlearnable and unteachable is nothing but a lazy fallacy, entertained only by those who have never taken the trouble to consider just how a practical job of thinking is really done."[2]

Brain research is providing new insights, notably that the structure of the brain is considerably more complex than previously imagined. The first breakthrough in understanding came when a neurosurgeon began treating patients with severe epilepsy in a new way. He severed the *corpus callosum*, the nerve fibers connecting the two hemispheres of the cerebral cortex, to relieve the symptoms of the disease. The separation made it possible to study the way each hemisphere functioned. The right hemisphere, it was learned, governs nonverbal, symbolic, and intuitive responses. The left hemisphere governs the use of language, logical reasoning, analysis, and the performance of sequential tasks.

Some popularizers of this research have taken it to mean there are "left-brained people" and "right-brained people," and a cottage industry has arisen to help people identify which they are and/or become what they are not. Most researchers regard this development as, at best, an oversimplification of the data. For example, Jerre Levy points out that none of the data "supports the idea that normal people function like split-brain patients, using only one hemisphere at a time," adding that the very structure of the brain implies profound integration of the two hemispheres, the *corpus callosum* connecting them and facilitating their arousal.[3]

William H. Calvin says that researchers who specialize in split-brain research (as he does) tend to regard the popularization "with something of the wariness which the astronomers reserve for astrology." He cites the "behavior and mental processes greater than and different from each region's contribution" as evidence of right/left integration.[4] Others underscore the fact that left-brain/right-brain research has been conducted with severely injured or surgically altered brains and not normal ones. In his Nobel lecture on the subject, for instance, Roger W. Sperry noted that "in the normal state the two hemispheres appear to work closely together as a unit, rather than one being turned on while the other idles."[5]

The extravagance of popularizers notwithstanding, neurophysiological research seems to parallel cognitive psychologists' earlier realization that the mind has two distinct phases—the *production* phase and the *judgment* phase—that complement each other during problem solving and decision making. Proficiency in thinking requires the mastery of all approaches appropriate to each phase and skill in moving back and forth between them. Let's examine each phase a little more closely, noting how good thinkers use each effectively.

The Production Phase

In this phase, which is most closely associated with creative thinking, the mind produces various conceptions of the problem or issue, various ways of dealing with it, and possible solutions or responses to it. Good thinkers produce both more ideas and better ideas than poor thinkers. They become more adept in using a variety of invention techniques, enabling them to discover ideas. More specifically, good thinkers tend to see the problem from many perspectives before choosing any one, to consider many different investigative approaches, and to produce many ideas before turning to judgment. In addition, they are more willing to take intellectual risks, to be adventurous and consider unusual ideas, and to use their imaginations.

In contrast, poor thinkers tend to see the problem from a limited number of perspectives (often just a single narrow one), to take the first approach that occurs to them, to judge each idea immediately, and to settle for only a few ideas. Moreover, they are overly cautious in their thinking, unconsciously making their ideas conform to the common, the familiar, and the expected.

The Judgment Phase

In this phase, which is most closely associated with critical thinking, the mind examines and evaluates what it has produced, makes its judgments, and, where appropriate, adds refinements. Good thinkers handle this phase with care. They test their first impressions, make important distinctions, and base their conclusions on evidence rather than their own feelings. Sensitive to their own limitations and predispositions, they double-check the logic of their thinking and the workability of their solutions, identifying imperfections and complications, anticipating negative responses, and generally refining their ideas.

In contrast, poor thinkers judge too quickly and uncritically, ignoring the need for evidence and letting their feelings shape their conclusions. Blind to their limitations and predispositions, poor thinkers trust their judgment implicitly, ignoring the possibility of flaws in their thinking.

GOOD THINKING IS A HABIT

It is frequently said that good thinkers are born, not made. Although there is an element of truth in this, the idea is essentially false. Some people have more talent for thinking than others, and some learn more quickly. As a result, over the years one person may develop thinking ability to a greater extent than another. Nevertheless, effective thinking is mostly a matter of habit. Research proves that the qualities of mind required to think well, the qualities we noted in our discussion of the production and judgment phases, can be mastered by anyone. It even proves that originality can be learned. Most important, it proves that you don't need a high IQ to be a good thinker.[6] E. Paul Torrance has shown that fully *70 percent* of all creative people score below 135 on IQ tests.[7]

The difficulty of improving your thinking depends on the habits and attitudes you have. Chances are you've had little or no direct training in the art of thinking before this, so you're bound to have acquired some bad habits and attitudes. This book will supply principles and techniques for you to master, and your instructor will supply the guidance. You must supply the most important ingredients: the desire to improve and the willingness to apply what you learn.

If at first the task of changing your habits and attitudes seems impossible, remember that a lot of other tasks seemed so, yet you mastered them: walking, for example, and eating without drooling food out of your mouth onto your high chair, swimming, hitting a baseball, and driving a car. The unfamiliar often seems daunting.

GETTING THE MOST FROM YOUR EFFORTS

At one time it was thought that the same occasions, places, and conditions of work are right for everyone. Today we know better. No two people are exactly alike in their needs. What works for one will not necessarily work for another. Mozart and Beethoven, for example, were both great composers, yet they worked very differently. Mozart thought out entire symphonies and scenes from operas in his head, without benefit of notes. Later he transcribed them onto paper. Beethoven, on the other hand, wrote fragments of notes in notebooks, often reworking and polishing them for years. His first ideas were so clumsy that scholars marvel at how he could have developed such great music from them.[8]

Imagine what would have happened if Mozart had followed Beethoven's approach, and vice versa. Surely Mozart's output would have been diminished. Given the unsuitability of another approach to his temperament, it might even have been choked off altogether. And Beethoven would have given the world trash.

It is not unreasonable to believe that there are thousands, perhaps millions, of people in the world today who have not begun to glimpse, let alone develop, their potential for achievement *simply because they are using work habits borrowed from someone else or fallen into by chance or force of circumstance.* Your best approach is not to assume that your work habits fit your needs but to experiment a little and find out what really works best for you. What you find may not make a dramatic difference, but even modest improvements in proficiency will continue to pay dividends over the years.

Consider Time. An hour of prime time will often get better results than two or three hours of the wrong time. When are you in the habit of doing your most important schoolwork? Early in the morning? Late at night? At midday? For the next week or two, try different times and note the effect on your work.

Consider Place. You can observe students studying in strange places: dormitory lounges, crowded cafeterias filled with people clanging and chattering, and snack bars (often next to a blaring jukebox). You've probably studied in some of these places, too, at one time or another, and for no other reason than that you happened to be there at the time an assignment had to be done. But that is not a good reason. If you need quiet to work efficiently, you should seek a quiet place—if not a dormitory room, then an empty classroom, a park bench, or a parked car. Of course, if you find that a busy place actually stimulates your thinking, by all means work there.

Consider Conditions. Thinkers throughout history have occasionally needed some strange stimuli. Poet Friedrich von Schiller needed a desk filled with rotten apples. Novelist Marcel Proust needed a cork-lined workroom. Dr. Samuel Johnson demanded a purring cat, an orange peel, and a cup of tea. But you'd do well not to become dependent on gimmicks or bizarre conditions, if for no other reason than that they're hard to maintain. You're better off trying such approaches as taking a walk or a brisk jog across campus before beginning work or playing music while you work.

A word of caution is in order here. Don't confuse what you like with what works best for you. You may, for example, enjoy being in the dormitory lounge in the early evening watching TV or listening to the stereo blare. But these might hinder more than help your efforts to think or write. Similarly, alcohol and drugs may make you feel good (temporarily, at least), but they are definitely counterproductive. Although the notion persists that such substances enhance creativity, researchers are almost unanimous in concluding that they have the reverse effect: They cloud and numb the mind.

USING FEELINGS TO ADVANTAGE

Feelings were greatly emphasized in the 1960s and early 1970s. "Do your own thing," "If it feels good, do it," and "Get in touch with your feelings" were the catchphrases of the time. In light of the neglect of feelings in previous decades, that emphasis was understandable, but it often took the form of a rejection of thought. The proper relationship of thoughts and feelings is harmonious, not mutually exclusive.

The contribution feelings can make to problem solving and decision making is immeasurable. Not only do feelings often yield the hunches, impressions, and intuitions that produce the answers we seek but they also, more importantly, provide the enthusiasm to undertake difficult challenges and persevere in them. Albert Einstein spent 7 years working out his theory of relativity; Thomas Edison spent 13 years perfecting the phonograph; Copernicus devoted more than 30 years to proving that the sun is the center of the solar system. And millions of men and women labor tirelessly to realize the most elusive of goals: victory over disease, poverty, ignorance, and inhumanity. Without deep and abiding feelings about the importance of their work, such people could not sustain their efforts.

The popular notion that only artists feel, that scientists and other practical people approach problems in computerlike fashion, has long been discredited by scholars.[9] Albert Einstein himself affirmed the role of intuition in science. "There is no logical way to the discovery of [complex scientific laws]," he explained. "There is only the way of intuition, which is helped by a feeling for the order lying behind the appearance."[10] And Arthur Koestler, who studied the lives of innumerable great scientists, observed, "In the popular imagination [they] appear as sober ice-cold logicians, electronic brains mounted on dry sticks. But if one were shown an anthology of typical extracts from their letters and autobiographies with no names mentioned, and then asked to guess their profession, the likeliest answer would be: a bunch of poets or musicians of a rather romantically naive kind."[11]

Of course, not all feelings are good. Some direct us in ways good sense would not have us go. From time to time even the mildest individuals may feel like responding violently to people they don't like, experience a strong urge for sexual contact with those who don't share the sentiment, or be overtaken by the impulse to steal something. For this reason, wisdom demands that we refuse to surrender ourselves to our feelings but instead examine them dispassionately and separate the worthy from the unworthy.

As you proceed through this course, try to become more aware of your feelings. Accept the challenge of finding your best and noblest feelings and allowing them to motivate you.

LEARNING TO CONCENTRATE

Many people have the notion that concentration means a constant, unbroken line of thought. They imagine that scientists, writers, inventors, and philosophers start from point A and move smoothly to point B without distraction. That notion is incorrect. Concentration is not so much something done to *prevent* distraction and interruption as it is something done to *overcome* distraction and interruption when they occur. To concentrate means to return our attention to our purpose or problem whenever it wanders.[12]

Concentrating is much like steering a car. When experienced drivers steer, they don't lock their hands on the wheel in one fixed position; they turn it slightly to the right and to the left to keep the car on course. Even on a straight road, the car stays on course only a small percentage of the time. Drivers must make constant adjustments, many of them almost imperceptible. Experienced drivers are not more talented than inexperienced ones; they have simply learned to make subtle corrections at the right time.

Similarly, the secret of efficient thinkers is not that they experience fewer distractions, but that they have learned to deal with them more quickly and more effectively than inefficient thinkers do. There is no magic in what effective thinkers do. You can learn it as they did, by practicing.

COPING WITH FRUSTRATION

All thinkers have their share of frustration: confusion, mental blocks, false starts, and failures happen to everyone. Good thinkers, however, have learned strategies for dealing with their frustration, whereas poor thinkers merely lament it—thus allowing themselves to be defeated by it. One important study of students' problem-solving processes revealed some interesting differences between good and poor problem solvers. Among them were the following:[13]

Good Problem Solvers	Poor Problem Solvers
Read a problem and decide how to begin attacking it.	Cannot settle on a way to begin.
Bring their knowledge to bear on a problem.	Convince themselves they lack sufficient knowledge (even when that is not the case).
Go about solving a problem systematically—for example, trying to simplify it, puzzling out key terms, or breaking the problem into subproblems.	Plunge in, jumping haphazardly from one part of the problem to another, trying to justify first impressions instead of testing them.
Tend to trust their reasoning and to have confidence in themselves.	Tend to distrust their reasoning and to lack confidence in themselves.
Maintain a critical attitude throughout the problem-solving process.	Lack a critical attitude and take too much for granted.

MAKING DISCUSSION MEANINGFUL[14]

At its best, discussion deepens understanding and promotes problem solving and decision making. At its worst, it frays nerves, creates animosity, and leaves important issues unresolved. Unfortunately, the most prominent models for discussion in contemporary culture—radio and TV talk shows—often produce the latter effects.

Many hosts demand that their guests answer complex questions with simple "yes" or "no" answers. If the guests respond that way, they are attacked for oversimplifying. If, instead, they try to offer a balanced answer, the host shouts, "You're not answering the question," and proceeds to answer it himself. Guests who agree with the host are treated warmly; others are dismissed as ignorant or dishonest. As often as not, when two guests are debating, each takes a turn interrupting while the other shouts, "Let me finish." Neither shows any desire to learn from the other. Typically, as the show draws to a close, the host thanks the participants for a "vigorous debate" and promises the audience more of the same next time.

Here are some simple guidelines for ensuring that the discussions you engage in—in the classroom, on the job, or at home—are more civil, meaningful, and productive than what you see on TV. By following these guidelines, you will set a good example for the people around you.

Whenever Possible, Prepare in Advance

Not every discussion can be prepared for in advance, but many can. An agenda is usually circulated several days before a business or committee meeting. And in college courses, the assignment schedule provides a reliable indication of what will be discussed in class on a given day. Use this advance information to prepare for discussion. Begin by reflecting on what you already know about the topic. Then decide how you can expand your knowledge and devote some time to doing so. (Fifteen or 20 minutes of focused searching on the Internet can produce a significant amount of information on almost any subject.) Finally, try to anticipate the different points of view that might be expressed in the discussion, and consider the relative merits of each. Keep your conclusions very tentative at this point so that you will be open to the facts and interpretations others will present.

Set Reasonable Expectations

Have you ever left a discussion disappointed that others hadn't abandoned their views and embraced yours? Have you ever felt offended when someone disagreed with you or asked you what evidence you had to support your opinion? If the answer to either question is yes, you probably expect too much of others. People seldom change their minds easily or quickly, particularly in the case of long-held convictions. And when they encounter ideas that differ from their own, they naturally want to know what evidence supports those ideas. Expect to have your ideas questioned, and be cheerful and gracious in responding.

Leave Egotism and Personal Agendas at the Door

To be productive, discussion requires an atmosphere of mutual respect and civility. Egotism produces disrespectful attitudes toward others—notably, "I'm more important than other people," "My ideas are better than anyone else's," and "Rules don't apply to me." Personal agendas, such as dislike for another participant or excessive zeal for a point of view, can lead to personal attacks and unwillingness to listen to others' views.

Contribute but Don't Dominate

If you are the kind of person who loves to talk and has a lot to say, you probably contribute more to discussions than other participants. On the other hand, if you are more reserved, you may seldom say anything. There is nothing wrong with being either kind of person. However, discussions tend to be most productive when everyone contributes ideas. For this to happen, loquacious people need to exercise a little restraint, and more reserved people need to accept responsibility for sharing their thoughts.

Avoid Distracting Speech Mannerisms

Such mannerisms include starting one sentence and then abruptly switching to another, mumbling or slurring your words, and punctuating every phrase or clause with audible pauses ("um," "ah,") or meaningless expressions ("like," "you know," "man"). These annoying mannerisms distract people from your message. To overcome them, listen to yourself when you speak. Even better, tape your conversations with friends and family (with their permission), then play the tape back and listen to yourself. And whenever you are engaged in a discussion, aim for clarity, directness, and economy of expression.

Listen Actively

When the participants don't listen to one another, discussion becomes little more than serial monologue—each person taking a turn at speaking while the rest ignore what is being said. This can happen quite unintentionally because the mind can process ideas faster than the fastest speaker can deliver them. Your mind may get tired of waiting and wander about aimlessly like a dog off its leash. In such cases, instead of listening to the speaker's words, you may think about her clothing or hairstyle or look outside the window and observe what is happening there. Even when you are making a serious effort to listen, it is easy to lose focus. If the speaker's words trigger an unrelated memory, you may slip away to that earlier time and place. If the speaker says something you disagree with, you may begin framing a reply. The best way to maintain your attention is to be alert for such distractions and to resist them. Strive to enter the speaker's frame of mind and understand each sentence as it is spoken and to connect it with previous sentences. Whenever you realize your mind is wandering, drag it back to the task.

Judge Ideas Responsibly

Ideas range in quality from profound to ridiculous, helpful to harmful, ennobling to degrading. It is therefore appropriate to pass judgment on them. However, fairness demands that you base your judgment on thoughtful consideration of the overall strengths and weaknesses of the ideas, not on your initial impressions or feelings. Be especially careful with ideas that are unfamiliar or different from your own because those are the ones you will be most inclined to deny a fair hearing.

Resist the Urge to Shout or Interrupt

No doubt you understand that shouting and interrupting are rude and disrespectful behaviors, but do you realize that in many cases they are also a sign of *intellectual insecurity*? It's true. If you really believe your ideas are sound, you will have no need to raise your voice or to silence the other person. Even if the other person resorts to such behavior, the best way to demonstrate confidence and character is by refusing to reciprocate. Make it your rule to disagree without being disagreeable.

PRELIMINARY THINKING STRATEGIES

At the end of this chapter, you will find three kinds of challenges. The first kind, warm-up exercises, are intended to provide an enjoyable way for you to experiment with ideas and limber up your thinking. The second kind are applications, which invite you to apply what you learned in the chapter to real-life problems and issues. Finally, the chapter has a composition/speech exercise that requires more extended analysis and more formal presentation of your findings.

The remainder of this chapter will explain seven helpful preliminary strategies that you can begin using immediately. Because most involve using writing in a way you may not be familiar with, we'll begin by clarifying what that way is.

Although writing is most commonly thought of as a way of expressing thoughts we have already formed, it is also an excellent tool for *discovering* and *clarifying* thoughts. You've probably had the experience of believing you have an idea clearly in mind and then finding out it is hopelessly muddled. It's a common experience. As Ernest Dimnet explains:

> Most men and women die vague about life and death, religion or morals, politics or art. Even about practical issues we are far from being clear. We imagine that other people know definitely their own minds about their children's education, about their own careers, or about the use they should make of their money. The notion helps us to imagine that we ourselves are only separated from decision on these important issues by the lightest curtain of uncertainty. But it is not so. Other people, like ourselves, live in perpetual vagueness. Like us they foolishly imagine they are thinking of some important subject when they are merely *thinking of thinking about it.*[15] [emphasis added]

The solution, Dimnet suggests, is to use the technique known as *freewriting.* It consists of focusing on a problem or issue, letting your mind produce whatever associations it will, and writing down the resulting ideas, without pausing to evaluate any ideas (lest you shut off the flow prematurely). This kind of writing is not intended to be read by anyone else, so the rules of composition do not apply. Nor do you have to worry about spelling or penmanship. A variation on freewriting is *listmaking.* Because it involves single words and phrases rather than sentences, it is more efficient than freewriting, which makes it the perfect way to capture those ideas that come suddenly and leave just as quickly.

Once you have recorded your ideas, you can sort them out, refine them, and express them in a way that will be meaningful to others. Generally, that will take the form of stating what you think and why you think it, as well as providing sufficient explanation to overcome any confusion your readers might have.

Following are seven worthwhile strategies to help you meet the challenges at the end of each chapter:

1. If the exercise consists of a single statement to be analyzed, read it again carefully. Be sure you understand what it says. Ask yourself, "Does this make sense?" If you find yourself answering with a firm "yes" or "no," decide precisely what makes you respond that way. Often, that will be what you should explain to your audience.

2. If words fail you at the outset, refuse to sit and stare at the page. If you took a dead-end street by accident, you wouldn't sit in your car staring at the dead-end sign; you'd turn the car around and try moving in another direction. Do the same with difficult challenges. One approach that works well with some problems is to use a diagram. If, for example, you were evaluating the reasoning "All dogs are animals. Fido is a dog. Therefore, Fido is an animal," you might diagram it this way:

   The diagram would suggest the way to explain your analysis:

   It is correct to classify dogs under the general heading *animals.* Moreover, this applies not just to some dogs but also to *all* dogs. There is no other category under which to classify dogs. Fido is correctly classified as a dog, so he must be an animal.

3. When the statement presents as fact something that is not factual, identify the error and explain how it invalidates the statement.

4. When the statement confuses two terms or ideas, identify the confusion and show its effect on the statement as a whole.

5. When the statement presents a conclusion as the only possible conclusion and other conclusions are also possible, present the other conclusions and demonstrate that they, too, are reasonable (perhaps more reasonable).

6. When the statement, or some part of it, is open to interpretation, use the if-then approach to analysis. Consider, for example, the statement "Everyone must die." Here's how the if-then approach works:

   The statement as it stands is ambiguous. *If* it is taken to mean "At present there is no known way for human beings to avoid death," *then* it is a statement of fact. But *if* it is taken to mean "There will never be a way for human beings to avoid death," *then* it is presumptuous. For, however unlikely such a development may seem, we cannot say for certain it will never occur.

   The if-then approach is also useful when you are uncertain of the facts. In other words, you might say, "I am uncertain of the facts in this matter, but *if* they are as stated, *then* the conclusion is sound because. . . . *If*, however, they are not as stated, *then* the conclusion is not sound because. . . ."

7. If the exercise consists of a dialogue, read it several times, each time for a different purpose. First, read it to understand the discussion in its entirety. Then read each person's comments individually, noting the progression of his or her thoughts and the degree of logical consistency. Finally, read for implications and assumptions; these are ideas that are not stated directly but are nevertheless identifiable by what *is* stated directly. (The dialogue in Sample Exercise 2, below, contains an unstated idea.)

SAMPLE EXERCISES AND RESPONSES

Each exercise you do will have its own particular details and will therefore demand a special response. For that reason, no one formula can be given for responding to the exercises. The following sample exercises and responses, though fairly typical, are illustrations of what can be done rather than models to be slavishly imitated.

Exercise 1

The Assignment: Analyze the following statement, deciding whether it is reasonable and, if so, to what degree. Explain your thinking thoroughly.

The results of a recent national examination reveal that 75 percent of America's high school students are below average in reading ability.

The Response:

I don't know if the statement is a factual one. But I can say that it may have different meanings, depending on how the word *average* is interpreted. And the various meanings affect the reasonableness of the statement.

Below average may mean "below a score that half the high school seniors have achieved in previous years." Or it may mean "below a score now regarded as an acceptable minimum." In either of these cases, the statement is a reasonable one and could very well be factual.

But there is a more technical definition of *below average*. It may mean "below the arithmetic mean (the score derived from dividing the total scores of all high school students by the total number of high school students)." I am not sure whether it is even mathematically possible that 75 percent could fall below the mean, but I do know that it is highly unlikely. So if this is what the statement is saying, it is not very reasonable.

Exercise 2

The Assignment: Read the following dialogue carefully. Then decide whether what is stated (or implied) makes sense. Explain your reasoning thoroughly.

JOHN: Do you think the masses really have any power in the United States today?

BILL: That depends on what groups you include in "the masses." Would you include professional people—doctors, lawyers, teachers . . . ?

JOHN: *Teachers?* They don't make that much money.

The Response:

John's last comment reveals the assumption that money is the basis for determining professional status. That assumption is unwarranted. If money were the measure, a lawyer with a small practice would not be considered a professional, but a plumber with a good business would be. If an apprentice clerk in a store inherited a large sum of money from his aunt, he would be a nonprofessional one day and a professional the next. No, a professional person is one engaged in one of the *professions:* those fields requiring a liberal arts or science education and some form of subsequent specialization. The amount of money a person earns is beside the point.

Exercise 3

The Assignment: Rowena has three unmarked glasses of different sizes: 3 ounces, 5 ounces, and 8 ounces. The largest glass is full. What can Rowena do to get 4 ounces of liquid into each of the larger two glasses?

The Response: After some initial difficulty trying to work the problem out in your head, you create a visual aid by drawing three glasses on a sheet of paper, as shown here. (You could have instead gotten three actual glasses of appropriate sizes.)

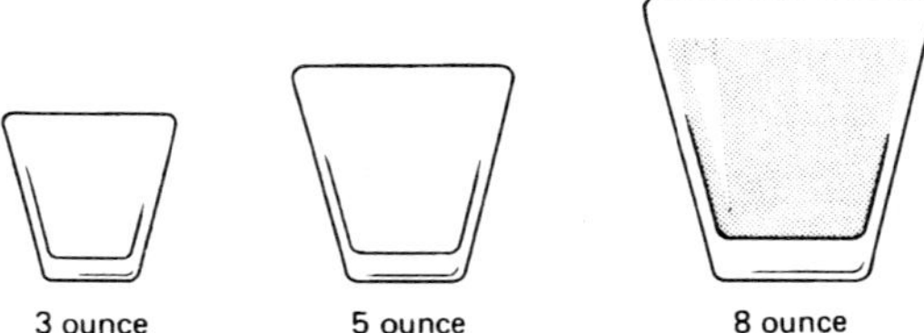

What next? You would pour some liquid into one of the empty glasses, actually or in your imagination. Which glass? It makes no difference. You would just get busy *doing*. If one approach failed, you'd try another.

Try this approach and see if you can solve this challenge by yourself. (You'll find the answer at the end of the chapter).

Warm-Up Exercises

1 Decide whether the reasoning that underlies the following statement is sound or unsound. Write a paragraph or two stating and explain-

ing your judgment. (If you have difficulty doing this assignment, consult the preliminary thinking strategies.)

> There's a possibility that the price of postage stamps will be raised again soon. I'll stock up on them now to avoid paying the higher price.

2 Follow the directions for Exercise 1.

> The sun has always risen in the past; therefore, it will rise tomorrow.

3 A young child is convinced that the time between two o'clock and three o'clock is longer than the time between one o'clock and two o'clock. Compose a brief explanation, with or without a diagram, that helps the child understand that the time isn't longer.

Applications

1 For each of the following statements, write a brief response (one or two sentences) stating your position and explaining why you hold it.

a. Violence is better than reason in dealing with dangerous situations.
b. Only the good die young.
c. It's human nature to be greedy.
d. Capital punishment is a deterrent to crime.
e. If people are unemployed, they must be lazy. There's a job for everyone who really wants to work.
f. Everyone has a value system of some kind.
g. We know ourselves better than others know us.
h. An unborn fetus is a human being.
i. If guns are outlawed, only outlaws will have guns.
j. Truth is an intensely personal matter: What is true for me is not necessarily true for you.
k. Winning isn't everything—it's the *only* thing.
l. Challenging another's opinion is a sign of intolerance.
m. Atheists are generally moral people.
n. Censorship is evil.
o. Black people are better athletes than white people.
p. The oil companies manipulate gasoline prices.
q. Getting your feet wet can cause a cold.
r. Homosexuals are as likely to control their sexual urges as are heterosexuals.

2 Read the following dialogue carefully, looking for flaws in thinking. If you find a flaw, identify it and explain what is wrong with it in sufficient detail to persuade someone who has read the passage but sees no flaw. If you find two or more flaws, decide which is most serious and limit your discussion to that one. If you find nothing wrong with

the thinking in the dialogue, explain why you agree with what is said. (If you have difficulty doing this assignment, consult strategy 7.)

SALLY: Norma, have you begun your composition yet, the one that's due tomorrow?

NORMA: No, I haven't. But I have done quite a bit of research on the topic. I have a few very interesting facts I plan to refer to. Have you done any reading?

SALLY: Not me. I want to do my own thing in my compositions—you know, be original.

NORMA: Really? Maybe I'd better not use those facts. They could work against me, I guess.

3 Follow the directions for Application 2.

HOMER: Excuse me, Professor Collins, may I speak to you for a minute?

PROF. C.: Sure, Homer. What can I do for you?

HOMER: It's about the test we had last week. You gave me a 40 on it.

PROF. C.: That's not a very good grade. Had you read all three chapters carefully?

HOMER: *Carefully?* I read each one four times, underlined every important detail, and then studied them for about 10 hours for three nights before the test. I took No-Doz and stayed up until 4:30 A.M. the night before the test.

PROF. C.: I see. That would surely seem to be more than adequate preparation. What do you think went wrong?

HOMER: I think the test was unfair. . . . I mean, it's not. . . . I know you wouldn't make a test unfair on purpose. I think you're a good teacher and all. Sociology is your field and I'm just an amateur, but after all that trying, I wouldn't have got a 40 if the test were fair.

4 Follow the directions for Application 2.

LILLIAN: Do you think parents should be told when their teenage daughters are given abortion counseling?

ROY: Absolutely. Parents are responsible for their children until they become of age. They have a right to be told.

LILLIAN: I'm not as sure as you. I can see how not telling them is a violation of their rights as parents, and the family has been weakened enough today without its being weakened further. But on the other hand, teenage girls are not just objects. They're people, and therefore, they have rights, such as the right to determine how their bodies will be used. And many times they can't talk to their parents about sex.

ROY: Nonsense. Parents care about their kids. They have their interests at heart more than anyone else, particularly some money-grabbing doctor or abortion-happy feminist. If kids really want to talk to their parents, there's nothing stopping them—except the possibility that they don't want to hear what their parents will say.

LILLIAN: Another thing bothers me, too. Why does the issue always focus on teenage girls rather than teenage boys?

ROY: Check with your local anatomist.

5 Follow the directions for Application 2.

GUY: Want to know what makes me sick? The tolerance our society has for transsexuals. I can't think of anything more disgusting than a person changing sexes to act out homosexual fantasies or to get more sexual satisfaction.

DARRELL: You obviously don't know much about transsexualism.

GUY: Don't tell me you excuse their perversion, too?

DARRELL: There's nothing to excuse. And you're mistaken in calling it a perversion. It's not.

GUY: What else can it be but a perversion? A man decides to be a woman, or vice versa. It's a mockery of nature. We are what we're born to be, and it's our responsibility to accept that. It ought to be against the law to tamper with nature the way they do.

6 The following passage is an excerpt from a student's letter home. Read it carefully. Then decide whether its reasoning is sound or unsound. State and explain your judgment in a paragraph or two, including whatever supporting material you believe will help persuade your reader.

> The one thing that really bugs me about my schedule this term is that required course, "Introduction to Literature." Some students may not know what their future career is. I do. It's to help you, Dad, with the business, and someday to take it over. If we sold books I could see the value of such a course. But literature surely isn't going to make me a better furniture store manager.

ISSUE FOR EXTENDED ANALYSIS

Following is a more comprehensive thinking challenge than the others in the chapter. Read the background note, the two opposing essays, and the class discussion.* Analyze what you have read, conduct additional research where appropriate, and formulate your assessment of the issue. Then write a composition that explains and supports your assessment. Remember that in addressing one issue, people often raise other issues. Also, keep in mind that the essays and discussion may contain erroneous statements and/or unsound arguments and may neglect important matters. Part of your challenge is to identify new issues as well as errors and omissions.

The Issue: Human Nature

This issue is an ancient one that has fascinated philosophers, scientists, and, most recently, social scientists. Of its many aspects, the one that we will focus on here is the question of whether people are by nature good. Traditional religious believers, notably Jews and Christians, answer "no," claiming that people have a natural predisposition, or at least a vulnerability, to evil. Some conservative Christians go further, arguing that humans are by nature "depraved." Secular humanists and humanistic psychologists tend to take the opposite view, claiming that people are born good and that any bad behavior they may engage in is attributable to social influences and conditions. (This view is borrowed from Romanticism, particularly from the ideas of Jean Jacques Rousseau.) Many current social controversies reflect this controversy over human nature.

The Essays

People Are Inherently Good
By Asanti Jones

Rousseau was insightful in noting that people are born good and, left to follow their natural inclinations and intuitions, will develop their potential and benefit themselves and those around them. A number of conclusions follow logically from this insight.

First, parents should not impose their beliefs and values on children but instead leave them free to develop their own. This is particularly so in

Nothing More Than Potential
By Inga Nowak

If people are inherently good, it makes sense not to burden them with regimens, rules, and regulations that hinder the natural expressions of their impulses. And the lifting of such burdens should begin at the earliest time of life—in childhood. On the other hand, if people are not inherently good—if goodness like wisdom is not inborn but acquired—then regimens, rules, and regulations are beneficial.

---

*Note that the essays and the discussions in this exercise, here and in subsequent chapters, are presented in the informal style typically encountered in nonscholarly, journalistic writing. Thus, quotations from authors and mentions of statistical data or other research materials are not accompanied by footnote citations, though in some cases they contain a reference to a book title. This approach creates a different, and in some ways more difficult, burden than that of more scholarly reading, but it is more reflective of everyday reading and discussion.

such matters as religion, politics, and morality. No one has a right to say what others should regard as right and proper. Each individual must choose for him/herself. And what each chooses, others should respect.

Secondly, schools should have as few regulations and formalities as possible. Courses should be suggested by teachers, but the final determination of what to study and how to do so should be the student's. If students find a lecture or other class exercise boring or irrelevant to their needs at the moment, they should be free to choose another activity. Moreover, any assessment of students' achievement should be made by the students themselves—just as they alone know what goals they should set, they alone know how well their have progressed toward reaching those goals.

If all people received such an upbringing, they would be healthy, happy, and successful. Unfortunately, few do, and the result is crime, drug and alcohol addiction, child and spouse abuse, and a host of other social problems. But it is a mistake to meet such problems with more laws and stricter punishment for infractions. The fault lies in society's failure to recognize the inherent goodness of people and to ensure their freedom to be themselves.

Only a foolish generation would answer such a vital question on the basis of wishful thinking. But that is just what the past couple of generations did. They installed permissivism in both home and school. They let children decide what to think about truth and falsity, right and wrong, beauty and ugliness. They discarded the idea of discipline and let students decide what they would learn and how they would learn it. They put self-esteem above self-control and eliminated instruction in civics and civility.

Exactly what has been the result of almost half a century of permissivism and self-indulgence? Social chaos. Parents have lost control of their children and have no idea of how to regain it. Teachers are frustrated in their attempts to impart knowledge and often fearful for their personal safety. Young people, intent on following their urges, are making life difficult for themselves and everyone around them, and are filled with resentment without knowing why.

It's about time America saw the notion that people are inherently good for the dangerous nonsense it is. People are not born good or evil but have the potential to be either. And which they become depends partly on the quality of the training they receive and partly on the choices they make.

Class Discussion

EDNA: Jones is right. The old saying "As the twig is bent, so grows the tree" supports his view. People, like twigs, start out straight. The bending is supplied by others.

WALLY: Jones's argument is a big cop-out. Efforts to escape personal responsibility are as old as history. They go all the way back to Adam, who blamed Eve, who in turn said the devil made her do it. Today's rapists, child molesters, thieves, and terrorists continue the tradition by blaming their victims. What is different today is that some prominent thinkers tend to side with the perpetrators.

EDNA: Do you deny that bad environments—slums, for example—are more crime-ridden and produce more lawbreakers than the suburbs?

WALLY: Not at all. But I also recognize that two children in the same family, exposed to identical influences, often turn out very differently. One will become a criminal, and the other, a law-abiding citizen; one a narcissist, the other an altruist; one a sinner, the other a saint.

EDNA: There are always exceptions. I'm talking about what happens as a general rule.

WALLY: If Jones were right, then more permissive ages would have fewer social problems than more restrictive ages. Yet over the last few decades, our society has become very permissive, and our social problems have *increased*.

EDNA: Don't kid yourself. The influences of parents, teachers, and other authority figures are every bit as strong today. They're just more subtle.

WALLY: I'm not saying kids aren't influenced by adults. I'm saying that they show the tendency to bad behavior way before such influence takes place. Children who are barely able to crawl display meanness and selfishness. Most parental guidance aims to correct already-existing bad tendencies.

Solutions to Sample Problems

THE THREE GLASSES PROBLEM

The key to solving this problem is to use one or more of the glasses as a measuring device. Here's how to proceed.

1. Fill the 3-ounce glass and empty it into the 5-ounce glass. Fill it a second time and empty as much as will fit into the 5-ounce glass. Now the 3-ounce

glass will contain 1 ounce of liquid, the 5-ounce glass 5 ounces, and the 8-ounce glass 2 ounces.

2. Empty the 5-ounce glass into the 8-ounce glass. Then empty the 3-ounce glass into the 5-ounce glass. Now the 3-ounce glass will be empty, the 5-ounce glass will contain 1 ounce of liquid, and the 8-ounce glass 7 ounces.
3. Fill the 3-ounce glass from the 8-ounce glass. Then empty the 3-ounce glass into the 5-ounce glass. Now the 3-ounce glass will be empty, and the 5- and 8-ounce glasses will each contain 4 ounces.

Notes

1. Arthur Koestler, *The Act of Creation* (New York: Macmillan, 1964), p. 173.
2. *Using Your Mind Effectively* (New York: McGraw-Hill, 1951), pp. vi–vii.
3. "Research Synthesis on Right and Left Hemispheres," *Educational Leadership* 40, no. 4 (January 1983): 66–71.
4. William H. Calvin, "Left Brain, Right Brain: Science or the New Phrenology," Chapter 10, of *The Throwing Madonna*, http://universe.com, 2001.
5. Accessed on 11/20/02 @ http://www.nobel.se/medicine/laureates/1981/sperry-lecture.html.
6. See, for example, Sidney Parnes, *Creative Behavior Guidebook* (New York: Scribner's, 1967), p. 32.
7. *Guiding Creative Talent* (Englewood Cliffs, NJ: Prentice-Hall, 1962), p. 5.
8. Brewster Ghiselin, *The Creative Process: A Symposium* (Berkeley: University of California Press, 1954), p. 115.
9. See, for example, J. Dewey, *Art as Experience* (New York: Milton Balch, 1934), p. 73.
10. Quoted in W. I. B. Beveridge, *The Art of Scientific Investigation* (New York: Norton, 1951), p. 56.
11. *Act of Creation*, p. 146.
12. This definition is Henry Hazlitt's, quoted in ibid., pp. 72–73.
13. Benjamin Bloom and Lois J. Broder, *Problem-Solving Processes of College Students* (Chicago: University of Chicago Press, 1950), pp. 25–30.
14. This section copyright © 2002 by MindPower, Inc. Used with permission.
15. *The Art of Thinking* (New York: Simon & Schuster, 1928), pp. 103–104.

Be a Critical Reader

You may be thinking, "This chapter doesn't apply to me. I read pretty fast and have excellent comprehension." But this chapter isn't about reading faster or merely understanding what you read. It is about deciding whether to accept or reject what the author says. Chances are you haven't had much training in this important aspect of reading.

In this chapter, you'll learn a four-step strategy for critical reading. You'll also receive tips for making important distinctions as you read.

Not long ago, while searching the Internet, I encountered a reference to an article describing "Pepper Power Bear Spray," which was created by a survivor of a grizzly bear attack for defense against bears, lions, and moose. The manufacturer promises "quick access and potent stopping power." If I were going camping in the deep woods, I thought to myself, I'd certainly feel safer if I had a good supply of that product.

Then my glance fell on the *very next* response to my search request. It read, "Bears attracted to repellent, researcher says." My curiosity aroused, I read the news article. It seems that though pepper spray can indeed stop a charging bear if sprayed in its face, it has the *opposite* effect if sprayed on clothing, camping equipment, or the ground around a campsite. A camper who sprayed it around his tent was soon surrounded by a bunch of brown bears. A pilot who sprayed it on his plane's pontoons returned to find them chewed up.

The lesson in that experience was don't believe everything you read in newspapers, books, magazines, or on the Internet. Unfortunately, many people have never learned this lesson. They erroneously assume that if something is published, it must be true. In reality, even honest, well-intentioned writers make mistakes; imperfection is an unavoidable part of being human.

The consequences of being misinformed by the printed word are not always as dramatic as being visited by a family of wild and presumably hungry beasts, but they are no less real. Every day people undermine their health, make disastrous investments or career moves, or harm their marriages by uncritically accepting something they've read. The best safeguard against such misfortunes is to develop the habit of *critical reading*.

CRITICAL READING DEFINED

Critical reading* is active, thoughtful reading, as opposed to passive acceptance of whatever appears on the printed page. Critical readers *evaluate* what they read, and their standard of judgment is not how closely the author's view matches their own, but whether it is accurate and reasonable. Consequently, critical readers are less vulnerable to deception and manipulation than other people.

Our age is not the first to realize the importance of critical reading. Almost 400 years ago, Francis Bacon warned about the danger of reading improperly. He advised people not to dispute an author's view nor to accept it uncritically, but to "weigh and consider" it. In the nineteenth century, British statesman Edmund Burke expressed the same view in more dramatic terms: "To read without reflection is like eating without digesting." The following explanation by a twentieth-century scholar expands on this idea:

> There is one key idea which contains, in itself, the very essence of effective reading, and on which the improvement of reading depends: *Reading is reasoning.* When you read properly, you are not merely assimilating. You are not automatically transferring into your head what your eyes pick up on the page. What you see on the page sets your mind at work, collating, criticizing, interpreting, questioning, comprehending, comparing. When this process goes on well, you read well. When it goes on ill, you read badly.[1]

Such intense mental activity is not required for everything you read. A bus schedule or a menu can be read with virtually no reflection; an encyclopedia article or light fiction requires relatively little evaluation. Critical reading is most relevant, and necessary, when the writing is intended to *persuade* you—that is, when the author argues for one perspective or opinion over others. Persuasive writing can be found in every subject—from politics, psychology, finance, religion, popular culture, and business management to sports, chess, and even gardening. Although persuasive writing is typically associated with editorials, opinion essays, and letters to editors, it may also be found in news reports and in textbooks. Wherever it is found, you are challenged to read critically.

---

*Don't be confused by the fact that the word *critical* is also used to mean "finding fault with." That is not the meaning intended here.

MAKING IMPORTANT DISTINCTIONS

A fundamental requirement for critical reading is making distinctions. The most important and most often overlooked ones are the following.

The Distinction Between the Person and the Idea

Your reaction to a sentence beginning "Adolf Hitler said . . ." would probably be very different from your reaction to one beginning "Winston Churchill said. . . ." In the first instance, you might not even continue reading. At the very least, you would read with great suspicion and be ready to reject what was said. There's nothing strange about that. You've learned things about Hitler and Churchill, and it's difficult to set this information aside. In one sense, you *shouldn't* set it aside. Yet, in another sense, you *must* set it aside to be a good thinker. After all, even a lunatic can have a good idea, and a genius will, on occasion, be wrong.

If you do not control your tendency to accept or reject ideas on the basis of who expresses them, your analysis of everything you read and hear is certain to be distorted. You will judge arguments on whether the speaker is of your race, religion, political affiliation, or generation. And consequently you might embrace nonsense and reject wisdom. Aristotle's contemporaries tell us he had very thin legs and small eyes, favored conspicuous dress and jewelry, and was fastidious in the way he combed his hair.[2] It's not hard to imagine some Athenian ignoramus muttering to friends the ancient Greek equivalent of "Don't pay any attention to what Aristotle says—he's a wimp."

To guard against confusing the person and the idea, be aware of your reactions to people and try compensating for them. That is, listen more carefully to people you are inclined to dislike and more critically to people you are inclined to like. Judge the arguments as harshly as you wish, but only on their merits as arguments.

The Distinction Between Matters of Taste and Matters of Judgment

There are two broad types of opinion: *taste* and *judgment*. They differ significantly. In matters of taste we may express our personal preferences without defending them. In matters of judgment, however, we have an obligation to provide evidence—that is, supporting material that provides a basis for our view. Only when evidence is sufficient in both quality and quantity to remove all reasonable doubt and establish certainty does it qualify as *proof*. Evidence may take a variety of forms, notably factual details, statistics, examples, anecdotes, quotations, comparisons, or descriptions.

Many people confuse taste and judgment. They believe their right to hold an opinion is a guarantee of the opinion's rightness. This confusion often causes them to offer inadequate support (or no support at all) for views that demand support. For example, they express judgments on such controversial issues as abortion, capital punishment, the teaching of evolution in the schools, mercy killing, discrimination in hiring, and laws concerning rape as if they were matters of taste rather than matters of judgment.

Keep in mind that whenever someone presents an opinion about the truth of an issue or the wisdom of an action—that is, whenever someone presents a judgment—you, as a critical thinker, have not only the right but also a duty to judge that opinion by the evidence. To be a careful thinker, you *must* do so.

The Distinction Between Fact and Interpretation

A *fact* is something known with certainty, something either objectively verifiable or demonstrable. An *interpretation* is an explanation of meaning or significance. Frequently, facts and interpretations are so intertwined that we have difficulty deciding where one leaves off and the other begins. Here is an example of such intertwining:

This paragraph presents facts from research conducted by others. (The author cites his source in a footnote.)	Poverty causes crime? According to James Q. Wilson and Richard Herrnstein, "During the 1960s, one neighborhood in San Francisco had the lowest income, the highest unemployment rate, the highest proportion of families with incomes under four thousand dollars a year, the least educational attainment, the highest tuberculosis rate, and the highest proportion of substandard housing. . . . That neighborhood was called Chinatown. Yet, in 1965, there were only five persons of Chinese ancestry committed to prison in the *entire* [emphasis added] state of California."
The first four sentences are factual statements. The final sentence is the author's interpretation.	Roxbury, Massachusetts, a predominantly black and impoverished area, sits next to South Boston, a predominantly white and impoverished area. Both contain the same percentage of single parent households, and public housing accounts for the same percentage of the population. Yet, the violent crime rate in Roxbury, the black area, is four times the rate of that in South Boston. If poverty caused crime, one would expect the numbers to be closer to equal.
This entire paragraph is the author's interpretation of the facts he presented in the previous paragraphs.	No, the formula is more likely the other way around: crime causes poverty. The more crime, the less incentive for businesspeople to locate businesses in

> that area. Store owners must charge consumers more to offset losses caused by theft and higher insurance premiums. Homeowners, apartment dwellers, and businesspeople pay increased security costs to combat the ever-present threat of theft or violent crime. *This* impoverishes neighborhoods.[3]

The danger in failing to distinguish between fact and interpretation is that you will regard uncritically statements that ought to be questioned and contrasted with other views. If the habit of confusing the two is strong enough, it can paralyze your critical sense.

The Distinction Between Literal and Ironic Statements

Not everything that is said is intended to be taken literally. Sometimes, a writer makes a point by saying the exact opposite of what is meant—that is, by using irony or satire. Suppose, for example, you encountered this passage in your reading:

> Congress is right in reducing the taxes of the wealthy more than those of the working classes. After all, wealthy people not only pay more into the treasury but they also have a higher standard of living to maintain. If the cost of soybeans has risen, so also has the cost of caviar; if the subway fare has increased, so has the maintenance cost of a Rolls-Royce and a Lear jet. If the government listens to the minor grumbling and whining of the unemployed, it surely should be responsive to the plight of the affluent.

On the surface, this certainly looks like a plea on behalf of the rich. But on closer inspection, it will be seen as a mockery of that plea. The clues are subtle, to be sure, but undeniable: the reference to the higher standard of living, the comparison of travel by Rolls-Royce or jet with travel by subway, the reference to the "plight" of the rich. Such tongue-in-cheek writing can be more biting and therefore more effective than a direct attack. Yet you must be alert to the subtlety and not misread it, or the message you receive will be very different from the message that has been expressed.

The Distinction Between an Idea's Validity and the Quality of Its Expression

The way an idea is expressed can influence people's reactions. This is why a mad leader like Hitler won a large popular following even among intelligent and responsible people and why Jim Jones's followers killed their children and committed suicide in Guyana. Impassioned, eloquent expression tends to excite a favorable response, just as lifeless, inarticulate, error-filled expression prompts a negative response. Compare these two passages:

> Ain't right to treat some folks good and others bad. If a man don't treat all equal, he ain't much of a man.
>
> To achieve success in a competitive world, you must honor the first principle of success: Treat well those people who can benefit you, and ignore the others.

The first passage may seem less appealing than the second. And yet it contains an idea most philosophers would enthusiastically endorse, whereas the second contains an idea most would find reprehensible. Careful thinkers are able to appraise the passages correctly because they are aware that expression can deceive. Such thinkers make a special effort to separate form from content before judging. Thus they are able to say, "This idea is poorly expressed but profound" and "This idea is well expressed but shallow."

The Distinction Between Language and Reality

Language is our principal means of understanding reality and communicating that understanding to others. Words come so naturally and become so closely associated with what they represent that we may unconsciously regard them as synonymous with reality. That can be a costly mistake. A people's language develops according to its insights and observations, and because no single group has equal insight into all dimensions of reality, no language is perfectly suited to express all realities. For example, Eskimos have many words for snow, each word denoting a certain kind of snow (heavy and wet versus light and fluffy, small and fine versus large and dense, and so on), so they can speak with much greater precision about snow than can English-speaking peoples. Similarly, the ancient Greeks had a number of words for love, each representing a distinct type of love (love of God, love of family, romantic or sexual love, and so forth), whereas we require our word *love* to bear an excessive burden and thereby create confusion in our discourse.

The word *self* is another good example of a term that is made to carry more meaning than it can bear. We say, "I made myself resist that triple chocolate truffle cake," "You really ought to give yourself a chance to get over one lousy relationship before entering another," and "Bill is not himself these days." In each of these constructions there seem to be two distinct selves: in the first, the one controlling and the one controlled; in the second, the giver and the receiver; and in the third, Bill and not-Bill. As Peggy Rosenthal has shown, the problem is not limited to informal, everyday expression but is found in psychological discourse as well:

> One thing [writers about psychology] often seem to have in mind is that *self* is a goal of some kind. But the kind varies. It can be the goal of what sounds like a treasure hunt (the familiar "finding of one's self"), a trip ("the long journey to achieve selfhood"), a vegetable ("the maturation of the self"), or a vaguely Aristotelian process ("self-actualization is actualization of a self"). Sometimes, though, *self* seems not to be a

> goal but to have goals of its own: "the [mature] self now expresses . . . its intentions and goals." . . . [It can even be] a sort of balloon that expands and contracts with our moods: there's "that enlargement of self that goes into feeling good," whereas "in despair we have a reduced sense of self."[4]

Rosenthal notes that some writers use *self* and *sense of self* interchangeably. "But how can this be?" she asks. "Can the sense, or awareness, of something be equal to the thing itself?" The ultimate confusion, she suggests, is found in a passage written by Carl Rogers in which he uses *self* to mean "both the considering agent and the object of consideration in the same sentence."[5]

The reality of the *self* would be no less complex if we had half a dozen words, each designating a single aspect, instead of merely one word, but our discourse would undoubtedly be less confusing and we might well achieve a deeper, more accurate understanding of that reality. In any case, keeping in mind the distinction between language and reality will help you approach both your thinking and your communication with appropriate care and humility.

A STRATEGY FOR CRITICAL READING

So much for the distinctions essential to critical reading. Now we'll consider a four-step critical reading strategy: *Skim, Reflect, Read,* and *Evaluate.* We'll examine each in turn.

Step 1: Skim

To skim is to glance at selected parts of a book or article in order to gain an overview of it. On average, skimming should take about 15 or 20 minutes for a book and 5 or 10 minutes for an article. When done effectively, skimming will not only make your reading easier and more effective; it will also save you time by sparing you the chore of *rereading* all or part of the work.

Skimming should answer these questions: *What issue is the author writing about? What is the author's position on this issue? What are the main divisions (subtopics) of the book or article? How much evidence does the author offer in support of his or her view? What type(s) of evidence?*

In the case of a book, skim the preface or introduction for a statement of the author's purpose in writing and essential message, the table of contents for the breakdown and sequence of the contents, the beginnings and ends of one or two chapters to learn whether the author provides previews or summaries (if they are provided, skim them for each chapter), and the endnotes and/or bibliography to see how well documented the book is and the kinds of sources the author has used. If time permits, skim the entire concluding chapter to learn what judgments and/or recommendations the author makes. Sometimes the final chapter will summarize the main argument presented in the book.

For articles, skim the introduction, the section headings, the first paragraph following each heading, and the conclusion.

Step 2: Reflect

As used here, *reflection* means examining your own views rather than the author's. Ask yourself: *What ideas do I have about this subject that could create a bias for or against the author's view and prevent me from giving it a fair hearing?*

Bias can occur in one of two ways. The more obvious way is to have thought carefully about the issue, considered the opposing views, and decided that the evidence supports one better than the others. Far from being shameful, this process is praiseworthy—the purpose of thinking, after all, is to form conclusions. But is it fair to *prejudge* one author's presentation on the basis of our prior conclusion about some *other* author's presentation? No. The author we are reading now may have compelling new evidence or may expose an error in our thinking. The only way we can be sure is to set aside our prior conclusion long enough to read fairly.

The other way in which bias can occur is more subtle, so subtle in fact that we may be unaware of it. Each of us has many ideas that we did not form for ourselves, ideas that slipped into our minds when we were not paying close attention. Such ideas include the ones our parents and teachers expressed while we were growing up, statements made by people on talk shows or characters in films, advertising jingles, and all our casual perceptions, impressions, hunches, and assumptions. Many of these ideas have no doubt faded, but others—notably the popular ones that we have heard repeated time and again—are still present and can impact our thinking. These repeated ideas may become so familiar and comfortable that we are inclined to defend them, even though we have never evaluated them and, for that reason, they are not really our own. Because this kind of bias is both unconscious and irrational, it can pose a greater problem than the more obvious kind.

The purpose of reflection is to become aware of both kinds of bias and to control them during the remaining steps.

Step 3: Read

If you have skimmed well, this step will be relatively easy. You will already know what the author is saying; you will also understand the sequence of the author's points and the kind and amount of evidence presented. Now your task is to deepen and refine your understanding. Read the entire work carefully, at a single sitting if possible. Keep a pen or pencil in hand while reading and underline the most important sentences. Try to limit your underlining to one sentence per several paragraphs. Where appropriate, add your questions and thoughts in the margin.

In the case of a book or a long article, it is a good idea to *summarize* what you have read. To do this, review the sentences you have marked as important. Consider how many sentences you can combine without changing the author's meaning. Next write your summary in complete sentences, keeping to the original phrasing and the original order of presentation as much as possible to avoid distortion. Then briefly note in your own words the evidence offered by the writer. Do not attempt to elaborate on the evidence as the author did, or your summary will be too long to be useful.

If you have summarized effectively, you should now have a brief version of the original work that is faithful in content yet much easier to analyze. A whole book can be reduced to several paragraphs in this way; a full-length magazine article, to seven or eight sentences or less. Whenever you summarize, however, keep in mind the danger of distortion and oversimplification. It is not only unfair but pointless to criticize an author for something he or she did *not* say.

Step 4: Evaluate

Begin by reading your summary carefully so that you grasp the author's main points AND the evidence offered for each. Then answer the following questions. (Note: Some questions will require you to reexamine the work itself and not just your summary of it. In such cases, your summary will help you determine in which chapter or section to look.)

Are any of the author's terms vague or ambiguous (open to more than one meaning)? In such cases, you will have to decide what meaning is implied.

Does the author use emotionally charged language as a substitute for evidence? Words like *harassment*, *terrorism*, *rape*, *censorship*, *diversity*, *multicultural*, *human rights*, *family values*, *justice*, *empowerment*, *freedom*, *liberty*, *rights*, and *choice* tend to evoke an emotional response. Persuasive writing may make us feel as well as think, but when it makes us feel *instead* of think, it is dishonest.

Is the author's evidence relevant to the issue? No matter how comprehensive and authoritative evidence may be, if it has no bearing on the issue under discussion, it does not deserve our consideration.

Did the author omit any significant evidence? Often, the weakness in an argument lies in what the author does *not* say. For example, let's say an author stated that several years ago, an American engineer and his wife visited the Congo, trying to find evidence of a dinosaurlike creature reportedly living there; and also that they returned with a picture that they said documented their sighting of the creature. Everything in the statement is correct.[6] However, one important detail is missing: the picture was severely underexposed and therefore worthless as documentation.

Are the author's examples and cases typical and comprehensive? The author's citation of some examples and cases does not necessarily establish the argument's validity. If the cases are extraordinary—exceptions rather than typical instances—they are worth very little. Similarly, if they represent one narrow aspect of the issue, they may not adequately support the author's argument.

If the author cites a scientific study, has it been replicated? The practice of the scientific community is to withhold endorsement of any researcher's findings until they have been independently confirmed. This is a wise approach, for some studies are proven to be "flukes."

If the author cites a survey, what organization designed and administered it? How large was the sample? Was it random? A survey that does not conform to established statistical principles is worthless as evidence.

Are the sources of information cited by the author still current? There is nothing necessarily wrong with old sources. Something written in 1800 may still be valid today. But later findings may have discredited older views.

Are the experts cited by the author authoritative and reliable? The fact of being well known does not make one an authority. A Nobel Prize winner in physics may be totally incompetent in psychology or government. And even if the person cited is an authority in the field in question, the view is open to question if the person has been guilty of unreliability (professional dishonesty, for example) in the past.

Do other experts agree with the experts cited by the author? In controversial matters, there is seldom any more agreement among experts than among nonexperts. A little investigation may reveal that the experts cited by the author hold the minority view!

What criticisms and counterarguments would someone who holds a different position make about this book or article? Nothing reveals the flaws on one side of an issue better than hearing the other side.

Does the author commit any errors in logic? For example, does the author overgeneralize, oversimplify, or assume facts not in evidence?

Is the author's conclusion about the evidence the most reasonable one, or is another conclusion more reasonable? Like the rest of us, authors sometimes yield to their biases and interpret evidence in a way that flatters their prior opinions. In such cases, an objective assessment of the evidence may produce a different conclusion.

As you no doubt realize, the answers to many of these questions are not likely to be found either in the book or article you are evaluating or in your own head. To answer them will require further investigation on your part. Be sure to conduct whatever investigation is necessary before making your final judgment.

EXPRESSING YOUR JUDGMENT

One mistake readers commonly make in evaluating a book or article is to assume that they must agree completely or disagree completely with the author. More often than not, the most reasonable response is to accept some parts of an author's argument, reject others, and perhaps be uncertain about still others. The following guidelines will assist you in expressing your judgment.

1. If you agree in part and disagree in part, explain exactly what your position is and support it carefully. Remember that good thinkers will judge your arguments as closely as you judge other people's arguments.

2. If some vagueness or ambiguity in the author's argument prevents you from giving a flat answer, don't attempt one. Rather, say, "it depends," and go on to explain. The if-then approach is very helpful in such cases. Here's how it works. Suppose someone had written, "A human being is an animal." You might respond as follows.

   <u>It depends</u> on what you mean by *animal.* <u>If</u> you mean *human being* is included in the broad classification *animal,* as opposed to *vegetable* or

mineral, then I agree. But if you mean a human being has nothing more than animal nature, no intellect and will that distinguish him or her from other members of the animal kingdom, then I disagree. I believe that . . .

3. If you must deal with conflicting testimony and cannot decide your position with certainty, identify the conflict and explain why you cannot be certain. If you believe that circumstances seem somewhat in favor of one side, explain those circumstances and why you are inclined to judge them as you do.

An example of conflicting testimony occurred some years ago in the highly publicized trial of Jack Henry Abbott. Abbott, who had spent 24 of his 37 years behind prison bars, was paroled after Norman Mailer arranged for Abbott's book, *In the Belly of the Beast*, to be published. Six weeks after his parole, Abbott stabbed a waiter in a dispute over the use of a restroom. Abbott testified that he thought the waiter had pulled a knife first and that he lunged forward with his knife in self-protection. A passerby, however, witnessed the incident and testified that the waiter had made what appeared to be a "conciliatory gesture" and turned to walk away when Abbott raced after him, reached over his shoulder, and stabbed him with "terrible ferocity," then taunted him as he lay dying.[7]

In this case, you might reasonably say that although you cannot be certain which testimony is correct, circumstances seem to favor the witness's testimony. You would go on to explain that Abbott's testimony was more likely than the witness's to be colored by emotion and self-interest.

These guidelines may seem to encourage evasion or straddling the fence. They are not intended to do so and should not be used for that purpose. Apply them when reasonableness demands a qualified answer, not in situations in which timidity prompts you to avoid answering.

A SAMPLE EVALUATION

To see how a typical evaluation might proceed, imagine you are evaluating a magazine article arguing that "inferior" people should be sterilized at puberty. You have completed the first three steps in the critical reading process and have summarized the author's argument as follows. (For reference purposes, the sentences and items of evidence are numbered.)

1. A serious world population problem exists today.
2. The ideal solution is for everyone to be responsible in deciding whether he or she should reproduce.
3. However, few people make that decision rationally—emotion overwhelms logic.
4. Moreover, the least talented and least intelligent are likely to have the most children.

5. In time, this tendency may set the process of evolution in reverse.
6. The best and most practical solution is to identify inferior people and force them to be sterilized at puberty.

As evidence in support of the argument, the article presented:

7. UN statistics on world population
8. Selected UN statistics on world poverty, illiteracy, and disease
9. A research study showing that more affluent, better-educated, higher-IQ couples tend to have fewer children
10. Quotations from geneticists showing the favorable genetic effects that would occur if only higher-IQ individuals were to reproduce
11. Quotations from medical authorities showing the benefits that would accrue to world health if people with hereditary diseases did not reproduce

Your evaluation of the argument and evidence might look like this (parenthetical numbers refer to the preceding statements and evidence).

Concerning the Clarity of the Argument:

Several terms are ambiguous. Do *talented* and *intelligent* (4) refer to the broad range of abilities or to some specific ones? People with mild mental impairment often possess considerable talent and intelligence if measured by a broad definition of the terms. Does the *process of evolution* (5) mean survival of the physically fit or the perpetuation of culture as we know it? And does *inferior people* (6) mean those with hereditary diseases, the mentally impaired, neurotics, nonconformists, or all of these?

Concerning the Questions Informed Critics Might Raise:

These are the most probable ones: Isn't it possible that forced sterilization might pose even worse dangers to civilization than a reversing of evolution (5)? Might it not lead to totalitarianism? Wouldn't a better and more practical solution (6) be to improve the distribution of wealth among nations, to find cures for disease, to share technology, and to expand educational opportunity (including education in birth control methods)?

Concerning the Kind and Quality of the Evidence:

One significant question about some of the evidence (10, 11) concerns how typical and comprehensive it is. Is the view expressed in the quotations one that is shared by most geneticists and medical authorities, or is it a minority position? An even more important question concerns the evidence that is omitted. Surely psychologists, sociologists, and historians could contribute to this issue. Some of the questions they could answer are these: What psychological effects would forced sterilization have on those subjected to it? A feeling of worthlessness, perhaps, or rage? What social behavior would be likely to result from such effects? Violence? Revolution? What historical precedents are there to help us measure the probable effects?

In light of these considerations, you might conclude that although the world population problem and the related concerns of poverty, illiteracy, and disease are serious and should be addressed, the idea of forced sterilization should be opposed—at least until its advocates clarify their terms and answer the important critical questions. If you were to make a formal response to the argument in an analytical paper or article, you would develop your ideas thoroughly, meeting the same standards you expect of others.

Warm-Up Exercises

1 Make up as many new words—*non*words like *garrumptive*—as you can to reflect people's moods. In each case, indicate the specific mood each word reflects. Be sure to list many possible words before choosing the *best one*.

2 Make up a new name for yourself (both first name and last), one that fits the special qualities you have or are striving for. Be sure to consider unusual names (Honor Trueblood, Rick Decent), and list many possibilities before choosing the best one.

3 Your young nephew is confused. He has learned "He who hesitates is lost" and "Haste makes waste." The sayings seem to oppose each other, and he wants to know which is right. Answer in a way he will understand.

Applications

1 Read the following dialogue carefully. Decide which statements are reasonable and which are not. Provide a brief explanation of why you consider any statement unreasonable.

[Scene: A college dormitory room. A bull session is in progress. George and Ed, freshmen at Proudly Tech, are discussing academic affairs with their sophomore roommate, Jake.]

GEORGE: When I arrived on campus last month, I went to see my adviser to get my freshman English course waived. I didn't get to first base with him. "Everyone takes freshman English," he said. "Everyone!" I'll bet he's got that line taped and just plays it whenever a student raises the question. It really burns me having to take that course. I can see it as a requirement for most students. But I earned straight B's in high school English. Why should I spend more time on that stuff in college?

ED: You're right, George. This place is like home—everybody's on your back making you do things you don't want to do. I should have gone to Bloomville State instead of to this dump.

JAKE: What's so great about Bloomville State?

ED: They let you take whatever courses you want. No required courses at all.

JAKE: Look, my uncle went there after the Vietnam War. He told me a lot about his college days. But he never mentioned that.

ED: It's true. Listen, there was this guy I was talking to at the bar in the train station when I was coming up here. He goes to Bloomville, and he told me they had no required courses.

GEORGE: That really bugs me. Straight B's. And still I've got to take this crappy course. . . .

JAKE: Listen, pal. You're lucky you were born talented in writing. I wish I had that gift. For me, nothing but D's and F's. Hopeless.

ED: Who'd you have for English, Jake?

JAKE: Crawford. An OK guy, I guess, but sort of scholarly. Talks over everybody's head, always quoting some writer or other.

ED: I've got Mr. Schwartz. What's the word on him?

JAKE: Three of my friends had him last year and two got B's and one a B+. A guy who grades like that has got to be a winner.

GEORGE: I'm glad somebody's luck held. Mine certainly didn't. For the two comps I've written so far, I've got a D+ and a C–.

JAKE: Who have you got?

GEORGE: Mr. Stiletto.

JAKE: He wasn't here last year.

GEORGE: I'll bet he's just out of graduate school. Or maybe he never went. At any rate, he sure has it in for me. Maybe he's prejudiced against Germans.

ED: Maybe you picked the wrong side of the issue to write on—you know, the one he disagrees with.

GEORGE: Hey, you may be right. The first topic was birth control, and I'm sure he's Catholic because I saw a little statue of Jesus on his car dashboard when his wife dropped him off outside the building last week. I wrote in favor of abortion. Wow. What a jerk I am. Hey, and come to think of it, that second comp. . . .

JAKE: I should have taken him for comp. I'm Catholic.

GEORGE: That second comp was on civil rights. And I know he's against blacks. The guy who sits next to me is black, and Stiletto really cut him down just because he was late a few times. And there's a black girl he always calls on for the tough questions. No wonder I got a C–.

JAKE: Wait till you guys take psych next year. I don't know if I'll be able to last till the end of the term. It's the boringest subject ever thought up. Professor Clifford walks in, opens his book, and begins reading from his notes in a low mumble: "Mmmm . . . Freud says . . . mmmmmm . . . Oedipus complex . . . repression . . . mmmmm." Deadliest stuff you ever heard. I'm glad I don't need another social science course. Those guys are really out of it.

ED: Doesn't he ever let you discuss what you read?

JAKE: Yeah, once in a while. Yesterday, for example, we were talking about some guy named Frankl, and Clifford said that according to this Frankl, boredom causes people more problems than distress does. Some kids in the class gave examples of how that's so—you know, there are always some guys looking to agree with the prof to make some points. . . .

ED & GEORGE: Yeah.

JAKE: . . . And so I raised my hand and said that that guy Frankl was all wet, that everybody knows that distress causes more problems than boredom. I told him that my own experience proved it because five years ago, when my father lost his job, my family really had to struggle for more than a year. We had problems, believe me, and they weren't caused by *boredom!*

GEORGE: What did he say to that?

JAKE: Well, he mumbled something about Frankl not meaning that. And then he started tossing around a lot of statistics and examples to try to get me confused. He couldn't corner me, though. I finally said, "Frankl's entitled to his opinion; I've got my own."

GEORGE: Hey, that's great. I bet he cursed you out under his breath. You really nailed him.

JAKE: Yeah, I guess I did. When I get mad, I can argue pretty good. Now I've just got to be careful he doesn't take it out on me in my grade.

ED: Say, fellas, I've got to cut out. I'm going to the library and prepare for tomorrow's English class.

GEORGE: What's your assignment?

ED: Oh, a piece by Orwell. We just have to read it and be ready to discuss it. I've read it five times already, but I can't find anything wrong with it, nothing to disagree with. I'll just have to read it again. Be seeing you.

2 Follow the directions for Application 1. In addition, decide what action you would recommend if you were a school board member. Explain why you think that action is best.

[Scene: The Alertia, Indiana, town hall. The members of the Alertia school board are meeting with a group of parents concerned about the school's new sex education program for seventh- and eighth-graders.]

CHAIR: I'd like to welcome the guests of the board to our regular meeting. As you all know, the board agreed to Ms. Jackson's request for an opportunity for those who wished to present their views on the school's new program in sex education. As we know, sex was around for quite a while before this program began, heh, heh. *[Silence]*

MS. SCHULTZ: It's exactly that sort of levity about this dangerous program that worries me.

CHAIR: I'm sorry, Ms. Schultz. I only meant that as a little joke.

MS. SCHULTZ: Well, there's nothing funny about a program that introduces raw sex into the minds of innocent young children.

MS. JACKSON: The reason we asked for this meeting is that we feel that what is taking place in sex education class goes beyond the bounds of decency.

CHAIR: Could you be more specific, please? Just what is taking place?

MS. JACKSON: Someone told me that Ms. Babette encouraged the students to touch each other freely to overcome any inhibitions they might have about sex. Can you deny that such encouragement goes beyond the bounds of decency?

CHAIR: No, I certainly wouldn't deny that. But . . .

MS. BROWN: I heard that last week she asked two students to come to the front of the room and demonstrate what petting means.

MS. GREEN: That doesn't surprise me a bit. She *does* have a sluttish manner, you know. Those miniskirts, that long hair. The way she talks to men is most provocative, positively lewd. If my daughter dressed and acted like that, I'd feel I had failed as a parent.

CHAIR: Ladies, please. We've got to have a little more order. Mr. Lessrow has had his hand up for some time.

MR. LESSROW: Thank you. Of course, I agree with the good ladies who have spoken thus far. But with all respect to them, I think they may be missing the real nature of this threat to the morals of our young people. We must not forget that those young people are the United States citizens of tomorrow. And let me ask you, just who will stand to profit if they are corrupted, if their preoccupation with the flesh stays them from their duties and obligations as citizens? Let me ask . . .

MEMBER 1: Who *will* stand to profit, Mr. Lessrow?

MR. LESSROW: I was getting to that point, sir. Who else but the Muslim extremists?

MEMBER 1: Are you suggesting that the Muslim extremists are in some way responsible for sex education in American schools, for the course in our school?

MR. LESSROW: I am saying precisely that. Sex education is a plot to lure our children into lives of lustful hedonism. It is a plot designed and supported by those who would overthrow our country. All a person needs to do is a little reading, have a little concern for the truth, and not be like these hothouse liberals who believe that the only real enemy is conservatives. The liberals are either misguided dupes of the extremists or willing accomplices.

MEMBER 2: Now that's surely a very extreme interpretation of . . .

MR. LESSROW: It's an extreme plot! Extreme situations demand extreme responses.

MEMBER 2: As I started to say, it's an extreme interpretation of a very complex issue. Surely we should be a little less quick to jump at every wild accusation, be a little more open-minded.

MS. SCHULTZ: A person should be open-minded while searching for the truth but not after finding it.

MS. JACKSON: I just can't understand how people can resist common sense. It should be clear enough to everybody—even to the teachers of this school—that when you bring sex into the classroom, you dignify it. When you encourage the young to talk about it openly in school, they'll talk about it openly out of school. And talking is a very short step away from acting. I for one don't want my teenagers to become promiscuous just because some so-called educators in this town persist in denying the obvious.

MS. OVERLOOK: I don't see the need for a sex education course in the first place. Surely, if parents know enough to raise their children in other respects, they are qualified to teach them about sex. Sex is a moral matter—and the school has no business butting into the moral upbringing of the young. The school should stick to the three R's and leave moral and spiritual matters to the home and church.

MS. SCHULTZ: If the school were as anxious to guard the innocence of the young as it is to fill their heads with sex ideas, perhaps our society wouldn't be slipping so badly today.

MEMBER 2: I'd like to go back to something Ms. Jackson said a few minutes ago about promiscuity. Ms. Jackson, no one wants to make teenagers promiscuous. The whole effect of the program in sex education, as I understand it, may be to prevent just that development. There is a great deal of emphasis on sex in advertising today and an increasing tendency toward frankness in the arts. The board had only a brief explanation of the objectives and approaches of this course, but we were told by the principal that the faculty committee that developed the course consulted numerous statistical studies, and every one showed that most young people receive very little direct, honest, and accurate information about sex. Despite appearances, he said, they're woefully ignorant, in many cases, about the facts of life. That is what the course and its teacher, Ms. Babette, are trying to overcome: misinformation and ignorance.

MS. GREEN: *[Turning to Ms. Brown and whispering]* It's obvious why he speaks that way. I've seen the way he looks at Ms. Babette. Those bachelors and their filthy minds.

MS. SCHULTZ: A course in sex education is a strange way of decreasing promiscuity. Why is it that since courses like this have been added to curricula around the country, the incidence of rape, out-of-wedlock pregnancy, and venereal disease has risen so dramatically?

MEMBER 2: I'm not sure I understand the point you are making. Are you suggesting that . . .

MS. SCHULTZ: I'm suggesting that I'm in favor of ridding our society of its preoccupation with sex. I confess I don't know quite how to do that. But I do know where to start. Right here in Alertia—by ridding our school of that course.

MR. LESSROW: *[Applauding vigorously]* My sentiments exactly. If we're not going to defeat our country's enemies, including those in Washington, at least we can stop their insidious campaign against our youth at home. I voted for you for the school board—probably most of us in this room did. We had confidence in your ability to act wisely, to do the right thing. You now know the facts in this matter. It's time to act on them. You can justify our confidence in you by demanding that that course be discontinued immediately.

CHAIR: *[After a minute or two of silence]* Well, I believe the board has a good idea of the nature of your concern about this course. If there are no more comments at this time, I'd like to thank you ladies and gentlemen for coming out tonight and to assure you that we will give your position our careful consideration. If the board members will remain, we'll continue with our meeting in a few minutes.

3 Evaluate the argument in the following letter to the editor, using the approach explained in this chapter. State your judgment and support it thoroughly.

Dear Editor:
I enjoyed your recent series of articles on religious views. I believe religious values occupy the central place in one's being. Today an increasing number of young people are giving up their religion because of the vocal skepticism of those who find religious values too restrictive. If more of us who do believe were as vocal, the young would surely see the relevance of religion and not be so easily deceived by those who wish to mislead them.

It is fashionable today among so-called humanists to place people's reason above religious faith. They say a person must follow his or her own lights, affirm what he or she believes is true. But are they really so open-minded and humble as that view makes them seem? I think not. For underneath that view lies the fact that they exalt their own judgment. When they accept the word of an authority, it is only because they agree with that authority. And they do not accept one authority without, by that very acceptance, rejecting other authorities. In short, they are superegotists who refuse to accept what transcends their understanding and who try to fit God into their understanding. Their efforts are in vain, for God will not fit into the finite mind. A god who can be understood by human beings is no god at all, but a poor imitation.

I do not believe that any intelligent, honest person can place his or her confidence in human intelligence and reason. Human learning is too sparse and fragmentary to warrant such trust. Human knowledge and understanding change all too quickly. Yesterday's theories gather dust in the attics of libraries, and history judges all things mercilessly. But the Bible, God's own word, remains. It stands as an immutable beacon to all who love the truth. One need only put aside his or her probing and questioning and doubting, become like the little children, and accept it.

Sincerely yours,

Mrs. Joan Truly

4 The following letter appeared in the *New York Times Magazine*.[8] Evaluate the argument it presents by using the approach explained in the chapter. State your judgment and support it thoroughly.

To the Editor:

As a man whose past is considerably peppered with the buckshot of imprisonment including four years at Attica prison, I am in a position to state that William R. Coons's article, "An Attica Graduate Tells His Story" (Oct. 10), is equipped with built-in blinders. The reader can look in only one direction: at the brutal guards, the butcher doctors, the unfeeling, unconscionable warden, etc. A cartoon, therefore, forms in the mind of the reader. He sees a huge, hairy monster, frothing fangs bared, labeled "Penal System" and crushing the life out of a ragged, pity-evoking figure labeled "Defenseless Convict."

I wonder why Mr. Coons omitted the worst handicap facing the inmate who is sincerely interested in rehabilitation—his own "brothers" in gray?

Contrary to what Mr. Coons would have the reader believe, prison populations are not made up solely of misunderstood, slightly tarnished angels unjustly sentenced to hundreds of years for merely stealing wormy apples.

Many—let me lean on that word—many convicts are incorrigible scum whose sole purpose in life closely parallels that of a demented crocodile. They wouldn't lead an honest life if guaranteed a thousand dollars per week and half of God's throne in the hereafter.

They are the ones who steal from their fellow inmates, who collect "protection money" from the weak and frightened, who force others with "shanks" pressed to their throats to commit homosexual acts, whose roaring animal voices fill the cell blocks until your brains vibrate from the obscene cacophony and you couldn't write your own name without misspelling it. They are the ones who will grip prison reform by the throat and choke it, exploit it, mangle and tramp on it until, in disgust, the administration rescinds it.

The first step toward lasting prison reform is to collect all the incorrigible scum, the human cockroaches who infest prison-populations, and place them in separate institutions. Let them prey on each other. Let them, if it comes to it, kill each other off . . . incurable cancers devouring each other.

Unless this step is taken, prison reform, however great and shining, will fade into the limbo of things that might have worked.

Name Withheld

ISSUE FOR EXTENDED ANALYSIS

Following is a more comprehensive thinking challenge than the others in the chapter.

THE ISSUE: THE IRAQ WAR

The central question about the Iraq war is "Was it *just*—that is, justified?" As George Weigel points out, classical just-war theory has six requirements. In question form, they might be expressed thus: *Is the cause for going to war just? Are the stated intentions for going to war defensible? Do the leaders of the nation going to war have the authority to do so? Is there a reasonable chance for the war effort to be successful? Will the good that the war accomplishes outweigh the harm that it does? Have less drastic means of achieving the desired outcome been exhausted? (In other words, does the particular war in question represent the last resort?)*

THE ESSAYS

The Iraq War Was Just
By Pedro Blanco

The infamous attack on "nine-eleven" took 3,000 innocent lives, and that alone was sufficient reason for the U.S. to go to war. True, the perpetrators wore no uniforms and carried no country's flag; they were, instead, a group of international thugs who sought sanctuary in various countries. But these facts in no way diminished the horror and injustice of their actions.

The Bush administration repeatedly tried to get international support,

The Iraq War Was Unjust
By Wendy Walker

All war is a failure or an abandonment of reason and is therefore an inappropriate response to difficulties between nations. Since violence can never be the solution to violence, all war must be considered evil. Some philosophers claim that, in rare circumstances, this form of evil may be unavoidable. The Iraq War, however, does not fall into this category because, to put it simply, there was nothing "just" about it.

both through the U.N. and through direct diplomacy with other nations, for the Iraq War. Some large and influential nations refused to support the war because, as was later revealed, they were profiteering from the Oil for Food program. And the U.N. had warned Iraq several times that noncompliance with its directives could have dire consequences. All the U.S. did was to carry out the threat that the U.N. was unwilling to carry out. And more than twenty other nations joined the U.S.

The main reason for singling out Iraq was the threat of Weapons of Mass Destruction (WMD). For a decade virtually all U.S. officials, including those in the Clinton administration, were convinced Saddam had WMD, and with good reasons—he had used them against his own citizens and most intelligence showed that he still had a huge stockpile. The fact that WMD could not be found after the war does not prove they didn't exist; Saddam could easily have sent them to Syria. In any case, the U.S. decision to go to war was made in good faith and on the best available intelligence. And it freed millions of people from tyranny.

Most important, the war was conducted so as to minimize harm to civilians. For the first time in military history, pinpoint bombing was used, and wherever possible, Iraq's infrastructure was spared. Finally, when Saddam was ousted, the U.S. did not attempt to colonize Iraq but helped the Iraqi people establish a democratic government. For all these reasons, and by any fair measure, the Iraq war was just.

To begin with, there was no provocation for the U.S. to invade Iraq. True, the attack on "9/11" claimed 3,000 innocent lives, but that outrage was perpetrated by a group of terrorists that, though they had bases in several nations, were formally aligned with none. There was never any proof that the terrorists acted on behalf of the nation of Iraq or, for that matter, that they had any more support for the attack from Iraq than from any other nation. Given that all of the terrorists on 9/11 were Saudis, a better case could have been made for a U.S. attack on Saudi Arabia.

Second, the Iraq War was not a "last resort," decided upon after all diplomatic avenues had been exhausted. It was a *first* resort. Moreover, the Bush administration did not bother to get either the support of the United Nations or the (required) consent of Congress. Instead, the administration acted hastily, recklessly, and unilaterally.

A third reason for considering the Iraq War unjust is that it was conducted inhumanely. Not only were hundreds of noncombatants killed, but prisoners were detained without the filing of formal charges and without benefit of legal counsel. Worse, there were credible charges of torture at the Guantanamo Bay prison camp and humiliation and sexual mistreatment at Abu Ghraib. (Disgusting photos documenting the latter abuse were circulated in the world press.)

Far from being a just war, the Iraq War was a stain on our national character.

Class Discussion

NICK: There's no such thing as a just war because all war violates the ethical requirement of loving our neighbors and treating them with kindness. The "just war" theory is simply a clever way of defending the indefensible.

MARGARET: War exists because human nature is flawed—that is, because people *and nations* don't always behave as they should. Whenever the leaders of one nation commit atrocities against their own people or acts of aggression against weaker nations, it is not only right and proper but also neighborly for other nations to wage war against the offenders.

AGNES: I believe the just war criteria need to be revised to cover the new forms of aggression that have arisen in recent decades. The aggressors no longer wear uniforms or represent specific countries. They don't march in columns or attack others openly but, rather, work to conduct their operations secretly. They rely on terror and make no distinction between enemy soldiers and innocent people. The kind of war they are waging calls for different kinds of responses.

NATHAN: I agree that the strong have an obligation to protect the weak and defenseless. But they can't just rush off to war willy-nilly the way the U.S. did in Iraq. They have to gain the cooperation of other nations.

MARGARET: The idea that the president made no effort to get the cooperation of other nations is false. He not only made efforts; he also got the support of more than 20 other nations. The only reason he failed to get the U.N. support for the war is that the representatives of some key nations were taking bribes from Saddam.

NATHAN: What about all the ballyhoo about WMD? The administration knew there were no such weapons—they manufactured the idea as an excuse to attack.

MARGARET: The term "Monday morning quarterback" fits Iraq war critics perfectly. They can tell you exactly how any "game" should have been played *after the game has been played.* It's easy to say the Bush administration should have known there were no WMD, but given the circumstances of the time, there was no way anyone could have known. Furthermore, to say the Bush administration manufactured the idea of WMD is irresponsible. Well before Bush came to office, President Clinton and virtually all other leaders of both political parties believed WMD existed.

Notes

1. Mursell, *Using Your Mind Effectively*, p. 217.
2. James Harvey Robinson, *The Mind in the Making* (New York: Harper & Brothers, 1921), p. 46.
3. Larry Elder, *The Ten Things You Can't Say in America* (New York: St. Martin's Press, 2000), pp. 44–45.
4. Peggy Rosenthal, *Words and Values: Some Leading Words and Where They Lead Us* (New York: Oxford University Press, 1984), p. 21.
5. Ibid., p. 22. Carl Rogers's sentence is as follows: "When the self is free from any threat of attack ... then it is possible for the self to consider these hitherto rejected perceptions, to make new differentiations, and to reintegrate the self in such a way as to include them."
6. "Photo of Dinosaur Needs Some Help," *Oneonta Star*, 29 December 1981, p. 2.
7. *Time*, 25 January 1982, p. 31.
8. *New York Times Magazine*, 7 November 1971, p. 30. © 1971 by the New York Times Company. Reprinted by permission.

The Basics

Issue, Conclusion, and Reason

REASONS IN STRICT ARGUMENTS

When critical thinkers hear a claim, the next move they make is to ask *why* they should believe that claim. For example:

> Claim: You should try to drive at or below 55 m.p.h.
> Critical thinker's question: Why?
> Reason offered: Statistics show that there are fewer fatalities when people drive at or below this speed.

That is an argument in the strict sense. The claim is supported by a reason. It's the bare bones of a strict argument, and it's just one point of view on the subject. The reason may not even be true. But still, it is an argument. Here is "argue" as it appears in both loose and strict cases:

> Loose case: Fritz argued that you should try to drive at or below 55 m.p.h.
> Strict case: Martina argued that you should try not to drive over 55 m.p.h., **because** statistics show that when people drive at or below that speed, fewer deaths occur.

The *issue* Fritz is arguing is whether you should drive at or below 55 m.p.h. Fritz *concluded* that you should not drive over 55 m.p.h. He gave no reason for his claim. Therefore it is a loose argument, a claim without a reason.

Loose arguments are perfectly acceptable and are made all the time (for instance, right now!). You need only recognize them as such so that you can go on to ask whether they require supportive reasons. Most of the time they do.

Martina argued that you should try not to drive over 55 m.p.h., because statistics show that when people drive at or below that speed, fewer deaths occur.

The *issue* she argued is whether you should try not to drive over 55 m.p.h. She argued for the *conclusion* that you should try not to drive over 55 m.p.h. The *reason* that she gave in support of her conclusion *is that* statistics show that when people drive at or below 55 m.p.h., fewer deaths occur. A reason, be it that of Martina or anyone else, is a claim presented to defend or to justify a belief in a conclusion.

If the notions of issue, conclusion, and reason are still fuzzy, the rest of this chapter is calculated to set you straight. If, on the other hand, you feel confident about these features, skip to the exercises at the end of the chapter and try your skill.

FOR THE ISSUE, THINK "WHETHER"

A crucial ingredient in paying close attention to an argument is trying to figure out what question is being talked about. This is the issue, which permits alternative conclusions and is best approached by thinking "whether." The following are some common phrases:

> The author **deals with the issue whether . . .**
> She **raised the question whether . . .**
> The **issue under discussion is whether . . .**

Everyone can find the issue in life-and-death matters. If someone were to walk into the room where you are now sitting and say, "Smoke is filling up the building," you would probably respond with something like, "What? Is there a fire?" You instantly seek out the significant question for you, namely, whether there is a fire and not just a hundred people smoking cigarettes, which may be the issue in the other person's mind. At the same time you are demanding to hear his conclusion ("Yes, there is a fire" or "No, there's no fire"). You thus make sure—before you run out of the building yelling—that you are not confusing your interpretation of the issue with the one the bearer of bad tidings has in mind. Better that both of you should run out of the building yelling!

It is in less than life-and-death matters that we should cultivate this same spirited interest. One very handy way of locating the issue is to say to yourself, "The issue is whether," and then fill in the ending with the author's or speaker's conclusion. Note that the issue is more precise than the topic, which is a word or phrase that is not in the form of a question. In the previous example the topic would be "smoke" or "smoky buildings," which is not helpful in arriving at any decision. In contrast, the issue you raised was whether there is a fire (another helpful issue might have been the factual question whether smoke was filling up the building).

Sometimes an author will come right out and tell us, "The question I'm going to address is whether abortion is right or wrong." Or, "at issue is whether there is better evidence for drinking coffee than tea." In other cases an author can rightly assume that we'll figure out what the issue is about without being told outright. When the argument is short, the presumption is that we can easily see what it's about; when the argument is long, say in a book or article, the issue is usually part of the title. Take for example, *Do Trees Have Standing?,* a clever title announcing the issue whether we have a moral obligation to forests. Whenever the argument is long and the issue is not part of the title, however, the author should come right out and say "**The issue is.**" Wherever the issue is found, in the title or in the body of the argument, it can always be found *embedded* in the conclusion, whether written or spoken. So it does not matter that you rarely find titles like *The Question Whether Abortion Is Right or Wrong,* but titles like *Abortion: Scourge of Society* or *Abortion: Every Woman's Right.* Both of these titles state conclusions, which happen to be opposed to each other.

Let's look at some further examples of conclusions; then I can show you an easy way to get at the issue when it's not stated outright.

HOW TO FIND THE CONCLUSION

The conclusion is the *decision* that the thinker has made about an issue. Unlike the issue, the conclusion of an argument is usually stated outright. It is often preceded by words just meant to let us know that this claim is the conclusion, the main point the person has been driving at. When, near the end of the argument, the author says, "In conclusion," or "In sum," or "Therefore," it is tantamount to saying, "This is that major idea that I, the author or speaker, want you to believe." A conclusion word is almost mandatory in a good argument, if that argument is longer than a paragraph. The most popular word used to indicate a conclusion is "therefore." Other words that may show a conclusion are "in sum" and "so." Here is an example for each of them:

> The weatherman said on the news this morning that it's going to rain today. In fact, when I walked outside I noticed that it was clouding up. **Therefore,** I'd better go back and get my umbrella.
>
> The critical thinking instructor is notorious for giving tough quizzes. **So** I should spend all day Saturday studying.
>
> The roof leaks, the floors are warped, the drains are clogged, the foundation is full of termites. **In sum,** this house needs a lot of work.

To get at the exact issue for these brief arguments, all you need do is substitute the word "whether" for the conclusion words.

> *Issue 1:* **whether** I'd better go back and get my umbrella
> Conclusion: Yes, I'd better go back and get my umbrella.
> *Issue 2:* **whether** I'd better spend all day Saturday studying
> Conclusion: Yes, I'd better.
> *Issue 3:* **whether** this house needs a lot of work
> Conclusion: Yes.

You can see by these examples how closely bound the issue and the conclusion are. Many people have a relatively easy time spotting conclusions, but it's harder for them to pull out the exact issue. This trick of exchanging the conclusion word for "whether" may help you to get started.

Perhaps you are wondering why you should bother pulling out issues when authors and people living their ordinary lives often don't. That's an excellent critical question! Compare seeing arguments in a "whether" vein with the notion of "maybe . . . and maybe not":

> **One could argue that** it is crucial for a critical thinker to start out by considering an argument in a balanced, "maybe . . . maybe not" stance. Digging the issue out of an argument brings alternative conclusions to the critical thinker's awareness. For instance, once a person becomes aware that an argument is about "**whether** I'd better spend all day Saturday studying," he or she is closer to the balanced start of "maybe I should study all day, but maybe I shouldn't," rather than being swayed too readily by the conclusion of the argument at hand to study all day. **Therefore,** extracting the issue from the argument is an important part of critical thinking.

Do you see the connection? If not, you're welcome to take issue with the argument.

Conclusions at the Beginning

We're not out of the woods with conclusions yet. Conclusions almost always begin with words like "therefore" and "so" when they occur at the end of an argument. But were you aware that the conclusion of an argument often occurs right at the *start*? When it does, there is no telltale word. Imagine starting an essay with "therefore"! Here is a typical example of an argument that starts with its conclusion:

> Eating crackers in bed is a bad idea. First of all, you probably don't need the calories. Moreover, when you turn out the light and lie down, there are all these sharp crumbs that attack you. Then, you have to get up, stumble around in the dark, find the light switch, and either sweep them onto the floor—which is messy—or locate and use a whisk broom and dustpan—which is tedious.

The ideas which follow the opening sentence are all reasons supporting the conclusion that eating crackers in bed is a bad idea. One way to see whether the first statement of any argument is the conclusion is by putting it at the end of the argument, preceded by "therefore," and seeing if that makes sense:

> Eating crackers in bed is a bad idea. First of all, you probably don't need the calories. Moreover, when you turn out the light and lie down, there are all these sharp crumbs that attack you. Then, you have to get up, stumble around in the dark, find the light switch, and either sweep them onto the floor (messy) or get and use a whisk broom and dustpan (tedious). *Therefore, eating crackers in bed is a bad idea.*

And it fits the sense of the argument. Notice what happens if you try this "therefore" test with one of the earlier arguments:

> The weatherman said on the news this morning that it's going to rain today. In fact, when I walked outside I noticed that it was clouding up. I'd better go back and get my umbrella. *Therefore the weatherman said on the news this morning that it's going to rain.*

It doesn't make sense. The weatherman doesn't say it's going to rain because I'd better go and get my umbrella. Only a megalomaniac would think so. That first sentence isn't the conclusion of this argument.

Try your new techniques on Mario's argument, next. Find the sentence you believe to be the conclusion, "test" it if you need to by putting it at the end with "therefore," then see if you can pull out the issue using the term "whether":

> I really deserve to go to the movies tonight. I did several loads of wash (even studying while I was at the laundromat), went to class, and worked all afternoon. (Therefore, ______________.)
>
> Mario's conclusion is that ______________.
>
> His reason is that ______________.
>
> Mario's issue is whether ______________.

The conclusion is almost always found at the very beginning or the end of an argument. In the clearest longer arguments it is found in both places.

VISUALIZE A STRUCTURE

Keep in mind that the basic structure of all arguments great and small is the same. The main issue is brought to a conclusion, with at least one reason to support that conclusion. This structure is really quite simple, and we're using it all the time (Figure 1).

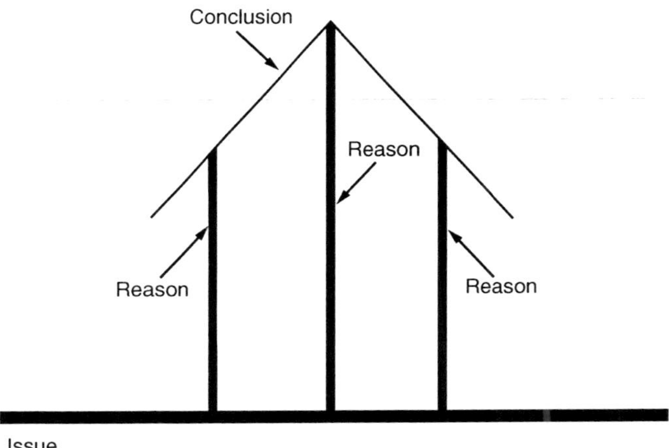

Figure 1 The Structure of an Argument

The house is not a universal symbol for arguments, but it does provide a way to visualize them. Some form of schematization helps you to see the argument more clearly. This visual analogy is full of helpful figures of speech: A house is called a "structure"; we often refer to well-structured and well-supported arguments. Both houses and arguments can "collapse." It's not good for arguments or houses to "shift" without due notice. Finally, both need to "rest on solid ground."

But why visualize arguments as structures in the first place? If you can readily locate the structure when reading most arguments, by all means don't bother with the visualizations. However, novice critical thinkers are in the habit of seeing the claims in an argument as separate pieces of lumber lying about rather than as parts of a whole. Or they will read an argument the way one should read a story ("this was said, and then this, and then that"). They thus give each sentence equal importance and often fail to see that certain types of sentences are always going to be more important than others. To overcome this "line-by-line" habit, *think of yourself as always on a mission in search of the issue, conclusion, and reasons.* If you have to reconstruct the major features of an argument in a visual form, you will be forced to literally see the reasons supporting the conclusion, the way posts hold up the roof of a house.

Let's try this with some day-to-day examples:

Annie: Do we need to go to the market this afternoon?
Bruno: No.
Annie: Why not?
Bruno: We have enough food to last until tomorrow.

The visual structure of this discussion is shown in Figure 2; the verbal structure is as follows:

> Annie: Do we need to buy food this afternoon? (*The issue* here is whether Annie and Bruno need to go to the market this afternoon.)
>
> Bruno: No (*Bruno's conclusion*). We have enough food to last until tomorrow (Bruno's reason for claiming that they don't need to go to the market).

Annie raised the issue in this case, and Bruno made the argument. Let's continue the dialogue. Can you spot the issue, conclusion, and reason or reasons?

> Bruno: Well, Annie, do you think we need to go to the market this afternoon?
>
> Annie: No. I'd like to take you out to dinner tonight. Besides, we can always borrow whatever we want from the people next door.

Bruno raised the same issue, and Annie came to the same conclusion that he did (no, we don't need to go to the market); but Annie gave different reasons to support her conclusion. So Annie made a different argument:

> Issue: Do Bruno and Annie need to buy food?
>
> Annie's conclusion: No.
>
> Annie's reasons: (1) She wants to take Bruno to dinner; (2) they can borrow whatever they need from the neighbors.

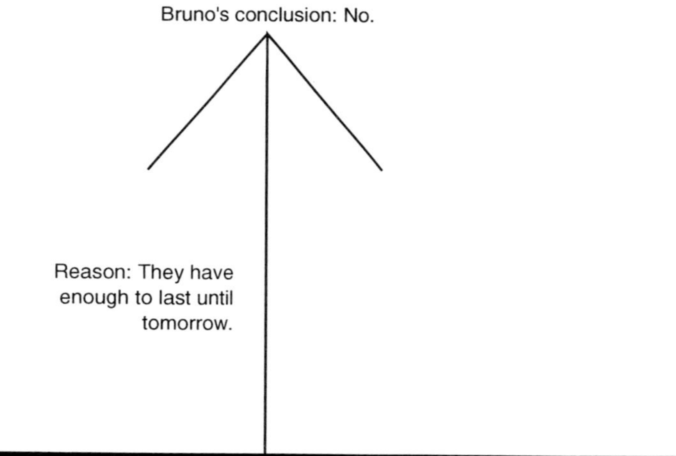

Figure 2 Bruno's Argument

Figure 3 is a visual comparison of Annie's and Bruno's arguments. Notice that since the issue of the arguments is the same, the houses are both on the same "block." In fact, thinking of different arguments on a subject as being like different houses on a block isn't a bad way to imagine arguments.

Of course, arguing doesn't require two people. One can make an entire argument to oneself, as often happens. Ask yourself whether you need to go to the market today, make a decision (your conclusion), and notice your reasons for deciding the way you did:

Issue: Do I need to go to the market today?
Your conclusion: ______________________________.
Your reason(s): ______________________________.

Next, draw a structure to represent your argument.

If you live a simple life, your conclusion was probably a straightforward yes or no, with one or two reasons. But what if you're not sure, or you think that maybe you'll need to go? Then "not sure" or "maybe" are your conclusions.

Here's an example of a person suffering through life's little aggravations. Hal is really not sure whether he should bother to go to the market, because he can't remember what's in his refrigerator. Then those are his conclusion and reason:

Hal's issue: Do I need to go to the market today?
Hal's conclusion: I'm not sure.
Hal's reason: I can't remember what's in my refrigerator.

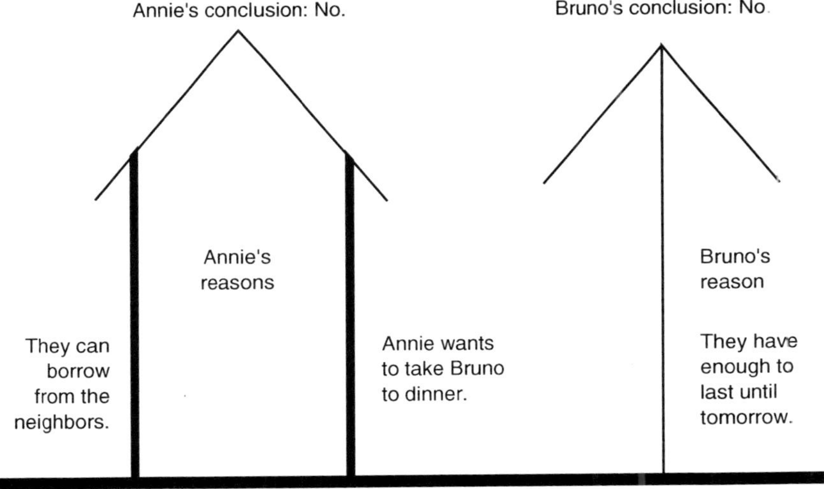

Figure 3 Annie's and Bruno's Arguments

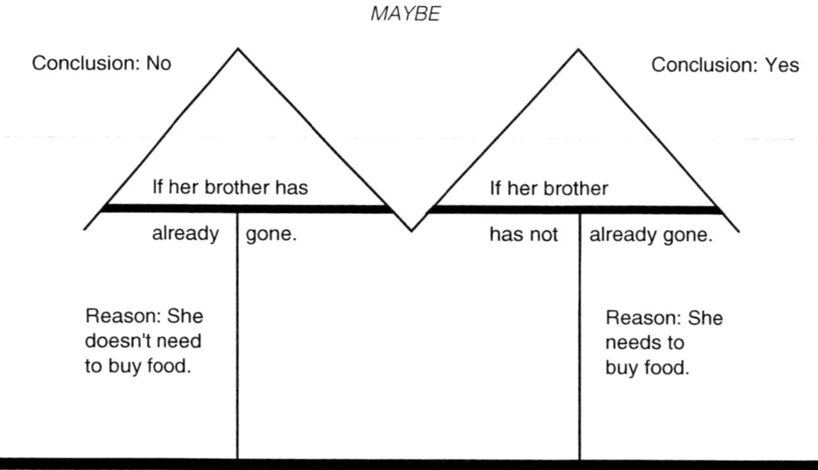

Figure 4 Agnes's Argument

People make literally thousands of arguments every day on the question of whether to go to the market. Here is an example of one of a myriad of "maybe" answers:

> Agnes: Let's see . . . do I need to stop by the market today?
> Agnes's conclusion: Maybe.
> Agnes's reasons: If my brother has already gone to the market, then I don't need to go, because he will buy whatever we need. If he hasn't gone yet, then I do need to go.

Agnes has come to a "double" conclusion (maybe yes, maybe no); she has one reason for going and another for not going, but she needs to know an additional fact before making her final decision. What is that fact?

She needs to know whether her brother has gone to the market already. Her decision **hinges on that fact.** Agnes's needed fact can be visualized as a beam in the ceiling of the argument structure (see Figure 4).

DO THE REASONS MAKE SENSE AS REASONS?

It's easy to get careless and just slap down some statement as the reason because it could be a reason in some argument. That won't work here. You have to take a few minutes to think about whether that statement you're writing down is the reason being offered *in the argument at hand.* Think of statements as analogous to pieces of lumber. Just as a board can be made a part of the wall or part of the ceiling, so a statement can be a reason or a conclusion. It depends on what the builder (arguer) decides to do with it.

You might want to say out loud, "The author concludes that . . . because," and see if what you've come up with makes any sense. If it doesn't, out of charity assume first that it may be your fault and look very carefully. Only then can you start wondering about the arguer's carefulness or sanity.

The following is an issue that most of us have to face. Al, the owner of a car 50,000 miles old, inspects the beloved object:

> Gee, I think I'd better get new tires for my car. With these threadbare tires I'm afraid I'll have a blowout on the freeway.

See if you can identify the issue, conclusion, and reason given by the car owner. Diagram the structure first, then analyze the language.

Al's issue is whether ________________________________.
His conclusion is ____________________________________.
His reasons are that _________________________________.

If you determined that the issue is whether Al should get new tires and his conclusion was yes; and if you wrote that his reason was that he's afraid that with his threadbare tires he'll have a blowout on the freeway, you've done well. If you decided that he gave two reasons, that his tires were threadbare and that he was afraid that he'd have a blowout, that's even better. But if you got it wrong, let's figure out how you can avoid the mistake in the future.

What, for example, if you had this:

> Al's issue: Whether with his threadbare tires he'll have a blowout on the freeway.
> Al's conclusion: Yes.
> Al's reason is that he thinks he'd better get new tires for his car.

Would Al have a blowout because he thinks he'd better get new tires? That would be a cosmic injustice to careful car owners; that's not Al's reasoning. You have to spend a couple of minutes pondering whether the reason makes sense. Say to yourself "Is that *really* the reason?" Most people who misidentify the reason just haven't stopped long enough to think it through.

BOOK TITLES AS CONCLUSIONS

Book titles offer the first clues about what a book will argue. The title of a book or article may give just the general topic, as opposed to specifying an issue within that topic. Let's inspect a few topic titles. Take, for example, a book entitled *Execution.* Notice that the issue is not clear: Is it a book about the incidence of execution, its rightfulness or wrongfulness, an evaluation of state-approved or gangland-style, or some bizarre how-to book? We'd have to look at the table of contents to see. Other topic titles: *On History, The Germans.* Here again, while the titles tell us the overall topic, we have no idea what the authors are concluding about history or about the Germans. For a precise issue, we must dig out an author's main conclusion and then place "whether" in front. In a well-written book, we need not dig deeply.

Often the title of a book or article contains the author's overall conclusion. When you pull the issues out of these title-conclusions it helps you to see that conclusions other than the ones the authors suggest are quite possible. Consider these examples: *You Can't Spoil Your Baby; I'm O.K.—You're O.K.; India: A Wounded Civilization; The Disappearance of Childhood; Winning Through Intimidation;* or *The Criminal as Victim.*

In these cases we know what the authors have concluded, but not why they have done so. From the last title we can infer that the author has concluded that the criminal is a victim, whereby we can helpfully turn this around to the issue of whether the criminal is a victim. But we don't yet know the author's argument. Why is the criminal a victim? Will the argument be that it's because of the criminal's environment or genetic makeup or some other cause? The answer to that question will have to come as a result of browsing through the book or reading it.

WRITING ABOUT SEVERAL RELATED ISSUES

Start to familiarize yourself with the following phrases for the main issue in complex arguments:

> **The central question** that must now be asked is . . .
> In my opinion, **the foremost issue is . . .**
> The **fundamental problem** that we must first solve is . . .

Once the main issue has been discussed, the reader must somehow be alerted that a second issue is going to be raised. For the issue that's second in importance (or for the one that is dealt with next), a paragraph could begin with the following:

> There is **a second problem.**
> **Subordinate to** this **main issue is the question whether . . .**

Each time the issue changes, the reader should be alerted:

> There is still **a third difficulty.**
> Of **further** importance is the **question whether . . .**

SOME DISTINCTIONS

Arguments involve decisions of two sorts: what to do and what to think. The examples in this chapter have been about what to do in day-to-day life, as opposed to what to think. Obviously, there is considerable overlap between what one does and what one thinks, but the general distinction is useful. Some students have trouble with arguments about what to think. If you are one of them, review the first part of this chapter, keeping in mind that the structure is the same in both types of argument.

Another distinction regarding arguments is between those that make claims about what *is* the case and those that make claims about what *should be* the case. While there are a few examples of purely factual or purely directive arguments, much argumentation that at first seems purely factual is actually directive as well. Does this chapter, for example, argue (in the loose sense) about what the basic features of formal argument are, or does it direct you on what they should be? Both, actually.

SUMMARY

There are three basic features of argumentation in the strict sense: An issue is brought to a conclusion with the support of at least one reason. These basic features may appear anywhere in an argument. Therefore the critical thinker must actively seek them out by asking questions.

> What is the author trying to have me think or do? That is, what is the author's conclusion? Tip-off terms may occur at the end of the paragraph: "therefore," "in conclusion," "to summarize." If not, the conclusion may well be at the beginning.
>
> What is the exact issue? Try replacing the "therefore" word with "whether."
>
> What are the reasons? If the word "reason" doesn't appear, look for "because"; whatever occurs after that word is a reason. See if it makes sense as a reason that supports the conclusion.
>
> If you can't find these telltale terms, and you know that the author is driving home a point, see if any of these synonyms is doing the work:

Therefore	**Because**
in short	since
so	for (before a clause)
it follows that	for the reason that
it is believed that	the source is
shows that	
indicates that	
proves that	
we may conclude that	
necessitates	

Don't forget to check for the conclusion at the beginning.

EXERCISES

1. The following are brief arguments about human nature expressed clearly and cleverly. Whether you agree or disagree, you might become intrigued by them.

   a. People often think they are in love when they are not: The excitement of an intrigue, the emotional flutter of gallantry, natural delight in being loved, and the difficulty of saying no, all these conspire to persuade them that they are feeling passionate when they are merely being flirtatious.[1]

      1. Diagram the structure.
      2. Analyze the language.

      The issue here is whether ______________________.
      The author concludes that ______________________.
      His reasons for making this argument are ______________________
      ______________________.

      The issue is whether people often wrongly think they are in love. **The author concludes that this is the case. His reasons are that** people confuse the excitement of an intrigue, the emotional flutter of gallantry, natural delight in being loved, and the difficulty of saying no for being in love (feeling passionate).

      The language of your analysis doubtless varied somewhat from that above. Don't be concerned, as long as you have stated your answers in complete, grammatical sentences and have used "issue," "reason," and "conclusion" for the correct ideas. Study the phrasing that is in boldface, however. Repeat it a number of times, and think about copying it in your essays to expand your repertoire of critical thinking phrases. You might even copy the language used in the foregoing example when writing out the exercise which follows.

   b. People hate injustice, not because it is inherently wrong, but because of the harm it does them.[2]

      1. Diagram the structure.
      2. Analyze the language. Provide a description of the basics, being careful to use the language of argument exemplified in boldface type. When you give the reason, be sure to say, "The reason is **that.**" Never write, "The reason is because"; it is redundant.

      It would be all right to ignore the statement, "It [injustice] is inherently wrong." You could also draw a falling wall-beam (a negation symbol is printed over it) to indicate that the author alleges that it is *not* the reason that people hate injustice (see Figure 5).

      Just be certain that you did not put down, "Injustice is inherently wrong" as the *author's* reason, even though it might be your reason and might be true. One of the most important tasks is to separate your opinion from that of the person who is presenting an argument.

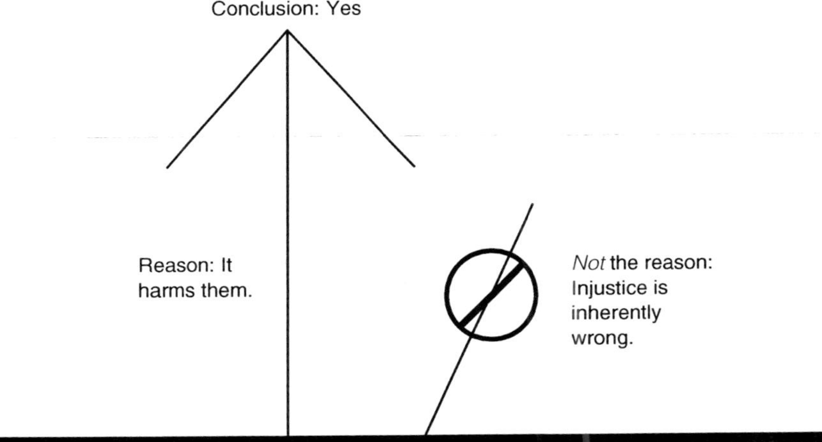

Figure 5 Identify What Is Not the Author's Reason

c. One of the most important things you must do as a critical thinker is to be aware of how your opinion differs from that of the person who is presenting you an argument. Otherwise, you will not learn this new opinion.

1. Diagram the structure.
2. Analyze the language.

The writer proposes the issue whether one of the most important things that you must do as a critical thinker is to distinguish your opinion from that of the person who is presenting an argument, **concluding that** this is the case, and **giving the reason that** otherwise you will not learn this new opinion. Notice that even though the reason contains a "not," it still is the author's reason, unlike the "injustice" example before it, in which the author was telling something that was *not* his reason.

Rule: If the word "not" goes in front of the word "because" or "reason," then it's not the reason. Otherwise, it is the reason. For example: He rewrote his essay not because he had to, but because he did not want to turn in shoddy work ("because he did not want to turn in shoddy work" being the reason argued). Mull over this distinction until it makes sense to you.

d. When we have grown tired of loving, we are delighted at the other's unfaithfulness, for that releases us from having to be faithful.[3]

Hint: Watch the issue. Don't make it broader than the arguer does.

1. Diagram the structure.
2. Analyze the language.

The issue under discussion is whether we are delighted at the other's unfaithfulness when we have grown tired of loving. **The author concludes in the affirmative, reasoning that** it releases us from having to be faithful. Your statement of the author's issue must include "when we have grown tired of loving." Otherwise you are stating that the author is claiming that we generally delight in others' unfaithfulness to us. The author has, however, **qualified his statement.**

2. You're on your own! Identify the issue, reason, and conclusion, using the pictorial structure if it helps.
   a. We should not take offense when people hide the truth from us, since so often we hide it from ourselves.[4]

      1. Diagram the structure.

      2. Analyze the language.
      The issue at hand is whether _____.
      The author concludes that _____.
      The reason offered is that _____.

   b. Little is needed to make a wise man happy, but nothing can content a fool. That is why nearly all men are miserable.[5]
   c. I don't trust him. We're friends.[6]

      Is this last example a strict argument or just two factual claims side by side? Why?

3. Which of the following are loose arguments; which are strict?
   a. I saw him tiptoe across the lawn and steal softly into the house. It was broad daylight.
   b. Since I'm not in the business of giving advice, I refused to tell him which career to choose.
   c. When the stock market is down, buy more stock. When it's up, sell.
   d. Thinking about how to spend your time most efficiently is of vital importance.
   e. Thinking about how to spend your time most efficiently is of vital importance, because that's the only way you'll accomplish your major goals in life.

      Answers: a. two loose arguments (just two claims, one not the reason for the other); b. strict argument; c. two loose arguments; d. loose argument; e. strict argument

4. What are the issue, conclusion, and reason(s) in the following two arguments?
   a. Should there be a law requiring motorcyclists to wear helmets? Many motorcyclists would argue "No." They object to a helmet law because the helmet reduces peripheral vision and hearing acuity. Another reason is that helmets interfere with the freedom of being completely exposed to the elements.
   b. Motorcycle accidents cause more than four thousand deaths and tens of thousands of brain injuries each year in the United States. In California alone $60 million to $100 million is taken from the public purse each year to pay medical bills of riders injured while they were not wearing helmets. So while some motorcyclists say, "Let those who ride decide," I would argue that "Those who pay should have the final say," a helmet law.

5. Analyze the following argument and locate the issue, conclusion, and reason(s).

   It seems that humans are not the only species that doesn't like to see two people doing the same thing but one of them gets a greater reward. In an article provocatively titled "Monkeys reject unequal pay," the authors offered evidence that brown capuchin monkeys refused to participate in a game set up by the researcher if they saw another monkey get a bigger reward than they did for doing the same thing as they did. (Sarah F. Brosnan & Frans B.M. de Waal, in *Nature:* Vol 425, September 18, 2003, p. 297).

6. Here is a hopeful argument for anyone looking for employment! Locate issue, conclusion, and reason(s).

   According to Jay Jamrog, executive director of the Human Resource Institute, roughly 43 percent of people now working will be eligible to retire in 2015. Although many of these people may choose to keep working, it is highly likely that millions will retire or reduce their hours to part-time. This opens the possibility of as many as 40 million available jobs in the United States at that time.

7. Try this argument for issue, conclusion, and reason(s).

   Wild salmon and swordfish may soon become extinct due to overfishing. The answer to this crisis is a tax on consumers of these and other fish. The tax revenues could go toward paying fishermen *not* to fish for a few years in order to give the salmon and swordfish populations time to recover.

READINGS

1. *Should we consider the welfare (interests) of animals as equal to that of humans? While admitting that "this suggestion may at first seem bizarre," Peter Singer makes a persuasive argument. What is his basic argument?*

The capacity for suffering and enjoying things is a prerequisite to having interests at all, a condition that must be satisfied before we can speak of interests in any meaningful way. It would be nonsense to say that it was not in the interests of a stone to be kicked along the road by a schoolboy. A stone does not have interests because it cannot suffer. Nothing that we can do to it could possibly make any difference to its welfare. A mouse, on the other hand, does have an interest in not being tormented, because it will suffer if it is.

If a being suffers, there can be no moral justification for refusing to take that suffering into consideration. No matter what the nature of the being, the principle of equality requires that its suffering be counted equally with the like suffering—insofar as rough comparisons can be made—of any other being. . . .

Racists violate the principle of equality by giving greater weight to the interests of members of their own race when there is a clash between their interests and the interests of those of another race. White racists do not accept that pain is as bad when it is felt by blacks as when it is felt by whites. Similarly, those I would call "specieists" give greater weight to the interests of members of their own species where there is a clash between their interests and the interests of those of other species. Human specieists do not accept that pain is as bad when it is felt by pigs or mice as when it is felt by humans.

That, then, is really the whole of the argument for extending the principle of equality to nonhuman animals.[7]

Analyze Singer's argument:
Singer raises the issue whether ________________________________.
He argues (concludes) that ____________________________________.
because ____.

2. *Philosopher Paul Weiss became curious about the deep love many people feel for sports. The book Sport: A Philosophic Inquiry was the result. Keep the following in mind as you read this excerpt from Weiss's book:*
   a. *Two of these paragraphs entail almost all factual claims; the third contains an argument. Which is which?*
   b. *One way to deal with a lot of closely related questions is to summarize them into one "umbrella" question.*
   c. *Look for the conclusion and then work backward (a good ploy most of the time).*

Athletes usually submit themselves, often with enthusiasm, rarely with reluctance, to long periods of training. They do not seem to mind having to engage repeatedly in dull exercises and tedious practice sessions. Nor do they seem to take amiss the need to control their appetites, even those that are imperious and insistent. Willingly, athletes sacrifice opportunities to be lax, give up occasions to be irresponsible, and put aside a desire simply to enjoy themselves. At times they risk injury, and in some cases death. Fatigue is a familiar. Sooner or later every one of them comes to know . . . defeat, and perhaps humiliation. [The athlete's] days are numbered, successes rarely momentous, and glories short-lived; [one] works hard and long to prepare . . . for what may end in dismal failure. Why?

Why are athletes ready to give up so much that is desirable to accept what involves a good deal of wasted motion and boredom? Why are they willing to risk making their inadequacies evident, instead of enjoying the struggle of others from afar, or instead of plunging into a game without concern for how they might fare? Why do they subject themselves to the demands of a severe disciplining? Why are they so ready to practice self-denial or to sacrifice their interest in other pursuits to prepare themselves for what may prove disastrous? Why are they so prone to accept advice, often from [others] not nearly so competent as they themselves are? Strong, with more than the normal amount of pride and impulsiveness, why do they docilely listen to criticism which is not infrequently phrased in brutal or scathing terms?

These questions are not often asked. But unless they are, we will not learn what it is that the athlete wants or . . . should get. The answer that I think should be accepted—[is that] sport attracts because it offers a superb occasion for enabling young [people] to be perfected . . . to have fine functioning bodies and thereby reveal [one dimension of what humans] can be and do.[8]

Analyze Weiss's argument.

NOTES

1. LaRochefoucauld, *Maxims,* trans. Leonard Tancock (New York: Penguin Books, 1981), p. 74.
2. *Ibid.,* p. 117.
3. *Ibid.*
4. *Ibid.,* p. 105.
5. *Ibid.,* p. 108.
6. Bertolt Brecht, quoted in Robert Byrne, ed., *The 1,911 Best Things Anybody Ever Said* (New York: Ballantine Books, a division of Random House, 1988). Byrne has increased the number of humorous and insightful quotes in *The 2,548 Best Things Anybody Ever Said* (New York: Fireside Books, 2002).
7. Peter Singer, *Practical Ethics,* 2nd ed. (New York: Cambridge University Press, 1993), pp. 57–58.
8. Paul Weiss, *Sport: A Philosophic Inquiry* (n.p.: Southern Illinois University Press, 1969), pp. 18–19. This book is, unfortunately, out of print. However, you can find a wealth of continuing arguments about this subject on the Web site of the International Association of the Philosophy of Sport: *http://icps.net.* Go to the link "Journal."

How to Create Alternative Arguments

The basic structure of argument consists of issue, conclusion, and reasons—three of the twelve basics. A fourth fundamental feature is distinction. That leaves eight. At this point, there is no "correct" next move. Having discovered the three basics in any argument, you could proceed to consider any of the remaining features next. You might, for example, immediately proceed to generate alternative arguments (Figure 1), or you might pursue one of the other areas of argument shown in Figure 2.

Alternative arguments give you a lot to work with. The novice critical thinker, when faced with an argument to critique, often worries, "I can't think of anything to say." In a few weeks you will suffer from the opposite problem, wondering which of many approaches to take.

Most important, alternative arguments broaden your perspective on the issue to a greater extent than the other remaining tools. Ultimately you will come to think of **critical thinking as the consideration of alternative arguments in light of their evidence.**

QUICK STARTS

Quick Start 1

The easiest way to get a second argument on an issue is to *oppose the conclusion* of the first and support that opposite conclusion with a reason:

> First argument: Students shouldn't underline in their textbooks, because they can sell them back to the bookstore for more money when the books have no writing in them.
>
> Second argument (oppose conclusion of first and back up with a reason): Students should underline in their textbooks, because doing so will help them to get better grades.

Now you try. Think up a strict argument, then oppose it.

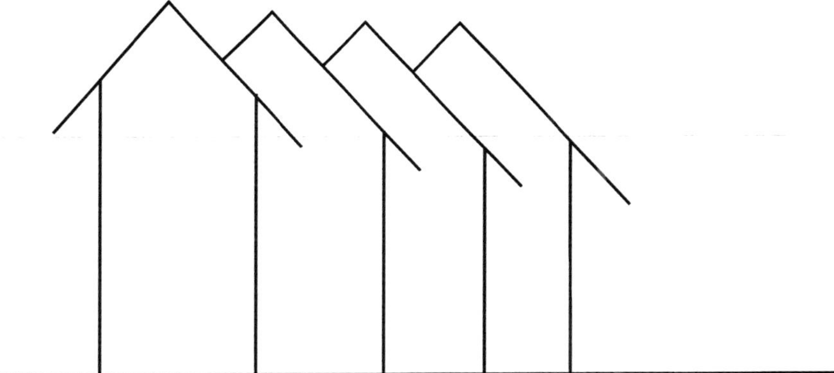

Figure 1 Generating Alternative Arguments

Quick Start 2

Another easy way to come up with a second argument is to *oppose the conclusion and oppose a reason* or reasons offered by the first:

> First argument: Students shouldn't underline in their textbooks, because they can sell them back to the bookstore for more money when the books have no writing in them.
>
> Second argument (oppose first conclusion and its reason): Students should underline in their textbooks, because once they've written their names in them, the bookstore buys them back at the same used price whether the students underline in them or not.

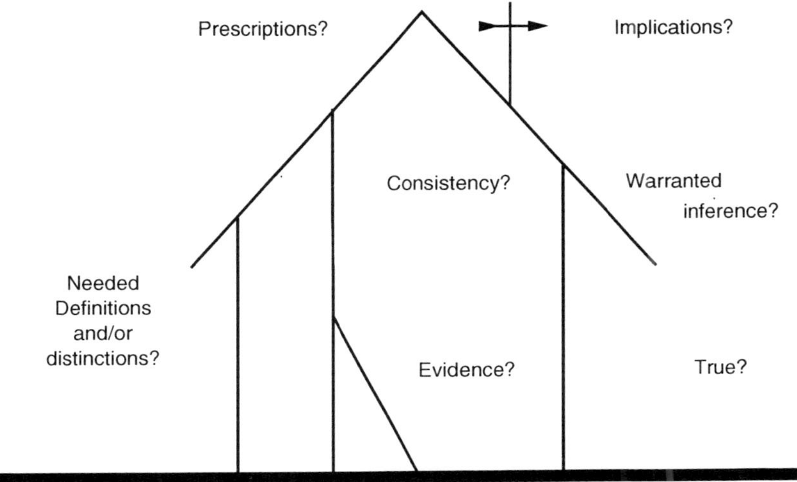

Figure 2 Areas of Argument

If the reasons for the foregoing arguments are true, questions still remain. For instance, we're still faced with the question whether students should write their names in their textbooks. But the issue has expanded, and the argument is making progress.

It would mean even more progress if the arguments could "speak directly to one another." Here, for instance, if underlining tends to help students get better grades (but how much better), should students go for better grades over a bigger refund (but how big is the refund)? We need to engage these arguments directly with one another to make the most enlightened decision about underlining textbooks. In the next two sections you'll see how to get arguments directly engaged in this way.

FACTORS FOR, FACTORS AGAINST

Say that someone argues that grades should be abolished because they create bad feelings in students who get poor marks. If a school were seriously considering eliminating grades, then students, school administrators, teachers, and even businesses would have to consider a great many factors before being in favor of it. Brainstorm for a few minutes, listing as many factors as you can in favor of abolishing grades, and then do the same against the idea. Don't forget to include favorable and unfavorable factors from the point of view of nonstudents. For the moment, put down everything you can think of, no matter how zany it sounds.

In thinking up these factors, you will be generating *reasons* which you could use in arguments for and against grades (see Figure 3). Now do the same for underlining in textbooks.

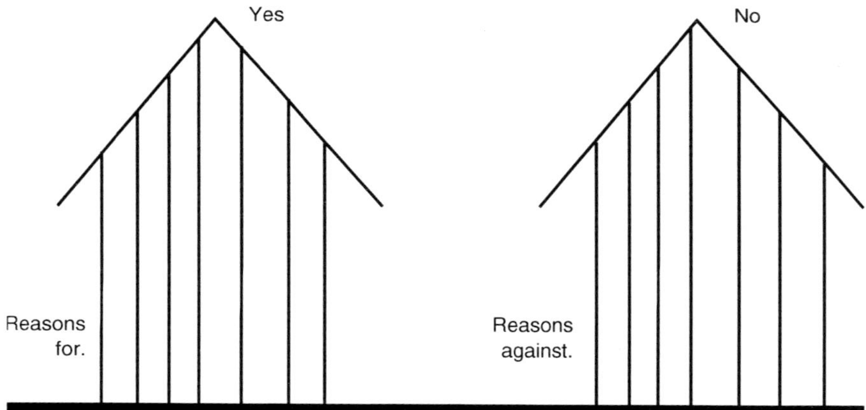

Figure 3 Generating Reasons

Winnow Out the Strongest Reasons

Do not censor yourself in coming up with factors, because sometimes a wild idea can lead you by association to a very good idea. In fact, sometimes the wild idea, upon further reflection, *is* a good idea. Many ideas considered nonsense in one century become common sense in the next.*

To prevent an argument from becoming unwieldy, it is best to reduce both sets of factors to the two or three strongest, most convincing reasons, in your opinion. If your wilder idea happens to convince you, by all means use it, and make it a convincing reason for others.

ENGULF AND DEVOUR

Here is a wonderful three-part technique for developing a sophisticated argument. Its "point, counterpoint, point" structure really engages opposing arguments:

1. **Strongest Reasons For** First, you make the strongest case you can for some position. First argue for, say, the importance of grades (or of an athletics requirement or capital punishment), offering your strongest reasons in support of this position.
2. **Strongest Reasons Against** Then you argue against grades, offering the strongest reasons you can to abolish grades (or against athletics requirement or capital punishment).
3. **Engulf and Devour the Second Argument** Taking the first position again, you argue that **even granting** the truth of the reasons offered in this second argument, say, against grades, the argument for grades is stronger because . . .

   "Engulf and devour" is a very powerful form of argumentation because the arguer acknowledges the opposing point of view at its best and goes on to show how the first argument is still better. The following argument in favor of brainstorming illustrates "engulf and devour."

Strongest reasons for: One of the best ways to get critical material is to play around with an argument, generating as many factors favorable or unfavorable to it as one can. Generating factors also helps the critical thinker to consider an issue in broad perspective, from many angles.

Strongest reasons against: **On the other hand, one could argue that** this method of generating arguments is inadvisable because it is dishonest. The honest approach would be to gather evidence before ever entertaining a factor as part of an argument.

Engulf and devour the second argument: **Yet even granting that** honesty in making arguments is necessary, it is possible to be honest and still to generate playfully as much of an argument as possible. One remains honest throughout this endeavor by realizing that the ideas so generated are

*Instances of ideas that when propounded seemed outlandish to most, but later drew millions of adherents: Christianity, Marxism, Einstein's theory of relativity (a wild idea winning general acceptance within twenty years, rather than a hundred); Freudian notions of the unconscious, neurosis, and repression; equality of the sexes.

> exploratory, not final. And it is arguable that surveying the whole landscape of factors, rather than limiting oneself to an immediately demonstrable few, will result in a fuller and, therefore, more honest argument. **Moreover, accepting that the second argument offered that** evidence plays a vital role in finally deciding whether a factor is a strong reason for accepting an argument, **the fact remains that** most critical thinkers, scientists included, advance by making an imaginative leap beyond the evidence at hand and then looking to see if evidence exists in support of the new idea. In sum, with arguments as well as in many areas of life, it is better to leap before you look.

You can see that this three-part argument is a lot stronger than the first part of the argument alone.

One final note: Engulf and devour is a two-way treat. Someone might come along saying " **even granting all that has been said** about leaping before one looks, **still,** careful investigation should precede all argumentation **because,** " thus engulfing and devouring this example whole!

If It's Better, Accept It for the Time Being

If in the course of making a strong opposing argument, the arguer becomes convinced of the opposing argument, the arguer has learned something. There should be no shame in that, only in obtusely refusing to budge from one's original position in the teeth of better reasons. (There is difference between deliberation, which allows you to gracefully embrace the opposite argument, and debate, which prohibits you from accepting the opposite argument under pain of "losing the debate.")

If you are in the middle of writing a paper and convince yourself of the opposite argument, just switch the placement of the argument and counterargument, enabling whichever position can engulf and devour to do so.

Of course, that second argument may persuade you intellectually while making you uneasy emotionally. Remember that in the interests of balance you can accept an argument provisionally—no cost, no obligation to act on it today.

A SIGNIFICANT EXCEPTION

In some cases one argument can engulf another, but many times this is not possible. You can't in conscience grant the truth of all of the reasons in an opposing argument. So engulfing is out. The next best approach is to try to think up the *strongest possible reason against* the argument. Again, generate a number of factors against a position and then winnow out the one or two most likely to change the opinion of a person who believed the position.

Take the issue of grade abolition. Say that someone has presented two strong factors in favor of abolition: (1) that many people would actually try harder, no longer feeling incompetent because of bad grades, and (2) that everyone would work for the correct reason, that is, the value of learning, rather than for an extrinsic reward.

Now, what is the strongest reason that can come up against those reasons? Another way of putting it is to ask, "What is the main reason that grades exist?" You may have thought of a better answer, but one answer is that grades are supposed to let both the individual and society (employers, graduate schools, and so on) know what level of skill an individual has attained in a given subject. This is, then, a factor in favor of grades. In countering the argument against grades, one could say:

> **However, in arguing that** grades should be abolished, the author **has failed to take the problem of** standards of preparedness **into account.**

or

> **The proponents of** grade abolition **must address the difficult necessity of** distinguishing those who are skilled from those who are not skilled in a subject.

Tactfully raising these important problems for the arguer is doing the arguer a great favor.

COUNTEREXAMPLE

This tack, of coming up with one significant exception, works especially well on arguments that at first seem so airtight as to be inevitable. Consider this argument about boredom:

> It's plain that boredom results from outside stimuli that are dull, repetitious, or tedious. People become bored because they are in such an environment.

Who could fight that argument? We've all been in such situations, and it's obvious that people get bored because they're in boring situations. But wait—just fool around trying to remember whether you've been in situations where boredom can't have occurred because of dull, outside stimuli. Rack your brain for a few minutes. Any ideas? If not, here's one approach. Think of any situations in which one person has been bored and another hasn't. We're searching for any exceptions to the claim that boredom has to come from dull, outside stimuli. Any situation in which some people get bored and others don't can be used to argue against the position that boring situations are just "out there" in the same way that boiling water is "out there" on the stove.

If you can think up such an exceptional case, you can use it to back up your counterargument:

> **On the contrary, one could argue that** boredom **does not result** from outside stimuli which are dull, repetitious, or tedious. **For instance,** ______________.

For instance, there are many people who would find a lecture on thermodynamics boring, while others would find it quite interesting.

Finding such exceptions can be a revelation. If you have always believed that a boring situation came from the outside world, attacked, and bored you, then you should now feel puzzled, wondering just how people do get bored. That puzzlement is good. It will lead you to deepen your awareness on the subject.

FALSE OR INSUFFICIENT REASONS

The first argument's reasons may be false, or they may be true but too flimsy to support the conclusion. Either of these factors is ruinous to an argument.

Examples of language used to criticize reasons:

> **It has been claimed that** the abolition of grades would result in greater efforts on the part of many students. **This argument does not hold because its reason is simply untrue. It is not the case that** students would try harder; if anything, a lot of students would stop trying entirely.

Taking the first argument's reasons head-on is a favored strategy when you are alone and trying to decide whether to accept an argument. It's easy to run the reasons through one's experience and past reasoning on the issue, coming to a decision. But accusing reasons of being false or flimsy is the least-favored method when arguing with someone else. The reason is due to the complexity of the human mind. Take the example of grades. The person who is convinced that grades should be abolished is probably already convinced of a lot of other things as well, perhaps that people are basically intellectually curious and that the carrot of academic enjoyment is better than the stick of bad grades. These other, deeper convictions beneath the argument at hand are assumptions. A person's reasons for accepting an argument are normally much more complicated than the argument at hand would lead one to believe. In addition, people like what they believe, and feel a personal stake in it.

The complexity of human reason and the commitment to belief are two reasons why "engulf and devour" is such a powerful argumentative tool. When it can be used, it leaves all the apparatus of the person's beliefs intact, while enlarging them.*

TIME OUT FOR FACT-FINDING OR EXPERIMENTATION

You probably realized while reading the example of grade abolition that you had no statistics that would help you to decide whether, in fact, abolishing grades would help students to work harder. You doubtless have your suspicions about the matter, but if you're arguing with someone of opposite suspicions, you're stuck.

One approach would be to suggest researching for past or present cases in which schools have abolished grades:

> **The author has argued that** the elimination of grades will improve student efforts. **If we are to seriously entertain this possibility, thorough research** of the effect of grade abolition on other schools similar to ours **must be undertaken.**

or

> **More facts must be gathered on the question whether** to abolish grades **before it can be decided.**

When past and present cases cannot be found, an arguer can call for experimentation. Consider these examples:

> **Only experimentation will decide the question whether** searching students on high school campuses for weapons will reduce the incidence of violence.
>
> At the moment, the answer remains controversial. **It might be resolved by further experimentation.**

Notice that the second writer has decided to be more cautious about the role experimentation will play in deciding the issue at hand.

BALANCE AND BELIEF

If you happen to agree with an argument, it's going to sound terrific. If you violently disagree, an argument will sound like it's full of holes and just terrible. Both of these tendencies are hard on balance, and mean that

*Big factor and significant exception also tend to enlarge the perspective of the other side, although not to as great an extent.

everyone has to work to be tougher on arguments with which they already agree, and more tender with those they initially feel opposed to. This may seem obvious, but it often gets lost in the flush of argument.

Don't infer that openness to counterarguments means to accept all arguments as equal. That would lead to *relativism,* the view that there is no ultimate truth. Openness to counterarguments is meant to defend against a different danger, that of *dogmatism,* the belief that one already has all the truth to be known on a subject. Dogmatism is the refusal to entertain a different point of view.

There is an intermediate, balanced view which has aided material as well as social progress—*progressivism.* It holds that the truth is real and that, thanks to the community of thinkers, we're getting closer to it on many issues. At the heart of progressivism is a willingness always to entertain counterarguments, even on positions on which near-certainty is felt. The distinction among these three beliefs is crucial. As Figure 4 indicates, relativism makes fresh information to be of little consequence, and dogmatism locks it out.

Obviously, you do not have to agree. I can't think of any alternatives beyond these three positions, but can you?

LOGOPHOBIA: THE FEAR OF ARGUING

If you slink away from an argument, it's often from fear that the conclusion is true. If that conclusion is right, you may feel that it could do violence to one or more of your deeply felt beliefs—and therefore violence could be done to you! So in a sheer panic of self-protection, you retreat.

Now, one can remain in permanent retreat or make a comeback—that is, get back into balance—either to make a counterargument or to defer making one. Let's make the case for the comeback. You may have noticed that the foregoing paragraph was an argument in favor of retreating. Imagine a second "you" talking to the "you" crouching in a corner:

> Look, you really should face up to this argument. No matter what happens, you stand to win, whether you become convinced by the argument or not.

Say that you give the argument your most sincere efforts but aren't convinced. Chances are that you've seen flaws in it that will help you to find more points to make your original belief even stronger. So by looking at a counterargument you have enriched your original argument.

On the other hand, assume that after giving the argument your sincerest efforts you find that you do become persuaded by that argument. You can easily define your experience as one of *changing* your beliefs as if having had violence done to your old belief. After all, the old

Progressivism: The truth is real, and we're on a never-ending journey towards it.

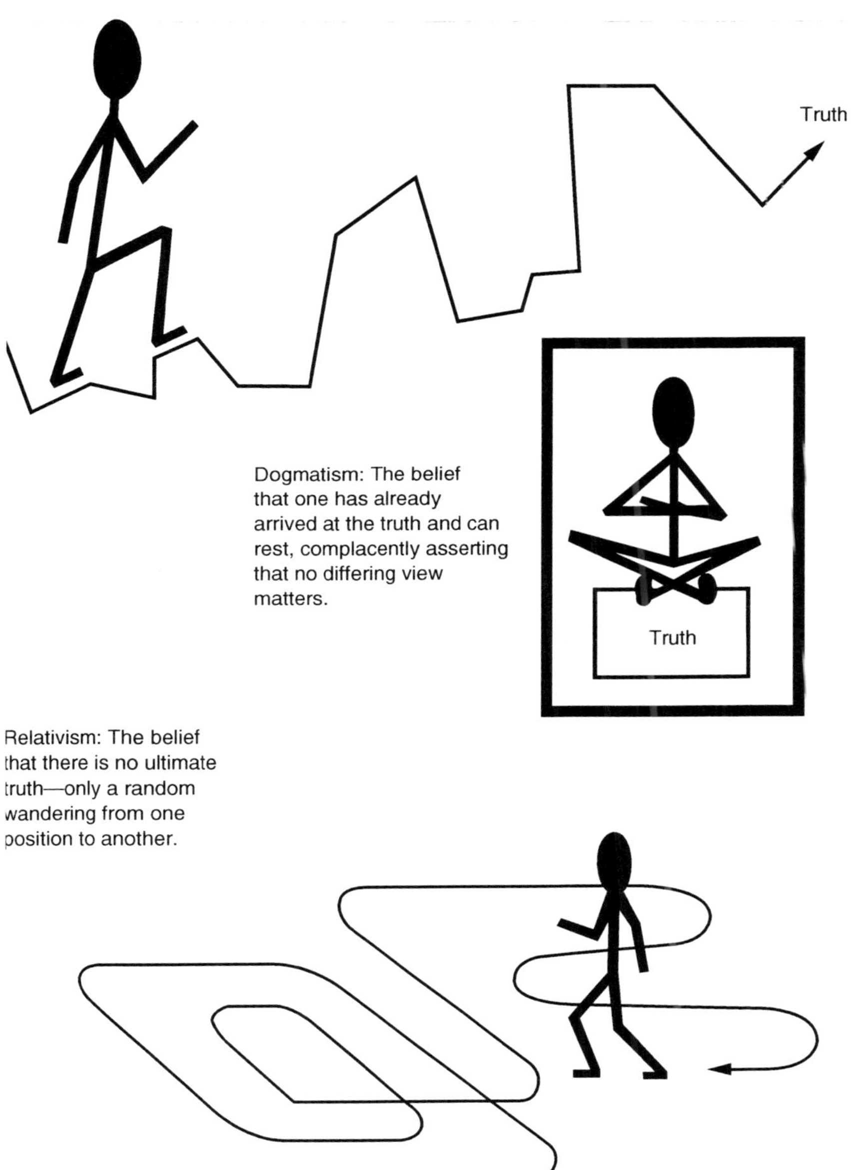

Figure 4 Three Beliefs

belief isn't dead—as long as you leave yourself open to persuasion, you can take back your old belief any time you decide that it is more convincing to you.

And just as violence is not really done to the belief, violence is not really done to you. It just seems that violence is going to be done to you, because you are experiencing fear that such a big belief change will turn you into an unknown quantity, maybe even cause you to lose your identity. It's true that your beliefs are an important part of you, but you are, in fact, more than the sum of your beliefs; you are a reasoning, feeling, many-faceted human being. And rather than the new belief having a power of its own that changes you, you, in fact, have been in charge all along, changing your belief! However, if you continue to hide over there, not making an informed choice between the belief you have and this one, you can hardly consider yourself in charge.

Remember, too, that you can always accept an argument *provisionally*—in fact you should. You can think, "I can't beat that argument at the moment, so I'll accept it for the time being. But I'm still uneasy with it, so I certainly won't act on it yet. But now I'm fascinated, so I will definitely keep thinking about it, and look for arguments others have made on the issue." Temporary acceptance pending further thought will not force you out into the street to act on that belief.

Welcome All Comers

If we can acquire the habit of seeing arguments as opportunities to acquire wisdom, with no possibility of "losing" an argument since we always "win" insight, it will be easy to cultivate a spirit of welcome for any ideas. Then no argument need scare us off—at least not for long. Or would you like to make the opposite argument? All you have to do is to turn the conclusion around, claiming, "No, there are some positions that should never even be considered. My reason(s) for saying this are that __________. For instance (strongest exception), __________.

A Horrifying Issue

What assertion could we practice on that would displease nearly everyone? How about the argument that torture is right under certain circumstances? The most offensive argument on the subject would probably be that we should be constantly torturing one another. But one couldn't construct a good foundation for that conclusion. I'll make do by arguing that torture under a few circumstances is right. Note that this argument is as persuasive as possible because the **strongest case** has been taken.

Torture is not only right but a positive obligation in certain very limited circumstances. By "torture" I mean the willful infliction of physical pain on another, unwilling person.	*delimit scope of argument definition*
The decison to torture another person is a grievous one. I would rule out almost all cases of torture as inhumane and therefore highly immoral. Yet consider this frightening scenario: A man has hidden a plutonium bomb somewhere in New York City. When captured, the man claims that the bomb will go off in half an hour, that all New Yorkers deserve to die, and that he will not tell where the bomb is.	*emphasize limited acceptability* *strongest case: death to millions over pain to one*
With millions of lives at stake, the police sergeant surely has the right to apply a bit of pressure, perhaps starting with the delicate fold of skin between the man's thumb and index finger and increasing the man's pain until he reveals the bomb's location.	*strongest case: recommend least pain necessary*
In fact, torture of this man will have the effect of saving his life as well as the lives the millions held in jeopardy. But consider this statement: "The right of one person to be free of pain is greater than the right of millions, even if that one person would take the lives of those millions of people." Doesn't that sound wrong? The right of many people to live is in fact greater than the right of one person to be temporarily free of pain, especially if that one person has put the millions in jeopardy.	*strongest case,* even for man tortured!

By "strongest case" you should recognize the significant exception, the most persuasive example that you can imagine. Then to respond to the argument, you might keep that strongest case in mind and generate an argument "engulfing and devouring"—claiming why, even in that strongest case, torture would still be wrong. For example,

> Don't accept even this compelling case. Once torture is permitted, where will the line be drawn? Should we torture one person who even *says* she's got a plutonium bomb and will hurt three people with it?

See? A strong case in the opposite direction.

Use Uneasiness to Generate Alternatives

If you dislike both the argument and the counterargument, use that dislike to propel yourself into creating alternative ways of dealing with an issue. In the case of a terrorist with a bomb, aren't the alternatives quite limited? Perhaps, but it would be better to assume that the alternatives are unlimited. Otherwise we wouldn't bother to think up alternatives, possibly missing some very important solutions to our problems. For example, consider how the Dutch have dealt with the terrorism that plagued their country several years ago. The terrorists were a few of the Moluccan immigrants to Holland from their islands near Indonesia. They wanted independence for their islands, which were once under Dutch rule but were overtaken by Indonesia in the 1950s. In the late 1970s the Dutch Moluccans hijacked trains and executed a number of people until the government came up with a unique alternative. Why not send some Moluccans back to visit their islands? First, they would see that their quarrel was with Indonesia, not Holland. Second, life in Holland compares very favorably with life in the Moluccas, so they would not even want to go back to live in the Moluccas. The Dutch paid the fare for perhaps 10 percent of the 40,000 Moluccans living in Holland. The terrorism has stopped.[1]

Obviously, this won't work in a number of other terrorist hot spots. But maybe *some as yet unthought alternative* would.

MISCELLANEOUS ADVICE

When you hear an argument, think "Yes, maybe so, but." For the fun of it try to generate a counterargument or at least some reasons why the argument at hand may not be complete. Try to think of instances that don't fit the argument. Take the reason and imagine some exception. Or make a strong opposite case. Try to imagine what the person is arguing—both for and against.

Ask yourself *whether the argument needs more* support in the form of *evidence or reasons;* perhaps the argument needs the support of different reasons. Don't forget that there are times when the opposite case is better just because it's closer to the truth.

SUMMARY

The following tactics were discussed in this chapter:

1. *Quick starts:* Oppose the conclusion, come up with a reason; oppose the conclusion and reason(s).
2. *Factors for and against:* Brainstorm for as many factors as possible on either side, then winnow them down to the best few.
3. *Engulf and devour:* Accept the opposing argument, offering more powerful reasons to accept your argument.

4. *A big factor, a significant exception, the strongest case:* Search for missing elements that the arguer has not taken into account.
5. *Faulty or flimsy reasons:* The first position's reasons are false or insufficient to support the argument.
6. *Call for more factual evidence or for experimentation.*

Although these are different approaches, they can overlap.

EXERCISES

1. Use one of the quick-start techniques on each of these arguments:
   a. Everyone should buy a few clothes every year because wearing something different adds spice to life.
   b. Fraternities and sororities are clubs whose sole purpose is to make their members feel superior to outsiders. These clubs should be banned from college campuses.
2. Factors for, factors against:
   a. Generate five reasons in favor of a flat, 15 percent federal income tax for every person and every business; then imagine five reasons against such an idea. Winnow the reasons on each side to two, then choose the strongest, explaining why it is strongest.
   b. Think of alternative ways, even zany ones, to tax people other than according to income.
   c. You should major in a subject you really love, not a subject that you think will guarantee you the best income later on.
   d. Women wear pants; therefore, men should wear skirts. You can find an entertaining article by a male reporter who wore a skirt in Brooklyn because the Constume Institute at the New York Metropolitan Museum of Art ran an exhibit called "Bravehearts: Men in Skirts" to point out the different cultural values we have regarding the clothing options of men versus women.[2]
3. Engulf and devour the following:
   a. It's a mistake to have children. They are expensive, difficult to train, and often end up ungrateful for parental efforts.
   b. Since no one can predict how the economy will be in ten years, one is better off spending money on desired items than saving it.
   c. Because it's so hard to get a job these days, there is no use trying to interview with prospective employers.
   d. It's impossible to eat "healthy" food because the standards for "healthy" keep changing. For instance, nutritionists used to advise against eating nuts because they had a lot of fat. Now, nuts and peanut butter are considered healthy foods. So you might as well give up and eat what you want.
4. Think up a strongest case against the following:
   a. People want only what they cannot have.
   b. Laughter is the best medicine.
   c. There is no use doing exercise to lose weight because you just want to eat more afterward.
   d. Argue against the claim that the screwdriver and the screw are the most important tools invented during the last thousand years (because they have affected so many of the things we use).[3]

5. Make up an argument in favor of dogmatism, then see if you can engulf and devour it. Do the same for relativism and progressivism.

READINGS

1. *The best arguments are those that give a counterargument and then show how the case being argued is better. Two examples follow. In each, pick out the argument and its opposing view.*

> Unhappily, biography has lately been overtaken by a school that has abandoned the selective [aspects of a person's life] in favor of the all-inclusive. . . . We are presented with the subject's life reconstructed day by day from birth to death, including every new dress or pair of pants, every juvenile poem, every journey, every letter, every loan, every accepted or rejected invitation, every telephone message, every drink at every bar. . . . I think this development is part of the anti-excellence spirit of our time that insists on the equality of everything and is thus reduced to the theory that all facts are of equal value and that the biographer or historian should not presume to exercise judgment. To that I can only say, if he cannot exercise judgment, he should not be in the business. A portraitist does not achieve a likeness by giving sleeve buttons and shoelaces equal value to mouth and eyes.[4]

Having grasped both arguments, do you agree with the author? One way to discover whether you agree would be to imagine that there exist two biographies about someone whom you greatly admire. One presents every known fact—"every drink at every bar"—about that person; the other biography tells only about the major events in that person's life along with what the biographer has decided are interesting details. Which would you prefer to read and why?

2. *The following are an argument and counterargument on the merits of an artist's career by Dame Janet Baker, a famous opera singer. Can you tell when the counterargument begins? Is her conclusion the same in both arguments? Notice that she is careful to define her major term.*

> If someone asked if my career has been "worth it," in other words worth the sacrifices made by me and members of my family, worth the separations, the agony of performing, of trying to keep perfectly fit, the undying battle against nerves, the strains and pitfalls of being a public figure, my honest answer would have to be "No."
>
> This sounds a terrible comment to make on a career which, in terms of the world, has been a highly successful one. I have done everything any singer could dream of, yet the moments when the musical rewards have equalled the price one has to pay for them have been few.
>
> But if someone were to ask me how I would choose to be born in order to learn about life, I would unquestionably reply, "As an artist." If it is, as many people suggest, a rather special privilege to be born one, the privilege lies in the opportunities such an existence provides for the individual to learn about himself; in the questions artistic life forces one to ask and try to answer; in the struggle to come to terms with performing and everything

implied by an act of heroism, which demands the baring of the soul before strangers, and public judgment of this act; in the choices to be made as a result of loving something more than oneself and serving that something with the greatest integrity one is capable of. Yes, in these terms, my career has been "worth it," a thousand times over.[5]

3. *Social historian Norbert Elias gives a counterargument to the normal accounts one might give for eating with a fork:*

> What is the real use of the fork? It serves to lift food that has been cut up to the mouth. Why do we need a fork for this? Why do we not use our fingers? Because it is "cannibal," as . . . the author of *The Habits of Good Society* said in 1859. Why is it "cannibal" to eat with one's fingers? That is not a question; it is self-evidently cannibal, barbaric, uncivilized, or whatever else it is called.
>
> But that is precisely the question. Why is it more civilized to eat with a fork?
>
> "Because it is unhygienic to eat with one's fingers." That sounds convincing. To our sensibility it is unhygienic if different people put their fingers into the same dish, because there is a danger of contracting disease through contact with others. Each of us seems to fear that the others are diseased. But this explanation is not entirely satisfactory. Nowadays we do not eat from common dishes. Everyone puts food into his mouth from his own plate. To pick it up from one's own plate with one's fingers cannot be more "unhygienic" than to put cake, bread, chocolate, or anything else into one's mouth with one's own fingers.
>
> So why does one really need a fork? Why is it "barbaric" and "uncivilized" to put food into one's mouth by hand from one's own plate? Because it is distasteful to dirty one's fingers, or at least to be seen in society with dirty fingers. The suppression of eating by hand from one's own plate has very little to do with the danger of illness, the so-called "rational" explanation. In observing our feelings toward the fork ritual, we can see with particular clarity that the first authority in our decision between "civilized" and "uncivilized" behavior at table is our feeling of distaste.[6]

NOTES

1. "Why Holland's South Moluccans Aren't Hijacking Trains Any More," *Wall Street Journal* (New York), May 24, 1984.
2. Michael Brick, "Guy in Skirt Seeks Sensitivity in Brooklyn," *New York Times*, Sunday, November 2, 2003, Section 9, pp.1, 11.
3. Witold Rybczynski, *One Good Turn: A Natural History of the Screwdriver and the Screw* (New York: Scribner, 2000).
4. Barbara W. Tuchman, *Practicing History* (New York: Alfred A. Knopf, 1981), p. 89.
5. Janet Baker, *Full Circle* (London: Julia MacRae Publishers, a division of Franklin Watts, 1982), pp. 52–53.
6. Norbert Elias, *The History of Manners: The Civilizing Process* (New York: Pantheon Books, a division of Random House, Inc., 1978), 1, pp. 126–27. This book was published again in 1993 under the title *The Civilizing Process*, by Blackwell Publishers, London.

Express the Problem or Issue

Imagine that a certain kind of question would help you produce many and varied kinds of solutions to problems. Imagine, too, that other questions would enable you to cut through confusion and get to the heart of controversial issues and that knowing those questions would make you a more confident and successful thinker.

The good news is that such questions do exist. This chapter identifies them and shows you how to use them.

This stage in the creative process is the one most often neglected. The reason is not that people decide to be stubborn and to proceed without having identified the best expression of the problem or issue. Rather, it is that they are convinced that the problem is self-evident and that it would be a waste of their valuable time to consider alternative ways of formulating it.

Such thinking is wrong. Like our first impressions of people, our initial perspectives on problems and issues are likely to be limited or superficial. We see no more than what we have been conditioned to see, and stereotyped notions block clear vision and crowd out imagination. Most important, all this happens without any alarms sounding, so we never realize it is occurring.

You can avoid this narrowness of perspective by developing the habit of expressing every problem or issue in as many different ways as you can. Before discussing the most effective forms of expression, we will note how to distinguish between problems and issues.

DISTINGUISHING PROBLEMS FROM ISSUES

Problems and issues differ in some respects. A problem is a situation that we regard as unacceptable; an issue is a matter about which intelligent, informed people disagree to some extent. Solving problems therefore means *deciding what action will change the situation for the best,* whereas resolving issues means *deciding what belief or viewpoint is the most reasonable.*

Whenever you are uncertain whether to treat a particular challenge as a problem or an issue, apply this test: Ask whether the matter involved tends to arouse partisan feelings and to divide informed, intelligent people. If it does not, treat it as a problem. If it does, treat it as an issue. Here are some sample problems: a student trying to study in a noisy dormitory, a child frightened by the prospect of being admitted to the hospital, a businesswoman dealing with subtle sexual harassment from her boss. And here are some sample issues: a public school teacher leading students in prayer in a public school classroom, a member of Congress proposing a cut in Social Security benefits for the elderly, an anthropologist stating that human beings are by nature violent.

Each of the situations in the first group is properly considered a problem because there is nothing about the situation itself that is likely to divide informed, intelligent people. Of course, someone, somewhere, might conceivably take an unusual view of a situation—for example, challenging the right of a student to a quiet dorm atmosphere—but that is likely to be a remote possibility. However, each of the situations in the second group is likely to provoke considerable disagreement because each involves *a matter that is itself controversial.*

EXPRESSING PROBLEMS

Both problems and issues are best expressed as questions, but the form of the question is different for each. The form most effective in expressing problems is the "How can . . . ?" form. Let's consider an actual case and see how this form applies. Some years ago, almost 7000 public schools around the country closed their doors because of declining enrollments, budget cuts, and inflation.[1] Here are the various ways school officials might have expressed this problem.

- How can school enrollments be increased?
- How can school budgets be reduced?
- How can the impact of inflation on education be lessened?
- How can school buildings best be used after the schools are closed?
- How can the unused space in school buildings be used to generate income so the school will not have to be closed?
- How can school buildings be used in evenings and on weekends to generate income?
- How can the empty buildings be used after the schools are closed?
- How can the unemployed teachers be used after the schools are closed?

Let's consider another problem, the drug problem, arguably the greatest social challenge of our time. Here are just a few of the many ways this problem can be expressed.

- How can people be taught to shun drugs?
- How can people be discouraged from dealing in drugs?
- How can celebrities be persuaded to use their influence to combat drug use?
- How can the media assist in the antidrug effort?
- How can individual citizens support the federal government's antidrug program?
- How can law enforcement agencies be made immune to corruption by drug lords?
- How can the support of drug-producing countries be enlisted?
- How can crops of drug-producing plants be spotted and destroyed before harvest?

There is room for disagreement about which expression of a problem is best. But there can be no disagreement that we are in a better position to make that decision, and to produce a creative solution, if we take the time to identify and consider all of the questions, because *each question opens a different avenue of thought.* The kinds of solutions for teaching people to shun drugs are very different from those for destroying drug crops.

EXPRESSING ISSUES

The question forms most effective in expressing issues are the "Is . . . ?" "Does . . . ?" or "Should . . . ?" forms. Using such questions, in the sense we are considering here, does not mean asking for simple facts. Rather, it means probing the central elements of dispute. To determine these elements, just note the main points each side uses in its arguments, and turn them into questions.

For example, in the abortion issue, the pro-life side argues that the fetus is a human being and therefore should be entitled to the protection of the law. The pro-choice side argues that a woman's body is hers alone and therefore she alone should have the right to decide the fate of her fetus. Thus, your expression of the issue would be

Is the fetus a human being?

Does the fetus deserve the protection of the law?

Is a woman's body hers alone?

Should a woman have the right to decide the fate of her fetus?

In the issue of capital punishment, the pro side argues that when a person has been convicted of a capital crime, the government has the right to decide whether he or she should live or die. The anti side argues that capital punishment constitutes cruel and unusual treatment and is therefore a violation of a person's constitutional rights. Thus, your expression of this issue would be

> Does the government have the right to decide whether someone convicted of a capital crime will live or die?
>
> Is capital punishment cruel and unusual treatment?
>
> Does capital punishment violate a person's constitutional rights?

The main points in an argument will be either directly expressed or at least clearly implied. They may, of course, be more numerous than those in the preceding examples.

The fact that "How can . . . ?" questions are the best kind for expressing problems and "Is . . . ?" "Does . . . ?" or "Should . . . ?" questions are best for expressing issues does not mean that other kinds of questions are without value. It means only that they have a different purpose than to focus a challenge. Questions that demand information—such as "Who?" "What?" "When?" and "Where?"—are useful in the investigating stage.* And questions that analyze—such as "Why?" and "How?"—are useful in the evaluation and refinement of ideas.

WHEN PROBLEMS BECOME ISSUES

It is possible to create a controversial issue where none existed. The way we express the problem (or, at a later stage, the specific solution we choose) may provoke serious objection. Consider, for example, the last expression of the drug problem: "How can crops of drug-producing plants be spotted and destroyed before harvest?" Even people strongly committed to the war on drugs might respond as follows: "Most of the plants used for drugs could be used for other purposes. It is morally wrong to destroy such plants, especially if they are found in foreign countries on the lands of poor farmers."

Concerned about the high number of dropouts in West Virginia high schools (a problem in other states as well), officials devised an ingenious way to keep students in school: taking away the driver's licenses of students aged 16 to 18 who miss classes. The school notified the Department of Motor Vehicles, which sent a letter telling the offender to return to school or surrender his or her license.[2] This solution, however, was controversial. Some people argued that it violated the rights of students or that it transferred jurisdiction over minors from the parents to an agency of the government.

Good thinkers are sensitive to the implications of both their questions and their assertions. Whenever your questions or assertions create an issue, address it immediately. In the case of destroying drug plants, that would mean asking, "Are there any situations in which it would be morally wrong to destroy such plants?" and resolving the matter. (If you decided the most reasonable answer was affirmative, of course, you would either revise or delete the question "How can

*When the subject is noncontroversial, "Is . . . ?" and "Does . . . ?" are also in this category.

crops . . . be spotted and destroyed?") And in the case of the West Virginia school action, it would mean asking, "Does this action violate the rights of students? Does it transfer jurisdiction from parents? Is doing so defensible?"

GUIDELINES FOR EXPRESSING PROBLEMS AND ISSUES

1. Identify the challenge. The moment you are aware that something you have experienced or read about is bothering you or that you are dissatisfied with some person, object, or situation (stage 1), examine the situation and raise your negative feeling to the conscious level. Ask yourself, "What exactly am I feeling? Sadness? Anger? Frustration? What is the source of this feeling?" Then decide whether what bothers you is best treated as a problem or as an issue.
2. Express the problem or issue. Using the appropriate form of questions— "How can ...?" for a problem, "Is . . . ?" "Does . . . ?" or "Should . . . ?" for an issue—express the problem or issue on paper rather than merely in your mind. There are two important reasons for writing your expressions. First, joining mental and physical effort and externalizing ideas often help clarify them. Second, as any composition teacher will verify, *the very act of writing an idea has a way of triggering other ideas.* Press yourself to produce as many expressions of the problem or issue as you can.
3. Refine your expression. After you have expressed the problem or issue in as many ways as you can, refine the expressions. That is, replace vagueness with exactness and general words with specific ones. An expression is too vague or general whenever you can't be sure what kind of solution it points to. For example, "How can the school enrollment problem be solved?" and "How can the drug problem be eliminated?" point nowhere in particular and therefore should be revised.

BENEFITS OF CAREFUL EXPRESSION

It Helps You Move Beyond the Familiar and Habitual

The first perspective that occurs to you will usually be slanted heavily toward familiar, habitual ways of seeing and interpreting experiences. Thus, it is more likely than later perspectives to reflect bad thinking habits: mine-is-better, face saving, resistance to change, conformity, stereotyping, and self-deception. Creativity is not likely to arise out of these habits.

It Keeps Your Thinking Flexible

Once you adopt a perspective, even tentatively, it becomes difficult to entertain a different one. This is especially true with issues. Once you have reached a position on an issue, even casually, without any real analysis, you will be tempted to become inflexible about it. Thus, you will have difficulty considering it further, even in light of dramatic new evidence.

To appreciate the speed with which you can "lock into" a perspective and the difficulty of entertaining another perspective once you do so, look closely at each of these pictures for at least a minute. Then continue reading.

In the left-hand figure, you should be able to see both an old woman and a young girl; in the right-hand figure, both a vase and two faces. In each case, many people see one image quite readily but have difficulty seeing the other until it is pointed out to them. (If you still haven't seen both, turn to the end of this chapter for assistance.) Once you have seen both, however, you are able to move back and forth between them freely and quickly. It is much the same with perspectives on issues. If you force yourself to entertain a variety of perspectives, you are better able to maintain flexibility.

It Opens Many Lines of Thought

Once you have settled on a perspective, you close off all but one line of thought. Certain kinds of ideas will occur to you, but only those kinds and no others. Thus, if the handicapped man who invented the motorized cart had defined his problem as "How to occupy my time while lying in bed" rather than "How to get out of bed and move around the house," he would never have conceived his invention.

Have you ever looked closely at the wheels on a railroad train? They are flanged. That is, they have a lip on the inside to prevent them from sliding off the track. Originally, train wheels were not flanged; instead, the railroad *tracks* were. Because the problem of railroad safety had been expressed as "How can the tracks be made safer for trains to ride on?" hundreds of thousands of miles of railroad track were manufactured with an unnecessary steel lip. Only when someone thought to redefine the problem as "How can the wheels be made to grip the track more securely?" was the flanged wheel invented.[3]

The tendency to limit the lines of thought that are considered is one of the reasons that breakthrough ideas take years, even centuries, to develop. The development of modern periodontal surgery is a case in point. Before the idea of recording human history was invented, some toothless, elderly person may have wondered, "How can I prepare food to make it edible without teeth?" Having asked the question, he or she may have hit upon the idea of pounding food with a rock to grind it into powder or paste. Later, history tells us, the ancient Etruscans asked, "How will we chew our food after our teeth have fallen out?" and proceeded to invent false teeth. But thousands of years passed before some dentist thought to ask, "How can we restore the gums to good health and make loose teeth more secure in the underlying bone?" and thereafter invented periodontal surgery. Undoubtedly, some creative person is at this very moment asking, "How can people's gums be permanently protected from disease?"

Keeping more than one line of thought open is especially urgent when dealing with issues. The human drive to make sense of things (a healthy drive, we should acknowledge) will often lead you to take sides too quickly in disputes. And once you have taken a side, ever afterward you are burdened with a powerful temptation to ignore all arguments and all evidence for the other side—indeed, to ignore the very questions that intellectual honesty requires you to ask.

For example, a strict creationist, who believes that the earth is only a few thousand years old, will tend to avoid pondering the question "Is it likely that scientific techniques for dating rocks and other materials are as inaccurate as my belief would suggest?" Similarly, a strict evolutionist, who attributes all that exists to strictly material causes, will tend to avoid pondering the question "Is it possible that a Supreme Being created the evolutionary process by which all things come into existence?" Surely both would be better thinkers for asking the questions they tend to ignore.

Keeping many lines of thought open when you address problems and issues can enable you to produce ideas that are ahead of your time and to avoid narrow-mindedness.

A SAMPLE PROBLEM

A situation that occurred some time ago in a college town illustrates the approach discussed here. Jean, a middle-aged woman, returned to college after many years to complete her degree. She was living off campus, in an apartment house. Directly below her apartment lived a young woman who played her stereo loud enough to reach Vladivostok with a favorable wind. At least it seemed that way to Jean. The sound and the woman's rudeness infuriated her. She pondered the problem and came up with these expressions of it.

How can I persuade her to turn it down?

How can I compel her to turn it down?

How can I frighten her into moving?

How can I escape the noise?

How can I bother her as much as she bothers me?

Deciding that the first expression of the problem was the best, Jean investigated how she might approach the woman. She tried to recall similarly difficult situations in the past that she had experienced or heard others tell about. Then she brainstormed the possible approaches she might take. After producing a generous number of ideas, she chose the best one, went to the woman, and tried it. It failed; the music continued to blare.

Disappointed, Jean looked at her list of expressions again and decided, probably because of her anger, that *compelling* might succeed where persuasion hadn't. She investigated again, produced ideas again, then selected and carried out not one, but two of them: reporting the matter to the apartment house's owner and registering a complaint with the police. The result was disheartening. The owner made a feeble appeal to the woman and the police gave her a half-hearted warning. After a day or two of quiet, the music blared again.

Now Jean decided her last expression of the problem was the best of the remaining ones. She gleefully listed dozens of hateful ideas for *bothering* the woman (including boring a hole in the floor and pouring water on the stereo). Then the insight came to her. An athletic woman, Jean loved to play tennis and jog. Why not use exercise as a weapon? So she did. She bought herself a jump rope and every morning, promptly at 4:00 A.M., she jumped rope in her bedroom—right over the sleeping woman's head. Wham, whump, thump. How sweet was revenge.

What happened next proved Jean's idea to be even more creative than she had realized. In a few days, the woman knocked on Jean's door and explained sheepishly that Jean's jumping was keeping her awake. Jean seized the opportunity and said, "I'll tell you what: I'll stop jumping rope if you'll turn the stereo down." The woman agreed, and the problem was solved.

A SAMPLE ISSUE

The following situation illustrates how the expression of an issue would differ from that of a problem.* You read a newspaper story explaining that a national chain of convenience stores has decided no longer to sell magazines with a sexual emphasis. The chain's decision, the story says, reflects increasing public objection to all forms of pornography. You decide to address the challenge implicit in this subject.

Your first step is to decide whether the subject should be considered a problem or an issue. Because pornography divides informed, intelligent people—some regarding it as harmless and others as harmful—you decide it is an issue. Next, you consider the essential elements of dispute found in the pro and con arguments concerning pornography. Those who believe pornography is harmless

*Because an adequate treatment of the issue illustrated here would demand greater space than is available, the discussion, unlike that of the sample problem, is limited to the expression of the issue.

often argue that (1) countries that take a liberal approach to the dissemination of pornography have no higher incidence of sex crimes than the United States, (2) looking at pornography provides a healthy release for sexual tension, and (3) the right of free speech applies to pornographers. On the other hand, those who believe pornography is harmful often argue that (4) it promotes a distorted view of sexuality and a negative view of women, and (5) it encourages irresponsible, immoral sexual behavior, including sadomasochism and sex between children and adults.

This consideration of the elements of dispute would lead you to the following expressions of the issue (the numbers correspond):

1. Is the incidence of sex crimes lower in countries that take a liberal approach to pornography?
2. Does looking at pornography provide a healthy release for sexual tension? In everyone? In certain people? Does the answer depend on the kind of pornography viewed?
3. Is the right of free speech applicable to pornographers?
4. Does pornography promote a distorted view of sexuality? A negative view of women? Does it do so for some people but not others? Is age a factor here?
5. Does all pornography encourage irresponsible, immoral sexual behavior, including sadomasochism and sex between children and adults? Does some pornography encourage these?

Careful exploration of these questions would prepare you to address the more general expression of the issue: Should the sale and distribution of pornography be in any way restricted?

Warm-Up Exercises

1 A hunter sees a squirrel on the trunk of a tall tree. The hunter approaches quietly, but the squirrel hears him and scampers to the other side of the tree. The hunter follows the squirrel around the tree, but the squirrel is very clever: it keeps moving at just the right pace to be on the side of the tree opposite the hunter. Around and around they move that way, on into the night. The question is: Does the hunter ever go around the squirrel? Explain your answer.

2 Is it possible for you to think of a city or a country that you have never been to? Explain your answer thoroughly.

3 Read the following dialogue carefully. Then state what you think Kenneth should say next to ensure that Karl will have no reasonable comeback.

KENNETH: Every circle has an inside and an outside.

KARL: I'll bet you can't prove that statement.

KENNETH: Sure, I can . . .

KARL: Remember, you said *every* circle. That's what you have got to prove.

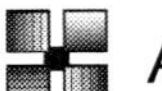

APPLICATIONS

Note: Do each of the following applications in this manner: First, express the problem or issue, using the guidelines explained in this chapter. Then investigate, as necessary, and produce as many ideas as you can to solve or resolve it. (Record all your thoughts as they occur to you, and be prepared to submit them to your instructor.) Finally, state which of your ideas you believe is best, and briefly explain why.

1 A Los Angeles woman and her husband were convicted of prostitution charges in an unusual case. The couple admitted accepting money from men for sexual favors, but they claimed that the sex acts were part of a religious ritual rather than prostitution. The husband testified he had a revelation from God to revive a 5000-year-old Egyptian religion. In his church, he explained, men's sins are absolved by having sex with the priestess, his wife.[4]

2 James Cook, president of the Thomas Alva Edison Foundation, noted that the number of patent applications in the United States had declined steadily and that a large number of the applications filed came from foreigners. He believed that the main reason for the apparent lack of interest in invention here was the poor image technology enjoyed, particularly among young people. He cited a UN study of the understanding level and appreciation of technology among the people of 19 industrialized countries. Japan scored first, the United States last.[5]

3 Hermione is a college student living in a dormitory room with two other women. Whenever she is trying to study, it seems, her roommates decide to have company, talk loudly, dance to the stereo, or do something else distracting. It's not that they *try* to bother Hermione, but the effect is the same.

4 Rocco is the manager of a movie theater. In recent years a number of competitors have cut into his business, and cable television and video rental stores have reduced the number of moviegoers still further. Rocco desperately needs to get more people to patronize his theater, particularly since he has begun to hear the owners talk of closing it and dismissing him if box office receipts don't improve.

5 Many authorities agree that one of the important reasons for the high divorce rate in this country is the naively romantic view of love many people have when they enter marriage.

6 Gail has always slept well, but lately, she has been waking up at about 3 A.M. and having trouble getting back to sleep.

ISSUE FOR EXTENDED ANALYSIS

Following is a more comprehensive thinking challenge than the others in the chapter.

THE ISSUE: JUDICIAL ACTIVISM

"Judicial activism" refers to the philosophy under which judges do not just interpret the law—in particular, the Constitution—but also, in effect, *revise* it. Supporters of such activism claim that the law—in particular, the Constitution—is a living entity that must be revised to fit new circumstances and insights. Opponents argue that the legislature alone should legislate and the courts should only decide whether a law is constitutional. The debate over this issue became especially heated during the George W. Bush administration, when some senators used the filibuster to prevent some of his federal court nominees from being voted on.

THE ESSAYS

Judicial Activism Is an Abomination
By Hannah Andersen

America has been blessed with bountiful natural resources, but the greatest resource of all is the U.S. Constitution. For over 200 years that document has provided us a finely balanced political system and a legal foundation that is the envy of the world. Today, however, the Constitution—and our liberty—are threatened by judicial activism. Thurgood Marshall, the late Supreme Court justice, expressed that philosophy simply: "You do what you think is right and let the law catch up."

As Mark Levin has documented in *Men in Black*, judicial activism has

A Blend of Old and New
By Benjamin Ward

The passing of time changes human understanding, and over the last 200 years, the changes have been astounding. When the U.S. Constitution was written, the biological and physical sciences were primitive, and the academic disciplines of psychology, sociology, and anthropology did not even exist. The insights since gained in those areas, as well as in philosophy and history, give us a much greater and deeper understanding of ourselves and our institutions.

Any suggestion that a 200-year-old treatise in physiology, astronomy, or physics should remain the standard led jurists to base their decisions on their personal opinion or international law rather than on the Constitution. In so doing, they have usurped the legislative function. For example, they have created "rights" that are nowhere to be found in the Constitution: notably, the "right" to abortion, to privacy in the bedroom, to affirmative action, to welfare assistance for illegal aliens, to flag burning, and to legal status (in U.S. courts) for enemy combatants.

But unlike members of Congress, federal jurists cannot be voted out of office—they serve for life. And that is exactly the problem. It is outrageous to have a small number of individuals decide for several million Americans what is fair and unfair, just and unjust, legal and illegal on the basis of *their personal desires and preferences.* The courts should be using a clear, objective standard that, Supreme Court Justice Antonin Scalia suggests, reflects the *original meaning* of the Constitution as it was written and as it was understood at that time. Any other approach is a violation of the founders' and our trust.

Judicial activism is not a Democrat-versus-Republican issue. It's between individuals in both parties who believe our country should be guided by the Constitution and individuals who prefer to be guided by the intellectual fashion of the day. President Franklin D. Roosevelt (a Democrat) was one of the former; as he argued, the job of the judiciary is to "do justice under the Constitution and not over it."

for contemporary judgments would be greeted with derision. I submit that the view that America's legal system should remain chained to the past is equally laughable and even more dangerous.

Today's jurists know everything that the authors of the Constitution knew about democracy and law. In addition they have 200 years' worth of knowledge that has accumulated since the founders' time. This reality is neither a credit to modern jurists nor a discredit to the founders, and it certainly does not imply any criticism of the Constitution. It is merely an acknowledgment that past ideas, however noble in their time, are inadequate to present situations.

Because society and the law evolve, today's jurists serve us best when they are guided but not constricted by the Constitution—in other words, when they blend the ideas in the Constitution with contemporary insights. Harvard law professor Lawrence Tribe argues that such *constructing* of legal interpretations is more honest than the more passive approach of *discovering* them, as long as the interpreter presents "a forthright account, incomplete and inconclusive though it might be, of why one deems his or her proposed construction of the text to be worthy of acceptance. . . ."

Class Discussion

HARRY: Mr. Ward's essay is right on the mark. His argument reveals the weakness of Hannah Andersen's old-fashioned view of the law.

EDWARD: Your own words betray the error of Ward's view. Law is not a matter of fashion, whether old or new. When it is made so, it becomes vulnerable to whatever nutty ideas happen to be popular.

HARRY: There's nothing "nutty" about keeping the Constitution up to date and having it reflect the latest insights of psychology, biology, and the other academic disciplines.

EDWARD: The problem with that perspective is that it's seldom possible to tell whether the latest idea is an insight or a fallacy until it has been tested. Besides, many of the supposed insights ignore the findings of the disciplines. The issue of abortion is a perfect example of this tendency. Geneticists have documented that human life begins at conception, yet in *Roe* v. *Wade* the Supreme Court embraced the pretense that it begins whenever a pregnant woman wishes it to begin.

EDWARD: You have to admit that it's anti-intellectual to cling to the views embodied in the Constitution, views that are now over 200 years old.

HARRY: The test of any idea is not how *old* but how *wise* it is. The U.S. Constitution is the most profound and practical set of ideas ever proposed for governing a nation. To swap it for the latest intellectual fad is not only absurd but dangerous.

Solutions to Sample Problems

THE YOUNG GIRL/OLD WOMAN PROBLEM

The young girl is looking away from you. You can see only the side of her face. The old woman is looking down, her chin touching the top of her chest.

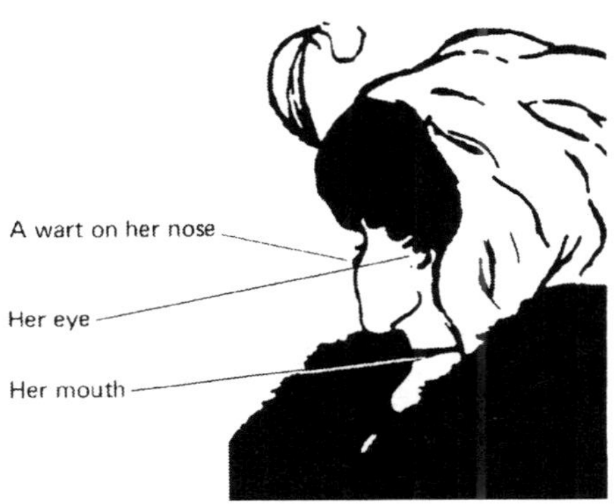

THE VASE AND FACES PROBLEM

To see the vase, focus on the white object against a background of shadow. To see two faces, imagine a bright light shining through a window and two people standing nose to nose, in silhouette.

Notes

1. Dan Kaercher, "School Closings: What Can Parents Do?" *Better Homes and Gardens,* August 1982, p. 17.
2. "No Pass, No Drive," *U.S. News & World Report,* 5 June 1989, p. 49.
3. George Iles, *Inventors at Work* (New York: Doubleday, Page, 1906), p. 370.
4. " 'Priestess' Is Convicted as Prostitute," *St. Petersburg Times,* 10 September 1989, p. 7A.
5. Interview on *Good Morning America,* 29 August 1980.

Investigate the Problem or Issue

It would be convenient if every problem or issue came in a kit containing all the information necessary to solve it. Unfortunately, that is seldom the case—we've got to search out the facts for ourselves.

In this chapter, you'll learn numerous sources of information and how to use them efficiently and imaginatively. You'll also learn how to conduct your own research whenever possible.

It may seem strange to learn that investigation is a creative stage. You may think of it as a dull, plodding effort involving very little thinking of any kind, let alone creative thinking. In part, that is right. The way many people actually carry out their investigation involves little or no thinking—which is why their investigation is so often unproductive.

Investigation, as we define it, means more than routinely getting the same information as everyone else. It means getting information others overlook by searching in ways and places that never occur to the uncreative. It means using our resourcefulness and originality, being imaginative in our search.

Not every problem you encounter requires significant investigation. If, for instance, you decide to go beyond grumbling and kicking your gym locker when the string in your sweatpants slips out, you can apply the creative process without using the investigative stage at all. You can identify the problem in a number of ways—"How can I insert the string again easily?" "How can I avoid having it slip out again in the future?" "How can I eliminate the need for a string?"—and then go directly to the third stage of the creative process: producing as many solutions to the problem as you can.

In many other cases, however, the investigative stage is a crucial step in the process. The scientists who developed the creative surgical procedure in response to periodontal disease first had to investigate the nature of the disease—that is, its cause, its progress from initial infection to tooth loss, and the various technological methods, medical tools, and approaches available to be used. In the case of unwanted graffiti, the invention of Graffiti Gobbler depended on (1) a knowledge of what techniques had been unsuccessfully tried and (2) a basic understanding of chemistry. "Inspiration," wrote Louis Pasteur, "is the impact of a fact on a well-prepared mind." The investigation stage provides the mental preparation.

Investigation is especially important in complex or controversial issues. In such matters, unless you know all the relevant facts, including the various viewpoints involved and the different lines of reasoning people follow, you are not likely to make sound judgments and develop workable solutions. A. E. Mander makes the point vividly:

> The fewer the facts [one] possesses, the simpler the problem seems to him. If we know only a dozen facts, it is not difficult to find a theory to fit them. But suppose there are five hundred thousand other facts known—but not known to us! Of what value then is our poor little theory which has been designed to fit, and which perhaps fits, only about a dozen of the five hundred thousand known facts![1]

Sometimes a single fact can make a significant difference, as in a study of multiple personality disorders that revealed that 97 percent of the victims had been abused as children.[2]

The point is not that you should feel daunted by difficult problems and issues and give up—that would certainly not help you to become a better thinker. It is that you should appreciate the importance of being thorough in your investigations and refusing to rush in, like the proverbial fool, where angels fear to tread.

WHAT TO LOOK FOR

Broadly speaking, the information necessary to solve problems or resolve issues consists of facts and informed opinions. Following are the most common sources of information.

Eyewitness Testimony

Such testimony is usually associated with the courtroom but in the more general sense it consists of any observation recounted by the person who made it. A report of what transpired at a committee meeting by someone who was present constitutes eyewitness testimony, as does the statement of someone who witnessed an automobile accident.

Eyewitness testimony is commonly thought to be highly reliable, but that is a misconception. Research has shown that perception can be clouded by a number of factors, including time of day, atmospheric conditions, emotional state, and degree of alertness. In addition, memories change over time, as Elizabeth Loftus explains:

> The "drawers" holding our memories are obviously extremely crowded and densely packed. They are also constantly being emptied out, scattered about, and then stuffed back into place. . . . As new bits of information are added into long-term memory, the old memories are removed, replaced, crumpled up, or shoved into corners. Little details are added, confusing or extraneous facts are deleted, and a coherent construction of the facts is gradually created that may bear little resemblance to the original event.[3]

Because eyewitness testimony may or may not be accurate, you should not accept it at face value. Instead, wherever possible, try to verify it.

Unpublished Report

This kind of information sometimes reflects real knowledge and sometimes merely hearsay. If you are familiar with the game "Rumor,"* you know that the more a story is told, the greater the likelihood of its being changed, often dramatically. Unpublished reports abound in e-mail. Even if you have only a few correspondents, you may receive a number of these reports every day. Sometimes they take the form of a warning to do or avoid doing something lest harm befall you or your computer. Often as not, they are false. Therefore, it is prudent to verify the accuracy of unpublished reports before accepting them or repeating them.

Published Report

This kind of information is found in books, magazines, professional journals, radio and television broadcasts, such reference works as encyclopedias, almanacs, and dictionaries, and (sometimes) on the Internet. When the information is documented in a footnote or endnote, as it sometimes is, you can check the original source for verification. If documentation is not provided, you should consider whether the author's and/or publisher's reputation for reliability is solid enough for you to trust the information. (Remember, too, that even trustworthy people can make mistakes.)

Expert Opinion

Expert opinion is generally much more trustworthy than most other sources of information because experts are better acquainted with the complexities of their subjects than laypeople and better able to distinguish typical incidents and events from nontypical ones. However, the knowledge explosion has made it more diffi-

*This game is played with a group of people. It begins with one person whispering a statement to the person next to him or her. That person then whispers the statement to the next person, and so on around the room. When the last person whispers it to the person who originated it, that final version is compared with the original statement.

cult to stay abreast of the developments even in a single area of a discipline, let alone an entire discipline. Thus, a person can be world renowned in one special area of his or her discipline yet uninformed about other areas. Before accepting expert opinion, it is best to (1) be sure the person is qualified in the *specific* area in question and (2) check to see whether or not the expert's view is shared by other experts. And never confuse celebrity with expertise.

Experiment

An experiment is a controlled procedure undertaken to test the validity of a hypothesis, a statement that predicts or explains phenomena or behavior. The researcher begins the experiment by formulating one or more hypotheses. Next, the researcher decides what behavior characteristics can be measured, rated, or scored; these characteristics are known as *variables*. Finally, the researcher constructs and conducts the experiment and analyzes the resulting data.

There are two broad categories of experiment: the laboratory experiment and the field experiment. The laboratory experiment has the advantage of controlled conditions, which permit more accurate determinations of cause and effect. However, it has the disadvantage of the experimenter unintentionally influencing the outcome. The results of a laboratory experiment can be trusted if it has been replicated by other researchers; the conclusions of a field experiment can be trusted if they have been independently confirmed.

In one well-known psychological experiment, Haney, Banks, and Zimbardo tested the hypothesis that the roles people choose or are assigned strongly influence the way they behave. The researchers had college students volunteer (for pay) to take part in a six-day "prison" experiment in the basement of a university building. Some students were randomly assigned to be "prisoners" and others were assigned to be "guards." In a relatively short time, the "prisoners" developed one or more emotional symptoms, including depression, helplessness, apathy, anger, and panic. The "guards" quickly adopted the characteristics common to prison workers. Some were kind and fair, but others were cruel and abusive, even when the "prisoners" gave them no reason to be so. When the experiment ended, all the "prisoners" were relieved, but most of the "guards" were disappointed: they had found their position of power enjoyable and were reluctant to relinquish it.[4]

In another well-known experiment, Solomon Asch tested the hypothesis that people will contradict their own perceptions and judgments if they are under group pressure to conform. Asch's experiment was quite simple. One by one, eight students were shown a sheet of paper containing a 10-inch line and three other lines marked A, B, and C. They were then asked which of the three other lines matched the 10-inch line. The correct answer was A, the other lines being obviously shorter or longer. Unknown to the eighth student, all the students who answered before had been secretly directed to choose line B. By the time the eighth student answered, the pressure to conform was strong. Predictably, a majority of students yielded to the pressure and gave the wrong answer.[5] In this experiment, as in the previous one, the researcher's hypothesis was validated.

Statistics

The term *statistics* refers, in the broadest sense, to quantified information. Used more narrowly, it means information obtained by accounting for every individual in a group. Examples of statistical information are the voting records of members of Congress, the patterns of immigration over the last 50 years, and the comparative incomes of various racial and ethnic groups. When carefully collected and honestly presented, statistical information is very reliable. In considering any statistical information, determine the completeness and currency of the data as well as the reputation of the statistician.

Survey

Like statistics, a survey produces quantified information. However, a survey is done with a *representative sample* of a group rather than with the entire group. A survey identifies the opinions, beliefs, or behaviors of a particular group of people, the technical name for which is a *population.* If the population is small enough, all members may be surveyed. However, if the population is too large, a more limited number, or *sample,* is surveyed. The sample must be representative of the total population, and to ensure that this is the case, researchers are required to take a systematic approach, selecting, for example, every tenth or twentieth or one-hundredth name on a list of members of the population. The actual survey may be mailed (or otherwise delivered) and self-administered, or it may be conducted in person or by telephone. Survey questions are typically fill-in or multiple-choice and designed to identify the subject's feelings, thoughts, or behaviors concerning the issue being investigated. For the survey to be valid, all questions must be clear, unambiguous, and free of bias.

Observational Study

As the name implies, this approach consists of closely examining an event or activity as it is taking place, for the purpose of understanding it and, in some cases, finding ways to improve it. The researcher may be either a participant or a bystander. In the latter role, his or her physical presence is not necessarily required; a videotape of the activity might suffice. For example, an executive charged with improving a company's customer service department might spend a week or so performing that job or, instead, arrange to videotape customer service staff interacting with customers. (The staff would, of course, be informed that they were being taped.) From this study, the executive would learn the kinds of situations customer service representatives are required to deal with, the variation in the time necessary to complete transactions, the difficulties and frustrations that accompany the job, and the relative effectiveness of the strategies employed to achieve customer satisfaction.

The conclusions reached by formal observation are generally reliable if (a) they were of sufficient duration to ensure that the group's behavior was not unusual, (b) the observer did not influence the group's behavior by his or her presence, and (c) the conclusions are not overgeneralized beyond the group observed to other groups that might be different.

Research Review

As the term implies, a research review draws together and compares the results of a number, often dozens or hundreds, of individual studies. Because it can reveal broad areas of agreement and disagreement among researchers, it is among the most valuable and reliable kinds of information, provided that it does not omit any relevant research.

Your Personal Experience

This is often the most vivid information because you know it intimately and have greater confidence in it. Unfortunately, that confidence could lead you to assume that an experience is typical when it might not be and to end your investigation prematurely. The best approach is to combine your personal experience with the other information rather than use it as a substitute.

Your personal experience may be more substantial and more relevant than you realize. This is especially so if, like many people, you regard every subject, and every aspect within a subject, as neatly and permanently separated from every other one. In that case, you might never dream of finding a scientific insight in a poem or a clue to an ethical problem in a math book. Yet many of the most creative insights come from just such unexpected places.

The forklift, for example, which makes it possible to move the heaviest objects effortlessly, was first conceived of when the inventor was standing in a bakery. He noticed how the doughnuts were lifted out of the oven on steel "fingers" and thought, "Why shouldn't that same idea work in the warehouse?"[6] Similarly, the idea of the printing press first occurred to Johannes Gutenberg while he was watching a winepress operating. He had long pondered how to achieve quicker book production; the current method was to carve words laboriously on blocks and then to rub paper against them. The winepress suggested the idea of transferring an image to paper by pressing an inked lead seal against it.[7]

What connection is there between a secretary's desk and an operating room? Or between the dolphins at Florida's Ocean World and the education of children with Down syndrome? "No connection at all," most people would say. And yet creative people have seen a very valuable connection. Surgeons are now using staples in place of sutures to save time and blood loss. And David Nathanson, a professor of psychology at Florida International University, has demonstrated that young people with Down syndrome learn to speak more quickly and remember words longer when they are placed in pools with trained dolphins. He got the idea for the experiment when he noticed that these children, who couldn't sit still and pay attention to a teacher, would play with a puppy for a quarter of an hour. Speculating on how this interest in animals could best be used in teaching, he decided to use dolphins.[8]

In addition to searching for connections among ideas you encounter now, you can also search for connections you overlooked in past experiences and observations. You surely have thousands of experiences classified under only one heading that could be classified under several. For example, you may have gone swimming as a child, got a little too far from shore, struggled, panicked, and almost drowned, until a friend saved you. That experience and the circumstances surrounding it are probably etched in your mind as *narrow escape from drowning*. But think of the other possible classifications: *effects of fear on performance, importance of children's obedience to parents, role of personal sacrifice in friendship*. By seeing more connections between past experiences and observations, you multiply your store of useful information.

The Experiences of People You Know

Other people's experiences can be as valuable to you as your own. To tap your friends' experiences, approach them skillfully, with questions that stimulate their thinking and assist them in remembering. Let's say your problem is how to overcome your fear of heights. You could ask a friend, "Have you ever been afraid of high places?" but that wouldn't be the best way to phrase the question. Any of your friend's fears might give you helpful information, so your first question should be broader. And you should be ready with subsequent questions to direct your friend's recall in ways that seem helpful to you. Here's how you might proceed:

YOU: Have you ever had a nagging fear you wanted to overcome?

FRIEND: I don't know . . . I guess so. Hmmm . . . *[Trying to remember something specific]*

YOU: *[Stimulating recall]* I mean, like a fear of being closed in; or dogs; or high places.

FRIEND: Yeah, when I was about 12. I can remember being terrified of the dogs on my paper route.

YOU: Tell me about it. How did you feel?

Later in the conversation, you would ask how the fear began and, more important, how your friend coped with and overcame it. You'd also ask whether he or she ever received any advice from others that proved helpful or knows any books and articles that speak to the question of overcoming fear. You might even share your fear with your friend and ask for a reaction.

Any time you try to draw on other people's experience in this way, keep two points in mind. First, some people are more helpful than others. You'll always do better asking a good thinker rather than a poor thinker or an open, talkative person rather than a shy, secretive one. Second, successful questioning depends not only on your ability to ask the right question at the right time but also on your willingness to listen at other times, to open yourself to the person's experience and not let other thoughts (even analytical ones) intrude.

It is also a good idea not to rely solely on your memory. Instead, get in the habit of taking notes. In most cases, this is better done soon after the conversation rather than during it because many people will be distracted if you write while they speak.

USING THE LIBRARY

Perhaps you think of the library as a gathering place for dull people, a place of little use to anyone who is lively and creative. That is a mistaken view. In fact, the library is best seen as *a formal meeting room for interviews with authorities not otherwise available.* That's precisely the way the very best thinkers regard it.

If your aversion to the library is based instead on the fear of lingering too long, you'll be pleased to learn that the people who use the library most often—professional writers, speakers, and scholars—have even more reason than you to save time. They often have difficult deadlines to meet. Efficiency is not just a matter of preference with them; it's a dollars-and-cents concern. Yet they don't avoid the library; they simply use it more effectively.

The first step in using the library as professionals do is to determine all the headings and subheadings that might apply to your subject. Because the information sought may appear under different headings in the library's various sources, this is an important step. Start by giving free rein to your imagination and listing as many headings as you can. For example, for *crime,* you may think of the subtopics *homicide, rape, shoplifting, kidnapping, vandalism,* and *burglary.* Next, expand your list of headings by consulting two sources available in most college libraries: the index volume of *Encyclopedia Americana* and the *Thesaurus of Psychological Index Terms,* a companion volume to *Psychological Abstracts.* You'll find such additional headings as *felonies, misdemeanors, antisocial behavior, behavior disorders, psychosexual behavior,* and *infanticide.*

Once you have determined the headings under which the information you are looking for is classified, get the information by using these simple and efficient approaches.

1. Consult a good encyclopedia for a broad overview of your subject. *Encyclopaedia Britannica* and *Encyclopedia Americana* are generally considered the best. Note important facts. In addition, note special terms that might be useful in further research.

2. Consult an almanac, a collection of miscellaneous facts and statistical information about a wide variety of subjects. On the subject of crime, for example, you can find information under as many as two dozen specific listings. Most almanacs are published once a year. Thus, you can obtain comparative data—say, for 1970, 1980, and 1990—quickly and easily.

3. Consult the appropriate indexes. Indexes do not present the information you are looking for, but they tell you where to find it and so save you much time and energy. The following are among the most generally useful indexes. (Your librarian will be able to suggest others.)

   - For information in nontechnical periodicals—*The Readers' Guide to Periodical Literature.*

- For information in specialized and technical publications—
  Applied Science and Technology Index
  Art Index
  Biography Index
  Biological and Agricultural Index
  Book Review Index
  Business Periodicals Index
  Education Index
  Engineering Index
  Essay and General Literature Index
  General Science Index
  Humanities Index
  Index to Legal Periodicals
  Magazine Index
  Music Index
  Philosopher's Index
  Psychological Abstracts
  Religion Index One: Periodicals
  Social Science Index
- For information in newspaper reports—the *New York Times Index*.
- For information in government publications—the *Monthly Catalog of United States Government Publications* and the *Monthly Checklist of State Publications*.

4. Consult computer databases and abstracting services. Data searches are easier than ever with modern information-retrieval technology. Your librarian can explain the databases available to you. Ask, too, about abstracting services such as *Sociological Abstracts, America: History and Life,* and *Dissertation Abstracts International.*

5. Consult the *subject index* of the card catalog for books on your subject. Use broad subject headings as well as narrow ones; often a book that treats a larger subject will have a chapter or two on your subject.

6. Obtain and read the books and articles that are most relevant to your subject. Though the number of books and articles you read will depend on the scope of your project, the first five steps of the process should be followed for all but the very briefest of treatments.

These reference works are only the basic ones. For that reason, it is important to remember that your most important resource in the library is the people who work there: the librarians and their assistants. They can suggest other research materials and help you expand your expertise.

USING THE INTERNET

In less than a decade the Internet has become one of the most popular and useful research tools. One important reason is that you don't have to leave home to access it. All you need is a computer and an Internet Service Provider (ISP). Then you just dial up the ISP, get online, and you're free to surf the Web. You can visit commercial sites, designated by .com; organizational sites (.org); government sites (.gov); and education sites (.edu).

The main challenge of using the Internet is finding the information you are looking for quickly and efficiently. If you happen to know the address of the Web site you are looking for, all you have to do is type it in the address box and hit "enter." (*Note:* It is essential that you get the address exactly right. Change a character or add a space and you'll end up nowhere, or somewhere unintended.) If you don't have a specific address, you will have to use a "search engine." One of the best is Google—the address is http://www.google.com. If you were to type that address into your ISP address box, you would get the Google home page shown in Figure 1. If you were to click on any of the blue words on that home page, a window would open, providing you with information on that topic.

Next, if you were to type in the term "media bias" in the search box and click on "Google Search," you would get a page like the one shown in Figure 2. Notice near the top right of the page that the search produced over 700,000 results and took 0.12 seconds. The page shown here contains only five of the ten results shown on the actual Web page. At the bottom of that page you can choose to access the next ten results, and so on. You can access any one of the items by clicking on its title. By clicking on "Cached" at the end of an item, you can get a snapshot of what Google found when it accessed the item. If you find an item is especially appropriate, you can click "Similar pages" at the end of the entry and get more focused results.

Use Google when you don't know which Web site is likely to provide the information you are seeking, or when you wish to expand your search. On the other hand, if you do know the most likely Web site, start your search there. Here are some special-purpose Web sites.

For Finding Hoaxes and Fake Viruses

If you've ever passed on an e-mail warning to your friends only to learn later that it was a hoax, you know how embarrassing the experience can be. By checking the following sites *before* you pass on the message, you can spare yourself that embarrassment:

http://www.snopes2.com (the best general-purpose site)

http://www.cdc.gov/search.htm (this is run by the Centers for Disease Control (CDC); when there, type "hoaxes" in the search box)

http://hq.mycio.com/dispHoax.asp?virus_k=99436 (this McAfee site helpful in detecting virus hoaxes)

http://www.fraud.org (The National Fraud Information Center site)

FIGURE 1 www.google.com, November 13, 2002, 11:00 a.m.

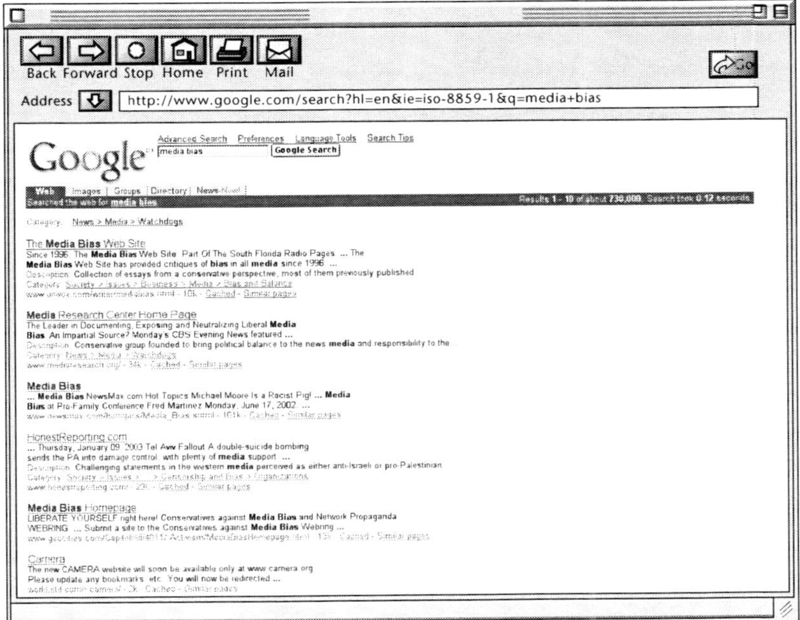

FIGURE 2 www.google.com, November 13, 2002, 11:02 a.m.

For Evaluating the Quality of a Web Site

http://www2.widener.edu/Wolfgram-Memorial-Library/webeval/eval1198/index.htm (an outstanding slide show by Jan Alexander and Marsha Ann Tate)

For Informed Opinion

Conservative

http://www.townhall.com (click on "columnists," and then click on any of the featured columns or on any name in the list of contributors)

http://www.jewishworldreview.com/ (click on any of the names in the "Insight" column on the home page)

Liberal

http://www.prospect.org (click first on "columnists" and then on "find other authors")

http://www.demsonline.net/home.htm (click on "links")

Varied

http://www.blueagle.com/index.html (this site lists 700 columnists, many cartoonists, and links to political Web sites)

For News

http://www.foxnews.com (the Fox News Channel site)

http://www.ap.org (the Associated Press site)

http://www.cnn.com (the CNN site)

For Reference Materials (including encyclopedias; thesauruses; dictionaries; collections of quotations; guides to English usage, religion, and literary history)

http://www.bartleby.com/reference/

http://www.infoplease.com (the Information Please site)

For Quotations on a Variety of Subjects

http://www.toinspire.com

For Legal Information

http://www.legalengine.com

For Health

http://www.nih.gov

http://www.medlineplus.gov

For General Up-to-Date Information on Search Engines

http://www.searchenginewatch.com

MAINTAINING A QUESTIONING PERSPECTIVE

When dealing with published ideas, particularly those of well-known authorities, you may be tempted to surrender your judgment. To let that happen is a mistake. Being human, authorities are subject to making the same errors as anyone else. They can, for example, be blinded by personal preferences, cling stubbornly to outmoded views, and suffer lapses in reasoning.

Even when they manage to avoid such elementary errors, they may miss important new developments in their field or related fields, or they may misinterpret the significance of such developments. Research is constantly being done in every field, and the findings of such efforts often overturn previous conclusions. For example, for years, expert medical opinion was in agreement that eating fats increased the risk of heart disease, that heavy salt consumption caused a rise in blood pressure, that the frequent consumption of eggs caused an increase in serum cholesterol, and that obesity in adulthood depended on childhood eating habits. Then new studies were published that challenged each of these conclusions and caused expert opinion to be modified.[9]

Complicating the matter further is the fact that new insights often take years to become general knowledge among the members of a profession. Psychologist Carol Tavris's excellent study *Anger: The Misunderstood Emotion,* which demolished the traditional assumption that venting hostility is beneficial, was published in 1982. Yet articles are still being written endorsing the earlier idea, the authors apparently oblivious of Tavris's work or irrationally committed to an erroneous view.

Accordingly, as important as it is to seek out authoritative opinion, it is equally important to maintain a questioning perspective. The best ways to do so are to consult several authorities of differing perspectives, to ask probing questions of each, and to compare their responses.

MANAGING AN INTERVIEW

Chances are, most of your investigation will be done in the library or on the Internet. But you may, on occasion, have the opportunity to interview an authority (for example, a professor on your campus who has done special research in the area you are investigating). In such cases, follow this basic rule: be considerate of the interviewee, who is donating valuable time and shouldn't be taken for granted. Here are some specific ways to show consideration.

1. Call or write ahead for an appointment. Explain exactly what you wish to discuss and how long you'll take. (Keep the time as brief as you can, preferably under half an hour.) Make yourself available at a time that fits the interviewee's schedule best.

2. Before the interview, make an effort to learn the fundamentals of the subject you will be discussing. If the subject is controversial, know the issues in dispute and have at least a general notion of the competing arguments.

3. Prepare your questions carefully in advance. Make them clear and brief. Try to avoid those that can be answered yes or no; they won't be very helpful. For instance, instead of asking, "Do you agree with the governor's position?" ask, "What is your reaction to the governor's statement?" If you are sufficiently informed about a view that opposes the interviewee's views, ask, "Dr. ___________ says such-and-such. How would you respond?" If you are insufficiently informed about opposing views, ask, "On what matters do those who oppose your view differ with you, and how would you respond to their disagreement?"

4. Anticipate the responses to your initial questions, and prepare follow-up questions to probe those responses you feel don't go far enough or don't address the points you wish addressed.

5. Arrive on time. When you begin the interview, get right to the point. Keep your questions crisp and clear. Avoid thinking ahead to your next question. Instead, listen carefully to the reply. If any of your interviewee's comments open up an aspect of the issue you did not consider but is worth pursuing, be sure to pursue it. However, try not to overstay your welcome.

6. If at all possible, don't make the person wait while you take notes. If you can't take shorthand or write rapidly in longhand, consider the possibility of taping the interview. (Always obtain permission to tape an interview. Never merely assume taping is acceptable to the other person.)

If an in-person interview is not possible, consider a telephone interview. Such an interview is conducted the same as the preceding, with two additional requirements. First, be sure to call or write in advance to determine when the interview will be most convenient. It is boorish to assume that because you are ready, your interviewee is, too. Second, remember that when conducting a telephone interview, it is especially important to speak clearly and to ask clear, concise questions.

AVOIDING PLAGIARISM[10]

Once ideas are put into words and published, they become "intellectual property," and the author has the same rights over them as he or she has over a material possession such as a house or a car. The only real difference is that intellectual property is purchased with mental effort rather than money. Anyone who has ever wracked his or her brain trying to solve a problem or trying to put an idea into clear and meaningful words can appreciate how difficult mental effort can be.

Plagiarism is passing off other people's ideas or words as one's own. It is doubly offensive in that it both steals and deceives. In the academic world, plagiarism is considered an ethical violation and is punished by a failing grade for a paper or a course, or even by dismissal from the institution. Outside the academy, it is a crime that can be prosecuted if the person to whom the ideas and words belong wishes to bring charges.

Some cases of plagiarism are attributable to intentional dishonesty, others to carelessness. But many, perhaps most, are due to misunderstanding. The instructions "Base your paper on research rather than on your own unfounded opinions" and "Don't present other people's ideas as your own" seem contradictory and may confuse you, especially if no clarification is offered. Fortunately, there is a way to honor both instructions and, in the process, to avoid plagiarism.

Step 1: When you are researching a topic, keep your sources' ideas separate from your own. Begin by keeping a record of each source of information you consult. For an Internet source, record the Web site address, the author and title of the item, and the date you visited the site. For a book, record the author, title, place of publication, publisher, and date of publication. For a magazine or journal article, record the author, title, the name of the publication, and its date of issue. For a TV or radio broadcast, record the program title, station, and date of transmission.

Step 2: As you read each source, note the ideas you want to refer to in your writing. If the author's words are unusually clear and concise, copy them *exactly* and put quotation marks around them. Otherwise, paraphrase—that is, restate the author's ideas in your words. Write down the number(s) of the page on which the author's passage appears. If the author's idea triggers a response in your mind—such as a question, a connection between this idea and something else you've read, or an experience of your own that supports or challenges what the author says—write it down and put brackets (not parentheses) around it so that you will be able to identify it as your own when you review your notes.

Here is a sample research record illustrating these two steps:

> **Adler, Mortimer J. *The Great Ideas: A Lexicon of Western Thought* (New York: Macmillan Publishing Co., 1992, pp. 867, 869)** Says that throughout the ages, from ancient Greece, philosophers have argued about whether various ideas are true. Says it's remarkable that most renowned thinkers have agreed about what truth is—"a correspondence between thought and reality." 867 Also says that Freud saw this as the scientific view of truth. Quotes Freud: "This correspondence with the real external world we call truth. It is the aim of scientific work, even when the practical value of that work does not interest us." 869 [I say true statements fit the facts; false statements do not.]

Whenever you look back on this record, even a year from now, you will be able to tell at a glance which ideas and words are the author's and which are yours. The first three sentences are, with the exception of the directly quoted part, *paraphrases* of the author's ideas. The fourth is a direct quotation. The final sentence, in brackets, is your own idea.

Step 3: When you compose your paper, work borrowed ideas and words into your writing by judicious use of quoting and paraphrasing. In addition, give credit to the various authors. Your goal here is to eliminate all doubt about which ideas and words belong to whom. In formal presentations, this crediting is done in footnotes; in informal ones, it is done simply by mentioning the author's name.

Here is an example of how the material from Mortimer Adler might be worked into a composition. (Note where the footnote is placed and the form that is used for it.) The second paragraph illustrates how your own idea might be expanded:

> Mortimer J. Adler explains that throughout the ages, from the time of the ancient Greeks, philosophers have argued about whether various ideas are true. But to Adler the remarkable thing is that, even as they argued, most renowned thinkers have agreed about what truth is. They saw it as "a correspondence between thought and reality." Adler points out that Sigmund Freud believed this was also the scientific view of truth. He quotes Freud as follows: "This correspondence with the real external world we call truth. It is the aim of scientific work, even when the practical value of that work does not interest us."[1]
>
> This correspondence view of truth is consistent with the common sense rule that a statement is true if it fits the facts and false if it does not. For example, the statement "the twin towers of New York's World Trade Center were destroyed on September 11, 2002" is false because they were destroyed the previous year. I may sincerely believe that it is true, but my believing in no way affects the truth of the matter. In much the same way, if an innocent man is convicted of a crime, neither the court's decision nor the world's acceptance of it will make him any less innocent. We may be free to think what we wish, but our thinking can't alter reality.
>
> [1]Mortimer J. Adler, *The Great Ideas: A Lexicon of Western Thought* (New York: Macmillan Publishing Co., 1992), pp. 867, 869.

CONDUCTING YOUR OWN RESEARCH

The approaches considered so far in this chapter constitute the first and most fundamental line of investigation—determining *what is already known*. In many cases, such an investigation will produce all the evidence you need to solve the problem or resolve the issue. Sometimes, however, you will need to go beyond what is already known and develop *new knowledge* by conducting your own research. Here are two suggestions.

Consider Doing a Survey

Among the survey topics that might be interesting to investigate on a college campus are students' attitudes toward cheating, the campus community's position on the issue of whether women's athletic teams should receive the same level of funding as men's teams, and the professors' attitudes toward open parking on campus.

Consider Doing an Observational Study

Examples of observational studies that would be appropriate on a college campus are a study of the dynamics of a committee meeting to determine areas of inefficiency and ineffectiveness, and a study of the flow of people through the campus cafeteria during peak volume periods to identify how and where bottlenecks occur.

Before you attempt either of these approaches, reread the explanation provided earlier in the chapter.

KEEPING CREATIVITY ALIVE

As crucial as the investigation stage is in the solution of many problems, it can threaten creativity. The more information you accumulate, the greater the potential for confusion. To keep creativity alive, you will have to overcome that confusion. Here is how to do so.

Whenever you are confused by the amount or complexity of the information you have obtained and have difficulty sorting it out, pause for a moment, look back at your statement of the problem (stage 2), and use that statement to decide what is relevant and what is not. If you are dealing with an especially difficult problem, you may have to use this approach many times. Even the best and most creative thinkers lose their bearings from time to time, but they don't allow themselves to become discouraged. They just find their bearings again and continue.

A large amount of information can also have a daunting effect on your confidence. The more you probe a problem, the more you are likely to realize its complexity. In time, you may find yourself thinking, "I didn't realize it would be this difficult. Maybe there is no solution. If other, more qualified people have been unable to find a solution, what business do I have trying?" When such thoughts occur, remind yourself that others may not have solved the problem precisely because they gave in to their feelings of apprehension—the ones that at this very moment threaten your creativity—or because, despite their expertise, they lacked the techniques for unlocking and applying their creativity. (After all, creativity is not a formal subject taught in most schools and colleges, so it is not surprising that otherwise educated people should be uninformed about it.) Remember, too, that whatever difficulties arise in thinking, there are effective methods for dealing with them, and your resources for producing creative responses to problems and issues are, as the next chapter will demonstrate, considerable.

WARM-UP EXERCISES

1 Read the following dialogue carefully. Then decide what you would say next if you were Veronica. Make your response so clear and effective that the matter would be settled.

PERRY: The only book a person ever needs to read is the Bible.

VERONICA: I don't agree. Other books surely have something to offer.

PERRY: Let me show you how wrong that is. If other books agree with the Bible, they are unnecessary. And if they disagree, they are irreligious and should be avoided.

2 Create as many new food recipes as you can. Include ingredients and preparation instructions.

3 Old toothbrushes are usually thrown in the trash. But are they really useless? Think of as many uses as you can for them.

Applications

1 Each of the following cases was reported in the news. Most readers undoubtedly viewed them narrowly, believing each was entirely irrelevant to any but the most obvious subject. Yet, to someone searching for more than surface connections, each case offers some interesting possibilities. For each of the following cases, list as many implied subjects or issues as you can. Be sure to specify what those implications are.

a. Some research findings suggest that personality differences among individuals are more a result of heredity than of environment. For example, University of Minnesota psychologists who studied 400 sets of adult twins found a strong genetic link for such qualities as anger, cautious behavior, and social-political religious conservatism. And a Pennsylvania State University study of 700 sets of twins estimated that environment counts for only 10 percent of personality differences.[11]

b. A 9-year-old boy known as Robert M. pointed a toy gun at a New York City bank teller and robbed her of $118. He was placed on two years' probation after his attorney argued he was only playacting during the robbery. Then, a year later, the same boy, with two accomplices, was arrested for stealing a sled from two boys at knifepoint.[12]

c. Three-year-old Chad Chancey was expected to be the youngest trial witness in Oklahoma's history. He was the only person with any knowledge of the events that took place the night his mother and sister were murdered. Chad reportedly heard a loud argument in the next room, women's screams, a sound he described as a loud handclap, then silence. He later identified the man who had been in the apartment that night from a police file photo. The defense attorney expressed concern that the child might be too young to separate fact from fantasy.[13]

d. In 1945, Charles Jamison was found badly wounded on a Boston dock. He carried papers identifying him as a first mate on the USS *Cutty Sark*. Yet no records could be found of the existence of such a ship, and all further investigations about the man revealed nothing. Interviews with him disclosed only that he had no family, had gone to sea at age 13, and believed his ship had been torpedoed. He remained in a Boston hospital until his death 30 years after his discovery on the dock.[14]

e. Dr. Martin Orne, a psychiatrist and an expert on memory and hypnosis, and Dr. Elizabeth Loftus, a psychologist and memory expert, presented information to the American Association for the Advancement of Science that suggested that using hypnotism to get witnesses to recall details of past events may be ill advised. Their research showed that memory may be unintentionally altered by the form of the hypnotist's questions. "If the hypnotist has certain beliefs," said Dr. Orne, "he will create memories in the subject's mind."[15]

f. A human fetus survived to full term after it was extracted from its mother's womb for surgery and then returned to the womb following surgery. The surgery, which took place in the twenty-fourth week of pregnancy, corrected a life-threatening urinary tract obstruction.[16]

2 Woebegone College is having a problem with grade inflation. The average grade submitted by many professors is a B+, even though the average entrance examination score of Woebegone's students has declined steadily over the past decade. It appears that work that would have received a C 10 or 15 years ago is now being given a B or B+. One effect has been that 60 percent of the student body is on the dean's list. Find the best expression of this problem. Then investigate it, as necessary, using the approaches explained in the chapter, and produce as many solutions as you can. (Record all your thoughts as they occur to you, and be prepared to submit them to your instructor.) Finally, state which of your solutions you believe is best, and briefly explain why.

3 Every so often, someone writes an article about the poor state of composition teaching, usually with a title such as "Why Dick and Jane Can't Write" or "The Scandal in the English Classroom." The public then gets excited and calls for a study of the problem, and the media explore methods of developing students' language skills. But no lasting creative solution to the problem ever seems to be found. Identify and solve this problem, following the directions in Application 2.

4 Alcohol and drug abuse are associated with crime in the streets, health problems, the breakdown of the family, and poor job performance. Identify and solve this problem, following the directions in Application 2.

5 In many states, the schools are financed primarily by property taxes. This system, of course, tends to favor wealthy areas over poor areas and often results in inequality of educational opportunity. Identify and solve this problem, following the directions in Application 2.

6 On the one hand, the federal government forbids cigarette advertising on radio and television and requires health warnings to be printed on every pack of cigarettes sold. On the other hand, the same government heavily subsidizes tobacco farming. Address this challenge, following the directions in Application 2.

7 The U.S. Patent and Trademark Office announced in 1987 that it considered "non-naturally occurring non-human multicellular living organisms, including animals, to be patentable subject matter. . . ." A year later a patent was issued to Harvard University for a new breed of genetically altered mice. Some people consider this scientific advancement. Others consider it a dangerous precedent.[17] Address this challenge, following the directions in Application 2.

ISSUE FOR EXTENDED ANALYSIS

Following is a more comprehensive thinking challenge than the others in the chapter.

The Issue: U.S. Foreign Aid

Every year the United States donates billions of dollars in cash, goods, and services to other countries. Many Americans believe our foreign aid programs are a shining example of our compassion and generosity. Others believe the programs not only fail to achieve their objectives but, in some cases, are *counter*productive.

The Essays

Expand U.S. Foreign Aid
By Mirra al-Nur

It is commonly believed that the United States is the most generous country in the world. This is simply not the case. Statistical comparisons of the foreign aid contributions of major industrialized countries consistently show the United States near last place. For example, in 2004, only one industrialized country (Italy) scored lower. Those scoring higher included Canada, Ireland, Finland, and even tiny Luxembourg!

End the Foreign Aid Fiasco
By Mary Robinson

America is the most generous country in history. We contribute money and services to countries stricken by earthquakes, hurricanes, tsumanis, and disease epidemics. We help countries ravaged by war. We even help restore countries with whom *we ourselves* have been at war—notably Nazi Germany and Imperial Japan after World War II.

Despite our generosity, however, we are the most hated country in the

If this fact is surprising, it is only because the ratings are based not on total dollars given but instead on what percentage of each country's gross national product (GNP) the contribution represents. That is a much more reasonable measure, and by it our contribution is embarrassingly low. After all, we are the richest and most powerful nation in the world. Our generosity is essential to overcoming the devastation of poverty and disease in the Third World.

To say that U.S. foreign aid should be increased is not to suggest that the existing model for that aid is perfect. The largest amounts of our aid now go to Egypt, Russia, and Israel. If they were to receive less, nations with more basic and serious problems could receive more. In addition, our aid programs tend to pay little attention to the use to which the aid is put and the effectiveness of distribution efforts. It would be wise for us not merely to trust the leaders of foreign countries to be honorable but to require verification.

We also should consider giving more of our aid in the form of technical assistance. There is much insight in the old saying, "Give a man a fish and you feed him for a day. Teach him to fish and you feed him for a lifetime."

But however much we may revise our aid model, we should increase its funding. A great nation should lead the world in generosity.

world. In the U.N. and elsewhere world leaders accuse us of lacking compassion and even of being bullies and imperialists. It is not uncommon to see the American flag and effigies of our leaders burned in public squares.

The fact that our efforts are so unappreciated would be reason enough to rethink our foreign aid policy. But there is an even better reason—our foreign aid is not working. This is not exactly a news flash. In 1986, in a research study titled "The Continuing Failure of Foreign Aid" James Bovard pointed out that "foreign aid has rarely done anything that countries could not have done for themselves. And it has often encouraged the recipient governments' worst tendencies." Bovard argues that in dumping free food in other countries, our Food for Peace program bankrupts local farmers. He also feels that the Agency for International Development (AID) helps corrupt governments take charge of entire industries and thus stifle private enterprise, strengthen their hold over the people, and block democratic movements.

The situation has actually gotten worse since he wrote those words. Dictators and their lackeys have become more sophisticated at diverting aid from their people to their own bank accounts or, worse, to the coffers of terrorists. The time has come to admit that foreign aid doesn't work and to end it. There are more than enough good uses to which our money can be put in this country.

Class Discussion

ALEXIS: I think al-Nur's view is more balanced than Robinson's. She admits that the aid could be divided more evenly among the recipient countries. And she acknowledges the problem of ensuring that the aid reaches the people it is intended to help. Yet she also points out the fact than the United States is providing far less aid than it could and should.

BRUCE: I applaud her balance, but when all is said and done, she is championing a failed program. I see no virtue in that. It's simply throwing good money after bad.

ALEXIS: The virtue lies in helping people in need. Acts of kindness are the cornerstone of religion and morality. In Judaism, they are known as *mitzvahs* (good deeds); in Buddhism, as metta (acts of loving kindness). And Jesus admonished his disciples that "whatever you do to . . . the least of my brethren, you do unto me."

BRUCE: It's true that religion urges, even demands, that *individual people* help neighbors in need. But to my knowledge no religion teaches that *governments* have any such responsibility.

ALEXIS: There are so many poor people and nations, and their needs are so great, that governmental aid is absolutely essential. Individuals couldn't meet the need even if they wanted to, and I'm not sure that a sufficient number of people want to.

BRUCE: You're mistaken. There are thousands of private aid programs, including many religious ones. Millions of people support those programs. And the programs do a more efficient and effective job in distributing aid than any government does.

Notes

1. *Logic for the Millions* (New York: Philosophical Library, 1947), p. 55.
2. "Child Abuse a Major Factor in Multiple Personalities," *Oneonta Star,* 31 October 1985, p. 5.
3. Elizabeth Loftus and Katherine Ketcham, *Witness for the Defense: The Accused, the Eyewitness, and the Expert Who Puts Memory on Trial* (New York: St. Martin's Press, 1991), p. 20.
4. Cited in Carole Wade and Carol Tavris, *Psychology,* 5th ed. (New York: Longman, 1998), pp. 656–657.
5. Cited in Wade and Tavris, pp. 672–673.
6. Parnes, *Creative Behavior Guidebook,* p. 40.
7. Koestler, *Act of Creation,* p. 123.
8. "Dolphins May Help Train Retarded Tots," *Binghamton Press,* 28 February 1982, p. 5a.
9. "America's Diet Wars," *U.S. News & World Report,* 20 January 1985, p. 62. See also "Obesity Depends on Genetics," *Oneonta Star,* 23 January 1986, pp. 1ff.

10. This section copyright © 2002 by MindPower, Inc. Used with permission.
11. Marilyn Elias, "Inborn Traits Outweigh Environment," *USA Today*, 9 August 1989, pp. 1Df.
12. "Bank Robber, 10, Back in Trouble," *Oneonta Star*, 13 February 1982, p. 1.
13. "Tot's Testimony Crucial in Murder Trial," *Binghamton Press*, 26 October 1975, p. 2.
14. "A Man Called Jamison," *New York Times*, 26 January 1975, sec. 4, p. 9.
15. "Expert Warns on Testimony...," *New York Times*, 10 January 1982, p. 44.
16. "Fetus Born Alive After...," *Binghamton Press*, 15 November 1981, p. 1a.
17. http://www.biotech.iastate.edu/Bioethics/forum/brody.htmlIntroduction, accessed 11/20/02.

Evaluate Your Argument on the Issue

In this chapter you will learn how to identify and overcome errors in reasoning. This is a special step that applies only to issues because resolving issues involves finding the most *reasonable* belief.

Two broad kinds of errors are examined—errors affecting the truth of your ideas and errors affecting the quality of your reasoning. A step-by-step approach to evaluating arguments is also included.

Because your main objective in addressing an issue is not to find the most effective action but to determine the most reasonable belief, your main task in refining an issue is to evaluate your argument to be sure that it is free of error. Two broad kinds of error must be considered. The first affects the *truth* of the argument's premises or assertions. The second affects the argument's *validity*—that is, the legitimacy of the reasoning by which the conclusion was reached. A sound argument is both true and valid.

ERRORS AFFECTING TRUTH

Errors affecting truth are found by testing the accuracy of the premises and the conclusion as individual statements. The first and most common error in this category is simple factual inaccuracy. If we have investigated the issue properly and have taken care to verify our evidence whenever possible, such errors should not be present. We will therefore limit our consideration to the more subtle and common errors:

- Either/or thinking
- Avoiding the issue
- Overgeneralizing
- Oversimplifying
- Double standard
- Shifting the burden of proof
- Irrational appeal

Either/Or Thinking

This error consists of believing that only two choices are possible in situations in which there are more than two choices. A common example of either/or thinking occurs in the creationism-versus-evolution debate. Both sides are often guilty of the error. "The biblical story of creation and scientific evolution cannot both be right," they say. "It must be either one or the other." They are mistaken. There is a third possibility: that there is a God who created everything but did so through evolution. Whether this position is the best one may, of course, be disputed. But it is an error to ignore its existence.

Either/or thinking undoubtedly occurs because, in controversy, the spotlight is usually on the most obvious positions, those most clearly in conflict. Any other position, especially a subtle one, is ignored. Such thinking is best overcome by conscientiously searching out all possible views before choosing one. If you find either/or thinking in your position on an issue, ask yourself, "Why must it be one view or the other? Why not both or neither?"

Avoiding the Issue

The attorney was just beginning to try the case in court when her associate learned that their key witness had changed his mind about testifying. The associate handed the attorney this note: "Have no case. Abuse the other side." That is the form avoiding the issue often takes: deliberately attacking the person with the opposing view in the hope that the issue itself will be forgotten. It happens with lamentable frequency in politics. The issue being debated may be, for example, a particular proposal for tax reform. One candidate will say, "The reason my opponent supports this proposal is clear: it is a popular position to take. His record is filled with examples of jumping on the bandwagon to gain voter approval." And so on. Of course, what the candidate says may be true of the opponent, and if it is, then it would surely be relevant to the issue of whether the opponent deserves to be elected. But it is not relevant to the issue at hand, the tax reform proposal.

Avoiding the issue may not necessarily be motivated by deceit, as the preceding examples are. It may occur because of unintentional misunderstanding or because of an unconscious slip to something irrelevant. But it is still error, regardless of its innocence. To check your reasoning, look closely at each issue, and ask whether your solution really responds to it. If it doesn't, make it do so.

Overgeneralizing

Overgeneralizing means taking a valid idea and extending it beyond the limits of reasonableness. Here are some examples.

- Women who have abortions are poor and unmarried.
- Politicians are corrupt.
- Conservative Christians are intolerant.
- Men have trouble expressing their feelings.

Each of these statements could be true at times. That is, we could find examples of poor, unmarried women who have had abortions; corrupt politicians; and so on. Yet, in each case, we could also find examples that do not fit the assertion. That is what makes these statements overgeneralizations. (The fact that your overgeneralizations do not take the most extreme form—stereotypes—should not make you complacent about correcting them. They still mar your arguments, usually significantly.)

To find overgeneralizations in your arguments, be alert to any idea in which *all* or *none* is stated or *implied.* (That is the case in each of the preceding four examples.) Occasionally, you will find a situation in which *all* or *none* is justified, but in the great majority of cases, critical evaluation will show that it is not. To correct overgeneralizations, decide what level of generalization is appropriate, and modify your statement accordingly. For example, in the four cases discussed, you would consider these possibilities:

Some Many Most All A specific number of	. . . women who have abortions are poor and unmarried.
Some Many Most All Certain types of	. . . politicians are corrupt.
Some Many Most All In certain cultural conditions	. . . conservative Christians are intolerant.
Some Many Most All In certain cultural conditions	. . . men are incapable of expressing their feelings.

Oversimplifying

There is nothing wrong with simplifying a complex reality to understand it better or to communicate it more clearly to others. Teachers simplify all the time, especially in grade school. Simplification is only a problem when it goes too far: when it goes beyond making complex matters clear and begins to distort them. At that point, it ceases to represent reality and *mis*represents it. Such oversimplification is often found in reasoning about causes and effects. Here are three examples of this error.

- The cause of the economic recession in the early 1980s was excessive welfare spending.
- The American Nazi Party has a beneficial effect on the intellectual life of the country. It reminds people of the constitutional rights of free speech and assembly.
- A return to public executions, shown on prime-time television, would make crime less glamorous and thus, in time, make us a less brutal, more civilized society.

These statements contain an element of truth (many authorities would say a very small element). Yet they do not fairly or accurately represent the reality described. They focus on one cause or effect as if it were the only one. In fact, there are others, some of them significant.

To find oversimplifications in your arguments, ask what important aspects of the issue your statements ignore. To correct oversimplifications, decide what expression of the matter best reflects the reality without distorting it.

Double Standard

Applying a double standard means judging the same action or point of view differently depending on who performs the action or holds the point of view. It can often be recognized by the use of sharply contrasting terms of description or classification. Thus we may attack a government assistance program as a welfare handout if the money goes to people we don't know or don't identify with but defend it as a necessary subsidy if it goes to our friends. Similarly, if one country crosses another's border with a military force, we may approve the action as a "securing of borders" or condemn it as "naked aggression," depending on our feelings toward the countries involved.

Be careful not to confuse the double standard with the legitimate judgment of cases according to their circumstances. It is never an error to acknowledge real differences. Accordingly, if you find you have judged a particular case differently from other cases of the same kind, look closely at the circumstances. If they warrant different judgments, you have not been guilty of applying a double standard. However, if they do not warrant different judgments—if your reasoning shows partiality toward one side—you have committed the error and should revise your judgment to make it fair.

Shifting the Burden of Proof

This error consists of making an assertion and then demanding that the opposition prove it false. This is an unreasonable demand. The person making the assertion has the burden of supporting it. Though the opposing side may accept the challenge of disproving it, it has no obligation to do so. Suppose, for example, you said to a friend, "Mermaids must exist," your friend disputed you, and you responded, "Unless you can disprove their existence, I am justified in believing in them." You have shifted the burden of proof. Having made the assertion about mermaids, you have the obligation to support it. To overcome this error in your arguments, identify all the assertions you have made but not supported, and provide adequate support for them. If you find you cannot support an assertion, withdraw it.

Irrational Appeal

This error bases your position on an appeal that is unreasonable. The most common forms of irrational appeal are the appeal to *common practice* ("Everyone does it"), the appeal to *tradition* ("We mustn't change what is long established"), the appeal to *fear* ("Awful things could happen"), the appeal to *moderation* ("Let's not offend anyone"), and the appeal to *authority* ("We have no business questioning the experts"). Of course, there is nothing necessarily wrong with defending common practice or tradition, warning about dangers, urging moderation, or supporting the views of experts. It is only when these appeals are used as *a substitute* for careful reasoning—when they aim at an audience's emotions rather than their minds—that they are misused. To correct irrational appeals, refocus your argument on the specific merits of your ideas.

ERRORS AFFECTING VALIDITY

Errors affecting validity do not occur within any individual premise or within the conclusion. They occur instead in the reasoning by which the conclusion is drawn from the premises. Therefore, to determine whether an argument is valid or invalid, we must examine the relationship between the premises and the conclusion. The logical principles governing validity are the substance of *formal logic,* the area of logic concerned with the various forms of argument. Since a detailed treatment of formal logic is beyond the scope of this book, we will focus on an essential error that commonly occurs in controversial issues: the *illegitimate conclusion.*

An illegitimate conclusion is one that does not follow logically from the premises preceding it. Before examining an illegitimate conclusion, let's first look at a *legitimate* one.

> Anything that shortens people's attention span harms their concentration. Television commercials shorten people's attention span. Therefore, television commercials harm people's concentration.

This conclusion is legitimate because if anything that shortens people's attention span harms concentration, and if television commercials do shorten that span, they therefore must harm people's concentration. Commercials, after all, are a thing, so they fit in the *anything* specified in the first premise. When we are checking for the validity of the reasoning, remember, we are not checking for the truth of the premises or conclusion. That concern is a separate matter. Thus even a ludicrous argument could be technically valid. Here is an example.

> Anything that gives people indigestion harms their concentration. Television commercials give people indigestion. Therefore, television commercials harm people's concentration.

Let's now look at some *illegitimate* conclusions and see what makes them so.

> All people who take courses significantly above their level of competency will surely fail. Samantha is taking a course well within her level of competency. Therefore, Samantha will surely pass.

Even if it were true that all people who take courses well above their competency level necessarily fail, this would not eliminate the possibility of other reasons for failure, reasons that apply to the competent as well as the incompetent. In other words, the first premise does not imply that *only* the incompetent will fail. Samantha may be extraordinarily proficient and still fail because she cuts classes and does not submit the required work.

Here is another example of an illegitimate conclusion.

> People who care about the environment will support the clean air bill now before Congress. Senator Boychik supports the clean air bill. Therefore, Senator Boychik cares about the environment.

The first premise of this argument says that people—all people*—who care about the environment will support the bill. However, it does not say that no one else will support the bill. Thus it leaves open the possibility that some who do not care will support it, perhaps for political reasons. Which group Boychik belongs to is unclear. Therefore, the conclusion is illegitimate.

Illegitimate conclusions also occur in hypothetical (if-then) reasoning. Of course, not all hypothetical reasoning is faulty. Here is an example of a *valid* hypothetical argument:

> *If* a person uses a gun in the commission of a crime, *then* he should be given an additional penalty. Simon used a gun in the commission of a crime. *Therefore,* Simon should be given an additional penalty.

*Though the premise says *people*, rather than *all people*, the sense of *all* is clearly conveyed. Usually, when no qualifying word or phrase—such as *some*, *many*, *the citizens of Peoria*—is present, we presume that the universal *all* is intended.

The first premise sets forth the conditions under which the additional penalty should be applied. The second presents a case that fits those conditions. The conclusion that the penalty should apply in that case is legitimate.

Here, in contrast, is an *illegitimate* conclusion.

> *If* a person uses a gun in the commission of a crime, *then* he should be given an additional penalty. Simon was given an additional penalty for his crime. *Therefore,* Simon used a gun in the commission of the crime.

Here the first premise sets forth one condition for an additional penalty. It does not exclude the possibility of *other* conditions carrying additional penalties. For this reason, we have no way of knowing whether Simon's additional penalty was for using a gun or for some other reason.

The following is another example of an *illegitimate* conclusion.

> If a person has great wealth, he can get elected. Governor Mindless got elected. Therefore, Governor Mindless has great wealth.

The first premise of this argument specifies one way of getting elected. There may be others, including endorsements from influential groups and skill in telling people what they want to hear. Did Governor Mindless get elected in this or in some other way? We can't be sure from the information given, so the conclusion is illegitimate.

Occasionally, an illegitimate conclusion in hypothetical arguments takes a slightly different form: the reversal of conditions. The following argument illustrates this.

> *If* the death penalty is reinstated, *then* the crime rate will drop. *Therefore,* if the rate of crime is reduced, the death penalty will be reinstated.

The error here is reversing what is not necessarily reversible. The clear implication in the first premise is that there is a cause-and-effect relationship between the reinstatement of the death penalty and a drop in the crime rate. To reverse that relationship makes the effect the cause, and vice versa. Such a reversal does not logically follow.

A SPECIAL PROBLEM: THE HIDDEN PREMISE

The expression of an argument in ordinary discussion or writing is not always as precise as our examples. The sentence order may vary; the conclusion, for example, may come first. In place of the word *therefore,* a variety of signal words may be used. *So* and *it follows that* are two common substitutes. Sometimes, no signal word is used. These variations make the evaluation of an argument a little more time-consuming, but they pose no real difficulty. There is, however, a variation that can cause real difficulty: the *hidden premise.* A hidden premise is a premise implied but not stated. Here is an example of an argument with a hidden premise. (Such an argument is known in logic as an enthymeme.)

Argument with Premise Hidden	**Same Argument, Premise Expressed**
Liberty means responsibility.	Liberty means responsibility.
That is why most men dread it.	Most men dread responsibility.
	Therefore, most men dread liberty.

There is nothing necessarily wrong with having a hidden premise. It is not an error. In the preceding case, the hidden-premise argument is from the writing of George Bernard Shaw. In either of the forms shown, the argument is perfectly valid. The only problem with hidden premises is that they obscure the reasoning behind the argument and make evaluation difficult. Accordingly, whenever a premise is hidden, it should be identified and expressed before the argument is evaluated.

Here are several more examples of hidden-premise arguments. Note how much easier it is to grasp the reasoning when the hidden premise is expressed.

Premise Hidden	**Premise Expressed**
Prostitution is immoral, so it should be illegal.	Everything immoral should be illegal. Prostitution is immoral. Therefore, it should be illegal.
Newspapers are a threat to democracy because they have too much power.	All agencies that have too much power are a threat to democracy. Newspapers have too much power. Therefore, newspapers are a threat to democracy.
If Brewster Bland is a good family man, he'll make a good senator.	If a person is a good family man, he'll make a good senator. Brewster Bland is a good family man. Therefore, Brewster Bland will make a good senator.
AIDS is a costly and, at this time, terminal disease. Therefore, health insurance companies should be able to suspend coverage when people contract AIDS.	Insurance companies should not have to provide coverage for costly terminal diseases. AIDS is a costly and, at this time, terminal disease. Therefore, health insurance companies should be able to suspend coverage when people contract AIDS.
Many celebrities believe that a 35,000-year-old spirit entity known as Ramtha speaks through channeler J. Z. Knight. Therefore, this belief is worthy of respect.	If many celebrities believe something, it is by that fact worthy of respect. Many celebrities believe that a 35,000-year-old spirit entity known as Ramtha speaks through channeler J. Z. Knight. Therefore, this belief is worthy of respect.

RECOGNIZING COMPLEX ARGUMENTS

Not all arguments can be expressed in two premises and one conclusion. Many are complex, involving a network of premises and conclusions. Moreover, some of these premises and conclusions may, like the hidden premises we have discussed, be unexpressed. Consider, for example, this argument.

> The communications and entertainment media have more influence on young people than parents and teachers do, so the media are more responsible for teenage pregnancy, drug and alcohol abuse, violence, and academic deficiency.

At first glance, only one premise may seem to be missing from this argument. Actually, it is a complex argument, and more is missing. Here is how it would be expressed if nothing were omitted.

> The agency that has the greatest influence on young people's attitudes and values bears the greatest responsibility for the behavior caused by those attitudes and values. Although parents and teachers used to have the greatest influence on young people's attitudes and values, the media now have a greater influence. In addition, the messages disseminated by the media generally oppose the lessons of home and school. Typical media messages—that each person creates his or her own morality, that self is more important than others, that restraint of one's urges is harmful, and that feelings are a more reliable guide than thought—tend to lead to impulsiveness and the demand for instant gratification and to create or aggravate such problems as teenage pregnancy, drug and alcohol abuse, violence, and academic deficiency. Therefore, the communications and entertainment media bear the greatest responsibility for these problems.

Here are two more examples of complex arguments. In each case, the argument is first expressed in the abbreviated form often used in everyday conversation and then in its complete logical form.

1. *Abbreviated:* The government wastes billions of tax dollars, so I'm not obligated to report all my income.

   Complete: The government wastes billions of tax dollars. Wasting tax dollars increases every individual's tax burden unnecessarily. I am a taxpayer, so the government is increasing my tax burden unnecessarily. Furthermore, when the government increases the taxpayers' tax burden unnecessarily, the taxpayers are not obligated to report all their income. Therefore, I'm not obligated to report all my income.

2. *Abbreviated:* People who lack control over their sexual urges are a threat to society, so homosexuals should be banned from the teaching profession.

> *Complete:* People who lack control over their sexual urges are a threat to society. Homosexuals lack control over their sexual urges. Therefore, homosexuals are a threat to society. Furthermore, people who are a threat to society should be banned from the teaching profession. Therefore, homosexuals should be banned from the teaching profession.

Recognizing that an argument is complex and, where necessary, expressing it more completely is a necessary step in argument analysis. But such recognition and expression do not complete the analysis. In other words, in each of our three examples, we now know what the complete argument is, but we do not yet know whether it is sound—that is, whether its premises are true and the reasoning from premises to conclusion is valid.

STEPS IN EVALUATING AN ARGUMENT

The following four steps are an efficient way to apply what you learned in this chapter—in other words, to evaluate your argument and overcome any errors in validity or truth that it may contain.

1. State your argument fully, as clearly as you can. Be sure to identify any hidden premises and, if the argument is complex, to express all parts of it.
2. Examine each part of your argument for errors affecting truth. (To be sure this examination is not perfunctory, play devil's advocate and *challenge* the argument, asking pointed questions about it, taking nothing for granted.) Note any instances of either/or thinking, avoiding the issue, overgeneralizing, oversimplifying, double standard, shifting the burden of proof, or irrational appeal. In addition, check to be sure that the argument reflects the pro and con arguments and is relevant to the scenarios you produced earlier.
3. Examine your argument for validity errors; that is, consider the reasoning that links conclusions to premises. Determine whether your conclusion is legitimate or illegitimate.
4. If you find one or more errors, revise your argument to eliminate them. The changes you will have to make in your argument will depend on the kinds of errors you find. Sometimes, only minor revision is called for—the adding of a simple qualification, for example, or the substitution of a rational appeal for an irrational one. Occasionally, however, the change required is more dramatic. You may, for example, find your argument so flawed that the only appropriate action is to abandon it altogether and embrace a different argument. On those occasions, you may be tempted to *pretend* your argument is sound and hope no one will notice the errors. Resist that hope. It is foolish as well as dishonest to invest time in refining a view that you know is unsound.

To illustrate how you would follow these steps, we will now examine two issues.

THE CASE OF PARENTS PROTESTING TV PROGRAMS

You have read a number of articles lately about protests over television commercials and programming. The protesters are mostly parents of school-aged children. They have spoken out either individually or through organizations they belong to, expressing concern that the values taught by school and home are being undermined by television. Specific complaints include the emphasis on sex and violence in television programming, the appeal to self-indulgence and instant gratification in commercials, and the promotion of "if it feels good, do it" in both programming and commercials. The protestors are urging concerned citizens to write to the companies that sponsor programs and threaten to boycott their products unless these offenses are eliminated.

Let's say you identify the main issue here as "Are parents justified in making such demands on companies?" After considering the matter and producing a number of ideas, you decide that the best answer is "No, they are not justified" and state your argument as follows.

> Only those who pay for television programming and advertisements are entitled to have a say about them. The companies alone pay. Therefore, the companies alone are entitled to have a say.

You examine your argument for validity errors and find that it contains none. Then you examine it for errors of truth or relevance. Playing devil's advocate, you ask, "*Do* the companies alone pay?" "How exactly is payment handled?" Not being sure, you ask a professor of business and learn that the sponsorship of television programs and other advertising are part of the overall product budget. You also learn that these costs, along with other costs of raw materials, manufacturing, and packaging, warehousing, and delivery, are reflected in the price of the product.

"Wait a minute," you reason. "If programming and other advertising costs are reflected in the price of the product, that means consumers are paying for every television show and every commercial. And if that's the case, parents (and other consumers) *are* entitled to have a say, make demands, and threaten boycotts." And so you revise your argument accordingly.

> Those who pay for television programming and commercials are entitled to have a say about them. Consumers pay. Therefore, consumers are entitled to have a say.*

In elaborating this argument you would, of course, address the important questions that flow from it, including this one: What guidelines does fairness suggest consumers follow in making such requests? Your answers to this and related questions should also be evaluated for reasonableness.

---

*Such a formal, logical ($a + b = c$) statement of your argument is essential when you are evaluating your reasoning. However, it is seldom appropriate for a central-idea statement in a piece of writing. In this case, your central-idea statement might be "Because consumers pay for television programming and commercials, they are entitled to make demands and threaten boycotts."

THE CASE OF THE MENTALLY IMPAIRED GIRLS

The parents of three girls with severe mental impairments brought court action seeking the legal right to make the decision to sterilize the girls. The larger issue here continues to be controversial. Let's say you express it as follows: "Should anyone have the right to make such a significant decision for another person?" After investigating the issue and producing a number of ideas, including the major pro and con arguments and several relevant scenarios, you state your argument thus:

> Those who have the child's interest at heart can be expected to judge wisely if they are properly informed. Most parents or guardians have the child's interest at heart. Therefore, most parents or guardians can be expected to judge wisely if they are properly informed. Furthermore, knowing whether the child will ever be able to meet the responsibilities of parenthood constitutes being properly informed. A qualified doctor can tell parents or guardians whether the child will ever be able to meet the responsibilities of parenthood. Therefore, a qualified doctor can properly inform parents.

You examine your argument (a complex one that cannot be expressed adequately in two premises and a conclusion) and decide that though it is valid and essentially true, it raises a serious question that should not be ignored. That question is "Would such a system provide sufficient protection for the child?" You address it by imagining a variety of situations that might easily arise, notably the following ones.

1. The parents are obsessed with the fear that their child will bring shame on them. They pressure the doctor to certify that their child will never be able to fulfill parental responsibilities even though that is not really the case. The doctor, though qualified to make an appropriate diagnosis, is unscrupulous and therefore willing to certify anything for a fee.
2. The parents are responsible and the doctor is not only qualified but above reproach morally. The decision is made to sterilize the child at age four. Several years later, medical science finds a way to overcome the child's mental impairment. The child becomes normal, but the sterilization cannot be reversed.

To prevent the first situation from occurring, you revise your argument to specify that certification be made by a board of physicians rather than a single physician. You might also decide the composition of the board. (All surgeons? One or more psychologists? An authority on mental retardation?) Unfortunately, there is no way to ensure that the second situation will not occur, but you decide there is a way to lessen the risk considerably. To that end you add to your argument the stipulation that no sterilization should be permitted before the onset of puberty.

Both this case and the case of parents protesting TV programming are offered to illustrate the *process* of evaluating your positions on issues rather than to promote the arguments contained in them. What is important is not that you agree with these arguments but that you recognize the value of evaluating your own.

WARM-UP EXERCISES

1 Willy Joe and Joe Willy are having a conversation of sorts:

WILLY JOE: There's no such thing as reality, man.

JOE WILLY: No way . . . like, I mean . . . it makes no sense that way. No, there's no way.

WILLY JOE: OK, man, you say there's a reality. So describe it to me.

JOE WILLY: Um . . . ah . . . uh . . .

WILLY JOE: You can't describe it, so it can't exist. Case closed.

How would you answer Willy Joe? Explain your thinking carefully.

2 One thing, at least, is indisputable about rock music: it produces groups with very creative names. But perhaps you can do even better. Think of as many creative names as you can for a rock group, names you've never heard before.

3 In Strangeville it was decided that the local barber should shave all those, and only those, who did not shave themselves. Did the barber shave himself? Explain your thinking thoroughly.

APPLICATIONS

1 Evaluate the three arguments presented in the section of this chapter entitled "Recognizing Complex Arguments"—that is, the arguments about media influence on young people, reporting income for tax purposes, and homosexuals in education. Decide whether each argument is sound, and explain your judgment.

2 Check each of the following arguments to be sure that it contains no hidden premises and, if it is a complex argument, that all parts are expressed. Revise each, as necessary, to make the expression complete. Then evaluate the argument and decide whether it is sound. Explain your judgment.

a. Having great wealth is a worthy goal because it is difficult to attain and many famous people have pursued it.

b. Low grades on a college transcript are a handicap in the job market, so teachers who grade harshly are doing students a disservice.

c. The Bible can't be relevant to today's problems; it was written many centuries ago and is filled with archaic phrasing.
d. It is dishonest to pretend to have knowledge one does not have, so plagiarism is more virtue than vice.
e. The credit card habit promotes careless spending, particularly among young people. Therefore, credit card companies should not be permitted to issue credit cards to anyone under age 21.
f. No one who ever attended this college achieved distinction after graduation. Marvin attends this college. Therefore, Marvin will not achieve distinction after graduation.
g. Drug dealing should not be a crime because it does not directly harm others or force them to harm themselves.
h. A mature person is self-directing, so parents who make all their children's decisions for them are doing their offspring a disservice.
i. There's no point in attending Professor Drone's class; all he does is lecture in a boring monotone.
j. Power must be evil because it can corrupt people.
k. If the theory of evolution is true, as scientific evidence overwhelmingly suggests, a human being is nothing more than an ape.
l. Rock musicians are contributing to the decline of language by singing in a slurred, mumbling manner.
m. If emphasis on error paralyzes effort, this college is paying my English professor to make it impossible for me to learn English.
n. Nuclear power is a threat to world peace. Nuclear energy stations generate nuclear power. So nuclear energy stations are a threat to world peace.
o. Lew Fairman is the best candidate for governor because he is in favor of the death penalty.
p. All religious authorities are concerned about the dangers of nuclear war. All politicians are concerned about the dangers of nuclear war. Therefore, all politicians are religious authorities.
q. The government should undertake a comprehensive censorship program because censorship eliminates undesirable books and films from the market.
r. If the Social Security system is further weakened, the elderly will have to fear poverty. Therefore, if the Social Security system is not further weakened, the elderly will not have to fear poverty.
s. Challenging other people's opinions is a sign of intolerance, so debating courses have no place on a college campus.
t. It's ridiculous to think that there will be fewer deaths if we ban handguns. Handguns don't kill people; *people* kill people.
u. The antiabortionists say that the fetus is human, but they have not proved it. Therefore, they have no reasonable basis for opposing abortion.

v. We must either defeat communism or be defeated by it. To be defeated by communism is unthinkable. Therefore, we must defeat communism.

w. There is no way that anyone can ever deserve to live better than her or his neighbors, so capitalism is an immoral economic system.

x. If an expectant mother drinks, smokes, takes drugs, or fails to get proper rest, she may damage her unborn child. Therefore, if an expectant mother does these things and her child is born with a defect or ailment that can be traced to them, the mother should face criminal charges.

y. Custom is a form of folk wisdom. In some parts of the world, it is customary for "bride buyers" to buy (or sometimes kidnap) young women from their parents and sell them to men looking for wives. Even though we might find this practice distasteful, it would be morally wrong for us to object to others' practicing it.

3 Identify, investigate (as necessary), and resolve each of the following issues. Be sure you do not just accept your reasoning uncritically. Evaluate it by using the approach explained on page 208. Then modify your argument as necessary and decide how you could most effectively demonstrate its soundness.

a. Radar detectors give speeders a warning so that they can slow down in time to avoid getting a ticket. Some people believe the detectors should be banned because they help people break the law. Others disagree, arguing that they should be able to protect themselves from the sneaky practices of highway patrols.

b. One proposal for combating the drug problem is government seizure of the property (cars, homes, etc.) of convicted drug dealers. One objection to this proposal is that such seizure could violate the rights of innocent parties, such as spouses and children.

c. Since smoking is not permitted at one's desk in many companies, significant time is presumably lost in unauthorized smoking breaks in restrooms or outside of buildings. A company could save itself that time, and the money it represents, by establishing a policy of hiring only nonsmokers. Predictably, of course, some people would consider such a policy discriminatory.

d. The practice of freezing embryos has been controversial since it was first announced by London test-tube baby pioneer Dr. Robert Edwards and a colleague in 1982. The idea then was to save the embryos for donation to infertile women at some later time.[1] Now, two decades later, the controversy has taken on a new dimension. Some members of Congress are pressing for federal funding research in which frozen embryos would be destroyed so that their stem cells could be used in the search for cures to diseases such as Parkinson's and Alzheimer's. The current administration is opposed to this use of federal funds.[2]

e. A number of states and many foreign countries have programs forcing alcoholics to receive treatment. A person arrested for drunken driving, for example, is required to receive treatment as a stipulation of probation. Or a welfare recipient will be threatened with loss of benefits if he or she does not comply. The programs range from individual therapy to group therapy to the taking of such drugs as Antabuse (which can make a person violently ill if he or she drinks within three days after ingesting it). There is sharp disagreement over such programs. Many feel they are a violation of civil rights.[3]

ISSUE FOR EXTENDED ANALYSIS

Following is a more comprehensive thinking challenge than the others in the chapter.

THE ISSUE: RACIAL/ETHNIC PROFILING

Racial/ethnic profiling operates on the premise that statistical analysis can identify, with considerable accuracy, individuals that are more likely than others to engage in criminal behavior. The controversy centers on whether that premise is true or false. Proponents say it is true; opponents say it is false and therefore that such profiling amounts to little more than stereotyping.

THE ESSAYS

Racial Profiling Is an Outrage
By Brian Costello

However well most white people understand racial profiling as an abstract category, they haven't a clue about racial profiling as a concrete reality. Consider these brief but typical scenarios.

- It's Saturday morning and a black executive dons a sweatsuit and drives off to the gym in his Lexus. A mile later he is stopped by a white policeman, who asks to see his license and the car's registration and then radios in to see if the vehicle has been stolen. (African-

Politically Correct Nonsense
By Joshua Levy

Some years ago in the Southwest, the FBI were in pursuit of a serial killer described by one near-victim as a short Hispanic male in his late twenties or early thirties. When an FBI spokesperson mentioned this description at a news conference, a reporter asked, "What would you say to Hispanics who take offense at your racial profiling?" The FBI agent, who happened to be black, gave the reporter a withering look and responded, "I'd say we're following the description we were given." Soon thereafter, the

Americans refer to this "offense" as DWB: driving while black.)

- A twenty-five-year-old Latino college student dressed in jeans and a leather jacket is walking to campus when he is stopped by detectives and "frisked." When they find nothing incriminating in his possession, they say, "We know you're dealing in drugs, and we'll be watching you."
- While shopping in a department store, two black teenagers are watched closely by the salespeople. As they pass from the cosmetics department to housewares and then to clothing, the teens are "stalked" by new observers. Clearly they are suspected of being shoplifters.

These situations, and their many variations, show racial profiling for what it really is—active discrimination against members of one race, culture, or ethnic group. Such profiling is rooted in negative stereotypes. In the first example, "black people are lower class and shouldn't be driving expensive cars"; in the second, "all Latinos are drug merchants"; and in the third, "black young people are more likely than whites to engage in shoplifting."

In America, we are supposed to be judged by our actions, not by the color of our skin or the style of our clothing, and certainly not by someone's delusion about our inherent badness. Racial profiling makes a mockery of this standard. It is un-American and should be abolished.

serial killer was found, and, not surprisingly, he fit that description.

That incident reveals how ridiculous all the politically correct blather about racial profiling really is. If a killer is described as Hispanic, should the police include black, white, and Asian males *and even females* in their search? Political correctness says yes; common sense says no.

Political correctness is also at work in airport security. In order to avoid offending the sensibility of people of Middle Eastern origin, random selection is used. For example, every tenth person passing through security is subjected to special screening. The people so selected may include elderly Americans and small children; meanwhile, a dozen Saudis and Iraqis and Palestinians will be allowed to pass without special screening.

Is it possible to misuse racial and ethnic profiling? Of course. But the solution to that problem is to punish misuse, not to abolish profiling. The latter response, which all too many people advocate, is an absurd overreaction that compromises both the ability of the police agencies to maintain law and order and the ability of security agencies to keep our nation secure.

Properly used, racial profiling is an invaluable tool for law enforcement and other security uses.

Class Discussion

REBECCA: Singling out people for suspicion just because they belong to a certain race or ethnic group is abhorrent.

NIGEL: What about situations like the ones described by Joshua Levy—situations in which the police have been given a description of a suspect? Is it wrong to limit their search to people who fit the description?

REBECCA: I suppose that wouldn't be wrong.

NIGEL: What would you say about situations in which specific descriptions are unavailable but statistical probability is high. For example, if a certain highway corridor is known to be a drug transport route and Hispanic gang members are known to be involved in the transport, would you approve stops and searches of vehicles driven by Hispanics?

REBECCA: I'd need to know more about the basis of the statistics. Consider this possibility: a variety of people have been involved in past trafficking, including blacks, whites, Asians, and Hispanics, but only Hispanics have been searched. In that case, the statistics would erroneously point only to Hispanics. My point is that statistics are sometimes biased and therefore an unacceptable basis of profiling.

NIGEL: That's an interesting but highly unlikely scenario.

REBECCA: You have no way of knowing that. Take, for example, the statistical fact that a disproportionately large number of prison inmates in this country are African-American. That *could* mean that a higher percentage of African-Americans are criminals. But it could just as easily mean that the police are prejudiced against African-Americans and therefore are more eager to arrest and prosecute them. Unless we can be sure which is the case, we should avoid using statistics as a basis for profiling.

NIGEL: I'm sure the people who use the statistics take such matters into consideration and use only valid statistics.

REBECCA: Sounds a lot like wishful thinking to me.

Notes

1. "Frozen Embryo Plan Stirs Uproar," *Oneonta Star,* 29 January 1982, p. 8.
2. http://www.aclj.org/news/nr_01096_thompson_stands_firm.asp, accessed 11/20/02.
3. "Compulsory Alcoholism Treatment Gaining," *New York Times*, 9 May 1982, p. 10.

Produce Ideas

So far our examination of the creative process has demonstrated how to recognize problems and issues, express them clearly, and gain essential insights into them. There is one additional stage in the creative process: producing possible solutions.

In this chapter you will learn the advantage of producing a wide range of solutions rather than settling for a few. You will also learn how to stimulate your imagination, how to be more original, and how to overcome the obstacles most common at this stage of creativity.

Imagine a pearl diver on an island in the South Seas. He pushes off his canoe from the shore, paddles out into the lagoon, dives deep into the water, picks an oyster off the bottom, surfaces, climbs into his boat, paddles to shore, and opens the shell. Finding nothing but an oyster inside, he sets off in his canoe again and begins paddling into the lagoon. "Wait a minute," you're probably thinking. "He's wasting an awful lot of time. The right way to do it is not to paddle back to shore with one oyster but to dive again and again, fill the canoe with oysters, and then return to shore."

You're right. Pearls are rare; a diver must open many oysters before finding one. Only a very foolish diver would waste time and energy making a separate trip for each oyster.[1] *And it's exactly the same with producing ideas.* Foolish people think of a single solution to a problem and then proceed as if that solution *had* to be creative. But creative ideas, like pearls, occur infrequently. So sensible people produce many ideas before expecting to find a creative one.

Researchers have found a clear relationship between the number of ideas produced and the quality of the ideas. The more ideas produced, the better the chances of having one or more good ones.[2] There are two reasons for this. The first is a matter of simple probability. Creative ideas are statistically uncommon. As Alfred North Whitehead explains, "The probability is that nine hundred and ninety-nine of [our ideas] will come to nothing, either because they are worthless in themselves or because we shall not know how to elicit their value; but we had better entertain them all, however skeptically, for the *thousandth* idea may be the one that will change the world."[3]

The second reason is that initial ideas are usually poorer in quality than later ideas. Just as water must run from a faucet for a while to be clear and free of particles, so thought must flow before it becomes creative. "Early ideas," Herbert Spencer warned, "are not usually true ideas."[4] Exactly why this is so is not known, but one very plausible hypothesis is that familiar and safe responses lie closest to the surface of our consciousness and therefore are naturally thought of first.[5] In any case, success in creative thinking depends on continuing the flow of ideas long enough to purge the common, habitual ones and produce the unusual and imaginative.

In dealing with problems, the ideas you should seek to produce are answers to the "How can . . . ?" questions you asked in expressing the problem. In dealing with issues, your ideas should be broader, including not only direct answers to your "Is (Are) . . . ?" "Does . . . ?" and "Should . . . ?" questions, but also all other ideas that can help you answer those questions. Not infrequently, the idea that provides a key to resolving an issue will seem, at first consideration, irrelevant.

STIMULATING YOUR IMAGINATION

Producing a large quantity of ideas is the first way to produce creative solutions, but it is not the only way. Another important way is to stimulate your imagination. Most people behave unimaginatively not because they lack imagination, but because they fear the reaction their ideas will receive. In time, they grow used to suppressing ideas that differ from the norm, ideas that might raise eyebrows. They do themselves a great disservice because creativity depends on imagination. "No great discovery is ever made without a bold guess," observed Sir Isaac Newton.[6] And Albert Einstein added, "I believe in imagination. . . . Imagination is more important than knowledge."[7]

It takes more than determination to stimulate your thoughts, of course, particularly if you have gotten into the habit of suppressing them. You'll need some strategies for activating your creative imagination. Following are seven effective strategies. Some will fit problems better than issues; others, the reverse.

1. Force uncommon responses.
2. Use free association.
3. Use analogy.
4. Look for unusual combinations.
5. Visualize the solution.
6. Construct pro and con arguments.
7. Construct relevant scenarios.

Force Uncommon Responses

We noted that common, familiar ideas tend to come first. Nothing can be done to avoid this pattern. Therefore, your best approach is to expect them, even encourage them, to free your mind for more original ideas. Begin by asking yourself what responses most people would think of. Write them all down. When you have produced a number of these, and you can't think of any others, ask yourself what responses others would probably *not* think of. Press yourself for as many as you can produce.

One predictable outcome of this effort is the listing of some outrageous or silly ideas. Chances are you will feel a little uncomfortable with such ideas. "How can they be helpful?" you'll think. "Problems and issues are serious matters—no room for foolishness here." *Resist that feeling.* Playfulness, as we saw, is one important characteristic of creative people; it contributes to their dynamism. There's nothing wrong with writing even the most ridiculous ideas on paper. Listing them is not the same as endorsing them; you can always cross them out later. But don't screen them out now; you might inadvertently discard an original insight in the process.

Don't misunderstand this advice. It doesn't mean you should try to be outrageous or ridiculous. It means you should tolerate being so when it occurs as a natural consequence of striving for uncommon ideas.

Use Free Association

Free association means letting one idea suggest another. It differs from forced response in that you are not directing your mind at all but giving it free rein, relaxing your control over it momentarily and observing what ideas and associations result. Some of them may be quite unexpected and may point out interesting and profitable directions. As with forced responses, you should not screen any associations as they occur to you. Rather, write them all for later examination. Often, what seems totally irrelevant when it occurs to you may later prove valuable.

A word of warning is in order. The purpose of this strategy is to help you retrieve relevant information you originally classified too restrictively. Because this strategy involves relaxing mental control and allowing your thoughts to drift, it can slip into aimless daydreaming. You should therefore use it as a variation on other strategies and not as a substitute for them.

Use Analogy

An analogy is a reference to one or more similarities between two otherwise very different things. An analogy might be made, for example, between a football halfback's broken-field running and the movements of a jaguar or cheetah.

The history of creative achievements documents the value of analogical thinking. Creative breakthroughs often occur when a person makes a connection between something outside his or her field. (This fact suggests the value of a broad education. Narrowness of training all too often breeds a narrowness of perspective that hinders creativity.) When Gutenberg observed a winepress in operation and conceived of the printing press and when the inventor of the forklift got his insight from the doughnut machine, they were using analogical thinking.

To use analogy in your thinking, simply ask what the problem or issue is like, what it reminds you of. Where appropriate, you may also ask more specific questions, such as "What does this *look* like (or sound, taste, smell, or feel like)?" or "What does this *function* like?"

Look for Unusual Combinations

Sometimes, the best solution to a problem will be to combine things not usually combined. The miner's cap (combining a flashlight and a protective hat), the wheelchair, and the clock radio are examples of how combinations result in invention. Perhaps the most common example of this kind of invention is the recipe. Every time a cook blends different ingredients to make a dish differently, he or she is inventing by combination. The first person to put a slice of mozzarella cheese on a veal cutlet invented veal parmigiana, and the ingenious person who couldn't afford veal and substituted a slice of meatloaf invented meatloaf parmigiana.

This same strategy works well in other kinds of creativity as well—finding solutions to social problems, for example. One problem of growing concern today is the increasing cost of our prison system. Someone wrestling with that problem might well consider combining prisons with factories—that is, having convicts work for private industry behind bars and be paid for their efforts, and reimbursing the taxpayers for the cost of the imprisonment. (The idea might even come through analogy, by noting that prisons sometimes resemble large factory complexes.)

Visualize the Solution

This strategy consists of imagining the problem solved and visualizing what it would look like then. For example, before the problem of automobile travel on snow- and ice-covered roads was solved, a man forced to drive in such conditions would have pictured in his mind not the reality of tires mired in snow or spinning on ice but the condition he *wished for:* wheels turning smoothly and tires biting into the snow and grasping the ice firmly. His imagination thus stimulated, he'd have asked himself, "What would those tires look like if they were able to perform the way I wish?" And he might just have visualized pieces of metal wrapped around the tire (chains) or spikes protruding from the tire to grip the road (studs).

Construct Pro and Con Arguments

This strategy, an essential one in dealing with issues, consists of listing all conceivable arguments that might be advanced on either side of the issue. To use it, simply address your expression(s) of the issue—"Is . . . ?" "Does . . . ?" or "Should . . . ?"—and list as many "yes" responses as you can, together with the reasoning that supports them, and as many "no" responses as you can, together with the reasoning for them. If, for example, the issue you examined was whether technology has had a positive or negative effect on human society, you would include these points, among others. (For the sake of brevity, supporting arguments are omitted.)

Positive-Effect Arguments	Negative-Effect Arguments
Has shortened the workweek, creating more leisure time for workers.	Has made many jobs very routine, increasing workers' boredom.
Has increased the variety of goods and services available.	Has decreased the quality of goods and services in many cases.
Has created many new skilled occupations.	Has eliminated many unskilled jobs.
Has increased the monetary reward to both employers and employees.	Has caused many workers to hate what they do for a living.
Has created the need for new kinds of education—vocational and technical.	Has undermined the role of the liberal arts in education.

An important warning: expect yourself to be biased, and expect your bias to affect your efforts to construct arguments. Unless you are perfectly neutral about the issue, an unlikely circumstance, at the very outset of this strategy you will believe one side of the issue to be right, and that belief will incline you to construct your list accordingly. In other words, consciously or unconsciously you will present more and better arguments for the side of the issue you prefer. The only safeguard against such bias is to *go out of your way to think of arguments that might be advanced on the other side of the issue.* If your investigation of the issue gave a fair hearing to both sides, this safeguard should not be too difficult to accomplish.

Construct Relevant Scenarios

We often tend to think of ideas exclusively as *assertions,* claims about what is or should be, such as "Respect for the rights of others is decreasing in our society" and "Ethics instruction belongs in the nation's schools." Those are ideas, to be sure, but so are *scenarios,* which are imaginatively conceived examples of situations and events that are relevant to the issue under consideration. Well-constructed scenarios have a special value that assertions lack: they represent reality itself and not just conclusions about reality.

Let's say that the issue you are analyzing concerns whether a woman must have offered "earnest resistance" to a man's sexual advances for a rape charge to be filed in the courts. (This was still a legal requirement in some states as recently as 1982.) Here are three scenarios you might construct.

- A woman has just returned from a date with a young man whom she has known for some time, has dated previously, and has had sexual intercourse with on several occasions. She invites him into her apartment and proceeds to engage in sexual foreplay. When he proposes that they have intercourse, she says "no" several times but does not stop him from performing the act.

- A woman is lying in a hospital bed, heavily sedated after experiencing a nervous breakdown. A male nurse realizes she is unable to resist his advances and so assaults her sexually.
- Walking from the campus library to her dormitory one evening, a college student passes through a dimly lighted wooded area. Suddenly, two men jump out at her, one brandishing a knife and warning that if she resists sexual intercourse with them, he will kill her. Fearing for her life, she submits.

A close reading of these scenarios will reveal the importance of constructing more than a single scenario and of taking care that those constructed cover the broad range of possibilities. All of these are believable—an indispensable qualification that every scenario must meet. However, they do not shed equal light on the issue of whether "earnest resistance" is a reasonable legal requirement. Taken alone, the first scenario might be considered to support an affirmative answer. Yet, as the other two make clear, such an answer would be shallow. Under the very plausible circumstances they present, the requirement of "earnest resistance" is quite unreasonable.

These seven strategies will give you significant help in activating your imagination. But don't expect to be able to use them smoothly right away. Give them time to become familiar. If you are inclined to give up after a few tries, remind yourself how awkward you felt the first time you dribbled a basketball or drove a car. That, too, seemed impossible to learn, but you mastered it. Whenever turning from one strategy to another confuses you, simply look back at your statement of the problem, regain your bearings, and continue producing ideas.

AIMING FOR ORIGINALITY

In the popular view, originality is a kind of genetic endowment. Either you have it or you don't, and if you don't have it, you have no hope of learning it. Research has demolished this idea. Like every other creative skill, *originality can be learned.* If you don't produce original thoughts, it is only because you have acquired the habit of being unoriginal. One study revealed that originality can be stimulated simply when the person knows it is expected.[8]

To achieve originality in your thinking, demand it of yourself. Remind yourself that there is nothing mysterious about originality; it lies just a step or two beyond the commonplace. Don't restrict your ideas to those you have heard or thought of before. Every time you address a problem and try to find solutions, stretch your mind a little, reach for thoughts a little more daring than you have entertained before.

There is one additional method that can help you be more original: *watch your fringe thoughts.* The term *fringe thoughts* was coined by Graham Wallas.[9] It means thoughts occurring on the edge or fringe of consciousness, much the same way objects appear on the periphery of our vision. When walking down the street or driving a car, we focus our gaze in one direction but continue to see objects outside that focus. When something unusual or unexpected appears there, we are able to turn our attention to it. Since original ideas often appear first on the fringe of consciousness, the more alert you are to what is happening there, the more original ideas you will discover.

WITHHOLDING JUDGMENT

Judgment is an essential part of thinking. Without it, we wouldn't be able to distinguish between good and bad solutions or select the best and most workable one. But the timing of our judgment can make all the difference. Most people don't time their judgment well: they are impulsive, evaluating ideas as soon as they are produced, sometimes even screening out certain ideas before they are fully conceptualized. At the first inkling of an idea, they say, "No, that's no good" or "This is silly" or "That can't be a solution."

Yet often, the most creative ideas are the ones that seem silliest at first. Rushing to judgment, therefore, causes some of the best ideas to be discarded—and the least creative ones to be approved mindlessly. Ironically, it ensures that people will be uncreative just when they want most to be creative.

Research has documented that thinkers who resist judging ideas during the idea-producing stage and who extend their effort to produce ideas beyond the point where they are tempted to stop are rewarded with a greater proportion of good ideas.[10] As you do the applications for this and subsequent chapters, and whenever you look for solutions to problems outside this course, don't allow yourself to judge any idea until after you have produced as many ideas as you can. Don't set artificial limits on the number of your ideas. When you find yourself thinking, "I've got 10 (or 20 or 30) ideas now—that's enough," remember that the best solution to the problem very likely lies 10 or 20 ideas beyond that point. It can be reached only by pressing on. Moreover, just to be sure you are not unconsciously setting limits on your thinking, look back occasionally at previous efforts—the applications you did in the last few chapters, for example—and decide whether you stopped producing ideas too soon.

OVERCOMING OBSTACLES

The three most common obstacles to the effective production of a large and varied number of ideas are thinker's block, vagueness and confusion, and inflexibility. Learning how to recognize each, and mastering a few simple responses, can prevent your problem-solving efforts from being frustrated.

Thinker's Block

Like writer's block, which prevents an author from putting words on the page, thinker's block prevents us from producing ideas. It makes us sit idle and grow increasingly nervous, waiting for ideas that do not come. Poor thinkers are not the only ones afflicted with thinker's block. Everyone experiences it from time to time. But good thinkers have learned that they needn't be victimized by it, that there are effective methods for dealing with it.

The best way is to minimize the chance of its occurring by doing something we have already discussed: *developing the habit of withholding judgment while you are producing ideas.* Every time you stop the flow of ideas to make a judgment, even if you stop for only a second or two, you run the risk of not being able to start again. On the other hand, the more you resist the temptation to stop and instead sustain your idea production, the less trouble thinker's block will cause you.

When it occurs despite your best efforts to avoid it, try one or more of the following approaches, in the order they are presented.

1. Look back at the ideas you have written. Read them carefully, concentrating on each as you read it. Usually, one of those ideas will suggest another that you have not written. As soon as it does, write it. Now that the ideas are flowing again, don't stop until you have to. It doesn't matter if the first few ideas are off target. You can gently direct the flow back to the problem or issue.
2. Run through the strategies for stimulating your imagination again. That is, force uncommon responses (however outrageous), use free association and analogy, look for unusual combinations, and so on through the list of strategies. You'll seldom get beyond the first or second strategy before the ideas are flowing again.
3. Copy your list of ideas over again and again, concentrating on each idea as you are writing it. Be alert to the appearance of a new idea on the fringe of your consciousness. This approach will keep you active and will prevent frustration and apprehension.
4. Walk away from the problem for a time (an hour, a day, a week). Return to it only when you can take a fresh look at it, unburdened of anxiety.
5. If all else fails, go back to the second stage of the process and consider other expressions of the problem or issue.

Vagueness and Confusion

Even the greatest thinkers experience this obstacle to problem solving. Einstein, for example, began considering the problem that led to his relativity theory when he was 16 years old. He struggled with it for seven years before reaching a solution. During that time he experienced vagueness, confusion, and puzzlement to the point of depression and despair.[11]

Whether this obstacle appears during the investigating stage or the idea-producing stage, it is most often caused by losing sight of the problem. The best way to overcome it is to *look back at your statement of the problem or issue and get your bearings.* In the beginning, you may have to stop the flow of ideas to take this backward look, but with a little practice, you will be able to do it without stopping the flow. You will merely slow it down a little. It's much like steering a car. A beginning driver often has to come to a complete stop to straighten the car's direction, but very soon, he or she learns to make slight corrections with the steering wheel while maintaining speed.

You will find this kind of mental steering easier to master if you write your expression of the problem on a card or sheet of paper and keep it handy while working on the problem.

Inflexibility

This obstacle is characterized by too many ideas of one type, with little or no variation. It is caused by unconsciously directing your thinking along one narrow line of thought. Whenever you find this obstacle in your work (a simple glance back over your ideas will reveal whether it is present), make a special effort to stimulate your imagination. Any of the seven strategies we discussed may be used, but the first two and the last—forcing uncommon responses, using free association, and constructing relevant scenarios—are especially helpful.

HOW INSIGHT OCCURS

The most dramatic experience of the idea-producing stage—indeed, of the entire creative process—is the arrival of an insight. The moment of insight has been described in many ways. One is the *Aha!* reaction, such as Archimedes experienced when he sat down in a tub of water, noticed the displacement of the water by the mass of his body, and instantly conceptualized the principle of specific gravity. "Eureka!" ("I have found it!") he is said to have shouted as he ran naked through the streets. (Apparently the law against indecent exposure was not well enforced then, or else he ran very fast. In any case, he seems to have escaped arrest.) Another way of describing the moment of insight is an intense feeling of satisfaction, such as we get when we find a missing puzzle piece. But perhaps the most common experience is sudden illumination, like the lightbulb glowing above the head of a cartoon character.

For some reason, many insights come during moments of rest. One of the building blocks of modern science, an idea called "the most brilliant piece of prediction to be found in the whole range of organic chemistry," occurred at such a time. Friedrich August von Kekulé lay dozing by the fire one day in 1865 and suddenly realized that the molecules of certain organic compounds were not open structures, but ring-shaped. Here's how he described the experience:

> I turned my chair to the fire and dozed. . . . Again the atoms were gambolling before my eyes. This time the smaller groups kept modestly in the background. My mental eye, rendered more acute by repeated visions of this kind, could now distinguish larger structures, of manifold conformation; long rows, sometimes more closely fitted together; all twining and twisting in snakelike motion. But look! What was that?

> One of the snakes had seized hold of its own tail, and the form whirled mockingly before my eyes. As if by a flash of lightning I awoke.[12]

The fact that many imaginative leaps have come during periods of leisure or rest has led to the misconception that insight comes without effort. Authorities on the creative process are in agreement that insight is not associated with idleness. (If it were, the village loafer would hold the record for creative achievement.) Nor does it arrive during any type of leisure. Rather, it arrives during the leisure that follows periods of intense activity, in which the thinker grapples with the problem or issue, is momentarily defeated by it, and turns away in frustration. Authorities theorize that the conscious mind then turns the problem over to the unconscious, which continues working. Insight comes from that effort.[13]

Sudden insights, like all dramatic experiences, tend to be more widely publicized and more memorable than everyday occurrences. However, the fact is that many, sometimes the vast majority, of creative solutions come about more quietly. They are the result of alertness to details and careful analysis of ideas. Such solutions, though they arrive without fanfare, are no less valuable for that. And they have one great advantage over sudden insights. We can, to a significant extent, *make* them happen.

A SAMPLE PROBLEM

You are a bill collector for a magazine. You have wasted countless hours in waiting rooms, hoping to see the magazine's debtors. But most secretaries have been instructed to let you wait until you get tired and leave. You examine the problem from all sides and consider a number of expressions of the problem. Finally, you decide that the best expression is "How can I get to see debtors despite their secretaries' refusal to let me do so?" Here is how your production of ideas might proceed.

You begin listing all your ideas. The first ones are outrageous, but that doesn't bother you. You know you shouldn't stop to evaluate them.

- Carry a shotgun and threaten the secretary.
- Threaten to kidnap the debtor's wife and kids.
- Bring an attack dog to the office.
- Scale the building and climb in the debtor's window.
- Tell the secretary you are the boss's brother or sister.
- Tie up the secretary and barge into the office.

You encounter thinker's block, so you apply one or more of the strategies recommended in the chapter for overcoming this obstacle. The ideas begin to flow again.

- Sweet-talk the secretary.
- Call and make an appointment first.
- Send a letter requesting payment.
- Fax the debtor repeatedly.

- Change jobs.
- Take a course in quick thinking.
- Cancel the debtor's subscription.
- Take legal action.
- Sit and wait until the office closes.
- Take an attorney with you.
- Send someone else to wait in your place.

At this point, you become confused; you believe you've lost sight of the problem. A glance back at the ideas you've just produced confirms this. They do not address the problem as you expressed it. You reread your expression and begin producing again.

- Bother the secretary.
- Give him or her a box of candy.
- Take him or her to lunch.
- Try bribery.
- Beg to see the debtor.
- Wait for the secretary to go to lunch and then barge in.

You run dry again, so you start once more with the first strategy, looking back over the ideas you have produced. Starting with the most recent, you read, "Wait for the secretary to go to lunch . . . beg to see the debtor, bribery. . . ." Suddenly you realize your inflexibility: you have slipped into producing ideas of the same type, with little or no variation. You try to stimulate your imagination, first by forcing uncommon responses. The ideas begin again.

- Pretend to be someone else.
- Catch the debtor outside the office.
- Bother the other people in the waiting room.
- Cause a disturbance.
- Be obnoxious.

The ideas stop once more, so you stimulate your imagination. When you fail to force uncommon responses, you turn to free association. Several of your ideas suggest a number of associations. Specifically, "Pretend to be someone else" suggests

- A telephone repairer
- A janitor
- A job applicant
- A police officer
- An office-supplies salesperson
- A priest or nun
- An electrician
- A newspaper reporter
- A magazine contest representative (to award a prize)
- A window washer

"Bother the secretary" suggests

- Ask to be announced every few minutes.
- Sit on the secretary's desk.
- Talk to him or her incessantly.

"Bother the other people in the waiting room" suggests

- Talk loudly about your recently contracted contagious disease.
- Tell everyone loudly that the debtor has been named in a paternity suit.
- Tell them the truth about the debtor's bill.

"Cause a disturbance" suggests

- Fall down and feign a seizure.
- Practice the tuba.
- Yell, "Fire!"
- Jump up and down on a whoopee cushion.
- Sing off-key.
- Pitch a tent (literally).
- Make howling noises.
- Put up signs saying, "This guy doesn't pay his bills."

"Be obnoxious" suggests

- Put on a horrible mask and fake blood.
- Rub your clothing with garlic and onions.
- Soak your clothes in skunk spray.

At this point, you'd have produced enough good ideas, including a number of creative ones, to stop producing and select your best one. (This selection, remember, will be tentative, pending your application of critical thinking.) Which idea would that be? A real bill collector, Andy Smulion of London, uses the very last one with great success. He soaks his clothes in skunk spray, walks quietly into the debtor's office, and hands the secretary a note saying, "I'll leave when you pay." Needless to say, he doesn't have to wait long.

A SAMPLE ISSUE

You read in the newspaper that the Television Information Office, an organization financed by the television industry, has issued a six-page research paper arguing that television is not the cause of declining reading scores in the nation's schools. The research paper claims that children's reading scores have more to do with "socioeconomic factors" than with the amount of television they watch and that heavy viewing doesn't cause reading problems but is the result of those problems. It states, "Children having difficulty with classroom study and with homework will turn to television . . . precisely because of their reading difficulties."[14]

You realize that this is a matter that informed people disagree about, so you approach it as an issue and decide that the best expression of it is "Is television viewing in any way a causative factor in declining reading scores?" After reading several scholarly articles in the library and interviewing an education professor and a reading-skills instructor (both of them on your campus), you develop ideas as follows.*

> The television industry financed the study, so it could be biased.
>
> The conclusion says television doesn't cause reading deficiencies. That makes me more suspicious, though it proves nothing.
>
> *[A move to interpretation]* The claim that reading scores have more to do with "socioeconomic factors" suggests that the disadvantaged are the only ones with reading problems. Yet that's not the case.
>
> Middle- and upper-class students' reading deficiencies must be caused by something else.
>
> What about reading problems causing heavy television viewing? Sounds odd, but the authorities I consulted agreed that it can happen.
>
> How exactly would this happen? Let's see . . .
>
> *[Now constructing a scenario]* Kids have trouble reading in school, grow frustrated, and so are motivated not to pick up a book but to escape. They come home, switch on the television set, and watch the evening away.
>
> It makes sense. In cases like this, reading deficiencies probably do cause excessive television viewing.
>
> *[Now playing devil's advocate]* But how are those kids any different from the average kid? Don't many good readers watch television just as much? If reading problems don't cause them to be enslaved by the boob tube, maybe they don't always cause poor readers to do so. Is it possible that the study is in error, that television viewing does cause reading problems, after all?
>
> What would have to happen in order for television viewing to be the cause? It would have to *precede* reading deficiencies. Kids would first have to be hooked on television. Let me get a clearer picture of the sequence.
>
> *[Now another scenario]* First, the TV viewing. When, exactly? In early childhood. How? The kid plays while a parent is busy. The parent leaves the

---

*The form and content of this sample do not reflect what you would typically do. You would undoubtedly list your ideas in fragmentary fashion so as not to interrupt the flow of thought; yet, for the sake of clarity, ideas are presented here in complete sentences. Moreover, your analysis would involve actually conducting investigations and then reflecting on each to generate more ideas, whereas here, because of space limitations, the investigations are only suggested. The emphasis here is not on research completeness but on the process by which one strategy leads to another and produces ideas.

> television set on as a kind of baby-sitter. The kid watches it, hour after hour, day after day, from age 1 to age 5. By the time the child begins learning to read, at age 6 or so, he or she has already watched thousands of hours of TV. . . .
>
> That's not only plausible, it's what actually happens in many cases. TV does exert influence in a child's life much earlier than formal education.
>
> *[Now an attempt to interpret]* What exactly is the influence of television? What happens on television that could affect reading?
>
> *[Now yet another scenario, this one of a typical television hour, during a soap opera]* The hour begins with a cluster of commercials, then for ten minutes or so moves back and forth among two or three story lines. Then there's another cluster of three or four commercials and perhaps a newsbreak before returning to the several story lines. . . .
>
> What does all of that translate into? Frequent shifts from scene to scene, frequent commercial breaks, frequent shifts of the viewer's attention, no demands on the mind, no difficulties or challenges—no wonder reading seems impossibly difficult by comparison.

At this point you will no doubt be inclined to conclude that television viewing is indeed a causative factor in declining reading scores. But before you can be fully confident that this is the correct conclusion, you will have to apply critical thinking and evaluate your thinking. The next chapter introduces the critical thinking process.

Warm-Up Exercises

1. Many performers drop their given names and take stage names that are easy to remember and that project a particular image. Thus, the cinema had Theda Bara (her last name was derived by reversing *Arab*) and Victor Mature. Wrestling has Hulk Hogan, and music had Prince (until he grew tired of the name). Think of as many creative stage names as you can. The image you aim to project may be macho male, female sex symbol, charming child, or any other you wish.
2. Think of as many creative names as you can for a restaurant. Consider all types of establishments, from the fancy high-priced variety to the lowly coffee shop, as well as all types of cuisines.
3. Most of us complain that we don't have enough closets. Yet we seldom use very efficiently the closet space we already have. Redesign your closet at home (or if you prefer, the one at college) to achieve maximum use of its space. Do "before" and "after" sketches of the closet.

Applications

For each of the following applications, find the best expression of the problem or issue, investigate it as necessary, and then produce as many ideas as you can, applying what you learned in this chapter. (Record all your thoughts as they occur to you, and be prepared to submit them to your instructor.) Finally, state which of your ideas you believe is best, and briefly explain why.

1 You've entered a snow sculpture contest. The most important judging criterion, according to the organizers of the contest, will be creativity. There is no special theme, nor are there any restrictions on size or form.

2 The problem of having the string slip out of your sweatpants can be expressed in a number of ways.

3 Newton's friends are a partying crowd. Almost every night, they are either having a party themselves, attending a party in someone's dorm room or apartment, or making the rounds of the local bars. Newton wants to do his best academically and would prefer to drink only on weekends—and even then only moderately. He'd like to explain this to his friends, but he's sure they wouldn't understand; they'd either try to pressure him into conforming or feel he was rejecting them.

4 You are the editor of the college newspaper. Your staff consists of two other people who limit their work to a few hours a week. To get the paper out each week, you've had to spend many more hours than your course load permits. On several occasions, you've stayed up all night and slept through the next morning's classes. You've tried putting ads in the paper to get more staff members, but no one answers them.

5 In some cultures, the elderly are greatly respected and made to feel important. Their views are considered especially valuable because they are formed out of a lifetime of experience. In our culture it is quite different. Most of those over 70 are regarded as having nothing to offer society.

6 Many people, notably students, believe that extracurricular activities in high school complement the curriculum and provide valuable opportunities for personal growth and achievement. Yet many communities are finding the cost of financing today's schools an intolerable burden and are looking for ways to reduce that cost. Some are deciding, reluctantly, that they must cut extracurricular activities (including varsity sports) from the school budget.

7 The American Lung Association is looking for ways to warn teenagers about the dangers of cigarette smoking. Assist the association.

8 Going to the hospital for the first time can be a frightening experience, particularly for small children. Think of as many ways as you can to make the children's ward of a hospital a nonthreatening, cheery place.

9 Some states still consider adultery a crime and can legally impose monetary fines or prison sentences on anyone convicted of it.

ISSUE FOR EXTENDED ANALYSIS

Following is a more comprehensive thinking challenge than the others in the chapter.

THE ISSUE: AFFIRMATIVE ACTION

There is little controversy about the theoretical concept of "affirmative action," which refers to any program that aims to achieve racial/ethnic balance in education and in the workplace by actively seeking out minority candidates. The controversy concerns some of the strategies certain programs have employed, notably "set asides," quotas, and various forms of preferential treatment. Some people believe such strategies are both necessary and fair; others strongly disagree.

THE ESSAYS

Affirmative Action: A Good Thing
By Lawrence Bertrand

However free of prejudice white people can be, they cannot understand the burden of slavery's legacy. Nor can they perceive how many slights, insults, and deprivations are *still* inflicted (whether intended or not) on black people. Thus, white people cannot fully appreciate the critical importance of affirmative action to the black community. To their credit, of course, many white people accept the testimony of spokespeople of the black community—notably Jesse Jackson and Al Sharpton—and vigorously support affirmative action.

End Affirmative Action
By Kimberly Jones

The government's affirmative action program was designed to achieve justice but instead has created a new injustice, not just to the white majority but also, and most significantly, to the black community it was intended to help.

Unlike civil rights and voting rights legislation, which is necessary to prevent racial discrimination, affirmative action is unnecessary and unfair. To begin with, it emphasizes people's race over more important considerations, including the role of effort in achievement, the ideal of merit, and the necessity of being qual-

The case for affirmative action rests on two amply-supported conclusions: it is necessary and fair. Why necessary? Because there is no other way for significant numbers of black citizens to make up for centuries of discrimination and the denial of educational and employment opportunities. Imagine a marathon race with many participants. Imagine, too, that 90% of the runners start at 9:00 A.M. but the remaining 10% are held back until 10:00 A.M. No matter how naturally gifted and determined the 10% may be, they will have no chance of winning the race.

The situation of those handicapped runners is analogous to that of black Americans in school and at work. They have entered the "competition" for education and employment that the only way for them to have a chance at "winning" is to have their handicap removed. Present opportunity is fine, but it does not restore the education and jobs black people could and should have had. Preferences alone ensure parity.

The second conclusion concerns the fairness of affirmative action. Some say it is manifestly *unfair* to allow black students to enter college with lower test scores than white students or to set aside a certain number of jobs for black applicants. They are mistaken. Extreme situations demand unusual responses, and no situation is as extreme as a history of slavery and discrimination. Affirmative action is therefore the fairest possible response to the situation of black Americans.

ified for a level of academic pursuit or a particular job. (Interestingly, the very idea of affirmative action ignores Martin Luther King, Jr.'s plea to value the content of a person's character more than the color of his or her skin.) By substituting entitlement for merit, affirmative action also robs black youth of the motivation to achieve and erodes their confidence and sense of self-worth.

Many people in the black community accept the notion that white liberal supporters of affirmative action are their friends and conservative critics of the program disrespect them. The truth is exactly the reverse. The real reason white liberals are so committed to affirmative action is one they won't express publicly: they don't think blacks are *capable* of making it in school or on the job without government assistance.

A number of distinguished black authors have recognized these facts and have spoken out strongly against affirmative action. Among those individuals are Ward Connerly, Walter Williams, William Raspberry, Thomas Sowell, and Shelby Steele. For example, in *Losing the Race* Berkeley professor John McWhorter argues academic underachievement among black students is not caused by lack of opportunity but by liberal conditioning that they are victims who don't have to conform to traditional academic standards.

Simply said, affirmative action does more harm than good and should be abolished.

Class Discussion

KAREN: I've heard all the arguments for affirmative action, but the one fact that stands out to me is that it gives one group of people preferential treatment. I think that is unfair, and I'm heartened to know that Martin Luther King, Jr. had the same view.

EMMA: How fair is it to have denied millions of black Americans the opportunities historically enjoyed by other Americans?

KAREN: It wasn't fair at all but the solution is not to treat other people unfairly. Doing that merely compounds the problem. The only real solution is to guarantee everyone equal opportunity. That was the original idea behind the Civil Rights movement. Affirmative action is a corruption of that idea.

EMMA: I agree that fairness to everyone is a worthy ideal. But that doesn't make up for past injustices.

KAREN: It doesn't make up for past injustices because it can't do so—the vast majority of the people who were treated unjustly are long dead. Giving preferences to their great-grandchildren in no way removes the injustice to them. It just transfers the injustice to another group and perpetuates it.

EMMA: Not really. Affirmative action is both a powerful symbol of the nation's regret and a spur to black success.

KAREN: Wrong on both counts. The symbol is an empty exercise in assuaging white guilt. And affirmative action doesn't spur black success—it creates a false sense of entitlement that hinders success. Jones cited a number of black authors who take that view.

EMMA: Those authors are traitors to their race.

KAREN: It's offensive for you, a white woman, to make such a judgment.

Notes

1. This analogy was first made by Zbigniew Pietraskinski, *The Psychology of Efficient Thinking*, trans. B. Jankowski (New York: Pergamon Press, 1969), p. 134.
2. Parnes, *Creative Behavior Guidebook*, p. 57.
3. Quoted in Osborn, *Applied Imagination*, p. 149.
4. Quoted in ibid., p. 151.
5. Parnes, *Creative Behavior Guidebook*, pp. 57–58.
6. Quoted in Beveridge, *Art of Scientific Investigation*, p. 143.

7. Quoted in Clarence D. Tuska, *Inventors and Inventions* (New York: McGraw-Hill, 1957), p. 88.
8. Parnes, *Creative Behavior Guidebook,* pp. 55–56.
9. *The Art of Thought* (New York: Harcourt, Brace, 1926), p. 139.
10. Parnes, *Creative Behavior Guidebook,* p. 57.
11. Max Wertheimer, *Productive Thinking* (New York: Harper & Brothers, 1945), pp. 169–173.
12. Quoted in Koestler, *Act of Creation,* p. 118.
13. See, for example, Hutchinson, *How to Think Creatively,* pp. 35–40.
14. "TV Fights Charges It Undercuts Reading," *Binghamton Press,* 29 November 1981, p. 1a.

The Role of Criticism

There are two phases to thinking: the *creative* phase, in which ideas are produced, and the *critical* phase, in which they are evaluated. Since then we have discussed the creative phase in detail. Now we turn our attention to the critical phase.

This chapter explains why critical thinking is necessary and gives you an overview of how critical thinking strategies are applied to problems and issues.

G. K. Chesterton once described a poet as a person with his head in the clouds and his feet on the ground. That description also fits good thinkers. They are able to entertain the boldest ideas, the undreamed-of solutions to problems—yet they are also able to fit their ideas to the exacting demands of reality. They are not only imaginative but practical as well. Now we will examine the latter, critical phase.

Critical thinking, as we define it here, means reviewing the ideas we have produced, making a tentative decision about what action will best solve the problem or what belief about the issue is most reasonable, and then evaluating and refining that solution or belief.

WHY CRITICISM IS NECESSARY

The role of criticism in problem solving is important for two reasons. First, no solution is ever perfect. However creative it may be, there is always room for improvement. Even the best ideas seldom occur in refined form. Like fine gems, they must be cleaned and polished before their potential worth is realized. Second, in many cases solutions cannot just be put into effect; they must first be approved by others. Ideas for the improvement of the office or factory, for example, may require the approval of an employer or supervisor. Ideas about overcoming difficulties in family relationships may depend on the cooperation of other family members. And creative solutions to social problems often require the support of government leaders or the endorsement of the voters. In such cases, the best idea in the world is of little value until others are persuaded of its worth.

Criticism is equally important in resolving issues. A viewpoint may seem eminently reasonable, the ideal ground for compromise between opposing views, yet contain subtle flaws. Sometimes these become evident only when the idea is translated into a course of action.

In the early 1970s, for example, in response to the issue of fairness in divorce settlements, the idea of "no-fault" divorce became law in California, and in subsequent years, in most other states. It was considered at the time an ingenious way to permit a marriage to be dissolved easily and fairly, without squabbling and bitter accusations. Later, many critics identified an effect of no-fault divorce that no one anticipated when it was instituted: the impoverishment of divorced women and their children.[1]

Although there can never be a guarantee that even the most thorough criticism will reveal every flaw in an idea, your responses to issues are more likely to be reasonable if you subject your ideas to rigorous evaluation before reaching a judgment. Critical thinking reduces your chance of error.

FOCUS ON *YOUR* IDEAS

The focus of this chapter is not on criticism of other people's solutions. It is rather on a much more difficult, even painful, criticism: that of *your own* solutions. Like everyone else, you are vulnerable to a variety of errors. You may receive inaccurate reports from others, including the media. In addition, you may misunderstand accurate reports, fall prey to rumor and hearsay, let emotion color your judgment, and suffer lapses in logic. For these reasons, the ideas you produce need criticism.

Ironically, though you are undoubtedly ready to criticize others' ideas freely, like most people you are probably blind to the need for criticism of your own thinking. There are several reasons for this. First, your ego is inclined against self-criticism. Once you have settled on an idea, you feel a proprietary interest in it. "It is mine," you tell yourself, "so it must be good." And once in that frame of mind, you are ready to defend the idea against all attack, even the attack that your own good judgment might mount against it. The situation is something like that of a dog with a bone. The dog will cling to it tenaciously and growl and snarl when anyone approaches, not because the bone is worth anything (it may long since have been chewed out), but simply because it is the dog's possession.

Another reason you will be reluctant to evaluate your own ideas is that their familiarity makes it difficult to see flaws in them. The longer you work on a problem or an issue, the more accustomed you become to its details. And once your effort yields a solution, you have usually got so close to the problem that it is difficult to distance yourself from it, to step back mentally from your solution and see it objectively.

OVERCOMING OBSTACLES TO CRITICAL THINKING

This blindness toward imperfections in your ideas will make it tempting to approach criticism of your ideas with, at best, mock analysis followed by a vigorous nod of approval. There are two ways you can safeguard against this mistake. The first is to say to yourself, before you begin to take a critical look at any idea, "I know this idea is going to look good to me and that I am going to feel it's pointless to look for flaws. That's natural. I thought of it, so I want it to be perfect. *But I'm going to disregard this reaction and force myself to examine it critically.*"

The second safeguard is to use your ego to advantage. Whenever you find yourself ready to stop evaluating your idea before you really should, reflect for a moment on how it would feel to have a serious flaw pointed out by someone else, particularly by someone you don't much care for. Visualize the situation; imagine yourself squirming with embarrassment and awkwardly offering face-saving excuses. Such a mental picture ought to motivate you to continue evaluating your idea.

APPLYING CURIOSITY

We know how curiosity increases awareness of problems and issues, enabling you to feel dissatisfactions and annoyances more consciously and to regard them more productively as challenges and opportunities. We know, too, that curiosity keeps your mind dynamic and contributes to the playfulness Einstein regarded as "the essential feature of productive thought." That same curiosity is also a valuable aid to critical thinking.

Perhaps you've had the experience of adding up a column of figures and getting the same answer—the *wrong* answer—again and again. Psychologists have long recognized that when we travel a particular mental route a second or third time, we often follow our earlier footsteps without realizing that we are doing so. That's what happened when you added up those figures. You had the impression that each new total was fresh and independent. In reality, though, you were trapped by your initial miscalculation.

That same kind of mistake can occur when you examine your ideas critically. You can look at an idea again and again and still not see its flaws. To be effective, you need to examine the idea from different perspectives. That's where curiosity comes in. By approaching criticism inquisitively—asking "How will my idea work when it is applied?" and "How will others react to it?"—you will increase your chances of finding the imperfections and complications that need to be addressed.

AVOIDING ASSUMPTIONS

To assume is to take something for granted, to expect that things will be a certain way because they have been that way in the past or because you want them to be that way. It's natural to make assumptions. Everyone makes them continually. You assume, for example, that your professor will be in class when class is scheduled, that the cafeteria will not serve lunch two hours early, that your car is safe from vandalism in the college parking lot, that the bank that has always cashed your checks will continue to do so, and that the elevator is really going up when the indicator says it is. Making such assumptions is reasonable, even if on occasion they prove to be incorrect.

Nevertheless, it is important to be careful about what you assume. And when you are evaluating and refining your ideas, you should make a special effort to identify assumptions you may not have detected previously. The reason is not only that unexpected outcomes can cause you embarrassment but also, and more important, that *what you take for granted you will not examine critically.* Assumptions obstruct the evaluation process.

It would be impossible to list all the assumptions it is possible to make. However, the following assumptions occur often enough, and interfere with critical thinking seriously enough, to warrant special mention.

1. *The assumption that others familiar with the problem or issue will share your enthusiasm for your ideas.* Although this might seem to be a reasonable expectation, it seldom is. The more familiar people are with a problem or issue, the more likely they are to have their own ideas.

2. *The assumption that small imperfections in your idea will not affect people's acceptance of it.* When other people's ideas differ from yours, they are likely to magnify flaws in your ideas without even realizing it because, subconsciously, they are looking for an excuse to reject your ideas. Small imperfections may provide that excuse.

3. *The assumption that if your idea is clear to you, it will be clear to others.* If you've ever sat in a classroom and heard a teacher offer an explanation that didn't make the slightest sense to you, you should appreciate the confusion this assumption can cause. *Your* understanding of what you are expressing does not constitute clarity. If you want the solution and its presentation to be clear, you must *construct* it to be so and not just assume that it is.

4. *The assumption that the people who stand to benefit most from your idea will accept it automatically without any persuasion on your part.* This assumption has caused creative people incalculable grief. For example, when Elias Howe invented the sewing machine, he knew it would be a boon to the garment industry by revolutionizing garment construction and making the clothing business much more profitable. He may very well have assumed that the mere unveiling of his invention would be sufficient to have the leaders of that industry praise it and him. But reality didn't match

that assumption. Howe couldn't get a single American firm interested enough to buy the machine. He was forced to go to England to find a favorable reception. To spare yourself disappointment, never assume that the value of your ideas will be universally recognized. Expect to have to persuade other people.

REFINING YOUR SOLUTIONS TO PROBLEMS

Refining your solutions means making good ideas even better—that is, making the results of your creative thinking more effective, more workable, more attractive. Although much of what you will be doing in this stage is finding flaws and complications, the emphasis is not negative but positive. Your aim is to *improve* your ideas.

Not every idea, of course, requires refinement. With the problem of the string that slips out of your sweatpants, for example, there is little or no need for refinement and no need to present the solution for others' approval. Once you have decided on a solution, you can just implement it. Most of the important problems and issues you will encounter, however, are more demanding.

The basic approach that follows will enable you to begin using these steps and developing skill in applying them even while you are studying each in greater depth. The approach consists of asking and answering these four questions.

1. How exactly will your solution be applied? List all steps and all important details.
2. What difficulties could arise in its implementation, and how would these best be overcome?
3. What reasons might others find for opposing this solution? What modifications could you make to overcome their opposition?
4. Who, specifically, will have to be persuaded of the merit of your solution? What kind of presentation would be most likely to persuade them?

A SAMPLE PROBLEM

You are the editor of the college newspaper. Your staff consists of two other people who limit their work to a few hours a week. To get the paper out each week, you've had to spend many more hours than your course load permits. On several occasions, you've stayed up all night and slept through the next morning's classes. You've tried putting ads in the paper to get more staff members, but no one answers them.

Let's say you identify the problem as "How to reward students for joining the staff." (This is one good expression of the problem, though not, of course, the only one.) Let's say further that after investigating the problem and producing a number of possible solutions, you chose *giving college credit to those who work on the paper* as the best one. You'd apply the critical approach as follows.

1. How exactly will your solution be applied?
   Here you'd have to decide and list the requirements for obtaining credit for the work. You'd also have to decide which department would grant credit, how much credit would be granted, and whether it would be elective credit or would fulfill some course requirement.

2. What difficulties could arise in its implementation, and how would these best be overcome?
   The most obvious difficulty would involve course requirements and the evaluation of student performance. Who would teach the course? Where? (In a classroom? In the newspaper office?) How could one, two, or three time periods per week satisfy the demands of producing the paper? How would the instructor evaluate performance? Would the editor have to meet a different standard than a reporter or a layout person? If so, how would the registrar clarify on each student's transcript what standard was met? These and other questions would have to be raised and answered satisfactorily.

3. Why might others resist this solution? What modifications could you make to overcome this resistance?
   Here you'd consider such reasons as the inappropriateness of the new course to any curriculum on campus (if the campus did not offer a journalism major), the lack of journalistic expertise among campus faculty, and the possible course overload the solution would represent for faculty.

4. Whom would you have to persuade of the solution's value? What kind of presentation would be most likely to persuade them?
   You'd surely have to persuade the college administration and the faculty, particularly the faculty of the department you are suggesting should teach the course.

REFINING YOUR POSITIONS ON ISSUES

Though the terms *problem* and *issue* both refer to disagreeable situations that challenge our ingenuity, an issue also tends to divide people into opposing camps, each sure that it is right and the opposition wrong. Whereas the aim of problem solving is to find the best course of action, the aim of issue resolving is to find the most reasonable belief, and so we express problems and issues differently and produce different kinds of ideas for each.

Now we will consider another difference. Your approach to refining your positions on issues is to decide not whether the idea works but whether it meets the tests of logic. Thus you must take the following steps.

1. State your argument. That is, state the belief you have decided to be most reasonable concerning the issue, and give your reasons for so deciding.
2. Examine your evidence for relevance, comprehensiveness, and reliability.
3. Examine your argument for flaws in reasoning—for example, errors of narrow perspective, confusion, or carelessness.

In cases where your aim is solely to form a reasonable belief and not to take any action about it, this approach will constitute refinement of the issue. However, in cases in which you wish not only to establish what belief is most reasonable but also to take action on that belief, you will next answer questions quite similar to those used for refining solutions to problems, questions designed to plan a course of action and then to evaluate it critically. Here are those questions.

> What action do you recommend be taken, and how exactly will it be taken? List all steps and important details.
>
> What difficulties could arise in taking this action, and how would they best be overcome?

To see how this approach works, let's consider a sample issue.

A SAMPLE ISSUE

Let's say that you are addressing the matter of the United States giving monetary aid to foreign governments that victimize their citizens and deny them their human rights and that you have expressed the main issue as "Is it morally right for the U.S. government to provide such aid?" Let's also say that your argument is as follows.

> It is morally wrong for the U.S. government to provide monetary aid to foreign governments that victimize their citizens and deny them their human rights because the United States is a democracy and holds that government exists for the good of the people and that the people are "endowed with certain unalienable rights." To support tyranny in this way, while preaching human rights, is hypocritical.

Next, you examine your argument for reasonableness and find only one serious flaw: the unwarranted assumption that giving monetary aid to such countries is *necessarily* supporting tyranny and therefore is hypocritical. On reflection, you decide that if the money actually assists needy people, giving it would represent the lesser of two evils and therefore a moral course of action. You modify your argument, replacing the last sentence with this one: "Giving monetary aid in such circumstances is justifiable only if the people would be worse off without it and no other effective way to help them can be found."

Taking Action on the Issue

Recognizing that your argument is a challenge to find a better approach than giving money to corrupt governments, you proceed with your critical thinking as follows:

What action do you recommend be taken, and how exactly will it be taken?

> Let's say that the action you choose is to give aid in the form of technological education and employment opportunities, with the stipulation that the governments end all victimization of the people. You would then detail the kinds of technological education and employment opportunities you have in mind. You would also decide whether the teachers and employers will be sponsored by our government, by private enterprise, or by a combination of the two. Finally, you'd detail any special employment conditions, including wages and benefits.

What difficulties could arise in taking this action, and how would they best be overcome?

> The most obvious difficulty would be policing the country's government—deciding how to ensure that it would end human rights violations. (This problem could be overcome by having a UN task force monitor the situation.) Another difficulty would be preventing the corrupt officials from using your plan in a manner you do not intend, such as by taking advantage of the new cheap labor for their own financial gain. (This difficulty could be overcome by the establishment of profit-sharing plans and cooperatives so that the people would enjoy the fruits of their labor.)

One final suggestion: If you ever become discouraged about imperfections and complications in your work—if you are inclined to say, "How can I ever be expected to work out all the flaws I discover? It's an impossible task!"—try this approach: Treat each significant imperfection or complication as a miniature problem, first finding the best expression, investigating it if necessary, and generating as many possible solutions as you can. Not every issue warrants such meticulous attention, but the more important ones will. And by using a familiar process to address them, you bolster your confidence, overcome discouragement, and stimulate your imagination.

WARM-UP EXERCISES

1 Old dishwashing liquid containers (the plastic ones that Dawn, Joy, and Ivory liquid come in) are usually discarded when empty. But perhaps they could be put to some use. Think of as many uses for them as you can.

2 A law student hired a tutor to help him with his law studies. He promised to pay for the tutor's services as soon as he passed his bar exam, set up practice, and won his first case. He subsequently passed the exam and set up practice, but a year passed and he still had not won a case. The tutor grew tired of waiting and sued him for payment. The young lawyer then wrote the tutor a letter and said, "If your suit against me goes to court and I win it, I won't have to pay you. And if I lose it, I still won't have to pay you, because the terms of our agreement (my winning my first case) will not have been met."[2] Do you agree with the young lawyer's reasoning? Explain thoroughly.

3 In the following dialogue, Lily admits she is confused. Perhaps Daisy is, too. Clear up the confusion for them.

DAISY: What is the meaning of life?

LILY: There is no one meaning.

DAISY: There's got to be. Otherwise, everyone makes his or her own, and that would create chaos.

LILY: No, everyone *decides* his or her own. Whatever a person says, that's it.

DAISY: Do you mean if I say the meaning of life is "Eat, drink, and be merry, for tomorrow we die," that *is* the meaning of life?

LILY: Yes, for *you* it is, though maybe not for me.

DAISY: That would mean that no one can be wrong in his or her view. And if that's the case, why is everyone so concerned about finding the meaning of life?

LILY: I don't know. That's always puzzled me.

1 Since you graduated from high school, you've been wondering what single improvement could be made in your school system between kindergarten and twelfth grade that would have the best and most lasting impact on students. Now you've come up with the answer: have the students be taught *how to think,* directly and systematically. Now take that idea and refine it.

2 You are a Hollywood film producer. You have just been tried in federal court for agreeing to buy five ounces of cocaine. The judge deferred final judgment of your case for a year but put you on probation and offered you this challenge: "If you put your talents to work fighting drug abuse by children, I will wipe your record clean." You feel remorse for your own drug use and resolve to meet the challenge. Identify and solve this problem; then refine your best solution.

3 Your older sister shares this personal problem with you: Her daughter is only a toddler, but before long, your sister will have to explain to her the value of honesty in daily life. Yet she herself is confused. Here's how she explains her dilemma to you: "Mom and Dad always told us that 'honesty is the best policy' in every case. Yet every other day, it seems, I read about workers who report corruption in their company or in government and then lose their jobs for their honesty. I want to give my daughter the best advice, and yet I'm not sure what the best advice is." Identify and solve your sister's problem; then refine your best solution.

4 Michael is very excited. He has just got his first job, delivering newspapers in a residential neighborhood. The only problem is that he has to pass several large dogs on his route, and he has been afraid of dogs for as long as he can remember. Identify and solve Michael's problem; then refine your best solution.

5 Millions of American adults are functionally illiterate. These people cannot decipher a bus, train, or airline schedule; write a letter; or fill out a job application. Such illiteracy is estimated to cost the United States billions of dollars annually in welfare and unemployment payments. With the federal government decreasing its aid to education, that cost is likely to increase. Apply your creative and critical thinking to this problem as you did in previous applications.

ISSUE FOR EXTENDED ANALYSIS

Following is a more comprehensive thinking challenge than the others in the chapter.

THE ISSUE: RELIGION IN SCHOOLS AND PUBLIC PLACES

Hardly a week goes by without some conflict about religion in schools being reported in the news. Many people believe that there is no reason to bar expressions or symbols of religion from public schools. Many others think such expressions and symbols are unconstitutional. Even the U.S. Supreme Court is divided on the issue, so it is understandable that many other Americans aren't sure what to think.

THE ESSAYS

Welcome Religion in Public Schools
By Bernard Hoffman

It's astounding that the same liberal establishment that is forever chanting odes to multiculturalism, diversity, tolerance, and inclusion is fanatical about banning any hint of religion from the public schools. Any hint of traditional Jewish or Christian religion, that is. (Buddhism, Wicca, and Santeria would probably pass muster.)

Liberals believe it is acceptable for students to dress in the costumes, sample the food, and even perform the various rituals of distant cultures but unacceptable for them to practice their own beliefs. Similarly, that it's fine for students to master the art of putting a condom on a cucumber and to memorize every last position specified in the Kama Sutra but not to learn the biblical perspective on sexuality. There's a word for such folderol: *insanity.*

One argument against the mention of religion in schools is that it is a divisive subject. That's phoney. There are dramatic differences of viewpoint in sociology, psychology, economics, history, and many other subjects, but we don't call those subjects divisive and we don't ban them from the schoolhouse. Besides, as attorney Jay Sekulow points out, federal courts begin the day with the words "God

Keep Religion Out of School
By Lisa Stepanowsky

The most sensible position on the issue of religion and public schools is to keep it out. That means no prayers, no Bible readings, no devotions, no after-school religious clubs. Not even a "moment of silence" at the beginning of the day—that is, after all, just religious exercise in disguise. Permitting it is like letting the proverbial camel's nose into the tent—before you know it, the whole camel is in.

Why is this the most sensible position on the issue? First, government and religion don't mix. That is why the Constitution forbids the "establishment" of religion. Second, religion causes dissension. Religious people can't even agree among themselves about who or what God is or the right way to worship. Back in the days when the "Our Father" was still being read in schools, Catholics and Protestants were at war over whose version should be used, and Jews were offended by both versions.

Finally, having religion in the schools is stressful for nonbelieving students. Conservative Christians argue that nonbelievers can simply stand or sit silently while others are praying, but this reasoning is specious. When school authorities permit religious expression, they are in effect save the United States and this Honorable Court," the Ten Commandments are displayed in U.S. Supreme Court, and the world hasn't ended as a result.

Another argument is that every religion has its own scriptures and no one should be given preference over the others. OK, so don't single out any one—let *all* be represented. Post the Ten Commandments alongside the Code of Hammurabi and whatever others there are. Display the Hebrew Scriptures, the New Testament, *and* the Koran. Problem solved.

To ask students to leave their religious beliefs at the schoolhouse door is like asking them to leave their minds and hearts there. That is a violation of common sense *and* their constitutional rights.

endorsing it and leaving nonbelieving students with the uncomfortable choice of denying their consciences or risking the displeasure of school authorities and the rejection of their peers. That rejection can take the form of ostracism, insults, threats, and even bodily injury.

An atheist pointed out to me recently that even Jesus was against religion in the schools. He cited Matthew 6:5–6, and he was correct. In that passage Jesus tells his disciples not to pray in public but to do so in secret, in the privacy of their homes. Christians would do well to heed Jesus' words and keep their religion to themselves.

Class Discussion

ED: It seems to me that students should be encouraged to express their deepest and most important thoughts, including their religious beliefs.

NORMAN: The problem is that students express their religious beliefs in a sectarian way. And the schools have to be *non*sectarian.

ED: When students express their views about UFOs, the Iraq war, the campus dress code, or any other controversial matter, they are being sectarian—that is, *partisan*. So why should they be held to a nonpartisan standard when they speak about religion?

NORMAN: Because religion is about faith rather than reason.

ED: The faith/reason distinction is bogus. Reasoning is involved in matters of faith—theological research depends no less on reasoning than does any other research. By the same token, faith is involved in reason—every act of reasoning involves the assumption that careful, logical thinking makes a difference.

NORMAN: For me, Stepanowsky's reference to Jesus' admonition to pray in secret is the most telling argument against religion in the schools. A related fact is that whenever the Gospels mention Jesus praying, they say he went off by himself. In other words, he opposed public prayer by his words and his personal example.

ED: That Scripture quote was taken out of context. Jesus was just admonishing his followers not to be hypocrites and make a big show of their piety. And the fact that he is described as praying in private tells us nothing about whether he also prayed in public.

Notes

1. See, for example, Lenore Weitzman, *The Divorce Revolution* (New York: Free Press, 1986).
2. Jepson, *Clear Thinking*, p. 194.

Problem Solving by Way of Review

Since critical thinking is the consideration of alternative arguments in light of their evidence, problem solving is the consideration of alternative *solutions* in light of their evidence. The solution is equivalent to the conclusion. This is lucky, because it enables us to enlarge the practicality of the book while reviewing its twelve basic features.

THE PROBLEM IS THE ISSUE

Say you're low on money, but you don't know whether to add more hours to your twelve-hours-per-week part-time job while going to school, fearing that working more might jeopardize your education. The initial problem-issue is, therefore, "Should I add more hours to my part-time job?" You have the *alternatives* yes and no to work out first. Write down the possible solutions, followed by the reasons for and against each.

> *Solution 1:* Yes, add hours to my job.
> Reason(s) working more is good: It would please my boss, who might give me a better recommendation; it would make me feel more independent; I could maintain contact with more people by working more.
> Reason(s) working more is bad: If I worked longer, I might become overtired and drop out of school.
> *Solution 2:* No, don't add hours to my job.
> Reason(s) not working more is good: I'd keep my time to study; I'd keep my time to enjoy myself; education is more important than money.
> Reason(s) not working more is bad: Being low on money is irritating and demoralizing.

ORDER THE REASONS

Pick the most urgent reason on each side and label it 1. A bit of thinking will show some reasons to be less significant. For example, more contact with people could be achieved by other activities less time-consuming than additional work, such as study groups or church groups. In fact, more work might not bring you into contact with more people than it does now. Moreover, getting a recommendation from the boss is presumably not nearly as important as finishing your education. And are you thinking important thoughts, studying, and enjoying yourself in the free time you have, or are you more often just passing time?

It is the reasons against on both sides that are the primary considerations in this case. What does it matter if education is more important than money if you get irritated by being low on money and drop out anyway? Yet the foremost worry on the other side creates a bind, because you might drop out of school from overwork. You are caught on the horns of a dilemma. But now you have a clearer idea of what your dilemma is, so you can work on it. The next stage is to define the dilemma.

DEFINE THE PARAMETERS

How low on money am I, exactly? So low that I can't pay for my necessities? How irritating and demoralizing is it? Irritating enough that I am distracted and thinking about it all the time, or just once or twice a day? Say that I can pay for the basics but am broke at the end of each month. And say that I am not thinking about it all the time but lately have noticed that I am worrying about it more often (five or six times a day).

BREAK GRIDLOCKS WITH EVIDENCE

Sometimes finding out how most people fare in similar situations can cast a surprising light. Consider this claim by Professor Alexander Astin, Director of the Higher Education Research Institute at the University of California Los Angeles, based on his educational research:

> One of the most interesting ways to keep students in college now is through jobs. Students who have part-time jobs while enrolled in college have a better chance of finishing than comparable students who have no jobs. This effect is particularly strong if the student lives on campus. Here we have a case where the facts clearly contradict the folklore: Having to work while attending college does not hamper the student's academic progress but rather enhances it. We should add a note of caution here, however. The beneficial effects of work diminish as the number of hours of work exceeds twenty, and if the student has a full-time job the effect is actually reversed: Students who have to work full-time have a decreased chance of finishing college in contrast to students who have no jobs. In short, it would appear that jobs represent a highly effective way of combating attrition, *provided* that the number of hours worked is limited to twenty per week.
>
> Students who work up to twenty hours per week tend to get better grades than students who don't work.[1]

Amazing—perhaps in setting up the problem as more work versus a better education, I have created a **false dichotomy.** It looks as though people are managing both. But a bit of caution is in order when considering the **nature of the evidence.** The authority is impeccable, but he had to make a correlational study. Persevering students and part-time jobs are strongly correlated, but ask yourself whether some other factor could be causing both of these results, for instance, love of work. Furthermore, might these working students be the kind of people who, even if they didn't work, would stay in school and get better grades to boot?

Consider this counterargument. On the other hand, what would be lost by trying it for a while? You could always bail out of the additional work if it got to be too much. So:

> *Solution 3:* On the premise that up to twenty hours of work doesn't seem to hurt the average student, one prescription would be to go ahead and add hours up to a total of twenty, if possible getting my boss to agree to let me go back to twelve hours if twenty prove too arduous.

SEEK ALTERNATIVES

So far there are three possible solution-conclusions. But we're just warming up. Brainstorming for a while might produce even better ideas to generate money. For instance:

1. Belt-tightening, budgeting. I am wasting some money now, for example, buying lunch and snacks instead of making them, and buying goods at full price instead of sale price. I compute that savings in these areas alone could add up to $100 per month.

   Solution 4: Make a realistic but lean budget and stay within it.

2. Borrowing. Is there some understanding friend or relative who would stand me to a loan, or even better, a scholarship were I to attain a certain grade point average?
3. Selling something I own. Do I own some things I don't particularly want? I should seriously consider whether I might want these valuables in the future! I'll hold off on heirlooms.
4. Getting a job with better pay. What else is there that I could do for more money per hour?* Thus I might either work twelve hours and get more money than at present, or work twenty hours and make a bundle.

   Solution 5: Check the want ads and all possible sources for jobs, applying for any likely sounding position.

There are many other places along the list where you could have written in a solution, but chose not to, because that solution—selling your

*Notice the **assumptions** that better jobs do in fact exist, that I am worthy of them and could get one, and that some of the ones I could get would be no more tiring than the one I now have.

motorcycle, for instance—didn't appeal immediately. Yet you now know that you can return to your list later, choose other options, or generate more.

THE GRAND SOLUTION

Make a list of the possible solutions:

Same hours at same job
More hours at same job
Add hours to total twenty
Budget
Check ads and apply for higher-paying jobs

Some of these solutions are mutually exclusive, others compatible. The first two are impossible to act on at the same time, but budgeting can occur with any of the others. It's such a good idea that you might pick it for sure. At this point a good critical question is "Would budgeting be enough?" For the sake of elaborating on the example, say no. You can also check the want ads, and since no harm and a lot of good can come of it, you could pick that solution too.

Now, if there are some possible jobs, you'll need to pursue them. Proceeding from the premise that you're already in school and working twelve hours per week, keeping the fewer hours for the time being will enable you to hunt for a better job. For the moment, therefore, you've eliminated the option of working longer at your present job. And **accepting** Astin's **inference** that working up to twenty hours per week is normally not academically harmful, you will look for jobs with a wider range of hours without worry that it will damage your education.

If you get a better offer you can take it outright; or if you would rather work for your present boss you can use your better offer as a bargaining chip to see if she might raise your hourly salary to match what you've been offered.

If, after four weeks (longer?), you can't get a different job, you can try the longer hours at the same job. If the longer hours turn out to be burdensome, you can go back to twelve per week, perhaps job hunting again. If that doesn't turn anything up, you can go back to your problem-solving list to seek other solutions.

As this problem turned out, here are all the presently conceived solutions for use in case of need:

Budget plus twelve hours at present job plus job hunt for one month to result in:
New higher-paying job or old job with higher pay. If not, then:
Old job with more hours plus budget. If unsatisfactory after one month, old job with twelve hours plus job hunt plus budget.

You'll see that with other problems, some solutions that make it to the grand finals are then eliminated. There is nothing more comforting than contingency planning.

KEEP AN OPEN MIND

Most important decisions are fraught with uncertainty. The **inference** that longer work hours don't hurt an education may be **unwarranted.** But on the **assumption** that money worries will continue, it is reasonable to try working more, based on Astin's **evidence.** The **implications** are uncertain too, but ideally they would include being happier, easier to live with, and more productive. On the other hand, maybe this is not the best solution, after all. The point is to keep an open mind, considering other options and possibilities as they occur.

Working systematically on solutions to major life problems requires a lot of thought and nerve. To fully explore a problem, write, revise, and think at some length. Doing so turns anxiety into an interesting challenge. Further, as with the dialogue and any creative thought, you shouldn't know where your ideas will take you; otherwise, there is no problem.

NOTE

1. Alexander W. Astin, "Strengthening Transfer Programs," in *Issues for Community College Leaders in a New Era,* George B. Vaughan and Associates, eds. (San Francisco: Jossey-Bass Publishers, 1983), p. 125. Continuing studies have shown as recently as 2001 that students who work 15 hours or fewer per week (5 hours fewer than Astin recommends) usually get higher grades, with the added bonuses of learning time management, organization, and office etiquette. See an article by Jennifer Grubb, Virginia Tech University, at *http://www.youngmoney.com/careers/071603_01.asp*

The Creative Process

Have you heard any of these sayings: "Creativity can't be learned," "The way to be creative is to ignore traditional ways of doing things," "It takes a high IQ to be creative," "Taking drugs enhances a person's creativity," or "Creativity is related to mental illness"? They've all been around for a long time. But guess what? *They're all wrong.*

This chapter sets the record straight about creativity. It also details the characteristics of creative people, provides an overview of the creative process, and offers a strategy you can use to develop and apply *your* untapped creative potential.

The human mind, as we have seen, has two phases. It both produces ideas and judges them. These phases are intertwined; that is, we move back and forth between them many times in the course of dealing with a problem, sometimes several times in the span of a few seconds. To study the art of thinking in its most dynamic form would be difficult at best. It is much easier to study each part separately. For this reason, we will focus first on the production of ideas and then turn to the judgment of ideas.*

Although everyone produces and judges ideas, the quality of the effort varies greatly from person to person. One individual produces a single common or shallow idea for each problem or issue and approves it uncritically, whereas another produces an assortment of ideas, some of them original and profound, and examines them critically, refining the best ones to make them even better. The terms *creative thinking* and *critical thinking*, as we will use them throughout the remaining chapters, refer to the latter kind of effort.

---

*Because it is impossible to separate the two completely, minor elements on judging will be included in our treatment of creativity, and vice versa.

KEY FACTS ABOUT CREATIVITY

Before the mid-1950s, creativity received little scholarly attention. Then one researcher examined more than 121,000 listings of articles recorded in *Psychological Abstracts* during the previous 23 years. He found that only 186 articles—less than two-tenths of 1 percent of the total—had any direct concern with creativity.[1] Since that finding, interest in creativity has increased considerably, and many books have been published on the subject.[2] Researchers have examined the lives of creative achievers, probed the creative process, and tested creative performance in every conceivable circumstance and at every age level.

Researchers' efforts have helped deepen our understanding of creativity and overcome the many misconceptions that for so long went unchallenged. You have undoubtedly been exposed to some of these misconceptions and therefore have developed some false impressions about what creativity is and how it works. Replacing those false impressions with facts is an important first step in developing your creative potential. The facts that follow are the most important ones. All are worth returning to and reflecting on from time to time.

"Doing Your Own Thing" Is Not Necessarily a Mark of Creativity. "For many people," George F. Kneller observes, "being creative seems to imply nothing more than releasing impulses or relaxing tensions. . . . Yet an uninhibited swiveling at the hips is hardly creative dancing, nor is hurling colors at a canvas creative painting."[3] Creativity does involve a willingness to break away from established patterns and try new directions, but it does not mean being different for the sake of being different or as an exercise in self-indulgence. It is as much a mistake to ignore the accumulated knowledge of the past as it is to be limited by it. As Alfred North Whitehead warned, "Fools act on imagination without knowledge; pedants act on knowledge without imagination."[4] Being creative means *combining* knowledge and imagination.

Creativity Does Not Require Special Intellectual Talent or a High IQ. The idea that highly creative people have some special intellectual ability lacking in the general population has been widely accepted for centuries. When the IQ test was devised, that idea was given new currency, and anyone who achieved less than a genius-level score (135 and above) was considered to have little or no chance for creative intellectual achievement.

However, when researchers began studying the lives of creative people and comparing IQ test performance with creativity test performance, they made two discoveries. They found that creativity depends not on the possession of special talents, but on the *use* of talents that virtually everyone has but most have never learned to use. In addition, they found that the IQ test was not designed to measure creativity, so a high score is no indication of creative ability, and a low score, no indication of its absence. In fact, they found that the great majority of creative achievers fell significantly below the genius level.[5]

The Use of Drugs Hinders Creativity. Although many people seem determined to resist this fact, it has long been acknowledged by those who have studied creativity. If liquor and other drugs have been such a boon to original thought, one researcher asks, why hasn't the corner saloon produced more creative achievers? No one, as yet, has answered this question satisfactorily. Nor is anyone likely to. The reason drugs harm creativity, Brewster Ghiselin explains, is that "their action reduces judgment, and the activities they provoke are hallucinatory rather than illuminating." What is needed, he argues, is not artificial stimulation of the mind, but increased control and direction.[6]

The use of drugs and liquor as stimulants is sometimes part of a larger misconception that might be termed the *bohemian mystique*. This misconception is the notion that a dissipated lifestyle somehow casts off intellectual restraints and opens the mind to new ideas. Eliot Dole Hutchinson offers an assessment that most researchers would endorse: "Narrow streets, shabby studios, undisciplined living, and artistic ballyhoo about local color may all have their place in pseudo artistry, but they have little to do with genuine creation. Nor is the necessary creative freedom clearly associated with them at all. Bohemianism squanders its freedom, returns from its hours of dissipation less effective. Creative discipline capitalizes its leisure, returns refreshed, reinvigorated, eager."[7]

Creativity Is an Expression of Mental Health. One common image of the creative person is reinforced by a number of low-budget horror films. That image depicts a wild-eyed mad scientist, shuffling nervously around a laboratory (pronounced *lab-or´-a-try* in an ominous tone of voice), rubbing hands together evilly and drooling. Many people really believe the image: They view *creative person* and *lunatic* as near synonyms. They are wrong.

In the following passage, Harold H. Anderson summarizes a leading psychological view concerning the relative sanity of creative people. (Endorsers include such respected thinkers as Erich Fromm, Rollo May, Carl Rogers, Abraham Maslow, J. P. Guilford, and Ernest Hilgard.)

> The consensus of these authors is that creativity is an expression of a mentally or psychologically healthy person, that creativity is associated with wholeness, unity, honesty, integrity, personal involvement, enthusiasm, high motivation, and action.
>
> There is also agreement that neurosis either accompanies or causes a degraded quality of one's creativity. For neurotic persons and persons with other forms of mental disease [who are, at the same time, creative] such assumptions as the following are offered: that these persons are creative in spite of their disease; that they are producing below the achievements they would show without the disease; that they are on the downgrade, or that they are pseudo creative, that is, they may have brilliant original ideas which, because of the neurosis, they do not communicate.[8]

CHARACTERISTICS OF CREATIVE PEOPLE

Studies of creative achievers have identified a number of characteristics they share.[9] The following characteristics are among the most prominent.

Creative People Are Dynamic. Unlike most people, creative people do not allow their minds to become passive, accepting, unquestioning. They manage to keep their curiosity burning, or at least to rekindle it. One aspect of this intellectual dynamism is *playfulness*. Like little children with building blocks, creative people love to toy with ideas, arranging them in new combinations, looking at them from different perspectives. It was such activity that Isaac Newton was referring to when he wrote, "I do not know what I may appear to the world; but to myself I seem to have been only like a boy playing on the seashore, and diverting myself in now and then finding . . . a smoother pebble or a prettier shell than ordinary whilst the great ocean of truth lay all undiscovered before me."[10]

Einstein was willing to speculate further. He saw such playfulness as "the essential feature in productive thought."[11] But whatever the place of playfulness among the characteristics of creative people, one thing is certain: it provides those people a richer and more varied assortment of ideas than the average person enjoys.

Creative People Are Daring. For the creative, thinking is an adventure. Because they are relatively free of preconceived notions and prejudiced views, creative people are less inclined to accept prevailing views, less narrow in their perspectives, and less likely to conform with the thinking of those around them. They are bold in their conceptions, willing to entertain unpopular ideas and seemingly unlikely possibilities. Therefore, like Galileo and Columbus, Edison and the Wright brothers, they are more open than others to creative ideas.

Their daring has an additional benefit: It makes them less susceptible to face-saving than others. They are willing to face unpleasant experiences, apply their curiosity, and learn from those experiences. As a result, they are less likely than others to repeat the same failure over and over.

Creative People Are Resourceful. Resourcefulness is the ability to act effectively and to conceptualize the approach that solves the problem—even when the problem stymies others and the resources at hand are meager. This ability is not measured by IQ tests, yet it is one of the most important aspects of practical intelligence. One dramatic example of this quality was reported in *Scientific American* more than half a century ago. A prisoner in a western state penitentiary escaped but was recaptured after a few weeks. The prison officials grilled him for days. "Where did you get the saw to cut through the bars?" they demanded. In time, he broke down and confessed how he had managed to cut the bars. He claimed he had picked up bits of twine in the machine shop, dipped them in glue and then in emery, and smuggled them back to his cell. Night after night for three months, he had "sawed" the one-inch-thick steel bars. The prison officials accepted his explanation, locked him up, and made sure he never visited the machine shop again.

That, however, is not the end of the story. One dark night about three and a half years later, the man escaped again, and the prison officials found the bars cut in exactly the same manner. Though he was never recaptured, the way he escaped is legendary in the underworld. He'd lied about using material from the machine shop the first time. He had been much more resourceful than that. He had used woolen strings from his socks, moistened them with spit, and rubbed them in dirt on his cell floor.[12]

Creative People Are Hardworking. "All problems," states William Gordon, "present themselves to the mind as threats of failure."[13] Only people who are unwilling to be intimidated by the prospect of failure, and who are determined to succeed no matter what effort is required, have a chance to succeed. (Even for them, of course, there is no guarantee of success.) Creative people are willing to make the necessary commitment. It was that commitment Thomas Edison had in mind when he said, "Genius is 99 percent perspiration and 1 percent inspiration"; so did George Bernard Shaw when he explained, "When I was a young man I observed that nine out of ten things I did were failures. I didn't want to be a failure, so I did ten times more work."

Part of creative people's industriousness is attributable to their ability to be absorbed in a problem thoroughly and to give it their undivided attention. But it is derived, as well, from their competitiveness, which is unlike most people's in that it is not directed toward other people but toward ideas. They take the challenge of ideas *personally*. Lester Pfister was such a person. He got the idea of inbreeding stalks of corn to eliminate weaker strains. He began with 50,000 stalks and worked by hand, season after season. After five years, he had only four stalks left, and he was destitute. But he had perfected the strain.[14] Where others would have succumbed to frustration and disappointment, he persevered because he was unwilling to accept defeat.

Creative People Are Independent. Every new idea we think of separates us from other people, and expressing the idea increases the separation tenfold. Such separation is frightening, especially to those who draw their strength from association with others and who depend on others for their identity. Such people are not likely to feel comfortable entertaining, let alone expressing, new ideas. They fear rejection too much. Creative people are different. This is not to say that they don't enjoy having the acceptance and support of others or that the possibility of losing friends doesn't bother them. It means that however much they may want acceptance and support and friendship, they don't need them the way others do. Instead of looking to others for approval of their ideas, they look within themselves.[15] For this reason, they are less afraid of appearing eccentric or odd, are more self-confident, and are more free to speak and act independently.

Knowing these five characteristics can help you develop your creative potential if you are willing to make the effort to acquire them—or if you already possess them, to reinforce them. It is never an easy task; old habits resist replacement. But even modest progress will make a difference in the quality of your thinking.

APPLYING CREATIVITY TO PROBLEMS AND ISSUES

The two broad applications of creativity that are of special concern to us are solving problems and resolving controversial issues. The terms *problem* and *issue* overlap considerably. Both refer to disagreeable situations that challenge our ingenuity, situations that have no readily apparent, satisfactory remedy. But an *issue* has an additional characteristic. It tends to divide people into opposing camps, each sure that it is right and the opposition wrong.

The most important ways to apply creativity to problems and issues include taking a novel approach, devising or modifying a process or system, inventing a new product or service, finding new uses for existing things, improving things, and inventing or redefining a concept. Let's look at some examples of each.

Taking a Novel Approach

D. B. Kaplan's, a Chicago delicatessen, approaches menu writing with its tongue well in cheek (and in some cases, in the sandwich). Items include Tongue Fu, the Italian Scallion, Chive Turkey, Ike and Tina Tuna, Dr. Pepperoni, the Breadless Horseman, Annette Spinachello, and Quiche and Tell. The ingredients are as creative as the names.

Humane Society inspectors who found two dogs in a closed car in brutal 92-degree heat used a novel approach in dealing with the dogs' owners. They offered them an alternative to being charged with cruelty to animals: spend an hour inside the closed car themselves in the same heat the dogs endured, while the dogs spent the hour in the air-conditioned Humane Society building.[16]

A judge in a Michigan divorce court took a novel approach to the issues of custody and the right to live in the family home. He awarded the house to the *children* until the youngest reached 18. The parents would take turns living in the house and paying the bills. (Both parents lived in the area, so this housing arrangement was workable.)[17]

To instill in students a sense of obligation to help those in need, Tulane University Law School set the unusual graduation requirement of performing at least 20 hours of volunteer legal work for the poor.[18]

The city of Venice, Italy, sits on a number of small islands in an Adriatic lagoon and has long been subject to periodic flooding. Now there is reason to fear that the rising sea level will eventually flood the city. The most publicized and widely accepted proposal to prevent this disaster is to build 79 moveable, hollow gates at the entrance to the lagoon. These gates could be filled with air and caused to rise up, preventing rising waters from flooding Venice. Not everyone accepts this novel plan, however. Some scientists say the gates' design is based on outdated tide tables, and thus the gates would eventually have to be replaced. And environmentalists have raised concerns about the increased pollution the gates could cause.[19]

Devising or Modifying a Process or System

The Dewey decimal system and the Library of Congress system are two techniques that were invented for classifying books. (Even more basic to learning, of course, is the invention known as the alphabet.)

In recent decades, a new surgical procedure has been devised for combating periodontal disease and making it possible for people to keep their teeth throughout their lives. The procedure involves cutting back diseased gum tissue and scraping accumulated plaque from the teeth. (Left untreated, periodontal disease can cause teeth to loosen and fall out.)

Over the years, several procedures have been developed for determining the health of a fetus. Both amniocentesis and chorionic villus sampling involve the extraction of amniotic fluid; ultrasound involves the bouncing of sound waves off the fetus to form an image.

Between the 1880s and the 1980s the principal tool of criminal investigation was the fingerprint. Since then it has been DNA testing. Every individual who ever lived has his or her own distinctive genetic makeup. A strand of hair or a spot of urine, saliva, or semen left at a crime scene can be compared with a DNA sample of a suspect and be a significant factor in determining guilt or innocence.[20]

Reacting to widespread criticism of the 1988 presidential campaign as superficial, a member of Congress from Indiana, Lee Hamilton, proposed a change in the traditional debating format. His idea was to have each candidate speak alone for an hour, presenting his or her ideas on a single issue and responding to in-depth questioning by a panel of experts. The presentations would be videotaped simultaneously for sequential televising at a later time.[21] (Unfortunately, the idea has not been implemented in subsequent presidential campaigns.)

Inventing a New Product or Service

In 1845, a man needed money quickly to pay a debt. "What can I invent to raise some money?" he thought. Three hours later, he had invented the safety pin. He later sold the idea for $400. Virtually all the products we use every day have similar, though perhaps less dramatic, stories. The hammer, the fork, the alarm clock, the electric blanket, the toothpaste tube, the matchbook—these and thousands of other products first occurred as ideas in a creative mind. And new ideas are occurring every day. Two you may not have heard of are Graffiti Gobbler, a chemical compound that can remove ink or paint from wood, brick, or steel,[22] and the Moto-Stand, a three-wheeled, upholstered, motorized truck invented by a man paralyzed from the chest down. The vehicle permits him to maneuver around the house in a standing position.[23]

The laundromat, the car wash, and the rent-a-car agency are examples of successful services that have been invented. When the rent-a-car service became quite expensive, some enterprising people invented rental services providing older, high-mileage cars in good working condition. (One such agency is called Rent-a-Wreck; another, Rent-a-Heap.) A public-spirited psychiatrist invented a service for insomniacs called Sleepline that offers an eight-minute recorded message ("Sleep is coming . . . slower . . . deeper . . .") to help people sleep.[24]

Finding New Uses for Existing Things

No matter how old something is, new uses can always be devised for it. Consider how many kinds of nails, nuts, bolts, and brushes have been developed from the original ideas. Even the water bed, a relatively new variation on the bed, has been given a new use: to simulate the warmth and protection of the womb for premature babies.[25] In some cases, apparently useless objects can be put to good use. For example, a St. Louis barber combines hair clippings with peat and other substances to form an unusually rich potting soil that he believes may help restore drought-ravaged soil in parts of Asia and Africa. And at least one college student devised a use for empty beer and soda cans: He punched holes in the top and bottom, ran heavy cord through them, and hung the cans in close rows as window curtains.

Agricultural crops have long been used for unusual purposes. Cotton lint, for example, is used to manufacture explosives, and ground-up tobacco is used for insecticide. Now scientists have found new uses for the largest surplus crop in the United States: corn. These uses include de-icing materials, adhesives, disposable bottles, and biodegradable garbage bags. Such creative ideas promise to reduce dependency on oil imports and to reduce pollution.[26]

New uses for the computer and the laser continue to multiply, such as this one that combines the two: A Cleveland firm markets a computer device that measures a person for a suit of clothing and then telephones the information to a factory where lasers cut the fabric.[27]

Improving Things

Far more patents are issued each year for improvements in existing things than for new inventions. There is a very good reason. Nothing of human invention is perfect; everything can be made better. Consider the development of the light, from the prehistoric torch to the latest flashlight, or that of the camera and the automobile.

Recent developments in the telephone, for example, include call block, call trace, priority call, return call, repeat call, and caller ID. Each of these features was developed in response to a particular need that was not being met by the existing equipment.

The use of creativity to improve things is nowhere more evident than in the computer industry. Every few months a significant breakthrough is announced in hardware or software, and minor improvements are constantly being made.

Inventing or Redefining a Concept

We tend to regard the many concepts that help us think and deal with reality as fixed and eternal. Yet that is not so. Concepts are invented, just as products and services are. The concepts of taxation and punishing criminals, for example, may be very old, but they were once new. Numerous other concepts are relatively recent. It is hard to imagine how mathematics could even be used without the concept of zero. Yet that concept was invented by a Hindu around A.D. 500. Similarly, the concept of the corporation originated in the sixteenth century, and our ideas of progress and worldly success in the seventeenth. The concept of the zip code is very recent.

The concept of childhood we are familiar with—as a stage of innocence with its own special characteristics—dates back only a few centuries. Before then, children were treated as little adults. The historian J. H. Plumb writes: "Certainly there was no separate world of childhood [in earlier times]. Children shared the same games with adults, the same toys, the same fairy stories. They lived their lives together, never apart. The coarse village festivals depicted by Bruegel, showing men and women besotted with drink, groping for each other with unbridled lust, have children eating and drinking with the adults."[28]

STAGES IN THE CREATIVE PROCESS

Being creative means more than *having* certain traits. It means *behaving creatively*, addressing the challenges we encounter with imagination and originality. In short, it means demonstrating skill in applying the creative process. Although authorities disagree over the number of stages in this process—some say three, others say four, five, or seven—the disagreement is not over substantive matters. It is merely over whether to combine activities under one heading or several. There is no real disagreement about the basic activities involved.[29]

For ease in remembering and convenience of application, we will view the creative process as having four stages: searching for challenges, expressing the particular problem or issue, investigating it, and producing a range of ideas. Each of these stages will be the subject of a separate chapter, but a brief overview of the process will enable you to begin using it right away.

The First Stage: Searching for Challenges

The essence of creativity is meeting challenges in an imaginative, original, and effective way. Often, challenges need not be sought out; they come to you in the form of obvious problems and issues. For example, if your roommate comes home night after night at 2 or 3 A.M., crashes into the room, and begins talking to you when you are trying to sleep, you needn't be very perceptive to know you have a problem. Or if you find yourself in the middle of a raging argument over whether abortion is murder, no one will have to tell you that you are addressing an issue.

However, not all challenges are so obvious. Sometimes, the problems and issues are so small or subtle that few people notice them; at other times, there are no problems and issues at all, only *opportunities to improve existing conditions*. Such challenges arouse no strong emotion in you, so you will not find them by sitting and waiting—you must look for them.

The first stage of the creative process represents the habit of searching for challenges, not at one specific time, but constantly. Its importance is reflected in the fact that you can be creative only in response to challenges that you perceive.

The Second Stage: Expressing the Problem or Issue

The objective in this stage is to find the best expression of the problem or issue, the one that will yield the most helpful ideas.* "A problem properly stated," noted Henry Hazlitt,[30] "is partly solved." Because different expressions open different avenues of thought, it is best to consider as many expressions as possible. One of the most common mistakes made in addressing problems and issues is to see them from one perspective only and thus to close off many fruitful avenues of thought.

Consider the prisoner deciding how to escape from prison. His first formulation of the problem was probably something such as "How can I get a gun and shoot my way out of here?" or "How can I trick the guards into opening my cell so I can overpower them?" If he had settled for that formulation, he would still be there (where he belonged). His ingenious escape plan could have been devised only as a response to the question "How can I cut through those bars without a hacksaw?"

Often, after expressing the problem or issue in a number of ways, you will be unable to decide which expression is best. When that happens, postpone deciding until your work in later stages of the process enables you to decide.

The Third Stage: Investigating the Problem or Issue

The objective of this stage is to obtain the information necessary to deal effectively with the problem or issue. In some cases, this will mean merely searching your past experience and observation for appropriate material and bringing it to bear on the current problem. In others, it will mean obtaining new information through fresh experience and observation, interviews with knowledgeable people, or your own research. (In the case of the prisoner, it meant closely observing all the accessible places and items in the prison.)

The Fourth Stage: Producing Ideas

The objective in this stage is to generate enough ideas to decide what action to take or what belief to embrace. Two obstacles are common in this stage. The first is the often unconscious tendency to limit your ideas to common, familiar, habitual responses and to block out uncommon, unfamiliar ones. Fight that tendency by keeping in mind that however alien and inappropriate the latter kinds of responses may seem, it is precisely in those responses that creativity is to be found.

The second obstacle is the temptation to stop producing ideas too soon. As we will see in a later chapter, research has documented that the longer you continue producing ideas, the greater are your chances of producing worthwhile ideas. Or as one writer puts it, "The more you fish, the more likely you are to get a strike."

There is one final matter to be clarified before you will be ready to begin practicing the creative process: How will you know when you get a creative

*In the case where there is no real problem or issue but only an opportunity to improve an existing condition, you would treat the situation *as if it were* problematic, saying, for example, "How can I make this process work even more efficiently?"

idea? By what characteristics will you be able to distinguish it from other ideas? A creative idea is an idea that is both imaginative and effective. That second quality is as important as the first. It's not enough for an idea to be unusual. If it were, then the weirdest, most bizarre ideas would be the most creative. No, to be creative an idea must work, must solve the problem or illuminate the issue it responds to. A creative idea must not be just uncommon—it must be *uncommonly good*. This is the standard you should apply when looking over the ideas you produced.

When you have produced a generous number of ideas, decide which seems to be the best. Sometimes that will be a single idea; other times it will be a combination of two or more ideas. At this point your decision should be tentative. Otherwise, you will be tempted to forgo the valuable critical thinking process by which ideas are *evaluated*.

WARM-UP EXERCISES

1 Four friends have a large garden in the following shape. They want to divide it into four little gardens the same size and shape, but they don't know quite how to do this. Show them.

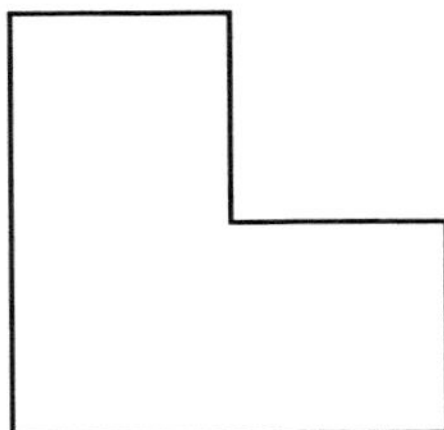

2 How many uses can you think of for old socks, stockings, or panty hose? Be sure to guard against setting unconscious restrictions on your thinking and to resist the temptation to settle for too few ideas.

3 Every change of season brings a new clothing fashion for men, women, and children. Invent as many new fashions as you can. (If you wish, you may include out-of-date fashions in your list, as long as they have not been popular in recent years.) Observe the cautions mentioned in Exercise 2.

APPLICATIONS

1 For each of the following problems, apply stages 2 through 4 of the creative process. Record all your thoughts as they occur, and be prepared to submit them to your instructor. When you have finished

with the last stage, state which of your solutions is best and briefly explain why.

a. Barney has early classes five days a week. Yet he has attended few of them because he just can't seem to wake up in the morning. If he doesn't find a solution to his problem soon, he'll surely flunk out of college.
b. The campus library has been losing articles from magazines and even pages from expensive books. Irresponsible students just tear them out, hide them in their book bags, and walk out of the library. But yesterday a student was caught leaving with ripped-out pages. Some of the library staff favor making an example of her by expelling her from school and pressing criminal charges against her. Others favor merely charging her for the mutilated books.
c. Virtually every building with a public bathroom has a graffiti problem. Even when the messages are not offensive, they create maintenance problems.
d. Shoplifting cuts deeply into store owners' profits. Owners and managers would welcome a solution to this problem.
e. Many elderly and handicapped people live lonely lives. No longer active in careers, they are often forgotten by former associates and neglected by family and friends. Many lack transportation to community affairs.

2 Think of the most unpleasant task you ever had to do. Use your creativity to make it more pleasant. Follow the directions given at the beginning of Application 1.

3 Think of your biggest pet peeve about other people, the thing they do that aggravates you most. Use your creativity to reduce or eliminate that aggravation. Follow the directions given at the beginning of Application 1.

ISSUE FOR EXTENDED ANALYSIS

Following is a more comprehensive thinking challenge than the others in the chapter.

THE ISSUE: OUTSOURCING U.S. JOBS

"Outsourcing" means exporting jobs overseas. The best-known instances of outsourcing are in the manufacturing sector—for example, most athletic shoes and many articles of clothing are made in Third-World or developing countries. Less well-known instances are in the technical and professional sectors—for example, computer technical support is done largely in India. Many Americans consider this a betrayal of American workers; others believe it is a boon to the economy; all agree it is the wave of the future.

The Essays

Outsourcing Is Unfair
By Kalif Ali

They called it "free trade" when it started a few decades ago. The idea was that outsourcing low-paying jobs like assembling garments would bring prosperity to Third-World countries and help us sell more of our goods overseas. The promise was that our higher-paying jobs would not be affected. But that promise was quickly forgotten. The flow of high-paying jobs out of America is increasing. A Forrester Research study estimates that by 2020 almost 3.5 billion more jobs, most of them white-collar and representing over $130 billion, will be outsourced.

At this very moment millions of jobs in machine tooling, steel processing, computer services, banking, medical services, aircraft design and manufacturing, insurance, graphic design, and engineering are performed offshore. Call for computer assistance, and you'll likely speak to someone in India. Go for an X-ray or an MRI, and it will be read by a radiologist in Japan or the Philippines. The list of countries participating include Canada, China, Sri Lanka, Pakistan, Burma, Hong Kong, Mexico, and Panama.

Some of the companies are American; others are multinational corporations, many based in America. All are obsessed with maximizing profits. Their greed has driven millions of Americans who had well-paying jobs into minimum-wage jobs or unem-

Outsourcing Is Fair
By Louie Lefebvre

For more than half a century, labor unions have had enormous power in America. In the beginning, they used that power to establish fair working conditions, pay schedules, and health and retirement benefits. But after achieving equity for their workers, they kept demanding more and more considerations from management. The unreasonableness of their demands is a main cause of the outsourcing phenomenon.

The unions depict corporate executives as greedy monsters totally without conscience or compassion. In reality, they are no different from the rest of us, except that the challenges they face are greater. They must control the costs and maintain work standards so that they can meet the often formidable challenge of international competition. Far from being their own bosses, they are answerable to their customers, who want the highest value at the lowest price, as well as to their stockholders, who want a profit on their investments.

Consider the case of Sudhakar Shenoy, CEO of Information Management Consultants, Inc., who had a choice of paying over $3 million for a job that could be done in India for less than $400,000. He chose India, as would any reasonable person. To do otherwise would have been a violation of his company's trust.

ployment. Lost, too, are their health insurance and retirement benefits. Taken together, these developments have created a massive burden on American taxpayers.

The impact on the countries receiving the American jobs is not much better. Because there are no labor unions and often no governmental regulations, workers often work in unsanitary sweatshops for 14 or 15 hours a day. The pay is meager and health care and retirement plans are nonexistent. In many cases, even children are forced to work in these slavelike conditions.

Far from being a boon, free trade and outsourcing of labor have proved to be a blight on rich and poor nations alike.

Critics complain that outsourcing puts Americans out of work, but that is a one-sided perspective. From the view of the other country, people are being employed. True, they may make only $2 a day compared with the $50 a day their American counterparts might make. But that $2 may be two or three times the average wage of other workers in their country. Moreover, that two dollars multiplied by millions of workers creates capitalism in entire countries and makes freedom and democracy possible. We Americans value those things for ourselves. Why should we deny them to others?

Outsourcing is a central feature of the new "global economy," and that economy is here to stay. American workers had better come to terms with that fact and find a way to live with it.

Class Discussion

ANNE: My main concern with outsourcing is that companies tend to choose the lowest-bidding countries; and those countries pay the lowest wages and have the worst working conditions. Many engage in child labor and even slave labor. Those practices are wrong, and American consumers should not be forced to support them. We should refuse to profit from other people's misery.

GIOVANNA: I'm sure the abuses you mention exist in other countries. They may even exist in our own. I agree we should make our concerns known. But we shouldn't ignore the greater benefits offered by outsourcing.

MARTIN: Some complain that computer manufacturers outsource their technical support operations to India. But I'm glad they do. I've had occasion to speak to many Indian technicians and have always found them polite, informed, and eager to help. That's more than I can say for many American technical support people.

GIOVANNA: People talk about buying American, but when it comes to their actual purchases, they aren't willing to pay the higher prices for American-made products. And I can't really blame them for bargain shopping.

MARTIN: I don't know whether the unions are at fault, as Louis Lefebvre says. But I do know that the current salaries and generous benefits being paid to American workers are making it increasingly difficult for American companies to compete in world markets.

ANNE: I can't see any merit in the wholesale abandonment of American workers. It seems to me that they have a *right* to keep their jobs, particularly if they've given 10, 20, or more years of faithful service to their employers. It's immoral to force them into unemployment or minimum-wage positions. The government should take control of the situation and prevent this travesty.

MARTIN: Competition has made America great. In countries that have replaced it with a government-controlled economy, the result has been chaos. That is why the old Soviet Union no longer exists. No, the only way for American companies to meet the challenge of world competition is to continue outsourcing. If they try to maintain their American work-forces, they'll eventually go out of business, have to lay off all their workers, and cease to contribute to the U.S. tax base. I can't see that as a solution for Americans.

BENJAMIN: Outsourcing seems to be a mixed blessing. On the positive side, it enables people in poor countries to raise their standard of living and thus reduces social unrest throughout the world. On the negative side, it causes America's standard of living to decline. Americans may be unenthusiastic about that fact, but from a global perspective, it is a worthwhile trade-off.

NOTES

1. Paul Smith, ed., *Creativity: An Examination of the Creative Process* (New York: Hastings House, 1959), p. 17.
2. The best source of current works (as well as important older works) is the *Journal of Creative Behavior.*
3. *The Art and Science of Creativity* (New York: Holt, 1965), p. 2.
4. Quoted in Parnes, *Creative Behavior Guidebook*, p. 7.
5. J. W. Getzels and P. W. Jackson, *Creativity and Intelligence* (New York: Wiley, 1962), pp. 21ff. Also Torrance, *Guiding Creative Talent*, pp. 5 and 63.
6. *Creative Process*, p. 9.
7. *How to Think Creatively* (Nashville: Abingdon-Cokesbury Press, 1949), p. 79.
8. "Creativity in Perspective," in Anderson, ed., *Creativity and Its Cultivation*, p. 258.
9. Good sources of studies include Getzels and Jackson, *Creativity and Intelligence*; Torrance, *Guiding Creative Talent*; and Parnes, *Creative Behavior Guidebook.*

10. Quoted in C. P. Curtis and F. Greenslet, eds., *The Practical Cogitator* (Boston: Houghton Mifflin, 1945), p. 231.
11. Quoted in William J. J. Gordon, *Synectics: The Development of Creative Capacity* (New York: Harper & Brothers, 1961), p. 116.
12. Joseph Rossman, *The Psychology of the Inventor* (Washington, DC: Inventors' Publishing Company, 1931), pp. 82ff.
13. Gordon, *Synectics,* p. 360.
14. Alex Osborn, *Applied Imagination* (New York: Scribner's, 1957), p. 196.
15. Getzels and Jackson, *Creativity and Intelligence,* p. 53.
16. "Couple Learns Golden Rule ...," *Oneonta Star,* 29 August 1981, p. 1.
17. "In Divorce, Kids Get the House," *Oneonta Star,* 20 January 1982, p. 1.
18. *Chronicle of Higher Education,* 12 December 1987, p. A2.
19. "Scientists Debate Wisdom of Plan to Save Venice from Flooding" a May 8 2002 news release posted on the American Geophysical Union's Web site, http://www .agu.org/sci_soc/prrl/prrl0218.html, accessed 11/19/02.
20. http://arbl.cvmbs.colostate.edu/hbooks/genetics/medgen/dnatesting/, accessed 11/19/02.
21. *Time,* 14 November 1988, p. 22.
22. "Grafitti Gobbler Gets Attention," *Oneonta Star,* 30 November 1981, p. 2.
23. "Crippled Inventor Is Standing Proud," *Oneonta Star,* 6 February 1982, p. 1.
24. "Trouble Sleeping? Call Up the Sandman," *Oneonta Star,* 7 July 1982, p. 1.
25. "Waterbabies," *Time,* 10 May 1982, p. 87.
26. "New Inventions from the Cornfield," *New York Times,* 10 January 1988, sec. 4, p. 36.
27. *U.S. News & World Report,* 7 March 1988, p. 53.
28. J. H. Plumb, "The Great Change in Children," *Horizon,* XIII (Winter, 1971), p. 7.
29. Hutchinson, *How to Think Creatively,* p. 38, for example, lists four stages, but one of them is "verification," which involves the process of solution refinement classified in this text as critical thinking.
30. Henry Hazlitt, *Thinking as a Science* (New York: E. P. Dutton & Co., 1966), p. 17.

Index

Page references followed by "f" indicate illustrated figures or photographs; followed by "t" indicates a table.

Student Workbook to Accompany

Delmar's Clinical Medical Assisting

WILBURTA (BILLIE) Q. LINDH, CMA
Current Instructor and Former Coordinator,
Medical Assisting Program
Highline Community College
Des Moines, Washington

CAROL D. TAMPARO, CMA-A, PhD
Coordinator, Medical Assistant and Paralegal
Programs, Highline Community College
Des Moines, Washington

MARILYN S. POOLER, RN, CMA-C, Med
Professor, Medical Assisting Department
Springfield Technical Community College
Springfield, Massachusetts

JOANNE U. CERRATO, BS, MT (ASCP), MA
Professor, Department Chairperson, and Program
Director, Clinical Laboratory Science Department
Springfield Technical Community College
Springfield, Massachusetts

Contributors

Lee Ann Chearney
Mary Kay Linge
Anne Pierce
Candace Levy, Ph.D.
Jenny Bolster, RN, CIC
Alison Molumby
Marianne LeVert
Melissa Johnson
Donna Baker, RN
Mary Fahsbender, DO.

an International Thomson Publishing company

Albany • Bonn • Boston • Cincinnati • Detroit • London • Madrid
Melbourne • Mexico City • New York • Pacific Grove • Paris • San Francisco
Singapore • Tokyo • Toronto • Washington

NOTICE TO THE READER

Publisher does not warrant or guarantee any of the products described herein or perform any independent analysis in connection with any of the product information contained herein. Publisher does not assume, and expressly disclaims, any obligation to obtain and include information other than that provided to it by the manufacturer.

The reader is expressly warned to consider and adopt all safety precautions that might be indicated by the activities described herein and to avoid all potential hazards. By following the instructions contained herein, the reader willingly assumes all risks in connection with such instructions.

The publisher makes no representation or warranties of any kind, including but not limited to, the warranties of fitness for particular purpose or merchantability, nor are any such representations implied with respect to the material set forth herein, and the publisher takes no responsibility with respect to such material. The publisher shall not be liable for any special, consequential, or exemplary damages resulting, in whole or part, from the readers' use of, or reliance upon, this material.

Produced by Publisher's Studio

Printed in the United States of America
For more information, contact:

Delmar Publishers
3 Columbia Circle, Box 15015
Albany, New York 12212-5015

International Thomson Publishing Europe
Berkshire House 168-173
High Holborn
London, WC1V 7AA
England

Thomas Nelson Australia
102 Dodds Street
South Melbourne, 3205
Victoria, Australia

Nelson Canada
1120 Birchmount Road
Scarborough, Ontario
Canada, M1K 5G4

International Thomson Editores
Campos Eliseos 385, Piso 7
Col Polanco
11560 Mexico D F Mexico

International Thomson Publishing GmbH
Konigswinterer Strasse 418
53227 Bonn
Germany

International Thomson Publishing Asia
221 Henderson Road
#05-10 Henderson Building
Singapore 0315

International Thomson Publishing—Japan
Hirakawacho Kyowa Building, 3F
2-2-1 Hirakawacho
Chiyoda-ku, Tokyo 102
Japan

2 3 4 5 6 7 8 9 10 XXX 03 02 01 00 99 98

Library of Congress Card No. 97-21697
ISBN: 0-8273-8526-9

Table of Contents

To the Learner

This workbook is designed to accompany *Delmar's Clinical Medical Assisting*. Using the textbook, study guide software, videos, CD-ROM and this workbook will provide you with the most creative and dynamic learning system available. This complete learning package will help reinforce all the essential competencies you will need to enter the field of medical assisting and become a highly skilled professional in today's multiskilled health care environment. In addition the workbook will challenge you to apply basic skills, use critical thinking abilities, and integrate your knowledge effectively.

WORKBOOK ORGANIZATION

Workbook chapters are divided into the following sections: Vocabulary Builder, Learning Review, Investigation Activity, Case Study, Skills Competency Assessments, and Evaluations of Chapter Knowledge.

Vocabulary Builder

Includes exercises designed to put vocabulary into situational or applied contexts and/or to build spelling skills. Exercises range from word scrambles, crossword puzzles, and word searches to matching and fill in the blank. Very often, vocabulary builder exercises will utilize simulation characters to create applied scenarios that put the key term in a situational workplace context that makes the meaning real and requires you to truly understand the term in usage—going beyond just supplying rote definitions.

Learning Review

These exercises cover the basic chapter content, reinforcing and applying your understanding of chapter content. Simulation characters are often used here to bring the information and place it in a working context for you to consider.

Investigation Activity

These activities take the you beyond the classroom walls. The activities include games, role-playing, research activities, self-tests that probe your response to issues related to chapter content or ability of certain skills (such as the "how observant are you" self-test in chapter 15: Introduction to the Medical Laboratory), therapeutic communication building exercises (such as the family medical history genogram exercise in chapter 5). These exercises help you develop a set of personal and professional viewpoints and ethical values that will help you build asuccessful career as a medical assistant, recognize health and medical issues faced by patients and in the community.

Case Study

These use simulation characters to apply chapter knowledge in a situational context requiring you to exhibit the proper clinical or administrative knowledge necessary to handle the situation and/or to examine the role of the medical assistant in a variety of situations and contexts.

In general, the workbook has been conceived to give you a creative and interpretive forum to apply your knowledge learned, not simply to repeat it to answer workbook questions. Realistic simulations appear throughout the workbook referencing characters referred to in the textbook, software, CD-ROM and videos. This gives the material a "real world" feel that comes as close as possible to your future experiences in an ambulatory setting. Clinical principles, such as those of infection control, are repeatedly reinforced through simulation exercises that require the ability to use your knowledge effectively and readily.

CHECKLIST SHEETS

By enrolling in a medical assisting program, you have chosen a special goal for yourself. Each step you master takes you closer to your ultimate goal. Remember that the longest journey begins with a single step, the steps you take are the lessons you study and the skills you practice!

This workbook provides two types of worksheets: Evaluation of Chapter Knowledge sheets and Skills Competency Assessment Checklists sheets. These sheets are designed to correlate with specific information and procedures discussed in *Delmar's Clinical Medical Assisting* textbook.

The Evaluation of Chapter Knowledge sheets are incorporated at the end of each chapter to review theoretical understanding and define competency, while at the same time incorporating essential interpersonal communication and professional skills. The evaluation and grading of these sheets can be done by self-evaluation, by another individual, or by instructor, and are based on a good, average, or poor checklist. If you perform poorly, the instructor may require re-evaluation at a future time.

The Skills Competency Assessment Checklist sheets are designed to set criteria or standards that should be observed while a specific procedure is being performed. They follow the same procedural steps as listed in the textbook. As you perform each procedure, the Evaluation Section of this sheet can be used to judge your performance. The instructor will use this sheet to evaluate your competency in performing this skill. A Skill Tracking sheet is also provided for you on page ix to use as an overview for all competency assessment checklists included in the workbook. This tracking sheet can serve as a table of contents for all checklists, as well as a guide to easily view your performance on the assessment checklists.

The format of the Skills Competency Assessment Checklist sheet is designed to provide specific conditions, standards, skill steps, and evaluation and documentation sections for essential skills necessary for an entry level medical assistant. The Competency Assessment Checklist sheet is organized as follows:

Conditions

These provide clues defining how and when to perform a task. Conditions should be stated in actual terms used in current medical practice. For example, when performing venipuncture, the tourniquet must be removed before removing the needle from the patient's vein.

Standards

Time and accuracy are very good measures of execution and performance. Where appropriate, the time standard pertains to how much time you will be allowed to complete a set of tasks. Accuracy entails how many times the task must be performed and the degree of correctness with which the task must be executed based on the conditions given for each skill. For some laboratory procedures, the exact time required for you to complete the procedure competently will vary according to your preparation and skill, the instructor's requirements, and the equipment and supplies available in the laboratory.

Skill Step Checklist

There are three columns provided for each step of a procedure. The first column includes a checkbox to indicate whether the task step was performed accurately, the second column indicates the point values assigned to each specific task, and the third column defines the specific task. A score for each procedure can easily be determined by dividing the total points earned by the total points possible and multiplying the results by 100. For example, if you earn 110 points out of 125 points possible, your score for that procedure would be:

$110 \div 125 = .88 \qquad .88 \times 100 = 88\%$

Evaluation Summary

This summary includes the actual time you need to complete the specific procedure and will be graded by your evaluator based on your performance of procedural steps and whether standards were met. Your instructor may also provide suggestions for improving your skills which can also be noted in this section.

Documentation

Charting is an extremely valuable part of a performing any medical procedure. This section will assist with hands-on charting exercises based on actual procedures performed. Including charting as a part of every Skill Competency Assessment will help you associate performing a procedure, then immediately charting it—which closely simulates the actual workplace environment.

GENERAL STUDY TIPS

Here are some tips to help you learn more effectively:

- Feel certain that each procedure and concept you master is an important step toward preparing your skills and knowledge for the workplace. The textbook, study guide software, student workbook, and instructor materials have all been coordinated to meet the core objectives. Review the textbook Objectives before you begin to study; they are a road map that will take you to your goal.
- Remember that you are the learner, so you can take credit for your success. The instructor is an important guide on this journey, and the text, workbook, software and clinical experiences are tools, but whether or not you use the tools wisely is ultimately up to you.
- Evaluate yourself and your study habits. Take positive steps toward improving yourself, and avoid habits that could limit your success. For example, do you let family responsibilities or social opportunities interfere with your study? If so, sit down with your family and plan a schedule for study that they will support and to which you will adhere. Find a special place to study that is free from distraction.

Because regulations vary from state to state regarding which procedures can be performed by a medical assistant, it will be important to check specific regulations in your state. A medical assistant should never perform any procedure without being aware of legal responsibilities, correct procedure, and proper authorization.

Enjoy your career in medical assisting!

SKILLS COMPETENCY ASSESSMENT TRACKING SHEET

Procededure No. and Title		Workbook Page No.	Date Assessment Completed & Competency Achieved			
			School Program Date/Initials	Externship Site 1 Date/Initials	Externship Site 2 Date/Initials	Externship Site 3 Date/Initials
EXAMPLE: 1–1	Medical Asepsis Handwash	###	2/23/97 MP	3/15/97 BG	4/20/97	
1–1	Medical Aseptic Handwash	11				
1–2	Instrument Sanitzation	13				
1–3	Removing Contaminated Gloves	15				
1–4	Instrument/Equipment Chemical Disinfection or Chemical Sterilization	16				
1–5	Wrapping Instruments for Sterilization in Autoclave	19				
1–6	Steam Sterilization of Instruments (Autoclave)	22				
5–1	Taking a Medical History	67				
6–1	Taking an Oral Temperature Using a Mercury Thermometer	80				
6–2	Taking an Oral Temperature Using a Disposable Oral Strip	82				
6–3	Taking an Oral Temperature Using a Digital Thermometer	84				
6–4	Obtaining an Aural Temperature Using a Tympanic Thermometer	86				
6–5	Taking a Rectal Temperature Using a Mercury Thermometer	88				
6–6	Taking a Rectal Temperature Using a Digital Thermometer	90				
6–7	Taking an Axillary Temperature	92				
6–8	Taking a Radial Pulse	94				
6–9	Taking an Apical Pulse	96				
6–10	Measuring the Respiration Rate	98				
6–11	Measuring a Blood Pressure	100				
6–12	Measuring Height	102				
6–13	Measuring Adult Weight	104				
7–1	Positioning Patient in the Supine Position	113				
7–2	Positioning Patient in the Dorsal Recumbent Position	114				
7–3	Positioning Patient in the Lithotomy Position	115				
7–4	Positioning Patient in the Fowler's Position	117				
7–5	Positioning Patient in the Knee-Chest Position	118				
7–6	Positioning Patient in Prone Position	120				
7–7	Positioning Patient in the Sims' Position	122				
7–8	Positioning Patient in the Trendelenburg Position	124				
7–9	Assisting with a Complete Physical Examination	125				
8–1	Chemical "Cold" Sterilization	135				
8–2	Applying Sterile Gloves	137				

SKILLS COMPETENCY ASSESSMENT TRACKING SHEET (cont'd)

Procededure No. and Title		Workbook Page No.	Date Assessment Completed & Competency Achieved			
			School Program Date/Initials	Externship Site 1 Date/Initials	Externship Site 2 Date/Initials	Externship Site 3 Date/Initials
8–3	Setting Up and Covering a Sterile Field	139				
8–4	Opening Sterile Packages of Instruments and Applying Them to a Sterile Field	141				
8–5	Pouring a Sterile Solution into a Cup on a Sterile Field	143				
8–6	Preparation of Patient Skin for Minor Surgery	146				
8–7	Assisting with Minor Surgery	147				
8–8	Suturing of Laceration or Incision Repair	150				
8–9	Dressing Change	152				
8–10	Suture Removal	154				
8–11	Application of Sterile Adhesive Skin Closure Strips	156				
8–12	Sebaceous Cyst Excision	158				
8–13	Incision and Drainage of Localized Infections	160				
8–14	Aspiration of Joint Fluid	162				
8–15	Hemorrhoid Thrombectomy	164				
10–1	Transferring Patient from Wheelchair to Examination Table	189				
10–2	Transferring Patient from Examination Table to Wheelchair	191				
10–3	Assisting the Patient to Stand and Walk	193				
10–4	Care of the Falling Patient	195				
10–5	Assisting a Patient to Ambulate with a Walker	197				
10–6	Teaching the Patient to Ambulate with Axillary Crutches	199				
10–7	Assisting a Patient to Ambulate with a Cane	201				
10–8	Range of Motion Exercises, Upper Body	203				
10–9	Range of Motion Exercises, Lower Body	206				
12–1	Administration of Oral Medications	226				
12–2	Administration of Subcutaneous, Intramuscular, and/or Intradermal Injections	228				
12–3	Withdrawing (Aspirating) Medication from a Vial	231				
12–4	Withdrawing (Aspirating) Medication from an Ampule	233				
12–5	Administering a Subcutaneous Injection	235				
12–6	Administering an Intramuscular Injection	237				
12–7	Administering an Intradermal Injection	239				
12–8	Reconstituting a Powder Medication for Administration	241				
12–9	"Z"-Track Intramuscular Injection Technique	243				

SKILLS COMPETENCY ASSESSMENT TRACKING SHEET (cont'd)

Procededure No. and Title		Workbook Page No.	Date Assessment Completed & Competency Achieved			
			School Program Date/Initials	Externship Site 1 Date/Initials	Externship Site 2 Date/Initials	Externship Site 3 Date/Initials
13–1	Measuring the Infant: Weight, Height, Head, and Chest Circumference	250				
13–2	Taking an Infant's Rectal Temperature with a Mercury or Digital Thermometer	253				
13–3	Taking an Apical Pulse on an Infant	256				
13–4	Measuring Infant's Respiration Rate	258				
13–5	Obtaining a Urine Specimen from an Infant or Young Child	260				
13–6	Instructing Patient in Self–Breast Examination	262				
13–7	Assisting with Gynecologic or Pelvic Examination and a Papanicolaou (Pap) Test	264				
13–8	Instructing Patient in Testicular Self-Examination	267				
13–9	Performing a Urinary Catheterization on a Female Patient	268				
13–10	Performing a Urine Drug Screening	271				
13–11	Assisting with Proctosigmoidoscopy	273				
13–12	Fecal Occult Blood Test	276				
13–13	Performing Visual Acuity Testing Using a Snellen Chart	278				
13–14	Measuring Near Visual Acuity	280				
13–15	Performing Color Vision Test Using the Ishihara Plates	282				
13–16	Performing Eye Instillation	284				
13–17	Performing Eye Patch Dressing Application	286				
13–18	Performing Eye Irrigation	288				
13–19	Assisting with Audiometry	290				
13–20	Performing Ear Irrigation	292				
13–21	Performing Ear Instillation	294				
13–22	Assisting with Nasal Examination	296				
13–23	Procedure for Obtaining a Throat Culture	297				
13–24	Performing Nasal Irrigation	299				
13–25	Performing Nasal Instillation	301				
13–26	Obtaining a Sputum Specimen	303				
13–27	Administer Oxygen by Nasal Cannula for Minor Respiratory Distress	305				
13–28	Instructing Patient in Use of Metered Dose Nebulizer	307				
13–29	Assisting with Spirometry	309				
13–30	Assisting with Plaster-of- Paris Cast Application	311				
13–31	Assisting with Cast Removal	313				
13–32	Assisting the Physician during a Lumbar Puncture	315				

SKILLS COMPETENCY ASSESSMENT TRACKING SHEET (cont'd)

Procededure No. and Title	Workbook Page No.	Date Assessment Completed & Competency Achieved			
		School Program Date/Initials	Externship Site 1 Date/Initials	Externship Site 2 Date/Initials	Externship Site 3 Date/Initials
13–33 Assisting the Physician with a Neurological Screening Examination	318				
14–1 Perform Twelve-Lead Electrocardiogram, Single Channel	327				
14–2 Perform Twelve-Lead Electrocardiogram, Three Channel	331				
14–3 Perform Holter Monitor Application	333				
15–1 Using the Microscope	349				
16–1 Finding a Vein in the Upper Arm	358				
16–2 Venipuncture by Syringe Procedure	360				
16–3 Venipuncture by Evacuated Tube System	363				
16–4 Venipuncture by Butterfly Needle System	366				
17–1 Hemoglobin Determination (Manual Method Using a Spectrophotometer)	375				
17–2 Hemoglobin Determination (Hemoglobin Analyzer)	378				
17–3 Microhematocrit	380				
17–4 White Blood Cell Count (Unopette Method)	382				
17–5 Red Blood Cell Count (Unopette Method)	385				
17–6 Preparation of a Differential Blood Smear Slide	388				
17–7 Staining a Differential Blood Smear Slide	390				
17–8 Differential Leukocyte Count	392				
17–9 Erythrocyte Sedimentation Rate	394				
18–1 Assessing Urine Volume	407				
18–2 Observing Urine Color	409				
18–3 Observing Urine Clarity	411				
18–4 Using the Refractometer to Measure Specific Gravity	413				
18–5 Performing a Urinalysis Chemical Examination	415				
18–6 Testing for Reducing Sugars	417				
18–7 Microscopic Examination of Urine Sediment	419				
18–8 Performing a Urinalysis	421				
19–1 Preparing a Bacteriological Smear	431				
19–2 Gram Stain	432				
19–3 Ziehl-Neelsen Stain	434				
19–4 Wet Slide and Hanging Drop Slide Preparations	436				
19–5 Specimen Inoculation and Dilution Streaking	438				
19–6 Broth Tube Inoculation	440				
19–7 Deep Inoculation/Slant	442				
20–1 Pregnancy Tests	441				
20–2 Slide Test for Infectious Mononucleosis	454				
20–3 Analyzing Semen	456				
20–4 Obtaining Blood Sample for Phenylketonuria (PKU) Test	458				

SKILLS COMPETENCY ASSESSMENT TRACKING SHEET (cont'd)

Procededure No. and Title	Workbook Page No.	Date Assessment Completed & Competency Achieved			
		School Program Date/Initials	Externship Site 1 Date/Initials	Externship Site 2 Date/Initials	Externship Site 3 Date/Initials
20–5 Obtaining Urine Sample for Phenylketonuria (PKU) Test	460				
20–6 Mantoux Test	462				
20–7 Measurement of Blood Glucose Using an Automated Analyzer	464				
20–8 Cholesterol Testing	466				

Medical Asepsis, Disease, and Infection Control

PERFORMANCE OBJECTIVES

During the last century, medical science, an improved standard of living, and public health measures have combined to reduce the incidence and mortality rates of infectious disease in the United States. Antibiotics and vaccines now protect much of the world from numerous ancient, deadly infectious diseases, including smallpox, measles, and tuberculosis. Because the world we live in, however, is teeming with pathogens, microorganisms that can cause disease, humankind is not, and indeed may never be, free from the threat of infectious diseases. Medical assistants who care for patients in an ambulatory care setting can help reduce the risk of infection to themselves, other health care professionals, patients, and visitors by adhering to the principles of infection control. Through the practice of medical and surgical asepsis as well as the observance of the Centers for Disease Control and Prevention's universal and standard precautions and transmission-based precautions, medical assistants will limit the presence of infectious agents, create barriers against transmission, and decrease their own and others' risks of contracting or transmitting infectious diseases.

EXERCISES AND ACTIVITY

Vocabulary Builder

A. *Fill in the blanks with the correct key vocabulary terms listed below.*

Infection control	Excoriated	Medical asepsis
Transmission	Microorganisms	Sanitization
Surgical asepsis	Epidemiology	Contaminated

______________________ is the study of the history, cause, and patterns of infectious diseases. Microscopic living creatures, also known as ______________________, that are capable of causing disease are called pathogens. The spread of infectious diseases can occur through direct contact, indirect contact, inhalation, ingestion, or blood-borne contact.

_____________________ refers to various methods, including the CDC's standard precautions, health care professionals use to eliminate or reduce the risk of _____________________ of infectious microorganisms from one person to another. _____________________ involves specific techniques used in the ambulatory care setting that are designed to destroy pathogens after they leave the body and to decrease the risk of spreading infection to others. _____________________ is also performed in the ambulatory care setting and involves techniques designed to maintain sterile conditions during procedures to prevent pathogens from entering a patient's body during an invasive procedure.

To reduce the risk that any item, including equipment, trays, and clothing, could be _____________________ or exposed to microorganisms or infectious material, various sterilization techniques are employed. Medically aseptic hand-washing techniques should be performed on a regular basis to ensure the reduction of pathogens spread by the hands. To reduce the risk of chapped, _____________________ skin, medical assistants can apply water-based antibacterial lotion to the hands after washing. Before instruments or other fomites are disinfected or sterilized, they must be scrubbed or cleaned to remove tissue, debris, or other impurities that may harbor pathogens, a process called _____________________.

B. *Match the following terms with the correct definitions.*

Amebic dysentery	Infectious agent	Pathogen
Blood-borne pathogen	Malaria	Scabies
Fomites	Palliative	Trichomoniasis

_____________________ 1. Infestation with a Trichomonas parasite, which may be transmitted through sexual intercourse.

_____________________ 2. Infectious skin disease caused by the itch mite, Sarcoptes scabiei, which is transmitted by direct contact with infected persons.

_____________________ 3. A pharmacological treatment agent for a viral infection is an example of an agent that relieves only symptoms of the disease instead of curing the infection.

_____________________ 4. A pathogen responsible for a specific infectious disease.

_____________________ 5. Infectious intestinal disease characterized by inflammation of the mucous membrane of the colon.

_____________________ 6. Any microorganism capable of causing disease found in blood or components of blood.

_____________________ 7. Infectious disease caused by protozoan parasites within red blood cells; transmitted to humans by female mosquitoes.

_____________________ 8. Substances that absorb and transmit infectious material, that is, contaminated items such as equipment.

_____________________ 9. Any disease-producing microorganism.

C. Write a brief definition for each key vocabulary term.

1. Resistance ____

____

2. Vaccine ____

____

3. Antibody ____

____

4. Immunoglobulins ____

____

5. Immunity ____

____

6. Disinfection ____

____

7. Antigen ____

____

Learning Review

1. The following are the common five stages of many infectious diseases. Place the stages in the proper order, starting with initial infection with a pathogen, and describe the identifying characteristics and symptoms associated with each.

Acute	Prodromal
Declining	Convalescent
Incubation	

Stage	Description
(1) ____________	____
(2) ____________	____
(3) ____________	____
(4) ____________	____
(5) ____________	____

2. For each vaccine, identify the disease for which the vaccine provides immunity and the route of vaccine administration.

Vaccine	Disease	Route of Administration
DTP	______	____________________
HBV	______	____________________
MMR	______	____________________
Hib	______	____________________
OPV	______	____________________

3. Health care professionals use many interventions to break the chain of infection transmission. For each intervention below, identify one of the five links of infection it is intended to break.

____________________ A. Hand washing.
____________________ B. Universal and standard precautions.
____________________ C. Rapid accurate identification of organisms.
____________________ D. Aseptic technique.
____________________ E. Recognition of high-risk patients.
____________________ F. Isolation.
____________________ G. Control of excretions and secretions.
____________________ H. Environmental sanitation.
____________________ I. Treatment of underlying disease.
____________________ J. Air flow control.
____________________ K. Trash and waste disposal.
____________________ L. Food handling.

4. A susceptible host is a person who is not resistant or immune to a pathogenic organism and is, therefore, able to contract the pathogenic organism and develop an infection.

A. List the five causes of susceptibility:

(1) ____________________
(2) ____________________
(3) ____________________
(4) ____________________
(5) ____________________

B. Susceptibility of a person depends upon several factors. For each example given, identify the correct factor of susceptibility.

____________________ (1) Dr. Angie Esposito is physically worn down by working double shifts at Inner City Health Care. While she loves the excitement of working intensely with patients in an urgent care setting, flu season is coming and Dr. Esposito is worried that she will succumb.

____________________ (2) Significantly overweight and a heavy smoker, Herb Fowler is prone to colds that just will not go away; Dr. Winston Lewis is treating Herb for a case of chronic bronchitis.

_______________ (3) Mary O'Keefe's three-year-old son, Chris, and several other members of his play group come down with chicken pox after playing with a child infected with the disease, caused by the varicella-zoster virus.

_______________ (4) Pneumocystis pneumonia is an infection common to patients who have a full-blown case of AIDS.

_______________ (5) Jim Marshall, stressed out by the pressure to complete an architectural design ahead of schedule and on a tight budget, is depressed and angry when he gets laid up with the flu and misses two days of work.

_______________ (6) Margaret Thomas's college-age niece is caught in an epidemic of scabies that sweeps through her dorm floor and places the students in temporary isolation until the outbreak is controlled.

_______________ (7) While vacationing at a remote spot in Mexico, Bill Schwartz eats almost a pound of shrimp at a local restaurant and the next day experiences severe diarrhea and vomiting. He is diagnosed with cholera, caused by the Vibrio cholerae bacterium harbored in the shellfish he had eaten.

5. Immunity is defined as the ability of the body to resist disease. Identify the correct terms or the specific form of immunity that may occur in response to specific antigens.

A. The immune response that involves T cells and B cells to attack viruses, fungi, organ transplants, or cancer cells is called _______________.

B. The immune response that produces antibodies to kill pathogens and recognize them in the future is called _______________.

C. The immunity that follows the administration of vaccines is called _______________.

D. The short-term immunity provided to a newborn that occurs when antibodies pass to a fetus from the mother is called _______________.

E. The immunity that results from contracting an infectious agent and experiencing either an acute or a subclinical infectious disease is called _______________.

F. The immunity achieved through administration of ready-made antibodies, such as gamma-globulin is called _______________.

6. For each infectious disease listed below, identify the agent of transmission (virus, bacteria, fungus, etc.), at least one route of transmission, and common symptoms.

A. AIDS

Agent: _______________

Transmission: _______________

Symptoms: _______________

____

____

____

B. TB

Agent: ______________________________

Transmission: ______________________________

Symptoms: ______________________________

____

____

____

C. Gastroenteritis

Agent: ______________________________

Transmission: ______________________________

Symptoms: ______________________________

____

____

____

D. Hepatitis B

Agent: ______________________________

Transmission: ______________________________

Symptoms: ______________________________

____

____

____

E. Chicken pox

Agent: ______________________________

Transmission: ______________________________

Symptoms: ______________________________

____

____

____

F. Influenza

Agent: ______________________________

Transmission: ______________________________

Symptoms: ______________________________

____

____

____

7. A. Describe three methods of medical asepsis used to reduce the presence of pathogens in an ambulatory care setting.

(1) ____

____

(2) ____

____

(3) ____

____

B. Place a checkmark next to each statement below that represents the appropriate use of medical asepsis in the ambulatory care setting.

______ (1) Joe Guerrero, CMA, washes his hands before performing the transfer of patient Lenore McDonell from the wheelchair to the examination table.

______ (2) Wanda Slawson, CMA, runs a clean sheet of disposable paper over the examination table to prepare the room for the next patient. She picks up the cloth gown patient Lydia Renzi leaves unused, still in its plastic protective covering, on a chair in the examination room and places it on the examination table for the next patient to use.

______ (3) After performing a venipuncture procedure on patient Leo McKay, Bruce Goldman, CMA, tells Leo he can just throw the gauze pad he has been holding on the venipuncture site in the trash can.

______ (4) Anna Preciado, CMA, moving quickly to assist a patient who may be about to faint, accidentally bumps into a sterile tray of instruments, knocking a scalpel and clamp onto the floor. The patient, who is bent over in front of Anna, picks the instruments up off the floor and places them back on the tray in the sterile field. "You dropped these," he says.

______ (5) After assisting in the removal of an infected sebaceous cyst from a patient, clinical medical assistant Audrey Jones cleans, dresses, and bandages the wound as directed by Dr. Winston Lewis. She then disposes of all contaminated items per OSHA guidelines, properly removes PPE, removes her gloves, and washes her hands.

C. For each item in part B (above) that does not reflect proper techniques of medical asepsis, explain what went wrong and how the error should be corrected.

____

____

____

____

8. ______________________ is a term used interchangeably for surgical asepsis. Living tissue surfaces, such as skin, cannot be sterilized. Name two examples of ways that skin can be rid of as many pathogens as possible before the use of a sterile covering.

(1) ____

____

(2) ____

____

9. A. For each instrument or item below, identify the method used for proper asepsis: chemical disinfection (CD), chemical sterilization (CS), or steam sterilization (SS) in an autoclave.

Match the following equipment with the correct aseptic method.

_____ (1) Glass thermometers
_____ (2) Wrapped surgical instruments
_____ (3) Stethoscopes
_____ (4) Fiber-optic endoscopes
_____ (5) Countertops
_____ (6) Wheelchairs
_____ (7) Gynecological instruments
_____ (8) Examination tables

B. Why are gynecological instruments sanitized separately from other external physical examination instruments before sterilization?

____

____

10. Identify and describe the most widely used method of sterilization in the ambulatory care setting.

____

____

____

____

11. A. List six general rules that ensure proper sterilization when using an autoclave.

(1) ____
(2) ____
(3) ____
(4) ____
(5) ____
(6) ____

B. Identify the recommended requirements for effective sterilization in an autoclave.

Temperature: ____________________

Time for sterilization of unwrapped items: ____________________

Time for sterilization of loosely wrapped items: ____________________

Time for sterilization of tightly wrapped items: ____________________

Frequency of draining of water and cleaning of autoclave: ____________________

Investigation Activity

Physicians are required to report cases of certain infectious diseases to the state Department of Public Health, which in turn sends these data to the Centers for Disease Control and Prevention. In the space provided below, list the five infectious diseases you believe physicians encountered most during the previous year in the state in which you live. Then elect one student volunteer to write, call, or visit your state's Department of Public Health to find out the five infectious diseases that actually were most prevalent that year in your state; obtain statistics regarding the outbreaks as well.

Suspected Five Most Common Infectious Diseases in Your State	*Actual Five Most Common Infectious Diseases in Your State*
Year: ________________	Year: ______________
1. ________________________________	1. ________________________________
2. ________________________________	2. ________________________________
3. ________________________________	3. ________________________________
4. ________________________________	4. ________________________________
5. ________________________________	5. ________________________________

Discuss the following:

1. Are you surprised at the specific diseases and the number of cases reported in your state? Why or why not? What populations are contracting the infectious diseases? Think about how infectious diseases are spread and if there are social or economic factors that might explain the presence or spread of disease.
2. What steps can people take at home, work, school, and other everyday settings to reduce their chance of exposure to infectious diseases?
3. What details of daily activity (general health, living or workplace conditions, attention to sanitation and cleanliness, exposure to populations at high risk for infection, etc.) might affect your personal risk of infection?

CASE STUDIES

Case 1

Michelle Richards, a medical assisting intern at the Northborough Family Medical Group of Drs. Winston Lewis and Elizabeth King, attends to patient procedures and examinations under the supervision of office manager Marilyn Johnson, CMA. Although Michelle is careful to follow all infection control methods during her observations, she has developed severe dermatitis on her hands. She is concerned that this condition, which has not responded to creams and lotions, is related to the latex gloves she wears during required procedures.

1. Discuss the possible causes of Michelle's symptoms.
2. Suggest a course of action that both addresses Michelle's condition and maintains the proper degree of asepsis.

Case 2

Liz Corbin, CMA, is responsible for maintaining and cleaning the autoclave at Inner City Health Care. Because this equipment is used every day to sterilize instruments used during procedures performed at the clinic, Liz cleans the inner chamber of the autoclave daily. Once a week, she gives the autoclave a thorough cleansing.

1. Describe Liz's daily cleaning procedure.
2. Describe the weekly cleaning procedure for the autoclave.
3. How important is proper maintenance and cleaning of the autoclave in the ambulatory care setting?

Case 3

One-year-old Marissa O'Keefe is a patient at the practice of Drs. Lewis and King. During her well-baby visit, Joe Guerrero, CMA, gives Marissa an MMR vaccine and is about to administer the scheduled fourth DTP immunization when her mother, Mary O'Keefe, voices concern about this vaccination. "I've read that the DPT shot can be dangerous and sometimes causes brain damage. Marissa had a fever after her last DPT, so I don't want to take any risks with this one. I don't think she should have this shot."

1. Should Joe administer the DPT shot to Marissa? How safe is the DPT shot? What is the ICD-9-CM diagnosis code for the DTP vaccination?
2. What is Joe's best therapeutic response to Mary?

SUPPLEMENTARY RESOURCES

Study Guide Disk: Additional practice exercises for this chapter are available on the study guide disk found in the back of the textbook.

Medical Assisting Videos: Appropriate content is available on Delmar's Medical Assisting Videos, 2nd ed., Tape 5, for the following topics:

Standard Precautions
Perform Medical Aseptic Procedure of Handwashing
Use Disposable Single-Contact Gloves (Putting On and Removing)
Personal Protective Equipment
Perform Medical Aseptic Procedures
Ultrasound Cleaners
Wrap and Autoclave an Article
Perform Surgical Aseptic Procedures

SKILLS COMPETENCY ASSESSMENT

Procedure 1–1: Medically Aseptic Handwash

Student's Name: ______________________________ Date: ____________

Objective: To reduce pathogens on the hands and wrist, decreasing direct and indirect transmission of infectious microorganisms.

Conditions: The student demonstrates the ability to reduce pathogens on the hands and wrists using the following equipment: sink, soap (bar soap discouraged), water-based antibacterial lotion, disposable paper towels, nail stick or brush.

Time Requirements and Accuracy Standards: 5 minutes. Points assigned reflect importance of step to meeting objective: Important = (5) Essential = (10) Critical = (15). Automatic failure results if any of the **critical** tasks are omitted or performed incorrectly.

STANDARD PRECAUTIONS:

SKILLS ASSESSMENT CHECKLIST

Task Performed	Possible Points	TASKS
❑	5	Removes all jewelry (except plain wedding band).
❑	5	*Rationale:* Jewelry can harbor microorganisms.
❑	5	Prepares disposable paper towel.
❑	5	Does not allow clothing or hands to touch sink.
❑	5	*Rationale:* Remembers sink is contaminated and touching sink with clothes or hands will contaminate them.
❑	10	Turns on faucet with a dry paper towel and adjusts water temperature to lukewarm.
❑	10	*Rationale:* Warm water makes better suds than cold water. Hot water may scald the skin.
❑	15	Wets hands and applies soap, rubbing into a lather.
❑	15	Washes all surfaces of the hands, interlacing the fingers and scrubbing between each finger.
❑	10	*Rationale:* Friction loosens debris and microorganisms.
❑	10	Rinses well, keeping hands and forearms pointed downward.
❑	5	*Rationale:* Prevents water from running down to the elbows, which are less contaminated than the hands.

SKILLS COMPETENCY ASSESSMENT — continued

Procedure 1–1: Medically Aseptic Handwash

Task Performed	Possible Points	TASKS
❑	10	Rinses hands and forearms, keeping them pointed downward.
❑	5	Washes wrists and forearms to height of possible contamination.
❑	5	Rinses hands, wrists, and forearms.
❑	10	Uses orange wood stick or brush for the first handwashing of the day.
❑	10	For the first handwashing of the day, or if hands are contaminated or excessively soiled, repeats hand-washing technique, rewetting hands and applying soap and following all other procedural steps.
❑	5	Dries hands, wrists, and forearms with disposable paper towels; does not touch towel dispenser; blots hands with towel instead of rubbing.
❑	10	If sink is not foot-operated, uses a clean disposable towel to turn off the water faucet.
❑	5	*Rationale:* Clean hands will become contaminated from the dirty sink.
❑	5	Discards paper towel in biohazard waste container.
❑	10	Repeats hand-washing procedure prior to and following each patient contact, procedure, or meal.
❑	5	Applies water-based antibacterial lotion to prevent chapped, excoriated skin.
❑	5	*Rationale:* Cracked skin allows microorganisms to gain entrance and cause infection.
❑	5	Completed the tasks within 5 minutes.
❑	15	Results obtained were accurate.

______	Earned	ADD POINTS OF TASKS CHECKED
205	Points	TOTAL POINTS POSSIBLE
______	SCORE	DETERMINE SCORE (divide points earned by total points possible, multiply results by 100)

Actual Student Time Needed to Complete Procedure: ____________

Student's Initials: ____________ Instructor's Initials: ____________ Grade: ____________

Suggestions for Improvement: ______________________________

Evaluator's Name (print) ______________________________

Evaluator's Signature ______________________________

Comments ______________________________

SKILLS COMPETENCY ASSESSMENT

Procedure 1–2: Instrument Sanitization

Student's Name: ______________________________ Date: ____________

Objective: To properly clean contaminated instruments to remove tissue or debris.

Conditions: The student demonstrates the ability to properly clean contaminated instruments using a sink (or ultrasonic cleaner), sanitizing agent, brush, disposable paper towels, disposable gloves, and biohazard waste container.

Time Requirements and Accuracy Standards: 5 minutes. Points assigned reflect importance of step to meeting objective: Important = (5) Essential = (10) Critical = (15). Automatic failure results if any of the **critical** tasks are omitted or performed incorrectly.

STANDARD PRECAUTIONS:

SKILLS ASSESSMENT CHECKLIST

Task Performed	Possible Points	TASKS
❑	5	Wears disposable gloves in accordance with OSHA standards.
❑	10	Rinses contaminated instrument immediately in water and disinfectant solution; rinses instrument again under running water.
❑	5	*Rationale:* Understands importance of rinsing instrument as quickly as possible after a procedure to help prevent debris from adhering to it.
❑	5	To carry contaminated instrument from one place to another to sanitize it, places instrument in a basin labeled "Biohazard."
❑	15	Scrubs each instrument well with detergent and water; scrubs under running water and scrubs any inside edges and all surfaces.
❑	10	Rinses well under hot water.
❑	5	*Rationale:* Understands that rinsing with hot water will remove residue and aid in the drying process while eliminating rust and water spots.
❑	5	After rinsing, places instruments on muslin or disposable paper towel until all instruments are scrubbed.
❑	10	*Rationale:* Understands danger of recontamination of instruments.

SKILLS COMPETENCY ASSESSMENT — continued

Procedure 1–2: Instrument Sanitization

Task Performed	Possible Points	TASKS
☐	10	Dries instruments with muslin or disposable paper towels.
☐	5	*Rationale:* Understands that wet instruments may rust or corrode.
☐	5	Completed the tasks within 5 minutes.
☐	15	Results obtained were accurate.

________	Earned	ADD POINTS OF TASKS CHECKED
105	Points	TOTAL POINTS POSSIBLE
________	SCORE	DETERMINE SCORE (divide points earned by total points possible, multiply results by 100)

Actual Student Time Needed to Complete Procedure: ____________

Student's Initials: ____________ Instructor's Initials: ____________ Grade: ____________

Suggestions for Improvement: ____

____

____

____

Evaluator's Name (print) ____

Evaluator's Signature ____

Comments ____

SKILLS COMPETENCY ASSESSMENT

Procedure 1–3: Removing Contaminated Gloves

Student's Name: ______________________________ Date: ____________

Objective: To remove and dispose of contaminated gloves in order to contain exposure.

Conditions: Student demonstrates the ability to remove and dispose of contaminated gloves using a biohazard waste receptacle.

Time Requirements and Accuracy Standards: 5 minutes. Points assigned reflect importance of step to meeting objective: Important = (5) Essential = (10) Critical = (15). Automatic failure results if any of the **critical** tasks are omitted or performed incorrectly.

STANDARD PRECAUTIONS:

SKILLS ASSESSMENT CHECKLIST

Task Performed	Possible Points	TASKS
☐	10	Grasps the palm of the used left glove with the right hand to begin removing the first glove, holding hands away from the body and pointed downward.
☐	15	Pulls off the used left glove and encases it in the right gloved hand.
☐	10	Holds the left glove that has been removed in the right gloved hand; inserts two fingers of the ungloved left hand between the right arm and the inside of the right glove.
☐	15	Turns the right dirty glove inside out over the other. One glove is now inside the other glove.
☐	15	Disposes of the inverted gloves into a biohazard waste receptacle.
☐	15	*Rationale:* Understands that biological waste should be placed in a red biohazard bag.
☐	10	Immediately washes hands thoroughly.
☐	5	Completed the tasks within 5 minutes.
☐	15	Results obtained were accurate.

________	Earned	ADD POINTS OF TASKS CHECKED
100	Points	TOTAL POINTS POSSIBLE
________	SCORE	DETERMINE SCORE (divide points earned by total points possible, multiply results by 100)

Actual Student Time Needed to Complete Procedure: ____________

Student's Initials: ____________ Instructor's Initials: ____________ Grade: ____________

Suggestions for Improvement: ______________________________

Evaluator's Name (print) ______________________________

Evaluator's Signature ______________________________

Comments ______________________________

SKILLS COMPETENCY ASSESSMENT

Procedure 1–4: Instrument/Equipment Chemical Disinfection or Chemical Sterilization

Student's Name: ______________________________ Date: __________

Objective: To achieve medical asepsis for instruments to be used during external physical examinations or procedures, such as thermometers (chemical disinfection), and to achieve surgical asepsis for instruments and equipment to be used during internal physical examinations or procedures, such as surgical instruments and proctological equipment (chemical sterilization).

Conditions: Student demonstrates the ability to achieve medical and surgical asepsis by appropriately and fully disinfecting or sterilizing instruments or equipment using an airtight container, disinfectant chemical solution, a timer or clock, distilled water for disinfection, sterile water for sterilization, disposable gloves, and a biohazard waste container.

Time Requirements and Accuracy Standards: 5 minutes. Points assigned reflect importance of step to meeting objective: Important = (5) Essential = (10) Critical = (15). Automatic failure results if any of the **critical** tasks are omitted or performed incorrectly.

STANDARD PRECAUTIONS:

SKILLS ASSESSMENT CHECKLIST

Task Performed	Possible Points	TASKS
		Chemical Disinfection
❑	10	Sanitizes instruments as shown in Procedure 1–2 that require medical aseptic chemical disinfection.
❑	5	*Rationale:* Sanitization must precede disinfection in order to remove debris. Understands that medical asepsis is not sterile and should not be used for instruments employed in invasive procedures requiring sterile technique.
❑	15	Reads the manufacturer's instructions on the original container of chemical disinfectant solution.
❑	5	*Rationale:* Is able to choose the chemical disinfectant solution with the specific preparation instructions and germicidal properties that best suits the needs of the ambulatory care setting.
❑	5	Puts on disposable gloves to prevent burning or irritation to the skin.
❑	15	Prepares solution as indicated by manufacturer.
❑	5	Writes own initials and date of opening or preparation directly on the container.
❑	10	Pours prepared solution into a container with an airtight lid, avoiding splashing.

Task Performed	Possible Points	TASKS
❑	5	*Rationale:* Understands that open containers can cause accidental inhalation of fumes or poisoning; splashing can cause skin, inhalation, or mucous membrane contact.
❑	10	Places sanitized instruments into solution, covering instruments completely; avoids splashing.
❑	5	*Rationale:* Understands that if instruments are not covered with solution, disinfection cannot occur.
❑	5	Closes lid of container.
❑	10	Labels container with name of solution, exposure time, and initials.
❑	15	Does not open or add additional instruments during disinfection period.
❑	5	*Rationale:* Understands that adding instruments during disinfection procedure limits effectiveness of the disinfectant solution.
❑	15	Waits required exposure time and lifts items from the container tray; rinses well under distilled water or tap water, according to the manufacturer's instructions.
❑	5	*Rationale:* Understands that using instruments without rinsing off chemical disinfectant solution can irritate the patient's skin and may corrode instruments over time, as solution is caustic.
❑	10	Removes instruments and places them on muslin or disposable paper towel.
❑	15	Dries instruments with muslin or paper towel.
❑	5	Properly discards used chemical disinfectant.
❑	5	Removes gloves.
❑	5	Stores instruments and/or equipment in a clean, dry area.
❑	5	Documents procedure.
		Chemical Sterilization
❑	10	Follows procedures for chemical disinfection above, beginning with the sanitization of instruments or equipment. Recalls that the difference between chemical disinfection and chemical sterilization is the type of solution used and the exposure time to the chemical solution.
❑	15	Reads the manufacturer's instructions for exposure time to achieve chemical sterilization.
❑	5	*Rationale:* Understands correct exposure time for sterilization is longer than time for disinfection.
❑	15	Following recommended exposure time, removes instruments with sterile transfer forceps to protect sterility. Rinses under sterile water.

SKILLS COMPETENCY ASSESSMENT — continued

Procedure 1–4: Instrument/Equipment Chemical Disinfection or Chemical Sterilization

Task Performed	Possible Points	TASKS
☐	15	Dries instrument with a sterile muslin towel.
☐	5	*Rationale:* Understands that wet instruments will contaminate a sterile field.
☐	15	Places the sterilized dry instrument on the sterile field with the sterile transfer forceps.
☐	5	Changes the solution as recommended by the manufacturer.
☐	5	Removes gloves.
☐	5	Documents the procedure.
☐	5	Completed the tasks within 5 minutes.
☐	15	Results obtained were accurate.

________	Earned	ADD POINTS OF TASKS CHECKED
305	Points	TOTAL POINTS POSSIBLE
________	SCORE	DETERMINE SCORE (divide points earned by total points possible, multiply results by 100)

Actual Student Time Needed to Complete Procedure: ____________

Student's Initials: ____________ Instructor's Initials: ____________ Grade: ____________

Suggestions for Improvement: ______________________________

Evaluator's Name (print) ______________________________

Evaluator's Signature ______________________________

Comments ______________________________

DOCUMENTATION

Record disinfected or sterilized instruments/equipment in the chemical disinfection/sterilization log book.

Date: ______________

Chemical Disinfection Documentation: ______________________________

____

Chemical Sterilization Documentation: ______________________________

____

Student's Initials: ______________

SKILLS COMPETENCY ASSESSMENT

Procedure 1–5: Wrapping Instruments for Sterilization in Autoclave

Student's Name: ______________________________ Date: ____________

Objective: To properly wrap sanitized instruments for sterilization in an autoclave.

Conditions: Student demonstrates the ability to properly wrap sanitized instruments for sterilization in autoclave using the following equipment: sanitized instruments, wrapping material (muslin or disposable wrapping paper), sterilization indicator, 2 × 2 gauze or cotton balls (if instrument has sharp edges), autoclave wrapping tape, and permanent marker or felt-tipped pen.

Time Requirements and Accuracy Standards: 5 minutes. Points assigned reflect importance of step to meeting objective: Important = (5) Essential = (10) Critical = (15). Automatic failure results if any of the **critical** tasks are omitted or performed incorrectly.

SKILLS ASSESSMENT CHECKLIST

Task Performed	Possible Points	TASKS
❑	10	Prepares a clean, dry, flat surface of adequate size to lay wrapping material.
❑	5	*Rationale:* Understands that a clean area reduces the risk of contamination.
❑	5	Selects two wraps of adequate size in which to wrap instruments.
❑	5	Places one square of wrapping material at an angle in front of the body on the dry surface with one corner pointed directly at the torso.
❑	5	Places the sanitized instruments or articles to be placed in the autoclave just below the center of the wrap.
❑	15	Opens instruments with hinges as wide as possible and places a 2 × 2 gauze or cotton ball in the opening.
❑	5	*Rationale:* Understands that instruments with hinged parts that are not spread wide open prior to autoclaving may not be properly sterilized.
❑	10	Places one sterilization indicator with the instrument.
❑	5	Brings corner of the wrap closest to the body up and over the article toward the center.
❑	5	Brings the tip of the same corner back toward the body until it reaches the folded edge, creating a fan-fold effect.
❑	5	Smooths edges of the fold; article remains completely covered.
❑	5	Folds one side edge toward the center line; fan-folds back to side and creases.

SKILLS COMPETENCY ASSESSMENT — continued

Procedure 1–5: Wrapping Instruments for Sterilization in Autoclave

Task Performed	Possible Points	TASKS
❑	15	Repeats previous step for the other side edge.
❑	5	Folds the package up from the bottom.
❑	5	Folds the top edge down and over the entire package.
❑	5	*Rationale:* Understands that if wrap does not cover the entire package, items must be unwrapped and rewrapped with a larger piece of wrapping material.
❑	15	To "wrap twice," places package into the center of a second wrap and repeats correct procedures for wrapping package within the second piece of wrapping material.
❑	5	*Rationale:* Wrap twice allows the outer wrap of a double-wrapped item to be removed so the inside wrapped item can be placed onto a sterile field.
❑	10	Tapes with autoclave tape across the point left exposed.
❑	5	*Rationale:* Understands that autoclave tape is not an indicator of sterilization or quality control, but only that the package has been through the autoclave.
❑	15	Labels the tape with names of instruments or type of pack, date of sterilization, and initials.
❑	5	*Rationale:* Understands that dating package provides a method for assessing its sterility over time.
❑	15	Immediately places wrapped instruments in autoclave after dating. If package is not placed immediately into the autoclave, waits to date package until just before autoclaving.
❑	5	Documents procedure.
❑	5	Completed the tasks within 5 minutes.
❑	15	Results obtained were accurate.

_______	Earned	ADD POINTS OF TASKS CHECKED
205	Points	TOTAL POINTS POSSIBLE
_______	SCORE	DETERMINE SCORE (divide points earned by total points possible, multiply results by 100)

Actual Student Time Needed to Complete Procedure: ____________

Student's Initials: ____________ Instructor's Initials: ____________ Grade: ____________

Suggestions for Improvement: ____

____

____

____

Evaluator's Name (print) ____

Evaluator's Signature ____

Comments ____

DOCUMENTATION

Record the label information for the instrument or type of pack wrapped.

Date: ____________

Label: ____

____

Student's Initials: __________

SKILLS COMPETENCY ASSESSMENT

Procedure 1–6: Steam Sterilization (Autoclave)

Student's Name: ______________________________ Date: ____________

Objective: To rid instruments for use in invasive procedures of all forms of microbial life.

Conditions: Student demonstrates the ability to rid instruments and other equipment of microorganisms using a steam sterilizer (autoclave), autoclave manufacturer procedure manual, and wrapped sanitized instrument packages with sterilization indicators placed inside (or unwrapped item if removed with sterile transfer forceps).

Time Requirements and Accuracy Standards: 15 minutes. Points assigned reflect importance of step to meeting objective: Important = (5) Essential = (10) Critical = (15). Automatic failure results if any of the **critical** tasks are omitted or performed incorrectly.

SKILLS ASSESSMENT CHECKLIST

Task Performed	Possible Points	TASKS
❑	5	Checks water level in reservoir; adds distilled water to "fill line."
❑	15	Loads packages into autoclave tray; allows three inches between packages; avoids stacking directly on top of other packages.
❑	10	**Jars:** Loads jars of dressings or cups on their sides, with tops ajar or loosely in place.
❑	10	**Packages:** Loads cloth or dressing packages vertically, three inches apart.
❑	15	**Unwrapped items:** Loads unwrapped items vertically, three inches apart, not allowing any item to touch another item.
❑	15	**Unwrapped instruments:** Loads unwrapped instruments flat with handles opened.
❑	5	Closes autoclave door and seals.
❑	15	Turns on autoclave and sets temperature to achieve 250–254° F (121° C) and 15 pounds of pressure according to the manufacturer's guidelines.
❑	10	When the temperature dial indicates that the proper temperature and pressure have been achieved inside the autoclave, begins necessary exposure time by setting timer.
❑	5	*Rationale:* Can identify proper length of exposure time required for wrapped instrument packages or trays, unwrapped items, and unwrapped items covered with cloth.
❑	5	Does not attempt to open the door during the autoclave cycle.
❑	10	Following completion of the autoclave cycle, exhausts steam pressure from the autoclave by following the manufacturer's instructions.
❑	10	Opens the door approximately 1 inch after the pressure gauge indicates zero (0) pressure and the temperature gauge indicates a decrease to at least 212° F. (Some autoclaves have a drying cycle, eliminating the need for opening the autoclave one inch.)

Task Performed	Possible Points	TASKS
☐	5	*Rationale:* Understands that injuries can occur if autoclave door is opened sooner.
☐	15	Allows contents to completely dry, ten to fifteen minutes.
☐	5	*Rationale:* Understands that if wet or damp packages are handled or placed on a countertop while warm, they will become contaminated by microorganisms.
☐	10	Removes wrapped contents with dry, clean hands and stores in clean, dry area reserved for sterilized packages only. If the outer wrapper is required to remain sterile, removes package with sterile transfer forceps and places on a sterile field or in a sterile storage area.
☐	10	Removes unwrapped contents with sterile transfer forceps; resanitizes and resterilizes the transfer forceps following use. (Sterile transfer forceps must have been sterilized immediately prior to or along with the unwrapped item.)
☐	5	Documents the procedure.
☐	10	Performs quality control by monitoring sterilization indicators with each use of sterilized instruments.
☐	15	Documents on a weekly basis sterilization indicator outcome in quality control log; dates and initials log entries.
☐	5	Completed the tasks within 15 minutes.
☐	15	Results obtained were accurate.

________	Earned	ADD POINTS OF TASKS CHECKED
225	Points	TOTAL POINTS POSSIBLE
________	SCORE	DETERMINE SCORE (divide points earned by total points possible, multiply results by 100)

Actual Student Time Needed to Complete Procedure: ____________

Student's Initials: ____________ Instructor's Initials: ____________ Grade: ____________

Suggestions for Improvement: ____________

Evaluator's Name (print) ____________

Evaluator's Signature ____________

Comments ____________

DOCUMENTATION

Document the procedure in the autoclave quality control log: ____________

____

____

____

Student's Initials: ____________

EVALUATION OF CHAPTER KNOWLEDGE

How has your instructor evaluated the knowledge you have gained?

Knowledge	**Instructor Evaluation** *Good*	*Average*	*Poor*
Defines key vocabulary terms correctly	_____	_____	_____
Identifies and understands the importance of infection control in the ambulatory care setting	_____	_____	_____
Observes universal and standard precautions	_____	_____	_____
Defines the five classifications of infectious organisms	_____	_____	_____
Describes the four stages of infectious diseases	_____	_____	_____
States and describes the four phases of immune response	_____	_____	_____
Understands the purpose of rapid sanitization of contaminated instruments	_____	_____	_____
Identifies four methods of sterilization	_____	_____	_____
Defines both surgical and medical asepsis	_____	_____	_____
Demonstrates ability to perform competent wrapping technique and proper operation of the autoclave with sanitized instrument packages	_____	_____	_____
States supplies and equipment used to achieve surgical asepsis when using an autoclave	_____	_____	_____
Performs accurate documentation of procedures	_____	_____	_____

Student's Initials: ______ Instructor's Initials: ______

Grade: _______

Federal Regulations and Guidelines

PERFORMANCE OBJECTIVES

While treating patients in the medical facility, health care professionals, including medical assistants, come into contact with blood and body fluids that may be highly infectious. To protect patients and health care providers from infection, medical asepsis or infection control measures are practiced to prevent and/or limit the spread of infection. State and federal agencies such as the Centers for Disease Control and Prevention (CDC), the Clinical Laboratory Amendments of 1988 (CLIA '88), and the Occupational Safety and Health Administration (OSHA) establish guidelines and regulations for health care providers and employers to follow in order to reduce the risk of transmission of infectious diseases. Medical assistants must understand the regulations set forth by these government agencies and implement them in the ambulatory care setting for the health and safety of patients and health care professionals. Medical assistants should practice standard and universal precautions, guidelines designed to protect all health care providers, patients, and visitors from a wide range of communicable diseases, with meticulous care to reduce the risk of spreading infection in the ambulatory care setting.

EXERCISES AND ACTIVITIES

Vocabulary Builder

A. Solve the crossword puzzle on the following page to identify key vocabulary terms that are used in relation to federal guidelines and regulations set to safeguard both patients and health care professionals and to reduce the risk of transmission of infectious diseases.

CLUES

Across

4. Guidelines established in 1985 by the Centers for Disease Control for the protection of health care workers from infectious diseases.
9. Term used to describe surgical techniques or procedures that penetrate healthy tissue.
10. Providing factual support through written information.
12. Contaminated items; items that have come in contact with patient blood and/or body fluids.
15. A written request for laboratory analysis to be performed on a specimen.
18. Commercially packaged materials containing supplies and equipment needed to clean a spill of biohazardous substances.
22. A material that has been in contact with body fluid and is capable of transmitting disease.

24. Rules set up and established to measure quality, weight, extent, or value.
27. The substance produced by the cells of glandular organs from materials in the blood.
28. A pathway of possible infection from pathogens present in the atmosphere.
29. Commercially packaged materials needed to perform laboratory tests.
30. Recognized as being outstanding.
32. To destroy by fire.
34. Federal government agency from which written CLIA '88 documents may be obtained.
38. Methods used to ensure reliable, accurate data.
39. To remove by suction.
40. To advance beyond established or proper limits.
43. A means of transmission of an infectious disease (such as HIV and HBV) via human blood.
45. Needles, scalpels, or other instruments capable of causing a penetrating or puncture wound of the skin.
47. Sample tests performed in a clinical laboratory to determine that a specific degree of accuracy is achieved.
48. To acquire through infection, as a disease.
50. Any refuse that contains infectious material that would pose a threat due to possible transmission of pathogenic microorganisms.
52. The body's strong line of defense against invading microorganisms.

Down

1. A pathway of possible infection from pathogens suspended in particles of liquid.
2. Personal protective equipment (PPE).
3. Measures used in the workplace that consist of physical equipment and mechanical devices to control employee exposure to bloodborne pathogens and OPIM.
5. A person who harbors a pathogenic organism and who is capable of transmitting the organism to others.
6. Guidelines released by the CDC in 1996, which represent the most current and comprehensive approach to infection control.
7. To make impure or unclean.
8. Conforming or adapting.
10. A written formal refusal.
11. Degree of difficulty.
13. Precautions issued by the CDC to be used in addition to standard precautions when caring for specific categories of patients.
14. A type of white blood cell that provides immunity.
16. An immune system unable to function normally due to the presence of a disease such as AIDS.
17. A system that maintains that personal protective equipment should be worn for contact with all body fluids whether or not blood is visible.
19. A system developed by CDC for grouping patients with infectious diseases, including strict, respiratory, protective, enteric, wound and skin, discharge, and blood.
20. A formal order to obey certain rules and regulations.
21. Payment.
23. Physical or mechanical devices that isolate or remove health hazards from the workplace.
25. Infections from any organisms that occur due to the possibility offered by the altered physiological state of the host.
26. A pathway of possible infection from pathogens present on surfaces.

33. The determination of the accuracy of an instrument by comparing the information provided with an accepted standard known to be accurate.
35. The elimination of waste products from the body.
36. Surgical puncture of the lumbar area of the intervertebral spaces to aspirate cerebral spinal fluid for laboratory analysis.
37. Removing a seriously ill patient or a patient with an infectious disease from others to reduce the risk of infection and to protect the patient.
38. Measures used to monitor the processing of laboratory specimens.
41. A barrier used in the laboratory to capture chemical vapors.
42. Any secretion or excretion from the human body.
44. An injury or wound.
46. Inspection with a microscope.
49. Infectious; able to overcome the host's defense mechanisms.
51. Used to describe a category of clinical laboratory tests that are simple, unvarying, and require a minimum of judgment and interpretation.

B. To test your spelling skill, unscramble the key vocabulary terms that follow. Then define each term in the space provided.

1. TANOECE ______________________________

____

____

2. SEGAI ______________________________

____

____

3. RADIQEUC CODMENIFIYMUNIEC MOREYNDS ______________________________

____

____

4. STONENCSEMIAI ______________________________

____

____

5. PATMIRHEEHCUTEOC TANGES ______________________________

____

____

6. RATMETDISI ______________________________

____

____

7. SONYEDPOC ______________________________

____

____

8. TELHY LOCOLAH ______________________________

____

____

9. RENCOSIF ______________________________

10. DOYEFAMEDLRH ______________________________

11. NUHAM FODENICIYIMUCENM SUVIR ______________________________

12. BINOLUGMISMOLUN ______________________________

13. CADIJUNE ______________________________

14. RELORAKEUH ______________________________

15. ALOHIC ______________________________

16. LAMDCIE PASSISE ______________________________

17. NESESM ______________________________

18. ALPENARERT ______________________________

19. GETNAPOH ______________________________

20. BOPMEYOTLH ______________________________

21. MOPLARYNU AMEDE ______________________________

22. MOSIUD HEYPOCOHIRTL ______________________________

23. TUSMUP ______________________________

24. RENTSETCASOIH ______________________________

25. TEARIVUNAC ______________________________

Learning Review

Fill in the blanks.

1. A. Universal Blood and Body Fluid Precautions, or universal precautions, were issued by the CDC in 1985 as a means of infection control to minimize the possibility of infection from ______________, ______________, and other ______________ diseases.

B. In 1996, the CDC released a new set of standard precautions, in addition to the universal precautions, for infection control that should now be used by all health care professionals for all patients. Standard precautions apply to what four sources of infection from the human body?

(1) ______________

(2) ______________

(3) ______________

(4) ______________

2. For each of the following situations, what guidelines of the universal and standard precautions should the medical assistant implement to practice effective medical asepsis?

A. Jaime Carrera, a construction worker, presents at Inner City Health Care with head wound that is bleeding profusely; his clothes and skin are covered with blood. Two workers accompany Jaime, and they are both covered with blood as well.

____

B. Lourdes Austen, a breast cancer survivor, presents for a flexible sigmoidoscopy, an endoscopy procedure.

____

C. (1) Audrey Jones, CMA, prepares to perform venipuncture on Maria Jover, a patient suspected of HIV infection.

(2) Audrey must dispose of the needle after performing venipuncture on Maria.

(3) Audrey properly disposes of gloves in a biohazard container.

D. Bruce Goldman, CMA, performs cardiopulmonary resuscitation (CPR) on a walk-in emergency patient at Inner City Health Care who collapses in the reception area.

E. Wanda Slawson, CMA, prepares to clean and sanitize the examination room after Dr. James Whitney completes emergency treatment of Jaime Carrera's head wound, an open laceration requiring stitches.

F. Karen Ritter, CMA, prepares urine and blood specimens collected for transport to an off-site laboratory for analysis.

G. While suffering a brief bout of dermatitis, administrative/clinical medical assistant Joe Guerrero is assigned to administrative office duties.

H. Ellen Armstrong, CMA, greets and correctly identifies patient Nora Fowler and prepares to initiate contact with the patient to obtain a blood pressure reading.

3. With the release of standard precautions in 1996, the CDC also introduced transmission-based precautions to be used in addition to standard precautions for patients diagnosed with or suspected of specific highly transmissible diseases.

For each of the following sets of symbols representing categories of transmission-based precautions, identify the pathway of infection for pathogens the precautions are designed to protect against. In each case, what special precautions are necessary to supplement standard precautions?

A. ______________________ Precautions

____

____

____

B. ______________________ Precautions

____

____

____

C. ______________________ Precautions

____

____

____

4. Persons infected with HIV or HBV remain infected for life. As carriers, infected persons are capable of transmitting the virus to others, even if they are asymptomatic. Name four ways these viruses are primarily transmitted:

(1) ____

____

(2) ____

____

(3) ____

____

(4) ____

____

5. The four categories of laboratory testing are waived, physician-performed microscopy tests (which are all waived tests), moderate-complexity tests, and high-complexity tests. All laboratories are required to register with CLIA '88 and receive certification to perform specific categories of tests within strict boundaries of compliance. Waived tests deliver simple unvarying results and require a minimum of judgment and interpretation. Name 10 waived tests.

(1) ____________________	(6) ____________________
(2) ____________________	(7) ____________________
(3) ____________________	(8) ____________________
(4) ____________________	(9) ____________________
(5) ____________________	(10) ____________________

6. CLIA '88 requires every facility that tests human specimens for diagnosis, treatment, and prevention of disease to meet specific federal requirements. Name five specific duties a medical assistant may perform that will impact the medical facility's compliance with CLIA '88 regulations.

(1) ____

____

(2) ____

____

(3) ____

____

(4) ____

____

(5) ____

____

7. A written chemical hygiene plan (CHP) is required of all medical facilities to comply with safety standards outlined by the Occupational Health and Safety Administration (OSHA). To comply with OSHA regulations, chemicals must be labeled using the National Fire Protection Association's color and number method.

A. *Match the colors below to the type of hazard each signifies.*

____ Blue	1. Fire
____ White	2. Reactivity
____ Yellow	3. Use of personal protective equipment (PPE)
____ Red	4. Health

B. *For each configuration listed, use the NFPA color and number method to describe the hazardous properties of each chemical.*

(1) CHEMICAL X: Red/2; Blue/3; Yellow/3; White/F.

____

____

____

(2) CHEMICAL Y: Red/0; Blue/1; Yellow/0; White/X.

____

____

____

(3) CHEMICAL Z: Red/1; Blue/2; Yellow/1; White/E.

____

____

____

8. The Bloodborne Pathogen Standard, effective in 1992, attempts to reduce the occupational-related cases of HIV and HBV infections among health care professionals. It covers all employees "reasonably anticipated" to come into contact with, as a result of performing their job duties, blood and other potentially infectious materials (OPIM) and seeks to limit exposure to pathogens.

Match each of the following components of the Bloodborne Pathogen Standard to a strategy used to implement it.

____ 1. Document exposure incident.
____ 2. Placed in a secondary container if the outside of the container is contaminated.
____ 3. Examples include needleless IVs, sharps disposal containers, and aerosol-free tubes.
____ 4. Go through training and cooperate; obey policies.
____ 5. Transported in bags that prevent soak-through or leakage.
____ 6. Epidemiology and symptoms of bloodborne disease.
____ 7. Records must be maintained for 30 years plus the duration of employment.
____ 8. Summary of contents of training program (kept for 3 years).
____ 9. Biohazard symbol and word *biohazard* must be visible.
____ 10. Prescription glasses may be fitted with solid side shields.
____ 11. Puncture-resistant, leak-proof, routinely replaced so there is no overflow.
____ 12. Training material must be appropriate for literacy and education level of employee.
____ 13. All human blood and OPIM are considered to be infectious.

A. Sharps containers
B. Protective clothing (component of PPE)
C. Labels
D. Work practice controls
E. Housekeeping
F. Methods of compliance
G. Medical records
H. Laundry
I. Training components
J. Exposure control plan
K. Engineering controls
L. Eye protection (component of PPE)

____ 14. Vinyl or latex are required for general use.
____ 15. Laundry personnel must use PPE and have a sharps container accessible.
____ 16. A list of job classifications where occupational exposure occurs.
____ 17. Contaminated equipment and surfaces must be cleaned as soon as feasible for obvious contamination or at the end of the work shift if no contamination has occurred.
____ 18. No eating, drinking, smoking, and so on in the work area.
____ 19. Lab coats are worn when a low-level risk for exposure is present.
____ 20. PPE, engineering and work practice controls, standard precautions, housekeeping.
____ 21. Given in accordance with the U. S. Public Health Service guidelines at no cost to employees. May be required for students to be admitted to college health programs as well as for externship.
____ 22. The standard applies to all occupational exposure to blood and OPIM, and includes part-time employees, designated first aiders, and mental health workers as well as exposed medical personnel.

M. Regulated waste containers (nonsharp)
N. Scope and application
O. Laundry facility
P. Training records
Q. Standard precautions
R. Gloves (component of PPE)
S. Hepatitis B vaccination
T. Employee responsibilities
U. Postexposure follow-up
V. Information and training

Investigation Activity

Material safety data sheets (MSDS) are compiled into a manual that must be kept on-site and made available to all employees. MSDS give information regarding any hazardous properties of chemical substances and are often supplied by the manufacturer when chemicals are ordered. MSDS manuals are required as a component of compliance with the OSHA standard for chemical exposure. In the ambulatory care setting, medical assistants come into contact with many substances that pose potential chemical hazards. Improper exposure to hazardous substances can cause illnesses, ranging from skin irritations to blindness to pulmonary edema. Substances range from ordinary office supplies (such as typewriter correction fluid) and essential cleansers (such as sodium hypochlorite or household bleach) to medical supplies (such as stains, ethyl alcohol, formaldehyde, fixatives, and preservatives), injectables (such as chemotherapeutic agents), and more.

As a class, come up with a list of chemical substances commonly found in the ambulatory care setting. Each student should select one substance. Then each student should perform research to identify a manufacturer who makes and supplies the substance. Write or call the manufacturer to obtain an MSDS and/or relevant information regarding the chemical substance's potential hazards. Using the National Fire Protection Association's color and number method for labeling to warn for potential hazards, configure a chemical hazard label for the substance based on the MSDS or hazard information supplied by the manufacturer.

Record information regarding the assigned chemical substance below.

Name of substance:______________________________

Purpose of substance in the ambulatory care setting: ______________________

____

Name of manufacturer: ______________________

Address: ______________________

____

____

Telephone: ______________________

Suggested NFPA label coding for chemical hazards of the substance:

Red: ______________ Yellow: ______________

Blue: ______________ White: ______________

CASE STUDY

Annette Samuels comes to Inner City Health Care experiencing flulike symptoms. Her skin and the whites of her eyes have a yellowish tone. Dr. Mark Woo examines the patient, assisted by Liz Corbin, CMA. It is discovered that Annette had her navel pierced at a local piercing and tattoo salon that recently opened in town. Mark suspects hepatitis B and asks Liz to perform venipuncture to obtain a blood sample for analysis to confirm the diagnosis.

Discuss the following:

1. What standard precautions will Liz employ to protect against infection while performing the venipuncture procedure?
2. What might have caused Annette's HBV infection? How can Mark help prevent the further spread of the hepatitis B infection to others at potential risk?
3. What regulation helps protect health care workers from HBV infection?

SUPPLEMENTARY RESOURCES

Study Guide Disks: Additional practice exercises for this chapter are available on the Study Guide disk found in the back of the textbook.

Medical Assisting Videos: Appropriate content is available on Delmar's Medical Assisting Videos, 2nd ed., for the following topics:

Tape 5: Standard Precautions
Perform Medical Aseptic Procedure of Hand Washing
Use Disposable Single-Contact Gloves
Personal Protective Equipment
Perform Medical Aseptic Procedures
Infections in the Office

Tape 12: Completion Procedures Following Injections
OSHA Regulations for Needles and "Sharps"
Accidental Needlesticks

EVALUATION OF CHAPTER KNOWLEDGE

How has your instructor evaluated the knowledge you have achieved?

Knowledge	Instructor Evaluation *Good*	*Average*	*Poor*
Understands and can implement			
Universal precautions	_____	_____	_____
Standard precautions	_____	_____	_____
Transmission-based precautions	_____	_____	_____
Knows routes of transmission for HIV/AIDS and HBV	_____	_____	_____
Identifies body fluids and OPIM	_____	_____	_____
Can identify government regulatory agencies responsible for setting standards	_____	_____	_____
Knows categories of testing and understands CLIA '88 requirements	_____	_____	_____
Understands components of OSHA's bloodborne standard	_____	_____	_____
Can define and identify PPE	_____	_____	_____
Understands the purpose and requirements of a chemical hygiene plan	_____	_____	_____
Understands the purpose of the MSDS manual and can apply NFPA system of chemical hazard labeling	_____	_____	_____
Knows procedures for proper disposal of infectious waste	_____	_____	_____
Can identify situations of potential risk of exposure to pathogens in the ambulatory care setting	_____	_____	_____

Student's Initials:_______ Instructor's Initials:_______

Grade: _______

Emergency Procedures and First Aid

PERFORMANCE OBJECTIVES

Medical assistants may encounter emergency situations and should be familiar with the various types of potential emergencies that may occur both within the ambulatory care setting and outside of the office environment. In the ambulatory care setting, primarily designed to see patients in non-emergency situations, a physician is usually available to provide emergency care. The ambulatory care setting also contains medical equipment and supplies to address emergency situations. The medical assistant, however, is often the first health care professional to interact with an emergency patient. The physician-employer will establish policies and procedures for emergency situations in an emergency policies and procedures manual for the ambulatory care setting that all employees, including medical assistants, will follow in emergency situations. The manual will be reviewed at regularly scheduled staff meetings. Emergency care is provided under the physician's instruction and according to the guidelines established in the emergency policies and procedures manual. Medical assistants must develop the essential skills of triaging emergency situations, that is, of recognizing emergency situations and correctly identifying the emergency measures that must be taken to provide immediate care. As with any health care professional, medical assistants should provide emergency care only within the scope of their knowledge and training. Medical assistants are encouraged to enroll in either a Red Cross or American Heart Association first aid and CPR program and take refresher courses at least every two years to update skills.

EXERCISES, EMERGENCY PROCEDURES, AND ACTIVITY

Vocabulary Builder

Identify each of the following key vocabulary terms as an emergency condition (EC), an emergency or first aid procedure performed by health care professionals (EP), emergency equipment (EQ), or an emergency service provided to assist in emergency situations (ES).

A. _____ A. First aid
_____ B. Triage
_____ C. Syncope

_____ D. Shock
_____ E. Wounds
_____ F. Crash tray or cart
_____ G. Heimlich maneuver
_____ H. Occlusion
_____ I. Universal emergency medical identification symbol and card
_____ J. Hypothermia
_____ K. Standard precautions
_____ L. Cardiopulmonary resuscitation (CPR)
_____ M. Sprain
_____ N. Emergency medical services (EMS)
_____ O. Fractures
_____ P. Splints
_____ Q. Strain
_____ R. Rescue breathing

B. Match each key vocabulary term given in part A with its definition listed below.

_____ 1. A break in a bone. There are several types, but all are classified as open or closed.

_____ 2. A tray or portable cart that contains medications and supplies needed for emergency and first aid procedures.

_____ 3. An injury to the soft tissue between joints, it involves the tearing of muscles or tendons and occurs often in the neck, back, or thigh muscles.

_____ 4. A break in the skin and/or underlying tissues, categorized as open or closed.

_____ 5. Closure of a passage.

_____ 6. An injury to a joint, often an ankle, knee, or wrist, that involves a tearing of the ligaments. Most are minor and heal quickly; others are more severe, include swelling, and may not heal properly if the patient continues to put stress on the affected joint.

_____ 7. A local network of police, fire, and medical personnel trained to respond to emergency situations. In most communities, the system is activated by calling 911.

_____ 8. Abdominal thrusts designed to overcome breathing difficulties in patients who are choking.

_____ 9. Identification sometimes carried by individuals to identify any health problems they might have.

_____10. Any device used to immobilize a body part. Often used by EMS personnel.

_____11. An extremely dangerous cold-related condition that can result in death if the individual does not receive care and if the progression of the condition is not reversed. Symptoms include shivering, cold skin, and confusion.

_____12. Fainting.

_____13. The immediate care provided to persons who are suddenly ill or injured, typically followed by more comprehensive care and treatment.

_____14. A condition in which the circulatory system is not providing enough blood to all parts of the body, causing the body's organs to fail to function properly.

_____15. The combination of rescue breathing and chest compressions performed by a trained individual on a patient experiencing cardiac arrest.

_____16. To assess patients' conditions and prioritize the need for care.

_____17. Performed in individuals in respiratory arrest, this is a mouth-to-mouth (using appropriate protective equipment) or mouth-to-nose procedure that provides oxygen to the patient until emergency personnel arrive.

_____18. Guidelines issued by the Centers for Disease Control and Prevention (CDC) in 1996 that combine many of the basic principles of universal precautions and body substance isolation techniques. These augmented 1996 guidelines represent the new requirements for infection control measures and are intended to protect health care professionals, patients, and visitors.

Learning Review

1. Keen observation skills are necessary to recognize potential emergency situations; medical assistants rely on sight, hearing, and even smell and must be acutely sensitive to unusual behaviors. To identify the nature of the emergency and respond effectively, what five things must the medical assistant do to triage, or assess, the patient's situation?

(1) ____________________

(2) ____________________

(3) ____________________

(4) ____________________

(5) ____________________

2. In an urgent care setting, two or more patients may present with emergency symptoms. The order in which emergency patients will receive care depends on the health care professionals' abilities to triage patients' symptoms to determine who needs care most urgently.

The following five patients present simultaneously on New Year's Eve at Inner City Health Care, an urgent care center. Office manager Walter Seals, CMA, is working the evening shift with Dr. Mark Woo. In what order will Walter and Mark triage the priority of treatment?

Number the patients 1 through 5 to correspond to the urgency of their conditions. For each patient, list the emergency conditions he or she is suffering from, in order of severity, and name the emergency procedures the health care team will initiate to treat the patient.

A. A patient presents with a gunshot wound to the leg that is bleeding severely. The patient is conscious but his pupils are dilated and he is unable to answer simple questions put to him by Walter and Dr. Woo. He cradles his right arm and will not let anyone touch it, though there is no immediate evidence of an open wound to the arm.

Urgency of Condition: ____________________

____

____

____

B. An elderly man, brought in by his grandson, complains of debilitating chest pains and nausea after eating a large family dinner. The man is a regular patient of Dr. Ray Reynolds, another physician at Inner City Health Care. The patient's medical record reveals that he suffers from a hiatal hernia, slipped disks, high blood pressure, and mild angina. His vital signs are within a normal range for his general physical condition. The man is walking and speaking with moderate distress and is extremely anxious.

Urgency of Condition: ______________________________

____

____

C. A young woman presents with her boyfriend. She appears to have multiple abrasions on her right palm and knee, with damage to the right knee and ankle joints sustained after a fall on in-line skates. Both joints are swollen and painful. She received the skates as a Christmas gift from her boyfriend.

Urgency of Condition: ______________________________

____

____

D. A man in his mid-thirties presents with the cotton tip of a cotton swab stuck in his ear canal. The tip became lodged in his ear while he was showering and dressing for a New Year's Eve party. Though the man feels a dull consistent pain in the ear, he says he has no trouble hearing. The outside of the ear appears normal and the man appears annoyed but not distressed.

Urgency of Condition: ______________________________

____

____

E. A young woman presents with a group of friends, all college students, with an eye injury sustained by a champagne cork. The cork, which had a metal covering over its tip, hit the patient's eye; the students bring the cork with them. The young woman's eye is red and tearing and she is experiencing severe pain in the eye.

Urgency of Condition: ______________________________

____

____

3. In administering emergency care in the ambulatory care setting, medical assistants and all health care professionals must follow standard precautions to protect themselves, their patients, and visitors. What five infection control measures can health care professionals follow to greatly reduce the risk of transmitting infectious disease when providing emergency care?

(1) ______________________________

(2) ______________________________

(3) ______________________________

(4) ______________________________

(5) ______________________________

4. The medical crash cart or tray contains emergency or first aid supplies and medications health care professionals commonly use in treating emergencies. Using a medical encyclopedia or reference such as the *Physician's Desk Reference* (PDR), describe the following emergency medications and identify potential uses for each. Remember that only a physician can order medications or treatment.

A. Lidocaine ______________________________

____

____

B. Verapamil ______________________________

____

____

C. Atropine ______________________________

____

____

D. Insulin ______________________________

____

____

E. Nitroglycerin ______________________________

____

____

F. Marcaine ______________________________

____

____

G. Diphenhydramine ______________________________

____

____

H. Diazepam ______________________________

____

____

5. Shock requires immediate medical attention. Progressive shock can reach an irreversible point and is life threatening. Shock occurs when the circulatory system is not providing enough blood to all parts of the body, causing the body's organs to function improperly.

For each of the patient symptoms or conditions below, identify the type of shock that is most likely.

______________________ A. Patient suffers heart attack.

_______________ B. Patient suffers severe infection following colon surgery.

_______________ C. Patient experiences syncope after witnessing a traumatic event.

_______________ D. Patient experiences reaction to food allergy.

_______________ E. Choking patient has extreme difficulty breathing.

_______________ F. A diabetic patient lapses into coma.

_______________ G. Patient suffers serious head trauma.

_______________ H. Accident victim suffers extreme loss of blood.

6. A common procedure for treating closed wounds is to RICE them. What do the letters of this acronym stand for?

R_______________ I_______________ C_______________ E_______________

7. A. Match each type of open wound to its defining characteristics.

A. Incision
B. Puncture
C. Laceration
D. Avulsion
E. Abrasion

_____ 1. A wound that pierces and penetrates the skin. This wound may appear insignificant but actually go quite deep.

_____ 2. These wounds commonly occur at exposed body parts such as the fingers, toes, and nose. Tissue is torn off and wounds may bleed profusely.

_____ 3. A wound that results from a sharp object such as a knife.

_____ 4. A painful wound that involves nerve endings. The epidermal layer of the skin is scraped away.

_____ 5. A wound that results in a jagged tear of body tissues and may contain debris.

B. For each type of wound, describe proper emergency concerns, care, and treatment.

Incision ____

____

____

Puncture ____

____

____

Laceration ____

____

____

Avulsion ____

____

____

Abrasion ____

8. Name three sources other than heat that can cause burns. For each, describe the proper emergency concerns, care, and treatment.

(1) ____

(2) ____

(3) ____

9. Musculoskeletal injuries, or injuries to muscles, bones, and joints, can be difficult to triage, especially for closed fractures. List five assessment techniques health care professionals can use to determine the seriousness of musculoskeletal injuries.

(1) ____

(2) ____

(3) ____

(4) ____

(5) ____

10. For each set of symptoms that follows, identify the most likely emergency condition and describe emergency concerns, care, and treatment.

______________ A. Off-color, cold skin with a waxy appearance.

______________ B. Hives, itching, lightheadedness.

______________ C. Cold, clammy skin; profuse sweating; abdominal cramps; headache; general weakness.

_______________ D. Lightheadedness, weakness, nausea, unsteadiness.

____

____

_______________ E. Moist, pale skin; drooling; lack of appetite; diplopia; full pulse.

____

____

_______________ F. Numbness in face, arm, and leg on one side of body; slurred speech; nausea and vomiting.

____

____

_______________ G. Fever, convulsions, clenched teeth.

____

____

_______________ H. Cold, clammy skin; anxiety; dilated pupils; weak pulse; rigid boardlike abdomen post-surgery for hysterectomy.

____

____

11. Identify the method of entry into the body for each of the following poisons:

_______________ A. Carbon monoxide.

_______________ B. Insect stingers.

_______________ C. Chemical pesticides used in the garden.

_______________ D. Spoiled food.

_______________ E. Poison oak.

_______________ F. Cleaning fluid fumes.

12. A. On a scale of 1 to 5, rate your personal comfort in regard to the following emergency situations medical assistants may find themselves involved with in an ambulatory or urgent care setting.

1. Extremely uncomfortable
2. Uncomfortable
3. Somewhat comfortable
4. Comfortable
5. Very comfortable

_____ Assisting in treatment of patients with injuries clearly sustained by an act of violence or abuse.

_____ Performing the Heimlich maneuver on an unconscious person.

_____ Administering CPR to a child.

_____ Administering back blows and thrusts to a conscious infant.

_____ Performing rescue breathing on someone who has poor personal hygiene.

_____ Bandaging the open wound of an HIV-infected person.

_____ Caring for a person experiencing a seizure.

_____ Administering care to a patient who faints after venipuncture.

_____ Administering care to a patient in extreme pain.

_____ Administering care to a patient who is verbally abusive or uncooperative.

B. On a scale of 1 to 5, rate your level of agreement with the statements that follow.

1. Never.
2. Occasionally.
3. Sometimes.
4. Most of the time.
5. All of the time.

_____ Life-threatening emergencies frighten me.

_____ I respond well under pressure.

_____ I am bothered by the sight of blood.

_____ I lose my temper easily, becoming openly frustrated and angry.

_____ I become frustrated and overwhelmed by feelings of helplessness in emergency situations.

_____ I remain calm and clear headed in emergency situations.

_____ I forget about myself completely and focus on the emergency victim.

_____ I am concerned about administering care in emergency situations where danger to myself may exist when giving such care.

_____ I am comfortable speaking to the family or friends of emergency victims.

Emergency Procedures

Emergency Procedure 1

Lenore McDonell, a wheelchair-bound woman in her early thirties, experiences a serious laceration to the right arm sustained from a fall while performing an independent transfer from the examination table to her wheelchair. Joe Guerrero, CMA, assists Dr. Winston Lewis in administering emergency care.

1. What standard precautions must the health care professionals follow before administering emergency treatment?

____

____

____

2. Joe and Dr. Lewis attempt to control Lenore's bleeding by applying a dressing and pressing firmly.

A. When the bleeding does not stop, what two actions do the health care professionals perform?

(1) ____

(2) ____

B. In the unlikely event that bleeding continues, what piece of medical equipment will the health care team use in substitution of a tourniquet? Why is this alternative equipment effective and widely used today?

3. The bleeding stops, and Joe applies a pressure bandage over the dressing.

A. This patient is prone to fractures and will need to be Xrayed. What is the next emergency procedure Dr. Lewis will perform? Why is this procedure necessary and what equipment will the physician and medical assistant require?

B. Before applying a sling, what do the health care professionals check to be sure that the medical equipment used has not been too tightly applied?

4. What standard precautions will the health care team follow after the emergency treatment of the patient is successfully completed?

5. What information will the health care team include in documenting the procedure for the patient's medical record?

Emergency Procedure 2

New patient Grace Fisher comes to the offices of Drs. Lewis and King for a well baby visit with Dr. Elizabeth King for infant Joseph Michael. In the reception area, the baby is fussy, and Grace picks him up and holds him at her chest, rocking and gently patting the baby's back. Suddenly, the baby's face becomes red; it begins to cough and wheeze. When the baby does not quickly resume normal breathing, Ellen Armstrong, CMA, alerts Dr. King over the office intercom. As Ellen takes the baby from a bewildered and frightened Grace to begin rescue breathing in a nearby empty examination room, she motions to co-worker Joe Guerrero, CMA, to accompany them to attend to the mother's needs.

1. What four steps will Ellen perform to initiate rescue breathing?
   (1) ______
   (2) ______
   (3) ______
   (4) ______

2. Ellen checks for a pulse at the brachial artery. The pulse is present but the baby seems to have increased difficulty breathing. What sequence of actions will Ellen follow next? How long should Ellen continue this sequence?

   ______

   ______

   ______

3. After 3 minutes the baby is still conscious and has a pulse but is no longer able to cough, cry, or breathe. Dr. King has joined Grace and Ellen in the examination room.

   A. What procedure does Dr. King initiate at this time?

   ______

   B. What four steps does Dr. King follow to perform this procedure?
   (1) ______
   ______
   (2) ______
   ______
   (3) ______
   ______
   (4) ______
   ______

   C. How long will Dr. King continue this procedure?

   ______

4. The infant, Joseph Michael, loses consciousness. Grace becomes hysterical.

   A. As she shakes the infant to check for consciousness, Dr. King gives what two instructions to Joe?
   (1) ______
   (2) ______

   B. Dr. King begins to administer what procedure? How long will Dr. King administer this procedure? What happens if the baby loses a pulse?

   ______

   ______

5. On the second set of back blows and thrusts after the baby loses consciousness, Dr. King sweeps a bead out of the baby's mouth. Joseph Michael begins to cough and cry. A bead from Grace's sweater had come loose and lodged in the baby's trachea. "We've caught this just in time," Dr. King announces to a grateful and relieved mother.

   What follow-up procedures will the health care team initiate?

   ___

   ___

   ___

6. What information will the health care team include in documenting the procedure in the infant's medical record? in Grace's medical record?

   A. *Joseph Michael Fisher:*

   ___

   ___

   ___

   ___

   B. *Grace Fisher:*

   ___

   ___

   ___

   ___

Emergency Procedure 3

Edith Leonard, a frail widow in her early seventies, participates in the knitting club at the local senior center. As she knits, Edith becomes restless and begins to rub her chest and massage her jaw. Her breathing becomes shallow. Bruce Goldman, CMA, who volunteers at the senior center, remembers Edith as a patient at Inner City Health Care, where he works. When Edith slumps in her chair, Bruce rushes over.

1. When Bruce calls Edith's name, she nods her head. However, Edith seems to have extreme difficulty breathing and her face is contorted with pain. What is Bruce's first action?

   ___

2. Edith is no longer breathing. What procedure should Bruce initiate? What steps does Bruce follow in performing the procedure?

   ___

   ___

   ___

   ___

   ___

3. Edith is still not breathing and no pulse is present.

   A. What procedure does Bruce initiate?

   ____

   ____

   B. What is the correct method to administer chest compressions?

   ____

   ____

   C. How many slow breaths will Bruce administer after completing the chest compressions?

   ____

   ____

   D. How many times will Bruce repeat the sequence of chest compressions and rescue breathing before again checking Edith's pulse?

   ____

   ____

4. Under what four conditions is it acceptable for Bruce to stop administering this technique of chest compressions and rescue breathing?

   (1) ____

   (2) ____

   (3) ____

   (4) ____

5. After 10 minutes, EMS personnel arrive and transport Edith to a local hospital.

   A. What standard precautions will Bruce practice at the senior center after EMS personnel have transported the patient from the scene of the emergency?

   ____

   ____

   ____

   B. What supplies and equipment would the medical assistant have used if this emergency had taken place in an ambulatory care setting?

   ____

   ____

   ____

Investigation Activity

Educating patients and the general community about the responsibility to be prepared for addressing emergency situations is one role the medical assistant can perform in the ambulatory care setting. Health care professionals should encourage patients to keep complete emergency reference information in an easily accessible place in the home. Furthermore, patients should be encouraged to receive training in first aid and emergency procedures, including cardiopulmonary resuscitation (CPR), and to learn about strategies for creating a safer home environment. Complete the sample emergency information sheet below with the resources closest to your home and essential medical information relevant to your family.

As a class, designate one student to contact each of the six resources listed—fire department, poison control center, police department, ambulance service, local hospital emergency department, and primary care physician's office—to ask about emergency procedures and services each provides and to obtain any literature that is available about preventing or treating emergencies. Bring the information to class for discussion.

EMERGENCY INFORMATION FOR THE ____________________ FAMILY

Address: ______________________________

____

Telephone: ______________________________

Emergency Medical Services (EMS): Dial 911. If 911 is busy or does not answer, dial "0" (Operator) and ask for help. TDD/TTY for the Hearing Impaired, dial 311.

Fire Department

Address: ______________________________

Telephone: ______________________________

Poison Control Center

Address: ______________________________

Telephone: ______________________________

Police Department

Address: ______________________________

____

____

Telephone: ______________________________

Ambulance Service

Name: ______________________________

Address: ______________________________

____

Telephone: ______________________________

Local Hospital Emergency Department

Name: ______________________________

Address: ______________________________

Telephone: ______________________________

Primary Care Physician

Name: ______________________________

Address: ______________________________

Telephone: ______________________________

Names and ages of family members and any medical conditions or medications emergency medical professionals should know about.

1. ______________________________

2. ______________________________

3. ______________________________

4. ______________________________

5. ______________________________

6. ______________________________

Person, not at the household address, who should be contacted in case of emergency.

Name: ______________________________

Address: ______________________________

____

Relationship to family: ______________________________

Telephone: ______________________________

CASE STUDY

Mary O'Keefe calls Dr. King's office in a panic. Ellen Armstrong, CMA, answers the telephone. "Oh my God, help me. I need Dr. King."

"This is Ellen Armstrong, CMA. Who is this calling and what is the situation?"

"It's my baby, oh God, get Dr. King."

"Dr. King is unavailable, but we can help you. Now, tell me your name."

"It's Mary O'Keefe. Help me, I think my baby is dead."

"Are you at home?"

"Yes."

"Good. Tell me what's happened."

"My son Chris pried the plug off an outlet and he's electrocuted himself!" Mary cries. "He's just lying there. I'm so scared; if I touch him will I electrocute myself? Oh my God, my baby, my baby. What should I do?"

Ellen, who has been writing the details on a piece of paper motions to Joe Guerrero, another CMA in the office, and hands him her notes. Joe immediately accesses the O'Keefe's address from the patient database and uses another telephone line to call EMS with the nature of the emergency situation and directions to the O'Keefe's residence. Meanwhile, Ellen remains on the line with Mary. Dr. King is on rounds at the hospital this morning and won't be in the office for at least another hour.

"Mary, we're calling EMS and they will be there as soon as possible. In the meantime, I'm going to need you to focus and answer my questions. Okay?"

Discuss the following.

1. What steps does the medical assistant take to triage the emergency situation?
2. What questions should Ellen ask Mary regarding the emergency situation? Based on Mary's answers, what instructions should Ellen give Mary to begin emergency treatment?
3. What should the medical assistant do after EMS arrives and takes over emergency care? What follow-up procedures are necessary?

SUPPLEMENTARY RESOURCES

Study Guide Disks: Additional practice exercises for this chapter are available on the Study Guide Disk found in the back of the textbook.

Medical Assisting Videos: Appropriate content is available on Delmar's Medical Assisting Videos, 2nd ed., for the following topics:

Tape 2: Triage Skills
Tape 5: Standard Precautions
Infections in the Office
Tape 10: Recognize Emergencies
Workplace Hazards and Material Safety Data Sheets
Emergency Use of Oxygen in the Office
Introduction to Airway Obstruction
Abdominal Thrust (Heimlich maneuver)
Obstructed Airway in an Unconscious Patient
Diabetic Emergencies
Bandaging

EVALUATION OF CHAPTER KNOWLEDGE

How has your instructor evaluated the knowledge you have gained?

Knowledge	Instructor Evaluation *Good*	*Average*	*Poor*
Recognizes emergency situations	_____	_____	_____
Understands need for emergency preparation and the function of emergency medical services (EMS)	_____	_____	_____
Possesses the ability to triage emergency cases in person and over the telephone	_____	_____	_____
Understands legal and health considerations of emergency caregiving	_____	_____	_____
Understands necessity of providing emergency care only within the scope of training and knowledge	_____	_____	_____
Can assemble a medical crash tray or cart	_____	_____	_____
Understands the use of standard precautions in emergency situations	_____	_____	_____
Identifies signs and symptoms of shock, types of shock, and treatment of shock	_____	_____	_____
Identifies classification and care of wounds	_____	_____	_____
Identifies dressings, bandages, and their applications	_____	_____	_____
Identifies first-, second-, and third-degree burns and burn care	_____	_____	_____
Identifies musculoskeletal injuries, including types of fractures and strategies for care	_____	_____	_____
Identifies heat- and cold-related illnesses and priorities for care	_____	_____	_____
Understands how poisons enter the body	_____	_____	_____
Identifies sudden illnesses such as syncope, seizures, diabetes, and hemorrhage	_____	_____	_____
Recognizes cerebral vascular accident (CVA) and priorities for immediate emergency care	_____	_____	_____
Recognizes heart attack and priorities for immediate emergency care	_____	_____	_____
Can identify and name steps for performing these emergency procedures:			
Control of bleeding	_____	_____	_____
Applying a splint	_____	_____	_____
Heimlich maneuver	_____	_____	_____
Rescue breathing	_____	_____	_____
Cardiopulmonary resuscitation (CPR)	_____	_____	_____

Student's Initials:_______ Instructor's Initials:____

Grade:_______

The Therapeutic Approach to the Patient with AIDS

PERFORMANCE OBJECTIVES

As a member of the health care team, the medical assistant will be involved in the care of patients with severe infectious diseases, including AIDS. In addition to providing medical, surgical, and psychological care, the health care team relies on the assets of empathy and compassion in building a strong therapeutic approach to the treatment and care of AIDS patients. As a source of information for AIDS patients and their families and significant others, medical assistants need to be sensitive, supportive, and respectful of people who are suffering from a controversial disease that challenges many strongly held cultural beliefs and attitudes. Medical assistants should strive to promote AIDS education and awareness by informing patients at high risk for contracting AIDS about preventive measures. It is important for medical assistants to remain impartial and professional, making AIDS patients as comfortable and confident as possible in the ambulatory care setting.

EXERCISES AND ACTIVITIES

Vocabulary Builder

Insert the proper key vocabulary terms into the paragraph on the following page.

acquired immunodeficiency syndrome (AIDS)
dementia
hemophilia
human immunodeficiency virus (HIV)
libido
living will
opportunistic infections
pathogens
physician's directive
psychomotor retardation
retroviruses
ribonucleic acid (RNA)

The incurable infectious disease ______________________________ involves a flaw in cell-mediated immunity; diagnosis depends on a number of indicator conditions, including a T4 cell count that has dropped below 200. The disease is caused by a virus transmitted from the secretions and excretions of blood from an infected person to the bloodstream of an uninfected person. The transmittor virus, ______________________, is a member of the class of ______________________ that carry genetic material in their ______________________. As T4 cells are destroyed, the body is left open to ______________________ such as toxoplasmosis and tuberculosis, that exist from an altered physiological state of the host and are caused by disease-producing microorganisms called ______________________. Two groups of people at high risk for infection are those suffering from ______________________ or another coagulation disorder, and those who have received transfusions with infected blood or blood products. As the disease progresses, the central nervous system is involved, which causes many symptoms, including a loss of sexual drive, or ______________________; mental disorientation and confusion, called ______________________; and/or a slowing of motor activity, called ______________________. Many patients with this devastating disease choose to protect their treatment preferences at end-of-life by completing a ______________________. This legal document is considered a ______________________, a document that gives physicians advance instructions regarding patients' treatment wishes in emergency and end-of-life situations, when they may not be able to speak for themselves.

Learning Review

1. For each of the stages of progression from HIV infection to a diagnosis of AIDS listed, describe the defining factors contributing to the presence or absence of disease, or epidemiology, of each.

(1) Initial infection with HIV ______________________

____

____

____

____

____

(2) Asymptomatic stage ______________________

____

____

____

____

____

(3) Symptomatic stage ______

(4) Diagnosis of AIDS ______

2. Name the three methods of transmission of HIV.

(1) ______

(2) ______

(3) ______

3. List the five population groups in which AIDS is most commonly diagnosed.

(1) ______

(2) ______

(3) ______

(4) ______

(5) ______

4. A. Common conditions appearing in people with AIDS include immunologic (IM), integumentary (IT), respiratory (R), gastrointestinal (GI), and central nervous system (CNS) manifestations. Identify the conditions listed below according to their categories of manifestation by placing the proper abbreviation ("IM," "IT," "R," "GI," or "CNS") in the spaces provided.

___ Night sweats
___ Visual changes
___ Poor wound healing
___ Fatigue
___ Low white blood cell count
___ Nausea and vomiting
___ Lymphadenopathy
___ Shortness of breath
___ Memory loss
___ Headache

B. Opportunistic infections appearing in people with AIDS include these types: protozoal (P), fungal (F), bacterial (B), and viral (V). AIDS patients can also develop various malignancies (M). Identify each of the following conditions by its correct classification as an infection or malignancy by placing the proper abbreviation ("P," "F," "B," "V," or "M") in the spaces provided.

___ Candidiasis
___ Herpes simplex
___ Nocardiosis
___ Cryptosporidiosis
___ Kaposi's sarcoma
___ Hodgkin's lymphoma
___ *Pneumocystis carinii*
___ Tuberculosis
___ Cryptococcosis
___ Cytomegalovirus

5. Name six physical symptoms of the psychological suffering experienced by AIDS patients.

(1)____________________
(2)____________________
(3)____________________
(4)____________________
(5)____________________
(6)____________________

6. On a scale of 1 to 5, rate your personal comfort in regard to the following situations medical assistants may find themselves involved with in an ambulatory care setting.

1. Extremely uncomfortable 2. Uncomfortable 3. Somewhat comfortable
4. Comfortable 5. Very comfortable

____ Assisting in the care of substance abusers and drug-addicted patients.
____ Performing venipuncture on patients with high-risk lifestyles.
____ Touching HIV-infected individuals during the course of routine physical examinations.
____ Educating high-risk patients about preventive measures.
____ Maintaining a professional and nonjudgmental attitude about patient lifestyles and potential behaviors.
____ Following standard precautions for infection control.
____ Assessing your openness about homosexuality and acceptance of homosexual patients or co-workers.
____ Discussing AIDS in an open and frank manner with patients and their family members and significant others.
____ Facing your own fears and concerns about HIV infection and AIDS.

Investigaton Activity

One nonmedical form of assistance that medical assistants can provide to AIDS patients is the referral to national and community-based AIDS organizations, programs, hotlines, and service groups where AIDS patients can gather information and explore resources on topics ranging from insurance, legal, and financial concerns to better communications with family members, friends, and significant others.

A. Write or call an AIDS organization or hotline to request information available to AIDS patients and to the general public about coping with the disease. Bring the information to class. As a class, or in smaller groups, examine the brochures you are sent and discuss their content. Decide which brochures contain the best information and seem to be the most effective to recommend to patients and their families and significant others. Here are two national sources:

National Health Information Center
Office of Disease Prevention and Promotion
U. S. Department of Human Services
P. O. Box 1133
Washington, DC 20013-1133
800-336-4797

National AIDS Hotline
Centers for Disease Control and Prevention
Atlanta, GA 30333
800-342-AIDS

B. List two community-based groups located in the area where you live that supply information and services to AIDS patients.

Name: ______________________	Name: ______________________
Address: ____________________	Address: ____________________
____________________________	____________________________
____________________________	____________________________
Phone: _____________________	Phone: _____________________

CASE STUDIES

In working with AIDS patients, medical assistants hone their personal coping skills, capitalizing on strengths, maintaining hope, and showing continued human care and concern. For each case scenario presented, answer the following questions:

1. What is the best therapeutic response of the medical assistant?
2. On what criteria do you base this response as the best therapeutic approach?

Case 1

Jaime Carrera, a Hispanic man in his late twenties, is brought to Inner City Health Care, an urgent care center, by co-workers when he injures his head in an accident at a construction site where he is working. His head is bleeding profusely. As Jaime's co-workers watch the health care team implement standard precautions for infection control, one of them, his own shirt and hands covered with Jaime's blood, pulls the medical assistant aside and whispers frantically, "What are you doing? Does he have AIDS?"

Case 2

Mary O'Keefe is a new patient of Dr. Elizabeth King. Mary is undergoing prenatal care. After several office visits, Mary approaches administrative medical assistant Ellen Armstrong, CMA, and sheepishly apologizes for asking what Mary calls a "paranoid" question. "Ellen, do Doctors Lewis and King treat AIDS patients at this practice? Normally, I wouldn't be concerned about the risk, but I'm pregnant, you know, and I worry about the baby being exposed."

Case 3

A. Liz Corbin, CMA, a young African-American woman, works part-time at Inner City Health Care, an urgent care center that sponsors a treatment program for AIDS patients. Liz works professionally and compassionately with the AIDS patients she encounters during her hours at the clinic. On one stressful afternoon, however, Liz seeks out office manager Walter Seals, CMA. Liz breaks down and cries after assisting in the examination of a patient infected with HIV who discovered that she is pregnant and may pass HIV to her unborn child. Liz's ambition is to someday attend medical school to become a pediatrician. "Walter, this disease is so unfair," Liz says passionately. "I just can't take it any more."

B. About a month later, Liz is again assisting in the examination of the pregnant female HIV-infected patient. After the physician leaves the examination room, the woman turns to Liz, takes her hand, and says, "How can I afford this medicine? Why is this happening to me and to my baby?"

SUPPLEMENTARY RESOURCES

Study Guide Disk: Additional practice exercises for this chapter are available on the study guide disk found in the back of the textbook.

Medical Assisting Videos: Appropriate content is available on Delmar's Medical Assisting Videos, 2nd ed., for the following topics:

Tape 1: Communication Skills
Tape 5: Infection Control and Universal Precautions
Apply Principles of Aseptic Technique and Infection Control
Standard Precautions
Infections in the Office
Tape 8: Taking a Patient History
Introduction to Health Promotion, Disease Prevention, and Self-Responsibility
Tape 12: OSHA Regulations for Needles and "Sharps"
Accidental Needlesticks

EVALUATION OF CHAPTER KNOWLEDGE

Evaluate your own strengths and weaknesses in administering a therapeutic approach to the patient with AIDS. Compare this evaluation to the one provided by your instructor.

Skills achieved:

	Student Self-Evaluation			Instructor Evaluation		
Skills	*Good*	*Average*	*Poor*	*Good*	*Average*	*Poor*
Ability to describe the epidemiology of HIV and AIDS in lay terms	____	____	____	____	____	____
Identifies population groups in which the AIDS diagnosis is commonly found	____	____	____	____	____	____
Recognizes psychological problems that accompany AIDS	____	____	____	____	____	____
Identifies personal fears or concerns about assisting in the care and treatment of AIDS patients	____	____	____	____	____	____
Ability to treat AIDS patients with empathy, impartiality, and respect	____	____	____	____	____	____
Possesses working knowledge of conditions, manifestations, opportunistic infections, and malignancies that may appear in AIDS patients	____	____	____	____	____	____
Recognizes the demands of providing therapeutic care for AIDS patients in the ambulatory care setting	____	____	____	____	____	____
Ability to avoid emotional burnout when caring for AIDS patients	____	____	____	____	____	____
Understands the use of standard precautions for infection control in protecting themselves from AIDS infection	____	____	____	____	____	____
Advocates AIDS education and methods of disease prevention for high-risk individuals	____	____	____	____	____	____

Student's Initials:____ Instructor's Initials:_____

Grade:_________

CHAPTER 5

Taking a Medical History

PERFORMANCE OBJECTIVES

The patient's medical history is an invaluable tool in helping the physician treat the patient effectively. When taking or updating patient medical histories, medical assistants must be as thorough and accurate in documentation as possible, while remaining respectful of the patient's emotional needs and right to privacy. Therapeutic communication skills, including, but not limited to, active listening, recognizing nonverbal cues, and adapting communication to the patient's ability to understand, are essential to the process of obtaining accurate and complete patient medical histories.

EXERCISES AND ACTIVITIES

Vocabulary Builder

Match each key vocabulary term to the example that best describes it.

A. Allergies
B. Chart
C. Chief complaint
D. Clinical diagnosis
E. Debridement
F. Differential diagnosis
G. Familial
H. Objective sign
I. Problem-Oriented Medical Record (POMR)
J. SOAP
K. Source-Oriented Medical Record (SOMR)
L. Subjective complaint

______ **1.** 3/10/xx CC: NVD × 4 days. T > 100° F × 2 days. Loss of appetite.

Decode this chart note: ____

____

A mistake is made in the chart note on the previous page. Three days should be listed instead of four. Using the proper procedure for notation, enter a correction to the chart note in the space provided below:

3/10/xx CC: NVD × 4 days. T > 100° F × 2 days. Loss of appetite.

______ **2.** Diseases or conditions with genetic links such as breast and colon cancers, coronary artery disease, diabetes mellitus, and hypertension.

______ **3.** Removal of dead or damaged tissue or foreign debris.

______ **4.** Mary O'Keefe calls Dr. King's office to schedule an emergency appointment and tells Ellen Armstrong, CMA, that her 3-year-old son Chris awakened during the night with a high fever and extreme pain in his right ear.

______ **5.** Dr. King examines 3-year-old Chris O'Keefe's right ear with an otoscope and observes that the ear is inflamed; the ear is also draining.

______ **6.** When a 19-year-old young woman comes into Inner City Health Care with extreme abdominal pain localized to the lower right quadrant, vomiting, slight fever, and loss of appetite, Dr. Whitney orders a CBC, a urinalysis, and an abdominal ultrasound to distinguish between possible diagnoses of acute appendicitis or an ovarian cyst that has become twisted.

Include proper insurance coding for each test Dr. Whitney has ordered, to be included on the patient's charge slip.

(1) ______________________________

(2) ______________________________

(3) ______________________________

What are the proper diagnosis codes for the two diagnoses Dr. Whitney is investigating for this emergency patient?

(1) ______________________________

(2) ______________________________

Will the physician code a diagnosis for the patient at this time? If so, what diagnosis will be used? If not, what kind of information will the physician code in place of a diagnosis?

____

____

______ **7.** Dr. Whitney confirms a diagnosis of acute appendicitis for the female emergency patient, based on subjective and objective information accumulated from the patient's history, the findings of the physical examination, and the results of the laboratory tests ordered.

______ **8.** A patient's file of medical history and treatment, kept by the physician.

______ **9.** A traditional form of charting that consists of a chronological set of notes for each visit, beginning with the patient's first visit.

______ **10.** Charting method that lists patient data in the following order: Subjective/Objective/Assessment/Plan.

_____ **11.** An acquired sensitivity to a substance (allergen) that does not normally cause a reaction.

_____ **12.** The most efficient way of recording chart notes, especially in multi-physician clinics or practices.

Learning Review

1. Every physician/patient interview is a cross-cultural one. List four questions a medical assistant might ask while taking a medical history that will help bridge social and cultural beliefs to obtain accurate information about a patient's condition that the physician will need to give proper care and treatment.

   (1) ______________________________

   (2) ______________________________

   (3) ______________________________

   (4) ______________________________

2. List the nine possible characteristics of patient chief complaints:

   (1) ____________________ (6) ____________________

   (2) ____________________ (7) ____________________

   (3) ____________________ (8) ____________________

   (4) ____________________ (9) ____________________

   (5) ____________________

3. Decode each component of the chart note excerpt listed below.

A.	7/15/xxxx	
B.	CC: lower abdominal pain × 1 wk c̄ ↑ malaise.	
C.	Wt. 135 Ht. 5′5″ T 99.8°F R 19 clear P 78 regular BP 134/82	
D	Pt describes ↑ urge to urinate c̄ burning sensation on urination; pressure in abdomen; lack of energy.	
E.	Past Med Hist	freq. UTIs dx Type II diabetes mellitus 1987; Rx Glynase 3 mg tab qd quit smoking 20 yrs ago weight ↓ 10lbs in last 2 yrs.
F.	Allergies	no known
G.	Family Hist	no Δ
H.	Habits	< 2 glasses wine per wk no smoking, regular exercise

A. ______________________________

B. ______________________________

C. ______________________________

D. ______________________________

E. ______________________________

F. ______________________________

G. ______________________________

H. ______________________________

4. After the history is taken by the medical assistant, the physician will perform a review of systems (ROS). In addition to the patient's general state of health, list ten body systems the physician will assess during the ROS.

(1) ____________	(6) ____________
(2) ____________	(7) ____________
(3) ____________	(8) ____________
(4) ____________	(9) ____________
(5) ____________	(10) ____________

Investigation Activity

It is important for the medical assistant to be aware of his or her own family medical history. Knowledge of diseases and conditions that occur within one's family can give a health care team invaluable information that may aid in a swift, accurate diagnosis and treatment of health problems. And, a knowledge of diseases and illnesses that "run" in families can give individuals an important head start in pursuing effective preventive measures.

Create your own family medical genogram. This genogram, or "family" tree, can be referenced quickly and easily and will reveal patterns of disease or illness within your family. You'll want to start by including four generations: yourself, your siblings (if any), your children (if any), your parents, and your grandparents. The genogram should only include individuals who are related to you by blood. Create the genogram using the following symbols recommended by the Task Force of the North American Primary Care Research Group:

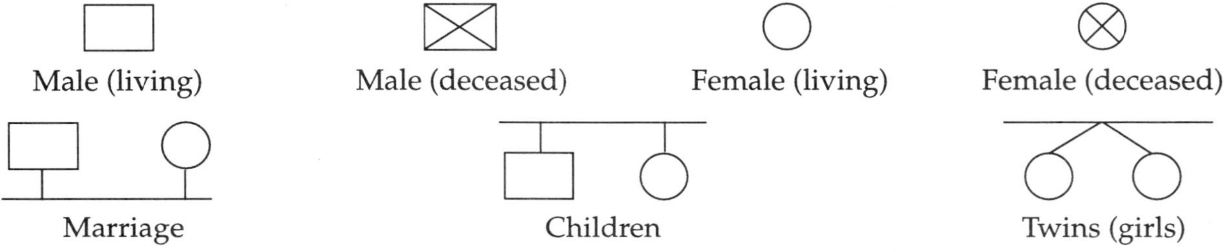

Within each symbol, fill in the relative's name and year of birth. Also include the year of death for those who are deceased. Underneath each symbol, write in as many diseases, conditions, or health care problems specific to that relative of which you are aware. For example, a relative may smoke, be overweight, or have had a heart attack. Use the completed genogram to evaluate your own health priorities and to adopt healthy lifestyle changes accordingly.

Here is a sample completed genogram for Martin Gordon and his sister Margaret.

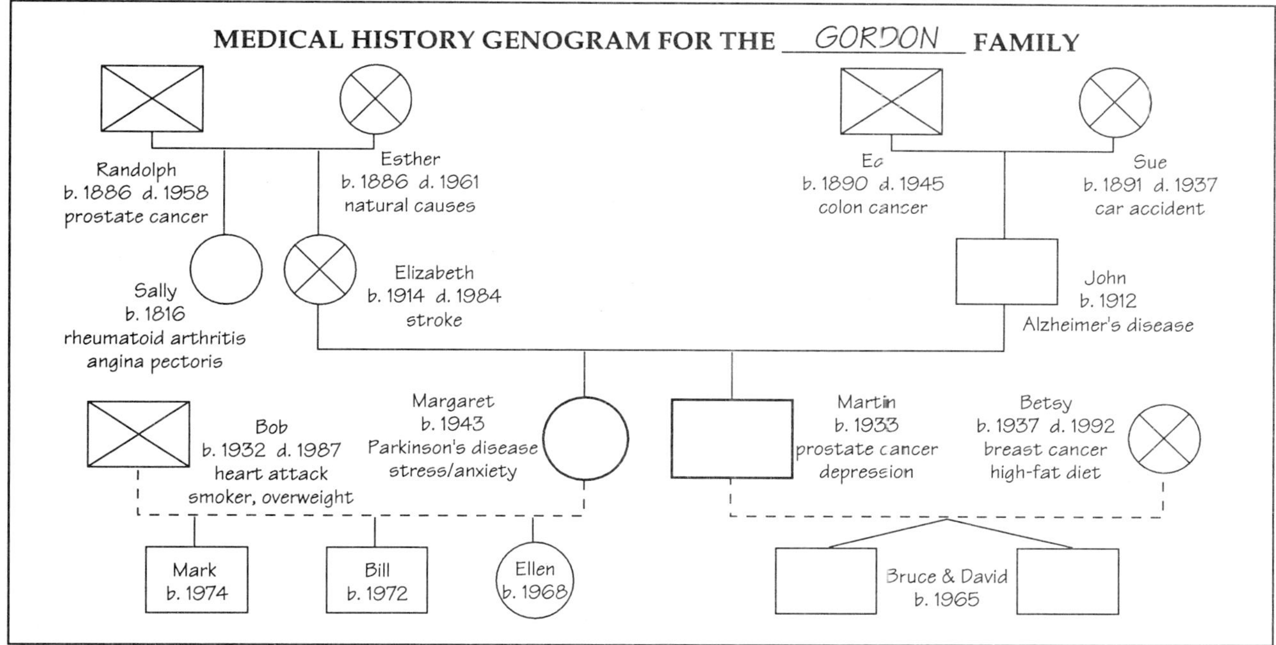

Complete the genogram below, which has been started, by entering symbols to represent your grandparents.

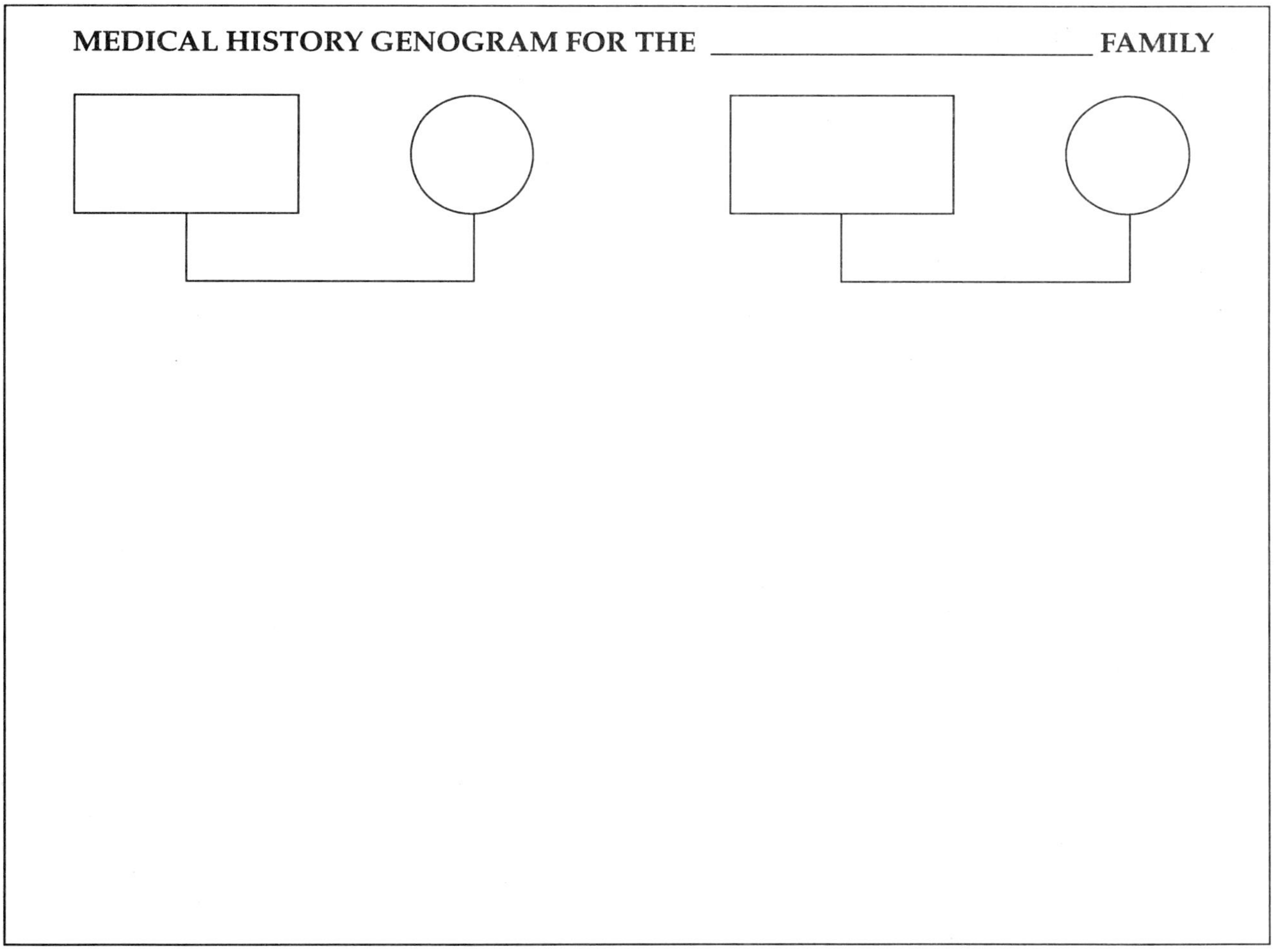

MEDICAL HISTORY GENOGRAM FOR THE ______________________ FAMILY

CASE STUDY

Nancy Catalina is a new patient of Dr. Esposito's at Inner City Health Care. Nancy, an 88-year-old Italian-born woman, comes to see Dr. Esposito at the urging of her granddaughter Leslie, who has set up the appointment for her. Nancy's primary care physician of thirty-five years has just retired; her only criteria for a new physician is that the physician must be of Italian descent.

When scheduling the appointment, Leslie notes to Liz Corbin, CMA, her grandmother's past medical history of mild angina pectoris, high blood pressure, hiatal hernia, and rheumatoid arthritis. On the day of the exam, Liz questions Nancy directly about her medical history. Nancy talks extensively about her aches and pains, moving back and forth in time between current problems and problems that took place as distant as forty years ago. In each case, a gentle reminder from her granddaughter brings Nancy back to a discussion of her present physical condition. Upon each reminder, Nancy acknowledges the difference between past and current events and admits she had gotten off track, though this is not readily apparent from her answers to Liz. It is clear that Leslie's knowledge of her grandmother's life and medical history makes it possible for Leslie to distinguish between events in Nancy's past and events in her present, guiding her back to the task at hand: taking a current medical history for the patient's permanent record.

Discuss the following:

1. What communications skills will Liz need to use to get the most accurate information from Nancy?
2. What can the manner in which this patient relates information reveal about her?
3. What effect does Nancy's granddaughter have on the process of taking the medical history? Is the effect beneficial or disruptive?

SUPPLEMENTARY RESOURCES

Study Guide Disk: Additional practice exercises for this chapter are available on the study guide disk found in the back of the textbook.

Medical Assisting Videos: Appropriate content is available on Delmar's Medical Assisting Videos, 2nd ed. Tape 8, for the following topics:

Interview and Take Patient History
Take an In-depth Patient History
Introduction to Health Promotion, Disease Prevention, and Self-Responsibility

SKILLS COMPETENCY ASSESSMENT

Procedure 5–1: Taking a Medical History

Student's Name: ______________________________ Date: ____________

Objective: To obtain a medical history from a patient new to the ambulatory care setting.

Conditions: To obtain a medical history from a new patient using the following equipment and supplies: patient history forms, clipboard, pens.

Time Requirements and Accuracy Standards: 15 minutes. Points assigned reflect importance of step to meeting objective: Important = (5) Essential = (10) Critical = (15). Automatic failure results if any of the **critical** tasks are omitted or performed incorrectly.

SKILLS ASSESSMENT CHECKLIST

Task Performed	Possible Points	TASKS
❑	5	Performs introductions. Confirms identity of new patient and escorts to examination room or private area.
❑	5	Makes eye contact and uses positive body language to put patient at ease.
❑	5	Explains purpose and importance of obtaining patient information. Asks questions on the form, trying to get as much information as possible without letting the patient deviate from the subject.
❑	10	Asks each question clearly. Makes sure patient understands all questions.
❑	15	Repeats the patient's answers when needed to confirm. Is specific in documentation of answers.
❑	10	Writes legibly using dark ink (blue or black).
❑	15	Rechecks the medical history form for completeness. Notes any additional information provided by the patient. Makes sure numbers, dates, spelling, and other information are accurate and legible.
❑	5	Prepares the patient for the review of systems and physical examination, if indicated.
❑	10	Documents the procedure.
❑	5	Completed the tasks within 15 minutes.
❑	15	Results obtained were accurate.

________	Earned	ADD POINTS OF TASKS CHECKED
100	Points	TOTAL POINTS POSSIBLE
________	SCORE	DETERMINE SCORE (divide points earned by total points possible, multiply results by 100)

SKILLS COMPETENCY ASSESSMENT — continued

Procedure 5–1: Taking a Medical History

Actual Student Time Needed to Complete Procedure: ____________

Student's Initials: ____________ Instructor's Initials: ____________ Grade: ____________

Suggestions for Improvement: ____

____

____

____

Evaluator's Name (print) ____

Evaluator's Signature ____

Comments ____

DOCUMENTATION

Chart the procedure in the patient's medical record.

Date: ____________________

Charting: ____

____

____

____

Student's Initials: ______________

EVALUATION OF CHAPTER KNOWLEDGE

How has your instructor evaluated the knowledge you have achieved?

Knowledge	**Instructor Evaluation** *Good*	*Average*	*Poor*
Understands the necessity and function of the medical history in patient treatment	______	______	______
Defines the parts of the medical history	______	______	______
Identifies and uses effective methods of interacting with patient	______	______	______
Obtains a medical history from patient	______	______	______
Explains different methods of charting/documentation	______	______	______
Defines SOAP and relates the function of this charting approach	______	______	______
Understands issues of cultural sensitivity in taking a medical history	______	______	______
Adapts communication to individuals' abilities to understand	______	______	______
Performs within ethical boundaries	______	______	______
Exhibits therapeutic communications skills	______	______	______
Documents accurately	______	______	______
Serves as liaison between physician and others	______	______	______

Student's Initials: ______ Instructor's Initials: ______

Grade: _______

CHAPTER 6

Vital Signs and Measurements

PERFORMANCE OBJECTIVES

One of the primary tasks of medical assistants is measuring patients' vital signs. The vital or cardinal signs—temperature, pulse, respiration (TPR) and blood pressure (B/P)—are important indicators of general health and must be measured and recorded with care. Because every individual's normal vital signs are different from those of every other person, the initial visit at any medical practice is usually used to record the patient's baseline vital signs. The baseline gives medical professionals an idea of what is normal for that patient and provides a point of comparison for use during future visits. For this reason, accuracy is especially important when recording vital signs at each patient's first visit. Medical assistants need to recognize factors that may influence the results of vital signs. Weight and height measurements may also be taken as further indications of the patient's condition. Aseptic techniques must be observed when taking patients' vital signs.

EXERCISES AND ACTIVITIES

Vocabulary Builder

Insert one of the following key vocabulary terms into each sentence describing a clinical situation.

Apnea
Arrhythmia
Baseline
Bradycardia
Bradypnea
Cheyne-Stokes
Diastole
Dyspnea
Emphysema
Eupnea
Frenulum
Hyperpnea
Hypertension
Hyperventilation
Hypotension
Hypoventilation
Orthopnea
Rales
Rhonchi
Stertorous
Stridor
Systole
Tachycardia
Tachypnea
Wheezes

1. Maria Jover comes to the office of Drs. Lewis and King complaining that she cannot breathe when she lies down. Joe Guerrero, CMA, notes ________________________ on her chart.

2. Winston Lewis, M. D., warns Herb Fowler that he is at risk of ________________________, a chronic pulmonary condition that causes destruction of air sacs in the lungs, if he does not quit smoking.

3. Liz Corbin, CMA, writes ________________________ on Annette Samuels's chart when she counts the patient's respiration rate at 35 breaths per minute.

4. A. "I'm so tired lately; I barely have the energy to get out of bed," Martin Gordon tells Audrey Jones, CMA, when he comes in for a regular exam. Audrey suspects moderate ________________________ and immediately takes Martin's blood pressure.

   B. Audrey's reading confirms that Martin's ________________________ measurement is 45 and alerts Dr. Elizabeth Lewis to the patient's possible problem.

5. As Bruce Goldman, CMA, measures young Henry Hansen's respiration rate, he hears the bubbling, crackling sound known as ________________________ each time Henry inhales.

6. Wanda Slawson, CMA, is taking Edith Leonard's temperature orally. She is careful to insert the thermometer in the side of Edith's mouth, just beside her ________________________ .

7. Marissa O'Keefe is rushed to see Elizabeth King, M. D., after swallowing a coin. Dr. King can clearly hear a crowing ________________________ when the toddler tries to inhale, so she knows that the obstruction is in the upper airway.

8. At a scheduled exam, Lenny Taylor's pulse is recorded at a regular 40 beats per minute: ________________________ .

9. Rhoda Au seems nervous and agitated during her first visit to Inner City Health Care, and Bruce Goldman, CMA, notes her respiration rate at over 35 breaths per minute. To ease her ________________________, he speaks to Rhoda calmly and has her breathe into a paper bag.

10. Audrey Jones, CMA, notices that Nora Fowler's breathing occasionally stops, then starts, as she measures it. Audrey is sure to tell Dr. King of her concern about this unexplained ________________________ .

11. Bruce Goldman, CMA, can hear a distinct snoring sound in the throat called ________________________, when he measures Leo McKay's respiration rate.

12. Jim Marshall's ________________________ measurement is a high 160 when Joe Guerrero, CMA, measures his blood pressure.

13. Dr. Winston Lewis takes careful note of Mr. Marshall's 160/100 blood pressure reading and discusses with him the dangers of ________________________ and the possible need of medication to control this condition.

14. Liz Corbin, CMA, notices an unusual breathing pattern in Cele Little: a period of apnea, then a deepening and quickening respiration rate, and finally a slowing rate and a return to apnea. Angie Esposito, M. D., diagnoses the pattern as the rare ________________________ .

15. On Bill Schwartz's recommendation, Jeffrey Karr visits Inner City Health Care for a physical. Since it is Jeffrey's first visit to the clinic, Ray Reynolds, M. D., is sure to order that ________________________ temperature, pulse, respiration, and blood pressure readings be taken.

16. Abigail Johnson's breathing is noticeably labored at one of her checkups. Joe Guerrero, CMA, notes this ______________________ on her chart.

17. Three-year-old Chris O'Keefe has had what seems to be a persistent chest cold for weeks. Audrey Jones, CMA, hears high-pitched ______________________ when he exhales, leading Dr. Winston Lewis to consider asthma instead.

18. David Kipperley visits Inner City Health Care for a persistent choking problem, but Wanda Slawson, CMA, notices that his breathing is shallow and his respiration rate is 10 breaths per minute. She alerts James Whitney, M. D., to this ______________________.

19. Audrey Jones, CMA, who has always been fond of patient Lenore McDonnell, is happy to note that Lenore's normal respiration indicates ______________________.

20. Dottie Tate's breath sounds are all normal, but her respiration is very slow—only 8 or 9 breaths per minute. This ______________________ worries Liz Corbin, CMA, so she notes it prominently on Dottie's chart.

21. While checking John O'Keefe's pulse, Joe Guerrero, CMA, notes a decided ______________________: a premature contraction or PVC.

22. Bill Schwartz is suffering from a persistent cough. Bruce Goldman, CMA, can hear a distinct snoring sound in the lungs when his listens to Bill's labored breathing. Dr. Ray Reynolds confirms that this ______________________ respiration may be related to the problem.

23. Juanita Hansen's resting pulse rate is 100 beats per minute. This ______________________ concerns Susan Rice, M. D., who orders a series of cardiac tests to try to find its cause.

24. Louise Kipperley comes to the clinic with a high fever. Wanda Slawson, CMA, confirms Louise's fast and deep respiratory rate, remembering that ______________________ is commonly seen in feverish patients.

Learning Review

1. Body temperature can be affected by many factors. An elevated or depressed body temperature may be a sign of disease or it may be normal for the person being examined.

   A. How is body heat produced? What part of the brain maintains the balance between the body's heat production and heat loss?

   ____

   ____

   B. List five processes that cause a body to lose heat. Then match each one to the example that best describes it.

   ___ 1. ______________________ ___ 4. ______________________

   ___ 2. ______________________ ___ 5. ______________________

   ___ 3. ______________________

A. Ellen Armstrong, CMA, climbs into a cold bed on a February night.

B. Anna Preciado, CMA, enjoys a good aerobic workout, which produces a full-body sweat.

C. On a trip to New York City, Bruce Goldman, CMA, attends a taping of the *Late Show with David Letterman*, known for its cold studio temperatures.

D. Karen Ritter, CMA, uses a portable fan to get through a temporary breakdown in the air-conditioning system on a July day at Inner City Health Care.

E. Liz Corbin, CMA, performs her daily routine of yoga breathing exercises.

C. List three factors that may increase body temperature.

(1)____________________________

(2)____________________________

(3)____________________________

D. List three factors that may decrease body temperature.

(1)____________________________

(2)____________________________

(3)____________________________

E. What is a synonym for *fever?* ____________________ List four categories of fevers. Then match each one to the examples that best describe it.

___ 1. ____________________________________

___ 2. ____________________________________

___ 3. ____________________________________

___ 4. ____________________________________

A. The patient's temperature fluctuates from 99° to 100° to 99°F.

B. The patient's temperature returns to normal for three days then rises again to 99.5°F.

C. The patient's temperature fluctuates from 99° to 98.4° to 99.3°F.

D. The patient's temperature fluctuates from 99.8° to 100°F for a period of two days.

2. A. Fill in the normal range of blood pressure for each of the following life stages.

Infant ____________________________________

Child, age 6 ________________________________

Child, age 10 _______________________________

Adolescent, age 16 ___________________________

Adult ____________________________________

B. How can each of the following factors affect a patient's blood pressure?

Blood volume ________________________________

____

Peripheral resistance __________________________

____

Vessel elasticity _____________________________

____

Condition of the heart muscle ______________________________

____

Name four other factors that can affect blood pressure.

(1)______________________ (3) ______________________

(2)______________________ (4) ______________________

C. What is the name of the sounds heard during blood pressure measurement?

______________ The sounds have five distinct phases. The act of listening for the sounds is called ______________. Identify each phase and explain what is happening in the body during that phase and what kind of sound is heard.

______________ A. This phase may be used to record the diastolic pressure in children and in those patients where a tapping sound is heard to zero.

____

____

______________ B. This phase occurs as the blood pressure cuff deflates.

____

____

______________ C. This phase is recorded as the diastolic pressure.

____

____

______________ D. This phase begins with the first sound heard and is used to determine the systolic reading of the blood pressure.

____

____

______________ E. If earlier phases are missed, this phase may be erroneously recorded as the systolic pressure.

____

____

3. A. Define hypertension. What are the four types of hypertension?

____

____

(1)______________________ (3) ______________________

(2)______________________ (4) ______________________

B. Define hypotension. What are three possible causes of hypotension?

____

____

(1)________________________________

(2)________________________________

(3) ________________________________

4. Fill in the normal pulse rate range for each of the following life stages.

Birth ________________________________

Infant (< 1 year) ________________________

Child age 1–7 __________________________

Child > age 7 __________________________

Adult ________________________________

5. Describe each of these common pulse abnormalities.

Bradycardia ____

Tachycardia ____

PVC ____

Sinus arrhythmia ____

6. Identify the name of each common pulse site described below and match the site to its proper location on the body by placing the correct letter in the spaces provided.

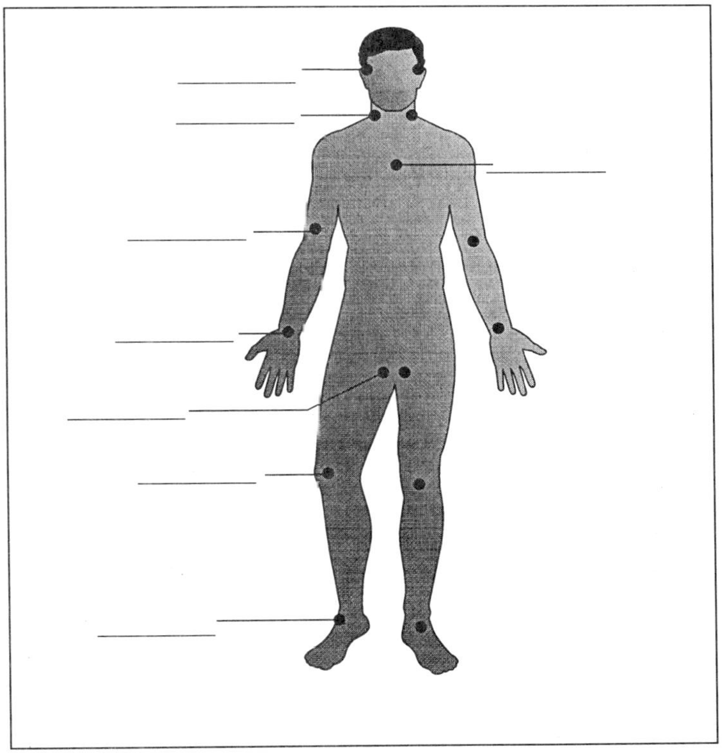

A. The site most commonly used for blood pressure readings.

____

____

B. The site used for leg blood pressure measurements to monitor circulation.

____

____

C. The site commonly used for infant pulse rates.

____

____

D. The site used in emergencies and when performing CPR.

____

E. The site used to control circulation or monitor bleeding from the head and scalp.

____

F. The site used to monitor lower limb circulation.

____

G. The site most commonly used to take a pulse rate.

____

H. The site used to control bleeding in the thigh.

____

7. Fill in the normal range of respiratory rates for each of the following life stages.

Infant ______________

Child age 1–7 ______________

Adult ______________

8. List the five abnormal breath sounds that may be heard during a check of the vital signs. Briefly describe how each may be recognized.

1. ______________
2. ______________
3. ______________
4. ______________
5. ______________

9. A. What are the four characteristics of the pulse? Define each.

(1) ______________

(2) ______________

(3) ______________

(4) ______________

B. What are the three characteristics of respiration? Define each.

(1) ______________

(2) ______________

(3) ______________

C. What is the normal ratio relationship of the respiration to the pulse rate? ______________

D. Determine how your pulse and respiration rates change during different physical activities. Chart your own pulse and respiration rates for each of the following.

(1) After 3 minutes at rest, seated in a straight-backed chair, feet resting on the floor, and hands resting on the thighs.

____

(2) After 3 minutes of marching in place at a comfortable pace.

____

(3) After 3 minutes of strong aerobic activity, such as jumping jacks or jogging in place.

___

(4) Note the variations in the characteristics of the pulse and respiration as your body moved from rest to strong activity.

___

___

(5) Calculate the ratio of respiration to pulse for your resting, active, and aerobic rates listed earler. Show your calculations in the spaces provided.

Rest Active Aerobic

___

Investigation Activity

Baseline vital signs can differ widely among healthy people. What is normal for one person may be an indication of illness for another. It is important for medical assistants to appreciate and understand these variations as well as the variations that different measurement methods can cause.

A. Choose one method of temperature measurement and use it to obtain baseline body temperatures for ten different people who are not suffering from any illnesses. Your subjects should be as varied as possible in age and other factors; be sure to include both males and females. Try to take each temperature at the same time of day. Fill in all of the information required in the chart below, using the proper method of recording temperatures.

Baseline Temperature Chart

Measurement Method Used: ___

Patient	Age	Gender	Time of Day	Temperature
A				
B				
C				
D				
E				
F				
G				
H				
I				
J				

What conclusions can you draw from this sample? ___

___

___

___

What other variables can you think of that might affect baseline body temperature? ________

____

____

____

B. Now take several temperature readings on one patient using each type of measurement equipment. Take the readings in sequence, all at one time. Fill in the chart below, using the proper method of recording temperatures.

Temperature Measurement Methods

Patient Age: __________ **Gender:** __________ **Time of Day:** __________

Method	Temperature
Mercury thermometer, oral	
Mercury thermometer, rectal	
Mercury thermometer, axillary	
Disposable strip thermometer, oral	
Digital thermometer, oral	
Tympanic thermometer, aural	

What conclusions can you draw from this experiment? ________________

____

____

____

Why do you think body temperature readings are affected by the methods used to measure them?

____

____

____

CASE STUDIES

As a medical assistant, you can expect to take patients' vital signs as a regular part of your work routine. You will have to make decisions about the equipment and methods used to make these measurements and answer patients' questions about each procedure. For each of the following scenarios, discuss the following.

1. What measurement method and/or site is the medical assistant most likely to use in this case, and why?
2. What is the medical assistant's best therapeutic response to the patient?

Case 1

Wayne Elder lives near Inner City Health Care in a group home for developmentally disabled adults. Wayne has a history of ear infections and colds in both ears. He visits the clinic one morning with dizziness and pain in his right ear. As Wanda Slawson, CMA, prepares to take Wayne's temperature, she learns that he drank a cup of hot coffee just before walking to the clinic. Wayne Elder asks, "How come you need to know what I ate? It's my ear that hurts."

Case 2

Henry Hansen is rushed to Inner City Health Care unconscious. He is bleeding profusely from a cut on his face. "He fell down the stairs," sobs Henry's mother, Juanita. Administrative medical assistant Karen Ritter alerts Dr. James Whitney, one of the clinic physicians, and calls 911 to summon emergency services personnel. The first thing clinical medical assistant Bruce Goldman does, after determining that Henry is breathing, is to take Henry's pulse. "What are you doing?" Juanita who is almost hysterical now, screams. "Why aren't you waking him up?"

Case 3

A. Abigail Johnson, who suffers from many of the problems of advancing age, including diabetes mellitus, is an elderly patient of Elizabeth King, M.D. A friendly woman, Abigail has a good rapport with everyone in the office—all of whom, she says, are "just like family"—and is eager to please the staff. One winter day she comes in with possible flu symptoms. As Audrey Jones, CMA, goes through the usual check of vital signs, Abigail audibly changes her breathing pattern, deepening and regularizing her respiration.

B. When Audrey asks Abigail to prepare for a weight measurement, Abigail says, "Oh, do we have to do that today? I'm just not up to it. Besides, I don't want to know how much I weigh right now. When I feel better, then I'll focus on losing more weight. You understand how I feel, don't you?"

SUPPLEMENTARY RESOURCES

Study Guide Disk: Additional practice exercises for this chapter are available on the study guide disk found in the back of the textbook.

Medical Assisting Videos: Appropriate content is available on Delmar's Medical Assisting Videos, 2nd ed., for the following topics:

Tape 6 Take Vital Signs
- Take and Record Oral Temperature Using a Glass Thermometer
- Take and Record Rectal Temperature
- Take and Record Oral Temperature Using an Electronic Thermometer
- Take and Record An Aural (Ear) Temperature
- Take and Record Axillary (Underarm) Temperature
- Take and Record a Radial Pulse
- Take and Record a Brachial Pulse (Infant)
- Use a Stethoscope to Take an Apical Pulse (Adult)
- Use a Stethoscope to Take an Apical Pulse (Infant)
- Take and Record Respiration

Tape 7 Take and Record Blood Pressure
- Measure Height and Weight Using an Upright Scale

SKILLS COMPETENCY ASSESSMENT

Procedure 6–1: Taking an Oral Temperature Using a Mercury Thermometer

Student's Name: ______________________________ Date: ____________

Objective: To obtain an oral temperature.

Conditions: The student demonstrates the ability to take an oral temperature using the following equipment and supplies: mercury thermometer, disposable thermometer sheaths, gloves, paper towels, biohazard waste container.

Time Requirements and Accuracy Standards: 10 minutes. Points assigned reflect importance of step to meeting objective: Important = (5) Essential = (10) Critical = (15). Automatic failure results if any of the **critical** tasks are omitted or performed incorrectly.

STANDARD PRECAUTIONS:

SKILLS ASSESSMENT CHECKLIST

Task Performed	Possible Points	TASKS
☐	5	Washes hands and follows standard precautions.
☐	5	Assembles equipment.
☐	5	Identifies patient and positions patient comfortably.
☐	10	Determines if patient has ingested hot or cold food or drink, or has smoked, in the previous half hour.
☐	5	*Rationale:* Understands that food ingestion or smoking can arbitrarily affect oral temperature reading.
☐	5	Explains procedure.
☐	10	Shakes thermometer until it reads below 96.0°F.
☐	5	Covers thermometer with sheath.
☐	5	Applies gloves.
☐	5	Inserts thermometer under patient's tongue to the side of the mouth.
☐	5	*Rationale:* Understands the anatomy of the tongue and the need to avoid the patient's frenulum.
☐	10	Instructs patient to close mouth around thermometer but not to place the teeth on it.
☐	5	*Rationale:* Understands the necessity of preventing air leakage and to avoid patient biting.
☐	15	Leaves in place for 3 to 5 minutes.

Task Performed	Possible Points	TASKS
❑	10	Removes thermometer from mouth, removing sheath and disposing it in a biohazard waste container.
❑	5	Holds thermometer at eye level and reads the result.
❑	5	Washes thermometer in cool water, rinses, dries, and places it on clean paper towel.
❑	5	Removes gloves and discards in a biohazard waste container.
❑	5	Washes hands.
❑	5	Places thermometer in disinfectant solution.
❑	5	*Rationale:* Understands that thermometer must remain in disinfectant solution for 30 minutes.
❑	15	Records temperature in patient chart and documents procedure.
❑	5	Completed the tasks within 10 minutes.
❑	15	Results obtained were accurate.

_________	Earned	ADD POINTS OF TASKS CHECKED
170	Points	TOTAL POINTS POSSIBLE
_________	SCORE	DETERMINE SCORE (divide points earned by total points possible, multiply results by 100)

Actual Student Time Needed to Complete Procedure: ____________

Student's Initials: ____________ Instructor's Initials: ____________ Grade: ____________

Suggestions for Improvement: ____________

Evaluator's Name (print) ____________

Evaluator's Signature ____________

Comments ____________

DOCUMENTATION

Chart the results in the patient's medical record.

Date: ____________

Charting: ____________

____

____

____

____

Student's Initials: ____________

SKILLS COMPETENCY ASSESSMENT

Procedure 6–2: Taking an Oral Temperature Using a Disposable Oral Strip

Student's Name: ______________________________ Date: __________

Objective: To obtain an oral temperature.

Conditions: The student demonstrates the ability to measure oral temperature using the following equipment and supplies: oral strip thermometer, gloves, biohazard waste container.

Time Requirements and Accuracy Standards: 5 minutes. Points assigned reflect importance of step to meeting objective: Important = (5) Essential = (10) Critical = (15). Automatic failure results if any of the **critical** tasks are omitted or performed incorrectly.

STANDARD PRECAUTIONS:

SKILLS ASSESSMENT CHECKLIST

Task Performed	Possible Points	TASKS
❑	5	Washes hands and follows standard precautions.
❑	5	Assembles equipment.
❑	5	Identifies patient and positions patient comfortably.
❑	10	Determines if patient has ingested hot or cold food or drink, or has smoked, in previous half hour.
❑	5	*Rationale:* Understands that food ingestion or smoking can arbitrarily affect oral temperature reading.
❑	5	Explains procedure.
❑	5	Applies gloves.
❑	10	Inserts oral strip thermometer under patient's tongue to the side of the mouth.
❑	5	*Rationale:* Understands the anatomy of the tongue and the need to avoid the patient's frenulum.
❑	10	Instructs patient to close mouth around thermometer but not to place the teeth on it.
❑	15	Leaves in place for 60 seconds.
❑	15	Removes thermometer and waits 10 seconds.
❑	5	*Rationale:* Understands that time is needed for strip to stabilize and record accurate temperature.

Task Performed	Possible Points	TASKS
❑	15	Reads temperature by locating the last dot that has changed color.
❑	10	Discards strip in a biohazard waste container.
❑	5	Removes gloves and discards in a biohazard waste container.
❑	5	Washes hands.
❑	10	Records temperature in patient chart and documents procedure.
❑	5	Completed the tasks within 5 minutes.
❑	15	Results obtained were accurate.

________	Earned	ADD POINTS OF TASKS CHECKED
165	Points	TOTAL POINTS POSSIBLE
________	SCORE	DETERMINE SCORE (divide points earned by total points possible, multiply results by 100)

Actual Student Time Needed to Complete Procedure: ____________

Student's Initials: ____________ Instructor's Initials: ____________ Grade: ____________

Suggestions for Improvement: ____

____

____

____

Evaluator's Name (print) ____

Evaluator's Signature ____

Comments ____

DOCUMENTATION

Chart the results in the patient's medical record.

Date: ____________

Charting: ____

____

____

____

Student's Initials: ________

SKILLS COMPETENCY ASSESSMENT

Procedure 6–3: Taking an Oral Temperature Using a Digital Thermometer

Student's Name: ______________________________ Date: __________

Objective: To obtain an oral temperature.

Conditions: The student demonstrates the ability to measure oral temperature using the following equipment and supplies: digital thermometer, probe covers, biohazard waste container.

Time Requirements and Accuracy Standards: 3 minutes. Points assigned reflect importance of step to meeting objective: Important = (5) Essential = (10) Critical = (15). Automatic failure results if any of the **critical** tasks are omitted or performed incorrectly.

STANDARD PRECAUTIONS:

SKILLS ASSESSMENT CHECKLIST

Task Performed	Possible Points	TASKS
❑	5	Washes hands.
❑	5	Assembles equipment.
❑	5	Identifies patient and positions patient comfortably.
❑	5	Determines if patient has ingested hot or cold food or drink, or has smoked in previous half hour.
❑	5	*Rationale:* Understands that food ingestion or smoking can arbitrarily affect oral temperature reading.
❑	5	Explains procedure.
❑	10	Selects blue probe.
❑	5	*Rationale:* Understands that blue probe is used for oral temperature taking with the digital thermometer.
❑	5	Covers probe with probe cover.
❑	10	Inserts probe under patient's tongue to the side of the mouth.
❑	5	*Rationale:* Understands the anatomy of the tongue and the need to avoid the patient's frenulum.
❑	10	Instructs patient to close mouth around thermometer but not to place the teeth on it.
❑	10	Leaves in place until beep is heard.

Task Performed	Possible Points	TASKS
❑	15	Removes thermometer and reads results on digital display.
❑	10	Discards probe cover in a biohazard waste container.
❑	5	Replaces digital thermometer in base holder.
❑	5	Washes hands.
❑	15	Records temperature in patient chart and documents procedure.
❑	5	Completed the tasks within 3 minutes.
❑	15	Results obtained were accurate.

_______	Earned	ADD POINTS OF TASKS CHECKED
155	Points	TOTAL POINTS POSSIBLE
_______	SCORE	DETERMINE SCORE (divide points earned by total points possible, multiply results by 100)

Actual Student Time Needed to Complete Procedure: ____________

Student's Initials: ____________ Instructor's Initials: ____________ Grade: ____________

Suggestions for Improvement: ____

Evaluator's Name (print) ____

____

____

____

Evaluator's Signature ____

Comments ____

DOCUMENTATION

Chart the results in the patient's medical record.

Date: ____________

Charting: ____

____

____

____

____

____

Student's Initials: ________

SKILLS COMPETENCY ASSESSMENT

Procedure 6–4: Obtaining an Aural Temperature Using a Tympanic Thermometer

Student's Name: ______________________________ Date: __________

Objective: To obtain an aural temperature using a tympanic thermometer.

Conditions: The student demonstrates the ability to measure aural temperature using the following equipment and supplies: tympanic thermometer, covers or ear speculum, waste container.

Time Requirements and Accuracy Standards: 2 minutes. Points assigned reflect importance of step to meeting objective: Important = (5) Essential = (10) Critical = (15). Automatic failure results if any of the **critical** tasks are omitted or performed incorrectly.

STANDARD PRECAUTIONS:

SKILLS ASSESSMENT CHECKLIST

Task Performed	Possible Points	TASKS
❑	5	Washes hands and follows standard precautions.
❑	5	Assembles equipment.
❑	5	Identifies patient and positions patient comfortably.
❑	5	Explains procedure.
❑	5	Places cover on thermometer.
❑	5	Sets thermometer to start.
❑	10	Gently places probe into ear canal, sealing it.
❑	5	*Rationale:* Understands that air leaks will occur and results will be inaccurate if ear canal is not sealed.
❑	10	Activates system.
❑	15	Waits until results are displayed on screen.
❑	5	Removes probe from ear.
❑	10	Discards cover into waste container by pressing release button.
❑	5	Washes hands.
❑	5	Replaces thermometer.
❑	10	Properly records temperature in patient chart and documents procedure.

Task Performed	Possible Points	TASKS
❑	5	Completed the tasks within 2 minutes.
❑	15	Results obtained were accurate.
________	Earned	ADD POINTS OF TASKS CHECKED
125	Points	TOTAL POINTS POSSIBLE
________	SCORE	DETERMINE SCORE (divide points earned by total points possible, multiply results by 100)

Actual Student Time Needed to Complete Procedure: ____________

Student's Initials: ____________ Instructor's Initials: ____________ Grade: ____________

Suggestions for Improvement: ____

____

____

____

Evaluator's Name (print) ____

Evaluator's Signature ____

Comments ____

DOCUMENTATION

Chart the results in the patient's medical record.

Date: ____________

Charting: ____

____

____

____

____

____

Student's Initials: ________

SKILLS COMPETENCY ASSESSMENT

Procedure 6–5: Taking a Rectal Temperature Using a Mercury Thermometer

Student's Name: ______________________________ Date: ____________

Objective: To obtain a rectal temperature using a mercury thermometer.

Conditions: The student demonstrates the ability to measure rectal temperature using the following equipment and supplies: rectal thermometer, sheath, lubricating jelly, gloves, clean paper towels, biohazard waste container.

Time Requirements and Accuracy Standards: 10 minutes. Points assigned reflect importance of step to meeting objective: Important = (5) Essential = (10) Critical = (15). Automatic failure results if any of the **critical** tasks are omitted or performed incorrectly.

STANDARD PRECAUTIONS:

SKILLS ASSESSMENT CHECKLIST

Task Performed	Possible Points	TASKS
❑	5	Washes hands.
❑	5	Assembles equipment.
❑	5	Identifies patient.
❑	5	Explains procedure.
❑	5	Removes patient's clothing from waist down, draping as needed to give patient privacy and warmth.
❑	5	Positions patient in Sims position.
❑	5	Places sheath on thermometer.
❑	10	Applies lubricating jelly to sheath.
❑	5	*Rationale:* Understands that lubrication makes insertion easier and increases patient safety.
❑	15	Spreads patient's buttocks and inserts thermometer into the rectum past the sphincter (1.5 inches in adults).
❑	15	Holds buttocks together, keeping thermometer in place, for 5 minutes.
❑	5	*Rationale:* Understands that patient movement can cause movement of thermometer and injury.
❑	5	Removes thermometer from rectum.
❑	10	Removes sheath and places in a biohazard waste container.

Task Performed	Possible Points	TASKS
❑	10	Reads thermometer.
❑	5	Washes, rinses, and dries thermometer and places it on a clean paper towel.
❑	5	Removes gloves, discarding in a biohazard waste container, and washes hands.
❑	5	Places thermometer in disinfectant solution in a container specifically for rectal thermometers.
❑	5	Offers tissues for patient to wipe anus, assists patient in dressing, and positions comfortably.
❑	15	Properly records temperature in patient chart and documents procedure.
❑	5	Completed the tasks within 10 minutes.
❑	15	Results obtained were accurate.
_______	Earned	ADD POINTS OF TASKS CHECKED
165	Points	TOTAL POINTS POSSIBLE
_______	SCORE	DETERMINE SCORE (divide points earned by total points possible, multiply results by 100)

Actual Student Time Needed to Complete Procedure: __________

Student's Initials: __________ Instructor's Initials: __________ Grade: __________

Suggestions for Improvement: ______________________________

Evaluator's Name (print) ______________________________

Evaluator's Signature ______________________________

Comments ______________________________

DOCUMENTATION

Chart the results in the patient's medical record.

Date: __________

Charting: ______________________________

____

____

____

____

____

Student's Initials: ________

SKILLS COMPETENCY ASSESSMENT

Procedure 6–6: Taking a Rectal Temperature Using a Digital Thermometer

Student's Name: ______________________________ Date: __________

Objective: To obtain a rectal temperature using a digital thermometer.

Conditions: The student demonstrates the ability to measure rectal temperature using the following equipment and supplies: digital thermometer with red probe, probe cover, lubricating jelly, gloves, biohazard waste container.

Time Requirements and Accuracy Standards: 2 minutes. Points assigned reflect importance of step to meeting objective: Important = (5) Essential = (10) Critical = (15). Automatic failure results if any of the **critical** tasks are omitted or performed incorrectly.

STANDARD PRECAUTIONS:

SKILLS ASSESSMENT CHECKLIST

Task Performed	Possible Points	TASKS
❑	5	Washes hands and applies gloves, following standard precautions.
❑	5	Assembles equipment.
❑	5	Identifies patient.
❑	5	Explains procedure.
❑	5	Removes patient's clothing from waist down, draping as needed to give patient privacy and warmth.
❑	5	Positions patient in Sims position.
❑	5	Places probe cover on red probe.
❑	5	*Rationale:* Understands that red probe is used for rectal temperature measurement.
❑	10	Applies lubricating jelly to probe cover.
❑	5	*Rationale:* Understands that lubrication makes insertion easier and increases patient safety.
❑	15	Spreads patient's buttocks and inserts thermometer into the rectum past the sphincter (1.5 inches in adults).
❑	15	Holds buttocks together, keeping thermometer in place, until beep is heard.
❑	5	*Rationale:* Understands that patient movement can cause movement of thermometer, inaccurate readings, and injury.
❑	10	Reads results on digital display.

Task Performed	Possible Points	TASKS
❑	5	Removes thermometer from rectum.
❑	10	Discards probe cover into a biohazard waste container by pushing release button.
❑	5	Replaces thermometer in base.
❑	5	Removes gloves, discarding in a biohazard waste container, and washes hands.
❑	5	Offers tissues for patient to wipe anus, assists patient in dressing, and positions comfortably.
❑	15	Properly records temperature in patient chart and documents procedure.
❑	5	Completed the tasks within 2 minutes.
❑	15	Results obtained were accurate.

________	Earned	ADD POINTS OF TASKS CHECKED
165	Points	TOTAL POINTS POSSIBLE
________	SCORE	DETERMINE SCORE (divide points earned by total points possible, multiply results by 100)

Actual Student Time Needed to Complete Procedure: ____________

Student's Initials: ____________ Instructor's Initials: ____________ Grade: ____________

Suggestions for Improvement: ____________

Evaluator's Name (print) ____________

Evaluator's Signature ____________

Comments ____________

DOCUMENTATION

Chart the results in the patient's medical record.

Date: ____________

Charting: ____________

____

____

____

____

____

Student's Initials: ________

SKILLS COMPETENCY ASSESSMENT

Procedure 6–7: Taking an Axillary Temperature

Student's Name: ______________________________ Date: __________

Objective: To obtain an axillary temperature using a mercury thermometer.

Conditions: The student demonstrates the ability to measure axillary temperature using the following equipment and supplies: mercury thermometer, sheath, Towelettes, paper towels.

Time Requirements and Accuracy Standards: 15 minutes. Points assigned reflect importance of step to meeting objective: Important = (5) Essential = (10) Critical = (15). Automatic failure results if any of the **critical** tasks are omitted or performed incorrectly.

STANDARD PRECAUTIONS: 

SKILLS ASSESSMENT CHECKLIST

Task Performed	Possible Points	TASKS
❑	5	Washes hands and follows standard precautions.
❑	5	Assembles equipment.
❑	5	Identifies patient.
❑	5	Explains procedure.
❑	10	Places sheath on thermometer.
❑	5	Asks patient to remove clothing from waist up, gowning as necessary to protect patient's privacy and warmth.
❑	5	Wipes axillary area with dry paper towel.
❑	5	*Rationale:* Understands that moisture in axilla will cause an inaccurate reading.
❑	5	Places thermometer in axilla.
❑	10	Asks patient to fold arm against chest.
❑	5	*Rationale:* Understands that this will keep thermometer in place, prevent air contact, and preserve an accurate reading.
❑	15	Leaves in place 10 minutes.
❑	10	Removes thermometer from axilla and discards sheath into a biohazard waste container.

Task Performed	Possible Points	TASKS
❑	5	Reads thermometer.
❑	5	Washes, rinses, and dries thermometer, placing it on a clean paper towel.
❑	5	Washes hands.
❑	5	Soaks thermometer in disinfectant solution.
❑	10	Properly records temperature in patient chart and documents procedure.
❑	5	Completed the tasks within 15 minutes.
❑	15	Results obtained were accurate.
	______	Earned ADD POINTS OF TASKS CHECKED
	140	Points TOTAL POINTS POSSIBLE
	______	SCORE DETERMINE SCORE (divide points earned by total points possible, multiply results by 100)

Actual Student Time Needed to Complete Procedure: ____________

Student's Initials: ____________ Instructor's Initials: ____________ Grade: ____________

Suggestions for Improvement: ____

____

Evaluator's Name (print) ____

Evaluator's Signature ____

Comments ____

DOCUMENTATION

Chart the results in the patient's medical record.

Date: ____________

Charting: ____

____

____

____

____

____

Student's Initials: ________

SKILLS COMPETENCY ASSESSMENT

Procedure 6–8: Taking a Radial Pulse

Student's Name: ______________________________ Date: __________

Objective: To obtain a pulse rate.

Conditions: The student demonstrates the ability to measure radial pulse rate using the following equipment and supplies: watch with second hand.

Time Requirements and Accuracy Standards: 2 minutes. Points assigned reflect importance of step to meeting objective: Important = (5) Essential = (10) Critical = (15). Automatic failure results if any of the **critical** tasks are omitted or performed incorrectly.

STANDARD PRECAUTIONS:

SKILLS ASSESSMENT CHECKLIST

Task Performed	Possible Points	TASKS
☐	5	Washes hands.
☐	5	Identifies patient.
☐	5	Explains procedure.
☐	5	Positions patient with wrist resting on his or her lap or on a table.
☐	10	Locates radial pulse with pads of first three fingers.
☐	10	Gently compresses radial artery so pulsations can be clearly felt.
☐	15	Counts pulsations for one full minute.
☐	15	Notes any irregularities in rhythm, volume, and arterial condition.
☐	5	Washes hands.
☐	10	Records pulse rate and any irregularities in patient chart, following the temperature reading, and documents procedure.
☐	5	Completed the tasks within 2 minutes.
☐	15	Results obtained were accurate.

______	Earned	ADD POINTS OF TASKS CHECKED
105	Points	TOTAL POINTS POSSIBLE
______	SCORE	DETERMINE SCORE (divide points earned by total points possible, multiply results by 100)

Actual Student Time Needed to Complete Procedure: ____________

Student's Initials: ____________ Instructor's Initials: ____________ Grade: ____________

Suggestions for Improvement: ____

____

____

____

Evaluator's Name (print) ____

Evaluator's Signature ____

DOCUMENTATION

Chart the results in the patient's medical record. This patient also has an aural temperature of 98.7°F taken with a tympanic thermometer.

Date: __________

Charting: ____

____

____

____

____

____

Student's Initials: ________

SKILLS COMPETENCY ASSESSMENT

Procedure 6–9: Taking an Apical Pulse

Student's Name: ______________________________ Date: ______________

Objective: To obtain an apical pulse rate.

Conditions: The student demonstrates the ability to measure apical pulse rate using the following equipment and supplies: stethoscope, watch with second hand.

Time Requirements and Accuracy Standards: 2 minutes. Points assigned reflect importance of step to meeting objective: Important = (5) Essential = (10) Critical = (15). Automatic failure results if any of the **critical** tasks are omitted or performed incorrectly.

STANDARD PRECAUTIONS:

SKILLS ASSESSMENT CHECKLIST

Task Performed	Possible Points	TASKS
❑	5	Washes hands.
❑	5	Assembles equipment.
❑	5	Identifies patient.
❑	5	Explains procedure.
❑	5	Asks patient to remove clothing from waist up, gowning as necessary to protect patient's privacy and warmth.
❑	5	Positions patient in supine position.
❑	5	*Rationale:* Understands that this provides easier access to apex of heart.
❑	10	Locates fifth intercostal space, midclavical, left off sternum.
❑	5	*Rationale:* Understands that this is the location of the apex of the heart.
❑	10	Places stethoscope on site and listens for lub-dub sound of heart.
❑	5	*Rationale:* Understands that each lub-dub pair equals one pulse.
❑	15	Counts pulse for 1 minute.
❑	5	Assists patient to sit up and dress.
❑	5	Washes hands.

Task Performed	Possible Points	TASKS
❑	15	Properly records pulse in patient chart, noting any arrhythmias, and documents the procedure.
❑	5	Completed the tasks within 2 minutes.
❑	15	Results obtained were accurate.

________	Earned	ADD POINTS OF TASKS CHECKED
125	Points	TOTAL POINTS POSSIBLE
________	SCORE	DETERMINE SCORE (divide points earned by total points possible, multiply results by 100)

Actual Student Time Needed to Complete Procedure: ____________

Student's Initials: ____________ Instructor's Initials: ____________ Grade: ____________

Suggestions for Improvement: ______________________________

____

____

____

Evaluator's Name (print) ______________________________

Evaluator's Signature ______________________________

DOCUMENTATION

Chart the results in the patient's medical record. This patient also has an axillary temperature of 98.7°F.

Date: ____________

Charting: ______________________________

____

____

____

____

____

Student's Initials: __________

SKILLS COMPETENCY ASSESSMENT

Procedure 6–10: Measuring the Respiration Rate

Student's Name: ______________________________ Date: ____________

Objective: To obtain an accurate respiration rate.

Conditions: The student demonstrates the ability to measure respiration rate using the following equipment and supplies: watch with second hand.

Time Requirements and Accuracy Standards: 2 minutes. Points assigned reflect importance of step to meeting objective: Important = (5) Essential = (10) Critical = (15). Automatic failure results if any of the **critical** tasks are omitted or performed incorrectly.

STANDARD PRECAUTIONS:

SKILLS ASSESSMENT CHECKLIST

Task Performed	Possible Points	TASKS
❑	5	Washes hands.
❑	5	Identifies patient.
❑	5	Positions the patient comfortably.
❑	15	For 1 minute, monitors and counts the rise and fall of the patient's chest wall: by observation alone, by holding the patient's arm across the chest and feeling for its rises and falls, or by placing a hand on the patient's shoulder and watching chest movements.
❑	5	Washes hands.
❑	15	Notes depth of breathing, rhythm, and breath sounds while counting.
❑	10	Records respiration rate in patient chart, along with any irregularities or sounds, and documents the procedure.
❑	5	Completed the tasks within 2 minutes.
❑	15	Results obtained were accurate.

________	Earned	ADD POINTS OF TASKS CHECKED
80	Points	TOTAL POINTS POSSIBLE
________	SCORE	DETERMINE SCORE (divide points earned by total points possible, multiply results by 100)

Actual Student Time Needed to Complete Procedure: ___________

Student's Initials: ___________ Instructor's Initials: ___________ Grade: ___________

Suggestions for Improvement: ___________

Evaluator's Name (print) ___________

Evaluator's Signature ___________

Comments ___________

DOCUMENTATION

Chart the results in the patient's medical record. This patient also has a rectal temperature of 99.4°F and a pulse rate of 72 beats per minute.

Date: ___________

Charting: ___________

Student's Initials: ______

SKILLS COMPETENCY ASSESSMENT

Procedure 6–11: Measuring a Blood Pressure

Student's Name: ______________________________ Date: ____________

Objective: To measure blood pressure.

Conditions: The student demonstrates the ability to measure blood pressure using the following equipment and supplies: stethoscope, sphygmomanometer, alcohol wipes.

Time Requirements and Accuracy Standards: 5 minutes. Points assigned reflect importance of step to meeting objective: Important = (5) Essential = (10) Critical = (15). Automatic failure results if any of the **critical** tasks are omitted or performed incorrectly.

STANDARD PRECAUTIONS:

SKILLS ASSESSMENT CHECKLIST

Task Performed	Possible Points	TASKS
☐	5	Washes hands.
☐	10	Assembles equipment, including a cuff of the appropriate size.
☐	5	*Rationale:* Understands that a cuff of the wrong size can give inaccurate results.
☐	5	Cleans stethoscope earpieces with alcohol wipe.
☐	5	Identifies patient.
☐	5	Explains procedure.
☐	10	Positions patient, preferably in a seated position, with feet flat on the floor and arm resting on lap or table.
☐	5	*Rationale:* Understands that crossed legs or an arm above heart level can give inaccurate results.
☐	5	Bares patient's upper arm, asking patient to remove clothing if necessary.
☐	5	Palpates brachial artery.
☐	10	Positions cuff bladder over the brachial artery, about two inches above the elbow.
☐	10	Palpates radial pulse and smoothly inflates cuff until pulse is no longer felt, noting this number.
☐	5	Deflates cuff quickly and allows arm to rest for 1 minute.
☐	5	Calculates peak inflation level.
☐	5	*Rationale:* Understands that this will ensure that an auscultatory gap is not missed.
☐	10	Determines that cuff is completely deflated.
☐	10	Positions stethoscope over brachial artery, holding in position with fingers only.
☐	10	Inflates cuff, smoothly and quickly, to peak inflation level.

Task Performed	Possible Points	TASKS
❑	15	Deflates cuff at 2 to 4 mm Hg per second.
❑	10	Listens for Korotkoff phase I, noting when it appears.
❑	5	Continues deflation, noting each Korotkoff phase.
❑	15	Notes point at which all sounds disappear, Korotkoff phase V.
❑	10	Continues deflating cuff at the same rate for at least 10 more mm Hg after sounds disappear.
❑	5	*Rationale:* Understands this will allow time for an auscultatory gap, should one be present.
❑	5	Deflates cuff quickly and removes it.
❑	5	Cleans stethoscope earpieces with alcohol wipe.
❑	5	Washes hands.
❑	10	Records measurement in patient chart and documents procedure.
❑	5	Completed the tasks within 5 minutes.
❑	15	Results obtained were accurate.

_______	Earned	ADD POINTS OF TASKS CHECKED
230	Points	TOTAL POINTS POSSIBLE
_______	SCORE	DETERMINE SCORE (divide points earned by total points possible, multiply results by 100)

Actual Student Time Needed to Complete Procedure: ____________

Student's Initials: ____________ Instructor's Initials: ____________ Grade: ____________

Suggestions for Improvement: ____

Evaluator's Name (print) ____

Evaluator's Signature ____

Comments ____

DOCUMENTATION

Chart the results in the patient's medical record. This patient also has an oral temperature of 98.6°F taken with an oral strip thermometer, a strong pulse of 62 beats per minute, and a respiratory rate of 15 breaths per minute.

Date: ____________

Charting: ____

____

____

____

Student's Initials: ____________

SKILLS COMPETENCY ASSESSMENT

Procedure 6–12: Measuring Height

Student's Name: ______________________ Date: __________

Objective: To obtain the height of a patient.

Conditions: The student demonstrates the ability to measure height using the following equipment and supplies: scale with measuring bar; paper towel.

Time Requirements and Accuracy Standards: 5 minutes. Points assigned reflect importance of step to meeting objective: Important = (5) Essential = (10) Critical = (15). Automatic failure results if any of the **critical** tasks are omitted or performed incorrectly.

STANDARD PRECAUTIONS:

SKILLS ASSESSMENT CHECKLIST

Task Performed	Possible Points	TASKS
❑	5	Washes hands.
❑	5	Identifies patient.
❑	5	Explains procedure.
❑	5	Instructs patient to remove shoes.
❑	5	Places paper towel on scale.
❑	10	Instructs patient to stand on the scale platform with back to measuring bar, looking straight ahead.
❑	5	*Rationale:* Understands that facial or eye injuries could result if patient faces the measuring bar, and that a more accurate result is obtained if patient looks straight ahead.
❑	5	Assists patient onto scale platform.
❑	5	*Rationale:* Understands that the movable platform could cause patient to lose balance if unassisted.
❑	10	Lowers measuring bar until headrest is positioned firmly atop patient's head.
❑	10	Assists patient in stepping off the scale, helping him or her to sit and replace shoes if necessary.
❑	15	Reads line where measurement falls.

Task Performed	Possible Points	TASKS
☐	5	Lowers measuring bar to original position.
☐	5	Washes hands.
☐	5	Records height in patient chart.
☐	5	Completed the tasks within 5 minutes.
☐	15	Results obtained were accurate.

_______	Earned	ADD POINTS OF TASKS CHECKED
120	Points	TOTAL POINTS POSSIBLE
_______	SCORE	DETERMINE SCORE (divide points earned by total points possible, multiply results by 100)

Actual Student Time Needed to Complete Procedure: __________

Student's Initials: __________ Instructor's Initials: __________ Grade: __________

Suggestions for Improvement: ______________________________

____

____

____

Evaluator's Name (print) ______________________________

Evaluator's Signature ______________________________

Comments ______________________________

DOCUMENTATION

Chart the results in the patient's medical record. This patient also has a rectal temperature of 99.9°F, a pulse rate of 75 beats per minute, a respiration rate of 25 breaths per minute, and a blood pressure reading in the left arm, while sitting, of 122/80. Sinus arrhythmia is noted in this patient.

Date: __________

Charting: ______________________________

____

____

____

____

____

Student's Initials: __________

SKILLS COMPETENCY ASSESSMENT

Procedure 6–13: Measuring Adult Weight

Student's Name: ______________________ Date: __________

Objective: To obtain the weight of the patient.

Conditions: The student demonstrates the ability to measure weight using the following equipment and supplies: balance beam scale; paper towel.

Time Requirements and Accuracy Standards: 5 minutes. Points assigned reflect importance of step to meeting objective: Important = (5) Essential = (10) Critical = (15). Automatic failure results if any of the **critical** tasks are omitted or performed incorrectly.

STANDARD PRECAUTIONS:

SKILLS ASSESSMENT CHECKLIST

Task Performed	Possible Points	TASKS
☐	5	Washes hands.
☐	5	Identifies patient.
☐	5	Explains procedure.
☐	5	Places paper towel on scale.
☐	5	Instructs patient to place any heavy items, including items in pockets, in a safe area provided.
☐	5	Instructs patient to remove shoes, jackets, and other outerwear.
☐	10	Assists patient onto scale platform, positioning patient in platform's center.
☐	5	*Rationale:* Understands that the movable platform could cause patient to lose balance if unassisted.
☐	5	Moves lower weight bar to estimated number (patient may be asked for approximate weight).
☐	5	Slides upper weight bar until balance beam point is centered.
☐	15	Reads weight, adding upper bar measurement to lower bar measurement.
☐	10	Assists patient in stepping off scale, helping him or her to sit and replace shoes if necessary and returning any other items.

Task Performed	Possible Points	TASKS
☐	5	Returns weights to 0.
☐	5	Washes hands.
☐	5	Records measurement in patient chart.
☐	5	Completed the tasks within 5 minutes.
☐	15	Results obtained were accurate.
______	Earned	ADD POINTS OF TASKS CHECKED
115	Points	TOTAL POINTS POSSIBLE
______	SCORE	DETERMINE SCORE (divide points earned by total points possible, multiply results by 100)

Actual Student Time Needed to Complete Procedure: ____________

Student's Initials: ____________ Instructor's Initials: ____________ Grade: ____________

Suggestions for Improvement: ____

____

____

Evaluator's Name (print) ____

Evaluator's Signature ____

Comments ____

DOCUMENTATION

Chart the results in the patient's medical record. This patient also has an oral temperature of 98.3°F; an apical pulse rate of 68 beats per minute; a respiration rate of 19 breaths per minute, with shallow breathing; a blood pressure reading in the right arm, while supine, of 132/78; and a height of 5 feet 7.5 inches.

Date: __________

Charting: ____

____

____

____

____

____

Student's Initials: ________

EVALUATION OF CHAPTER KNOWLEDGE

Evaluate your own strengths and weaknesses in the measurement of vital signs and your understanding of their ramifications. Compare this evaluation to the one provided by your instructor.

	Student Self-evaluation			Instructor Evaluation		
Knowledge	*Good*	*Average*	*Poor*	*Good*	*Average*	*Poor*
Ability to define and describe key terms relating to temperature, pulse, respiration, and blood pressure readings	____	____	____	____	____	____
Understands normal and abnormal body temperatures as well as factors that affect temperature	____	____	____	____	____	____
Identifies various types of thermometers and knows procedures for their care, storage, and use	____	____	____	____	____	____
Knows anatomical locations of pulse sites and procedures for obtaining pulse rate at each one	____	____	____	____	____	____
Identifies normal and abnormal pulse rates, including common arrhythmias	____	____	____	____	____	____
Understands procedure for obtaining respiration rate	____	____	____	____	____	____
Identifies normal and abnormal respiration rates and breath sounds	____	____	____	____	____	____
Ability to use blood pressure equipment and understand measurement procedures	____	____	____	____	____	____
Identifies normal and abnormal blood pressure readings, including factors that affect it	____	____	____	____	____	____
Understands procedures for obtaining height and weight measurements	____	____	____	____	____	____
Ability to accurately record all measurements on patient chart	____	____	____	____	____	____

Student's Initials: ______ Instructor's Initials: ______

Grade: ______

The Basic Physical Examination

PERFORMANCE OBJECTIVES

The medical assistant assists the physician in the physical examination of patients, commonly performing duties related to patient preparation and examination room preparation. Medical assisting students can use this workbook chapter to explore the standard routine of a physical examination and the standard sequence of events that occur during the examination, allowing for variations due to physician preference, type of practice, and the patient's chief complaint. By assisting the physician with professionalism and accuracy, medical assistants make vital contributions to physicians' abilities to make accurate diagnoses and formulate treatment plans based on patients' medical histories, physical examinations, and accurate results of laboratory tests and diagnostic procedures. Medical assistants observe aseptic technique and standard precautions as required during physical examinations. At all times, proper empathy and respect for the patient is shown.

EXERCISES AND ACTIVITIES

Vocabulary Builder

Identify the key vocabulary term most appropriate for each example from a patient's physical examination.

ataxia	pallor	vertigo
bruits	pyorrhea	vitiligo
cyanosis	scleroderma	
jaundice	symmetry	
labyrinthitis	tinnitus	

____________________ 1. During a physical examination of Louise Kipperley, a 48-year-old female, Dr. Esposito checks Louise's face for tight and atrophied skin.

____________________ 2. Leo McKay comes to Inner City Health Care with mouth pain. Dr. Reynolds examines Leo's mouth for dental hygiene and for this condition, which is the discharge of pus from the gums around the teeth.

______________________ 3. Medical assistant Liz Corbin observes the gait of Geraldine Potter, a 36-year-old woman diagnosed with multiple sclerosis. Geraldine's gait is lurching and unsteady, with her feet widely placed.

______________________ 4. Annette Samuels is diagnosed with HBV by Dr. Mark Woo. Annette contracted the virus from an infected needle used to pierce her navel. Among Annette's symptoms, noted by Dr. Woo during his physical examination, was a distinct yellowing of Annette's skin and the whites of her eyes.

______________________ 5. Lenny Taylor, an elderly man suffering from Alzheimer's disease, is brought to Inner City Health Care by his son George. Apparently, Lenny had gotten lost in a park near his home and had been wandering for hours in the cold. Dr. Whitney observes a bluish color in the beds of Lenny's fingernails and toenails and on his lips, tongue, and the mucous membranes lining the inside of his mouth.

______________________ 6. After performing a routine venipuncture procedure on patient Rhoda Au, Bruce Goldman, CMA, notices that all color has drained from Rhoda's face.

______________________ 7. Abigail Johnson's 28-year-old granddaughter Lucy comes in for an examination with Dr. King after observing white patches of depigmentation on her hand. "Is this what Michael Jackson had?" she asks Dr. King.

______________________ 8. While performing a complete physical examination on patient Rowena Lawrence, Dr. King listens for abnormal sounds from vital organs while auscultating her abdomen.

______________________ 9. During a routine physical examination of Lenore McDonnell, a young woman confined to a wheelchair, Dr. Lewis checks for the correspondence in size, shape, and position of body parts on opposite sides of her body.

______________________ 10. Mary O'Keefe brings her 3-year-old son Chris to see Dr. King when he exhibits a high fever and pain in his ear. The toddler, diagnosed with otitis media, keeps placing his hands over his ears and crying, "Mommy, stop noise."

______________________ 11. Rowena Lawrence's 6-year-old daughter Felicia, diagnosed with a case of the mumps, returns with her mother for a re-
and ______________________ examination with Dr. Lewis when the child experiences a sensation that the room is spinning, caused by inflammation of the labyrinth.

Learning Review

1. Match the correct method of examination used by a physician to the entry that best describes it.

Auscultation	Observation or Inspection
Percussion	Manipulation
Palpation	Mensuration

_______________ A. Upon his physical examination of Charles Williams, Dr. Winston Lewis looks at the patient to assess his general health, posture, body movements, skin, mannerisms, and care in grooming while verbally reviewing Charles's medical history with him.

_______________ B. Dr. Mark Woo uses a stethoscope to listen to the bowel sounds accompanying peristalsis.

_______________ C. Dr. King performs range of motion exercises on patient Margaret Thomas, suspected of Parkinson's disease.

_______________ D. Dr. Rice taps Edith Leonard's chest to feel and hear the hollow quality expected from clear lungs.

_______________ E. During Marissa O'Keefe's well-baby visit, chest and head circumference measurements are recorded in the patient's medical record.

_______________ F. When Leo McKay comes to Inner City Health Care with acute stomach pains, Dr. Reynolds feels his stomach and abdomen for irregularities in size, texture, and condition of vital organs.

2. For each procedure listed below, identify the most likely examination position that will be required during the physician's examination. Use a medical encyclopedia for reference, if necessary.

_______________ A. Urinary catheterization

_______________ B. Auscultation for borborygmi, the audible bowel sounds that are a normal part of the digestive process.

_______________ C. Colposcopy to observe the cervix under magnified illumination for evidence of precancerous cells, followed by a cone biopsy for laboratory analysis.

_______________ D. Hemorroids are removed through implementation of a proctoscope and banding instrument.

_______________ E. Percutaneous renal biopsy to aid in diagnosis of a suspected case of glomerulonephritis.

_______________ F. An ECG is performed on an elderly woman with angina pectoris.

_______________ G. A variation of this position is used for patients suffering from shock.

_______________ H. Proctoscopy to investigate a suspected case of proctitis, inflammation of the rectum.

3. Identify each entry below as a piece of medical equipment (ME), a laboratory procedure (LP), a part of the human body (BP), or a patient illness or condition (PI). Then, identify the correct component or sequence of the physical examination the entry relates to.

		Component or Sequence of Physical Examination
____	A. Sphygmomanometer	____________________
____	B. Aphonia	____________________
____	C. Lymph nodes	____________________
____	D. Edema	____________________
____	E. Tonometer	____________________
____	F. Anal fissures	____________________
____	G. Emphysema	____________________
____	H. Pharyngeal mirrors	____________________
____	I. Scrotum	____________________
____	J. Areola	____________________
____	K. Electrocardiography	____________________
____	L. Kyphosis	____________________
____	M. Dysphasia	____________________
____	N. Urinalysis	____________________
____	O. Achilles tendon	____________________
____	P. Tympanic membrane	____________________
____	Q. Acidosis	____________________

Investigation Activity

One of the medical assistant's chief duties in assisting physicians with the physical examinations of patients is patient preparation. Patient preparation includes patient explanation and preparation, positioning, draping, vital signs, specimen collection, such as urine and blood, and electrocardiogram (ECG). The medical assistant needs to demonstrate the ability to accurately triage patient conditions in order to prepare the patient properly for the physician's examination.

Write the following patient chief complaints on index cards. Divide the class into partners, one partner taking the role of the medical assistant and the other the role of the patient. The "patient" chooses an index card with a chief complaint listed on it. The chief complaint is not revealed to the student taking the role of the medical assistant. The medical assistant must then question the patient to determine the chief complaint, assess the patient's general condition, and prepare the patient for the physician's physical examination. Make note of any laboratory tests the physician may order for this patient and what supplies would be needed.

As a further challenge for the medical assistant, the student taking the role of the patient can also draw a card listing an emotion, a physical characteristic, or a personality characteristic—unrelated to the patient's chief complaint—that will test the medical assistant's triage and communication skills even more. Be creative and add your own ideas to the lists below.

Chief Complaints and Possible Diagnoses

- Vomiting and severe pain in or around one eye, blurred vision (glaucoma)
- Pain on urination with watery mucus discharge (nonspecific urethritis)
- Cough, fever, chest pain, shortness of breath (pneumonia)
- Lethargy, muscle weakness, cramps, slow heart rate, hair loss (hypothyroidism)
- Headache, nausea, dizziness, impaired mental processes; severe breathlessness, cough, and phlegm production (mountain sickness and high-altitude pulmonary edema)
- Abnormal or heavy menstrual bleeding with lower back pain during menstruation (endometriosis)
- Headache with severe pain on one side, nausea, flashing lights create vision disturbance before headache begins (migraine)
- Fever, rash of purple spots, dislike of strong light, pain on bending head forward (meningitis)
- Constipation, regular use of laxatives (overuse of laxatives)
- Inability to concentrate, low sex drive, recurrent headaches (depression)

Patient Characteristics

The patient is

- Aggressive but not rude; asks a lot of questions
- Shy, will not maintain eye contact
- Deaf, communicates by lip-reading and handwritten exchanges
- Unable to concentrate, does not seem to understand or follow directions well
- Complaining constantly
- Confined to a wheelchair
- Making a joke out of everything, but in a nice way
- Distrustful of the medical assistant
- Speaks broken English
- Evasive and does not want to reveal information
- Cooperative and good-natured
- Depressed
- In a great deal of pain
- Fatigued
- Worried
- Trying to self-diagnose and get the medical assistant to confirm the self-diagnosis

CASE STUDY

Rowena Lawrence brings her 5-year-old son Bobby to Inner City Health Care with a suspected case of the mumps contracted from his sister Felicia. As Bruce Goldman, CMA, helps the child remove his clothing, leaving only his underwear, the child becomes increasingly fearful and begins to cry. Rowena's gentle reprimand to "Hush up and do what you're told," makes the boy cry harder. It is obvious that the child is uncomfortable and feverish.

Discuss the following:

1. What can the medical assistant do to calm the child and make him more comfortable?
2. What is Bruce's therapeutic response?

SUPPLEMENTARY RESOURCES

Study Guide Disk: Additional practice exercises for this chapter are available on the study guide disk found in the back of the textbook.

Medical Assisting Videos: Appropriate content is available on Delmar's Medical Assisting Videos, 2nd ed., Tape 8, for the following topics:

Clean Examination Table and Countertop
Assist Physician with Examination and Treatments
Position and Drape the Patient
Role of the Medical Assistant During the Examination
Introduction to Health Promotion, Disease Prevention, and Self-Responsibility

SKILLS COMPETENCY ASSESSMENT

Procedure 7–1: Positioning Patient in the Supine Position

Student's Name: ______________________ Date: __________

Objective: To safely and properly assist patient into supine position for examination of anterior surface of the body from head to toe.

Conditions: The student demonstrates the ability to position the patient in the supine position for examination using the following equipment and supplies: examination table, drape, gown.

Time Requirements and Accuracy Standards: 2 minutes. Points assigned reflect importance of step to meeting objective: Important = (5) Essential = (10) Critical = (15). Automatic failure results if any of the **critical** tasks are omitted or performed incorrectly.

STANDARD PRECAUTIONS:

SKILLS ASSESSMENT CHECKLIST

Task Performed	Possible Points	TASKS
☐	5	Washes hands and follows standard precautions.
☐	5	Assembles supplies.
☐	5	Assists patient to sit on the end of the examination table.
☐	10	Assists patient to lie back on table while pulling out the table extension. Supports patient's feet and back while extending foot of table.
☐	5	Covers patient with drape from shoulders to ankles.
☐	5	Places small pillow under patient's head.
☐	10	Upon completion of procedure, assists patient to seated position (allows patient to remain seated to prevent orthostatic hypotension).
☐	5	Pushes table extension back into place while supporting patient's feet.
☐	15	Once patient is stable (checks color or patient's skin, checks pulse), gives further instructions as required.
☐	5	Completed the tasks within 2 minutes.
☐	15	Results obtained were accurate.

______	Earned	ADD POINTS OF TASKS CHECKED
85	Points	TOTAL POINTS POSSIBLE
______	SCORE	DETERMINE SCORE (divide points earned by total points possible, multiply results by 100)

Actual Student Time Needed to Complete Procedure: __________

Student's Initials: __________ Instructor's Initials: __________ Grade: __________

Suggestions for Improvement: ______________________

Evaluator's Name (print) ______________________

Evaluator's Signature ______________________

Comments ______________________

SKILLS COMPETENCY ASSESSMENT

Procedure 7–2: Positioning Patient in the Dorsal Recumbent Position

Student's Name: ______________________________ Date: ____________

Objective: To safely and properly assist patient to dorsal recumbent position for pelvic or rectal examination; urinary catheterization; and head, chest, or neck examination.

Conditions: The student demonstrates the ability to position patient in the dorsal recumbent position using the following equipment and supplies: examination table, drape, gown.

Time Requirements and Accuracy Standards: 2 minutes. Points assigned reflect importance of step to meeting objective: Important = (5) Essential = (10) Critical = (15). Automatic failure results if any of the **critical** tasks are omitted or performed incorrectly.

STANDARD PRECAUTIONS:

SKILLS ASSESSMENT CHECKLIST

Task Performed	Possible Points	TASKS
❑	5	Washes hands and follows standard precautions.
❑	5	Assists patient to sit on the end of the examination table.
❑	10	Assists patient to lie back on table; extends the foot of the table while supporting the patient's feet and back.
❑	5	Assists patient to bend knees and place feet flat on the surface of the table.
❑	5	Covers patient with drape (diamond shape) from shoulders to ankles.
❑	5	Places small pillow under patient's head.
❑	5	Upon completion of procedure, assists patient to seated position while pushing table extension back into place and supporting patient's feet.
❑	10	Has patient sit at end of table for a few minutes to prevent dizziness.
❑	15	Once patient is stable (checks color of patient's skin, checks pulse), gives further instructions as required.
❑	5	Completed the tasks within 2 minutes.
❑	15	Results obtained were accurate.

________	Earned	ADD POINTS OF TASKS CHECKED
85	Points	TOTAL POINTS POSSIBLE
________	SCORE	DETERMINE SCORE (divide points earned by total points possible, multiply results by 100)

Actual Student Time Needed to Complete Procedure: ____________

Student's Initials: ____________ Instructor's Initials: ____________ Grade: ____________

Suggestions for Improvement: ______________________________

Evaluator's Name (print) ______________________________

Evaluator's Signature ______________________________

Comments ______________________________

SKILLS COMPETENCY ASSESSMENT

Procedure 7–3: Positioning Patient in the Lithotomy Position

Student's Name: ______________________________ Date: ____________

Objective: To safely and properly assist patient in lithotomy position for pelvic or rectal examination or for urinary catheterization.

Conditions: The student demonstrates the ability to position patient in the lithotomy position using the following equipment and supplies: examination table, drape, gown.

Time Requirements and Accuracy Standards: 5 minutes. Points assigned reflect importance of step to meeting objective: Important = (5) Essential = (10) Critical = (15). Automatic failure results if any of the **critical** tasks are omitted or performed incorrectly.

STANDARD PRECAUTIONS:

SKILLS ASSESSMENT CHECKLIST

Task Performed	Possible Points	TASKS
☐	5	Washes hands and follows standard precautions.
☐	5	Has patient disrobe from waist down and put on gown.
☐	5	Assists patient to sit on the end of the examination table. Covers patient's lap and legs with drape.
☐	5	Assists patient to lie back on table while supporting patient's feet and back and extending foot of table.
☐	15	Positions stirrups level with the table and approximately one foot from edge of table. Locks stirrups into position.
☐	5	*Rationale:* Facilitates patient examination and ensures patient safety.
☐	5	Has patient move as close to edge of examination table as possible.
☐	10	Assists patient to bend knees and place feet in stirrups. Moves drape to diamond shape to ensure privacy.
☐	5	Places small pillow under patient's head.
☐	5	Upon completion of procedure, extends foot extension of table.
☐	5	Assists patient to slide toward head of table and place legs on foot extension.

SKILLS COMPETENCY ASSESSMENT — continued

Procedure 7–3: Positioning Patient in the Lithotomy Position

Task Performed	Possible Points	TASKS
❑	5	Assists patient to seated position while replacing foot extension.
❑	10	Has patient sit at end of table for a few minutes to prevent dizziness.
❑	15	Once patient is stable (checks color of patient's skin, checks pulse), gives further instructions as required.
❑	5	Completed the tasks within 5 minutes.
❑	15	Results obtained were accurate.

________	Earned	ADD POINTS OF TASKS CHECKED
120	Points	TOTAL POINTS POSSIBLE
________	SCORE	DETERMINE SCORE (divide points earned by total points possible, multiply results by 100)

Actual Student Time Needed to Complete Procedure: ____________

Student's Initials: ____________ Instructor's Initials: ____________ Grade: ____________

Suggestions for Improvement: ____

____

____

____

Evaluator's Name (print) ____

Evaluator's Signature ____

Comments ____

SKILLS COMPETENCY ASSESSMENT

Procedure 7–4: Positioning Patient in the Fowler's Position

Student's Name: ______________________________ Date: __________

Objective: To safely and properly assist patient into the Fowler's position for examination of upper body and head; often used for patients with cardiovascular or respiratory problems.

Conditions: The student demonstrates the ability to position patient in the Fowler's position using the following equipment and supplies: examination table, drape, gown.

Time Requirements and Accuracy Standards: 2 minutes. Points assigned reflect importance of step to meeting objective: Important = (5) Essential = (10) Critical = (15). Automatic failure results if any of the **critical** tasks are omitted or performed incorrectly.

STANDARD PRECAUTIONS:

SKILLS ASSESSMENT CHECKLIST

Task Performed	Possible Points	TASKS
❑	5	Washes hands and follows standard precautions.
❑	5	Provides gown and assists to disrobe if necessary.
❑	5	Assists patient to sit on the end of the examination table. Covers lap and legs with drape.
❑	5	Assists patient to slide back on table leaning on back rest.
❑	5	Supports patient's feet while extending foot of table.
❑	10	Positions head of table at a 90° angle (45° for Semi-Fowler's).
❑	5	Covers patient with drape from shoulders to ankles.
❑	5	Upon completion of procedure, replaces foot extension.
❑	10	Has patient sit at end of table for a few minutes to prevent dizziness.
❑	15	Once patient is stable (checks color of patient's skin, checks pulse), gives further instructions as required.
❑	5	Completed the tasks within 2 minutes.
❑	15	Results obtained were accurate.
______	Earned	ADD POINTS OF TASKS CHECKED
90	Points	TOTAL POINTS POSSIBLE
______	SCORE	DETERMINE SCORE (divide points earned by total points possible, multiply results by 100)

Actual Student Time Needed to Complete Procedure: __________

Student's Initials: __________ Instructor's Initials: __________ Grade: __________

Suggestions for Improvement: ______________________________

Evaluator's Name (print) ______________________________

Evaluator's Signature ______________________________

Comments ______________________________

SKILLS COMPETENCY ASSESSMENT

Procedure 7–5: Positioning Patient in the Knee-Chest Position

Student's Name: ______________________________ Date: ____________

Objective: To safely and properly assist patient in knee-chest position for examination of the rectum, sigmoid colon, and in some instances, the vagina.

Conditions: The student demonstrates the ability to position patient in the knee-chest position using the following equipment and supplies: examination table, drape, gown.

Time Requirements and Accuracy Standards: 5 minutes. Points assigned reflect importance of step to meeting objective: Important = (5) Essential = (10) Critical = (15). Automatic failure results if any of the **critical** tasks are omitted or performed incorrectly.

STANDARD PRECAUTIONS:

SKILLS ASSESSMENT CHECKLIST

Task Performed	Possible Points	TASKS
❑	5	Washes hands and follows standard precautions.
❑	5	Has patient completely undress. Provides gown.
❑	5	Instructs patient to sit on the end of the examination table with drape open over lap and legs.
❑	5	Instructs patient to lie back on table while supporting patient's feet and back and extending foot of table.
❑	5	Waits until physician is ready to begin examination to assist patient into knee-chest position.
❑	5	*Rationale:* Because this is an embarrassing and uncomfortable position for the patient, it is best to wait until the physician is ready to begin the examination.
❑	10	Assists patient to turn onto abdomen by turning the patient toward the medical assistant, being careful to stay in the center of the table to avoid a fall. Medical assistant places her/his left hand on the patient's back for support and guides the patient toward her/him. Adjusts drape.
❑	10	Assists patient to rise to knees by helping patient bend at the hips to place the chest on the table; keeps patient covered with drape.

Task Performed	Possible Points	TASKS
❑	10	Ensures that patient's arms are bent to each side of the head with hands placed under the head. If this position is uncomfortable, has patient rest on the elbows. Adjusts drape from shoulders to ankles.
❑	10	Upon completion of procedure, assists patient to lie flat on abdomen. Then, assists patient to turn onto the back (patient turns toward medical assistant) and return to seated position.
❑	10	Has patient sit at end of table for a few minutes to prevent dizziness.
❑	15	Once patient is stable (checks patient's skin color, checks pulse), gives further instructions as required.
❑	5	Completed the tasks within 5 minutes.
❑	15	Results obtained were accurate.
_________	Earned	ADD POINTS OF TASKS CHECKED
115	Points	TOTAL POINTS POSSIBLE
_________	SCORE	DETERMINE SCORE (divide points earned by total points possible, multiply results by 100)

Actual Student Time Needed to Complete Procedure: ____________

Student's Initials: ____________ Instructor's Initials: ____________ Grade: ____________

Suggestions for Improvement: ______________________________

____

____

____

Evaluator's Name (print) ______________________________

Evaluator's Signature ______________________________

Comments ______________________________

SKILLS COMPETENCY ASSESSMENT

Procedure 7–6: Positioning Patient in Prone Position

Student's Name: ______________________ Date: __________

Objective: To safely and properly position the patient into the prone position for examination of the posterior aspect of the body, including the back, spine, or legs.

Conditions: The student demonstrates the ability to position the patient in the prone position using the following equipment and supplies: examination table, drape, gown.

Time Requirements and Accuracy Standards: 2 minutes. Points assigned reflect importance of step to meeting objective: Important = (5) Essential = (10) Critical = (15). Automatic failure results if any of the **critical** tasks are omitted or performed incorrectly.

STANDARD PRECAUTIONS:

SKILLS ASSESSMENT CHECKLIST

Task Performed	Possible Points	TASKS
❑	5	Washes hands and follows standard precautions.
❑	5	Has patient undress. Provides gown.
❑	5	Assists patient to sit on the end of the examination table. Places drape over lap and legs.
❑	5	Assists patient to lie back on table while supporting patient's feet and back and extending foot of table.
❑	10	Assists patient to turn toward the medical assistant, then onto abdomen, being careful to stay in center of table to avoid a fall. Places pillow under patient's feet and head.
❑	5	Adjusts patient's drape from shoulders to ankles.
❑	10	Upon completion of procedure, assists patient to turn toward the medical assistant. Then, assists patient to seated position.
❑	10	Has patient sit at end of table for a few minutes to prevent dizziness.
❑	15	Once patient is stable (checks patient's skin color, checks pulse), gives further instructions as required.

Task Performed	Possible Points	TASKS
❑	5	Completed the tasks within 2 minutes.
❑	15	Results obtained were accurate.
________	Earned	ADD POINTS OF TASKS CHECKED
90	Points	TOTAL POINTS POSSIBLE
________	SCORE	DETERMINE SCORE (divide points earned by total points possible, multiply results by 100)

Actual Student Time Needed to Complete Procedure: ____________

Student's Initials: ____________ Instructor's Initials: ____________ Grade: ____________

Suggestions for Improvement: ____

____

____

____

Evaluator's Name (print) ____

Evaluator's Signature ____

Comments ____

SKILLS COMPETENCY ASSESSMENT

Procedure 7–7: Positioning Patient in the Sims' Position

Student's Name: ______________________________ Date: ____________

Objective: To safely and properly assist patient into Sims', or lateral, position for rectal examination, rectal temperature, proctoscopy, sigmoidoscopy, for an enema, and in some instances, for vaginal examination.

Condition: The student demonstrates the ability to position patient in the Sims' position using the following equipment and supplies: examination table, drape, gown.

Time Requirements and Accuracy Standards: 2 minutes. Points assigned reflect importance of step to meeting objective: Important = (5) Essential = (10) Critical = (15). Automatic failure results if any of the **critical** tasks are omitted or performed incorrectly.

STANDARD PRECAUTIONS:

SKILLS ASSESSMENT CHECKLIST

Task Performed	Possible Points	TASKS
☐	5	Washes hands and follows standard precautions.
☐	5	Has patient undress. Provides gown.
☐	5	Assists patient to sit on the end of the table. Places drape over lap and legs.
☐	10	Assists patient to lie back on table while supporting patient's feet and back and extending foot of table.
☐	10	Assists patient to turn toward the medical assistant onto the left side with the left arm behind the body, placing body weight on the chest. Adjusts drape.
☐	10	Assists patient to slightly flex left knee and flex right knee to a 90° angle for support.
☐	10	Ensures that patient's right arm is bent in front of body with hand toward head at an angle to provide support.
☐	5	Adjusts drape from shoulders to ankles creating triangle or diamond shape.
☐	10	Upon completion of procedure, instructs patient to turn toward the medical assistant, then onto back, then into seated position.
☐	10	Has patient sit at end of table for a few minutes to prevent dizziness.

Task Performed	Possible Points	TASKS
☐	15	Once patient is stable (checks patient's skin color, checks pulse), gives further instructions as required.
☐	5	Completed the tasks within 2 minutes.
☐	15	Results obtained were accurate.
	_______	Earned ADD POINTS OF TASKS CHECKED
	115	Points TOTAL POINTS POSSIBLE
	_______	SCORE DETERMINE SCORE (divide points earned by total points possible, multiply results by 100)

Actual Student Time Needed to Complete Procedure: ____________

Student's Initials: ____________ Instructor's Initials: ____________ Grade: ____________

Suggestions for Improvement: ____

____

____

____

Evaluator's Name (print) ____

Evaluator's Signature ____

Comments ____

SKILLS COMPETENCY ASSESSMENT

Procedure 7–8: Positioning Patient in the Trendelenburg Position

Student's Name: ______________________________ Date: ____________

Objective: To safely and properly assist patient into Trendelenburg position for certain abdominal surgical procedures.

Condition: The student demonstrates the ability to position the patient in the Trendelenburg position using the following equipment and supplies: examination table, drape, gown.

Time Requirements and Accuracy Standards: 2 minutes. Points assigned reflect importance of step to meeting objective: Important = (5) Essential = (10) Critical = (15). Automatic failure results if any of the **critical** tasks are omitted or performed incorrectly.

STANDARD PRECAUTIONS:

SKILLS ASSESSMENT CHECKLIST

Task Performed	Possible Points	TASKS
❑	5	Washes hands and follows standard precautions.
❑	5	Assists patient to undress. Provides gown.
❑	5	Assists patient to sit on the end of the table. Places drape over lap and legs.
❑	5	Assists patient to lie back on table, with head at headboard. Adjusts drape.
❑	10	Ensures that patient's feet are flexed over the end of the table.
❑	5	May lower the head of table to a 45° angle, if necessary.
❑	5	Adjusts drape from shoulders to ankles to ensure privacy.
❑	10	Upon completion of procedure, assists patient to return to seated position.
❑	10	Allows patient to sit at end of table for a few minutes to prevent dizziness.
❑	15	Once patient is stable (checks patient's skin color, checks pulse), gives further instructions as required.
❑	5	Completed the tasks within 2 minutes.
❑	15	Results obtained were accurate.

______	Earned	ADD POINTS OF TASKS CHECKED
95	Points	TOTAL POINTS POSSIBLE
______	SCORE	DETERMINE SCORE (divide points earned by total points possible, multiply results by 100)

Actual Student Time Needed to Complete Procedure: __________

Student's Initials: __________ Instructor's Initials: __________ Grade: __________

Suggestions for Improvement: ______________________________

Evaluator's Name (print) ______________________________

Evaluator's Signature ______________________________

Comments ______________________________

SKILLS COMPETENCY ASSESSMENT

Procedure 7–9: Assisting with a Complete Physical Examination

Student's Name: ______________________________ Date: __________

Objective: To assist the physician in a complete physical examination.

Conditions: The student demonstrates the ability to assist the physician in a complete physical examination using the following equipment and supplies: urine specimen bottle, laboratory request forms, balance beam scales, Snellen chart, patient gown and drape, thermometer, stethoscope, sphygmomanometer, examination lights, penlights, ophthalmoscope, tonometer, otoscope, tuning fork, nasal speculum, tongue depressors, laryngeal and pharyngeal mirrors, tape measure, percussion hammer, safety pins, cotton balls, kidney-shaped basin, gloves, lubricant, tissues, alcohol swabs, gauze sponges, biohazard and regular waste containers.

Time Requirements and Accuracy Standards: 15 minutes. Points assigned reflect importance of step to meeting objective: Important = (5) Essential = (10) Critical = (15). Automatic failure results if any of the **critical** tasks are omitted or performed incorrectly.

STANDARD PRECAUTIONS:

SKILLS ASSESSMENT CHECKLIST

Task Performed	Possible Points	TASKS
❑	5	Washes hands.
❑	5	Assembles equipment.
❑	10	Places instruments in easily accessible sequence for physician's use, making efficient use of time and space.
❑	5	Greets and identifies patient.
❑	5	Explains procedure to patient.
❑	5	*Rationale:* Explains procedure to obtain patient cooperation and allay apprehension.
❑	5	Reviews medical history with patient (see Procedure 5–1).
❑	5	*Rationale:* Reviewing medical history ensures that information is complete and current.
❑	15	Takes and records patient's vital signs, visual acuity, and hearing test results.
❑	10	Obtains a urine specimen (see chapter 18 for urine collection procedures).
❑	10	Obtains all required blood samples (see chapter 16, procedures 16–1 through 16–4, for blood specimen collection procedures and chapter 17, procedures 17–1 through 17–9, for blood analysis procedures).
❑	10	Obtains electrocardiogram if directed by physician (see Procedures 14–1 and 14–2).
❑	10	Provides patient with appropriate gown and drape.

SKILLS COMPETENCY ASSESSMENT — continued

Procedure 7–9: Assisting with a Complete Physical Examination

Task Performed	Possible Points	TASKS
❑	5	Assists patient to disrobe completely; explains where the opening for the gown is to be placed.
❑	5	*Rationale:* Assists patient in maintaining modesty, privacy, and warmth.
❑	5	Assists patient in sitting at the end of the table; drapes patient's lap and legs to maintain patient's modesty.
❑	5	Informs physician when patient is ready.
❑	5	When the physician arrives, remains by the patient ready to assist him or her and/or physician.
❑	5	Positions patient in a seated or supine position for the head, throat, eye, ear, and neck examination.
❑	5	Turns off lights to allow pupils to dilate for retinal examination, if necessary.
❑	5	Hands the physician instruments as required (some physicians will not require the medical assistant to hand the instruments).
❑	5	Has patient maintain the seated position for auscultation of the chest and heart and examination of the posterior aspect of the body.
❑	5	Maintains a quiet atmosphere to enhance the ability of the physician in hearing heart and lung sounds.
❑	5	*Rationale:* Understands that a quiet environment is necessary to accurately hear heart and lung sounds.
❑	5	Assists the patient into a supine position and drapes patient for examination of the chest. For female patients, see Procedure 30-7: Instructing Patient in Self-Breast Examination.
❑	5	Maintains patient in supine position and drapes patient for abdominal and extremities examinations.
❑	5	Gynecological examination may then be performed for female patients (see Procedure 30–6: Assisting with Gynecologic or Pelvic Examination and a Papanicolaou (Pap) Test). Assists patient into lithotomy position for gynecological and rectal examination.
❑	5	Testicular examination performed and rectal area examined for lesions and for size of prostate for male patients.
❑	5	Assists patient into Sims' position, if a more comprehensive rectal examination is necessary.
❑	5	Upon completion of the examination, assists patient to seated position and allows patient to sit at end of table for a few minutes to recover from any dizziness.
❑	5	Assures patient stability (checks color of skin, checks pulse) before allowing patient to stand up.

Task Performed	Possible Points	TASKS
❑	5	Assists patient in dressing; provides privacy.
❑	15	Charts any notes or patient instructions per physician's orders.
❑	5	Escorts patient to physician's office for discussion of examination results.
❑	5	Puts on disposable gloves.
❑	5	Disposes of gown and drape in a biohazard waste container.
❑	5	*Rationale:* Proper disposal prevents microorganism cross-contamination from patient body secretions.
❑	5	Disposes of contaminated materials in a biohazard container.
❑	5	*Rationale:* Prevents cross-contamination from bloodborne microorganisms and OPIM.
❑	5	Removes table paper and disposes in a biohazard waste container.
❑	5	*Rationale:* Prevents microorganism cross-contamination.
❑	5	Disinfects counters and examination table with a solution of 10 percent bleach.
❑	5	*Rationale:* Prevents microorganism cross-contamination by blood and OPIM.
❑	10	Cleans, sanitizes, disinfects, or sterilizes reusable instruments as instructed.
❑	5	Removes gloves, discards them in a biohazard waste container.
❑	5	*Rationale:* Prevents microorganism cross-contamination by blood and OPIM.
❑	5	Washes hands.
❑	10	Replaces table paper and equipment in preparation for the next patient.
❑	5	Completed the tasks within 15 minutes.
❑	15	Results obtained were accurate.

________	Earned	ADD POINTS OF TASKS CHECKED
300	Points	TOTAL POINTS POSSIBLE
________	SCORE	DETERMINE SCORE (divide points earned by total points possible, multiply results by 100)

Actual Student Time Needed to Complete Procedure: ____________

Student's Initials: ____________ Instructor's Initials: ____________ Grade: ____________

Suggestions for Improvement: ________________________________

Evaluator's Name (print) ________________________________

Evaluator's Signature ________________________________

Comments ________________________________

EVALUATION OF CHAPTER KNOWLEDGE

How has your instructor evaluated the knowledge you have achieved?

Knowledge	Instructor Evaluation *Good*	*Average*	*Poor*
Understands six methods used in physical examinations	_____	_____	_____
Demonstrates ability to place patients in eight positions used for physical examinations	_____	_____	_____
Understands draping techniques and the importance of patient privacy	_____	_____	_____
Identifies instruments and supplies necessary for examination of various body parts	_____	_____	_____
Identifies basic components of the physical examination	_____	_____	_____
Identifies sequence followed during a routine physical examination	_____	_____	_____
Recalls method of examination, instruments used, and positions for examination of at least eight body parts	_____	_____	_____
Understands quality control techniques and guidelines	_____	_____	_____
Observes all standard precautions and applies principles of aseptic technique	_____	_____	_____
Documents accurately, maintaining medical records and completing requisition forms	_____	_____	_____
Prepares patient for procedure	_____	_____	_____
Respects patient and attends to patient's emotional needs during physical examination	_____	_____	_____
Prepares and maintains examination and treatment areas	_____	_____	_____

Student's Initials: ______ Instructor's Initials: ______

Grade: _______

CHAPTER 8

Assisting with Minor Surgery

PERFORMANCE OBJECTIVES

Minor surgery is often performed in the ambulatory care setting by a physician with the help of a medical assistant. Medical assistants must be knowledgeable about surgical asepsis and sterile principles, surgical instruments, suture materials, surgical supplies and equipment, and basic surgery setup. Medical assistants should also know how to prepare patients for minor surgery, provide patient care, and assist the physician during common minor surgical procedures performed in the ambulatory care setting.

EXERCISES AND ACTIVITIES

Vocabulary Builder

A. Unscramble the following vocabulary words. Write the correct word in the space next to each scrambled word.

1. mmationinfla ____________________
2. ineepinephr ____________________
3. turealig ____________________
4. diumso xidedrohy ____________________
5. bechilens ____________________
6. thesiaanes ____________________
7. tabedine ____________________
8. lversi ratenit ____________________
9. propisoyl holcoal ____________________
10. drohygen ideoxper ____________________
11. turesstric ____________________

12. nusatet ________________________________

13. calsurgi sispesa ____________________________

B. Match the vocabulary words below with their correct definitions.

______ 1. Allergies

______ 2. Antibacterial

______ 3. Approximate

______ 4. Bandage

______ 5. Cautery

______ 6. Contamination

______ 7. Dressings

______ 8. Infection

______ 9. Informed Consent

______ 10. Liquid Nitrogen

______ 11. Mayo Stand/Instrument Tray

______ 12. Ratchets

______ 13. Surgery Cards

______ 14. Suture

______ 15. Swaged

A. To bring together the edges of a wound.

B. A written reference for surgeries and procedures.

C. Gauze or other material applied directly to a wound to absorb secretions and for protection.

D. When a surgical needle is attached to length of suture material.

E. Surgical material or thread; may describe the act of sewing with the surgical thread and needle.

F. Being sensitive to a normally harmless substance that causes an autoimmune reaction.

G. An invasion of pathogens into living tissue.

H. A voluntary agreement to have a procedure or surgery after a patient has been informed about the risks and benefits.

I. A portable metal tray table used for setting up sterile fields for minor surgery and procedures.

J. Capable of destroying bacteria.

K. Commonly and incorrectly referred to as "dry ice," it is a very volatile freezing agent used to destroy unwanted tissue such as warts.

L. The locking mechanisms on the handles of many surgical instruments.

M. The destruction of tissue by burning.

N. Gauze or other material applied over dressing to protect and immobilize.

O. To make something unclean, often used to describe a sterile area being made "unsterile" or exposing a clean area to a pathogenic substance.

LEARNING REVIEW/CASE STUDY

1. Identify each entry below as an example that follows strict sterile principles or an example in which the sterile area, field, or tray is contaminated by writing "sterile" or "contaminated" in the spaces provided.

______________ A. Bruce Goldman, CMA, collects used instruments handed to him by Dr. Mark Woo during a minor surgical procedure to excise an infected sebaceous cyst by placing the instruments in a separate container or area out of view of the patient.

______________ B. Ellen Armstrong, CMA, sets up a sterile field for a minor surgical procedure. After setting up the field, she remembers that a sterile solution is required and leaves the room to obtain the solution to be poured into a sterile cup.

______________ C. Wanda Slawson, CMA, removes a dressing from a wound on a patient's arm and reaches over the sterile field to discard the used dressing in a biohazard waste container she has placed on the other side of the sterile field she set up for the procedure.

______________ D. Patient Edith Leonard will not stop talking and asking questions as Liz Corbin, CMA, removes sutures from a small wound on Edith's arm sustained during a recent fall. The medical assistant is careful to time her responses to Edith so she is not talking when she is working directly over the sterile field.

______________ E. Anna Preciado, CMA, applies sterile gloves in preparation to assist Dr. Lewis with a minor surgical procedure. During the procedure, she comforts the patient and assists the physician as required. When Anna's hands are not in use, she keeps them down at her sides, careful not to touch her gloved hands to her clothing or any other nonsterile item.

For each example above that represents a contamination of a sterile area, field, or tray, describe what went wrong and describe the correct sterile guidelines for each circumstance.

____

____

____

____

2. Identify each action that follows as an action appropriate to medical aseptic hand-washing technique (MAH), or surgical aseptic hand-washing technique (SAH).

_____ A. do not apply lotion

_____ B. glove for protection

_____ C. 2–3 minute duration

_____ D. scrub nails with brush and clean under each nail with cuticle stick

_____ E. apply lotion

_____ F. wash hands and wrists, and forearms to the elbows

_____ G. hands held down during rinsing

_____ H. 5–6 minute duration

3. Audrey Jones, CMA, will assist Dr. Lewis in suturing a long, deep, gaping laceration in Lenore McDonnell's leg, sustained when she fell while performing a wheelchair transfer from a car to the sidewalk on her campus. Audrey must prepare the examination room and assemble a sterile surgical tray for the physician's suturing procedure.

   A. From the selection that follows, identify each instrument by name. In the space below the instrument, give a brief description of what it is used for. Then, choose the correct instruments Audrey will need to prepare a sterile surgical tray for Dr. Lewis's suturing of the lacerated wound by placing an "X" in the appropriate boxes.

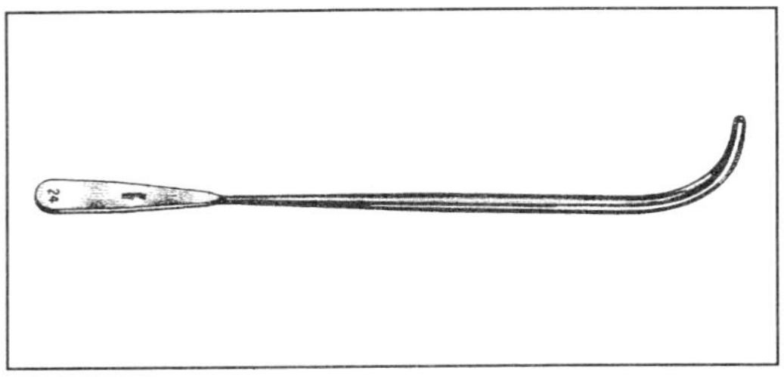

❑ A. ________________________

Purpose: ________________________

____

____

____

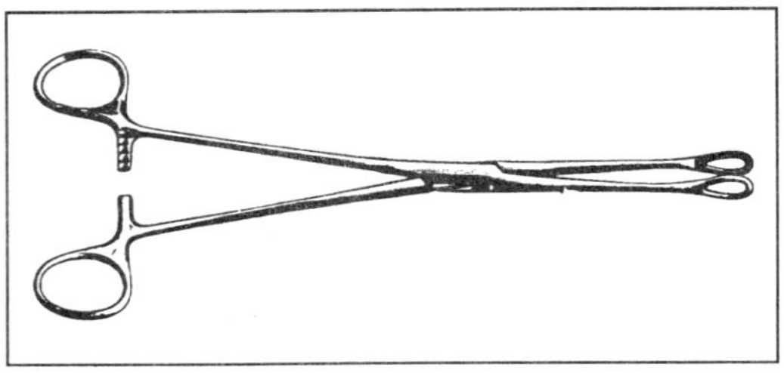

❑ B. ________________________

Purpose: ________________________

____

____

____

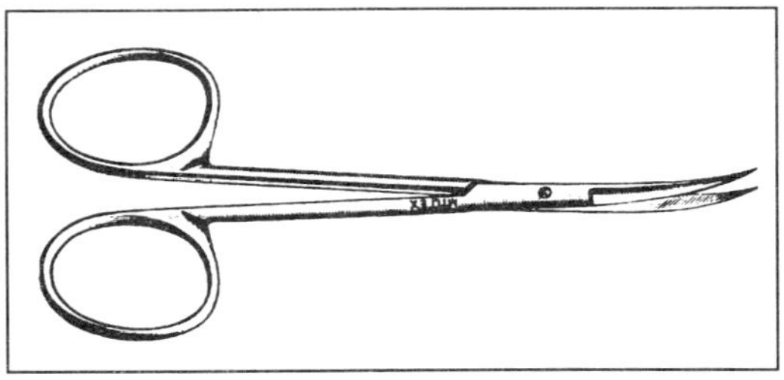

❑ C. ________________________

Purpose: ________________________

____

____

____

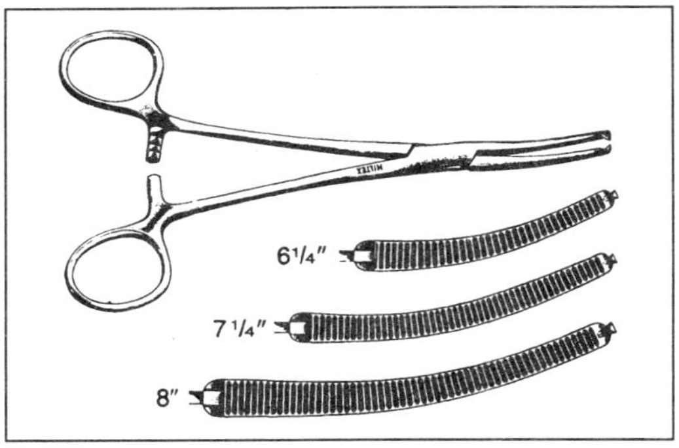

❑ D. ________________________

Purpose: ________________________

____

____

____

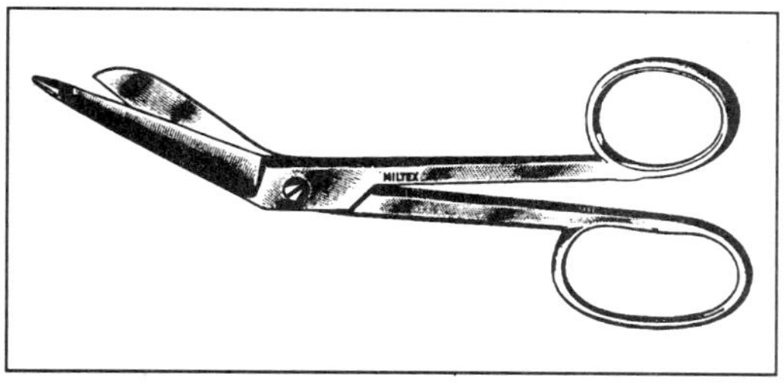

❑ E. ____________________

Purpose: ____________________

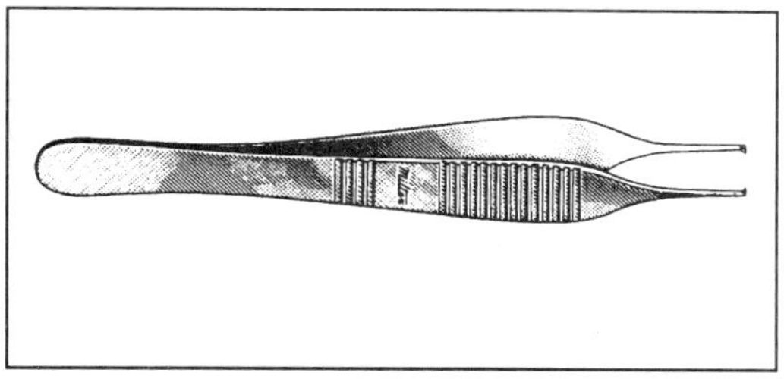

❑ F. ____________________

Purpose: ____________________

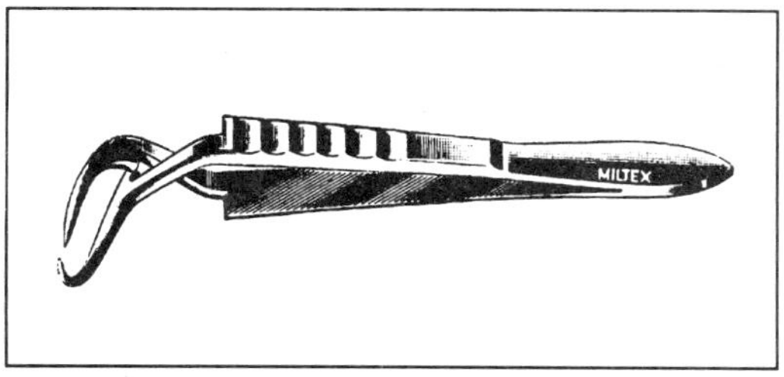

❑ G. ____________________

Purpose: ____________________

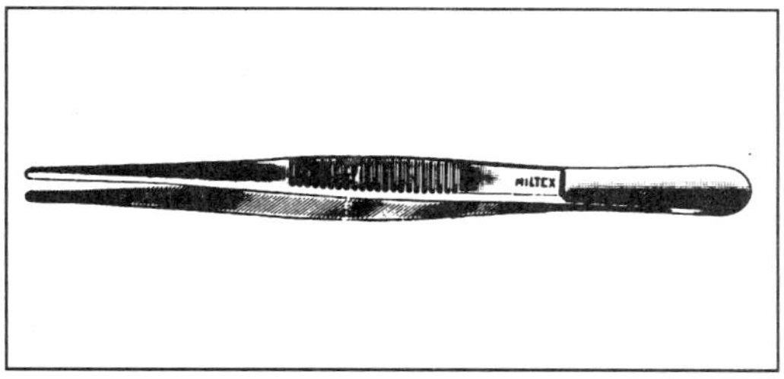

❑ H. ____________________

Purpose: ____________________

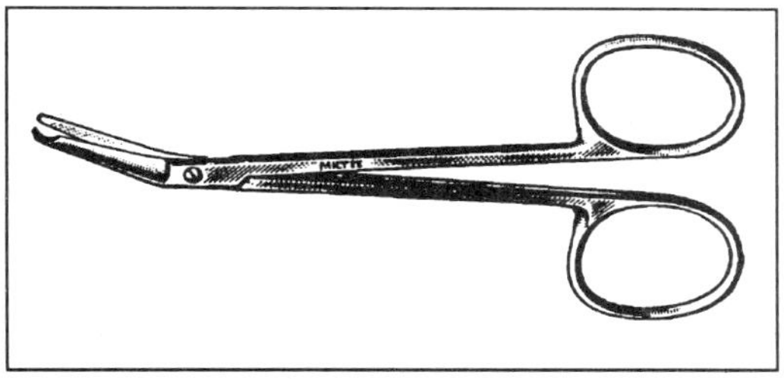

❑ I. ____________________

Purpose: ____________________

B. What other equipment will Audrey need to place on the sterile surgical tray for the physician's suturing of the lacerated wound? ____________________

What supplies will be needed for the side table? ____________________

C. When is suturing recommended? ____________________

What benefit does suturing provide the patient? ______________________________

____

Why must be done before a lacerated wound may be sutured? Why? ______________

____

4. When Lenore McDonnell returns to the physician's office to have sutures removed from her leg, Dr. Lewis checks the wound for the degree of healing and instructs Audrey Jones, CMA, to remove the sutures.

   A. From the selection of instruments shown in exercise #3A, which four will Audrey require for the suture removal procedure?

   (1) ______________________ (3) ______________________

   (2) ______________________ (4) ______________________

   B. What other equipment and supplies will Audrey assemble?

   ____

   ____

   ____

   C. What technique will Audrey use to perform the removal of the sutures?

   ____

   ____

   ____

   D. After removing the sutures, what additional patient care will Audrey give? Why?

   ____

   ____

   ____

SUPPLEMENTARY RESOURCES

Study Guide Disk: Additional practice exercises for this chapter are available on the study guide disk found in the textbook.

Medical Assisting Videos: Appropriate content is available on Delmar's Medical Assisting Videos, 2nd ed., for the following topics:

Tape 5: Set a Sterile Field
- Open a Sterile Pack
- Open a Peel Pack
- Use Disposable Trays of Instruments
- Perform Surgical Aseptic Procedures

Tape 6: Take Vital Signs

Tape 8: Assist Physician with Examination and Treatments
- Position and Drape the Patient
- Role of the Medical Assistant During the Examination

SKILLS COMPETENCY ASSESSMENT

Procedure 8–1: Chemical "Cold" Sterilization

Student's Name: ______________________________ Date: ____________

Objective: To sterilize heat-sensitive items such as fiber-optic endoscopes and delicate cutting instruments using an appropriate chemical solution.

Condition: The student demonstrates the ability to sterilize heat-sensitive items such as fiber-optic endoscopes and delicate cutting instruments using an appropriate chemical solution such as Cidex Steris System® (Percacetic acid) and the following equipment and supplies: airtight container, timer, sterile water, gloves (heavy-duty), sterile towel, plastic-lined sterile drapes.

Time Requirements and Accuracy Standards: 5 minutes. Points assigned reflect importance of step to meeting objective: Important = (5) Essential = (10) Critical = (15). Automatic failure results if any of the **critical** tasks are omitted or performed incorrectly.

STANDARD PRECAUTIONS:

SKILLS ASSESSMENT CHECKLIST

Task Performed	Possible Points	TASKS
❑	10	Sanitizes items that require chemical sterilization (see Procedure 21–4). Rinses and dries items.
❑	5	*Rationale:* Recalls that debris and body proteins must be scrubbed from items prior to sterilization.
❑	5	Reads manufacturer's instructions on original container of chemical sterilization solution.
❑	5	*Rationale:* Understands that each brand of chemical sterilization solution has specific preparation instructions and germicidal properties. Keeps solution in original container to avoid accidental poisoning.
❑	5	Puts on gloves.
❑	5	*Rationale:* Understands that heavy-duty gloves help protect from sharp items puncturing the skin and from harsh chemicals.
❑	10	Prepares solution as indicated by manufacturer, places the date of opening or preparation on the container, and initials it.
❑	5	*Rationale:* Following the manufacturer's instructions ensures sterility.
❑	5	Pours solution into a container with an airtight lid; avoids splashing.
❑	5	*Rationale:* Understands that chemicals should not be left exposed to open air in order to prevent evaporation and loss of potency, exposure to environmental contaminants, accidental inhalation, or poisoning. Splashing may cause injury to skin or mucous membranes.

SKILLS COMPETENCY ASSESSMENT — continued

Procedure 8–1: Chemical "Cold" Sterilization

Task Performed	Possible Points	TASKS
❑	10	Places sanitized and dried items into the solution, completely submersing item(s). Avoids splashing when placing items into airtight container.
❑	5	*Rationale:* Understands that total immersion is necessary for sterilization to be achieved.
❑	5	Closes lid of containers, labels with name of solution, exposure time required per manufacturer, and initials.
❑	5	*Rationale:* Understands that exposure time is the required time indicated by the manufacturer to achieve sterility.
❑	10	Does not open lid or add additional items during the processing time.
❑	5	*Rationale:* Understands that adding to the container interrupts the sterilization process and limits effectiveness of the chemical.
❑	15	Follows the recommended processing time, lifts item(s) from the container using sterile gloved hands or sterile transfer forceps. Holds item carefully above sterile basin and pours copious amounts of sterile water over it and through it (endoscopes) until adequately rinsed of chemical solution.
❑	5	*Rationale:* Items, once they are processed, are sterile and must be handled appropriately. Chemicals are rinsed from both the outside and inside of equipment (endoscopes) because they can be caustic to tissues.
❑	10	Holds item(s) upright for a few seconds to allow excess sterile water to drip off.
❑	10	Places the sterile item on a sterile towel, which has been placed on a sterile field, and dries it with another sterile towel. Removes the towel used for drying from the sterile field. Plastic-lined sterile drapes are used for the sterile field.
❑	5	*Rationale:* Plastic-lined sterile drapes create a barrier to prevent moisture from drawing contaminants from the metal surgical instrument tray or countertop up into the sterile area. The wet towel used to dry the endoscope is removed to prevent contamination.
❑	5	Completed the tasks within 5 minutes.
❑	15	Results obtained were accurate.

________	Earned	ADD POINTS OF TASKS CHECKED
165	Points	TOTAL POINTS POSSIBLE
________	SCORE	DETERMINE SCORE (divide points earned by total points possible, multiply results by 100)

Actual Student Time Needed to Complete Procedure: ____________

Student's Initials: ____________ Instructor's Initials: ____________ Grade: ____________

Suggestions for Improvement: ____________________________________

Evaluator's Name (print) ____________________________________

Evaluator's Signature ____________________________________

Comments ____________________________________

SKILLS COMPETENCY ASSESSMENT

Procedure 8–2: Applying Sterile Gloves

Student's Name: ______________________________ Date: ____________

Objective: To provide direction on how to apply sterile gloves without compromising sterility.

Conditions: The student demonstrates the ability to apply sterile gloves without compromising sterility using a packaged pair of sterile gloves.

Time Requirements and Accuracy Standards: 5 minutes. Points assigned reflect importance of step to meeting objective: Important = (5) Essential = (10) Critical = (15). Automatic failure results if any of the **critical** tasks are omitted or performed incorrectly.

STANDARD PRECAUTIONS:

SKILLS ASSESSMENT CHECKLIST

Task Performed	Possible Points	TASKS
❑	5	Removes rings and watches. Washes hands using surgical asepsis.
❑	5	*Rationale:* Understands that jewelry can snag gloves, interfering with barrier protection.
❑	10	Inspects glove package for tears or stains.
❑	5	*Rationale:* Torn or stained gloves are not sterile and must be disposed of or used for nonsterile purpose.
❑	10	Places the glove package on a clean, dry, flat surface above waist level.
❑	5	*Rationale:* A contaminated surface would compromise sterility of the sterile package.
❑	10	Peels open the package taking care not to touch the sterile inner surface of the package. Does not allow the gloves to slide beyond the sterile inner border.
❑	15	Opens the gloves with the cuffs toward the body, the palms of the gloves face up, and the thumbs pointing outward. Turns the package around, being careful not to reach over the sterile area or touch the inner surface or the gloves, if the gloves are not positioned properly.
❑	15	Grasps the inner cuffed edge of the opposite glove with the index finger and thumb of the nondominant hand. Picks the glove straight up off the package surface without dragging or dangling the fingers over any nonsterile area.
❑	5	*Rationale:* This method prevents the outer glove from becoming contaminated.

SKILLS COMPETENCY ASSESSMENT — continued

Procedure 8–2: Applying Sterile Gloves

Task Performed	Possible Points	TASKS
❑	15	Slides the hand carefully into the glove with the palm up on the dominant hand. Does not allow the outside of the glove to come into contact with anything. Always holds the hands above the waist and away from the body.
❑	5	*Rationale:* Understands that palm-up orientation keeps glove sterile in the palm area if it rolls slightly on the back of the hand.
❑	15	Picks up the glove for the remaining hand with the gloved hand by slipping four fingers under the outside of the cuff. Lifts the second glove up, keeping it held above the waist and away from the body. Does not allow the glove to drag across the package or touch nonsterile surfaces.
❑	5	*Rationale:* Understands that outside of the other glove is sterile and may only be touched by another sterile surface.
❑	15	Slips the second hand into the glove with the palm up. Does not allow the outside of the gloves to touch nonsterile skin.
❑	15	Adjusts the gloves on the hands as needed, but avoids touching the wrist area. Keeps gloved hands above the waist and away from the body. Does not touch nonsterile surfaces with gloved hands.
❑	5	Completed the tasks within 5 minutes.
❑	15	Results obtained were accurate.

_______	Earned	ADD POINTS OF TASKS CHECKED
175	Points	TOTAL POINTS POSSIBLE
_______	SCORE	DETERMINE SCORE (divide points earned by total points possible, multiply results by 100)

Actual Student Time Needed to Complete Procedure: ____________

Student's Initials: ____________ Instructor's Initials: ____________ Grade: ____________

Suggestions for Improvement: ____

____

____

____

Evaluator's Name (print) ____

Evaluator's Signature ____

Comments ____

SKILLS COMPETENCY ASSESSMENT

Procedure 8–3: Setting Up and Covering a Sterile Field

Student's Name: ______________________________ Date: ____________

Objective: To set up and cover a sterile field.

Conditions: The student demonstrates the ability to use disposable sterile field drapes or sterile towels to isolate a sterile area or field as well as to cover the sterile field for use in minor office surgery and procedures using the following equipment and supplies: 2 disposable sterile field drapes or 2 sterile towels (muslin or linen with water-repellent finish), Mayo instrument tray/stand, sterile transfer forceps.

Time Requirements and Accuracy Standards: 10 minutes. Points assigned reflect importance of step to meeting objective: Important = (5) Essential = (10) Critical = (15). Automatic failure results if any of the **critical** tasks are omitted or performed incorrectly.

STANDARD PRECAUTIONS: 

SKILLS ASSESSMENT CHECKLIST

Task Performed	Possible Points	TASKS
❑	5	Washes hands.
❑	10	Sanitizes and disinfects a Mayo instrument tray.
❑	5	Selects an appropriate disposable sterile field drape and places drape package on a clean, dry, flat surface, or removes a fan-folded sterile cloth towel from a canister using sterile forceps.
❑	5	*Rationale:* Sterile field drapes are fan-folded and positioned within the package to facilitate ease of use. Sterile towels are fan-folded and positioned within the canister for ease of use.
❑	10	If using disposable drape, peels open the package exposing the fan-folded drape. Turns package if necessary so cut corners of drape face toward the body. Or, removes sterile towel from canister using sterile transfer forceps.
❑	5	*Rationale:* The drape or towel will naturally unfold as it is lifted so care must be taken to ensure than it is lifted quickly and allowed to unfold without touching a nonsterile area.
❑	10	With thumb and forefinger of one hand, carefully grasps the top cut corner without touching the rest of the drape or towel and picks up the drape or towel high enough to assure that as it unfolds it does not drag across a nonsterile area.
❑	10	Holds the drape or towel above waist level and away from the body and grasps the opposing corner so both corners along the short edge of the drape are held.

SKILLS COMPETENCY ASSESSMENT — continued

Procedure 8–3: Setting Up and Covering a Sterile Field

Task Performed	Possible Points	TASKS
❑	15	Keeps the drape or towel above waist level and away from the body and reaches over the Mayo tray with the drape or towel. Takes care that the lower edge does not drag across the tray.
❑	5	*Rationale:* Sterile principle states that sterile items should be kept above the waist.
❑	15	Gently pulls the drape or towel toward the body as it is laid onto the tray. If adjusting to center on tray, does not touch the center of the drape or towel, or reach over the sterile field, but walks around or reaches underneath the tray to move it or make adjustments.
❑	5	*Rationale:* Understands that edges hanging over the tray are not sterile.
❑	15	Repeats procedure with a second drape or towel. Instead of pulling the drape toward the body, which would necessitate reaching over the sterile field, applies the covering drape or towel by holding it up in front of the field. Adjusts the lower edge so it is even with the lower edge of the field drape or towel. With a forward motion, carefully lays the cover over the sterile field.
❑	5	*Rationale:* Understands that reaching over sterile field will contaminate the tray.
❑	5	Completed the tasks within 10 minutes.
❑	15	Results obtained were accurate.

________	Earned	ADD POINTS OF TASKS CHECKED
140	Points	TOTAL POINTS POSSIBLE
________	SCORE	DETERMINE SCORE (divide points earned by total points possible, multiply results by 100)

Actual Student Time Needed to Complete Procedure: ____________

Student's Initials: ____________ Instructor's Initials: ____________ Grade: ____________

Suggestions for Improvement: ____

____

____

____

Evaluator's Name (print) ____

Evaluator's Signature ____

Comments ____

SKILLS COMPETENCY ASSESSMENT

Procedure 8–4: Opening Sterile Packages of Instruments and Applying Them to a Sterile Field

Student's Name: ______________________________ Date: ____________

Objective: To open sterile packages of surgical instruments and supplies and place them onto a sterile field using sterile technique.

Conditions: The student demonstrates the ability to open sterile packages of surgical instruments and supplies and place them onto a sterile field with sterile technique using the following equipment and supplies: Mayo instrument tray, sterile field drapes (2) or sterile towels (2), sterile gloves, wrapped-twice sterile surgical instruments, prepackaged sterile surgical supplies.

Time Requirements and Accuracy Standards: 10 minutes. Points assigned reflect importance of step to meeting objective: Important = (5) Essential = (10) Critical = (15). Automatic failure results if any of the **critical** tasks are omitted or performed incorrectly.

STANDARD PRECAUTIONS:

SKILLS ASSESSMENT CHECKLIST

Task Performed	Possible Points	TASKS
❑	5	Assembles supplies.
❑	5	Washes hands and sets up sterile field.
❑	10	Positions package of surgical instruments on palm of nondominant hand with outer envelope flap on top to facilitate opening the pack while protecting the sterile contents.
❑	5	*Rationale:* This will facilitate opening the pack while protecting the sterile contents.
❑	10	Grasps the taped end of the top flap and opens the first flap away from them. Does not touch the inside of the flap.
❑	10	Grasps just the folded back tips of the side flaps and pulls the right-sided flap to the right. Then pulls the left-sided flap to the left, taking care not to reach over the package.
❑	5	*Rationale:* Understands that pulling the tips of the flaps toward each side allows the inner portion of the package to be exposed without contamination.
❑	10	Pulls the last flap toward them by grasping the folded-back tip, taking care not to touch the inner contents of the package.
❑	5	*Rationale:* Understands that this method avoids reaching over the inner contents of the package.
❑	10	Gathers all of the loose edges together to obtain a snug covering over their nondominant hand. Closes their covered hand over the inner package and carefully applies the inner package to the sterile field.

SKILLS COMPETENCY ASSESSMENT — continued

Procedure 8–4: Opening Sterile Packages of Instruments and Applying Them to a Sterile Field

Task Performed	Possible Points	TASKS
❑	5	*Rationale:* Understands that gathering loose edges prevents dragging across the sterile field.
❑	15	Opens peel-apart packages using sterile techniques by grasping both edges of the flaps and pulling them apart in a rolling down motion, keeping both hands together. Gradually exposes the sterile item between the two peel-apart edges. Offers the sterile inner contents to the sterile-gloved physician or applies it to the sterile field using a flipping motion, taking care not to contaminate either the package contents or the field.
❑	15	Applies sterile gloves. Arranges instruments and supplies in an organized and logical manner according to the physician's preference. Points all handles toward the user. Separates instruments as much as possible within the space of the field so entanglement of instruments is not a problem.
❑	10	Applies the sterile field cover.
❑	5	*Rationale:* A sterile cover will need to be applied if the surgical tray will not be used immediately, needs to be moved, or if the medical assistant leaves the tray unattended.
❑	5	Completed the tasks within 10 minutes.
❑	15	Results obtained were accurate.

________	Earned	ADD POINTS OF TASKS CHECKED
145	Points	TOTAL POINTS POSSIBLE
________	SCORE	DETERMINE SCORE (divide points earned by total points possible, multiply results by 100)

Actual Student Time Needed to Complete Procedure: ____________

Student's Initials: ____________ Instructor's Initials: ____________ Grade: ____________

Suggestions for Improvement: ________________________________

____

____

____

Evaluator's Name (print) ________________________________

Evaluator's Signature ________________________________

Comments ________________________________

SKILLS COMPETENCY ASSESSMENT

Procedure 8–5: Pouring a Sterile Solution into a Cup on a Sterile Field

Student's Name: ______________________________ Date: ____________

Objective: To pour a sterile solution into a cup on a sterile tray in a sterile manner.

Conditions: The student demonstrates the ability to pour a sterile solution into a cup on a sterile tray in a sterile manner using the following equipment and supplies: covered sterile surgical tray with a sterile cup in upper-right corner, container of sterile solution.

Time Requirements and Accuracy Standards: 2 minutes. Points assigned reflect importance of step to meeting objective: Important = (5) Essential = (10) Critical = (15). Automatic failure results if any of the **critical** tasks are omitted or performed incorrectly.

SKILLS ASSESSMENT CHECKLIST

Task Performed	Possible Points	TASKS
☐	5	Transports the surgical tray into the surgical area before pouring the solution. Or: the surgical tray can be set up for immediate use in the surgical area.
☐	5	*Rationale:* Understands that solution may tip and spill during transport.
☐	5	Reads the label of the solution container and checks the expiration date.
☐	5	*Rationale:* To avoid pouring the wrong solution or using an outdated solution.
☐	10	Removes the cap from the solution container taking care not to touch the inner surface of the cap. Places the cap upside down on a nonsterile surface to avoid touching the inner surface of the cap with a nonsterile surface. Holds the cap right side up when it is held in the hand.
☐	5	*Rationale:* Understands that touching the inside of the cap with the hand or a nonsterile surface will contaminate the inside of an otherwise sterile container.
☐	15	Reads the label again to assure accuracy. Places palm over the label to protect the label from stains. Pours a small amount of the solution into a bowl or cup that is outside of the sterile field. If the sterile tray is set up in the surgical area, solution can be poured prior to covering the surgical tray with a sterile drape or towel.
☐	5	*Rationale:* This action cleanses container lip. NOTE: If the surgical tray is set up in the surgical area, the solution can be poured prior to voering the surgical ray with a sterile drape or towel.
☐	10	Pulls back carefully on the upper-right corner of the tray cover to expose the cup. Takes care to touch only the corner tip of the cover and to not reach over the exposed field.

SKILLS COMPETENCY ASSESSMENT — continued

Procedure 8–5: Pouring a Sterile Solution into a Cup on a Sterile Field

Task Performed	Possible Points	TASKS
❑	5	*Rationale:* Reaching over the sterile field or touching the underside of the cover will contaminate the sterile surgical tray.
❑	15	Approaches from the corner of the tray, and using the cleansed side of the lip of the container, pours the needed amount of solution into the sterile cup. Takes precautions to avoid splashing, spilling, reaching over the field, or touching any of the sterile surfaces.
❑	5	*Rationale:* Prevents contaminants from "wicking" from the metal tray into the sterile field. Polylined sterile field drapes will create a barrier.
❑	5	Replaces the cap of the solution container using sterile technique.
❑	10	Replaces the corner of the drape cover using sterile technique or covers with a sterile drape or towel.
❑	5	Completed the tasks within 2 minutes.
❑	15	Results obtained were accurate.
______	Earned	ADD POINTS OF TASKS CHECKED
125	Points	TOTAL POINTS POSSIBLE
______	SCORE	DETERMINE SCORE (divide points earned by total points possible, multiply results by 100)

Actual Student Time Needed to Complete Procedure: ____________

Student's Initials: ____________ Instructor's Initials: ____________ Grade: ____________

Suggestions for Improvement: ____

____

____

____

Evaluator's Name (print) ____

Evaluator's Signature ____

Comments ____

SKILLS COMPETENCY ASSESSMENT

Procedure 8–6: Preparation of Patient Skin for Minor Surgery

Student's Name: ______________________________ Date: __________

Objective: To remove as many microorganisms as possible from the patient's skin prior to surgery.

Conditions: The student demonstrates the ability to remove as many microorganisms as possible from the patient's skin prior to surgery using the following equipment and supplies: absorbent pad, drape, disposable prep kit (includes: antiseptic soap, several sponges, razor, and a container for water), sterile water, antiseptic solution, sterile bowl, sterile gloves for medical assistant and physician (2 pairs).

Time Requirements and Accuracy Standards: 10 minutes. Points assigned reflect importance of step to meeting objective: Important = (5) Essential = (10) Critical = (15). Automatic failure results if any of the **critical** tasks are omitted or performed incorrectly.

STANDARD PRECAUTIONS:

SKILLS ASSESSMENT CHECKLIST

Task Performed	Possible Points	TASKS
❑	5	Washes hands. Assembles equipment.
❑	5	Identifies patient. Explains the procedure, provides privacy, and drapes patient if appropriate.
❑	10	Provides good light source.
❑	5	Positions patient for comfort and preparation of site exposure.
❑	5	Washes hands.
❑	5	Protects area under preparation site with an absorbent pad.
❑	10	Puts on sterile gloves.
❑	10	Applies antiseptic soap (Betadine) with 4 × 4 sponges, beginning at operative site and moving outward in a circular motion from the center to away from the center of the prepared area.
❑	5	*Rationale:* Move from cleaner to least-clean areas to prevent contamination.
❑	5	Discards used sponges as necessary.

SKILLS COMPETENCY ASSESSMENT — continued

Procedure 8–6: Preparation of Patient Skin for Minor Surgery

Task Performed	Possible Points	TASKS
❑	15	Holds skin taut and uses razor to shave hair away from operative site, following hair growth pattern to prevent accidental nicks, which can cause infection.
❑	15	When hair has been removed, scrubs again in a circular fashion for about two to five minutes.
❑	10	Rinses shaved area with sterile water and dries with a sterile 4 × 4 gauze sponge.
❑	5	Covers with a sterile towel; instructs patient to not touch the area.
❑	5	Pours antiseptic solution (Betadine) into the sterile bowl. Physician will put on sterile gloves and using a sterile 4 × 4 gauze sponge will paint the operative site with the antiseptic solution. Lets dry, drapes patient with sterile drapes, and commences with the surgical procedure.
❑	5	Completed the tasks within 10 minutes.
❑	15	Results obtained were accurate.

_______	Earned	ADD POINTS OF TASKS CHECKED
135	Points	TOTAL POINTS POSSIBLE
_______	SCORE	DETERMINE SCORE (divide points earned by total points possible, multiply results by 100)

Actual Student Time Needed to Complete Procedure: ____________

Student's Initials: ____________ Instructor's Initials: ____________ Grade: ____________

Suggestions for Improvement: ____

____

____

____

Evaluator's Name (print) ____

Evaluator's Signature ____

Comments ____

SKILLS COMPETENCY ASSESSMENT

Procedure 8–7: Assisting with Minor Surgery

Student's Name: ______________________ Date: __________

Objective: To maintain sterility during minor surgical procedures that require surgical excision of a neoplasm.

Conditions: The student demonstrates the ability to maintain sterility during minor surgical procedures that require surgical excision of a neoplasm using the following equipment and supplies. Mayo stand: needles and syringe, Betadine solution, gauze sponges, scalpel and blades, dissecting scissors, operating scissors, forceps that hold the drapes or 4 sterile towels and 4 clamps, hemostats (2 curved and 2 straight), thumb forceps, suture material, tissue forceps, needle holder, skin retractor, transfer forceps. Side table: sterile gloves, labeled biopsy containers with formalin, appropriate laboratory requisition, anesthesia, alcohol wipes, dressing tape, bandages, biohazard container.

Time Requirements and Accuracy Standards: Time varies according to patient's condition and length of time required by the physician to complete the procedure. Points assigned reflect importance of step to meeting objective: Important = (5) Essential = (10) Critical = (15). Automatic failure results if any of the **critical** tasks are omitted or performed incorrectly.

STANDARD PRECAUTIONS:

SKILLS ASSESSMENT CHECKLIST

Task Performed	Possible Points	TASKS
❑	5	Checks room for readiness and equipment for cleanliness.
❑	5	Washes hands.
❑	5	Sets up side table of nonsterile items.
❑	5	*Rationale:* Understands that nonsterile items will contaminate a sterile field.
❑	10	Performs surgical asepsis handwash.
❑	15	Sets up sterile field on a Mayo stand or on a clean, dry, flat surface. • Uses a commercially prepared sterile setup that is appropriate for the surgical procedure. Opens the setup creating a sterile field with the inside of the sterile wrap. Adds other articles such as instruments or supplies as needed by using sterile transfer forceps or peel-apart packages that can be opened in a sterile fashion. *or* • Removes a sterile fan-folded towel from a canister of sterile towels using sterile transfer forceps. Holds one edge of the sterile towel and allows it to become unfolded by gently shaking it. Grasps the other edge and gently places the towel on the Mayo stand from the farthest side to the side nearest the body. Adds sterile articles.
❑	10	Applies sterile gloves. Arranges instruments according to use.

SKILLS COMPETENCY ASSESSMENT — continued

Procedure 8–7: Assisting with Minor Surgery

Task Performed	Possible Points	TASKS
❑	10	Covers the sterile field with a sterile towel if not being used immediately. Gently places towel from the side nearest the body to the side farthest away from the body.
❑	5	Identifies patient, explains the procedure, and prepares the patient.
❑	5	Prepares patient's skin (see Procedure 8–6).
❑	15	Removes the sterile cover from the sterile setup as the physician applies sterile gloves. Lifts the towel by grasping the tip of the corner farthest away from the body and lifting toward the body. Does not allow arms to pass over sterile field.
❑	15	Assists the physician as necessary, being certain to follow the principles of surgical asepsis. The physician will inject local anesthetic, apply Betadine or another antiseptic to the surgical site, apply sterile drapes, and begin the surgery.
❑	15	The medical assistant will assist the physician during surgery in the following manner: • Holds the vial of anesthesia while the physician withdraws the appropriate dose. • Adjusts the instrument tray and equipment around the physician. • Assures a good light source. • Comforts and supports the patient emotionally. • Assists with the surgery as directed by the physician (sterile gloves must be worn). • Hands instruments to the physician and receives used instruments from the physician and places them in a basin or container out of the patient's sight. • Holds biopsy container to receive specimen being excised, if necessary. • Does not contaminate the inside of the container. • Holds the cover facing down. Tightly places cover on the container. • Assists with or applies sterile dressing to the operative site.
❑	5	Assists patient as necessary.
❑	15	Handles the specimen container with disposable gloves as recommended by standard precautions. Assures that the container is tightly covered, labeled with the patient's name, date, type, and source of specimen and sent to the laboratory recommended by the appropriate laboratory requisition.
❑	15	Cleans surgical or examination room while wearing appropriate personal protective equipment (PPE). • Disposes of used sponges in biohazard container and knife blades and other disposable sharps in puncture-proof sharps container. • Rinses used surgical instruments; soaks, sanitizes, and sterilizes for reuse. • Removes gloves and other PPE and disposes of per OSHA guidelines.

Task Performed	Possible Points	TASKS
☐	5	Washes hands.
☐	5	Documents in the patient's record that the specimen was sent to the laboratory.
☐	5	Completed the tasks within the time constraint identified by the instructor.
☐	15	Results obtained were accurate.
________	Earned	ADD POINTS OF TASKS CHECKED
185	Points	TOTAL POINTS POSSIBLE
________	SCORE	DETERMINE SCORE (divide points earned by total points possible, multiply results by 100)

Actual Student Time Needed to Complete Procedure: ____________

Student's Initials: ____________ Instructor's Initials: ____________ Grade: ____________

Suggestions for Improvement: ______________________________

____

____

____

Evaluator's Name (print) ______________________________

Evaluator's Signature ______________________________

Comments ______________________________

DOCUMENTATION

Chart the procedure in the patient's medical record.

Date: ____________________

Charting: ______________________________

____

____

Student's Initials: ____________

SKILLS COMPETENCY ASSESSMENT

Procedure 8–8: Suturing of Laceration or Incision Repair

Student's Name: ______________________________ Date: ____________

Objective: To assist the physician in wound cleaning and suture repair of a laceration or incision-type wound.

Conditions: The student demonstrates the ability to assist the physician in wound cleaning and suture repair of a laceration or an incision-type wound, using the following equipment and supplies. Surgical tray: syringe and needle for anesthetic, hemostats (curved), Adson or tissue forceps, Iris scissors (curved), suture material and needle, needle holder, gauze sponges. Side table: anesthetic, as ordered by the physician, dressings, bandages, tape, splint/brace/sling (optional), sterile gloves.

Time Requirements and Accuracy Standards: 10 minutes. Points assigned reflect importance of step to meeting objective: Important = (5) Essential = (10) Critical = (15). Automatic failure results if any of the **critical** tasks are omitted or performed incorrectly.

STANDARD PRECAUTIONS:        

SKILLS ASSESSMENT CHECKLIST

Task Performed	Possible Points	TASKS
❑	5	Washes hands.
❑	10	Identifies the patient and explains the procedure. Checks for signed consent forms.
❑	5	Reassures and comforts the patient as needed.
❑	15	Assesses cause of wound and its severity. • Determines any known allergies and last tetanus booster • Identifies any health concerns to avoid possible complications • Soaks wound in an antiseptic solution as ordered by the physician • Cleans and dries wound • Positions patient comfortably, lying down
❑	5	Assists the physician as needed.
❑	5	Supports the patient as needed.
		Postoperative Care
❑	5	Applies sterile gloves.
❑	5	Cleans area around the wound.
❑	5	Dresses/bandages/splints wound following the physician's preference.
❑	5	Removes gloves, washes hands.

Task Performed	Possible Points	TASKS
❑	15	Checks patient's vital signs.
❑	15	Explains wound care to the patient (and caregiver) and provides written instructions, including symptoms of infection.
❑	5	Assists the patient with any concerns or questions.
❑	5	Arranges for follow-up appointment and medication, as ordered.
❑	10	Disposes of supplies per OSHA guidelines. Cleans room, sanitizes instruments, sterilizes for reuse.
❑	5	Washes hands; documents the procedure.
❑	5	Completed the tasks within 10 minutes.
❑	15	Results obtained were accurate.

________	Earned	ADD POINTS OF TASKS CHECKED
140	Points	TOTAL POINTS POSSIBLE
________	SCORE	DETERMINE SCORE (divide points earned by total points possible, multiply results by 100)

Actual Student Time Needed to Complete Procedure: ____________

Student's Initials: ____________ Instructor's Initials: ____________ Grade: ____________

Suggestions for Improvement: ________________________________

Evaluator's Name (print) ________________________________

Evaluator's Signature ________________________________

Comments ________________________________

DOCUMENTATION

Chart the procedure in the patient's medical record.

Date: ____________________

Charting: ________________________________

____

____

Student's Initials: ____________

SKILLS COMPETENCY ASSESSMENT

Procedure 8–9: Dressing Change

Student's Name: ______________________________ Date: ____________

Objective: To remove a wound dressing and apply a dry sterile dressing.

Conditions: The student demonstrates the ability to remove a wound dressing and apply a dry sterile dressing using the following equipment and supplies. Sterile field: several sterile gauze sponges and other dressing material as needed, sterile bowl with Betadine solution, sterile dressing forceps. Side area: nonsterile gloves, sterile gloves, container of hydrogen peroxide or sterile water, cotton-tipped applicators, sterile adhesive strips (optional), antibacterial ointment/cream as ordered, tape, bandage scissors (2), waterproof waste bag, biohazard waste container.

Time Requirements and Accuracy Standards: 10 minutes. Points assigned reflect importance of step to meeting objective: Important = (5) Essential = (10) Critical = (15). Automatic failure results if any of the **critical** tasks are omitted or performed incorrectly.

STANDARD PRECAUTIONS:    

SKILLS ASSESSMENT CHECKLIST

Task Performed	Possible Points	TASKS
❑	5	Washes hands.
❑	10	Prepares sterile field. Adds gauze sponges, bowl with solution, and forceps.
❑	5	Positions a waterproof bag away from sterile area.
❑	5	Pours Betadine solution into sterile bowl.
❑	5	Identifies the patient and explains the procedure.
❑	5	Reassures and comforts the patient as needed.
❑	5	Loosens tape on dressing or cuts off bandage if necessary.
❑	5	Puts on nonsterile gloves or uses forceps.
❑	10	Removes bandage carefully, places in biohazard waste container. Does not pass over sterile field.
❑	15	Removes dressing, taking care not to cause stress on the wound. If stuck to the wound, pours small amounts of sterile water or hydrogen peroxide over dressing; allows to soak for a short time. Removes dressing when loose enough to remove without resistance.
❑	10	Places used dressing in waterproof bag without touching inside or outside of bag.
❑	10	Assesses wound and notes any drainage or signs of infection. Removes and discards gloves in waterproof bag.

Task Performed	Possible Points	TASKS
❑	10	Washes hands, applies sterile gloves.
❑	5	Cleans the wound with Betadine solution.
❑	5	Disposes of used gauze in waterproof bag.
❑	10	Using forceps, applies sterile gauze sponge (s) to wound.
❑	5	Removes gloves and disposes of in waterproof bag.
❑	5	Secures dressing with adhesive tape, roller bandage, or elastic bandage.
❑	5	Disposes of waterproof bag in biohazard container.
❑	5	Washes hands.
❑	15	Documents procedure and describes wound appearance (i.e., discharge, signs of infection, healing, etc.)
❑	5	Completed the tasks within 10 minutes.
❑	15	Results obtained were accurate.
______	Earned	ADD POINTS OF TASKS CHECKED
175	Points	TOTAL POINTS POSSIBLE
______	SCORE	DETERMINE SCORE (divide points earned by total points possible, multiply results by 100)

Actual Student Time Needed to Complete Procedure: ____________

Student's Initials: ____________ Instructor's Initials: ____________ Grade: ____________

Suggestions for Improvement: ____

Evaluator's Name (print) ____

Evaluator's Signature ____

Comments ____

DOCUMENTATION

Chart the procedure in the patient's medical record.

Date: ____________________

Charting: ____

____

____

Student's Initials: ____________

SKILLS COMPETENCY ASSESSMENT

Procedure 8–10: Suture Removal

Student's Name: ______________________________ Date: ____________

Objective: To remove sutures from a healed minor surgical wound (as per physician).

Conditions: The student demonstrates the ability to remove sutures from a healed minor surgical wound (as per physician) using the following equipment and supplies: gauze sponges, biohazard waste container, tape, suture removal kit (suture scissors or staple remover and thumb forceps), sterile latex gloves, Betadine solution or wash.

Time Requirements and Accuracy Standards: 10 minutes. Points assigned reflect importance of step to meeting objective: Important = (5) Essential = (10) Critical = (15). Automatic failure results if any of the **critical** tasks are omitted or performed incorrectly.

STANDARD PRECAUTIONS:

SKILLS ASSESSMENT CHECKLIST

Task Performed	Possible Points	TASKS
❑	5	Identifies patient. Washes hands.
❑	5	Opens suture removal kit.
❑	10	Applies sterile gloves.
❑	10	Uses thumb forceps to gently pick up one knot of a suture. Pulls gently upward.
❑	15	Uses suture removal scissors to cut one side of the suture as close to skin as possible.
❑	5	*Rationale:* This technique ensures that the suture will be pulled out from under the skin, avoiding contamination of the wound.
❑	15	Removes all sutures in the same manner, noting number of sutures removed. Disposes of the sutures on a sterile gauze sponge.
❑	5	Examines the wound to be sure all sutures have been removed.
❑	5	Applies Betadine solution to area.
❑	5	Applies dry sterile dressing if ordered by physician.
❑	5	Removes gloves. Disposes of used items per OSHA guidelines.
❑	5	Washes hands.
❑	15	Checks patient's vital signs.

Task Performed	Possible Points	TASKS
❑	10	Explains wound care; provides written instructions.
❑	5	Arranges follow-up appointment if necessary.
❑	5	Documents the procedure.
❑	5	Completed the tasks within 10 minutes.
❑	15	Results obtained were accurate.

________	Earned	ADD POINTS OF TASKS CHECKED
145	Points	TOTAL POINTS POSSIBLE
________	SCORE	DETERMINE SCORE (divide points earned by total points possible, multiply results by 100)

Actual Student Time Needed to Complete Procedure: ____________

Student's Initials: ____________ Instructor's Initials: ____________ Grade: ____________

Suggestions for Improvement: ____

____

____

____

Evaluator's Name (print) ____

Evaluator's Signature ____

Comments ____

DOCUMENTATION

Chart the procedure in the patient's medical record.

Date: ________________________

Charting: ____

____

____

Student's Initials: ______________

SKILLS COMPETENCY ASSESSMENT

Procedure 8–11: Application of Sterile Adhesive Skin Closure Strips

Student's Name: ______________________________ Date: ____________

Objective: To approximate the edges of a wound after the removal of sutures. Sometimes used in lieu of sutures or to give additional support along with sutures.

Conditions: The student demonstrates the ability to approximate the edges of a wound after the removal of sutures using the following equipment and supplies. Surgical tray: suture removal instruments, sterile adhesive skin closure strips, Iris scissors (straight), tincture of benzoin (optional) in sterile cup, sterile cotton-tipped applicators (for tincture of benzoin). Side area: sterile gloves, dressings, bandages, tape.

Time Requirements and Accuracy Standards: 5 minutes. Points assigned reflect importance of step to meeting objective: Important = (5) Essential = (10) Critical = (15). Automatic failure results if any of the **critical** tasks are omitted or performed incorrectly.

STANDARD PRECAUTIONS:

SKILLS ASSESSMENT CHECKLIST

Task Performed	Possible Points	TASKS
❑	5	Identifies the patient and explains the procedure. Positions patient comfortably.
❑	5	Washes hands and applies gloves.
❑	5	Removes bandages and dressings.
❑	5	Cleans and dries wound.
❑	10	Removes sutures (as per physician's orders).
❑	5	Assesses the need for skin closure strips and alerts the physician as indicated.
❑	10	Removes gloves, washes hands, opens container of tincture of benzoin, applies sterile gloves.
❑	10	Applies tincture of benzoin to edges of wound if directed. Uses sterile cotton-tipped applicator, taking care not to let it come into contact with the actual wound.
❑	15	Removes strips from packaging one at a time. Applies one end of a skin closure strip to one side of the wound. Places the first strip over the center of the wound.
❑	10	Secures the end to the skin by carefully pressing.
❑	10	Stretches the strip across the edge of the wound and secures it on the other side in the same manner. The motion should bring the edges together without puckering the skin.
❑	10	Applies the next two closure strips at halfway points between the first strip and each end of the wound.

Task Performed	Possible Points	TASKS
❑	15	Continues in this manner until the edges are approximated.
		Postoperative care
❑	5	Dresses and bandages if necessary.
❑	5	Disposes of used items per OSHA guidelines.
❑	5	Removes gloves and washes hands.
❑	15	Checks the patient's vital signs.
❑	15	Explains wound care to the patient (and caregiver) and provides written instructions, including symptoms of infection.
❑	5	Assists the patient with any concerns or questions.
❑	5	Arranges for follow-up appointment and medication, as ordered.
❑	5	Documents the procedure.
❑	5	Completed the tasks within 5 minutes.
❑	15	Results obtained were accurate.

_______	Earned	ADD POINTS OF TASKS CHECKED
195	Points	TOTAL POINTS POSSIBLE
_______	SCORE	DETERMINE SCORE (divide points earned by total points possible, multiply results by 100)

Actual Student Time Needed to Complete Procedure: ____________

Student's Initials: ____________ Instructor's Initials: ____________ Grade: ____________

Suggestions for Improvement: ____

Evaluator's Name (print) ____

Evaluator's Signature ____

Comments ____

DOCUMENTATION

Chart the procedure in the patient's medical record.

Date: ____________________

Charting: ____

____

____

Student's Initials: ____________

SKILLS COMPETENCY ASSESSMENT

Procedure 8–12: Sebaceous Cyst Excision

Student's Name: ______________________________ Date: ____________

Objective: To remove an inflamed or infected sebaceous cyst. To remove a sebaceous cyst that is not inflamed or infected but is located on an area of the body where the cyst is unsightly or where it may become irritated from rubbing.

Conditions: The student demonstrates the ability to assist in the removal of an inflamed or infected sebaceous cyst or to remove a sebaceous cyst that is not inflamed or infected using the following equipment and supplies. Surgical tray: syringe/needle for anesthesia, Iris scissors (curved), mosquito hemostat (curved), scalpel blades and handle, suture material with needle, Mayo scissors (curved). Side area: skin prep supplies, tissue forceps (2), gauze sponges (many), needle holder, fenestrated drape, antiseptic solution (Betadine), gloves (sterile and nonsterile), personal protective equipment, anesthesia as directed, dressing, bandages, tape, specimen container/requisition (optional), biohazard waste container, extra gauze squares, safety razor (optional), alcohol pledgets, culturette (optional).

Time Requirements and Accuracy Standards: Time varies according to patient's condition and the time required by the physician to complete the procedure. Points assigned reflect importance of step to meeting objective: Important = (5) Essential = (10) Critical = (15). Automatic failure results if any of the **critical** tasks are omitted or performed incorrectly.

STANDARD PRECAUTIONS:

SKILLS ASSESSMENT CHECKLIST

Task Performed	Possible Points	TASKS
❑	10	Washes hands. Identifies the patient and explains the procedure.
❑	5	Reassures and comforts the patient as needed.
❑	15	Determines any known allergies and last tetanus booster. Checks for signed consent form.
❑	5	Identifies any health concerns to avoid possible complications.
❑	5	Positions the patient comfortably, lying down.
❑	5	Performs the skin preparation, as directed.
❑	5	Wears appropriate PPE if cyst is infected.
❑	5	*Rationale:* Purulent material may drain out of the wound.
❑	15	Assists physician to inject the anesthesia by holding the vial while the physician withdraws the appropriate amount of anesthesia. Continues to assist while the physician incises the cyst, removes it, and sutures the surgical incision. The physician will place the specimen in a container with a preservative to be sent to the pathology lab for analysis.
❑	5	Supports patient during surgery.

Task Performed	Possible Points	TASKS
		Postoperative Care
❑	5	Applies sterile gloves.
❑	5	Cleans area around the wound.
❑	5	Dresses and bandages, as directed.
❑	5	Disposes of items per OSHA guidelines. Removes gloves.
❑	5	Washes hands.
❑	15	Checks the patient's vital signs.
❑	15	Explains wound care to the patient (and caregiver) and provides written instructions, including symptoms of infection.
❑	5	Assists the patient with any concerns or questions.
❑	5	Arranges for follow-up appointment and medication, as ordered.
❑	5	Documents the procedure.
❑	5	Completed the tasks within the time constraint identified by the instructor.
❑	15	Results obtained were accurate.

______	Earned	ADD POINTS OF TASKS CHECKED
165	Points	TOTAL POINTS POSSIBLE
______	SCORE	DETERMINE SCORE (divide points earned by total points possible, multiply results by 100)

Actual Student Time Needed to Complete Procedure: ____________

Student's Initials: ____________ Instructor's Initials: ____________ Grade: ____________

Suggestions for Improvement: ____

Evaluator's Name (print) ____

Evaluator's Signature ____

Comments ____

DOCUMENTATION

Chart the procedure in the patient's medical record.

Date: ______________________

Charting: ____

____

____

Student's Initials: ______________

SKILLS COMPETENCY ASSESSMENT

Procedure 8–13: Incision and Drainage of Localized Infections

Student's Name: ______________________________ Date: __________

Objective: To incise and drain an abscess or other localized infection.

Conditions: The student demonstrates the ability to assist in the incision and drainage of localized infections using the following equipment and supplies. Surgical tray: syringe/needle for anesthesia, scalpel blades and handle, thumb forceps, mosquito hemostat (optional), gauze sponges (many), fenestrated drape, tissue forceps (2), Mayo scissors, Iris scissors, antiseptic solution, such as Betadine in a sterile cup. Side area: skin prep supplies, gloves (sterile and nonsterile), personal protective equipment, anesthesia as directed, dressing, bandages, tape, specimen container with preservative/requisition (optional), biohazard waste container, extra gauze sponges, Iodoform gauze wick or penrose drain, alcohol pledget, antiseptic solution, culturette (optional).

Time Requirements and Accuracy Standards: Time varies according to patient condition and the time required by the physician to complete the procedure. Points assigned reflect importance of step to meeting objective: Important = (5) Essential = (10) Critical = (15). Automatic failure results if any of the **critical** tasks are omitted or performed incorrectly.

STANDARD PRECAUTIONS:

SKILLS ASSESSMENT CHECKLIST

Task Performed	Possible Points	TASKS
❑	5	Washes hands.
❑	5	Identifies the patient and explains the procedure.
❑	5	Reassures and comforts the patient as needed.
❑	15	Determines any known allergies and last tetanus booster.
❑	15	Checks for signed consent form.
❑	5	Identifies any health concerns to avoid possible complications.
❑	5	Positions the patient comfortably, lying down.
❑	5	Puts on PPE.
❑	15	Performs the skin preparation as directed.
❑	15	Assists the physician as needed to inject the anesthesia by holding the vial while the appropriate amount is aspirated for injection. The physician will incise the abscess and either Iodoform gauze or a penrose drain will be inserted into the wound to encourage drainage.
❑	5	Supports the patient as needed.

Task Performed	Possible Points	TASKS
		Postoperative Care
❑	5	Applies sterile gloves.
❑	5	Cleans area around the wound.
❑	10	Dresses and bandages as directed. Several thicknesses of dressing material may be needed to absorb exudate.
❑	5	Disposes of items per OSHA guidelines. Removes gloves, washes hands.
❑	15	Checks the patient's vital signs.
❑	15	Explains wound care to the patient (and caregiver) and provides written instructions such as apply warm moist compresses to wound. Explains to watch for symptoms of infection.
❑	5	Assists the patient with any concerns or questions.
❑	5	Arranges for follow-up appointment and medication, as ordered.
❑	10	Documents the procedure.
❑	5	Completed the tasks within the time constraint identified by the instructor.
❑	15	Results obtained were accurate.

_______	Earned	ADD POINTS OF TASKS CHECKED
180	Points	TOTAL POINTS POSSIBLE
_______	SCORE	DETERMINE SCORE (divide points earned by total points possible, multiply results by 100)

Actual Student Time Needed to Complete Procedure: ____________

Student's Initials: ____________ Instructor's Initials: ____________ Grade: ____________

Suggestions for Improvement: ____

Evaluator's Name (print) ____

Evaluator's Signature ____

Comments ____

DOCUMENTATION

Chart the procedure in the patient's medical record.

Date:____________________________

Charting: ____

____

____

Student's Initials:________________

SKILLS COMPETENCY ASSESSMENT

Procedure 8–14: Aspiration of Joint Fluid

Student's Name: ______________________________ Date: __________

Objective: To remove excess synovial fluid from a joint following injury.

Conditions: The student demonstrates the ability to assist the physician in removing excess synovial fluid from a joint following injury using the following equipment and supplies. Surgical tray: syringe/needle for anesthesia, gauze sponges, sterile basin for aspirated fluid, fenestrated drape (optional), syringe/needle for drainage. Side area: skin prep supplies, gloves (sterile and nonsterile), personal protective equipment, anesthesia as directed, cortisone medication as directed, culturette (optional), pathology requisition, specimen container, biohazard waste container, extra gauze sponges (sterile, unopened), alcohol pledgets, dressing and bandages.

Time Requirements and Accuracy Standards: Time varies according to patient condition and the time required by the physician to complete the procedure. Points assigned reflect importance of step to meeting objective: Important = (5) Essential = (10) Critical = (15). Automatic failure results if any of the **critical** tasks are omitted or performed incorrectly.

STANDARD PRECAUTIONS:

SKILLS ASSESSMENT CHECKLIST

Task Performed	Possible Points	TASKS
☐	5	Washes hands.
☐	5	Identifies the patient and explains the procedure. Reassures and comforts the patient as needed.
☐	15	Determines any known allergies and last tetanus booster.
☐	15	Checks for signed consent form. Identifies any health concerns to avoid possible complications.
☐	5	Positions the patient comfortably, lying down.
☐	5	Puts on PPE if needed.
☐	5	Performs the skin preparation as directed.
☐	15	Assists the physician by holding the vial as anesthesia is aspirated. The physician will insert the needle into the synovial sac and aspirate fluid with the syringe. The aspirated fluid will be put into a sterile bowl as the syringe fills with fluid. The process continues until excess fluid is removed.
☐	5	Supports the patient as needed.
		Postoperative care
☐	5	Applies sterile gloves.
☐	5	Cleans area around the wound.

Task Performed	Possible Points	TASKS
☐	10	Dresses and bandages as directed.
☐	5	Disposes of items per OSHA guidelines. Removes gloves.
☐	5	Washes hands.
☐	15	Checks the patient's vital signs.
☐	15	Explains wound care to the patient (and caregiver) and provides written instructions, including symptoms of infection.
☐	5	Assists the patient with any concerns or questions.
☐	5	Arranges for follow-up appointment and medication, as ordered.
☐	10	Sends labeled specimen to the pathology lab, if directed.
☐	5	Documents the procedure.
☐	5	Completed the tasks within the time constraint identified by the instructor.
☐	15	Results obtained were accurate.

_______	Earned	ADD POINTS OF TASKS CHECKED
180	Points	TOTAL POINTS POSSIBLE
_______	SCORE	DETERMINE SCORE (divide points earned by total points possible, multiply results by 100)

Actual Student Time Needed to Complete Procedure: ____________

Student's Initials: ____________ Instructor's Initials: ____________ Grade: ____________

Suggestions for Improvement: ______________________________

Evaluator's Name (print) ______________________________

Evaluator's Signature ______________________________

Comments ______________________________

DOCUMENTATION

Chart the procedure in the patient's medical record.

Date: ______________________

Charting: ______________________________

____

____

Student's Initials: ______________

SKILLS COMPETENCY ASSESSMENT

Procedure 8–15: Hemorrhoid Thrombectomy

Student's Name: ______________________________ Date: ____________

Objective: To excise inflamed hemorrhoids.

Conditions: The student demonstrates the ability to assist the physician in excising inflamed hemorrhoids using the following equipment and supplies. Surgical tray: syringe/needle for anesthesia, mosquito hemostat (curved), sterile basin, gauze sponges, fenestrated drape. Side area: skin prep supplies, gloves (sterile and nonsterile), personal protective equipment, anesthesia as directed, biohazard waste container, extra gauze sponges, soft absorbent pad (similar to sanitary napkin), T-bandage (to hold pad in place).

Time Requirements and Accuracy Standards: Time varies according to patient's condition and the time required by the physician to complete the procedure. Points assigned reflect importance of step to meeting objective: Important = (5) Essential = (10) Critical = (15). Automatic failure results if any of the **critical** tasks are omitted or performed incorrectly.

STANDARD PRECAUTIONS:

SKILLS ASSESSMENT CHECKLIST

Task Performed	Possible Points	TASKS
❑	5	Washes hands.
❑	5	Identifies the patient and explains the procedure. Reassures and comforts the patient as needed.
❑	15	Determines any known allergies and last tetanus booster.
❑	15	Checks for signed consent form.
❑	10	Identifies any health concerns to avoid possible complications.
❑	10	Positions the patient comfortably, according to physician preference; usually lithotomy position is used.
❑	5	Assists with adequate draping for patient comfort.
❑	5	Applies PPE if necessary.
❑	5	Performs the skin preparation as directed.
❑	10	Assists the physician to aspirate the appropriate amount of local anesthesia. The physician will excise the hemorrhoids with a scalpel and remove the clot within with a hemostat forceps.
❑	5	Supports the patient as needed.
		Postoperative Care
❑	10	Applies sterile gloves.

Task Performed	Possible Points	TASKS
❑	10	Assists the physician in placing the soft absorbent pad against the wound. It may be held in place with a T-shaped bandage.
❑	5	Disposes of used items per OSHA guidelines. Removes gloves and washes hands.
❑	5	Assists the patient as needed.
❑	15	Checks the patient's vital signs.
❑	15	Explains wound care to the patient (and caregiver) per physician. Sitting in a tub of warm water is soothing and aids healing. Provides written instructions, including signs of complications such as excessive bleeding or pain.
❑	5	Assists the patient with any concerns or questions.
❑	5	Arranges for follow-up appointment and medication, as ordered.
❑	5	Documents the procedure.
❑	5	Completed the tasks within the time constraint identified by the instructor.
❑	15	Results obtained were accurate.

________	Earned	ADD POINTS OF TASKS CHECKED
185	Points	TOTAL POINTS POSSIBLE
________	SCORE	DETERMINE SCORE (divide points earned by total points possible, multiply results by 100)

Actual Student Time Needed to Complete Procedure: ____________

Student's Initials: ____________ Instructor's Initials: ____________ Grade: ____________

Suggestions for Improvement: ____________

Evaluator's Name (print) ____________

Evaluator's Signature ____________

Comments ____________

DOCUMENTATION

Chart the procedure in the patient's medical record.

Date: ____________

Charting: ____________

____

____

Student's Initials: ____________

EVALUATION OF CHAPTER KNOWLEDGE

How has your instructor evaluated the knowledge you have achieved?

	Instructor Evaluation		
Knowledge	*Good*	*Average*	*Poor*
Defines surgical asepsis and differentiates between surgical asepsis and medical asepsis	_____	_____	_____
Lists basic rules to follow to protect sterile areas	_____	_____	_____
Explains the sizing standards of suture material and the criteria used to select the most appropriate type and size	_____	_____	_____
Is able to identify and describe the intended use of a wide variety of surgical instruments	_____	_____	_____
Demonstrates the ability to select the most appropriate type of dressings for a given situation	_____	_____	_____
States advantages and disadvantages of Betadine, Hibeclens, isopropyl alcohol, and hydrogen peroxide when each is used as a skin antiseptic	_____	_____	_____
Defines anesthesia and explains the advantages and disadvantages of epinephrine as an additive to injectable anesthetics	_____	_____	_____
Recalls preoperative issues to be addressed in patient preparation and education	_____	_____	_____
Identifies postoperative concerns to be addressed with the patient and the caregiver	_____	_____	_____
Demonstrates procedure for applying sterile gloves	_____	_____	_____
Demonstrates ability to set up a surgical tray, including laying the field, supplies and instruments, pouring a sterile solution, using transfer forceps, and covering the sterile tray	_____	_____	_____
Explains what is meant by alternative surgical methods	_____	_____	_____
Documents accurately	_____	_____	_____
Attends to patient's emotional needs	_____	_____	_____

Student's Initials: ______ Instructor's Initials: ______

Grade: _______

CHAPTER 9

Nutrition in Health and Disease

PERFORMANCE OBJECTIVES

Nutrition is the study of the intake of nutrients into the body and how the body uses these nutrients. A proper balance of nutrients is required for optimum health. As individuals progress through each stage of the life span, their diets must be modified to adapt to the body's changing needs. Particular disease states may also require a change from a normal diet to control the progress of the disease and help return the patient to good health. Medical assistants who recognize the type and quantity of nutrients required to maintain good health and who understand how the diet should be changed in response to various disease states or to changes in physical development can use their knowledge of nutritional principles to encourage patients to adopt healthy, nutritional habits. Addressing the patient's eating habits and concerns also helps ensure that the patient will comply with the physician's treatment plan regarding diet and nutrition. Medical assisting students can use this chapter to learn about the vital importance of good nutrition in promoting and maintaining health.

EXERCISES AND ACTIVITIES

Vocabulary Builder

A. Vitamins are a class of nutrients in which each specific vitamin has a function entirely of its own. These complex molecules are required by the body in minute quantities. What are the two functions of vitamins in the body?

(1) ____________________

(2) ____________________

B. *Identify the correct chemical name for each vitamin listed. Then describe what each vitamin does in the body to promote good health.*

____________________ A. One of the B-complex vitamins, also called nicotinic acid

____

_______________ B. Vitamin B_1

____

_______________ C. Vitamin E

____

_______________ D. Vitamin D

____

_______________ E. One of the B-complex vitamins, also called folacin

____

_______________ F. Vitamin A

____

_______________ G. Vitamin B_{12}

____

_______________ H. Vitamin C

____

_______________ I. Vitamin B_2

____

_______________ J. Vitamin B_6

____

C. *Fill in the blank with the correct key vocabulary term from the list below.*

Absorption	Diuretics	Metabolism
Amino acids	Electrolytes	Nutrients
Antioxidant	Elimination	Nutrition
Basal metabolic rate (BMR)	Extracellular	Oxidation
Calories	Fat-soluble	Preservatives
Catalyst	Glycogen	Processed foods
Cellulose	Homeostasis	Saturated fats
Coenzyme	Ingestion	Trace minerals
Digestion	Major minerals	Water soluble

1. Artificial flavors, colors, and _______________, chemicals that keep food fresh longer, are nonnutritive substances commonly added to processed foods.
2. _______________ is the study of the intake of nutrients into the body and how the body processes and uses these nutrients.
3. Toxicity is most likely to occur with _______________ vitamins because they are stored in tissues composed of lipids and in the liver and are not carried easily into the bloodstream.

4. The best source of complete proteins are meats and animal products such as milk and eggs; complete proteins contain all eight of the essential ______________.
5. Beverages that contain caffeine and alcohol, which are ______________, will cause the body to increase urinary output and lose water. These substances should be avoided when performing activities, such as a good physical workout, and entering environments, such as an airplane passenger cabin, that promote dehydration.
6. A ______________ is a nonprotein substance that acts with a catalyst to facilitate chemical reactions in the body.
7. ______________ is the process of the digestive system involving the transfer of nutrients from the gastrointestinal tract into the bloodstream.
8. Chlorine (Cl) is a mineral with an important ______________ function, one that takes place outside the cells of body tissues in the spaces between layers or groups of cells.
9. The total of all changes, or energy, chemical and physical, that takes place in the body is called ______________.
10. Some minerals are considered ______________ in that they become ionized and carry a positive or negative charge; these minerals must be carefully balanced in the body.
11. ______________ begins at the mouth with chewing and progresses through the gastrointestinal tract to the small intestine.
12. ______________ are ingested substances that help the body maintain a state of homeostasis.
13. The process of ______________ maintains a constant internal environment of the human body, including such functions as heartbeat, blood pressure, respiration, and body temperature.
14. A ______________ facilitates chemical reactions by speeding up the reaction time without the need for a high energy output.
15. It is always important to analyze the nutritional labels on ______________ purchased in the supermarket.
16. Lard is one example of ______________, which have been found to raise the level of fats and cholesterol in the blood and are hydrogenated, or contain hydrogen.
17. The ability to reduce ______________ is a characteristic of vitamin E that has led some researchers to suggest that vitamin E may slow the aging process, although its true effectiveness has not yet been demonstrated.
18. The excretion of waste through the anus is called ______________, the final step of the digestive process.
19. The amount of energy a substance is able to supply is measured in large ______________.
20. Potassium is one of the seven ______________ found in the body.

21. Vitamins that are ___________________________ must be constantly ingested to maintain proper blood levels, as these vitamins are not easily stored in the body.
22. Vitamin E is a fat-soluble vitamin that belongs to a group of compounds called ___________________________, which counteract the damaging effects of oxidation. Beta-carotene is another substance in this group.
23. Despite their name, ___________________________ are vital to body functioning, and include molybdenum and fluorine.
24. ______________________ begins the digestive process when we put food in our mouths to eat.
25. Children, pregnant women, and people with a lean body mass will have a higher ___________________________ because it takes more energy to fuel the muscles than it does to store fat.
26. A type of carbohydrate, ___________________________, is derived from a plant source and supplies fiber in the human diet.
27. Ingested only in small quantities, ___________________________ is an important carbohydrate form for storage of glucose in the body.

Learning Review

1. Identify each organ of the digestive system in the diagram below. Describe the healthy functioning of each organ in the space provided. Then, using a medical dictionary or encyclopedia, look up each organ and list one common disorder that would adversely affect the digestive process.

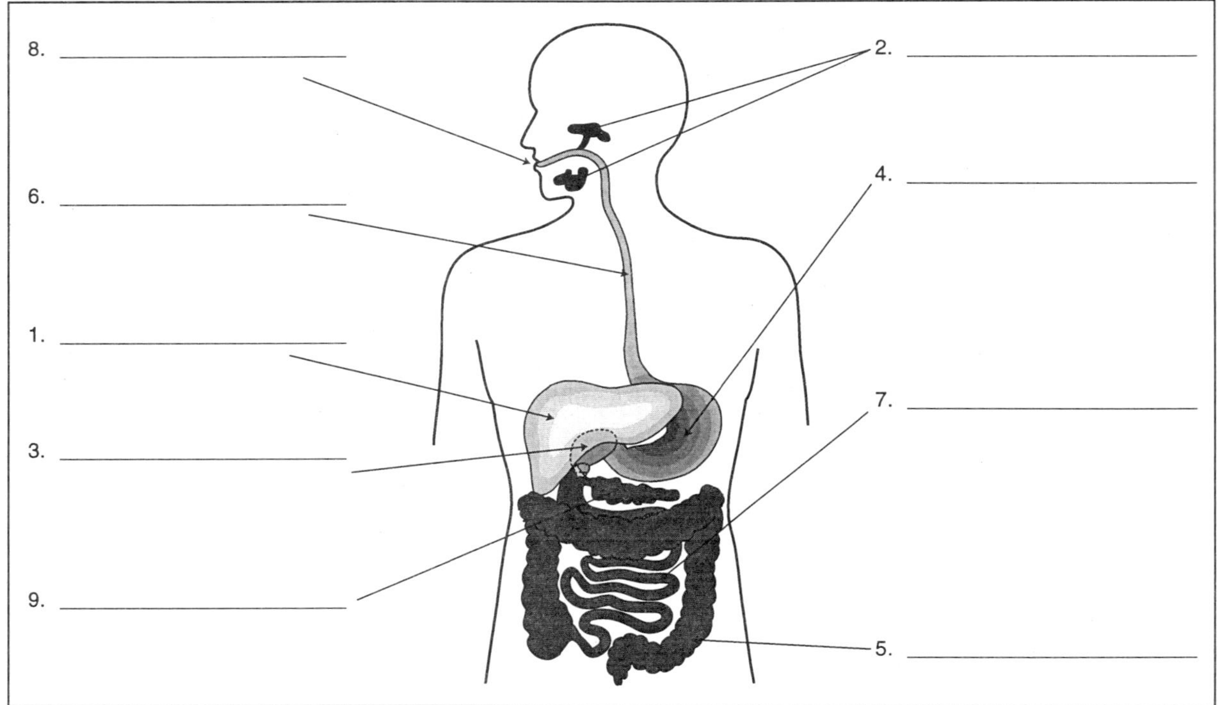

(1) Healthy function: ____________________
____________________ Common disorder: ____________________

(2) Healthy function: ____________________
____________________ Common disorder: ____________________

(3) Healthy function: ____________________
____________________ Common disorder: ____________________

(4) Healthy function: ____________________
____________________ Common disorder: ____________________

(5) Healthy function: ____________________
____________________ Common disorder: ____________________

(6) Healthy function: ____________________
____________________ Common disorder: ____________________

(7) Healthy function: ____________________
____________________ Common disorder: ____________________

(8) Healthy function: ____________________
____________________ Common disorder: ____________________

(9) Healthy function: ____________________
____________________ Common disorder: ____________________

2. A. Nutrients are divided into two groups: those that provide energy and those that do not.

Identify the nutrients listed below as providing energy or not providing energy by checking the appropriate box.

Energy	No Energy	
❑	❑	(1) Vitamins
❑	❑	(2) Carbohydrates
❑	❑	(3) Fiber
❑	❑	(4) Minerals
❑	❑	(5) Lipids (Fats)
❑	❑	(6) Proteins
❑	❑	(7) Water

B. What three chemical elements do carbohydrates, fats, and proteins all contain?

(1) ____________ (2) ____________ (3) ____________

C. Name the most important dietary complex carbohydrate. ____________________

D. Name the only true essential fatty acid in the human diet. ____________________

E. What additional chemical element does protein alone contain? ____________________

F. When the body does not have enough carbohydrates or fats in supply as an energy source, what happens and what effect does this have on the body? ____________________

____

G. What does the acronym PEM stand for, and what usually occurs with this deficiency?

____

____

H. Name two diseases associated with deficiencies in protein.

(1) ____________________ (2) ____________________

3. A. List two distinct ways in which minerals differ from vitamins.

(1) ____________________

(2) ____________________

B. For each food source, list the mineral or minerals that each provides.

(1) Eggs ____________________

(2) Milk ____________________

(3) Cheese ____________________

(4) Salmon ____________________

(5) Bananas ____________________

(6) Green vegetables ____________________

4. For each of the following, identify the substance as a water-soluble vitamin (WSV), fat-soluble vitamin (FSV), a major mineral (MM), or a trace mineral (TM). Then match the substance to the response that best fits its character or properties.

____ 1. Sulfur
____ 2. Vitamin B_{12}
____ 3. Iron
____ 4. Vitamin K
____ 5. Sodium
____ 6. Pyridoxine
____ 7. Iodine
____ 8. Biotin
____ 9. Retinol
____ 10. Vitamin D

____ A. This substance works with potassium to maintain proper water balance and proper pH balance; the two also are involved in nervous muscular conduction and excitability.

____ B. This substance is part of the pigment rhodopsin found in the eye and is responsible in part for vision, especially night vision.

____ C. This substance is vital to life because of its role in the heme molecule, which carries oxygen to every cell in the body.

____ D. Rickets and osteomalacia are diseases caused by deficiencies in this substance; when deficiencies occur, usually in childhood, malformation of the skeleton is seen.

____ E. This member of the B-complex, along with pantothenic acid, is generally responsible for energy metabolism.

____ F. Because this substance is only found in foods from animal sources, such as liver, kidney, and dairy products, pernicious anemia, the result of deficiencies, may be a problem for some vegetarians.

____ G. This substance, found in rice, beans, and yeast, is important to protein metabolism.

____ H. This substance is a component of one of the amino acids and is found in protein; it is also involved in energy metabolism.

____ I. About half of the body's requirement for this substance is fulfilled through synthesis by intestinal bacteria; bile is required for its absorption into the bloodstream.

____ J. This substance is only found in the thyroid hormones; without it, the thyroid gland would be unable to regulate the overall metabolism of the body.

5. A. List six types of fiber that are carbohydrates.

(1) ____________________ (3) ____________________

(2) ____________________ (4) ____________________

(3) ____________________ (6) ____________________

B. What important fiber is not a carbohydrate? ____________________

Americans generally do not consume enough fiber. How much fiber should be consumed each day? ____________ Why does brown rice contain more fiber than white rice? ____________________

6. A. What happens when the body takes in more calories than will be expended by the body as energy? ____________________

What happens when the body uses more energy than the calories it takes in will produce?

____

What is the ideal percentage of total calories that should be consumed as carbohydrates, fats, and proteins? Carbohydrates: ________ Fats: ________ Proteins: ________

B. An 8-fluid-ounce serving of 1% fat soy milk contains 110 calories with 2 grams of total fat, 20 grams of total carbohydrates, and 4 grams of total protein. Calculate the total number of calories from each energy nutrient; show your calculations in the spaces provided below.

Number of calories from fat: ______ Number of calories from carbohydrates: ______
Number of calories from protein: ______

Now calculate the percentage of total calories due to each energy nutrient.

Percent of calories from fat: ______ Percent of calories from carbohydrates: ______
Percent of calories from protein: ______

C. Compare the percentages of total Calories due to fat, carbohydrates, and protein found in soy milk to the percentages you calculated for one serving of peanut butter in your textbook's critical thinking question # 9.

Percent of Total Calories	Peanut Butter	Soy Milk
Fat		
Carbohydrates		
Protein		

How do the percentages relate to the ideal percentages for optimum energy balance in the body? ______________________________

____

____

7. Dr. Elizabeth King has confirmed that patient Mary O'Keefe is pregnant with her third child.

A. Name two minerals that Mary must increase amounts of in her diet.

(1) ______________ (2) ______________

B. Name three reasons why a woman needs to increase her intake of nutrients and calories when she is pregnant.

(1) ______________ (2) ______________ (3) ______________

C. What dietary supplement usually needs to be added to a baby's diet? ______________

8. When helping patients modify their diets, medical assistants need to be knowledgeable about the nutrients in the food we eat. The nutritional analysis label on the back or side of a food package is helpful when figuring out the levels of fat, cholesterol, sodium, carbohydrates, protein, and vitamins contained in a particular food.

A. The percent of daily values listed on a label report the amount of a nutrient obtained by eating how many servings of a product? ______________ The percentages are based on a ______________ calorie diet. The listing for total carbohydrates is broken down into what two additional listings? (1) ______________ (2) ______________

Which type of carbohydrate is more beneficial and why? ______________

____

A patient should look for a food product in which the sodium content is relatively low. What is the greatest number of milligrams of sodium a person should eat each day? ______________

What is the total amount of cholesterol a person should eat each day? ______________

Why is a high-fiber diet important? ______________

____

____

B. Compare the nutrition food label from a box of muesli with fruit, nuts, and seeds, to the label from a package of pretzel snacks. Which is more nutritious and why? Note that one serving of the muesli, ½ cup or 55 grams, is roughly equivalent to two servings of pretzels, 14 pretzels or 60 grams.

Muesli

Nutrition Facts

Serving Size: 1/2 cup (55g)
Servings Per Container: about 8

Amount Per Serving	Cereal	Cereal + 125 mL Vitamin A & D fortified skim milk
Calories	210	250
Calories from Fat	30	35
	% Daily Value**	
Total Fat 3g*	**5%**	**5%**
Saturated Fat 0.5g	**3%**	**3%**
Cholesterol 0mg	**0%**	**0%**
Sodium 30mg	**1%**	**4%**
Total Carbohydrate 40g	**13%**	**15%**
Dietary Fiber 5g	**21%**	**21%**
Sugars 13g		
Protein 6g		
Vitamin A	0%	8%
Vitamin C	8%	8%
Calcium	4%	20%
Iron	35%	35%
Vitamin D	0%	10%
Thiamine	35%	40%
Riboflavin	25%	35%
Niacin	2%	2%
Vitamin B_6	15%	20%
Folate	10%	10%
Pantothenic Acid	4%	10%

*Amount in Cereal. One half cup skim milk contributes an additional 40 calories, 65 mg sodium, 6g total carbohydrate (6g sugars), and 4g protein.

**Percent Daily Values are based on a 2,000 calorie diet. Your daily values may be higher or lower depending on your calorie needs.

	Calories	2,000	2,500
Total Fat	Less than	65g	80g
Sat Fat	Less than	20g	25g
Cholesterol	Less than	300mg	300mg
Sodium	Less than	2,400mg	2,400mg
Total Carbohydrate		300g	375g
Dietary Fiber		25g	30g

Calories per gram:
Fat 9 • Carbohydrate 4 • Protein 4

Pretzels

Nutrition Facts

Serving Size: 7 Pretzels (30g)
Servings Per Container: 9.4

Amount Per Serving	
Calories 120	
	Calories from Fat 10
	% Daily Value*
Total Fat 1g	**2%**
Saturated Fat 0g	**0%**
Cholesterol 0g	**0%**
Sodium 360mg	**15%**
Total Carbohydrate 24g	**8%**
Dietary Fiber 1g	**4%**
Sugars 1g	
Protein 3g	

Vitamin A 0% Σ Vitamin C 0%
Calcium 0% Σ Iron 2%

*Percent Daily Values are based on a 2,000 calorie diet. Your daily values may be higher or lower depending on your calorie needs:

		Calories 2,000	2,500
Total Fat	Less than	65g	80g
Sat Fat	Less than	20g	25g
Cholesterol	Less than	300mg	300mg
Sodium	Less than	2,400mg	2,400mg
Total Carbohydrate		300g	375g
Dietary Fiber		25g	30g

Calories per gram:
Fat 9 Σ Carbohydrate 4 Σ Protein 4

Ingredients: Unbleached Wheat Flour, Water, Corn Syrup, Partially Hydrogenated Vegetable Oil (Soybean), Yeast Salt, Bicarbonates and Carbonates of Sodium.

9. Compare the advantages and disadvantages of the following diets: U. S. southern, Jewish, and Japanese.

Investigation Activity

Many of the foods we eat today are processed foods. We rely on the labels on the cans, bottles, and boxes lining grocery store shelves to tell us what nutrients are inside. However, many of us do not actually read the labels, but instead use the shape or color of a package or advertisements to make our decisions about purchasing food products.

Go into your family kitchen and choose your three favorite food or beverage products—anything from milk to salsa to fruit juice, frozen macaroni and cheese, or ice cream. Base your choices on the foods that are the best tasting and most satisfying, ones you purchase frequently at the grocery store. Remove the nutrition facts labels from each product and tape or glue them in the spaces below.

Product Name: ____________ Product Name: ____________ Product Name: ____________

Now look for one food or beverage item in your kitchen that attracted you solely on the basis of the product's packaging. Remove the nutrition facts label from the product and tape or glue it in the space provided.

Product Name: ___________________________

What is it about this packaging that attracts you to the product? Describe the package.

____

____

____

What kind of mood does the packaging put you in?

____

____

____

What does the packaging suggest about the product? For example, is the packaging trying to look healthy, fun, wholesome, convenient, traditional? Does the product inside the package live up to its packaging promise?

____

____

____

Does the packaging make any claims or promises? If so, what are they?

____

____

____

Is this product nutritious? Give your analysis of the information on the nutrition facts label.

____

____

____

CASE STUDY

Lourdes Austen, a breast cancer survivor, regularly attends a support group for breast cancer patients and survivors held once a month. Lourdes finds the group a great source of encouragement, information, and support—a safe place to discuss her feelings and concerns about breast cancer. The group is planning a session to talk about nutrition issues, and Lourdes asks clinical medical assistant Audrey Jones if she would like to attend the meeting with her to contribute to the group's discussion. With permission from office manager Marilyn Johnson and Lourdes's physician Dr. Elizabeth King, Audrey attends the meeting. The group members are enthusiastic and ask Audrey many questions, including the following. "Why is good nutrition important for cancer patients?" "I don't have much of an appetite any more and get nauseous all the time. What can I do?" "I keep hearing about those macrobiotic diets? Are they any good? Should I try them?"

Discuss the following:

1. What information can Audrey give in answer to the question regarding the importance of good nutrition for cancer patients?
2. What suggestion can Audrey offer to patients who have no appetite, nausea, or vomiting?
3. What can Audrey tell the group about macrobiotic diets?
4. What is the role of the medical assistant in attending the breast cancer support group meeting?

SUPPLEMENTARY RESOURCES

Study Guide Disk: Additional practice exercises for this chapter are available on the study guide disk found in the back of the textbook.

Medical Assisting Videos: Appropriate content is available on Delmar's Medical Assisting Videos, 2nd ed., Tape 8, for the following topics:

Take an In-Depth Patient History

Introduction to Health Promotion, Disease Prevention, and Self-Responsibility

EVALUATION OF CHAPTER KNOWLEDGE

How has your instructor evaluated the knowledge you have gained?

Knowledge	Instructor Evaluation *Good*	*Average*	*Poor*
Understands the role of the digestive system and the four processes that take place in the digestive system	_____	_____	_____
Knows the seven basic nutrient types and how each contributes to a healthy diet	_____	_____	_____
Understands the relationship and balance between the three energy nutrients	_____	_____	_____
Understands the difference between water-soluble and fat-soluble vitamins and how vitamins contribute to a healthy diet	_____	_____	_____
Identifies major and trace minerals	_____	_____	_____
Can interpret the information on the nutrition labels of processed foods	_____	_____	_____
Understands the need for diets to be modified in response to life cycle changes and disease states	_____	_____	_____

Student's Initials: _______ Instructor's Initials: _______

Grade: ________

Rehabilitation Medicine

PERFORMANCE OBJECTIVES

Rehabilitation medicine is a field of medicine that specializes in both preventing disease or injury and restoring patients' physical function, using a combination of physical and mechanical agents to aid in the diagnosis and treatment. The goal of rehabilitation medicine is to help restore the functions that have been affected by a patient's condition. The role of the medical assistant is to assist the physician or rehabilitation therapist in enabling a patient to regain normal or near-normal function after an illness or injury. A medical assistant might assist a patient in learning to safely ambulate following a period of sedentary recuperation; in learning the correct use of assistive devices, such as crutches, a cane, or a walker; or in performing therapeutic exercises. Range of motion exercises, designed to maintain a patient's joint mobility, are often performed by the medical assistant. In addition to therapeutic exercise, a variety of therapeutic modalities such as heat, cold, light, electricity, and water can be used as part of the patient's rehabilitation program, and the medical assistant should be familiar with how these modalities act on the body and understand the safety precautions associated with each. It is very important for the medical assistant to understand the goals and objectives of the rehabilitation program designed by the physician or therapist. A medical assistant's duties in the field of rehabilitation medicine often involve physical strength and coordination, such as when performing wheelchair transfers. It is important to follow proper procedures at all times to protect both the patient and the medical assistant from injury. Therapeutic communication between medical assistants and rehabilitation patients is essential to providing encouragement and support for patients who face difficult, uncomfortable, or frustrating physical challenges.

EXERCISES AND ACTIVITIES

Vocabulary Builder

A. Rehabilitation Medicine Terminology

Match each of the following key vocabulary terms to the example that best describes it.

A. Vasoconstriction
B. Thermotherapy
C. Muscle testing
D. Contractures
E. Goniometer
F. Body mechanics
G. Atrophy
H. Rehabilitation medicine
I. Goniometry
J. Ambulation
K. Gait
L. Ultrasound
M. Activities of daily living (ADL)
N. Hemiplegia
O. Range of motion (ROM)
P. Modality
Q. Cryotherapy
R. Gait belt
S. Vasodilation
T. Assistive devices

_____ **1.** Patient Lenore McDonell, confined to a wheelchair since early childhood, receives continuing physical therapy to minimize the effects of any decrease of ability or size in her legs caused by inactivity.

_____ **2.** Clinical medical assistant Anna Preciado enjoys working with patients to help them restore their bodies to normal or near-normal function following an illness or injury. Her interest has led her to pursue advanced training in this field of medical discipline.

_____ **3.** When examining a new patient, a physical therapist must determine which of the physical agents, such as heat, cold, light, water, and electricity, will be most beneficial in treating the patient's condition.

_____ **4.** As Margaret Thomas, diagnosed with Parkinson's disease, began to develop balance problems and difficulties in walking, her physical therapist prescribed the use of high-frequency sound waves to generate heat in the deep tissue of her right leg, producing a therapeutic effect.

_____ **5.** Cold applications are used to constrict blood vessels and slow or stop the flow of blood to an area.

_____ **6.** Lenny Taylor, suffering the early stages of dementia from Alzheimer's, works with an occupational therapist to practice methods of making everyday tasks easier to perform.

_____ **7.** Heat is a modality that creates a therapeutic effect by causing blood vessels to dilate, thereby increasing circulation to an area and speeding up the healing process.

_____ **8.** When construction worker Jaime Carrera suffers a shoulder injury on the job, Dr. James Whitney performs this process for assessing the motion, strength, and task potential of the muscle group, tendons, and associated tissues.

_____ **9.** Joe Guerrero, CMA, instructs patient Martin Gordon on the correct method of ambulating while using a three-point gait and axillary crutches.

_____ **10.** Dr. Winston Lewis recommends this heat modality to help relieve Herb Fowler's chronic lower back pain, caused by strain on the back muscles created by the patient's overweight condition.

_____ **11.** When patient Dottie Tate comes to Inner City Health Care complaining of a sore back and several recent falls, clinical medical assistant Bruce Goldman secures a gait belt around Dottie's waist and asks her to walk across the room. Staying a step behind her and slightly to the side, Bruce carefully observes Dottie's progress when performing this task.

_____ **12.** As a muscle atrophies, shrinking and losing its strength, joints become stiff and develop these deformities. Without constant exercise, the musculoskeletal system deteriorates.

_____ **13.** Dr. Susan Rice recommends that patient Dottie Tate begin to use a walker at home to prevent further falls. Bruce Goldman, CMA, secures this safety device around Dottie's waist and positions her inside the walker as he gives her verbal instructions to begin the procedure of learning to ambulate with a walker.

_____ **14.** Elderly patient Abigail Johnson is afraid that because she has diabetes mellitus she is at increased risk for stroke. "I don't want to end up a vegetable and a burden to my family," she tells Dr. Elizabeth King, "all paralyzed on one side like that."

_____ **15.** Clinical medical assistant Joe Guerrero employs this practice of using certain key muscle groups together with correct body alignment to avoid injury when assisting patient Lenore McDonell in performing a transfer from her wheelchair to the examination table.

_____ **16.** Margaret Thomas's neurologist uses this instrument to measure the angle of her shoulder joint's range of motion during a follow-up examination for Parkinson's disease.

_____ **17.** Dr. Mark Woo chooses this cold modality to treat the sprained wrist of an emergency patient, reducing inflammation.

_____ **18.** Canes, walkers, and crutches are examples of walking aids.

_____ **19.** When lying flat with arms at the sides, the average person should be able to move from a 20° hyperextension of the elbow joint to a 150° flexion.

_____ **20.** A physical therapist uses the measurement of joint motion to help evaluate a patient's range of motion.

B. Joint Movement Terminology

Unscramble each term of joint movement to reveal the correct spelling. Then match the term to its correct definition.

A. CIUDBANOT _______________

B. SIONTXEEN _______________

C. VSOIREEN _______________

D. RSIONHTXEEENYP _______________

E. TIONNOARP _______________

F. VRSEINNOI _______________

G. TATORION _______________

H. XELIONF _______________

I. PINUSITAON _______________

J. SRDOXELFIINO _______________

K. ARPNTLA XELIONF _______________

L. UCTIONADD _______________

M. UMDIONTCUCRIC _______________

_____ **1.** Moving the arm so the palm is up.

_____ **2.** Moving a body part outward.

_____ 3. Straightening of a body part.

_____ 4. Motion toward the midline of the body.

_____ 5. Moving a body part inward.

_____ 6. Turning a body part around its axis.

_____ 7. A position of maximum extension, or extending a body part beyond its normal limits.

_____ 8. Motion away from the midline of the body.

_____ 9. Circular motion of a body part.

_____ 10. Moving the arm so the palm is down.

_____ 11. Moving the foot downward at the ankle.

_____ 12. Moving the foot upward at the ankle joint.

_____ 13. Bending of a body part.

Learning Review

1. Some patients require assistive devices in order to ambulate. Three broad types of assistive devices are listed below. For each assistive device, name the various styles available and one identifying feature of each style. Also, name the physical conditions each style is best suited to be used with as part of a physician's treatment plan.

CANES

(1) ____

____

(2) ____

____

(3) ____

____

WALKERS

(1) ____

____

(2) ____

____

CRUTCHES

(1) ____

____

(2) ____

____

(3) ____

____

2. Therapeutic exercise helps patients restore their bodies, protect their bodies from further damage, and prevent against the development of respiratory and circulatory complications caused by inactivity. Medical assistants need to understand the goals and objectives of therapeutic exercise programs. Patients will need support and encouragement to stick to their programs.

   Name four types of exercise programs that are employed for therapeutic or preventative purposes. Then match each one to the example that best describes it.

   ____ 1. ______________________________

   ____ 2. ______________________________

   ____ 3. ______________________________

   ____ 4. ______________________________

   A. Patient Jim Marshall, suffering a sports injury to the muscles surrounding the knee, performs exercises in a therapy pool.

   B. Lourdes Austen performs self-directed exercises at home to improve the range of motion and increase strength in her left arm, following lumpectomy and axillary lymph node dissection.

   C. Lenore McDonell, confined to a wheelchair and unable to move her legs voluntarily, works regularly with a physical therapist to avoid atrophy and contractures in the legs and to improve overall circulation.

   D. Jaime Carrera, recovering from a shoulder injury, rebuilds upper body strength with a daily regimen of push-ups: first against the wall and then on the floor.

3. A. List six precautionary measures that should be observed when performing range of motion exercises on a patient.

   (1) ______________________________

   ____

   (2) ______________________________

   ____

   (3) ______________________________

   ____

   (4) ______________________________

   ____

   (5) ______________________________

   ____

   (6) ______________________________

   ____

B. For each illustration below, identify the range of motion exercise being performed.

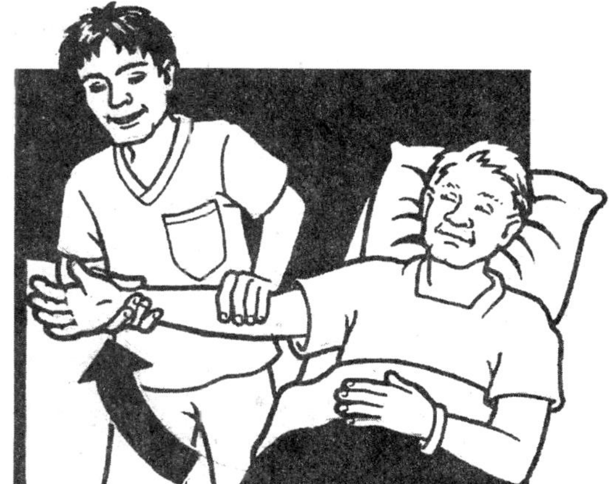

1. ________________________________ 2. ________________________________

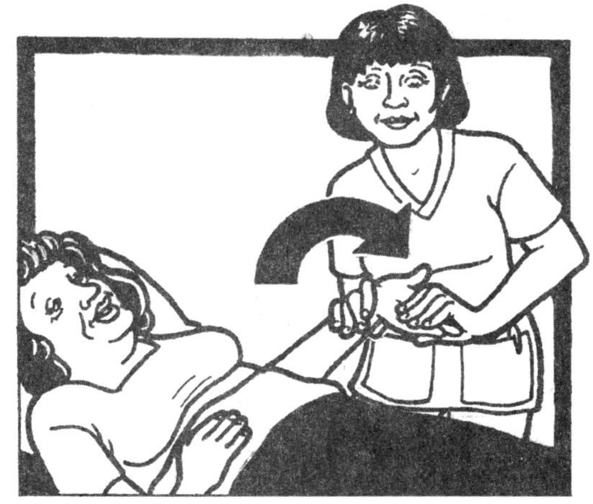

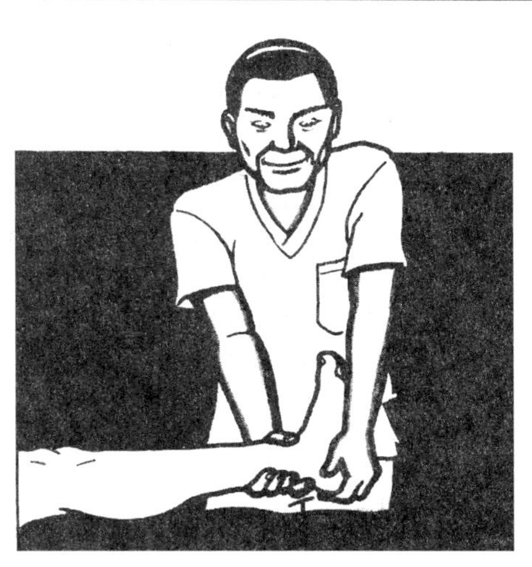

3. ________________________________ 4. ________________________________

4. Therapeutic exercise is not the only way to treat painful joints or tissues. Many patients respond well to the therapeutic modalities of heat and cold, thermotherapy and cryotherapy. List six precautions that medical assistants must take when applying heat or cold modalities.

(1) ____

____

(2) ____

____

(3) ____

____

(4) ____

____

(5) ____

____

(6) ____

____

5. Identify each modality listed below as either a dry heat therapy (DHT), a moist heat therapy (MHT), a moist cold therapy (MCT) or a dry cold therapy (DCT) by placing the proper letters in the space provided. Then identify whether the modality can be performed at home by the patient, with or without caregiver assistance, or whether the modality must be performed in a clinical setting under the supervision of a health care professional. List any special precautions or concerns.

_______ A. Ice pack ______________________________

____

_______ B. Paraffin wax bath ______________________________

____

_______ C. Cold compress ______________________________

____

_______ D. Hot water bottle ______________________________

____

_______ E. Hot compress ______________________________

____

_______ F. Whirlpool bath ______________________________

____

_______ G. Heating pad ______________________________

____

_______ H. Hot soak of one extremity ______________________________

____

_______ I. Hot pack ______________________________

____

_______ J. Total body immersion in a Hubbard tank ______________________________

____

6. For each of the following, identify the proper temperature and correct amount of time the modality should be administered to the patient.

A. Aquamatic K-Pad for an elderly patient ______________________________

B. Paraffin wax bath for a patient with rheumatoid arthritis ______________________________

C. An ice pack for a patient with an ankle sprain ______________________________

D. Hot water bottle for an adult patient ______________________________

E. A hot compress to drain pus from a patient's skin infection ______________________________

F. Hot soak of the arm and hand for a patient with osteoarthritis ______________________________

7. How do ultrasound waves travel best? What are the special concerns of ultrasound treatment, how long can ultrasound be administered, and who is authorized to perform ultrasound procedures on patients?

____

____

____

____

Investigation Activity

It is important to remember that patients undergoing rehabilitative medicine may be coping with the consequences of a serious accident or illness. Patients may no longer be able to perform activities of daily living, and they may feel frustrated, angry, or depressed at this loss of ability. Other patients, however, may have a strong sense of willpower and determination. Individuals will react differently. Similarly, friends and family members who serve as caregivers may be more or less willing, physically able, or temperamentally inclined to assist the patient in maintaining a program of rehabilitative care and treatment. The medical assistant can serve as an educator for the patient and caregiver, instructing both in methods that can make treatment easier and increase the chances of success. The medical assistant is also a strong source of support and encouragement.

Using a family member or friend in the role of caregiver, the student should play the role of a patient who has recently suffered a serious accident and is unable to walk or use his or her right arm and hand. Substitute a kitchen chair for a wheelchair placed in a stationary position with the breaks locked. Remain in the chair while the caregiver helps you put on a change of clothing, eat a full meal, and make a telephone call. Be alternately feisty or polite, determined or depressed, mentally focused or unable to concentrate; gauge the reaction of your caregiver to each emotional standpoint.

Consider the following.

1. How can an understanding of proper body mechanics and methods for assisting patients help caregivers and their loved ones who are suffering some kind of physical restriction? How easily did you and your caregiver perform each task?
2. What emotions did both you and your caregiver display? How did the encouragement or lack of encouragement displayed on either side affect the success of each task?
3. Ask your caregiver to write a brief paragraph or two describing the experience and how he or she felt about assisting you.

CASE STUDIES

Medical assistants must practice good body mechanics to protect themselves and their patients from injury. Often called on to lift heavy objects, perform patient transfers, and assist patients in ambulation, medical assistants need to know how to execute their duties safely and efficiently.

For each situation below, discuss the following.

1. What is the best action of the medical assistant?
2. What is the best therapeutic response of the medical assistant?
3. Could the situation have been avoided? If so, how? If not, why not?

Case 1

Ellen Armstrong, CMA, performs the annual task of assembling and moving inactive patient files into a storage filing area for safekeeping. It is the end of the day and Ellen is tired and eager to finish the job; this task has never been one of Ellen's favorites. When she gets to filling the last of three cartons of files, Ellen moves the carton to a shelf, about shoulder-high, in the storage room. She returns and decides to take both of the remaining cartons in one trip. Fatigued, she bends at the waist to pick them up.

Case 2

After explaining the procedure to the patient and her son, Wanda Slawson, CMA, performs the transfer of Mary Craig, an elderly blind patient with diabetes mellitus who is suffering from atrophy of the legs, from a car to a wheelchair in the parking lot of Inner City Health Care. Unfortunately, because of Mary's position in the car, the patient must be transferred with her weaker side closest to the wheelchair. The patient panics during the transfer and throws her arms around Wanda's neck as she is lifting and pivoting Mary to the right to position her in the wheelchair. The patient's son John rushes forward to grab onto his mother.

Case 3

Dr. Susan Rice asks Bruce Goldman, CMA, to instruct patient Dottie Tate in the use of a walker to prevent further falls at home. Dottie is silent as Dr. Rice leaves the examination room and Bruce proceeds to set the walker correctly. However, when Dottie sees that Bruce must once again put Dottie in a gait belt for her protection—the belt was used earlier in the examination to assess Dottie's ability to ambulate—the patient gets feisty. She is visibly tired and ready to go home. "I'll learn to use the walker if I have to, but I won't wear that infernal contraption. It makes me feel like a baby. And it's such a bother. Who wants to go through all that? We just don't need it."

SUPPLEMENTARY RESOURCES

Study Guide Disk: Additional practice exercises for this chapter are available on the study guide disk found in the back of the textbook.

Medical Assisting Videos: Appropriate content is available on Delmar's Medical Assisting Videos, 2nd ed., Tape 9, for the following topics:

- Introduction to Body Mechanics
- Body Mechanics
- Transfer Wheelchair to Examination Table and Back
- Ultrasound Procedures
- Rehabilitative Care
- Passive Range of Motion Exercises
- Instructing Patients with Special Needs

SKILLS COMPETENCY ASSESSMENT

Procedure 10–1: Transferring Patient from Wheelchair to Examination Table

Student's Name: ______________________________ Date: __________

Objective: To safely transfer a patient from a wheelchair to an examination table

Conditions: The student demonstrates the ability to transfer a patient from a wheelchair to an examination table using the following equipment and supplies: wheelchair, examination table, gait belt, stool with rubber tips and a handle for gripping.

Time Requirements and Accuracy Standards: 5 minutes. Points assigned reflect importance of step to meeting objective: Important = (5) Essential = (10) Critical = (15). Automatic failure results if any of the **critical** tasks are omitted or performed incorrectly.

STANDARD PRECAUTIONS:

SKILLS ASSESSMENT CHECKLIST

Task Performed	Possible Points	TASKS
❑	5	Washes hands.
❑	5	Identifies patient, introduces self, explains procedure.
❑	10	Places the wheelchair next to the examination table and locks the brakes.
❑	5	*Rationale:* Understands that patient must be placed on his or her strongest side nearest the examination table to allow him or her to balance on that leg during transfer.
❑	5	Places the gait belt securely around the patient's waist. Tucks excess under belt.
❑	5	Moves the wheelchair footrests up and out of the way. Has patient place feet firmly on floor.
❑	5	Positions the stool in front of the examination table as close to the wheelchair as possible and instructs the patient to move to the edge of the wheelchair.
❑	15	Stands directly in front of the patient with feet slightly apart. Bends at the hips and knees, grasps the gait belt, and instructs the patient to place both hands on the armrests of the wheelchair.
❑	5	*Rationale:* If patient does not have strength in the arms to push upward, instructs the patient to rest hands at sides.
❑	10	Gives a signal and lifts the gait belt upward, pushing with the knees. If patient has strength in the good leg, ask patient to push up with that leg and both arms.
❑	15	Grasps gait belt and instructs the patient to step onto the stool with the foot closest to the examination table, pivoting so the patient's back is to the examination table. Makes sure the buttocks are slightly higher than the bed. Supports patient's outer leg with the leg furthest from the examination table.

SKILLS COMPETENCY ASSESSMENT — continued

Procedure 10–1: Transferring Patient from Wheelchair to Examination Table

Task Performed	Possible Points	TASKS
❑	5	Instructs patient to grasp stool handle and place other hand on examination table.
❑	5	Eases the patient to a seated position on examination table.
❑	5	Places the patient in proper examination position on the table.
❑	5	Moves the wheelchair and stool out of the way.
		Modification: Two-Person Transfer
❑	5	Places gait belt snugly around the patient's waist and tucks excess end under the belt.
❑	5	One person stands in front of the patient and the other to the side, next to the examination table.
❑	10	Both persons grasp the gait belt from underneath. Has patient place both hands on the wheelchair armrests.
❑	10	On one person's signal, both persons pull the patient upward. Has patient push up with both hands, if upper body strength is sufficient; if not, asks patient to rest arms at sides.
❑	15	Person nearest the examination table moves wheelchair out of the way, while the other pivots the patient and has the patient place the stronger leg on the stool. Asks patient to grasp the stool handle, if upper body strength is sufficient.
❑	5	On one person's signal, both persons lift the patient onto the examination table.
❑	5	Places the patient in the proper examination position on the table.
❑	5	Completed the tasks within 5 minutes.
❑	15	Results obtained were accurate.

_______	Earned	ADD POINTS OF TASKS CHECKED
	Points	TOTAL POINTS POSSIBLE SINGLE 105 DOUBLE 75
_______	SCORE	DETERMINE SCORE (divide points earned by total points possible, multiply results by 100)

Actual Student Time Needed to Complete Procedure: ____________

Student's Initials: ____________ Instructor's Initials: ____________ Grade: ____________

Suggestions for Improvement: ____________

Evaluator's Name (print) ____________

Evaluator's Signature ____________

Comments ____________

SKILLS COMPETENCY ASSESSMENT

Procedure 10–2: Transferring Patient from Examination Table to Wheelchair

Student's Name: ______________________________ Date: ____________

Objective: To safely transfer a patient from the examination table to a wheelchair

Conditions: The student demonstrates the ability to transfer a patient safely from the examination table to a wheelchair using the following equipment and supplies: wheelchair, stool with rubber tips and gripping handle, gait belt, examination table.

Time Requirements and Accuracy Standards: 5 minutes. Points assigned reflect importance of step to meeting objective: Important = (5) Essential = (10) Critical = (15). Automatic failure results if any of the **critical** tasks are omitted or performed incorrectly.

STANDARD PRECAUTIONS:

SKILLS ASSESSMENT CHECKLIST

Task Performed	Possible Points	TASKS
❑	5	Washes hands.
❑	5	Identifies the patient and explains procedure.
❑	15	Positions the wheelchair next to the examination table and locks the brakes.
❑	5	*Rationale:* Places wheelchair close to the patient's strongest side, so the patient can transfer weight to strong leg and foot when stepping down.
❑	5	Positions the stool next to the wheelchair.
❑	10	Assists the patient to rise to a seated position; places the gait belt snugly around the patient's waist and tucks excess end under the belt.
❑	15	Places one arm under the patient's arm and around the patient's shoulders, and the other arm under the patient's knees. Pivots the patient so the legs are dangling over the side of the examination table.
❑	15	Keeps a hand on the patient, moves directly in front of patient and grasps the patient by placing hands under gait belt. Plants feet shoulder's width apart and bends knees to have a greater base of support.
❑	10	Gives signal and pulls the patient slightly forward so the patient's feet come down onto the stool. Instructs the patient to push off examination table and grasp the stool handle for support.
❑	10	Still grasping gait belt, instructs the patient to step to the floor with the strong leg, pivoting at the same time so the patient's back is to the wheelchair.

SKILLS COMPETENCY ASSESSMENT — continued

Procedure 10–2: Transferring Patient from Examination Table to Wheelchair

Task Performed	Possible Points	TASKS
☐	5	Has the patient grasp the armrests of the wheelchair.
☐	5	Bends from knees and hips and lowers the patient into the wheelchair, making sure the patient is seated comfortably.
☐	5	Lowers footrests and places the patient's feet on them.
☐	5	Completed the tasks within 5 minutes.
☐	15	Results obtained were accurate.

_______	Earned	ADD POINTS OF TASKS CHECKED
130	Points	TOTAL POINTS POSSIBLE
_______	SCORE	DETERMINE SCORE (divide points earned by total points possible, multiply results by 100)

Actual Student Time Needed to Complete Procedure: ____________

Student's Initials: ____________ Instructor's Initials: ____________ Grade: ____________

Suggestions for Improvement: ____

Evaluator's Name (print) ____

Evaluator's Signature ____

Comments ____

SKILLS COMPETENCY ASSESSMENT

Procedure 10–3: Assisting the Patient to Stand and Walk

Student's Name: ______________________________ Date: ____________

Objective: To help a patient ambulate safely.

Conditions: The student demonstrates the ability to help a patient stand and walk safely using the following equipment and supplies: gait belt and chair or wheelchair.

Time Requirements and Accuracy Standards: 5 minutes. Points assigned reflect importance of step to meeting objective: Important = (5) Essential = (10) Critical = (15). Automatic failure results if any of the **critical** tasks are omitted or performed incorrectly.

STANDARD PRECAUTIONS:

SKILLS ASSESSMENT CHECKLIST

Task Performed	Possible Points	TASKS
		One Person Assist with Ambulation
❑	5	Washes hands.
❑	10	Identifies the patient and explains procedure.
❑	15	Locks the brakes on the wheelchair if the patient is using one; places the patient's feet on the floor and moves the foot plates out of the way.
❑	15	Instructs the patient to slide forward in the chair; places the gait belt around the patient's waist and tucks excess under the belt.
❑	5	Stands directly in front of the patient, grasps the gait belt from underneath and assists the patient to stand on signal; instructs the patient to push up on the armrests of the wheelchair.
❑	15	Steadies the patient and watches for balance, strength, and skin color. Takes pulse, if necessary.
❑	5	*Rationale:* Can triage, or assess, the patient's physical state, looking for signs of potential unsteadiness or syncope, for example.
❑	5	If the patient is steady, proceeds by standing slightly behind and to the side of the patient's weaker side.
❑	10	Grasps the gait belt with one hand and places the other on the patient's bent arm for support. Gait belt is grasped with the fingers under the belt, palm up and elbow bent.
❑	5	Starts with the same foot as the patient and keeps in step with the patient.
❑	15	Documents the procedure; includes, date, time, duration of ambulation, response of patient, and instructions given. Initials report.
❑	5	Completed the tasks within 5 minutes.
❑	15	Results obtained were accurate.

________	Earned	ADD POINTS OF TASKS CHECKED
125	Points	TOTAL POINTS POSSIBLE
________	SCORE	DETERMINE SCORE (divide points earned by total points possible, multiply results by 100)

SKILLS COMPETENCY ASSESSMENT — continued

Procedure 10–3: Assisting the Patient to Stand and Walk

Task Performed	Possible Points	TASKS
		Modification: Two-Person Assist with Ambulation
❑	45	Performs the first four steps of the One-Person Assist Procedure.
❑	5	Has a person stand on either side of the patient. Grasps the gait belt from underneath with one hand, and places the other hand on the patient's back for support.
❑	5	During ambulation, both persons remain on either side of the patient and slightly behind. Both persons grasp the gait belt throughout the ambulation.
❑	15	Documents procedure including date, time, duration of ambulation, response of the patient, and instructions given. Initials report.
❑	5	Completed the tasks within 5 minutes.
❑	15	Results obtained were accurate.

______	Earned	ADD POINTS OF TASKS CHECKED
90	Points	TOTAL POINTS POSSIBLE
______	SCORE	DETERMINE SCORE (divide points earned by total points possible, multiply results by 100)

Actual Student Time Needed to Complete Procedure: ____________

Student's Initials: ____________ Instructor's initials: ____________ Grade: ____________

Suggestions for Improvement: ____________

Evaluator's Name (print) ____________

Evaluator's Signature ____________

Comments ____________

DOCUMENTATION

Chart the procedure in the patient's medical record.

Date: ____________

Charting for One-Person Assist: ____________

____

____

____

Charting for Two-Person Assist: ____________

____

____

Student's Initials: ________

SKILLS COMPETENCY ASSESSMENT

Procedure 10–4: Care of the Falling Patient

Student's Name: ______________________________ Date: ____________

Objective: To help the patient fall safely in order to avoid injury.

Conditions: The student demonstrates the ability to help the patient fall safely to avoid injury using the following equipment and supplies: gait belt already secured to patient.

Time Requirements and Accuracy Standards: 5 minutes. Points assigned reflect importance of step to meeting objective: Important = (5) Essential = (10) Critical = (15). Automatic failure results if any of the **critical** tasks are omitted or performed incorrectly.

SKILLS ASSESSMENT CHECKLIST

Task Performed	Possible Points	TASKS
❑	15	Keeps a firm hand on the gait belt.
❑	5	*Rationale:* Clothing can shift, providing an unstable handhold.
		Falling backward
❑	15	If the patient falls backward, widens stance to become a better base of support. Student allows the patient to fall against his or her body and guides the patient to the floor.
❑	5	Calls for assistance and takes the patient's pulse.
________		Points 40
		Falling to either side
❑	15	If the patient falls to either side, student steadies the patient back onto the feet by moving his or her foot in the direction in which the patient is falling.
❑	10	Asks whether the patient would like to stop the ambulation session; checks the patient for signs of fatigue. If necessary, calls for assistance and takes the patient's pulse.
________		Points 25
		Falling forward
❑	15	Supports the patient around the middle if the patient falls forward. Steps forward with outer leg and gently lowers the patient to the floor while protecting the patient from injury.
❑	10	Calls for assistance and takes the patient's pulse.
❑	15	Has the patient examined by a nurse or doctor before moving the patient again.
❑	15	Documents the fall in an incident report.
________		Points 55

SKILLS COMPETENCY ASSESSMENT — continued

Procedure 10–4: Care of the Falling Patient

Task Performed	Possible Points	TASKS	
❑	5	Completed the tasks within 5 minutes.	
❑	15	Results obtained were accurate.	
______		Points 20	
______		Earned	ADD POINTS OF TASKS CHECKED
	140	Points	TOTAL POINTS POSSIBLE
______		SCORE	DETERMINE SCORE (divide points earned by total points possible, multiply results by 100)

Actual Student Time Needed to Complete Procedure: ____________

Student's Initials: ____________ Instructor's Initials: ____________ Grade: ____________

Suggestions for Improvement: ____________

Evaluator's Name (print) ____________

Evaluator's Signature ____________

Comments ____________

DOCUMENTATION

Chart the procedure in the patient's medical record.

Date: ________

Charting: ____________

Student's Initials: ________

SKILLS COMPETENCY ASSESSMENT

Procedure 10–5: Assisting a Patient to Ambulate with a Walker

Student's Name: ______________________________ Date: __________

Objective: To help a patient ambulate safely and independently with a walker.

Conditions: The student demonstrates the ability to help a patient ambulate independently and safely with a walker using the following equipment and supplies: walker, gait belt.

Time Requirements and Accuracy Standards: 10 minutes. Points assigned reflect importance of step to meeting objective: Important = (5) Essential = (10) Critical = (15). Automatic failure results if any of the **critical** tasks are omitted or performed incorrectly.

STANDARD PRECAUTIONS:

SKILLS ASSESSMENT CHECKLIST

Task Performed	Possible Points	TASKS
❑	5	Washes hands.
❑	5	Identifies the patient and explains procedure.
❑	5	Applies the gait belt snugly around the patient's waist and tucks excess under belt.
❑	10	Checks the walker to be sure the rubber suction tips are secure on all the legs; checks the handrests for rough or damaged edges. Tightens all adjustments.
❑	10	Checks to make sure the patient is wearing good walking shoes with a rubber sole.
❑	5	Checks the height of the walker.
❑	5	*Rationale:* Walker must be adjusted to the correct position for the patient's height.
❑	5	Positions the patient inside the walker and instructs the patient to hold onto the handles while keeping the walker in front of the body.
❑	5	Stands behind and slightly to the side of the patient.
❑	15	Instructs the patient to lift the walker and place all four legs of the walker out in front so the back legs are even with the patient's toes.
❑	15	Instructs the patient to lean forward and transfer weight so that the patient steps into the walker, first with the stronger leg, then with the weaker leg. Makes sure the patient brings the stronger leg past the weaker leg.
❑	10	Monitors the patient carefully, alert to signs of fatigue in the patient. Stands ready to catch the patient in the event of a fall.

SKILLS COMPETENCY ASSESSMENT — continued

Procedure 10–5: Assisting a Patient to Ambulate with a Walker

Task Performed	Possible Points	TASKS
☐	10	If the walker has rollers, watches the patient roll the walker ahead a comfortable distance from the body, then walk into it. The patient can also walk normally with a rolling walker by simply rolling it in front and leaning into the gait, using the walker for support.
☐	15	Documents the date, time, duration of ambulation, response of the patient, and instructions given. Initials the report.
☐	5	Completed the tasks within 10 minutes.
☐	15	Results obtained were accurate.

______	Earned	ADD POINTS OF TASKS CHECKED
140	Points	TOTAL POINTS POSSIBLE
______	SCORE	DETERMINE SCORE (divide points earned by total points possible, multiply results by 100)=

Actual Student Time Needed to Complete Procedure: ______________

Student's Initials: ______________ Instructor's Initials: ______________ Grade: ______________

Suggestions for Improvement: ______________________________

Evaluator's Name (print) ______________________________

Evaluator's Signature ______________________________

Comments ______________________________

DOCUMENTATION

Chart the procedure in the patient's medical record.

Date: __________

Charting: ______________________________

____

____

____

____

____

Student's Initials: ________

SKILLS COMPETENCY ASSESSMENT

Procedure 10–6: Teaching the Patient to Ambulate with Axillary Crutches

Student's Name: ______________________________ Date: __________

Objective: To teach the patient how to ambulate safely using axillary crutches.

Conditions: The student demonstrates the ability to teach the patient how to ambulate safely using axillary crutches with the following equipment and supplies: axillary crutches and gait belt.

Time Requirements and Accuracy Standards: 10 minutes. Points assigned reflect importance of step to meeting objective: Important = (5) Essential = (10) Critical = (15). Automatic failure results if any of the **critical** tasks are omitted or performed incorrectly.

STANDARD PRECAUTIONS:

SKILLS ASSESSMENT CHECKLIST

Task Performed	Possible Points	TASKS
☐	5	Washes hands.
☐	5	Identifies the patient and explains procedure.
☐	10	Assembles the axillary crutches and makes sure they are in good condition and good working order.
☐	15	Checks the measurement of the crutches.
☐	10	Applies the gait belt; assists the patient to stand and places the crutches under the patient's armpits.
☐	15	Instructs the patient to carry weight completely on the hands and not on the armpits.
☐	10	Instructs the patient to put all weight on the good leg and bend the weak leg slightly so it will not drag on the floor while walking.
☐	5	Assists the patient with the required gait.
☐	15	Teaches the patient how to inspect the crutches daily for safety. • Check wing nuts. • Check crutch tips for wear and tear. • Check foam pads of hand grips and armpit rests for tears. • Wear comfortable shoes, preferably with rubber soles. • Never use crutches on waxed floors or loose rugs.
☐	5	Washes hands.

SKILLS COMPETENCY ASSESSMENT — continued

Procedure 10–6: Teaching the Patient to Ambulate with Axillary Crutches

Task Performed	Possible Points	TASKS
❑	15	Documents the date, time, duration of ambulation, and instructions given. Initials the report.
❑	5	Completed the tasks within 10 minutes.
❑	15	Results obtained were accurate.
________	Earned	ADD POINTS OF TASKS CHECKED
130	Points	TOTAL POINTS POSSIBLE
________	SCORE	DETERMINE SCORE (divide points earned by total points possible, multiply results by 100)

Actual Student Time Needed to Complete Procedure: ____________

Student's Initials: ____________ Instructor's Initials: ____________ Grade: ____________

Suggestions for Improvement: ____________

Evaluator's Name (print) ____________

Evaluator's Signature ____________

Comments ____________

DOCUMENTATION

Chart the procedure in the patient's medical record.

Date: ________

Charting: ____________

____

____

____

____

____

Student's Initials: ______

SKILLS COMPETENCY ASSESSMENT

Procedure 10–7: Assisting a Patient to Ambulate with a Cane

Student's Name: ______________________________ Date: ____________

Objective: To teach patients how to walk safely with a cane.

Conditions: The student demonstrates the ability to teach patients how to walk safely with a cane using the following equipment and supplies: appropriate cane for patient, gait belt.

Time Requirements and Accuracy Standards: 5 minutes. Points assigned reflect importance of step to meeting objective: Important = (5) Essential = (10) Critical = (15). Automatic failure results if any of the **critical** tasks are omitted or performed incorrectly.

STANDARD PRECAUTIONS: 

SKILLS ASSESSMENT CHECKLIST

Task Performed	Possible Points	TASKS
❑	5	Washes hands.
❑	5	Ascertains what type of cane the patient will be using and assembles the equipment.
❑	10	Identifies the patient and explains procedure.
❑	10	Checks the cane to be sure the bottom has a rubber suction tip(s).
❑	10	Applies the gait belt snugly around the patient's waist and assists the patient to a standing position.
❑	10	Places the cane 6 inches in front and slightly to the side of the foot of the strong leg. Adjusts the cane so the handle is at the level of the patient's hip joint.
❑	5	*Rationale:* Knows the proper angle to which the patient's elbow should be flexed during weightbearing.
❑	15	Instructs the patient to move the cane forward 10 to 18 inches, depending on the patient's ability.
❑	15	Instructs the patient to move the weak leg forward while transferring body weight to the cane.
❑	15	Instructs the patient to move the strong leg forward past the cane.
❑	5	Follows along behind and to the side of the patient's weak side.
❑	5	Washes hands.

SKILLS COMPETENCY ASSESSMENT — continued

Procedure 10–7: Assisting a Patient to Ambulate with a Cane

Task Performed	Possible Points	TASKS
❑	15	Documents the date, time, duration of ambulation, response of the patient, and instructions given. Initials report.
❑	5	Completed the tasks within 5 minutes.
❑	15	Results obtained were accurate.

________	Earned	ADD POINTS OF TASKS CHECKED
145	Points	TOTAL POINTS POSSIBLE
________	SCORE	DETERMINE SCORE (divide points earned by total points possible, multiply results by 100)

Actual Student Time Needed to Complete Procedure: ____________

Student's Initials: ____________ Instructor's Initials: ____________ Grade: ____________

Suggestions for Improvement: ______________________________

Evaluator's Name (print) ______________________________

Evaluator's Signature ______________________________

Comments ______________________________

DOCUMENTATION

Chart the procedure in the patient's medical record.

Date: __________

Charting: ______________________________

____

____

____

____

____

Student's Initials: ________

SKILLS COMPETENCY ASSESSMENT

Procedure 10-8: Range of Motion Exercises, Upper Body

Student's Name: ______________________________ Date: ____________

Objective: To maintain or increase joint mobility in a patient's upper extremities and to prevent contractures.

Conditions: The student demonstrates the ability to perform range of motion exercises to maintain or increase joint mobility in a patient's upper body. This procedure is best done with the patient in the supine position. Repeat each motion several times.

Time Requirements and Accuracy Standards: 15 minutes. Points assigned reflect importance of step to meeting objective: Important = (5) Essential = (10) Critical = (15). Automatic failure results if any of the **critical** tasks are omitted or performed incorrectly.

STANDARD PRECAUTIONS:

SKILLS ASSESSMENT CHECKLIST

Task Performed	Possible Points	TASKS
		PREPROCEDURE TASKS
❑	5	Washes hands.
❑	10	Identifies the patient and explains procedure.
		PROCEDURE TASKS
		Shoulder Flexion
❑	5	Keeps the patient's arm straight and holds the arm at the wrist and elbow.
❑	10	Lifts the patient's arm straight over the patient's head until it rests flat on the bed or table above the patient's head.
❑	5	Bends the patient's elbow if there is not enough room on the bed.
❑	5	Brings the arm back to the patient's side.
		Shoulder Abduction and Adduction
❑	10	Keeps the patient's arm straight by the patient's side with the palm of the hand facing up; supports the arm at the wrist and elbow.
❑	5	Keeps the patient's arm straight; brings it out at a right angle to the patient's body.
❑	10	Brings the arm back to the patient's side. Keeping the arm straight, brings it across the patient's body.
❑	5	Returns the patient's arm to a position parallel to the body.

SKILLS COMPETENCY ASSESSMENT — continued

Procedure 10–8: Range of Motion Exercises, Upper Body

Task Performed	Possible Points	TASKS
		Internal and External Shoulder Rotation
❑	5	Brings the patient's arm out at a right angle from the body.
❑	5	Bends the elbow at a right angle and keeps the patient's upper arm on the bed.
❑	10	Keeping the patient's arm at a right angle, presses down on the shoulder with one hand while holding the patient's wrist with the other.
❑	5	Moves the hand gently back until it touches the bed next to the patient's head.
❑	5	Brings the patient's hand back down until the palm of the patient's hand touches the bed.
		Elbow Flexion and Extension
❑	10	Holding the patient's arm by the patient's side, palm up, flexes and extends the elbow.
		Wrist Extension and Flexion
❑	5	Supports the patient's arm above the wrist.
❑	5	Holding the palm of the patient's hand, extends the patient's wrist, then straightens it.
❑	10	Places hand over the patient's hand while supporting the patient's wrist; bends or flexes the hand.
		Wrist Inversion and Eversion
❑	5	Grasps the patient's wrist with one hand and grasps the patient's hand with the other.
❑	5	Slowly bends the patient's hand toward the patient's body, then away from the body.
		Wrist Supination and Pronation
❑	5	Grasps the patient's wrist with one hand and grasps the patient's hand with the other.
❑	5	Slowly turns the patient's hand toward the patient's feet, then toward the face.
		Finger Flexion and Extension
❑	10	Supports the patient's wrist with one hand. Covers the patient's fingers with the other hand and curls them over to make a fist.
❑	5	Uncurls the patient's fingers and straightens them.

Task Performed	Possible Points	TASKS
		Finger and Thumb Abduction and Adduction
❑	10	Holds the patient's hand flat; pulls each finger away from the thumb, then pulls the finger back straight.
❑	5	Pulls the thumb away from the rest of the fingers, then pulls it back straight.
		Thumb Opposition
❑	5	Supports the patient's hand.
❑	5	Touches each finger with the patient's thumb.
		POSTPROCEDURE TASKS
❑	15	Documents the date, time, limbs given ROM, and response of the patient. Initials report.
❑	5	Completed the tasks within 15 minutes.
❑	15	Results obtained were accurate.

______	Earned	ADD POINTS OF TASKS CHECKED
225	Points	TOTAL POINTS POSSIBLE
______	SCORE	DETERMINE SCORE (divide points earned by total points possible, multiply results by 100)

Actual Student Time Needed to Complete Procedure: ____________

Student's Initials: ____________ Instructor's Initials: ____________ Grade: ____________

Suggestions for Improvement: ____

Evaluator's Name (print) ____

Evaluator's Signature ____

Comments ____

DOCUMENTATION

Chart the ROM procedure indicated by the instructor in the patient's medical record.

Date: __________

Charting: ____

____

____

____

____

Student's Initials: ________

SKILLS COMPETENCY ASSESSMENT

Procedure 10–9: Range of Motion Exercises, Lower Body

Student's Name: ______________________________ Date: ____________

Objective: To maintain or increase joint mobility in the patient's lower extremities and to prevent contractures.

Conditions: The student demonstrates the ability to maintain or increase joint mobility in the lower extremities and to prevent contractures. This procedure is best done with the patient in the supine position. Repeat each movement several times.

Time Requirements and Accuracy Standards: 15 minutes. Points assigned reflect importance of step to meeting objective: Important = (5) Essential = (10) Critical = (15). Automatic failure results if any of the **critical** tasks are omitted or performed incorrectly.

STANDARD PRECAUTIONS:

SKILLS ASSESSMENT CHECKLIST

Task Performed	Possible Points	TASKS
		PREPROCEDURE TASKS
❑	5	Washes hands.
❑	10	Identifies the patient and explains procedure.
		PROCEDURE TASKS *Hip Abduction and Adduction*
❑	5	Supports the patient's knee and ankle.
❑	10	Keeping the patient's leg straight, moves the entire leg away from the body.
❑	15	Moves the patient's leg back, toward the midline of the body.
		Hip and Knee Flexion and Extension
❑	5	Supports the patient's knee and ankle.
❑	15	Bends the patient's knee and raises it as far toward the patient's chest as the patient's tolerance and comfort will allow.
❑	10	Lowers and straightens the patient's leg.
		Hip Rotation
❑	5	Supports the patient's leg at the knee and ankle.
❑	10	Rolls the patient's leg in a circular motion, away from the body.
❑	10	Rolls the patient's leg in a circular motion, toward the body.

Task Performed	Possible Points	TASKS
		Ankle Dorsiflexion and Plantar Flexion
❑	10	Keeps the patient's leg flat on the bed, with the knee slightly bent if more comfortable for the patient. Grasps the patient's ankle with one hand and the heel of the patient's foot with the other.
❑	10	With the hand holding the patient's heel, flexes the patient's foot and rests the bottom of the patient's foot against the student's forearm, keeping the elbow straight.
❑	10	Dorsiflexes the ankle by pushing the patient's foot toward the patient's knee with student's arm.
❑	5	Returns the foot to its flexed position against the student's forearm.
❑	10	Keeping one hand on the patient's ankle, plantar flexes the ankle by drawing the foot down toward the foot of the bed.
		Foot Inversion and Eversion
❑	5	Grasps the patient's ankle with one hand and the arch of the foot with the other.
❑	5	Turns the patient's foot inward.
❑	10	Returns the patient's foot to the midline, then gently turns it outward.
		Toe Flexion and Extension
❑	10	Holds the patient's ankle in one hand and places fingers over the patient's toes with the other hand.
❑	5	Bends the toes, then straightens them.
		Toe Abduction and Adduction
❑	5	Moves each toe one at a time away from the second toe.
❑	5	Moves each toe one at a time toward the second toe.
		POSTPROCEDURE TASKS
❑	15	Documents the date, time, limbs given ROM, and response of the patient. Initials the report.
❑	5	Completed the tasks within 15 minutes.
❑	15	Results obtained were accurate.

________	Earned	ADD POINTS OF TASKS CHECKED
225	Points	TOTAL POINTS POSSIBLE
________	SCORE	DETERMINE SCORE (divide points earned by total points possible, multiply results by 100)

SKILLS COMPETENCY ASSESSMENT — continued

Procedure 10–9: Range of Motion Exercises, Lower Body

Actual Student Time Needed to Complete Procedure: ____________

Student's Initials: ____________ Instructor's Initials: ____________ Grade: ____________

Suggestions for Improvement: ____

Evaluator's Name (print) ____

Evaluator's Signature ____

Comments ____

DOCUMENTATION

Chart the procedure indicated by the instructor in the patient's medical record.

Date: __________

Charting: ____

____

____

____

____

____

Student's Initials: ________

EVALUATION OF CHAPTER KNOWLEDGE

How has your instructor evaluated the knowledge you have gained?

Knowledge	Instructor Evaluation *Good*	*Average*	*Poor*
Knows the definition of rehabilitation medicine and its importance in patient care	_____	_____	_____
Understands the importance of correct posture and body mechanics and how to safely transfer patients and lift or move large objects using correct body mechanics	_____	_____	_____
Knows how to care for the falling patient	_____	_____	_____
Knows how to help a patient safely stand and walk	_____	_____	_____
Knows the three types of assistive devices and how to teach patients to ambulate using each	_____	_____	_____
Understands how to measure patients for axillary crutches	_____	_____	_____
Describes the ambulation gaits used with crutches	_____	_____	_____
Understands the function of joint range of motion and how to measure joint movement	_____	_____	_____
Understands how therapeutic exercise is used in rehabilitation medicine and knows the types of therapeutic exercises	_____	_____	_____
Knows the definitions of the body movements used in range of motion exercises	_____	_____	_____
Knows the types of therapeutic modalities, can explain how the body reacts to each, and can describe the situation in which each modality would be used	_____	_____	_____
Understands how ultrasound works			

Student's Initials: _______ Instructor's Initials: _______

Grade: ________

Basic Pharmacology

PERFORMANCE OBJECTIVES

A comprehensive understanding of pharmacology, the study of drugs, is essential to medical assistants in the ambulatory care setting. Medical assistants must have a working knowledge of basic pharmacology—including uses, sources, forms, and delivery routes of drugs—and an understanding of governmental laws that oversee the distribution and administration of medications. Medical assistants should also demonstrate the ability to recognize drug classifications and identify actions that will allow them to caution patients in the use of both prescription and nonprescription medications. Medical assistants must also be able to access medical resources and reference books for information pertaining to pharmaceutical products, including drug classification, routes, forms of storage, and side effects and contraindications. It is essential that medical assistants also have the skills to recognize the signs of drug abuse and misuse and to effectively follow the procedures delegated to instances of suspected patient mishandling of drugs. It is important to remember, however, that only a licensed physician may prescribe medications.

EXERCISES AND ACTIVITIES

Vocabulary Builder

A. *Match the following key vocabulary terms listed in Column A with their corresponding definitions listed in Column B.*

Column A	Column B
A. Abuse	_____ 1. Term used to describe when a licensed practitioner gives a written order to be taken to a pharmacist to be filled.
B. Administer	_____ 2. An allergic hypersensitivity reaction of the body to a foreign protein or drug.
C. Anaphylaxis	_____ 3. To give the medication to the patient to be used at another time.

D. Contraindication _____ 4. The study of drugs; the science dealing with the history, origin, sources, physical and chemical properties, uses, and effects of on living organisms.

E. Dispense _____ 5. To give a medication to a patient by mouth, injection, or any other method of delivery.

F. Pharmacology _____ 6. Any symptom or circumstance that an otherwise approved form of treatment is inadvisable.

G. Prescribe _____ 7. The misuse of legal and illegal drugs.

B. *Insert the proper terms into the spaces provided in the following text, which discusses medical uses of drugs, name of drugs, and sources of drugs.*

Therapeutic	Synthetic	Chemical
Gene splicing	Genetically engineering	Generic
Curative	Plant	Animal
Replacement	Mineral	Diagnostic
Preventive or prophylactic	Trade or brand	

A drug is a medicinal substance that may be used to vary or modify the functions of a living being. Of the five basic medical uses for drugs, antibiotics are an example of ____________________ drugs, agents used for the killing or removal of the causative agent of a disease. An immunizing agent is an example of a ____________________ drug, one used to stave off or abate the severity of a disease. Another medical use for drugs is used in the treatment of a condition to provide symptomatic relief. This is known as ____________________. Insulin and hormones are examples of this medical use of drugs, known as ____________________. A fifth basic medical use of drugs is used in conjunction with radiology and allows physicians to pinpoint the location of diseases manifestations. This usage is known as ____________________.

As essential to the medical assistant as the knowledge of basic uses for drugs is the knowledge of the names of drugs. The majority of drugs have three types of names. The ____________________ name is the drug's official name assigned by the U.S. Adopted Names Council. Aspirin is an example of this type of name. The drug's ____________________ name describes its molecular structure and identification of its chemical structure. Acetylsalicylic acid is an example of this type of name. Ecotrin is an example of a ____________________ name, which is registered by the U.S. patent office and approved for usage by the U.S. Food and Drug Administration.

Medical assistants must also have a comprehensive understanding of the five basic sources of drugs. The source of digitalis, the dried leaf of a foxglove plant, is an example of a ____________________ source. Insulin, a hormone derived from the pancreas of cows and hogs, is an example of a drug derived from an ____________________ source. Drugs that are artificially prepared in pharmaceutical laboratories are known as ____________________ drugs. Synthetically prepared sulfur, used in pharmaceutical products (such as certain bacteriostatic drugs), is an example of a drug derived from a ____________________ source. One of the latest sources for drugs has been provided by ____________________. Using a technique called ____________________, scientists are able to create hybrid forms of life that can treat certain diseases; interferon for cancer treatment is an example of this process.

Learning Review

Circle the correct response for each multiple choice question below.

1. All drugs available for legal use are controlled by the
   A. Federal Food, Drug, and Cosmetic Act.
   B. The Council on Pharmacy of the American Medical Association.
   C. Controlled Substance Act of 1970.

2. Federal law requires that at the end of the work day, controlled substances that are used and the premises
   A. must be locked in a physician's office by a physician.
   B. must be removed from the building and stored in a government-appointed storage space.
   C. must be counted, verified by two individuals, and recorded on an audit sheet.

3. An inventory record of Schedule II drugs must be submitted to the Drug Enforcement Agency (DEA) every
   A. week.
   B. year.
   C. two years.

4. An example of drug requiring a prescription is
   A. the antibiotic penicillin.
   B. the antihistamine Benadryl.
   C. the analgesic acetaminophen.

5. An example of an over-the-counter (OTC) drug is
   A. the analgesic ibuprofen.
   B. the vasodilator nitroglycerin.
   C. the antitussive codeine.

6. When a drug acts on the area to which it is administered it has what is known as a:
   A. systemic action.
   B. remote action.
   C. local action.

7. The four principal factors that affect drug action are absorption, distribution, biotransformation, and
   A. elimination.
   B. interaction.
   C. contraindication.

8. By law, outdated and expired controlled substances must be
   A. handed over to your local law enforcement agency.
   B. thrown away.
   C. returned to the pharmacy.

9. Patients need to realize that OTC drugs can
   A. interact with other drugs and cause undesirable or adverse reactions or complications.
   B. mask symptoms and exacerbate an existing condition.
   C. both A and B.

10. The most frequently used routes of administering medication are
   A. inhalation and sublingual.
   B. parenteral and inhalation.
   C. oral and parenteral.

11. Under federal law, physicians who prescribe, administer, or dispense controlled substances must register with the DEA (Drug Enforcement Agency) and renew their registration as required by state law. Describe the five schedules of classification for controlled substances and give an example for each.

Schedule I ______________________________

______________________________ Example: ______________

Schedule II ______________________________

______________________________ Example: ______________

Schedule III ______________________________

______________________________ Example: ______________

Schedule IV ______________________________

______________________________ Example: ______________

Schedule V ______________________________

______________________________ Example: ______________

12. For each of the following, identify whether the drug involved is an over-the-counter medication (OTC) or a prescribed medication (PM). What patient guidelines for proper use are illustrated in each example?

_____ A. Nora Fowler insists that Dr. Winston Lewis cannot help her rheumatoid arthritis and that simple ibuprofen is all she needs. Nora buys bulk generic bottles of ibuprofen at the drugstore for her rheumatoid arthritis and takes as many as she needs to help ease the painful inflammation in her joints and tissues.

____

____

_____ B. When Jim Marshall experiences extreme stress while finishing the architectural designs for a new office building in the community, his girlfriend offers him a tablet or two of Lorazepam, a benzodiazepine drug used to treat anxiety and insomnia. "Here, Dr. King gave me these, and they work great," she says. "You can't drive when you take this stuff, though. Oh, and these pills are about two years old, but I'm sure they'll still work fine."

____

____

_____ C. At the slightest sniffle or sneeze, Lenore McDonell takes the strongest multisymptom cold medication she can find. Her philosophy: "I might as well knock it out of my system."

____

____

_____ D. Abigail Johnson hates taking so many medications. So every now and then, when she feels especially good, Abigail just decides to stop taking the antihypertensive drug that is part of Dr. Elizabeth King's treatment plan to control Abigail's high blood pressure. On a bad day, she'll take an extra pill.

____

____

_____ E. Wayne Elder is susceptible to recurrent colds and ear infections. Wayne's symptoms are hard to control because he'll almost always stop taking the antibiotics when he starts to feel better and he doesn't finish the entire regimen recommended by Dr. Lewis.

____

____

13. Proper disposal of drugs is important because expired drugs can be harmful. Identify the proper manner of disposing of each of the following forms of drugs.

A. Liquids and ointments ______________________________

B. Powdered drugs must be ______________________________

C. Pills and capsules must be ______________________________

D. Vials and ampules must be ______________________________

E. Outdated and expired controlled substances must be ______________________________

F. What happens if a medication is removed from its container but not used? For example, a patient refuses novocaine before a minor dental procedure. ______________________________

____

14. A. What factor in determining the route selection for administering a medication is illustrated by each example below and why?

(1) A patient diagnosed with insulin-dependent diabetes mellitus performs three self-injections of insulin daily, according to the physician's treatment plan.

____

(2) Chemotherapeutic drugs are used to attack cancer cells that may be traveling throughout a patient's body and usually they are administered intravenously.

____

(3) A patient in a nursing home in the end stages of Parkinson's disease is bedridden, has trouble swallowing, and suffers from dementia. The patient, who is also suffering from angina as a result of poor blood circulation, is prescribed a nitroglycerin transdermal system instead of a sublingual dosage, to be held under the tongue, or a time-released capsule to swallow.

____

B. The most frequently used routes of administering medication are oral and parenteral. List seven additional routes of administration.

(1) ____________________ (5) ____________________

(2) ____________________ (6) ____________________

(3) ____________________ (7) ____________________

(4) ____________________

C. Name three recently developed systems of drug delivery. Describe each and note their specific advantages.

(1) ______________________________

____

(2) ______________________________

____

(3) ______________________________

____

15. A. List four examples of the ways in which drugs may be classified, or arranged, in groups.

(1) ______________________________

(2) ______________________________

(3) ______________________________

(4) ______________________________

B. For each drug action, identify the correct drug classification. Then list one example of a drug contained in each class.

Action	Drug Classification	Example
(1) Controls or stops bleeding		
(2) Prevents or relieves nausea and vomiting		
(3) Neutralizes acid		
(4) Lowers blood pressure		
(5) Reduces fever		
(6) Loosens and promotes normal bowel elimination		
(7) Prevents conception		
(8) Kills or destroys malignant cells		
(9) Prevents or relieves diarrhea		
(10) Produces a calming effect without causing sleep		

16. The *Physicians' Desk Reference* (PDR) is an invaluable resource and one of the most widely used publications in the medical industry. The annually updated publication is usually available in most clinics and medical offices. It provides medical professionals with practical information about thousands of medications and includes other useful data, such as lists of drugs new to the market and those that have been discontinued. It is essential that medical assistants become familiar with the publication and learn how to access the wealth of information stored within.

Use the PDR to locate the pertinent information for each of the following scenarios. Then identify the drug's source or method of production.

A. Herb Fowler, Dr. Winston Lewis's patient, calls complaining of nausea, a symptom he believes may be a negative reaction to the Chronulac Syrup Dr. Lewis recently prescribed for Herb's chronic constipation. Using the *PDR*, locate the following information.

Chronulac Syrup's generic name: ______________________________

The sugar Chronulac Syrup contains: ______________________________

Identify the drug's source or method of production: ______________________________

B. Another patient of Dr. Lewis's, Michael Zamboni, has recently been diagnosed with insulin-dependent Type II diabetes. Dr. Lewis prescribes Humulin. Using the *PDR*, find the following information.

Humulin's generic name: ______________________________

The animal source Humulin is derived from: ______________________________

Identify the drug's source or method of production: ______________________________

C. Susan Marshall, a new patient of Dr. Elizabeth King's, acquired a high-pressure job about one month ago. Recently, she has been complaining of stomach upset, which has been attributed to her stressful job and poor eating habits. Dr. King orders prescription-strength Pepcid for Susan. Using the *PDR*, locate the following information.

Pepcid's generic name: ______________________________

Pepcid's active ingredient: ______________________________

Identify the drug's source or method of production: ______________________________

D. Camille Saunders, another patient of Dr. King's, has been taking Ortho-Tri-Cyclen, an oral contraceptive, for six months. It has just been discovered that Camille has epilepsy. Using the *PDR*, locate the following information.

Does Ortho-Tri-Cyclen have any known contraindications to any drugs used in the treatment of epilepsy, and if so, which drugs?

____

____

Identify the drug's source or method of production: ______________________________

Investigation Activity

Most individuals have a bathroom medicine chest with an assortment of over-the-counter and prescription drugs. Some are taken regularly, such as acetaminophen. Some are taken under the care and supervision of a physician in response to a specific illness or condition, with the remainder of the prescription left to sit on the shelf—codeine cough syrup is an example. Assess your own family's medicine chest. Choose three over-the-counter medications your family commonly uses and list them in the charts provided, along with the information requested.

Name of Product:	
Indications:	
Form of Drug and Dosage:	
Directions for Adults:	
Side effects:	
Contraindications:	

Name of Product:	
Indications:	
Form of Drug and Dosage:	
Directions for Adults:	
Side effects:	
Contraindications:	

Name of Product:	
Indications:	
Form of Drug and Dosage:	
Directions for Adults:	
Side effects:	
Contraindications:	

1. Where are medications stored in your home? Are they stored in more than one location? Is your medicine cabinet orderly or disorganized?

____

____

____

2. Are there children in your household? Are drugs properly stored so children cannot reach them? What methods can be used to keep drugs away from children?

____

____

3. How often do you clean out your medicine cabinet at home? How does your family dispose of medications? Why is maintaining an orderly medicine cabinet in the home important?

____

____

____

CASE STUDY

While Anna Preciado, a clinical medical assistant newly hired at the offices of Drs. Lewis and King, is performing her shift duties, she notices a fellow employee exhibiting strange behavior. Audrey

Jones, CMA, is usually the model of efficiency. Since Anna began working at the Northborough Family Medical Group, she has always known Audrey to be alert, friendly, and able to handle difficult clinical situations with grace under pressure. Lately, however, when Anna asks Audrey questions, Audrey seems irritable and easily confused. Anna also notices Audrey exhibiting a sloppy technique during routine clinical procedures. Anna is disturbed by Audrey's erratic behavior, but does not mention anything to anyone. After all, Anna is new to the job. But while counting the contents of the controlled substance cabinet in preparation for the end of her shift, Anna notices that a bottle of Phenobarbital is missing. Anna knows that office manager Marilyn Johnson will arrive shortly to verify and record the inventory count. Anna is now worried that perhaps Audrey is to blame for the missing drugs but is afraid of jumping to conclusions and of angering Audrey. Anna knows Audrey is in the staff lounge preparing to leave for a dinner break.

Discuss the following:

1. What is Anna's first action under the circumstances? Should she confront Audrey?
2. What special responsibilities do health care professionals, including medical assistants, have regarding the misuse or abuse of legal or illegal drugs?

SUPPLEMENTARY RESOURCES

Study Guide Disk: Additional practice exercises for this chapter are available on the study guide disk found in the back of the textbook.

Medical Assisting Videos: Appropriate content is available on Delmar's Medical Assisting Videos, 2nd ed., for the following topics:

Tape 2 Dispose of Controlled Substances in Compliance With Government Regulations
Perform Within Ethical Boundaries
Tape 11 Prepare and Administer Medication As Directed By Physician
Tape 12 Prepare and Administer Parenteral Medications

EVALUATION OF CHAPTER KNOWLEDGE

Evaluate your comprehension of basic pharmacology, including uses, sources, forms, and the delivery routes of drugs; the intent of the law regarding controlled substances and other medications; and your knowledge of the classifications and actions of drugs.

Compare this evaluation with the one provided by your instructor.

	Student Self-Evaluation			**Instructor Evaluation**		
Knowledge	*Good*	*Average*	*Poor*	*Good*	*Average*	*Poor*
Has a working knowledge of basic pharmacology, including knowing five basic uses and five basic sources for drugs and has the ability to recall three types of drug names and give examples of each	_____	_____	_____	_____	_____	_____
Able to prepare and administer medications as directed by a physician	_____	_____	_____	_____	_____	_____
Able to maintain medication records in relation to the prescription, administration, and dispensation of drugs	_____	_____	_____	_____	_____	_____
Documents medications accurately	_____	_____	_____	_____	_____	_____
Understands what the Federal Food, Drug, and Cosmetic Act and Controlled Substance Act of 1970 entails	_____	_____	_____	_____	_____	_____
Able to handle, store, and dispose of controlled substances in compliance with governmental regulations	_____	_____	_____	_____	_____	_____
Can define the law in terms of administering, prescribing, and dispensing drugs	_____	_____	_____	_____	_____	_____
Able to name the seven major sections (including the four most commonly used) of the *PDR*	_____	_____	_____	_____	_____	_____
Able to describe principal actions of drugs and at least three undesirable reactions	_____	_____	_____	_____	_____	_____
Able to list emergency drugs and supplies	_____	_____	_____	_____	_____	_____
Able to list commonly abused drugs and recognize their effects	_____	_____	_____	_____	_____	_____

Student's Initials: _____ Instructor's Initials: _____

Grade: _____

Dosage Calculations and Medication Administration

PERFORMANCE OBJECTIVES

To safely administer medications to patients, medical assistants must possess a fundamental knowledge of pharmacology, have the ability to calculate doses of medication, and be competent in various methods of medication administration, including oral and parenteral. Medical assistants must also be aware of the legal and ethical aspects of medication administration. It is the responsibility of all health care professionals to provide care only within the scope of practice of their training and knowledge, and within legal and ethical boundaries. Only a physician has the legal authority to prescribe medications for patients. Medical assistants prepare and administer medications as directed by the physician, accurately documenting and reporting according to the facility's established policies and procedures. All standard precautions and OSHA guidelines are observed to protect health care professionals, patients, and visitors from the transmission of pathogens.

EXERCISES AND ACTIVITIES

Vocabulary Builder

Supply a brief definition for each key vocabulary term.

1. Apnea ____________________
2. BSA ____________________
3. Hypoxemia ____________________
4. Meniscus ____________________
5. Nomogram ____________________
6. Parenteral ____________________
7. Precipitate ____________________
8. Taut ____________________
9. Unit Dose ____________________
10. Wheal ____________________

Learning Review

1. The prescription is a written legal document that gives directions for compounding, dispensing, and administering a medication to a patient. In the spaces below, "decode" the physicians' written prescriptions for medication in lay person's terms and answer the questions that follow.

A. Dr. King prescribes an adult dosage for a fever.

L&K LEWIS & KING, MD
2501 CENTER STREET
NORTHBOROUGH, OH 12345

Name Lourdes Austin

Address 821 Spring Lane, Apt. 12 Date 3/1/--

℞

Dilantin 100 mg tab
#90
Sig 100 mg p.o. tid

Generic Substitution Allowed Elizabeth King M.D.
Dispense As Written ______ M.D.
REPETATUR 0 1 2 3 p.r.n.
☑ LABEL

How many grains are in each dose? ______

______

How days of medication are dispensed? __

______

B. Dr. Lewis prescribes a child's dosage for an ear infection.

L&K LEWIS & KING, MD
2501 CENTER STREET
NORTHBOROUGH, OH 12345

Name Felicia Lawrence

Address 362 Owen's View Way Date 3/1/--

℞

Amoxicillin 250 mg/5cc
150cc
Sig 5cc p.o. tid

Generic Substitution Allowed Winston Lewis M.D.
Dispense As Written ______ M.D.
REPETATUR 0 1 2 3 p.r.n.
☑ LABEL

Perform the conversion:

______5 cc = ______ teaspoons

How many doses are included in the amount dispensed? ______

2. A. Identify the following measures as weight (W) or volume (V). Then name the measure each abbreviation stands for and what system of measurement it belongs to.

Weight	Volume	Abbreviation	Measure	System
❑	❑	Gm		
❑	❑	gr		
❑	❑	qt		
❑	❑	tbsp		
❑	❑	mL		
❑	❑	fldr		
❑	❑	gt		
❑	❑	µg		

B. Perform the following conversions:

(1) 4 tsp = ________ mL

(2) 3.5 in = ________ cm

(3) 1,200 mg = ________ Gm

(4) 30 mg = ________ gr

(5) 8 mL = ________ gtt

C. What are proportions? How are proportions useful in calculating dosages of medication?

3. A. Identify the type of syringe typically used for each of the following; list the size and calibration as well.

(1) Venipunture: ________________________

(2) Insulin administration: ________________________

(3) Allergy testing: ________________________

B. For each syringe-needle combination below, identify the most likely parenteral route: Subcutaneous injection (SC), Intramuscular injection (IM), or Intradermal injection (ID). Also identify the proper angle of injection.

		Angle of injection
_____	1. 3-cc syringe/22G, 1 1/2 inch needle	____________
_____	2. 1-cc syringe/25G, 5/8 inch needle	____________
_____	3. U-100 (1cc)/26G, 1/2 inch needle	____________
_____	4. 3-cc syringe/25G, 5/8 inch needle	____________

Investigation Activity

Under the law, health care professionals who administer medications are expected to be knowledgeable about the drugs they administer and the effects the drug(s) may and/or will have on the patient.

A. List three medications that are commonly prescribed to patients in the ambulatory care setting.

Three commonly prescribed medications:

(1) ________________ (2) ________________ (3) ________________

B. Choose one of the medications listed above and research it, consulting the *PDR*, a medical encyclopedia, and a nurse's drug reference. Complete the chart on the next page.

<table>
<tr><td colspan="2">Drug name (generic and brand)</td></tr>
<tr><td>Action</td><td>Uses</td></tr>
<tr><td>Contraindications</td><td>Warnings when indicated</td></tr>
<tr><td>Adverse reactions</td><td rowspan="2">Common dosages and routes</td></tr>
<tr><td>Implications for patient care</td></tr>
<tr><td>Patient teaching</td><td>Special considerations</td></tr>
</table>

CASE STUDY

Louise Kipperley comes to the urgent care center at Inner City Health Care when she experiences the third severe migraine headache in only one month. The headache has lasted two days and Louise has experienced symptoms of nausea and vomiting. Dr. Rice gives written orders to administer Imitrex 25 mg IM stat, along with a prescription for the patient to fill and use at home. Liz Corbin, CMA, makes a medicine card from the physician's order sheet of Louise's medical record and prepares the stat dosage for Louise according to the correct procedure for administering oral medications. Liz is about to transport the medication to Louise in examination room #3 when she reads the physician's written order for Louise, which calls for 25 mg IM stat. The written prescription is for Imitrex every 4 hours as needed. Liz discards the dosage she has prepared for the patient and instead gives Louise Dr. Rice's prescription and tells her to have it filled immediately.

Discuss the following:

1. What medication error has Liz made? What effect will the error likely have on the patient?
2. What should Liz do? What standard procedures should be followed when a medication error occurs?

SUPPLEMENTARY RESOURCES

Study Guide Disk: Additional practice exercises for this chapter are available on the study guide disk found in the back of the textbook.

Medical Assisting Videos: Appropriate content is available on Delmar's Medical Assisting Videos, 2nd ed., for the following topics:

Tape 2: Practice Risk Management Measure to Prevent Professional Liability
- Dispose of Controlled Substances in Compliance With Government Regulations
- Perform Within Ethical Boundaries

Tape 5: Infections in the Office

Tape 11: Prepare and Administer Medication As Directed By Physician
- Administer Oral Medications

Tape 12: Prepare and Administer Parenteral Medications
- Cartridge Injection Systems
- Safety Syringe
- Withdraw Parenteral Medication from Vial
- Initial Procedures Common To All Injections
- Administer Intramuscular Injections
- Administer Subcutaneous Injections
- Administer Intradermal Injections
- Completion Procedures Following Injections
- OSHA Regulations for Needles and "Sharps"
- Accidental Needlesticks

SKILLS COMPETENCY ASSESSMENT

Procedure 12–1: Administration of Oral Medications

Student's Name: ______________________________ Date: __________

Objective: To correctly administer an oral medication after receiving a physician's order.

Conditions: The student demonstrates the ability to correctly administer an oral medication after receiving a physician's order, and using the following equipment and supplies: proper medication, medicine card, water, milk, or juice for patient.

Time Requirements and Accuracy Standards: 10 minutes. Points assigned reflect importance of step to meeting objective: Important = (5) Essential = (10) Critical = (15). Automatic failure results if any of the **critical** tasks are omitted or performed incorrectly.

STANDARD PRECAUTIONS: 

SKILLS ASSESSMENT CHECKLIST

Task Performed	Possible Points	TASKS
❑	5	Verifies the physician's order.
❑	15	Follows the "Six Rights" (see textbook Figure 12–10A).
❑	5	Performs medical asepsis hand wash.
❑	5	Works in a well-lighted, quiet, clean area.
❑	5	Assembles equipment and supplies.
❑	15	Obtains the correct medication using the medicine card.
❑	15	Compares the medication label with the medicine card (first time).
❑	10	Checks the expiration date.
❑	15	Calculates dosage, if necessary.
❑	15	Correctly prepares: • Multiple dose solid medication • Unit dose medication • Liquid medication
❑	15	Compares medicine label with medicine card (second time).
❑	15	Returns medication to shelf and checks label (third time).
❑	5	Properly transports the medicine.
❑	5	Identifies the patient and explains the procedure.

Task Performed	Possible Points	TASKS
☐	10	Assesses patient. Takes vital signs if indicated.
☐	5	Assists patient to a comfortable position.
☐	10	Provides water, milk, or juice (unless contraindicated).
☐	15	Administers the medication. Makes sure the patient takes the medicine.
☐	10	Provides for the patient's safety by observing the patient for any adverse reactions.
☐	5	Documents the procedure in the patient's chart using the medicine card.
☐	5	Cares for equipment and supplies according to OSHA guidelines.
☐	5	Washes hands.
☐	5	Completed the tasks within 10 minutes.
☐	15	Results obtained were accurate.

______	Earned	ADD POINTS OF TASKS CHECKED
230	Points	TOTAL POINTS POSSIBLE
______	SCORE	DETERMINE SCORE (divide points earned by total points possible, multiply results by 100)

Actual Student Time Needed to Complete Procedure: ______________

Student's Initials: ______________ Instructor's Initials: ______________ Grade: ______________

Suggestions for Improvement: ______________________________

Evaluator's Name (print) ______________________________

Evaluator's Signature ______________________________

Comments ______________________________

DOCUMENTATION

Chart the procedure in the patient's medical record.

Date: __________

Charting: ______________________________

____

____

____

____

Student's Initials: ________

SKILLS COMPETENCY ASSESSMENT

Procedure 12–2: Administration of Subcutaneous, Intramuscular, and/or Intradermal Injections

Student's Name: ______________________________ Date: ____________

Objective: To properly administer subcutaneous, intramuscular, and/or intradermal injections.

Conditions: The student demonstrates the ability to properly administer subcutaneous, intramuscular, and/or intradermal injections using the following equipment and supplies: medication, as ordered by the physician, and medicine card, appropriately sized needle-syringe unit, antiseptic wipes, disposable gloves, sharps container.

Time Requirements and Accuracy Standards: 10 minutes. Points assigned reflect importance of step to meeting objective: Important = (5) Essential = (10) Critical = (15). Automatic failure results if any of the **critical** tasks are omitted or performed incorrectly.

STANDARD PRECAUTIONS: 

SKILLS ASSESSMENT CHECKLIST

Task Performed	Possible Points	TASKS
☐	10	Verifies the physician's order. Makes out medicine card taking information from physician's order sheet in the patient record.
☐	15	Follows the "Six Rights."
☐	5	Performs medical asepsis hand wash. Adheres to OSHA guidelines.
☐	5	Works in a well-lighted, quiet, clean area.
☐	10	Obtains the appropriate syringe-needle unit and alcohol swab.
☐	15	Obtains the correct medication.
☐	15	Compares the medication label with the medicine card (first time).
☐	10	Checks expiration date on medicine.
☐	15	Calculates dosage, if necessary.
☐	5	Prepares syringe-needle unit for use.
☐	5	Withdraws medication from container.
☐	15	Compares medicine label with the medicine card (second time).
☐	15	Places filled syringe-needle unit on the medicine tray with medicine card. Checks the medication label with the medicine card (third time).

Task Performed	Possible Points	TASKS
❑	5	Correctly transports the medicine to the patient.
❑	5	Identifies the patient. Explains the procedure.
❑	5	Assesses the patient. Puts on gloves.
❑	5	Prepares the patient for the injection (drapes, positions, allays apprehension).
❑	10	Selects an appropriate injection site. Follows a rotating schedule, if appropriate.
❑	10	Cleanses the injection site with a sterile antiseptic swab. Uses a circular motion, working from the center out to about two inches beyond the planned injection site.
❑	5	Allows the skin to dry.
❑	5	Administers the injection (aspirates to be certain needle is not in a blood vessel). Immediately disposes of syringe-needle unit in a puncture-proof sharps container.
❑	10	Massages injection site unless contraindicated (insulin, Imferon, heparin).
❑	5	Observes the patient for signs of difficulty.
❑	5	Inspects the injection site for bleeding, applies Band-Aid if necessary.
❑	5	Properly disposes of used equipment and supplies. Removes gloves.
❑	5	Performs medical asepsis hand wash.
❑	10	Correctly documents the procedure.
❑	5	Completed the tasks within 10 minutes.
❑	15	Results obtained were accurate.

________	Earned	ADD POINTS OF TASKS CHECKED
150	Points	TOTAL POINTS POSSIBLE
________	SCORE	DETERMINE SCORE (divide points earned by total points possible, multiply results by 100)

Procedure to follow should the medical assistant sustain an accidental needlestick after the injection:

Task Performed	Possible Points	TASKS
❑	10	Thoroughly washes the site where the stick occurred.
❑	5	Cleanses the skin with an antiseptic.
❑	15	Reports the incident.
❑	10	Documents the incident and retains a copy of the incident report.
❑	15	Obtains medical attention and is tested for HBV and HIV.

SKILLS COMPETENCY ASSESSMENT — continued

Procedure 12–2: Administration of Subcutaneous, Intramuscular, and/or Intradermal Injections

Task Performed	Possible Points	TASKS
❑	10	Fills out appropriate OSHA paperwork (200 form).

_______	Earned	ADD POINTS OF TASKS CHECKED
65	Points	TOTAL POINTS POSSIBLE
_______	SCORE	DETERMINE SCORE (divide points earned by total points possible, multiply results by 100)

Actual Student Time Needed to Complete Procedure: ____________

Student's Initials: ____________ Instructor's Initials: ____________ Grade: ____________

Suggestions for Improvement: ____

Evaluator's Name (print) ____

Evaluator's Signature ____

Comments ____

DOCUMENTATION

Chart the procedure in the patient's medical record.

Date: __________

Charting: ____

____

____

____

____

____

Student's Initials: ________

SKILLS COMPETENCY ASSESSMENT

Procedure 12–3: Withdrawing (Aspirating) Medication from a Vial

Student's Name: ______________________________ Date: __________

Objective: To withdraw (aspirate) medication from a vial.

Conditions: The student demonstrates the ability to withdraw (aspirate) medication from a vial into a syringe for parenteral injection using the following equipment and supplies: medication order, medicine card, appropriate syringe and needle with cover, vial of medication, antiseptic wipes or sponges, disposable gloves, puncture-proof sharps container.

Time Requirements and Accuracy Standards: 10 minutes. Points assigned reflect importance of step to meeting objective: Important = (5) Essential = (10) Critical = (15). Automatic failure results if any of the **critical** tasks are omitted or performed incorrectly.

STANDARD PRECAUTIONS:

SKILLS ASSESSMENT CHECKLIST

Task Performed	Possible Points	TASKS
❑	15	Reads the medication order and assembles equipment. Checks for the "Six Rights." Reads the vial label by holding it next to the medicine card (first time).
❑	5	Washes hands, applies gloves.
❑	10	Selects the proper size needle and syringe for the medication and the route. If necessary, attaches the needle to the syringe.
❑	15	Checks the vial label against the medicine card (second time).
❑	5	Removes the metal or plastic cap from the vial. If the vial has been opened previously, cleans the rubber stopper by applying a disinfectant wipe in a circular motion.
❑	5	Removes the needle cover, pulling it straight off.
❑	15	Injects air into the vial as follows: • Holds the syringe pointed upward at eye level. Pulls back the plunger to take in a quantity of air equal to the ordered dose of medication. • Holds the vial upright (inverted) according to personal preference. Takes care not to touch the rubber stopper. • Inserts the needle through the rubber stopper of the vial. Injects air by pushing in the plunger.
❑	15	Withdraws the medication: Holds the vial and syringe steady. Pulls back on the plunger to withdraw the measured dose of medication. Measures accurately. Keeps the tip of the needle below the surface of the liquid to prevent air from entering the syringe. Keeps syringe at eye level.
❑	10	Checks the syringe for air bubbles. Removes air bubbles by tapping sharply on the syringe.
❑	5	Removes the needle from the vial. Replaces the sterile needle cover.

SKILLS COMPETENCY ASSESSMENT — continued

Procedure 12–3: Withdrawing (Aspirating) Medication from a Vial

Task Performed	Possible Points	TASKS
❑	15	Checks the vial label against the medicine card (third time).
❑	5	Places the filled needle and syringe on a medicine tray or cart with an antiseptic wipe and the medicine card. The dose is now ready for injection.
❑	5	Returns multiple-dose vials to the proper storage area (cabinet or refrigerator). Disposes of unused medication in a single-dose vial according to facility procedure. (Disposal of a controlled substance must be witnessed and the proper forms signed.)
❑	5	Discards used syringe-needle unit immediately after use in a sharps container.
❑	5	Removes gloves and disposes in biohazard waste container.
❑	5	Washes hands.
❑	5	Documents the procedure.
❑	5	Completed the tasks within 10 minutes.
❑	15	Results obtained were accurate.

______	Earned	ADD POINTS OF TASKS CHECKED
165	Points	TOTAL POINTS POSSIBLE
______	SCORE	DETERMINE SCORE (divide points earned by total points possible, multiply results by 100)

Actual Student Time Needed to Complete Procedure: ____________

Student's Initials: ____________ Instructor's Initials: ____________ Grade: ____________

Suggestions for Improvement: ____________

Evaluator's Name (print) ____________

Evaluator's Signature ____________

Comments ____________

DOCUMENTATION

Chart the procedure in the patient's medical record.

Date: ________

Charting: ____________

____

____

____

Student's Initials: ________

SKILLS COMPETENCY ASSESSMENT

Procedure 12–4: Withdrawing (Aspirating) Medication from an Ampule

Student's Name: ______________________________ Date: ____________

Objective: To withdraw (aspirate) medication from an ampule.

Conditions: The student demonstrates the ability to withdraw (aspirate) medication from an ampule into a syringe for parenteral injection using the following equipment and supplies: medicine tray, medicine card, ampule of medication, alcohol wipes, sterile gauze sponges, sharps container, sterile needle-syringe unit, gloves.

Time Requirements and Accuracy Standards: 5 minutes. Points assigned reflect importance of step to meeting objective: Important = (5) Essential = (10) Critical = (15). Automatic failure results if any of the **critical** tasks are omitted or performed incorrectly.

STANDARD PRECAUTIONS:

SKILLS ASSESSMENT CHECKLIST

Task Performed	Possible Points	TASKS
❑	10	Checks the physician's order. Writes out medicine card.
❑	5	Washes hands and gathers equipment. Puts on gloves.
❑	15	Obtains ampule of medication. Reads label and checks medicine card for correct medication, dose, route, and time (first time). Checks medication expiration date.
❑	5	Flicks ampule of medication, using a sharp flick of the wrist to force all of the medication down below the neck of the ampule into the body of the ampule.
❑	5	*Rationale:* Understands that if some medication remains trapped in ampule, an incorrect dosage may be administered to the patient.
❑	15	Thoroughly disinfects the neck with an alcohol swab. Checks label (second time).
❑	5	*Rationale:* Understands that ampule neck must be disinfected, as it may come into contact with the needle when the needle is inserted into the ampule.
❑	10	Wipes dry the neck of the ampule with a sterile gauze. Completely surrounds the ampule with the gauze and forcefully snaps off the top of the ampule by pushing the top away from the body.
❑	15	Sets opened ampule on medicine tray. Checks label (third time).
❑	15	With prepared sterile syringe-needle unit, aspirates the required dose into syringe. Covers needle with sheath and transports on the medicine tray to the patient.
❑	5	Identifies patient and administers medication.

SKILLS COMPETENCY ASSESSMENT — continued

Procedure 12–4: Withdrawing (Aspirating) Medication from an Ampule

Task Performed	Possible Points	TASKS
❑	5	Discards syringe-needle unit into sharps container. Discards alcohol swabs and gauze in biohazard waste container.
❑	5	Washes hands.
❑	5	Documents procedure.
❑	5	Completed the tasks within 5 minutes.
❑	15	Results obtained were accurate.

________	Earned	ADD POINTS OF TASKS CHECKED
140	Points	TOTAL POINTS POSSIBLE
________	SCORE	DETERMINE SCORE (divide points earned by total points possible, multiply results by 100)

Actual Student Time Needed to Complete Procedure: ____________

Student's Initials: ____________ Instructor's Initials: ____________ Grade: ____________

Suggestions for Improvement: ________________________________

Evaluator's Name (print) ________________________________

Evaluator's Signature ________________________________

Comments ________________________________

DOCUMENTATION

Chart the procedure in the patient's medical record.

Date: __________

Charting: ________________________________

____

____

____

____

____

Student's Initials: _______

SKILLS COMPETENCY ASSESSMENT

Procedure 12–5: Administering a Subcutaneous Injection

Student's Name: ______________________________ Date: ____________

Objective: To correctly administer a subcutaneous injection.

Conditions: The student demonstrates the ability to correctly administer a subcutaneous injection after receiving a physician's order, using the following equipment and supplies: medication ordered by physician, medicine card, appropriately sized needle-syringe unit, antiseptic wipe, disposable gloves, sharps container.

Time Requirements and Accuracy Standards: 5 minutes. Points assigned reflect importance of step to meeting objective: Important = (5) Essential = (10) Critical = (15). Automatic failure results if any of the **critical** tasks are omitted or performed incorrectly.

STANDARD PRECAUTIONS:

SKILLS ASSESSMENT CHECKLIST

Task Performed	Possible Points	TASKS
❑	10	Verifies the physician's order. Makes out a medicine card.
❑	15	Follows the "Six Rights."
❑	5	Performs medical asepsis hand wash. Adheres to OSHA guidelines.
❑	5	Works in a well-lighted, quiet, clean area.
❑	5	Obtains the appropriate equipment and supplies.
❑	15	Obtains the correct medication.
❑	15	Compares the medication label with the medicine card (first time).
❑	15	Checks expiration date on medicine.
❑	15	Calculates dosage, if necessary.
❑	15	Correctly prepares the parenteral medication.
❑	15	Compares medication label with the medicine card (second time).
❑	5	Replaces medication in an appropriate area (shelf, refrigerator). Compares the medication label (third time).
❑	5	Correctly transports the medicine to the patient.
❑	5	Identifies the patient. Explains the procedure.
❑	5	Assesses the patient. Puts on gloves.
❑	5	Prepares the patient for the injection (drapes, positions, allays apprehension).
❑	15	Checks label for third time.
❑	15	Selects an appropriate injection site.
❑	15	Correctly cleanses the site using a circular motion starting with the injection site and moving outward to a two-inch diameter. Allows skin to dry.

SKILLS COMPETENCY ASSESSMENT — continued

Procedure 12–5: Administering a Subcutaneous Injection

Task Performed	Possible Points	TASKS
❑	5	Removes needle guard.
❑	10	Grasps skin to form a one-inch fold.
❑	15	Inserts needle quickly at a 45-degree angle.
❑	15	Aspirates to be certain needle is not in a blood vessel.
❑	10	Slowly injects the medicine.
❑	5	Correctly removes the needle and syringe.
❑	5	Immediately disposes of needle and syringe in a sharps container.
❑	15	Covers site. Massages (unless contraindicated), as with insulin, Imferon, and heparin.
❑	5	Removes gloves and washes hands.
❑	5	Provides for patient's safety.
❑	5	Documents the procedure.
❑	5	Completed the tasks within 5 minutes.
❑	15	Results obtained were accurate.

________	Earned	ADD POINTS OF TASKS CHECKED
315	Points	TOTAL POINTS POSSIBLE
________	SCORE	DETERMINE SCORE (divide points earned by total points possible, multiply results by 100)

Actual Student Time Needed to Complete Procedure: ____________

Student's Initials: ____________ Instructor's Initials: ____________ Grade: ____________

Suggestions for Improvement: ________________________________

Evaluator's Name (print) ________________________________

Evaluator's Signature ________________________________

Comments ________________________________

DOCUMENTATION

Chart the procedure in the patient's medical record.

Date: __________

Charting: ________________________________

____

____

____

Student's Initials: ________

SKILLS COMPETENCY ASSESSMENT

Procedure 12–6: Administering an Intramuscular Injection

Student's Name: ______________________________ Date: __________

Objective: To correctly administer an intradermal injection.

Conditions: The student demonstrates the ability to correctly administer an intradermal injection after receiving a physician's order, using the following equipment and supplies: medication as ordered by physician, with medication card, appropriately sized needle-syringe unit, antiseptic wipe, disposable gloves, sharps container.

Time Requirements and Accuracy Standards: 5 minutes. Points assigned reflect importance of step to meeting objective: Important = (5) Essential = (10) Critical = (15). Automatic failure results if any of the **critical** tasks are omitted or performed incorrectly.

STANDARD PRECAUTIONS:

SKILLS ASSESSMENT CHECKLIST

Task Performed	Possible Points	TASKS
☐	10	Verifies the physician's order. Makes out a medicine card.
☐	15	Follows the "Six Rights."
☐	5	Performs medical asepsis hand wash. Adheres to OSHA guidelines.
☐	5	Works in a well-lighted, quiet, clean area.
☐	5	Obtains the appropriate equipment and supplies.
☐	15	Obtains the correct medication.
☐	15	Compares the medication label with the medicine card (first time). Checks expiration date.
☐	15	Calculates dosage, if necessary.
☐	15	Correctly prepares the parenteral medication.
☐	15	Compares medicine label with the medicine card (second time).
☐	15	Replaces medication on an appropriate shelf and compares medication label with medicine card (third time).
☐	5	Correctly transports the medicine to the patient.
☐	5	Identifies the patient. Explains the procedure.
☐	5	Assesses the patient. Puts on gloves.
☐	5	Prepares the patient for the injection (drapes, positions, allays apprehension).
☐	10	Selects an appropriate injection site.
☐	10	Correctly cleanses the site using a circular motion and covering a two-inch diameter. Allows the skin to dry.
☐	5	Removes needle guard.

SKILLS COMPETENCY ASSESSMENT — continued

Procedure 12–6: Administering an Intramuscular Injection

Task Performed	Possible Points	TASKS
❑	5	Stretches the skin taut, pulling it tight.
❑	10	Using a dart-like motion, inserts needle to the hub at a 90-degree angle.
❑	5	Releases the skin.
❑	15	Aspirates to check for blood.
❑	5	Injects the medicine slowly.
❑	5	Correctly removes the needle and syringe.
❑	10	Immediately disposes of needle and syringe in a sharps container.
❑	15	Covers site. Massages (unless contraindicated), as with insulin, Imferon, and heparin.
❑	5	Disposes of equipment. Removes gloves.
❑	5	Washes hands.
❑	5	Observes the patient for signs of difficulty.
❑	5	Provides for patient's safety.
❑	5	Documents the procedure.
❑	5	Completed the tasks within 5 minutes.
❑	15	Results obtained were accurate.

______	Earned	ADD POINTS OF TASKS CHECKED
290	Points	TOTAL POINTS POSSIBLE
______	SCORE	DETERMINE SCORE (divide points earned by total points possible, multiply results by 100)

Actual Student Time Needed to Complete Procedure: ____________

Student's Initials: ____________ Instructor's Initials: ____________ Grade: ____________

Suggestions for Improvement: ______________________________

Evaluator's Name (print) ______________________________

Evaluator's Signature ______________________________

Comments ______________________________

DOCUMENTATION

Chart the procedure in the patient's medical record.

Date: ________

Charting: ______________________________

____

Student's Initials: ______

SKILLS COMPETENCY ASSESSMENT

Procedure 12–7: Administering an Intradermal Injection

Student's Name: ______________________________ Date: ____________

Objective: To correctly administer a intradermal injection.

Conditions: The student demonstrates the ability to correctly administer an intradermal injection after receiving a physician's order, using the following equipment and supplies: medication as ordered by physician, with medicine card, appropriately sized needle-syringe unit, antiseptic wipe, disposable gloves, sharps container.

Time Requirements and Accuracy Standards: 5 minutes. Points assigned reflect importance of step to meeting objective: Important = (5) Essential = (10) Critical = (15). Automatic failure results if any of the **critical** tasks are omitted or performed incorrectly.

STANDARD PRECAUTIONS:

SKILLS ASSESSMENT CHECKLIST

Task Performed	Possible Points	TASKS
☐	5	Verifies the physician's order. Makes out a medicine card.
☐	15	Follows the "Six Rights."
☐	5	Performs medical asepsis hand wash. Adheres to OSHA guidelines.
☐	5	Works in a well-lighted, quiet, clean area.
☐	5	Obtains the appropriate equipment and supplies.
☐	15	Obtains the correct medication.
☐	15	Compares the medication label with the medicine card (first time). Checks expiration date.
☐	15	Calculates dosage, if necessary.
☐	15	Correctly prepares the parenteral medication.
☐	15	Compares medication label with the medicine card (second time).
☐	15	Replaces medication on appropriate shelf and compares medication label with medicine card (third time).
☐	10	Correctly transports the medicine to the patient.
☐	10	Identifies the patient. Explains the procedure.
☐	5	Assesses the patient. Puts on gloves.
☐	5	Prepares the patient for the injection (drapes, positions, allays apprehension).
☐	5	Selects a site on the anterior forearm, two to three inches below the antecubital fossa.
☐	5	Correctly cleanses the site using a circular motion and covering a two-inch diameter. Allows the skin to dry.
☐	5	Removes needle guard.

SKILLS COMPETENCY ASSESSMENT —continued

Procedure 12–7: Administering an Intradermal Injection

Task Performed	Possible Points	TASKS
☐	10	Pulls the skin tissue taut.
☐	15	Carefully inserts the needle at a 10- to 15-degree angle, beveled upward about ⅛ inch. **Does not aspirate.**
☐	15	Steadily injects the medicine. Produces a wheal, or slight elevation of the skin.
☐	5	Correctly removes the needle.
☐	5	Immediately disposes of needle and syringe in a sharps container.
☐	15	Covers site. Does not massage. Disposes of equipment. Removes gloves.
☐	5	Washes hands.
☐	5	Observes the patient for signs of difficulty.
☐	5	Provides for patient's safety.
☐	5	Documents the procedure.
☐	5	Completed the tasks within 5 minutes.
☐	15	Results obtained were accurate.

________	Earned	ADD POINTS OF TASKS CHECKED
275	Points	TOTAL POINTS POSSIBLE
________	SCORE	DETERMINE SCORE (divide points earned by total points possible, multiply results by 100)

Actual Student Time Needed to Complete Procedure: ____________

Student's Initials: ____________ Instructor's Initials: ____________ Grade: ____________

Suggestions for Improvement: ____________________________________

Evaluator's Name (print) ____________________________________

Evaluator's Signature ____________________________________

Comments ____________________________________

DOCUMENTATION

Chart the procedure in the patient's medical record.

Date: __________

Charting: ____________________________________

____

____

____

Student's Initials: ________

SKILLS COMPETENCY ASSESSMENT

Procedure 12–8: Reconstituting a Powder Medication for Administration

Student's Name: ______________________________ Date: __________

Objective: To reconstitute drugs supplied in a powdered (dry) form to a liquid for injection.

Conditions: The student demonstrates the ability to reconstitute drugs supplied in a powdered (dry) form to a liquid for injection using the following equipment and supplies: medication, as ordered by the physician, and medicine card, diluent, two appropriately sized needles and syringe units, antiseptic swabs, disposable gloves, sharps container.

Time Requirements and Accuracy Standards: 5 minutes. Points assigned reflect importance of step to meeting objective: Important = (5) Essential = (10) Critical = (15). Automatic failure results if any of the **critical** tasks are omitted or performed incorrectly.

STANDARD PRECAUTIONS:

SKILLS ASSESSMENT CHECKLIST

Task Performed	Possible Points	TASKS
❑	5	Prepares the needle-syringe unit in preparation for reconstituting powder medication.
❑	10	Removes tops from diluent and powder medication containers and wipes with alcohol swabs.
❑	15	Inserts the needle of a sterile needle-syringe unit through the rubber stopper on the vial of diluent that has been cleansed with an antiseptic swab. The needle-syringe unit should have an amount of air in it equal to the amount of diluent to be withdrawn.
❑	15	Withdraws the appropriate amount of diluent to be added to the powder medication. Covers the sterile needle on the syringe containing appropriate amount of diluent.
❑	15	Adds this liquid to the powder medication that has been cleansed with an antiseptic swab.
❑	10	Removes needle and syringe from vial with powder medication and diluent and discards into sharps container.
❑	15	Rolls the vial between the palms of the hands to completely mix together the powder and diluent. Labels the multiple dose vial with the dilution or strength of the medication prepared, the date and time, and the expiration date, and initials.
❑	10	Withdraws the desired amount of medication with a second sterile needle and syringe.
❑	10	Flicks away any air bubbles that cling to side of syringe.
❑	10	Has the medicine tray with reconstituted medication ready for transport to the patient.
❑	5	Proceeds to administer an intramuscular injection to the patient (see Procedure 12–6).

SKILLS COMPETENCY ASSESSMENT — continued

Procedure 12–8: Reconstituting a Powder Medication for Administration

Task Performed	Possible Points	TASKS
❑	5	Documents the procedure.
❑	5	Completed the tasks within 5 minutes.
❑	15	Results obtained were accurate.

_______	Earned	ADD POINTS OF TASKS CHECKED
145	Points	TOTAL POINTS POSSIBLE
_______	SCORE	DETERMINE SCORE (divide points earned by total points possible, multiply results by 100)

Actual Student Time Needed to Complete Procedure: ____________

Student's Initials: ____________ Instructor's Initials: ____________ Grade: ____________

Suggestions for Improvement: ________________________________

Evaluator's Name (print) ________________________________

Evaluator's Signature ________________________________

Comments ________________________________

DOCUMENTATION

Record information included on the multiple dose vial of prepared reconstituted medication.

Date: ____________

Label: ________________________________

Document the intramuscular injection in the patient's medical record.

Date: ____________

Charting: ________________________________

____

____

Student's Initials: ________

SKILLS COMPETENCY ASSESSMENT

Procedure 12–9: "Z"-Track Intramuscular Injection Technique

Student's Name: ______________________________ Date: __________

Objective: To correctly administer a "Z"-track intramuscular injection.

Conditions: The student demonstrates the ability to correctly administer a "Z"-track intramuscular injection after receiving a physician's order, using the following equipment and supplies: medication ordered by physician and medication card, appropriately sized needle-syringe unit, antiseptic wipe, disposable gloves, sharps container.

Time Requirements and Accuracy Standards: 5 minutes. Points assigned reflect importance of step to meeting objective: Important = (5) Essential = (10) Critical = (15). Automatic failure results if any of the **critical** tasks are omitted or performed incorrectly.

STANDARD PRECAUTIONS:

SKILLS ASSESSMENT CHECKLIST

Task Performed	Possible Points	TASKS
❑	10	Verifies the physician's order. Makes out a medicine card.
❑	15	Follows the "Six Rights."
❑	5	Performs medical asepsis hand wash. Adheres to OSHA guidelines.
❑	5	Works in a well-lighted, quiet, clean area.
❑	5	Obtains the appropriate equipment and supplies.
❑	15	Obtains the correct medication.
❑	10	Compares the medication label with the medicine card (first time).
❑	10	Checks expiration date.
❑	5	Calculates dosage, if necessary.
❑	15	Correctly prepares the parenteral medication.
❑	10	Compares medicine label with the medicine card (second time).
❑	10	Replaces medication on shelf and compares medication label with medicine card (third time).
❑	5	Correctly transports the medicine to the patient.
❑	5	Identifies the patient. Explains the procedure.
❑	5	Assesses the patient. Puts on gloves.
❑	5	Prepares the patient for the injection (drapes, positions, allays apprehension).
❑	10	Selects an appropriate injection site.
❑	10	Correctly cleanses the site using a circular motion and covering a two-inch diameter. Allows the skin to dry.
❑	5	Removes needle guard.

SKILLS COMPETENCY ASSESSMENT — continued

Procedure 12–9: "Z"-Track Intramuscular Injection Technique

Task Performed	Possible Points	TASKS
❑	10	Pulls the skin laterally 1½ inches away from the injection site.
❑	15	Inserts needle quickly, using a dartlike motion at a 90° angle. Maintains "Z" position.
❑	15	Aspirates to check for blood.
❑	10	Slowly injects medication.
❑	10	Waits ten seconds before removing needle to allow medication to begin to be absorbed.
❑	10	Removes needle and syringe at same angle of insertion.
❑	15	Releases traction of the "Z" position to seal off the needle track. Prevents medication from reaching the subcutaneous tissues and the surface of the skin.
❑	15	Immediately disposes of needle-syringe unit in a sharps container.
❑	5	Covers site. Does not massage. Removes gloves. Washes hands.
❑	5	Observes patient for signs of difficulty.
❑	5	Provides for the patient's safety.
❑	5	Documents the procedure.
❑	5	Completed the tasks within 5 minutes.
❑	15	Results obtained were accurate.

________	Earned	ADD POINTS OF TASKS CHECKED
300	Points	TOTAL POINTS POSSIBLE
________	SCORE	DETERMINE SCORE (divide points earned by total points possible, multiply results by 100)

Actual Student Time Needed to Complete Procedure: ____________

Student's Initials: ____________ Instructor's Initials: ____________ Grade: ____________

Suggestions for Improvement: ____

Evaluator's Name (print) ____

Evaluator's Signature ____

Comments ____

DOCUMENTATION

Chart the procedure in the patient's medical record.

Date: __________

Charting: ____

____

Student's Initials: _______

EVALUATION OF CHAPTER KNOWLEDGE

How has your instructor evaluated the knowledge you have achieved?

Knowledge	**Instructor Evaluation** *Good*	*Average*	*Poor*
Discusses legal and ethical implications of medication administration	_____	_____	_____
Describes medication order	_____	_____	_____
Describes the parts of a prescription	_____	_____	_____
Defines drug dosage	_____	_____	_____
States information contained on a medication label and can discuss the significance of the information	_____	_____	_____
Understands ratios and proportions	_____	_____	_____
Able to use metric, household, and apothecaries' systems of measurement and convert between metric and apothecary systems	_____	_____	_____
Understand units of medication dosage	_____	_____	_____
Correctly calculates adult and child dosages	_____	_____	_____
Lists guidelines to follow when preparing and administering medications	_____	_____	_____
Describes safe disposal of syringes, needles, and biohazardous materials	_____	_____	_____
Describes site selection for administration of injections	_____	_____	_____
Understands allergenic extracts	_____	_____	_____
Describes inhalation medication and its administration	_____	_____	_____
Exhibits therapeutic communication skills in administering medications to patients and attends to patients' emotional needs	_____	_____	_____
Documents accurately	_____	_____	_____
Complies with governmental regulations in the administration and disposal of controlled substances	_____	_____	_____
Possesses the ability to competently prepare and administer oral and parenteral medications as directed by a physician	_____	_____	_____

Student's Initials: _____ Instructor's Initials: _____

Grade: _______

Medical Specialty Examinations and Procedures

PERFORMANCE OBJECTIVES

Patients with complaints specific to a particular body system or body part need specialized care. Medical assistants assist the physician with many clinical procedures that are an integral component of specialty examinations. Medical assistants who are employed in a specialist's office or a setting that treats a variety of patient problems will need additional skills and ongoing training to stay proficient in the most current, technologies and treatments used to provide quality care to patients. Medical assisting students should use this workbook chapter to become familiar with specialty and body system examinations and with the appropriate clinical procedures in pediatrics; the female reproductive system; the male reproductive system; urology; endoscopy; sensory; the respiratory system; the musculoskeletal, neurological, and circulatory systems; blood and lymph; and the integumentary system.

EXERCISES AND ACTIVITIES

Vocabulary Builder

Find the key vocabulary terms in the word search puzzle.

Akinesia
Alimentary canal
Alveoli
Aphasia
Appendicular skeleton
Aseptic
Auricle
Axial skeleton
Biopsy
Bronchi
Carbuncle
Choroid layer
Closed Fracture
Comedone
Demyelination
Dislocation
Equilibrium
Erythema
External respiration
Furuncle
Gait
Hydronephrosis
Ingestion
Internal respiration
Lesion
Malabsorption
Nebulizer
Obturator
Occluder
Ophthalmoscope
Optic nerve
Ossicle
Otoscope
Oval window
Peripheral nerve
Polycystic
Spirometry
Stratum corneum
Vesicle

```
N Q R I U P G U P I F P B I Y W Q W N N E B O V S E G B D I M C D C Z G S Q
R J N X E K B A O C V P I Y T X I H O N B R O J N E O G I K L I H I W A T C
F E O Z G I Q Y L O Q G M J P Z Y I Q G Q I T B Y G H W M O S F A T Y I R P
E E D P P M S O Y M P J W X U D S L S M X B J U T J J G V L P P V P X T A O
V L S U O Q W L C T V H R W R E V F K O A T P S V U H H O K U S F E D Y T E
M C C W L A D S Y W T J T O L J D A E L U K X A W O R C B F L X Y S I L U L
F I P N S C W J S J H H N H E V R E N C I T P O X I A A X L H F W A O B M B
K R V N U Q C K T V G E O U A E T W R I V C Q I E T T V T I Q F Z F G C C V
I U T Y Q B N O I S P Z A T C L N T B V O J W D I E A F P O P F G R H L O S
E A L Y Q F R S C H L F O R M X M R K R T C U O O N O X H Z R F N O O E R F
A L I M E N T A R Y C A N A L V D O R I Q S N S J V C R J P M Y R S P X N R
M D B D C D B O C V F N O T E L E K S R A L U C I D N E P P A O E V D T E H
U B U T H R S X R E J S N O U S O Z X C Y F V D P E J W M S I D D S P E U Q
B Z K R O I V E P P J O J U I B S D M R O F Z F C L A Y G D F T B L W R M Y
Y T C N S C Z O U B T C S B H W S M E J W P R M I B U L L R Z H U C M N S N
Y N C U J I C R X E I N Y V G V I P U Q U J E F M G I A A V C O C T F A W O
K H I O L S Z Z L A B I K N O M C G I T U G N H Q C Y C I F U R U N C L E I
I L P U O N X E B Y Z W Z K Q F L Y J R H I J T S E T V E X U E Y U V R F T
E W B T I E K S Z J S I S R C Y E V B R O K L E R U F I F Y U X S L M E W P
C E O N P S C J T S M C Z D O K Z W N D J M O I R H R U P X P Q W Y D S U R
N R B K L G F G K V D Q Y D M U N Z M O W T E E B G M V V Q E Z J T C P V O
V Q M A H C E V R E N L A R E H P I R E P G F T D R H K Q R Z U O C S I Y S
N O I T S E G N I P I Y M V D O K Q O N V V V D R J I X K Z O L N B J R Q B
I X Y F F S E V D L S R G T O R A H P J R T O J Q Y I U R B S Q M I B A M A
A H L L I T P T C B Y K G H N B B J V X E L C I S E V U M N Y H A K D T T L
E R Y T H E M A X F Y T A Z E W H A I S E N I K A D X Y A P H A S I A I S A
O V A L W I N D O W D E M Y E L I N A T I O N Z J B I Z Q L M B Y Y F O O M
I N T E R N A L R E S P I R A T I O N G M T M Y I L O E V L A C F B T N K I
```

Learning Review/Case Study

Mary O'Keefe has called for an emergency appointment for her 3-year-old son Chris for an examination with Dr. King because he awakened during the night with a high fever and severe pain in his right ear, which is draining.

1. Ellen Armstrong, CMA, must prepare the examination room for the patient. Based on Chris's symptoms, what equipment will Ellen want to assemble for Dr. King's physical examination of Chris? List the equipment in the order it will most likely be used in the examination.

____

____

____

____

2. When Mary O'Keefe arrives with her son, Ellen takes them to examination room #2 and prepares the patient for Dr. King's physical examination. Ellen tells Mary that Dr. King will be examining Chris's ear and may want to take some laboratory tests. Ellen takes and records the child's vital signs:

   T 102.1°F; P 115 (AP) bounding, sinus arrhythmia; R 28 rhonci; 76/42/0, rt. arm, sitting.

   A. Explain the meaning and significance of each vital sign measurement, including the method and equipment used.

Temperature: ______________________________

Pulse: ______________________________

Respiration: ______________________________

Blood Pressure: ______________________________

B. Chris is fussy and disagreeable, but not uncooperative, while Ellen takes his vital signs. What can a medical assistant do to facilitate the measurement of a fussy child's vital signs?

____

____

3. Ellen assists Dr. King with her physical examination of the patient. After assessing the vital sign measurements taken by the medical assistant, Dr. King examines Chris's ear and lungs. A swab of fluid discharge is taken from the patient's ear. What is the role of the medical assistant during the physician's examination of this patient?

____

____

____

____

4. Dr. King makes a clinical diagnosis of otitis media for this patient and orders laboratory testing to be performed on the patient's specimen.

A. What criteria are necessary for a physician to make a clinical diagnosis?

____

B. What is otitis media? Why are children more likely at risk for this condition? How is otitis media commonly treated? What patient education can the health care team offer? *Consult a medical reference or encyclopedia for help in answering this question.*

____

____

SUPPLEMENTARY RESOURCES

Study Guide Disk: Additional practice exercises for this chapter are available on the study guide disk found in the back of the textbook.

Medical Assisting Videos: Appropriate content is available on Delmar's Medical Assisting Videos, 2nd ed., for the following topics:

Tape 6: Take Vital Signs
Take and Record Rectal Temperature
Take and Record a Brachial Pulse (infant)
Use a Stethoscope to Take an Apical Pulse (infant)

Tape 7: Take and Record Blood Pressure
Weigh and Measure an Infant
Growth Chart As a Screening Procedure
Vision Screen
Using an Audiometer to Perform a Hearing Screen

Tape 8: Take an In-Depth Patient History
Clean Examination Table and Countertops
Assist Physician With Examination and Treatments
Position and Drape the Patient
Role of the Medical Assistant During the Examination
Introduction to Health Promotion, Disease Prevention, and Self-Responsibility
Testicular Self-Examination
Breast Self-Examination

Tape 11: Prepare and Administer Medication As Directed By Physician
Administer Eye Medications
Administer Ear Medications
Administer Sub-Lingual Medications
Administer Rectal Suppositories
Topical Applications
Transdermal Patch Applications

SKILLS COMPETENCY ASSESSMENT

Procedure 13–1: Measuring the Infant: Weight, Height, Head, and Chest Circumference

Student's Name: ______________________________ Date: ____________

Objective: To obtain an accurate measurement of an infant's weight, height, head, and chest circumference.

Conditions: The student demonstrates the ability to obtain an accurate measurement of an infant's weight, height, head, and chest circumference for medical records and screen for growth abnormalities using the following equipment and supplies: infant scale, paper protector, flexible measuring tape, growth chart, patient's chart, pen, ruler, biohazard waste container.

Time Requirements and Accuracy Standards: 10 minutes for each measurement. Points assigned reflect importance of step to meeting objective: Important = (5) Essential = (10) Critical = (15). Automatic failure results if any of the **critical** tasks are omitted or performed incorrectly.

STANDARD PRECAUTIONS:

SKILLS ASSESSMENT CHECKLIST

Task Performed	Possible Points	TASKS
Measuring Infant's Weight		
❑	5	Washes hands. Explains procedure to parent(s).
❑	5	Undresses infant (including the diaper). Discards soiled diaper in biohazard waste container.
❑	10	Places all weights to left of scale to check balance.
❑	5	Places a clean utility towel on scale, checks balance scale for accuracy, being sure to compensate for the weight of the towel.
❑	5	*Rationale:* The paper helps protect against transmission of microorganisms and provides warmth for the infant, as the scale will be cool.
❑	10	Gently places infant on his or her back on the scale. Places own hand slightly above the infant's body to ensure safety.
❑	5	*Rationale:* Safeguards infant from falling.
❑	15	Places the bottom weight to its highest measurement that will not cause the balance to drop to the bottom edge.
❑	15	Slowly moves upper weight until the balance bar rests in the center of the indicator. A balanced scale will provide an accurate weight. Reads the infant's weight while he or she is lying still.
❑	15	Returns both weights to their resting position to the extreme left.
❑	10	Gently removes infant and applies fresh diaper. (Parent can help with diapering and holding infant.)
❑	5	Discards used protective paper towel per OSHA guidelines.
❑	5	Sanitizes scale.
❑	5	Washes hands.
❑	10	Documents results according to office policy (pounds and ounces or kilograms) on growth chart, patient's chart, and parent's booklet, if available. Connects dot from previous examination with a ruler to complete graph.

Task Performed	Possible Points	TASKS
❑	5	Completed the tasks within 10 minutes.
❑	15	Results obtained were accurate.

________	Earned	ADD POINTS OF TASKS CHECKED
145	Points	TOTAL POINTS POSSIBLE
________	SCORE	DETERMINE SCORE (divide points earned by total points possible, multiply results by 100)

Measuring Infant's Length/Height

Task Performed	Possible Points	TASKS
❑	5	Washes hands. Explains procedure to parent(s).
❑	5	Removes infant's shoes.
❑	15	Gently places infant on his or her back on the examination table. If the pediatric table has a headboard, asks parent to hold infant's head against (end) headboard of table at zero mark of ruler while medical assistant places infant's heels against footboard. Gently straightens infant's back and legs to line up along ruler. Uses right hand as a guide, if there is no footboard (to place infant's feet against). If necessary, gently places left hand over the infant's legs at the knees to secure the him or her in place and straightens legs so the recumbent length can be read from the head to the heel.
❑	5	*Rationale:* Sometimes it is difficult to straighten the infant's legs.
❑	15	Reads length in inches or centimeters from measuring device.
❑	5	Washes hands.
❑	10	Documents measurement on growth chart, patient's chart, and parent's booklet if available. Connects dot from previous examination with a ruler to complete graph.
❑	5	Completed the tasks within 10 minutes.
❑	15	Results obtained were accurate.

________	Earned	ADD POINTS OF TASKS CHECKED
80	Points	TOTAL POINTS POSSIBLE
________	SCORE	DETERMINE SCORE (divide points earned by total points possible, multiply results by 100)

Measuring Infant's/Child's Head Circumference

Task Performed	Possible Points	TASKS
❑	5	Washes hands and explains procedure to parent(s).
❑	5	Talks to infant to gain cooperation. Infant may be held by parent or may lie on examination table for procedure. Older children of two or three years may stand or sit if they will remain still.
❑	15	Places the measuring tape snugly around the head from the occipital protuberance to the supra-orbital prominence.
❑	15	Reads the measurement in either inches (to nearest ½ inch) or centimeters (to nearest 0.01 cm).
❑	5	Washes hands.
❑	10	Documents results according to office policy on growth chart, patient's chart, and parent's booklet if available. Connects dot from previous examination with a ruler to complete graph.
❑	5	Completed the tasks within 10 minutes.
❑	15	Results obtained were accurate.

________	Earned	ADD POINTS OF TASKS CHECKED
75	Points	TOTAL POINTS POSSIBLE
________	SCORE	DETERMINE SCORE (divide points earned by total points possible, multiply results by 100)

SKILLS COMPETENCY ASSESSMENT — continued

Procedure 13–1: Measuring the Infant: Weight, Height, Head, and Chest Circumference

Task Performed	Possible Points	TASKS
Measure Infant's Chest Circumference		
❑	5	Washes hands and explains procedure to parent(s).
❑	15	Uses one thumb to hold tape measure with zero mark against the infant's chest at the midsternal area. With the other hand, brings the tape around/under the back to meet the zero mark of the tape in front. Takes the measurement of the chest just above the nipples with the tape fitting around the infant's chest under the axillary region. Asks the parent or another medical assistant for assistance in holding the infant still, if necessary. Takes the measurement when the child is breathing normally and during the resting phase between respirations.
❑	15	Reads measurement to the nearest 0.01 cm or 1/16 inch.
❑	5	Washes hands.
❑	5	Documents results in patient's chart.
❑	5	Completed the tasks within 10 minutes.
❑	15	Results obtained were accurate.

_______	Earned	ADD POINTS OF TASKS CHECKED
65	Points	TOTAL POINTS POSSIBLE
_______	SCORE	DETERMINE SCORE (divide points earned by total points possible, multiply results by 100)

Actual Student Time Needed to Complete Procedure: ____________

Student's Initials: ____________ Instructor's Initials: ____________ Grade: ____________

Suggestions for Improvement: ____

Evaluator's Name (print) ____

Evaluator's Signature ____

Comments ____

DOCUMENTATION

Record the height, weight, head and chest circumference measurements in the patient's medical record.

Date: __________

Charting: ____

____

____

____

____

Student's Initials: _______

SKILLS COMPETENCY ASSESSMENT

Procedure 13–2: Taking an Infant's Rectal Temperature with a Mercury or Digital Thermometer

Student's Name: ______________________ Date: __________

Objective: To obtain a rectal temperature using a mercury or digital thermometer.

Conditions: The student demonstrates the ability to obtain a rectal temperature using the following equipment and supplies: mercury rectal thermometer (red tip) and sheath or digital thermometer (red probe) and probe cover, lubricating jelly, 4 × 4 gauze sponges, gloves, biohazard waste container.

Time Requirements and Accuracy Standards: 10 minutes. Points assigned reflect importance of step to meeting objective: Important = (5) Essential = (10) Critical = (15). Automatic failure results if any of the **critical** tasks are omitted or performed incorrectly.

STANDARD PRECAUTIONS:

SKILLS ASSESSMENT CHECKLIST

Task Performed	Possible Points	TASKS
		Using Mercury Thermometer
❑	5	Washes hands. Assembles equipment.
❑	5	Identifies patient. Explains procedure to parent(s) to gain assistance and cooperation.
❑	5	Removes infant's diaper and discards in biohazard waste container.
❑	10	Positions infant in a prone position having parent or another medical assistant safeguard infant.
❑	10	Places sheath on thermometer.
❑	5	*Rationale:* Sheath prevents microorganism cross-contamination.
❑	10	Places lubricant on a 4 × 4 gauze sponge and places tip of thermometer in lubricant.
❑	5	*Rationale:* Facilitates insertion of thermometer.
❑	5	Applies gloves.
❑	15	Spreads infant's buttocks, inserts thermometer gently into the rectum past the sphincter; for an infant, this is ½ inch.
❑	15	Holds buttocks together while holding the thermometer. If necessary, restrains infant movement by placing own arm across the infant's back. Parent can immobilize infant's legs.
❑	5	*Rationale:* Ensures infant's safety and comfort.
❑	15	Holds in place for five minutes. Does not let go of the thermometer.

SKILLS COMPETENCY ASSESSMENT — continued

Procedure 13–2: Taking an Infant's Rectal Temperature with a Mercury or Digital Thermometer

Task Performed	Possible Points	TASKS
❑	5	*Rationale:* Movement by infant can cause thermometer to move and can injure infant.
❑	5	Removes thermometer from rectum. Has parent attend to infant.
❑	5	Removes sheath and places in biohazard container.
❑	5	Reads thermometer.
❑	5	Washes, rinses, and dries thermometer. Places on clean paper towels.
❑	5	Removes gloves, discards in biohazard waste container. Washes hands.
❑	15	Places thermometer in a disinfectant solution for rectal thermometers.
❑	5	Assists parent in dressing infant if necessary.
❑	15	Records on the patient chart appropriately as a rectal temperature.
❑	5	Completed the tasks within 10 minutes.
❑	15	Results obtained were accurate.
	_______	Earned ADD POINTS OF TASKS CHECKED
	195	Points TOTAL POINTS POSSIBLE
	_______	SCORE DETERMINE SCORE (divide points earned by total points possible, multiply results by 100)
		Using Digital Thermometer
❑	5	Washes hands. Assembles equipment.
❑	5	Identifies patient. Explains procedure to parent(s) to gain assistance and cooperation.
❑	5	Removes infant's diaper and discards in biohazard waste container.
❑	10	Positions infant in a prone position having parent or another medical assistant safeguard infant.
❑	10	Places sheath on thermometer.
❑	5	*Rationale:* Sheath prevents microorganism cross-contamination.
❑	10	Places lubricant on a 4 × 4 gauze sponge and places tip of thermometer in lubricant.
❑	5	*Rationale:* Facilitates insertion of thermometer.
❑	5	Applies gloves.
❑	15	Spreads infant's buttocks, inserts thermometer gently into the rectum past the sphincter; for an infant, this is ½ inch.

Task Performed	Possible Points	TASKS
❑	15	Holds buttocks together while holding the thermometer. If necessary, restrains infant movement by placing own arm across the infant's back. Parent can immobilize infant's legs.
❑	5	*Rationale:* Ensures infant's safety and comfort.
❑	5	Holds digital thermometer in place until the beep is heard.
❑	5	Reads results on digital display window.
❑	5	Removes thermometer from rectum.
❑	5	Discards probe cover into biohazard waste container by pressing the eject button on probe end.
❑	5	Replaces thermometer on holder base.
❑	5	Removes gloves, discards in biohazard waste container, and washes hands.
❑	5	Assists patient in dressing and positions as necessary.
❑	15	Records on the patient chart appropriately as a rectal temperature.
❑	5	Washes hands.
❑	5	Completed the tasks within 10 minutes.
❑	15	Results obtained were accurate.

_______	Earned	ADD POINTS OF TASKS CHECKED
175	Points	TOTAL POINTS POSSIBLE
_______	SCORE	DETERMINE SCORE (divide points earned by total points possible, multiply results by 100)

Actual Student Time Needed to Complete Procedure: ____________

Student's Initials: ____________ Instructor's Initials: ____________ Grade: ____________

Suggestions for Improvement: ____

Evaluator's Name (print) ____

Evaluator's Signature ____

Comments ____

DOCUMENTATION

Record the rectal temperature in the patient's medical record.

Date: __________

Charting: ____

____

____

Student's Initials: _______

SKILLS COMPETENCY ASSESSMENT

Procedure 13–3: Taking an Apical Pulse on an Infant

Student's Name: ______________________________ Date: ____________

Objective: To obtain an apical pulse rate.

Conditions: The student demonstrates the ability to obtain an apical pulse rate using the following equipment and supplies: stethoscope, watch with second hand, alcohol wipes.

Time Requirements and Accuracy Standards: 2 minutes. Points assigned reflect importance of step to meeting objective: Important = (5) Essential = (10) Critical = (15). Automatic failure results if any of the **critical** tasks are omitted or performed incorrectly.

STANDARD PRECAUTIONS:

SKILLS ASSESSMENT CHECKLIST

Task Performed	Possible Points	TASKS
❑	5	Washes hands. Assembles equipment.
❑	5	Identifies patient. Explains procedure to parent.
❑	5	Assists in disrobing infant, if necessary.
❑	10	Provides a drape for infant's warmth, if necessary.
❑	5	Positions the infant in a supine position or seated in the parent's lap.
❑	5	*Rationale:* Understands the supine position may offer easier access to apex of heart if the child is calm.
❑	15	Locates the fifth intercostal space, midclavicular line, left of sternum.
❑	10	Places warmed stethoscope on the site and listens for the lub-dup sound of the heart.
❑	15	Counts the pulse for one minute; each lub-dup equals one heartbeat or pulse.
❑	5	Washes hands.
❑	5	Records the pulse in the infant's chart with the designation of (AP) to denote method of obtaining the pulse.
❑	10	Notes any arrhythmias.
❑	5	Assists patient, and parents, as needed.
❑	5	Cleans earpieces and diaphragm of stethoscope with alcohol wipes.
❑	5	*Rationale:* Prevents cross-contamination of microbes between patients.

Task Performed	Possible Points	TASKS
☐	5	Washes hands again.
☐	5	Completed the tasks within 2 minutes.
☐	15	Results obtained were accurate.

________	Earned	ADD POINTS OF TASKS CHECKED
135	Points	TOTAL POINTS POSSIBLE
________	SCORE	DETERMINE SCORE (divide points earned by total points possible, multiply results by 100)

Actual Student Time Needed to Complete Procedure: ____________

Student's Initials: ____________ Instructor's Initials: ____________ Grade: ____________

Suggestions for Improvement: ____________

Evaluator's Name (print) ____________

Evaluator's Signature ____________

Comments ____________

DOCUMENTATION

Record the apical pulse in the patient's medical record. This patient also has a rectal temperature of 37.5°C.

Date: ________

Charting: ____________

Student's Initials: ________

SKILLS COMPETENCY ASSESSMENT

Procedure 13–4: Measuring Infant's Respiration Rate

Student's Name: ______________________________ Date: ____________

Objective: To measure the infant's respiration rate.

Conditions: The student demonstrates the ability to measure the infant's respiratory rate using the following equipment and supplies: watch with second hand. The most accurate respiration rate is taken immediately before or after the pulse rate.

Time Requirements and Accuracy Standards: 2 minutes. Points assigned reflect importance of step to meeting objective: Important = (5) Essential = (10) Critical = (15). Automatic failure results if any of the **critical** tasks are omitted or performed incorrectly.

STANDARD PRECAUTIONS:

SKILLS ASSESSMENT CHECKLIST

Task Performed	Possible Points	TASKS
☐	5	Washes hands. Identifies the patient.
☐	5	Positions infant in a supine position.
☐	15	Places own hand on the infant's chest to feel the rise and fall of the chest wall for one minute.
☐	15	Notes depth, rhythm, and breath sounds while counting.
☐	5	Washes hands.
☐	10	Records respiration rate in patient chart, noting any irregularities and sounds.
☐	5	Completed the tasks within 2 minutes.
☐	15	Results obtained were accurate.

________	Earned	ADD POINTS OF TASKS CHECKED
75	Points	TOTAL POINTS POSSIBLE
________	SCORE	DETERMINE SCORE (divide points earned by total points possible, multiply results by 100)

Actual Student Time Needed to Complete Procedure: ______________

Student's Initials: ______________ Instructor's Initials: ______________ Grade: ______________

Suggestions for Improvement: ____

Evaluator's Name (print) ____

Evaluator's Signature ____

Comments ____

DOCUMENTATION

Record the respiration rate in the patient's medical record. This patient has a rectal temperature of 99°F and an apical pulse of 114 beats per minute with no arrhythmias.

Date: __________

Charting: ____

____

____

Student's Initials: ________

SKILLS COMPETENCY ASSESSMENT

Procedure 13–5: Obtaining a Urine Specimen From an Infant or a Young Child

Student's Name: ______________________________ Date: __________

Objective: To obtain a specimen of urine from an infant or a young child.

Conditions: The student demonstrates the ability to obtain a specimen of urine from an infant or a young child by using the following equipment and supplies: urine collection bag, laboratory request form, gloves, washcloth, soap, water, towel, biohazard waste container.

Time Requirements and Accuracy Standards: 10 minutes. Points assigned reflect importance of step to meeting objective: Important = (5) Essential = (10) Critical = (15). Automatic failure results if any of the **critical** tasks are omitted or performed incorrectly.

STANDARD PRECAUTIONS:

SKILLS ASSESSMENT CHECKLIST

Task Performed	Possible Points	TASKS
❑	5	Washes and gloves hands following standard precautions. Assembles equipment.
❑	5	Identifies patient and explains procedure to parent(s).
❑	5	Instructs parent to remove diaper.
❑	10	Washes and dries perineal area.
❑	5	*Rationale:* Understands that cleaning the area reduces the microorganism level and provides a better-quality urine specimen.
❑	15	Applies collection bag, secures with adhesive tabs. • Females: spreads perineum, places bag over labia • Males: places bag over penis and scrotum
❑	5	Replaces diaper carefully.
❑	5	Frequently checks bag for urine.
❑	5	Removes bag carefully after specimen has been collected.
❑	15	Prepares specimen as required. Sends to laboratory in a specimen container with a requisition or processes the specimen in the POL.
❑	5	Removes gloves and discards in biohazard waste container. Washes hands.
❑	5	Records collection in patient's chart.

Task Performed	Possible Points	TASKS
❑	5	Completed the tasks within 10 minutes.
❑	15	Results obtained were accurate.
______	Earned	ADD POINTS OF TASKS CHECKED
105	Points	TOTAL POINTS POSSIBLE
______	SCORE	DETERMINE SCORE (divide points earned by total points possible, multiply results by 100)

Actual Student Time Needed to Complete Procedure: ____________

Student's Initials: ____________ Instructor's Initials: ____________ Grade: ____________

Suggestions for Improvement: ______________________________

Evaluator's Name (print) ______________________________

Evaluator's Signature ______________________________

Comments ______________________________

DOCUMENTATION

Record the urine collection in the patient's medical record.

Date: ____________________

Charting: ______________________________

____

____

Student's Initials: ____________

SKILLS COMPETENCY ASSESSMENT

Procedure 13–6: Instructing Patient in Breast Self-Examination

Student's Name: ______________________________ Date: ____________

Objective: To properly instruct a woman in the procedure for performing a breast self-examination.

Conditions: The student demonstrates the ability to properly instruct a woman in the procedure for performing a breast self-examination using the following equipment and supplies: breast model, breast self-exam pamphlets.

Time Requirements and Accuracy Standards: 5 minutes. Points assigned reflect importance of step to meeting objective: Important = (5) Essential = (10) Critical = (15). Automatic failure results if any of the **critical** tasks are omitted or performed incorrectly.

SKILLS ASSESSMENT CHECKLIST

Task Performed	Possible Points	TASKS
		Medical assistant instructs the patient in the following steps involved in breast self-examination while in a warm bath or shower
❑	5	Examine breasts in a warm bath or shower.
❑	5	*Rationale:* Warm water softens skin and hands glide easily.
❑	10	Using the flat pads of the three middle fingers and moving in a circular motion, use the right hand to examine the left breast and the left hand to examine the right breast. Begin at the top outside edge using a circular, clockwise motion, examining every part of each breast, ending at the nipple.
❑	15	Check for lumps, thickening, and anything that is different from previous exams.
		Medical assistant instructs the patient in the following steps involved in breast self-examination in front of a mirror
❑	5	Inspect the breasts with arms at sides.
❑	5	Raise arms high overhead.
❑	5	Look for any change in contour of each breast.
❑	15	Observe for swelling, hard lump(s), dimpling of skin (orange skin), or changes in nipple (retracting, swelling, or discharge).
❑	5	Rest both hands on hips and press down while flexing chest muscles.
		Medical assistant instructs the patient in the following steps involved in breast self-examination while lying down
❑	5	Place a pillow or towel under right shoulder with the right hand behind the head to examine the right breast.

Task Performed	Possible Points	TASKS
❑	15	With left hand and fingers flat, press gently in small circular motions, starting at the top of the breast and moving toward the nipple. Examine every part of the right breast tissue.
❑	5	Repeat the procedure on the left breast, using a pillow or towel under the left shoulder and examine using the right hand.
❑	5	Squeeze the nipple of each breast gently between thumb and index finger.
❑	10	Report any abnormalities to the physician.
❑	15	Medical assistant answers any questions the patient has about breast self-examination during instructions. Any questions the medical assistant cannot answer are referred to the physician.
❑	5	Medical assistant checks that patient has received a breast self-examination pamphlet.
❑	5	Completed the tasks within 5 minutes.
❑	15	Results obtained were accurate.

________	Earned	ADD POINTS OF TASKS CHECKED
150	Points	TOTAL POINTS POSSIBLE
________	SCORE	DETERMINE SCORE (divide points earned by total points possible, multiply results by 100)

Actual Student Time Needed to Complete Procedure: ____________

Student's Initials: ____________ Instructor's Initials: ____________ Grade: ____________

Suggestions for Improvement: ______________________________

Evaluator's Name (print) ______________________________

Evaluator's Signature ______________________________

Comments ______________________________

DOCUMENTATION

Chart the procedure in the patient's medical record.

Date: ____________________

Charting: ______________________________

____

____

Student's Initials: ____________

SKILLS COMPETENCY ASSESSMENT

Procedure 13–7: Assisting with Gynecologic or Pelvic Examination and a Papanicolaou (Pap) Test

Student's Name: ______________________ Date: __________

Objective: To assist the physician in collecting cervical cells for laboratory analysis for early detection of malignant cells of the cervix, assess the health of the reproductive organs, and to detect diseases leading to early diagnosis and treatment.

Conditions: The student demonstrates the ability to assist the physician in collecting cervical cells for laboratory analysis using the following equipment and supplies: two pairs of nonsterile gloves, two to three frosted end glass slides, vaginal speculum (plastic or metal), basin of warm water, long cotton-tipped applicator or cytology brush, cervical scrapers, fixative, light source, drape sheet, marking pencil, lubricant, slide holder, lab requisition, urine specimen container, tissues, biohazard waste container.

Time Requirements and Accuracy Standards: 10 minutes. Points assigned reflect importance of step to meeting objective: Important = (5) Essential = (10) Critical = (15). Automatic failure results if any of the **critical** tasks are omitted or performed incorrectly.

STANDARD PRECAUTIONS:

SKILLS ASSESSMENT CHECKLIST

Task Performed	Possible Points	TASKS
❑	5	Washes hands and assembles necessary supplies near patient.
❑	10	Requests that patient empty her bladder. (Instructs patient to save urine specimen and provide specimen container if ordered by physician.)
❑	5	*Rationale:* Understands that an empty bladder facilitates examination of the uterus and provides a specimen for urinalysis.
❑	5	Provides patient with gown and requests her to completely undress.
❑	5	Explains procedure to patient.
❑	15	Instructs patient to sit at end of table when ready. Drapes patient for privacy. Correctly labels the frosted end of the slide with a marking pencil to include patient's name and cite of specimen collection.
❑	5	Encourages patient to breathe slowly and deeply through the mouth during exam.
❑	5	*Rationale:* Understands that slow, deep breathing allows for relaxation of the pelvic muscles and for easier insertion of vaginal speculum.
❑	5	Warms stainless steel vaginal speculum with warm water or places on a heating pad. Does not lubricate speculum.

Task Performed	Possible Points	TASKS
❑	5	*Rationale:* Understands that lubricant would obscure exfoliated cervical cells when Pap test is performed.
❑	5	Hands speculum and spatula or cytology brush to physician.
❑	5	Applies gloves.
❑	10	Holds slides for physician to apply smear of exfoliated cells, one for vaginal (v), one for cervical (c), and one for endocervical (e), in that order.
❑	10	Sprays fixative over each slide within ten seconds at a distance of about six inches. Allows to dry for at least ten minutes.
❑	5	*Rationale:* Fixing slides preserves cell appearance and avoids contamination of cells. Understands that slides must be fixed before they dry to maintain cell appearance and that getting too close with the spray may destroy or damage cells.
❑	10	Places lubricant on physician's gloved fingers without touching gloves, for bimanual and rectal exams. The physician will insert the index and middle fingers into the vagina. The other hand is placed on the lower abdomen. The size, shape, and position of the uterus and ovaries are palpated.
❑	5	The physician will insert one gloved finger into the rectum to check the tone of the rectal and pelvic muscles. Hemorrhoids, rectal fissures, or other lesions may be palpated.
❑	5	Assists patient to wipe genitalia and rectum.
❑	15	Helps patient to a seated position, allowing her to rest awhile. Checks her pulse and skin color.
❑	5	*Rationale:* Understands that some patients, especially the elderly, can experience orthostatic hypotension.
❑	5	Discards disposable supplies per OSHA guidelines. If stainless steel speculum was used, soaks in cool water. Sanitizes and sterilizes as soon as it is convenient.
❑	5	Removes gloves and washes hands.
❑	5	Assists patient down and off the table if necessary.
❑	5	Instructs patient to dress. Informs patient of how and when test results will be reported to her.
❑	15	Prepares laboratory requisition (cytology request) form. Includes physician name and address, date, source of specimen, patient's name, address, date of last menstrual period (LMP), and hormone therapy. Places slides in slide container, attaches requisition to container, and sends to laboratory.
❑	5	Documents that test is performed and slide has been sent to reference laboratory in the patient's chart.

SKILLS COMPETENCY ASSESSMENT — continued

Procedure 13–7: Assisting with Gynecologic or Pelvic Examination and a Papanicolaou (Pap) Test

Task Performed	Possible Points	TASKS
❑	5	Completed the tasks within 10 minutes.
❑	15	Results obtained were accurate.

_______	Earned	ADD POINTS OF TASKS CHECKED
200	Points	TOTAL POINTS POSSIBLE
_______	SCORE	DETERMINE SCORE (divide points earned by total points possible, multiply results by 100)

Actual Student Time Needed to Complete Procedure: ___________

Student's Initials: ___________ Instructor's Initials: ___________ Grade: ___________

Suggestions for Improvement: ___________

Evaluator's Name (print) ___________

Evaluator's Signature ___________

Comments ___________

DOCUMENTATION

Chart the procedure in the patient's medical record.

Date: ___________

Charting: ___________

____

____

Student's Initials: ___________

SKILLS COMPETENCY ASSESSMENT

Procedure 13–8: Instructing Patient in Testicular Self-Examination

Student's Name: ______________________ Date: __________

Objective: To provide a patient with the correct procedure for performing testicular self-examinations.

Conditions: The student demonstrates the ability to provide a patient with information concerning testicular self-screening for the presence of a painless mass in the scrotum using the following equipment and supplies: testicular self-examination card.

Time Requirements and Accuracy Standards: 5 minutes. Points assigned reflect importance of step to meeting objective: Important = (5) Essential = (10) Critical = (15). Automatic failure results if any of the **critical** tasks are omitted or performed incorrectly.

SKILLS ASSESSMENT CHECKLIST

Task Performed	Possible Points	TASKS
		Medical assistant instructs the patient in the following steps involved in testicular self-examination
❑	5	Patient should examine his testicles in a warm shower.
❑	5	*Rationale:* Warmth causes the scrotal skin to relax.
❑	10	Examine each testicle separately with both hands.
❑	15	Place the index and middle fingers underneath the testicle and the thumbs on top. Roll the testicle gently between the fingers.
❑	10	Locate the epididymis. Look for swelling or changes in the scrotal area.
❑	5	*Rationale:* Understands that patient must be instructed in the location and size of the epididymis, as a lump can be similar in size and patient must be able to distinguish the two.
❑	15	Provides a chart to the patient that illustrates the testes and epididymis. Medical assistant also provides the patient with a testicular self-examination card and encourages the patient to report anything unusual to the physician.
❑	5	Completed the tasks within 5 minutes.
❑	15	Results obtained were accurate.

______	Earned	ADD POINTS OF TASKS CHECKED
85	Points	TOTAL POINTS POSSIBLE
______	SCORE	DETERMINE SCORE (divide points earned by total points possible, multiply results by 100)

Actual Student Time Needed to Complete Procedure: __________

Student's Initials: __________ Instructor's Initials: __________ Grade: __________

Suggestions for Improvement: ______________________

Evaluator's Name (print) ______________________

Evaluator's Signature ______________________

Comments ______________________

SKILLS COMPETENCY ASSESSMENT

Procedure 13–9: Performing a Urinary Catheterization on a Female Patient

Student's Name: ______________________ Date: __________

Objective: To perform urinary catheterization to obtain a sterile urine specimen for analysis or to relieve urinary retention.

Conditions: The student demonstrates the ability to obtain a sterile urine specimen for analysis or to relieve urinary retention using the following equipment and supplies: catheter kit (commercially available), sterile gloves, antiseptic solution, waxed paper bag, lubricant, sterile cotton balls, sterile urine container with label, sterile 2 × 2 gauze sponges, forceps, sterile absorbent plastic pad, sterile catheter (size and type as ordered by physician), biohazard waste container, laboratory requisition form.

Time Requirements and Accuracy Standards: 10 minutes. Points assigned reflect importance of step to meeting objective: Important = (5) Essential = (10) Critical = (15). Automatic failure results if any of the **critical** tasks are omitted or performed incorrectly.

STANDARD PRECAUTIONS:

SKILLS ASSESSMENT CHECKLIST

Task Performed	Possible Points	TASKS
❑	5	Instructs patient to breathe slowly and deeply during procedure.
❑	5	*Rationale:* Understands that slow, deep breathing helps the patient relax the abdominal and pelvic muscles and facilitates easier insertion of catheter.
❑	5	Washes hands and assembles supplies.
❑	5	Identifies the patient and explains the procedure. Places catheter kit on Mayo stand near the patient.
❑	5	Provides adequate lighting. Has patient disrobe below the waist; provides a drape.
❑	5	Positions patient into a dorsal recumbent position on an exam table.
❑	5	*Rationale:* Understands that dorsal recumbent position allows for access to the urinary meatus.
❑	10	Drapes patient with sheet exposing only external genitalia.
❑	5	Opens outer wrapping of sterile kit.
❑	10	Places sterile absorbent plastic pad under patient's buttocks. Places catheter tray between patient's legs.
❑	5	Asks patient to keep knees apart.
❑	5	*Rationale:* This position provides a good view of the urinary meatus.

Task Performed	Possible Points	TASKS
❑	5	Washes hands and puts on sterile gloves.
❑	5	Pours antiseptic solution over three cotton balls in an appropriate compartment of the kit.
❑	5	Opens urine specimen container.
❑	15	Applies sterile lubricant to a gauze sponge and places tip of catheter in lubricant and other end of catheter in sterile basin.
❑	15	Reminds patient to breathe slowly. Spreads labia with nondominant hand. Dominant hand remains sterile. With dominant hand and sterile forceps, wipes genitalia with each of the three antiseptic-soaked cotton balls, with a front-to-back motion. First, wipes the right labia using front-to-back motion. Discards cotton ball into waxed paper bag that is placed away from sterile area. Second, wipes the left labia, repeating procedure, and last, wipes down the center, discarding cotton ball after each wipe. Discards forceps. Continues to hold labia apart until catheter is inserted.
❑	5	*Rationale:* Knows that holding labia open will keep urinary meatus from becoming contaminated from labia while inserting catheter.
❑	15	Using sterile gloved hand, picks up catheter and holds it about three to four inches from lubricated end.
❑	15	Gently inserts lubricated tip of catheter into urinary meatus approximately six inches or until urine begins to flow. Moves nondominant hand to hold catheter in place.
❑	10	Interrupts urine flow by clamping off.
❑	5	*Rationale:* Understands that this will stop the flow of urine while the specimen container is positioned.
❑	10	Positions end of catheter into urine specimen container.
❑	10	Collects specimen by releasing clamp and collecting approximately 60 mL of urine.
❑	5	Allows remaining urine to flow into basin until flow ceases. Pinches catheter closed.
❑	5	Removes catheter gently and slowly.
❑	5	Dries area with remaining cotton balls.
❑	5	Tightens lid on the urine specimen container.
❑	5	Removes procedure items.
❑	5	Positions patient for comfort. Assists patient in sitting up or relaxing in a horizontal recumbent position. After a rest period, helps patient sit on edge of table. Checks patient's color and pulse.
❑	5	Discards disposable items per OSHA guidelines.

SKILLS COMPETENCY ASSESSMENT — continued

Procedure 13–9: Performing a Urinary Catheterization on a Female Patient

Task Performed	Possible Points	TASKS
❑	15	Labels specimen container and attaches to completed laboratory requisition form if collecting specimen for analysis.
❑	5	Assists patient from exam table.
❑	5	Cleans room and table. Removes gloves and discards in biohazard waste container. Washes hands.
❑	15	Documents procedure in patient's chart, including the amount of urine collected. Documents that specimen was sent to outside laboratory (if appropriate).
❑	5	Completed the tasks within 10 minutes.
❑	15	Results obtained were accurate.

________	Earned	ADD POINTS OF TASKS CHECKED
280	Points	TOTAL POINTS POSSIBLE
________	SCORE	DETERMINE SCORE (divide points earned by total points possible, multiply results by 100)

Actual Student Time Needed to Complete Procedure: ____________

Student's Initials: ____________ Instructor's Initials: ____________ Grade: ____________

Suggestions for Improvement: ______________________________

Evaluator's Name (print) ______________________________

Evaluator's Signature ______________________________

Comments ______________________________

DOCUMENTATION

Chart the procedure in the patient's medical record, including the amount of urine collected.

Date: ____________________

Charting: ______________________________

____

____

Student's Initials: ____________

SKILLS COMPETENCY ASSESSMENT

Procedure 13–10: Performing a Urine Drug Screening

Student's Name: ______________________________ Date: ____________

Objective: To accurately obtain a urine specimen from a patient to screen for traces of drugs.

Conditions: The student demonstrates the ability to accurately obtain a urine specimen from a patient to screen for traces of drugs using the following equipment and supplies: Urine Drug Kit (provide at least two choices), gloves, biohazard waste container.

Time Requirements and Accuracy Standards: 5 minutes. Points assigned reflect importance of step to meeting objective: Important = (5) Essential = (10) Critical = (15). Automatic failure results if any of the **critical** tasks are omitted or performed incorrectly.

STANDARD PRECAUTIONS:

SKILLS ASSESSMENT CHECKLIST

Task Performed	Possible Points	TASKS
❑	15	Asks patient to show a photo ID and has patient sign a consent form, keeping copies for the patient file.
❑	5	*Rationale:* Only the person scheduled to take the test will be able to do so.
❑	5	Washes hands and explains procedures to the patient.
❑	10	Supplies at least two collection kits and allows the patient to choose one of them.
❑	15	Has patient remove unnecessary outer garments, empty pockets, and wash and dry hands.
❑	5	*Rationale:* Patient is not given the opportunity to substitute another specimen.
❑	15	Instructs patient to collect at least 40 mL of urine in the collection container.
❑	5	Puts on gloves. Records temperature of specimen, volume, and any contamination.
❑	5	*Rationale:* Understands that a fresh urine specimen will have a temperature of at least 98.6° F.
❑	15	Labels specimen and has patient initial specimen lid.
❑	15	Seals tamper-proof specimen kit bag and has patient initial.
❑	15	Secures sample in a locked container until pickup.
❑	15	Has collector and donor sign off on the test collection procedure to document that all procedural steps were followed.

SKILLS COMPETENCY ASSESSMENT — continued

Procedure 13–10: Performing a Urine Drug Screening

Task Performed	Possible Points	TASKS
❑	5	Removes gloves and disposes in biohazard waste container. Washes hands.
❑	5	Documents procedure in patient's chart.
❑	5	Completed the tasks within 5 minutes.
❑	15	Results obtained were accurate.

_______	Earned	ADD POINTS OF TASKS CHECKED
170	Points	TOTAL POINTS POSSIBLE
_______	SCORE	DETERMINE SCORE (divide points earned by total points possible, multiply results by 100)

Actual Student Time Needed to Complete Procedure: __________

Student's Initials: __________ Instructor's Initials: __________ Grade: __________

Suggestions for Improvement: ______________________________

Evaluator's Name (print) ______________________________

Evaluator's Signature ______________________________

Comments ______________________________

DOCUMENTATION

Chart the procedure in the patient's medical record.

Date: ______________________

Charting: ______________________________

____

____

Student's Initials: ______________

SKILLS COMPETENCY ASSESSMENT

Procedure 13–11: Assisting with Proctosigmoidoscopy

Student's Name: ______________________________ Date: ____________

Objective: To assist the physician in assessing the status of the sigmoid colon and the rectum for signs of disease such as tumors, polyps, ulcerations, hemorrhoids, or rectal bleeding.

Conditions: The student demonstrates the ability to assist the physician with proctosigmoidoscopy using the following equipment and supplies: sigmoidoscope with obturator (either a flexible fiberoptic sigmoidoscope or a rigid sigmoidoscope), sterile biopsy forceps, patient gown, sterile specimen container with preservative, laboratory requisition form, tissues, biohazard waste container, patient drape, small pillow, anoscope, rectal speculum, insufflator, suction machine and tip, probe with bulb tip, gloves, finger cots, long cotton applicators, lubricating jelly, basin of water, 4 × 4 gauze sponges.

Time Requirements and Accuracy Standards: 15 minutes. Points assigned reflect importance of step to meeting objective: Important = (5) Essential = (10) Critical = (15). Automatic failure results if any of the **critical** tasks are omitted or performed incorrectly.

STANDARD PRECAUTIONS:

SKILLS ASSESSMENT CHECKLIST

Task Performed	Possible Points	TASKS
❑	5	Washes hands and prepares equipment and supplies.
❑	15	Checks the lights on the illuminated instruments for loose bulbs by turning the bulb clockwise. Turns the switch to the "on" position to verify the light is working, then turns light off.
❑	10	Labels specimen container with patient's name, address, date, and source.
❑	5	Checks to see that obturators are correctly positioned.
❑	5	Has a basin ready to receive used instruments.
❑	5	Prepares a basin of water to rinse out suction pump.
❑	15	Tests suction machine.
❑	15	Prepares patient. Makes sure patient has been properly prepared; that is, necessary laxative taken, enema administered, and adequate results obtained from enema.
❑	15	Identifies patient. Verifies consent form has been signed. Explains procedure to the patient to promote relaxation and reduce apprehension.
❑	5	Asks patient to empty bladder and saves specimen (if required).
❑	5	*Rationale:* Understands that an empty bladder facilitates examination and is more comfortable for the patient.
❑	5	Asks patient to disrobe and put on gown.

SKILLS COMPETENCY ASSESSMENT — continued

Procedure 13–11: Assisting with Proctosigmoidoscopy

Task Performed	Possible Points	TASKS
❑	5	Assists patient into the knee-chest position or the Sims' lateral position, which assures accessibility to the rectum and sigmoid colon. Some physicians use proctologic tables that tilt the patient into the knee-chest position.
❑	5	*Rationale:* Understands that the abdominal contents tip forward and away from the pelvic area, making it easier to insert the sigmoidoscope.
❑	10	Drapes the patient and places small towel directly over the anus and under the perineal area or uses a fenestrated drape over the anus.
❑	5	Applies gloves and assists the physician during examination.
❑	5	Places lubricant on physician's gloves for digital examination.
❑	5	Warms metal scope by placing in warm water for a few minutes.
❑	10	Lubricates scope tip.
❑	10	Plugs in scope when physician is ready to use.
❑	5	*Rationale:* Understands that plugging the scope in too soon allows the light source to get too hot, which may harm the patient.
❑	5	Reminds the patient to take slow deep breaths to promote relaxation of muscles to facilitate insertion of the sigmoidoscope.
❑	10	Attaches inflation bulb; attaches light source.
❑	5	Observes patient throughout procedure. Provides support and reassurance.
❑	5	Takes instruments from physician as needed.
❑	5	Passes long cotton-tipped applicators to the physician and assists with suction equipment.
❑	5	Places suction tubing in basin of water.
❑	5	Places instruments in basin.
❑	10	Assists with collection of biopsy by handing biopsy forceps to the physician. Does not touch inside of specimen container. Receives and cares for specimen; labels properly.
❑	5	*Rationale:* Sterile container will become contaminated if the inside is touched and may cause inaccurate results.
❑	5	Cleans patient's anus with tissue.
❑	5	Removes gloves, washes hands.
❑	15	Assists patient to supine position after examination. Does not let patient rise too rapidly because of the possibility of dizziness. Checks patient's blood pressure.

Task Performed	Possible Points	TASKS
❑	5	*Rationale:* Understands that vagal nerve stimulation may cause shocklike symptoms, or that orthostatic hypotension can occur from lying flat for an extended period.
❑	5	Assists patient to dress if needed.
❑	5	Applies gloves. Transports specimen with completed lab requisition form.
❑	15	Cleans room and equipment following OSHA guidelines. Flexible sigmoidoscope should be sanitized and subjected to cold sterilization according to manufacturer's directions. Metal (rigid) sigmoidoscope must be sanitized and sterilized in the autoclave.
❑	5	Removes gloves and washes hands.
❑	5	Documents procedure in patient's chart. If specimen is taken, documents that it has been sent to the laboratory. Also documents the patient's blood pressure reading and any unusual circumstances or patient reactions.
❑	5	Completed the tasks within 15 minutes.
❑	15	Results obtained were accurate.

_______	Earned	ADD POINTS OF TASKS CHECKED
305	Points	TOTAL POINTS POSSIBLE
_______	SCORE	DETERMINE SCORE (divide points earned by total points possible, multiply results by 100)

Actual Student Time Needed to Complete Procedure: ____________

Student's Initials: ____________ Instructor's Initials: ____________ Grade: ____________

Suggestions for Improvement: ____

Evaluator's Name (print) ____

Evaluator's Signature ____

Comments ____

DOCUMENTATION

Chart the procedure in the patient's medical record.

Date: ____________________

Charting: ____

____

____

Student's Initials: ______________

SKILLS COMPETENCY ASSESSMENT

Procedure 13–12: Fecal Occult Blood Test

Student's Name: ______________________ Date: __________

Objective: To test feces for occult blood.

Conditions: The student demonstrates the ability to test feces for occult blood using the following equipment and supplies: three guaiac slide test kits, prepared fecal slides from patient, occult blood developer, kit reference card, gloves, biohazard waste container.

Time Requirements and Accuracy Standards: 5 minutes. Points assigned reflect importance of step to meeting objective: Important = (5) Essential = (10) Critical = (15). Automatic failure results if any of the **critical** tasks are omitted or performed incorrectly.

STANDARD PRECAUTIONS:

SKILLS ASSESSMENT CHECKLIST

Task Performed	Possible Points	TASKS
❑	10	Checks expiration dates on occult slides.
❑	5	*Rationale:* Understands that outdated slides can give an inaccurate reading.
❑	5	Identifies the patient.
❑	5	Fills out all information on the front flap of all three slides.
❑	15	Explains stool collection process to patient: • Keep slides at room temperature away from sunlight, which destroys the effectiveness of the guaiac paper and may give inaccurate results. • Open the front flap of the first slide. • Use one end of the wooden applicator to apply a thin smear of the stool sample from the toilet to Box " A." (Patient should not collect sample during menstrual period or if hemorrhoids are present.) • Repeat the procedure using the other end of the applicator, taking a specimen from a different section of the same stool and applying a thin smear to Box " B." (Occult blood may be distributed differently throughout the bowel movement.) • Dispose of the applicator in a waste container. • Close the cover after air-drying slide overnight. • Date the front flap. • Repeat the process with the next two bowel movements, on subsequent days.
❑	5	Provides the patient with an envelope to return the slides to the physician's office.
❑	5	Documents that the test kit and instructions were given to the patient.

Developing the fecal occult slide

The medical assistant will be responsible for developing the slides to determine the results when the patient returns the fecal occult samples to the office. The medical assistant should develop the results as soon as possible. Although most slides may be stored for up to fourteen days before developing, the patient may have already stored them for several days. Test results are important to ensure prompt treatment should a problem be discovered.

Task Performed	Possible Points	TASKS
❑	5	Checks the expiration date on the developer.
❑	5	Applies gloves.
❑	5	Opens the window flap on the back of the slide.
❑	15	Applies two drops of the developer to each Box "A" and "B", directly over each smear.
❑	15	Interprets the results within thirty to sixty seconds. Records the results.
❑	5	Looks for a blue halo appearing around the perimeter of the specimen, indicating a positive reaction.
❑	15	Performs the quality control procedure by processing the positive and negative monitor strip on each slide to confirm the test system is functional. If quality control is not functional, rechecks expiration dates on slide and developer. Repeats test, if necessary.
❑	5	Disposes of all supplies according to OSHA guidelines.
❑	5	Removes gloves and disposes in biohazard waste container. Washes hands.
❑	5	Documents results in patient's chart.
❑	5	Completed the tasks within 5 minutes.
❑	15	Results obtained were accurate.

_______	Earned	ADD POINTS OF TASKS CHECKED
150	Points	TOTAL POINTS POSSIBLE
_______	SCORE	DETERMINE SCORE (divide points earned by total points possible, multiply results by 100)

Actual Student Time Needed to Complete Procedure: ____________

Student's Initials: ____________ Instructor's Initials: ____________ Grade: ____________

Suggestions for Improvement: ____________________________

Evaluator's Name (print) ____________________________

Evaluator's Signature ____________________________

Comments ____________________________

DOCUMENTATION

Record the results of the fecal occult blood test in the patient's medical record.

Date: ____________________

Charting: ____________________________

____

____

Student's Initials: ____________

SKILLS COMPETENCY ASSESSMENT

Procedure 13–13: Performing Visual Acuity Testing Using a Snellen Chart

Student's Name: ______________________________ Date: __________

Objective: To perform a visual screening test to determine a patient's distance visual acuity.

Conditions: The student demonstrates the ability to perform a visual screening test to determine a patient's distance visual acuity using the following equipment and supplies: Snellen eye chart placed at eye level (appropriate for age and reading ability of patient), pointer, occluder, alcohol wipes.

Time Requirements and Accuracy Standards: 10 minutes. Points assigned reflect importance of step to meeting objective: Important = (5) Essential = (10) Critical = (15). Automatic failure results if any of the **critical** tasks are omitted or performed incorrectly.

STANDARD PRECAUTIONS:

SKILLS ASSESSMENT CHECKLIST

Task Performed	Possible Points	TASKS
❑	5	Washes hands and assembles equipment.
❑	10	Prepares a well-lighted room, free from distractions and with a distance mark twenty feet from the eye chart.
❑	5	Explains the procedure to the patient. Tests patients with their glasses on or contact lenses in, unless otherwise indicated by the physician.
❑	10	Instructs the patient to stand behind the mark and cover the left eye with the occluder. Instructs the patient to keep the left eye open under the occluder and not to apply pressure to the eyeball.
❑	5	*Rationale:* Keeps patient from squinting when reading the chart.
❑	15	Stands next to the chart and points to row 3, instructing the patient to read each letter with the right eye, verbally identifying each letter read. Goes to line 2 or line 1 if patient is unable to read line 3.
❑	5	*Rationale:* Pointing helps patient focus on one row of letters at a time.
❑	15	Records the results at the smallest line the patient can read with two or less errors. Allows the patient to repeat the line to verify accuracy. Records vision as right eye, left eye, both eyes (Examples: OD 20/25; OS 20/20; OU 20/20).
❑	5	*Rationale:* Can state that visual acuity is recorded as a fraction, with the top number indicating the distance the patient stands from the chart and the bottom number indicating the distance from which a person with normal vision can read that row of letters.

Task Performed	Possible Points	TASKS
❑	5	Records the patient's reaction during the test, such as leaning forward, squinting or straining, or tearing eyes.
❑	5	*Rationale:* These patient reactions may indicate an eye problem.
❑	5	Uses the same procedure to test the left eye.
❑	5	Wipes occluder with alcohol. Washes hands. Records the results.
❑	5	Completed the tasks within 10 minutes.
❑	15	Results obtained were accurate.

_______	Earned	ADD POINTS OF TASKS CHECKED
115	Points	TOTAL POINTS POSSIBLE
_______	SCORE	DETERMINE SCORE (divide points earned by total points possible, multiply results by 100)

Actual Student Time Needed to Complete Procedure: ____________

Student's Initials: ____________ Instructor's Initials: ____________ Grade: ____________

Suggestions for Improvement: ________________________________

Evaluator's Name (print) ________________________________

Evaluator's Signature ________________________________

Comments ________________________________

DOCUMENTATION

Record results in the patient's medical record.

Date:________________________

Charting: ________________________________

____

____

____

Student's Initials:______________

SKILLS COMPETENCY ASSESSMENT

Procedure 13–14: Measuring Near Visual Acuity

Student's Name: ______________________________ Date: ____________

Objective: To obtain the near vision of the patient.

Conditions: The student demonstrates the ability to obtain the near vision of the patient using the following equipment and supplies: appropriate near visual acuity chart, 3 × 5 cards or occluder.

Time Requirements and Accuracy Standards: 15 minutes. Points assigned reflect importance of step to meeting objective: Important = (5) Essential = (10) Critical = (15). Automatic failure results if any of the **critical** tasks are omitted or performed incorrectly.

STANDARD PRECAUTIONS: 

SKILLS ASSESSMENT CHECKLIST

Task Performed	Possible Points	TASKS
❑	5	Washes hands.
❑	10	Identifies patient. Explains procedure to patient; provides occluder. Positions patient in a comfortable position.
❑	15	Positions the near visual acuity fourteen inches from the patient by measuring with a tape measure.
❑	5	*Rationale:* Measuring the distance with a tape measure ensures accurate results.
❑	5	Has patient lightly (no pressure) cover the left eye with the occluder.
❑	5	*Rationale:* Understands that applying pressure will cause blurring of the eye to be tested next.
❑	15	Has patient read the paragraphs printed on the card.
❑	15	Notes the visual acuity for that eye when the patient has reached a line where more than two mistakes are made (allows the patient to repeat the line to verify acuity).
❑	5	Repeats the process to measure the left eye.
❑	5	Repeats the process to measure both eyes.
❑	5	Records the result in the patient chart.
❑	5	Discards the 3 × 5 card or disinfects the occluder to prevent microorganism cross-contamination.
❑	5	Washes hands.

Task Performed	Possible Points	TASKS
❑	5	Records results.
❑	5	Completed the tasks within 15 minutes.
❑	15	Results obtained were accurate.

_______	Earned	ADD POINTS OF TASKS CHECKED
125	Points	TOTAL POINTS POSSIBLE
_______	SCORE	DETERMINE SCORE (divide points earned by total points possible, multiply results by 100)

Actual Student Time Needed to Complete Procedure: __________

Student's Initials: __________ Instructor's Initials: __________ Grade: __________

Suggestions for Improvement: ____________________

Evaluator's Name (print) ____________________

Evaluator's Signature ____________________

Comments ____________________

DOCUMENTATION

Record near visual acuity test results in the patient's medical record.

Date: ____________________

Charting: ____________________

____

____

Student's Initials: __________

SKILLS COMPETENCY ASSESSMENT

Procedure 13–15: Performing Color Vision Test Using the Ishihara Plates

Student's Name: ______________________________ Date: ____________

Objective: To assess a patient's ability to distinguish between the colors red and green.

Conditions: The student demonstrates the ability to assess a patient's ability to distinguish between the colors red and green using the following equipment and supplies: Ishihara plates (1–12).

Time Requirements and Accuracy Standards: 10 minutes. Points assigned reflect importance of step to meeting objective: Important = (5) Essential = (10) Critical = (15). Automatic failure results if any of the **critical** tasks are omitted or performed incorrectly.

STANDARD PRECAUTIONS:

SKILL ASSESSMENT CHECKLIST

Task Performed	Possible Points	TASKS
❑	5	Explains that the purpose of the test is to determine if the patient has a color vision deficiency.
❑	5	Shows patient plate number 12 as an example of the test process.
❑	5	*Rationale:* With normal vision, plate number 12 can be easily identified.
❑	5	Washes hands and assembles the equipment in a room lighted by daylight.
❑	5	*Rationale:* Understands that direct sunlight or electric light may produce errors in the results because of an alteration in the appearance of shades of color.
❑	15	Holds each plate 75 cm or 30 inches from the patient and tilts each so the plane of each plate is at right angles to the line of the patient's vision.
❑	15	Records the number given by the patient on each plate.
❑	10	Assesses the patient's readings and records.
❑	5	*Rationale:* Knows that ten or more plates read correctly indicates normal color vision.
❑	15	Keeps test plates covered when not in use to avoided fading of color plates from exposure to sunlight, which can lead to inaccurate test interpretation.
❑	5	Completed the tasks within 10 minutes.
❑	15	Results obtained were accurate.

________	Earned	ADD POINTS OF TASKS CHECKED
105	Points	TOTAL POINTS POSSIBLE
________	SCORE	DETERMINE SCORE (divide points earned by total points possible, multiply results by 100)

Actual Student Time Needed to Complete Procedure: ____________

Student's Initials: ____________ Instructor's Initials: ____________ Grade: ____________

Suggestions for Improvement: ____

Evaluator's Name (print) ____

Evaluator's Signature ____

Comments ____

DOCUMENTATION

Chart the procedure in the patient's medical record.

Date: ______________________

Charting: ____

____

____

Student's Initials: ______________

SKILLS COMPETENCY ASSESSMENT

Procedure 13–16: Performing Eye Instillation

Student's Name: ______________________________ Date: ______________

Objective: To treat eye infections, soothe irritation, anesthetize, and dilate pupils.

Conditions: The student demonstrates the ability to treat eye infections, soothe irritation, anesthetize, and dilate pupils using the following equipment and supplies: sterile eye dropper, sterile ophthalmic medication as ordered by the physician (either drops or ointment), sterile cotton balls, sterile water or sterile normal saline, sterile gloves. Use separate medication for each eye, if both are affected.

Time Requirements and Accuracy Standards: 5 minutes. Points assigned reflect importance of step to meeting objective: Important = (5) Essential = (10) Critical = (15). Automatic failure results if any of the **critical** tasks are omitted or performed incorrectly.

STANDARD PRECAUTIONS: 

SKILLS ASSESSMENT CHECKLIST

Task Performed	Possible Points	TASKS
❑	5	Washes hands. Assembles supplies.
❑	15	Checks medication carefully as ordered by the physician, including expiration date. Reads label three times.
❑	10	Identifies patient. Explains procedure to the patient and informs the patient that instillation may temporarily blur vision.
❑	10	Positions the patient in a seated or lying down position. Instructs the patient to stare at a fixed spot during instillation of the drops.
❑	15	Puts on sterile gloves, moistens two to three sterile cotton balls with sterile water or sterile normal saline.
❑	5	Wipes the affected eye from the inner to outer canthus to remove any exudate that may be present.
❑	5	Prepares medication using either drops or ointment.
❑	10	Has the patient look up to the ceiling and expose the lower conjunctival sac of the affected eye by using fingers over a tissue to pull down.
❑	15	Places the number of drops ordered in the center of the lower conjunctival sac or a thin line of ointment in the lower surface of the eyelid, being careful not to touch the eyelid, eyeball, or eyelashes with the tip of the medication applicator. Replaces dropper in bottle to avoid contamination.
❑	5	Has the patient close the eye and roll the eyeball.

Task Performed	Possible Points	TASKS
❑	5	*Rationale:* Understands that rolling the eyeball helps distribute medication evenly.
❑	5	Blots excess medication from eyelids with cotton ball from inner to outer canthus.
❑	5	Disposes of supplies. Washes hands.
❑	5	Records procedure in patient's chart.
❑	5	Completed the tasks within 5 minutes.
❑	15	Results obtained were accurate.

________	Earned	ADD POINTS OF TASKS CHECKED
135	Points	TOTAL POINTS POSSIBLE
________	SCORE	DETERMINE SCORE (divide points earned by total points possible, multiply results by 100)

Actual Student Time Needed to Complete Procedure: ____________

Student's Initials: ____________ Instructor's Initials: ____________ Grade: ____________

Suggestions for Improvement: ____________

Evaluator's Name (print) ____________

Evaluator's Signature ____________

Comments ____________

DOCUMENTATION

Chart the procedure in the patient's medical record.

Date: ____________

Charting: ____________

____

____

____

Student's Initials: ____________

SKILLS COMPETENCY ASSESSMENT

Procedure 13–17: Performing Eye Patch Dressing Application

Student's Name: ______________________________ Date: ____________

Objective: To apply a sterile eye patch.

Conditions: The student demonstrates the ability to apply a sterile eye patch using the following equipment and supplies: tape, sterile eye patch, sterile gloves.

Time Requirements and Accuracy Standards: 10 minutes. Points assigned reflect importance of step to meeting objective: Important = (5) Essential = (10) Critical = (15). Automatic failure results if any of the **critical** tasks are omitted or performed incorrectly.

STANDARD PRECAUTIONS:

SKILLS ASSESSMENT CHECKLIST

Task Performed	Possible Points	TASKS
❑	5	Washes hands and assembles supplies.
❑	5	Identifies patient. Explains the procedure. Positions the patient in a seated position.
❑	15	Instructs the patient to close both eyes during the application of the patch. Prepares sterile area by opening the sterile package and using the inside of the package as a sterile field. Applies sterile gloves.
❑	15	Places the patch over the affected eye using sterile gloves.
❑	10	Secures the patch with three to four strips of transparent tape diagonally from mid-forehead to below the ear.
❑	5	Removes gloves. Washes hands.
❑	5	Documents the procedure and provides verbal and written care instructions to the patient.
❑	5	Completed the tasks within 10 minutes.
❑	15	Results obtained were accurate.

_______	Earned	ADD POINTS OF TASKS CHECKED
80	Points	TOTAL POINTS POSSIBLE
_______	SCORE	DETERMINE SCORE (divide points earned by total points possible, multiply results by 100)

Actual Student Time Needed to Complete Procedure: ____________

Student's Initials: ____________ Instructor's Initials: ____________ Grade: ____________

Suggestions for Improvement: ____________

Evaluator's Name (print) ____________

Evaluator's Signature ____________

Comments ____________

DOCUMENTATION

Chart the procedure in the patient's medical record.

Date: ____________

Charting: ____________

____

____

____

Student's Initials: ____________

SKILLS COMPETENCY ASSESSMENT

Procedure 13–18: Performing Eye Irrigation

Student's Name: ______________________________ Date: ____________

Objective: To irrigate the patient's affected eye for any of the following reasons: a. to cleanse a foreign object; b. to cleanse a discharge; c. to cleanse chemicals; d. to apply antiseptic; e. to apply heat.

Conditions: The student demonstrates the ability to irrigate the patient's affected eye using the following equipment and supplies: sterile irrigation solution as ordered by the physician, sterile bulb syringe (rubber), kidney-shaped basin to catch irrigation solution, sterile cotton balls, sterile gloves, biohazard waste container, towel, pillow. Use separate medication for each eye if both eyes are irrigated.

Time Requirements and Accuracy Standards: 10 minutes. Points assigned reflect importance of step to meeting objective: Important = (5) Essential = (10) Critical = (15). Automatic failure results if any of the **critical** tasks are omitted or performed incorrectly.

STANDARD PRECAUTIONS:

SKILLS ASSESSMENT CHECKLIST

Task Performed	Possible Points	TASKS
❑	5	Washes hands and assembles supplies.
❑	5	Identifies patient. Explains the procedure to the patient. Positions the patient in the supine position.
❑	15	Checks expiration date on solution bottle. Checks medication label three times. Warms solution to body temperature (98.6° F).
❑	10	Tilts head toward affected eye. Places towel on patient's shoulder. Places basin beside the affected eye.
❑	5	*Rationale:* Understands that tilting head toward affected eye allows solution to flow from affected eye into basin without causing cross-contamination of the unaffected eye. Basin acts as a catch receptacle for solution.
❑	15	Pours sterile solution into a sterile container.
❑	15	Puts on sterile gloves.
❑	5	Moistens two to three cotton balls with irrigation solution and cleans the eyelids and eyelashes of the affected eye from inner to outer canthus. Discards after each wipe.
❑	5	Exposes the lower conjunctiva by separating the eyelid with index finger and thumb.
❑	5	Has the patient stare at a fixed spot.

Task Performed	Possible Points	TASKS
❑	15	Irrigates the affected eye with sterile solution by resting the sterile bulb syringe on the bridge of the patient's nose, being careful not to touch the eye or conjunctival sac with the syringe tip. Allows the stream to flow from the inside canthus to the outer corner of the eye.
❑	5	*Rationale:* This avoids cross-contamination of the unaffected eye from the flow of solution.
❑	5	Dries the eyelid and eyelashes with sterile cotton balls following the irrigation.
❑	5	Discards supplies in biohazard waste container if discharge or exudate is present.
❑	5	Removes gloves. Washes hands. Documents procedure.
❑	5	Completed the tasks within 10 minutes.
❑	15	Results obtained were accurate.

________	Earned	ADD POINTS OF TASKS CHECKED
140	Points	TOTAL POINTS POSSIBLE
________	SCORE	DETERMINE SCORE (divide points earned by total points possible, multiply results by 100)

Actual Student Time Needed to Complete Procedure: ____________

Student's Initials: ____________ Instructor's Initials: ____________ Grade: ____________

Suggestions for Improvement: ______________________________

Evaluator's Name (print) ______________________________

Evaluator's Signature ______________________________

Comments ______________________________

DOCUMENTATION

Chart the procedure in the patient's medical record.

Date: ____________________

Charting: ______________________________

____

____

____

Student's Initials: ____________

SKILLS COMPETENCY ASSESSMENT

Procedure 13–19: Assisting with Audiometry

Student's Name: ________________________________ Date: ____________

Objective: To assist in testing patient for hearing loss.

Conditions: The student demonstrates the ability to assist in testing patient for hearing loss using the following equipment and supplies: audiometer with headphones, quiet room.

Time Requirements and Accuracy Standards: 15 minutes. Points assigned reflect importance of step to meeting objective: Important = (5) Essential = (10) Critical = (15). Automatic failure results if any of the **critical** tasks are omitted or performed incorrectly.

STANDARD PRECAUTIONS:

SKILLS ASSESSMENT CHECKLIST

Task Performed	Possible Points	TASKS
❑	5	Washes hands and assembles equipment and supplies.
❑	5	Prepares room. Holds test in a room without outside noises.
❑	5	*Rationale:* Understands that outside interference can cause inaccurate test results, especially in the lower frequencies, which are more difficult to hear.
❑	15	Explains procedure to patient. • Explains the use and purpose of the audiometer and explains that the test measures the frequency of sound waves and the ability of the patient to hear various frequencies of sound waves (one frequency at a time). • Explains that when the patient hears a new frequency, the tester is signaled.
❑	5	Positions patient in a comfortable sitting position. Has patient put on headphones. Does the procedure on each ear separately.
❑	15	If the medical assistant has been thoroughly trained to do the procedure, the physician will allow the medical assistant to perform the audiometry. Starts the audiometer at low frequency. Has patient indicate when the sound is heard and plots it on the audiogram.
❑	15	Increases the frequencies gradually, until completed.
❑	5	Checks the other ear in the same manner.
❑	15	Gives the results to the physician for interpretation.
❑	5	Cleans equipment following manufacturer's instructions. Washes hands.
❑	5	Documents procedure on patient's chart.

Task Performed	Possible Points	TASKS
☐	5	Completed the tasks within 15 minutes.
☐	15	Results obtained were accurate.

______	Earned	ADD POINTS OF TASKS CHECKED
115	Points	TOTAL POINTS POSSIBLE
______	SCORE	DETERMINE SCORE (divide points earned by total points possible, multiply results by 100)

Actual Student Time Needed to Complete Procedure: ______________

Student's Initials: ______________ Instructor's Initials: ______________ Grade: ______________

Suggestions for Improvement: ______________________________

Evaluator's Name (print) ______________________________

Evaluator's Signature ______________________________

Comments ______________________________

DOCUMENTATION

Chart the procedure in the patient's medical record.

Date: ______________________

Charting: ______________________________

____

____

____

Student's Initials: ______________

SKILLS COMPETENCY ASSESSMENT

Procedure 13–20: Performing Ear Irrigation

Student's Name: ______________________________ Date: ____________

Objective: To perform an ear irrigation to relieve inflammation, to remove cerumen, discharge, or foreign materials from the ear canal as directed by the physician.

Conditions: The student demonstrates the ability to perform ear irrigation as directed by the physician using the following equipment and supplies: irrigation solution, as ordered by the physician, warmed to body temperature (98.6° F), ear syringe or bulb, ear basin or emesis basin, basin for warmed solution, towel, cotton balls, otoscope.

Time Requirements and Accuracy Standards: 10 minutes. Points assigned reflect importance of step to meeting objective: Important = (5) Essential = (10) Critical = (15). Automatic failure results if any of the **critical** tasks are omitted or performed incorrectly.

STANDARD PRECAUTIONS: 

SKILLS ASSESSMENT CHECKLIST

Task Performed	Possible Points	TASKS
❑	5	Washes hands and assembles equipment.
❑	5	Identifies patient. Explains the procedure and informs the patient that during the procedure a minimal amount of discomfort and dizziness may be experienced, caused by solution coming into contact with the tympanic membrane.
❑	5	Places the patient in a sitting position and uses an otoscope to visualize the affected ear.
❑	10	Cleanses the outer ear with a wet cotton ball moistened with irrigation solution.
❑	5	Tilts the head toward the affected ear.
❑	10	Gently pulls the auricle upward and back to straighten the ear canal.
❑	10	Tilts the patient's head slightly forward and to the affected side to allow solution to flow into basin by force of gravity.
❑	5	Places towel on the patient's shoulder on the affected side.
❑	5	Places the ear basin under the affected ear and has the patient hold the basin in place.
❑	15	Checks label of solution three times for correctness and also checks the expiration date of the solution.
❑	15	Pours the solution into a basin and fills the syringe with the warmed irrigation solution as prescribed by the physician. Uses about 30 cc to 50 cc of solution at a time.
❑	5	Once again cleanses the outer ear with a cotton ball moistened with irrigation solution.
❑	10	Straightens the external auditory canal by pulling back and upward on the auricle for adults.
❑	15	Expels air from syringe and gently inserts the syringe tip into the affected ear, being careful not to insert too deeply. Does not occlude external auditory canal. Directs the flow of the solution upward toward roof of canal.

Task Performed	Possible Points	TASKS
❑	5	*Rationale:* Understands that this will avoid injury to the tympanic membrane, prevent occlusion of external auditory canal, and allow solution to drain out.
❑	5	Repeats the irrigation, allowing the solution to drain from the ear, noting the return. Allows for free flow of return each time.
❑	5	Dries the outer ear and views the inner ear with the otoscope to verify the procedure has removed or dislodged the foreign body.
❑	5	Notifies the physician that the procedure has been completed. Removes the ear basin and towel.
❑	10	Has patient lie on affected side on exam table for ear to continue draining.
❑	5	Provides dry cotton balls to the patient to catch any further drainage, if directed by the physician.
❑	5	Disposes of supplies. Washes hands.
❑	5	Documents the procedure, noting return and amount.
❑	5	Provides post-care instructions to patient: Report any pain or dizziness to the physician. Do not insert any foreign object (i.e., cotton applicator) into the ear canal.
❑	5	Completed the tasks within 10 minutes.
❑	15	Results obtained were accurate.

______	Earned	ADD POINTS OF TASKS CHECKED
190	Points	TOTAL POINTS POSSIBLE
______	SCORE	DETERMINE SCORE (divide points earned by total points possible, multiply results by 100)

Actual Student Time Needed to Complete Procedure: __________

Student's Initials: __________ Instructor's Initials: __________ Grade: __________

Suggestions for Improvement: ______________________________

Evaluator's Name (print) ______________________________

Evaluator's Signature ______________________________

Comments ______________________________

DOCUMENTATION

Chart the procedure in the patient's medical record.

Date: ____________________

Charting: ______________________________

____

____

Student's Initials: __________

SKILLS COMPETENCY ASSESSMENT

Procedure 13–21: Performing Ear Instillation

Student's Name: ______________________ Date: __________

Objective: To perform ear instillation to soften impacted cerumen, fight infection with antibiotics, or relieve pain.

Conditions: The student demonstrates the ability to perform ear instillation using the following equipment and supplies: otic medication, as prescribed by the physician, sterile ear dropper, cotton balls, gloves.

Time Requirements and Accuracy Standards: 5 minutes. Points assigned reflect importance of step to meeting objective: Important = (5) Essential = (10) Critical = (15). Automatic failure results if any of the **critical** tasks are omitted or performed incorrectly.

STANDARD PRECAUTIONS:

SKILLS ASSESSMENT CHECKLIST

Task Performed	Possible Points	TASKS
☐	5	Washes hands and assembles supplies.
☐	15	Identifies patient. Explains procedure to the patient. Positions patient to either lie on unaffected side or in seated position with head tilted toward unaffected ear to facilitate flow of medication.
☐	15	Checks otic medication three times against the physician's order and checks the expiration date of the medication.
☐	5	*Rationale:* Understands that only otic medication can be used in the ear.
☐	10	Draws up the prescribed amount of medication.
☐	15	Gently pulls the top of the ear upward and back for adults, or pulls earlobe downward and backward for children.
☐	10	Instills prescribed dose of medication (number of drops) by squeezing rubber bulb on dropper into the affected ear.
☐	10	Has the patient maintain the position for about five minutes to retain medication.
☐	5	Inserts moistened cotton ball into external ear canal for fifteen minutes, when instructed by the physician.
☐	5	*Rationale:* Understands that a moistened cotton ball will not absorb medication and will help retain medication in the ear.
☐	5	Disposes of supplies. Washes hands. Documents procedure.
☐	5	Completed the tasks within 5 minutes.

Task Performed	Possible Points	TASKS
❑	15	Results obtained were accurate.

________	Earned	ADD POINTS OF TASKS CHECKED
120	Points	TOTAL POINTS POSSIBLE
________	SCORE	DETERMINE SCORE (divide points earned by total points possible, multiply results by 100)

Actual Student Time Needed to Complete Procedure: ____________

Student's Initials: ____________ Instructor's Initials: ____________ Grade: ____________

Suggestions for Improvement: ________________________________

Evaluator's Name (print) ________________________________

Evaluator's Signature ________________________________

Comments ________________________________

DOCUMENTATION

Chart the procedure in the patient's medical record.

Date:____________________

Charting: ________________________________

____

____

____

Student's Initials:______________

SKILLS COMPETENCY ASSESSMENT

Procedure 13–22: Assisting with Nasal Examination

Student's Name: ______________________________ Date: ____________

Objective: To assist the physician with the nasal examination when looking for polyps, engorged superficial blood vessels, and the possible removal of a foreign body.

Conditions: The student demonstrates the ability to assist the physician with the nasal examination using the following equipment and supplies: nasal speculum, light source, gloves, bayonet forceps, kidney basin.

Time Requirements and Accuracy Standards: 15 minutes. Points assigned reflect importance of step to meeting objective: Important = (5) Essential = (10) Critical = (15). Automatic failure results if any of the **critical** tasks are omitted or performed incorrectly.

STANDARD PRECAUTIONS:

SKILLS ASSESSMENT CHECKLIST

Task Performed	Possible Points	TASKS
❑	5	Washes hands and assembles supplies.
❑	15	Identifies patient. Explains the procedure to the patient. • When a foreign object is involved, instructs the patient not to blow the nose or to attempt to remove the object because this could cause tissue damage or push the object deeper into the nasal passage.
❑	5	Places the patient in a seated position. Reassures the patient.
❑	5	Hands the physician equipment and supplies as needed.
❑	5	Cleans equipment and disposes of supplies per OSHA guidelines. Washes hands.
❑	5	Documents procedure noting foreign object, if applicable.
❑	5	Completed the tasks within 15 minutes.
❑	15	Results obtained were accurate.

________	Earned	ADD POINTS OF TASKS CHECKED
60	Points	TOTAL POINTS POSSIBLE
________	SCORE	DETERMINE SCORE (divide points earned by total points possible, multiply results by 100)

Actual Student Time Needed to Complete Procedure: ____________

Student's Initials: ____________ Instructor's Initials: ____________ Grade: ____________

Suggestions for Improvement: ______________________________

Evaluator's Name (print) ______________________________

Evaluator's Signature ______________________________

Comments ______________________________

SKILLS COMPETENCY ASSESSMENT

Procedure 13–23: Procedure for Obtaining a Throat Culture

Student's Name: ______________________________ Date: ____________

Objective: To obtain secretions from the nasopharnyx and tonsillar area in order to incubate for means of identifying a pathogenic microorganism.

Conditions: The student demonstrates the ability to obtain a throat culture using the following equipment and supplies: tongue depressor, culture tube with applicator stick or commercially prepared culture collection system, label and requisition form, gloves and mask.

Time Requirements and Accuracy Standards: 5 minutes. Points assigned reflect importance of step to meeting objective: Important = (5) Essential = (10) Critical = (15). Automatic failure results if any of the **critical** tasks are omitted or performed incorrectly.

STANDARD PRECAUTIONS:

SKILLS ASSESSMENT CHECKLIST

Task Performed	Possible Points	TASKS
❑	10	Identifies patient and explains procedure. Has patient in a seated position. Adjusts good light source.
❑	5	Washes hands. Gathers equipment. Applies mask and gloves.
❑	5	Removes sterile applicator from culture tube.
❑	5	Asks patient to open mouth widely. Depresses tongue with tongue depressor.
❑	15	Swabs the back of the throat and the tonsillar area.
❑	5	*Rationale:* Is certain to obtain a good sample of secretions or exudate from the very back of the throat, paying special attention to redness, rawness, or pustules.
❑	5	Takes separate culture from each side of the throat, if directed by the physician.
❑	10	Removes applicator stick and places in culture tube(s).
❑	5	Removes tongue blade and discards in biohazard waste container.
❑	15	Pushes the applicator stick into the culture medium until the medium compartment is punctured and growth medium is released.
❑	5	*Rationale:* Understands that this keeps the sample alive, because the medium contains nutrients similar to human tissues.
❑	5	Assures patient comfort.
❑	15	Labels culture tube(s) and sends to outside laboratory or processes the specimen according to agency policy.

SKILLS COMPETENCY ASSESSMENT — continued

Procedure 13–23: Procedure for Obtaining a Throat Culture

Task Performed	Possible Points	TASKS
❑	5	Removes gloves and masks. Washes hands.
❑	5	Documents procedure.
❑	5	Completed the tasks within 5 minutes.
❑	15	Results obtained were accurate.

_______	Earned	ADD POINTS OF TASKS CHECKED
135	Points	TOTAL POINTS POSSIBLE
_______	SCORE	DETERMINE SCORE (divide points earned by total points possible, multiply results by 100)

Actual Student Time Needed to Complete Procedure: __________

Student's Initials: __________ Instructor's Initials: __________ Grade: __________

Suggestions for Improvement: ______________________________

Evaluator's Name (print) ______________________________

Evaluator's Signature ______________________________

Comments ______________________________

DOCUMENTATION

Chart the procedure in the patient's medical record.

Date: ____________________

Charting: ______________________________

____

Student's Initials: ______________

SKILLS COMPETENCY ASSESSMENT

Procedure 13–24: Performing Nasal Irrigation

Student's Name: ______________________________ Date: ____________

Objective: To perform nasal irrigation to remove a foreign body, relieve inflammation, or increase drainage.

Conditions: The student demonstrates the ability to perform nasal irrigation using the following equipment and supplies: bulb-tip syringe, emesis basin, basins for irrigation solution, towels, nonsterile gloves.

Time Requirements and Accuracy Standards: 10 minutes. Points assigned reflect importance of step to meeting objective: Important = (5) Essential = (10) Critical = (15). Automatic failure results if any of the **critical** tasks are omitted or performed incorrectly.

STANDARD PRECAUTIONS:

SKILLS ASSESSMENT CHECKLIST

Task Performed	Possible Points	TASKS
❑	5	Washes hands and assembles supplies.
❑	5	Identifies patient. Explains the procedure to the patient.
❑	10	Warms irrigation solution to 98.6° F.
❑	10	Positions patient in a seated position with head slightly tilted to facilitate nasal drainage.
❑	5	Places towel across patient's chest and shoulders to absorb solution that may splash.
❑	5	Has the patient hold the emesis basin under the nose.
❑	5	Pours warmed irrigation solution into a basin and withdraws the irrigating solution into the bulb syringe.
❑	15	Inserts the tip of the syringe into the affected nostril and gently squeezes the bulb. Does not occlude nostril.
❑	5	Repeats until the required amount of solution has been used.
❑	5	Assists the patient when complete. Gives the patient a towel to wipe the face.
❑	15	Instructs the patient not to blow the nose for five minutes after the procedure, as blowing the nose could force solution into the sinuses or ears.
❑	5	Disposes of supplies per OSHA guidelines. Washes hands.
❑	5	Documents the procedure.
❑	5	Completed the tasks within 10 minutes.

SKILLS COMPETENCY ASSESSMENT — continued

Procedure 13–24: Performing Nasal Irrigation

Task Performed	Possible Points	TASKS
❑	15	Results obtained were accurate.

______	Earned	ADD POINTS OF TASKS CHECKED
115	Points	TOTAL POINTS POSSIBLE
______	SCORE	DETERMINE SCORE (divide points earned by total points possible, multiply results by 100)

Actual Student Time Needed to Complete Procedure: ____________

Student's Initials: ____________ Instructor's Initials: ____________ Grade: ____________

Suggestions for Improvement: ____

Evaluator's Name (print) ____

Evaluator's Signature ____

Comments ____

DOCUMENTATION

Chart the procedure in the patient's medical record.

Date: ______________________

Charting: ____

____

____

____

Student's Initials: ______________

SKILLS COMPETENCY ASSESSMENT

Procedure 13–25: Performing Nasal Instillation

Student's Name: ______________________________ Date: __________

Objective: To provide medication to the nose as ordered by the physician.

Conditions: To perform nasal instillation as ordered by the physician, using the following equipment and supplies: medication as ordered by physician, medicine dropper, cotton balls or 2 × 2 gauze sponges.

Time Requirements and Accuracy Standards: 5 minutes. Points assigned reflect importance of step to meeting objective: Important = (5) Essential = (10) Critical = (15). Automatic failure results if any of the **critical** tasks are omitted or performed incorrectly.

STANDARD PRECAUTIONS:

SKILLS ASSESSMENT CHECKLIST

Task Performed	Possible Points	TASKS
❑	5	Washes hands and assembles equipment.
❑	10	Identifies patient and explains procedure. Positions the patient with the head lower than the shoulders.
❑	5	Instructs patient to keep head tilted back during the procedure to allow medication to cover the nasal tissues.
❑	15	Draws medication into dropper after checking medication three times and checking expiration date.
❑	15	Places the dropper over the center of the affected nostril. Takes care not to touch the inside of the nostril.
❑	5	*Rationale:* Understands that touching the inside of the nostril will lead to contamination of the dropper and possible injury to the patient's mucosa.
❑	5	Repeats the procedure for the other nostril, if required.
❑	5	Instructs patient to remain in position for five minutes.
❑	5	Provides cotton balls or gauze sponges to the patient when the patient returns to seated position. Instructs patient to not blow nose.
❑	5	*Rationale:* Medication may still drain from the nostrils.
❑	5	Disposes of supplies per OSHA guidelines; washes hands; documents procedure.
❑	5	Completed the tasks within 5 minutes.

SKILLS COMPETENCY ASSESSMENT — continued

Procedure 13–25: Performing Nasal Instillation

Task Performed	Possible Points	TASKS
❑	15	Results obtained were accurate.

________	Earned	ADD POINTS OF TASKS CHECKED
100	Points	TOTAL POINTS POSSIBLE
________	SCORE	DETERMINE SCORE (divide points earned by total points possible, multiply results by 100)

Actual Student Time Needed to Complete Procedure: ____________

Student's Initials: ____________ Instructor's Initials: ____________ Grade: ____________

Suggestions for Improvement: ____

Evaluator's Name (print) ____

Evaluator's Signature ____

Comments ____

DOCUMENTATION

Chart the procedure in the patient's medical record.

Date:____________________________

Charting: ____

____

____

____

Student's Initials:________________

SKILLS COMPETENCY ASSESSMENT

Procedure 13–26: Obtaining a Sputum Specimen

Student's Name: ______________________________ Date: ____________

Objective: To collect a quality sputum specimen for laboratory analysis to assist in diagnosing disease.

Conditions: The student demonstrates the ability to collect a quality sputum specimen for laboratory analysis using the following equipment and supplies: tissues, small plastic bag to deliver specimen to laboratory, sterile sputum container and label, laboratory requisition, nonsterile gloves, goggles, gown, biohazard waste container.

Time Requirements and Accuracy Standards: 5 minutes. Points assigned reflect importance of step to meeting objective: Important = (5) Essential = (10) Critical = (15). Automatic failure results if any of the **critical** tasks are omitted or performed incorrectly.

STANDARD PRECAUTIONS:

SKILLS ASSESSMENT CHECKLIST

Task Performed	Possible Points	TASKS
❑	5	Washes hands, assembles supplies, and labels container.
❑	15	Identifies patient. Explains procedure to the patient. Instructs patient that if specimen must be collected at home, the container must be closed, labeled with date, time, and patient's name. Tells patient to collect three specimens on three different days if specimen is to be collected for AFB (acid-fast bacillus). Encourages patient to drink plenty of fluids.
❑	5	*Rationale:* Increased fluid intake keeps mucus moist.
❑	10	Puts on gloves, goggles, and gown.
❑	15	Instructs patient to cough deeply and to expectorate directly into the sterile container. Tells patient to take several deep breaths in order to cough up sputum and not saliva.
❑	5	*Rationale:* Understands that cough must be deep because this will bring up secretions from the lungs and bronchial tubes.
❑	15	Secures the top of the container. Fills out laboratory requisition and secures it to the specimen container. Delivers to laboratory within thirty minutes after collection.
❑	5	Disposes of supplies per OSHA guidelines. Washes hands.
❑	5	Documents the procedure.
❑	5	Completed the tasks within 5 minutes.

SKILLS COMPETENCY ASSESSMENT — continued

Procedure 13–26: Obtaining a Sputum Specimen

Task Performed	Possible Points	TASKS
❑	15	Results obtained were accurate.

_________	Earned	ADD POINTS OF TASKS CHECKED
100	Points	TOTAL POINTS POSSIBLE
_________	SCORE	DETERMINE SCORE (divide points earned by total points possible, multiply results by 100)

Actual Student Time Needed to Complete Procedure: ____________

Student's Initials: ____________ Instructor's Initials: ____________ Grade: ____________

Suggestions for Improvement: ____________

Evaluator's Name (print) ____________

Evaluator's Signature ____________

Comments ____________

DOCUMENTATION

Chart the procedure in the patient's medical record.

Date: ____________

Charting: ____________

____

____

____

Student's Initials: ____________

SKILLS COMPETENCY ASSESSMENT

Procedure 13–27: Administer Oxygen By Nasal Cannula for Minor Respiratory Distress

Student's Name: ______________________________ Date: ____________

Objective: To provide a low dose of concentrated oxygen to a patient during periods of respiratory distress (e.g., chronic obstructive pulmonary disease).

Conditions: The student demonstrates the ability to administer oxygen by nasal cannula for minor respiratory distress using the following equipment and supplies: portable oxygen tank with stand, disposable nasal cannula with connecting tube, flowmeter, pressure regulator.

Time Requirements and Accuracy Standards: 5 minutes. Points assigned reflect importance of step to meeting objective: Important = (5) Essential = (10) Critical = (15). Automatic failure results if any of the **critical** tasks are omitted or performed incorrectly.

STANDARD PRECAUTIONS:

SKILLS ASSESSMENT CHECKLIST

Task Performed	Possible Points	TASKS
☐	5	Washes hands.
☐	15	Identifies patient. Explains procedure to patient. • Demonstrates the position of the nasal prongs of the cannula into the nose. Shows how they face upward and the tab rests above the upper lip. • Describes how to clear the oxygen cylinder valve by turning it counterclockwise. • Explains that oxygen supports combustion and that a fire can start with oxygen in use. Instructs that friction, static electricity, or a lighted cigarette or cigar can cause ignition.
☐	15	Opens the cylinder one full turn, counterclockwise. Checks the pressure gauge.
☐	5	*Rationale:* Understands that this will determine the amount of pressure in the cylinder.
☐	10	Attaches the nasal cannula to the tubing and then to the flowmeter.
☐	15	Adjusts the flow rate according to the physician's order.
☐	10	Checks for oxygen flow through the cannula.
☐	5	Places the tips of the cannula into the nares no more than one inch.
☐	5	Adjusts the tubing around the patient's ears and secures it under the chin.
☐	5	Answers patient's questions.
☐	5	Washes hands.
☐	5	Documents the procedure.

SKILLS COMPETENCY ASSESSMENT — continued

Procedure 13–27: Administer Oxygen By Nasal Cannula for Minor Respiratory Distress

Task Performed	Possible Points	TASKS
❑	5	Completed the tasks within 5 minutes.
❑	15	Results obtained were accurate.

_______	Earned	ADD POINTS OF TASKS CHECKED
120	Points	TOTAL POINTS POSSIBLE
_______	SCORE	DETERMINE SCORE (divide points earned by total points possible, multiply results by 100)

Actual Student Time Needed to Complete Procedure: ____________

Student's Initials: ____________ Instructor's Initials: ____________ Grade: ____________

Suggestions for Improvement: ____________

Evaluator's Name (print) ____________

Evaluator's Signature ____________

Comments ____________

DOCUMENTATION

Chart the procedure in the patient's medical record.

Date: ____________

Charting: ____________

____

____

____

Student's Initials: ____________

SKILLS COMPETENCY ASSESSMENT

Procedure 13–28: Instructing Patient in Use of Metered Dose Nebulizer

Student's Name: ______________________________ Date: ____________

Objective: To instruct a patient in the correct use of a handheld nebulizer, a device that delivers a fine mist of medication, with or without the use of oxygen, to the respiratory tract, including the lungs.

Conditions: The student demonstrates the ability to instruct a patient in the correct use of a handheld nebulizer using the following equipment and supplies: handheld nebulizer containing medication ordered by the physician.

Time Requirements and Accuracy Standards: 10 minutes. Points assigned reflect importance of step to meeting objective: Important = (5) Essential = (10) Critical = (15). Automatic failure results if any of the **critical** tasks are omitted or performed incorrectly.

STANDARD PRECAUTIONS:

SKILLS ASSESSMENT CHECKLIST

Task Performed	Possible Points	TASKS
❑	5	Washes hands and assembles equipment.
❑	10	Identifies patient.
❑	15	Demonstrates the use of the equipment to the patient, then has the patient repeat the demonstration.
❑	5	Instructs the patient to exhale fully.
❑	10	Instructs the patient to hold the nebulizer upside down and close the mouth, lips, and teeth around the mouthpiece.
❑	10	Instructs the patient to tilt the head back, take a deep breath and at the same time push the bottle against the mouthpiece.
❑	10	Instructs the patient to continue to inhale until the lungs are full.
❑	5	Has patient remove the mouthpiece and slowly exhale.
❑	5	Repeats procedure if the physician has ordered more than one dose.
❑	5	Washes hands.
❑	15	Documents that patient is given written instructions for use and maintenance (clean the inhaler by rinsing mouthpiece in warm water) and that use of the nebulizer has been demonstrated.
❑	5	Completed the tasks within 10 minutes.

SKILLS COMPETENCY ASSESSMENT — continued

Procedure 13–28: Instructing Patient in Use of Metered Dose Nebulizer

Task Performed	Possible Points	TASKS
☐	15	Results obtained were accurate.

________	Earned	ADD POINTS OF TASKS CHECKED
115	Points	TOTAL POINTS POSSIBLE
________	SCORE	DETERMINE SCORE (divide points earned by total points possible, multiply results by 100)

Actual Student Time Needed to Complete Procedure: ____________

Student's Initials: ____________ Instructor's Initials: ____________ Grade: ____________

Suggestions for Improvement: ____

Evaluator's Name (print) ____

Evaluator's Signature ____

Comments ____

DOCUMENTATION

Chart the procedure in the patient's medical record.

Date: ____________________________

Charting: ____

____

____

____

Student's Initials: ________________

SKILLS COMPETENCY ASSESSMENT

Procedure 13–29: Assisting With Spirometry

Student's Name: ______________________________ Date: ____________

Objective: To prepare a patient for spirometry to obtain optimum test results.

Conditions: The student demonstrates the ability to prepare a patient for spirometry to obtain optimum test results using the following equipment and supplies: spirometer, disposable mouthpiece.

Time Requirements and Accuracy Standards: 10 minutes. Points assigned reflect importance of step to meeting objective: Important = (5) Essential = (10) Critical = (15). Automatic failure results if any of the **critical** tasks are omitted or performed incorrectly.

STANDARD PRECAUTIONS: 

SKILLS ASSESSMENT CHECKLIST

Task Performed	Possible Points	TASKS
❑	5	Washes hands and assembles equipment.
❑	15	Identifies the patient. Explains the parameters needed for successful completion of the test. • Instructs patient to refrain from the use of bronchodilators for 24 hours prior to test. • Explains that patient must inhale deeply and quickly and exhale quickly and forcibly until no air can be expelled. • Explains to the patient that maximum effort is required for accurate test results.
❑	15	Explains the procedure and equipment to the patient. • Allows the patient to breathe into the machine to become acquainted with the equipment. • Reinforces the importance of good posture during the process. • Explains that when blowing into the mouthpiece, the lips must seal tightly around it.
❑	5	Places the patient in a comfortable position (seated/standing).
❑	10	Instructs the patient not to bend at the waist when blowing into the mouthpiece.
❑	10	Reinforces the inhalation process (deep breaths to fill the lungs to maximum capacity).
❑	10	Instructs the patient to continue to blow into the mouthpiece until instructed to stop.
❑	5	Is supportive and encouraging throughout the test.
❑	5	Washes hands.
❑	5	Attends to patient's needs.

SKILLS COMPETENCY ASSESSMENT — continued

Procedure 13–29: Assisting with Spirometry

Task Performed	Possible Points	TASKS
❑	15	Places the test results on the patient's chart, after review by the physician.
❑	5	Completed the tasks within 10 minutes.
❑	15	Results obtained were accurate.

________	Earned	ADD POINTS OF TASKS CHECKED
120	Points	TOTAL POINTS POSSIBLE
________	SCORE	DETERMINE SCORE (divide points earned by total points possible, multiply results by 100)

Actual Student Time Needed to Complete Procedure: ____________

Student's Initials: ____________ Instructor's Initials: ____________ Grade: ____________

Suggestions for Improvement: ____

Evaluator's Name (print) ____

Evaluator's Signature ____

Comments ____

DOCUMENTATION

Chart the procedure in the patient's medical record.

Date: ______________________

Charting: ____

____

____

____

Student's Initials: ______________

SKILLS COMPETENCY ASSESSMENT

Procedure 13–30: Assisting With Plaster-of-Paris Cast Application

Student's Name: ______________________________ Date: ____________

Objective: To assist physician in cast application.

Conditions: The student demonstrates the ability to assist the physician in cast application using the following equipment and supplies: plaster bandage roll or synthetic tape, container of 75° F water, which is lined with plastic or cloth to catch loose plaster, water, stockinette (3-inch width for arms, 4-inch for leg casts), webril (sheet wadding), bandage, scissors, rubber gloves, sponge rubber for padding.

Time Requirements and Accuracy Standards: 15 minutes. Points assigned reflect importance of step to meeting objective: Important = (5) Essential = (10) Critical = (15). Automatic failure results if any of the **critical** tasks are omitted or performed incorrectly.

STANDARD PRECAUTIONS:

SKILLS ASSESSMENT CHECKLIST

Task Performed	Possible Points	TASKS
❑	5	Provides the patient with an explanation of the procedure.
❑	5	Answers any questions about the injury or cast application within the scope of the medical assistant's training.
❑	5	Washes hands and assembles the equipment and supplies.
❑	5	Positions the patient in a seated position or as required by the physician.
❑	5	Puts on gloves.
❑	10	Cleans and dries the area to be casted, as directed by the physician. Charts any areas of bruising, redness, or open areas.
❑	5	*Rationale:* Knows that appropriate documentation of skin condition is needed to assist in the evaluation of the extremity at a later time.
❑	10	Pads bony prominence with sponge rubber to protect from pressure.
❑	5	Provides the correct width of stockinette for the area on which cast is being applied.
❑	5	*Rationale:* Knows that if stockinette is too large it will form creases, creating possible injury to tissues.
❑	5	Provides physician with correct width of webril.
❑	5	*Rationale:* Knows that webril provides protection to the patient's skin preventing pressure sores, and that folds in the padding could lead to irritation of the skin.
❑	10	Places the bandage in the container of warm water for five seconds. Removes from water and gently squeezes to remove excess water. Does not wring.
❑	5	Assists with the application of cast material as requested by the physician.
❑	5	Reassures patient, as needed.

SKILLS COMPETENCY ASSESSMENT — continued

Procedure 13–30: Assisting With Plaster-of-Paris Cast Application

Task Performed	Possible Points	TASKS
❑	15	After cast application, reviews cast care instructions and provides written instructions for cast care and isometric exercises (if prescribed by the physician). Reinforces any precautions given by the physician. Instructs patient in how to cover cast when bathing. Provides patient with dietary information for bone healing.
❑	5	*Rationale:* Understands that reviewing possible complications with the patient enhances the immediate reporting of circulatory impairment and infection.
❑	5	Discards water down the sink drain, being cautious to keep plaster on the plastic or cloth. Discards plaster in trash receptacle.
❑	5	Clears work area. Removes gloves and washes hands.
❑	10	Schedules patient for next appointment to have cast checked.
❑	15	Documents the procedure, including skin condition prior to cast application.
❑	5	Completed the tasks within 15 minutes.
❑	15	Results obtained were accurate.

_______	Earned	ADD POINTS OF TASKS CHECKED
165	Points	TOTAL POINTS POSSIBLE
_______	SCORE	DETERMINE SCORE (divide points earned by total points possible, multiply results by 100)

Actual Student Time Needed to Complete Procedure: ____________

Student's Initials: ____________ Instructor's Initials: ____________ Grade: ____________

Suggestions for Improvement: ______________________________

Evaluator's Name (print) ______________________________

Evaluator's Signature ______________________________

Comments ______________________________

DOCUMENTATION

Chart the procedure in the patient's medical record.

Date: ____________________

Charting: ______________________________

____

____

Student's Initials: ____________

SKILLS COMPETENCY ASSESSMENT

Procedure 13–31: Assisting With Cast Removal

Student's Name: ______________________________ Date: __________

Objective: To assist the physician with the removal of a cast.

Conditions: The student demonstrates the ability to assist the physician with the removal of a cast using the following equipment and supplies: cast cutter, cast spreader, bandage scissors, bag for disposal of cast materials.

Time Requirements and Accuracy Standards: 10 minutes. Points assigned reflect importance of step to meeting objective: Important = (5) Essential = (10) Critical = (15). Automatic failure results if any of the **critical** tasks are omitted or performed incorrectly.

STANDARD PRECAUTIONS:

SKILLS ASSESSMENT CHECKLIST

Task Performed	Possible Points	TASKS
❑	5	Washes hands.
❑	10	Explains the cast removal process to the patient. Explains that the cutter vibrates and does not spin and that some pressure and warmth may be experienced.
❑	5	*Rationale:* Explaining procedure allays patient's fears about being cut with the blade.
❑	5	Reassures the patient that skin color and muscle tone will improve with therapy.
❑	5	Hands the physician the equipment, as requested.
❑	15	After procedure, provides patient with written instructions for post-care.
❑	5	Cleans equipment. Washes hands.
❑	15	Documents cast removal and appearance of body part from which cast was removed.
❑	5	Completed the tasks within 10 minutes.
❑	15	Results obtained were accurate.

_______	Earned	ADD POINTS OF TASKS CHECKED
85	Points	TOTAL POINTS POSSIBLE
_______	SCORE	DETERMINE SCORE (divide points earned by total points possible, multiply results by 100)

SKILLS COMPETENCY ASSESSMENT — continued

Procedure 13–31: Assisting With Cast Removal

Actual Student Time Needed to Complete Procedure: ____________

Student's Initials: ____________ Instructor's Initials: ____________ Grade: ____________

Suggestions for Improvement: ____

Evaluator's Name (print) ____

Evaluator's Signature ____

Comments ____

DOCUMENTATION

Chart the procedure in the patient's medical record.

Date:____________________

Charting: ____

____

____

____

Student's Initials:______________

SKILLS COMPETENCY ASSESSMENT

Procedure 13–32: Assisting the Physician During a Lumbar Puncture

Student's Name: ______________________________ Date: ____________

Objective: To assemble supplies and position the patient for removal of cerebrospinal fluid from the lumbar area, which will be sent to the laboratory for analysis.

Conditions: The student demonstrates the ability to assist the physician during a lumbar puncture using the following equipment and supplies: drape, xylocaine 1%–2%, sterile syringe and needle for anesthetic, sterile gloves, disposable sterile lumbar puncture tray to include skin antiseptic with applicator, Band-Aid, spinal puncture needle, three test tubes with corks or tops, drape, manometer, laboratory requisition, examination light.

Time Requirements and Accuracy Standards: 15 minutes. Points assigned reflect importance of step to meeting objective: Important = (5) Essential = (10) Critical = (15). Automatic failure results if any of the **critical** tasks are omitted or performed incorrectly.

STANDARD PRECAUTIONS:

SKILLS ASSESSMENT CHECKLIST

Task Performed	Possible Points	TASKS
❑	15	Reinforces physician's explanation of the procedure and answers questions. Reviews post-spinal tap instructions, including: • The patient should remain in a prone position for two to three hours to allow tissues to close over the puncture site and to minimize cerebrospinal fluid leakage. • Reinforce the need to increase fluid intake, as this helps replace fluid loss. • Report any severe headaches or alterations in neurological status (paralysis, numbness, tingling, and so on).
❑	15	Verifies that the patient has signed a consent form.
❑	5	Instructs the patient to empty the bladder and bowel.
❑	15	Washes hands and sets up sterile field for the physician.
❑	10	Cleans the puncture site with antiseptic soap and water. Rinses.
❑	10	Positions the patient in a lateral recumbent position with the back at the edge of the exam table and a small pillow under the head.
❑	5	*Rationale:* Understands that patient's alignment of the spine is best achieved in a horizontal position.
❑	5	Drapes patient for warmth and privacy.
❑	10	Has the patient draw the knees up to the abdomen and grasp onto knees, flexing chin on chest.

SKILLS COMPETENCY ASSESSMENT — continued

Procedure 13–32: Assisting the Physician During a Lumbar Puncture

Task Performed	Possible Points	TASKS
❑	5	*Rationale:* Understands that this position allows for easier needle insertion into the subarachnoid space of the spinal cord, because this position widens the space between the lumbar vertebrae.
❑	15	The physician will swab the puncture site with an antiseptic such as Betadine.
❑	5	The physician drapes the area with a fenestrated drape.
❑	15	Assists physician to aspirate anesthetic.
❑	10	Helps the patient maintain this position until the needle has reached the subarachnoid space.
❑	5	*Rationale:* Understands that patient movement could produce trauma to the spinal cord area.
❑	15	Reminds patient to breathe evenly, not to hold breath or talk, since this may interfere with the pressure reading.
❑	5	At the physician's direction, has the patient straighten the legs.
❑	5	*Rationale:* Understands that muscle tension can give false pressure reading.
❑	5	The physician will apply a Band-Aid to the puncture site after the procedure is completed. Assists patient into a prone position to rest for two to three hours, or as directed by the physician.
❑	5	Applies gloves. Caps specimens tightly. Labels samples with date and numbers CSF #1, #2, #3.
❑	5	Sends the specimen to the laboratory with the appropriate laboratory requisition. Stores in incubator.
❑	5	Cleans area using standard precautions. Removes gloves. Washes hands.
❑	10	Documents procedure in patient's chart, noting that specimen will be sent to a reference laboratory, and notes any patient problems or unusual occurrences.
❑	5	Completed the tasks within 15 minutes.
❑	15	Results obtained were accurate.

_______	Earned	ADD POINTS OF TASKS CHECKED
220	Points	TOTAL POINTS POSSIBLE
_______	SCORE	DETERMINE SCORE (divide points earned by total points possible, multiply results by 100)

Actual Student Time Needed to Complete Procedure: ______________

Student's Initials: ______________ Instructor's Initials: ______________ Grade: ______________

Suggestions for Improvement: ____

Evaluator's Name (print) ____

Evaluator's Signature ____

Comments ____

DOCUMENTATION

Chart the procedure in the patient's medical record.

Date: ______________________________

Charting: ____

____

____

____

Student's Initials: __________________

SKILLS COMPETENCY ASSESSMENT

Procedure 13–33: Assisting the Physician With a Neurological Screening Examination

Student's Name: ______________________________ Date: ____________

Objective: To determine a patient's neurological status.

Conditions: The student demonstrates the ability to assist in determining a patient's neurological status using the following equipment and supplies: percussion hammer, safety pin, material for odor identification, cotton ball, tuning fork, flashlight, tongue blade, ophthalmoscope.

Time Requirements and Accuracy Standards: 10 minutes. Points assigned reflect importance of step to meeting objective: Important = (5) Essential = (10) Critical = (15). Automatic failure results if any of the **critical** tasks are omitted or performed incorrectly.

STANDARD PRECAUTIONS:

SKILLS ASSESSMENT CHECKLIST

Task Performed	Possible Points	TASKS
❑	5	Washes hands and assembles equipment.
❑	15	Identifies patient. Informs the patient that the purpose of the exam is to assess the response to pain and touch reflexes and other neurological functions. Explains that the physician will use several supplies to test the function of each cranial nerve and to test the reflexes and coordination of the patient.
❑	15	Performs a mental status examination when taking the patient's medical history by observing the following: when taking patient's history, pays special attention to level of awareness, memory, cognition, and mood; notes if behavior is appropriate for the circumstances when the patient answers questions during the history-taking.
❑	10	The physician will evaluate the cranial nerve functions by using the results of the visual acuity tests, as well as results of other tests.
❑	5	Assists the patient as needed during the exam.
❑	5	Cleans equipment per standard precautions and washes hands.
❑	10	Documents patient problems, such as disorientation, confusion, or forgetfulness that are evident when taking the patient's history.
❑	5	Completed the tasks within 10 minutes.

Task Performed	Possible Points	TASKS
❑	15	Results obtained were accurate.

________	Earned	ADD POINTS OF TASKS CHECKED
85	Points	TOTAL POINTS POSSIBLE
________	SCORE	DETERMINE SCORE (divide points earned by total points possible, multiply results by 100)

Actual Student Time Needed to Complete Procedure: ____________

Student's Initials: ____________ Instructor's Initials: ____________ Grade: ____________

Suggestions for Improvement: ____________

Evaluator's Name (print) ____________

Evaluator's Signature ____________

Comments ____________

DOCUMENTATION

Chart the procedure in the patient's medical record.

Date: ____________

Charting: ____________

____

____

____

Student's Initials: ____________

EVALUATION OF CHAPTER KNOWLEDGE

How has your instructor evaluated the knowledge you have achieved?

Knowledge	Instructor Evaluation *Good*	*Average*	*Poor*
Describes pediatric care, including measuring height, weight, head, chest circumference, and vital signs	_____	_____	_____
Lists supplies needed for a gynecological examination with and without a Pap test	_____	_____	_____
Discusses the importance of self-breast and self-testicular examinations and describes how each is performed	_____	_____	_____
Describes how to perform urinary catheterization on a female patient	_____	_____	_____
States proper protocol when collecting urine for drug screening	_____	_____	_____
Describes patient preparation for occult blood testing	_____	_____	_____
Discusses patient instructions for the upper GI series, a barium enema, and a cholescystogram	_____	_____	_____
Differentiates between an instillation and an irrigation	_____	_____	_____
Discusses the different types of visual acuity tests and how to use each appropriately	_____	_____	_____
Explains the medical assistant's role when assisting with audiometry	_____	_____	_____
Describes how to perform a nasal irrigation	_____	_____	_____
Describes the proper use of a metered dose nebulizer	_____	_____	_____
Discusses the role of the medical assistant during spirometry	_____	_____	_____
Explains the medical assistant's role in cast application and cast removal and the guidelines for cast care	_____	_____	_____
Lists items required by the physician for a neurological exam and explains the medical assistant's role in assisting in the exam	_____	_____	_____
Identifies patient education information for sputum collections	_____	_____	_____
Explains oxygen administration using a nasal cannula	_____	_____	_____
Applies principles of aseptic technique and observes standard precautions for infection control	_____	_____	_____
Properly prepares patients for procedures	_____	_____	_____
Performs selected tests that assist the physician with diagnosis and treatment	_____	_____	_____
Properly prepares and administers medications as directed by the physician	_____	_____	_____
Maintains medical records and documents accurately	_____	_____	_____
Exhibits therapeutic communications skills in interaction with patients and attends to patients' emotional needs	_____	_____	_____
Communicates at the level proper for the receiver's ability to understand	_____	_____	_____

Student's Initials: ______ Instructor's Initials: ______

Grade: _______

Electrocardiography

PERFORMANCE OBJECTIVES

Electrocardiography is a noninvasive, safe, and painless procedure many physicians include as part of a complete physical examination. An electrocardiogram (ECG) measures the amount of electrical activity produced by the heart and the time it takes for the electrical impulses to travel through the heart during each heartbeat. The ECG is used in conjunction with other laboratory and diagnostic tests to assess total cardiac health. During an electrocardiogram, the medical assistant is responsible for patient preparation; patient education; operation of the electrocardiograph; elimination of artifacts; mounting, labeling, and placing the ECG reading in the patient's medical record; and proper maintenance and care of the equipment. It is important that the medical assistant perform electrocardiograms skillfully and accurately.

EXERCISES AND ACTIVITIES

Vocabulary Builder

Across

2. A series of X-rays of a blood vessel(s) following injection of a radiopaque substance.
5. The part of the heart cycle in which the heart is in contraction.
6. The flat, horizontal line that separates the various waves of the ECG cycle.
10. Chemical substance that enhances the conduction of electrical activity.
11. Conversion of a pathological cardiac rhythm (arrhythmia) to normal sinus rhythm.
12. Local and temporary lack of blood to an organ or a part due to obstruction of circulation.
16. Procedure used to obtain cardiac blood samples, detect abnormalities, and determine intracardiac pressure.
23. Heated slender wire of the electrocardiograph that melts the wax off the ECG paper during the recording.
24. Graphic record usually of an event that changes with time, as with the electrical activity of the heart.

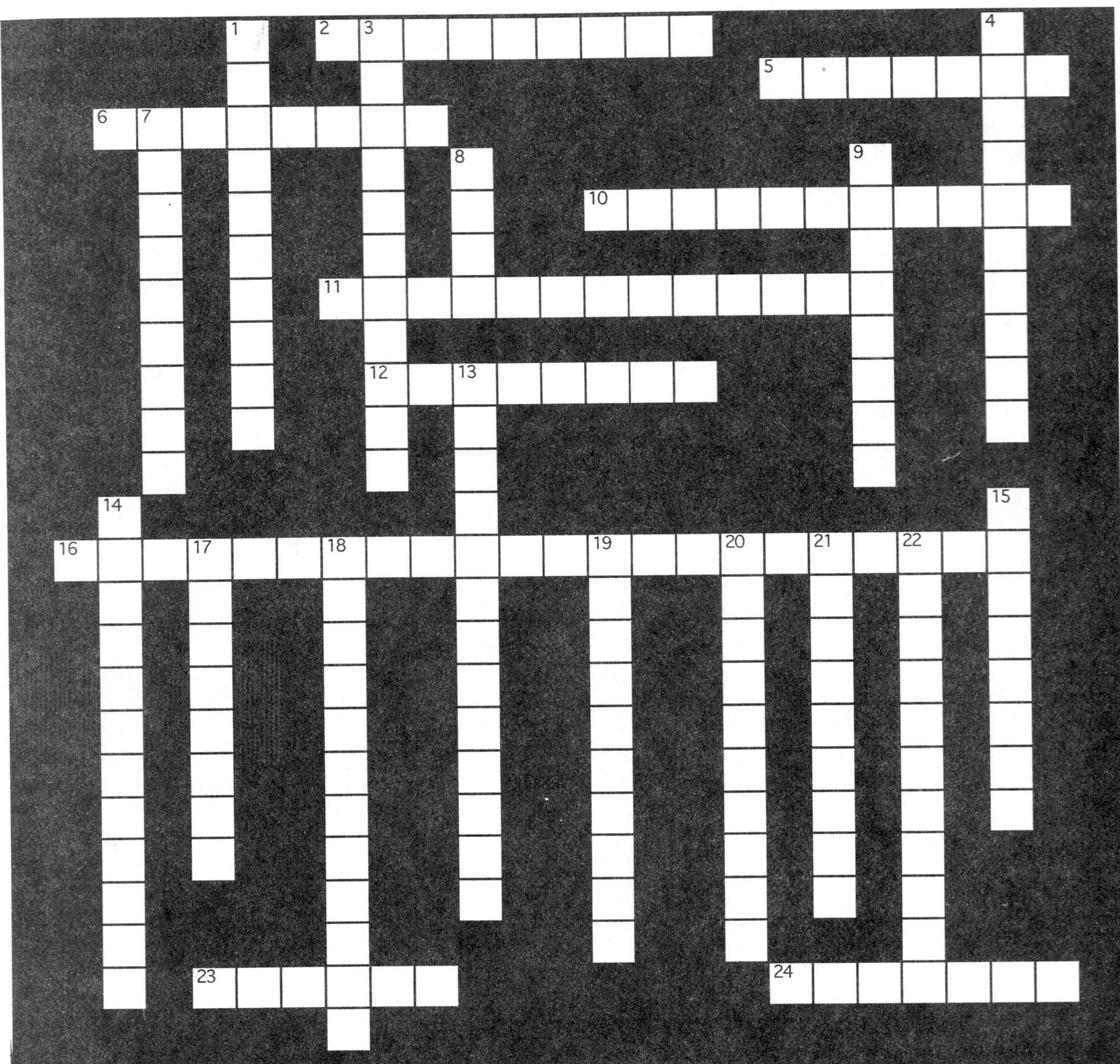

Down

1. Pertaining to the area on the anterior surface of the body overlying the heart.
3. Procedures that do not require entering the body or puncturing the skin.
4. Sensor used to conduct electricity from the body to the electrocardiograph.
7. To add or increase.
8. An electrocardiograph record. Consists of limb and chest.
9. Process of applying in sequence a portion of each of the twelve leads of the ECG recording onto a document placed in the patient's chart.
13. Applications of electric current to the heart, directly or indirectly, to alter a disturbance in cardiac rhythm.
14. Mechanism in the electrocardiograph that changes the voltage into a mechanical motion for recording purposes.

15. Having or pertaining to a one-pole process.
17. The normal period in the cardiac cycle during which the myocardial fibers lengthen, the heart dilates, and the cavities fill with blood.
18. One complete heartbeat.
19. During an ultrasound procedure, this device picks up echoes and converts them to electrical energy.
20. An area of tissue in an organ or a part that becomes necrotic following cessation of blood supply.
21. Amount, extent, size, abundance, or fullness.
22. Having equal electrical potentials; represented on the ECG as the baseline.

Learning Review

1. List five reasons why electrocardiography is performed.

(1) ____________________

(2) ____________________

(3) ____________________

(4) ____________________

(5) ____________________

2. A. The first three leads recorded on a standard ECG are Lead I, Lead II, and Lead III. These are ____________________ leads because each of them uses two limb electrodes that record simultaneously.

For each lead, what electrical activity of the heart is recorded? Draw it on each figure.

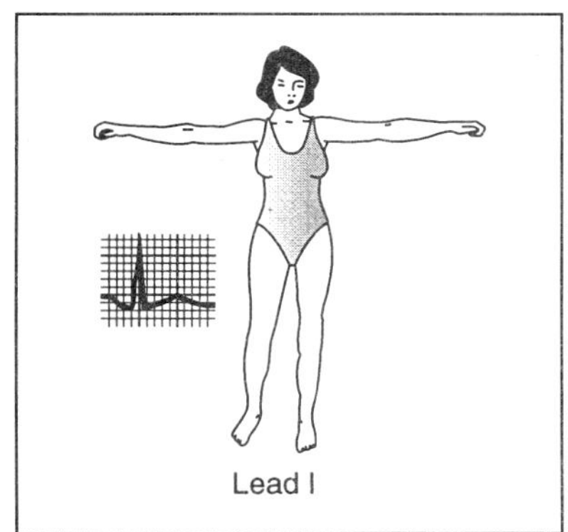

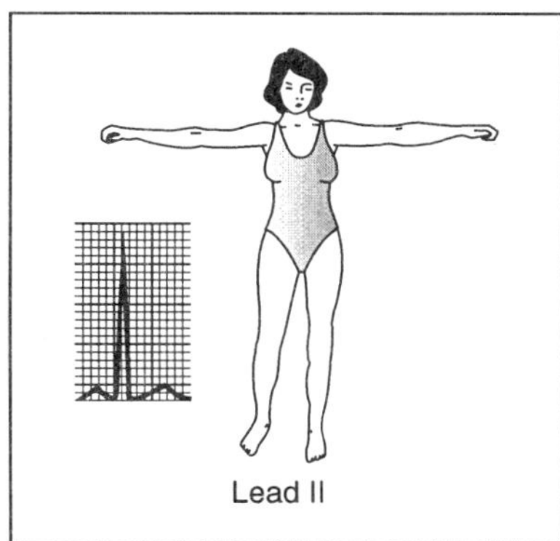

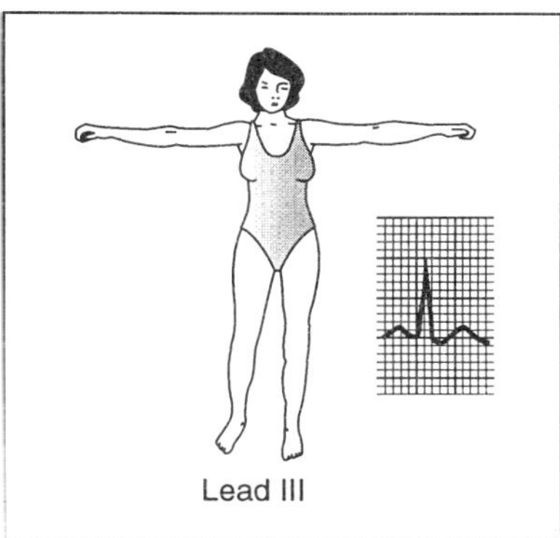

Lead I records electrical activity between the ____________ and ____________.

Lead II records electrical activity between the ____________ and ____________.

Lead III records electrical activity between the ____________ and ____________.

B. The next group of leads recorded on a standard ECG are augmented leads, designated, aVR, aVL, and aVF. These are ____________________ leads.

For each lead, what electrical activity of the heart is recorded? Draw it on each figure.

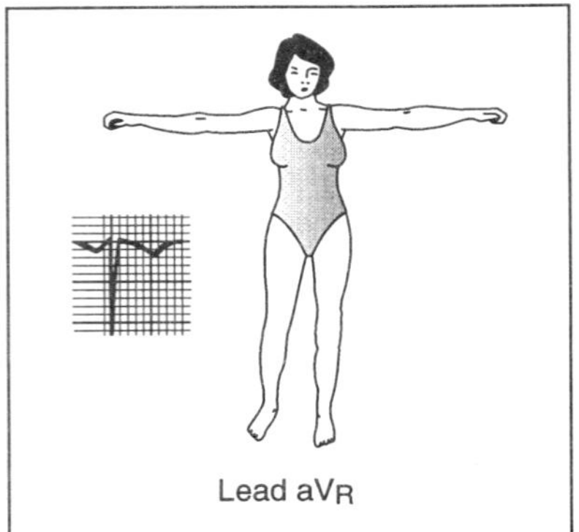
Lead aVR

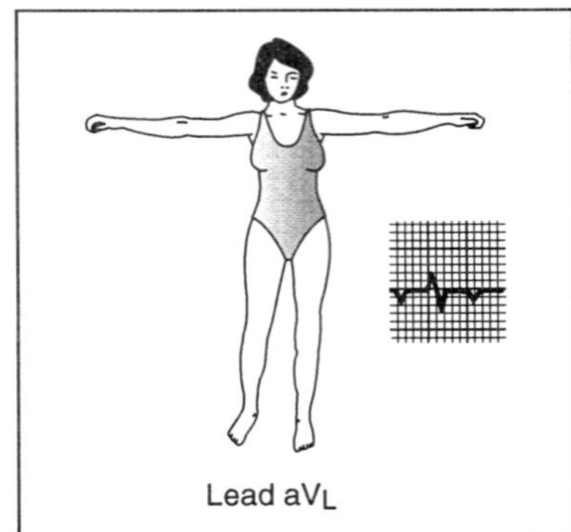
Lead aVL

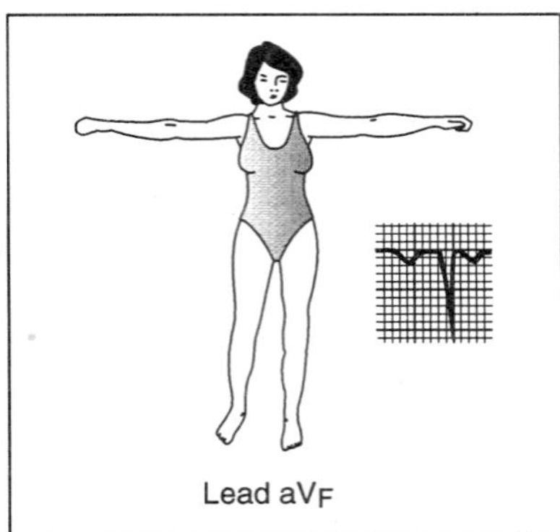
Lead aVF

Lead aVR records electrical activity from ______________________________.

Lead aVL records electrical activity from ______________________________.

Lead aVF records electrical activity from ______________________________.

C. The remaining six leads of the standard 12-lead ECG are the chest leads or ______________ leads. These leads are ________________ in polarity.

For these leads, what electrical activity of the heart is recorded? Where are the leads placed on the body?

Chest leads record the heart's electrical impulse from

____

____

____

____

3. Artifacts are unusual and unwanted activity in the ECG tracing not caused by the electrical activity of the heart. Match each circumstance below to the artifact ECG tracing it would produce and identify the type of artifact in the space provided.
   A. A broken patient cable or lead wire has become detached from an electrode.
   B. The patient sings to himself or herself during the ECG procedure.
   C. The patient uses body lotion.
   D. The lead wires are crossed and do not follow the patient's body contour.

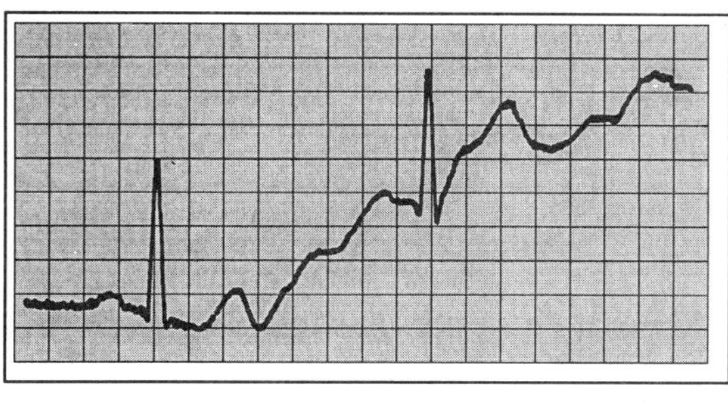

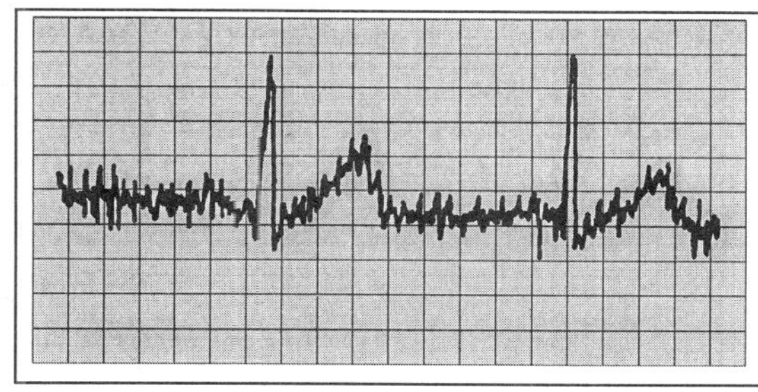

_____1. Type of artifact:

____

_____2. Type of artifact:

____

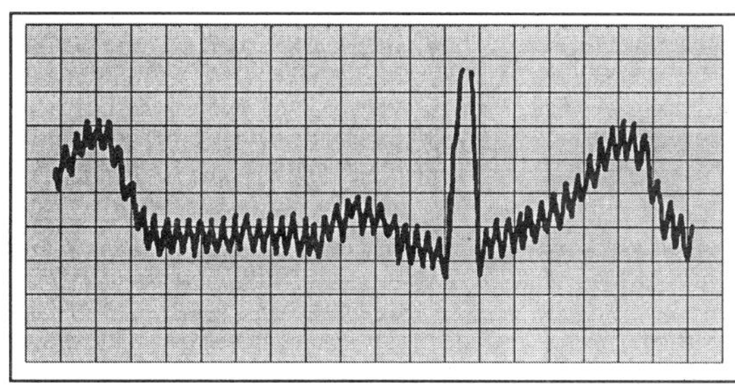

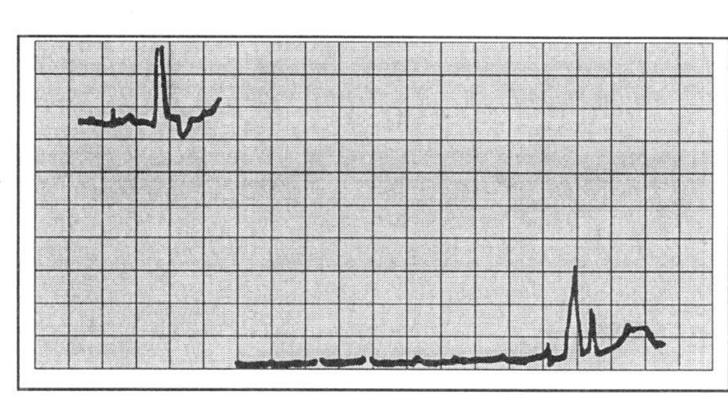

_____3. Type of artifact:

____

_____4. Type of artifact:

____

Investigation Activity

Myocardial infarctions (heart attacks) are the number one cause of death in the United States today. Changes in lifestyle and diet can help protect us from the risk of cardiovascular disease. As patient educators, medical assistants can encourage patients to develop heart-healthy habits.

A. Designate student volunteers to contact the American Heart Association, the National Institutes of Health, The American Association of Retired Persons, and The American Medical Association for information about the risk of heart disease and preventive measures individuals can take. Ask for information about any research studies that have been conducted with regard to measures that promote heart health. What are the results of the studies?

B. Contact a traditional insurance carrier and an HMO or managed care organization to ask about coverage offered for preventive health measures such as cardiovascular exercise programs or techniques to help people stop smoking and ask them to send literature on any cardiovascular health programs or studies in which they are involved.

C. Contact local organizations, such as a local senior citizen's center, health club, hospital, or anti-smoking group for information about cardiovascular health programs available to individuals on a community level.

Bring the information to class; compare and discuss the literature and make a class list of the most effective preventive measures patients can follow to prevent heart disease.

CASE STUDY

Jim Marshall, a prominent local architect in his late thirties, stays in good physical condition, works out regularly at the gym, and maintains a low-fat, low-cholesterol, low-sodium diet. Aggressive and ambitious, Jim enjoys pushing his mind and body to the limit. His favorite sports are skiing and sailing. At work, Jim is a perfectionist who puts in long hours and demands the same of his employees. Lately, though, Jim is more aware of the high-stress lifestyle he is leading and is worried about his family history of heart failure and diabetes. During periods of high physical exertion, Jim experiences mild chest pain and palpitations. Dr. Lewis prescribes an exercise tolerance test for Jim.

Discuss the following:

1. What is an exercise tolerance test? How is it performed?
2. Under what conditions would the test be discontinued?
3. At the conclusion of the test, what patient care is given? What special instructions for home care should the patient observe?
4. What is the proper insurance coding for the patient's exercise tolerance test or cardiovascular stress test? Is the code a diagnosis or procedures code?

SUPPLEMENTARY RESOURCES

Study Guide Disk: Additional practice exercises for this chapter are available on the study guide disk found in the back of the textbook.

Medical Assisting Videos: Appropriate content is available on Delmar's Medical Assisting Videos, 2nd ed., for the following topics:

Tape 15: Run an Electrocardiogram and Record the Results
Mounting and ECG Tracing
ECG Artifacts and Interference
Holter Monitor

SKILLS COMPETENCY ASSESSMENT

Procedure 14–1: Perform Twelve-Lead Electrocardiogram, Single Channel

Student's Name: ______________________________ Date: ____________

Objective: To perform a twelve-lead electrocardiogram, single channel.

Conditions: The student demonstrates the ability to obtain an accurate, graphic, artifact-free reading of the electrical activity of the patient's heart so that the physician may identify arrhythmias; estimate damage caused by MI; assess effects of cardiac medication; determine if electrolyte imbalance is present; identify cardiac ischemia; and determine the effects of hypertension or other disorders on the heart. The student uses the following equipment and supplies: examination or ECG table with pillow and sheet or blanket, patient gown, single-channel electrocardiograph with patient cable wires, electrolyte (gel, lotion, paste, or presaturated pads), ECG tracing paper, metal electrodes, rubber straps, gauze squares, and a mounting form.

Time Requirements and Accuracy Standards: 15 minutes. Points assigned reflect importance of step to meeting objective: Important = (5) Essential = (10) Critical = (15). Automatic failure results if any of the **critical** tasks are omitted or performed incorrectly.

STANDARD PRECAUTIONS:

SKILLS ASSESSMENT CHECKLIST

Task Performed	Possible Points	TASKS
❑	5	Performs tracing in a quiet, warm, and comfortable room away from electrical equipment that may cause artifacts.
❑	5	*Rationale:* Patient is less apprehensive in a quiet atmosphere. Alternating current (AC) interference is minimized when ECG is performed away from electrical equipment.
❑	10	Washes hands, gathers equipment, identifies the patient, and explains the procedure to the patient.
❑	5	*Rationale:* Following these universal steps minimizes transmission of microorganisms and reassures patient.
❑	5	Has the patient remove clothing from the waist up and uncover lower legs (stockings must be removed but socks may be worn); provides a sheet or blanket for privacy and warmth. Places the patient in a supine position on the examination table with arms and legs supported.
❑	5	*Rationale:* All four limbs and chest must be uncovered for proper electrode placement. Electrodes must be placed on bare skin for optimum conductivity of electricity.
❑	5	Explains that the procedure is painless and explains why it is necessary not to move or talk during the procedure.
❑	5	*Rationale:* Patient cooperation ensures good quality tracing.

SKILLS COMPETENCY ASSESSMENT — continued

Procedure 14–1: Perform Twelve-Lead Electrocardiogram, Single Channel

Task Performed	Possible Points	TASKS
❑	10	Places the electrocardiograph with the power cord pointing away from the patient. Does not allow the cable to go underneath the table.
❑	5	*Rationale:* This helps reduce AC interference.
❑	15	Applies the limb electrodes by first connecting the rubber straps to the tabs on the electrodes; applies a pea-size dab of electrolyte to the electrode; applies the electrodes to the fleshy parts of the four limbs; rubs the electrolytes into the patient's skin; makes sure the lead connectors of the electrodes are pointing toward the feet; pulls the rubber straps around the limb until they just meet, then pulls tighter one more hole and secures.
❑	5	*Rationale:* A more stable connection with the lead wires is possible when the lead connectors point to the feet. Electrolyte rubbed into the patient's skin helps ensure a good contact between the electrode and the skin. Straps applied too tightly or too loosely can cause artifacts. By applying electrodes to the fleshy part of the limbs, artifacts are minimized.
❑	10	Welch cup chest electrode • Applies electrolyte to chest position. Rubs the edge of each cup in the electrolyte, securing the cups in position by squeezing the bulb end of the cup to create suction on the skin of the chest wall.
❑	15	Welch cup chest electrode with a single channel non-automatic machine • Places chest lead V-1 in position, along with the first 6 leads: I, II, III, aVR, aVL, and aVF, and records. • Turns machine to "AMP OFF" and positions next V lead. Adjusts stylus. Turns machine to "AMP ON" and records six to eight inches of the V lead. Turns machine to "AMP OFF." • Repeats procedure until each V lead is manually positioned and recorded.
❑	10	Tightly connects the lead wires to the electrodes; makes sure to connect the correct lead wires to the correct electrodes; makes sure the lead wires follow the patient's body contour.
❑	5	*Rationale:* Following body contour minimizes artifacts.
❑	5	Makes sure the patient cable is supported either on the table or the patient's abdomen; plugs the patient cable into the electrocardiograph.
❑	5	Turns instrument to ON position.

Task Performed	Possible Points	TASKS
❑	10	Makes sure the lead selector switch is on STD; centers the stylus; makes sure the record switch is on Run. Checks the standardization for the instrument by quickly pressing the standardization button; makes sure the standardization mark is 10 mm or 10 small squares high.
❑	5	*Rationale:* Standardization ensures a dependable and accurate tracing.
❑	15	Centers the stylus and runs about four to five inches of each lead I, II, and III by placing the record switch on Run and turning the lead selector switch appropriately. • Makes sure the stylus and recording are near the center of the paper while recording. Adjusts using position control knob, if necessary. • Watches for artifacts and corrects if present. • Determines if a change in standard or stylus position is needed by observing the amplitude of the R wave.
❑	10	Continues with leads aVR, aVL, aVF, and records about four to five inches of each lead by turning the lead selector to the appropriate position.
❑	15	Records six to eight complexes of each of the V leads by turning the lead selector control to the appropriate position.
❑	10	Places another standardization at the end of the tracing by putting the lead selector on STD and depressing the button; runs the tracing through the instrument and turns the machine to the OFF position; removes the tracing from the instrument and immediately labels with patient's name, date, and time of day; initials; unplugs power cord.
❑	5	Disconnects the lead wires and removes the rubber straps and electrodes from the patient.
❑	5	Cleans patient's skin to remove paste or gel electrolyte.
❑	5	Assists patient as needed.
❑	5	Provides physician with uncut tracing.
❑	5	Cleans and returns equipment per OSHA guidelines.
❑	5	Washes hands.
❑	5	Documents procedure.
❑	5	Cuts and mounts the tracing, remembering to handle it correctly; labels appropriately and places in patient's record.
❑	5	Completed the tasks within 15 minutes.

SKILLS COMPETENCY ASSESSMENT — continued

Procedure 14–1: Perform Twelve-Lead Electrocardiogram, Single Channel

Task Performed	Possible Points	TASKS
❑	15	Results obtained were accurate.

________	Earned	ADD POINTS OF TASKS CHECKED
225	Points	TOTAL POINTS POSSIBLE
________	SCORE	DETERMINE SCORE (divide points earned by total points possible, multiply results by 100)

Actual Student Time Needed to Complete Procedure: ____________

Student's Initials: ____________ Instructor's Initials: ____________ Grade: ____________

Suggestions for Improvement: ____

Evaluator's Name (print) ____

Evaluator's Signature ____

Comments ____

DOCUMENTATION

Chart the procedure in the patient's medical record.

Date: ______________________

Charting: ____

____

____

Student's Initials: ________________

SKILLS COMPETENCY ASSESSMENT

Procedure 14–2: Perform Twelve-Lead Electrocardiogram, Three Channel

Student's Name: ______________________________ Date: ____________

Objective: To perform a twelve-lead electrocardiogram, three channel

Conditions: The student demonstrate the ability to obtain an accurate, graphic, artifact-free reading of the electrical activity of the patient's heart so that the physician may identify arrhythmias, estimate damage caused by MI, assess effects of cardiac medication, determine if electrolyte imbalance is present, identify cardiac ischemia, and determine the effects of hypertension on or other disorders of the heart. The student uses the following equipment and supplies: examination or ECG table with pillow and sheet or blanket, patient gown, three-channel automatic electrocardiograph with patient cable wires, disposable electrodes, ECG tracing paper, gauze squares, and mounting form.

Time Requirements and Accuracy Standards: 10 minutes. Points assigned reflect importance of step to meeting objective: Important = (5) Essential = (10) Critical = (15). Automatic failure results if any of the **critical** tasks are omitted or performed incorrectly.

STANDARD PRECAUTIONS:

SKILLS ASSESSMENT CHECKLIST

Task Performed	Possible Points	TASKS
❑	10	Washes hands; gathers equipment; identifies patient and explains procedure.
❑	5	Has patient remove clothing from the waist up and uncover lower legs. Places patient in supine position on examination table with arms and legs supported.
❑	5	Explains that procedure is painless and why the patient must not talk or move during the procedure. Places electrocardiograph appropriately.
❑	10	Prepares patient's skin for disposable electrode attachment; if patient's skin is oily, wipes electrode area with alcohol and lets dry.
❑	15	Applies electrodes firmly to fleshy parts of limbs; points tabs of electrodes attached to arms in a downward position, tears off electrodes attached to legs in an upward position.
❑	5	*Rationale:* Tab position allows for better connection and keeps lead wire pulling to a minimum.
❑	10	Locates chest sites and applies electrodes with tabs pointing in a downward position.
❑	10	Connects lead wires to the electrodes with alligator clips.
❑	10	Plugs patient cable into machine; supports patient cable to avoid pulling or tangling.
❑	10	Turns on the ECG; enters patient data by keying it into machine.
❑	5	Presses AUTO for automatic and runs the ECG to obtain the tracing; watches for artifacts and takes the appropriate steps to eliminate them, should they occur.
❑	5	Disconnects the lead wires and removes the electrodes from the patient; disposes of the electrodes.

SKILLS COMPETENCY ASSESSMENT — continued

Procedure 14–2: Perform Twelve-Lead Electrocardiogram, Three Channel

Task Performed	Possible Points	TASKS
❑	5	Assists patient as needed.
❑	5	Provides physician with uncut tracing.
❑	5	Cleans and returns equipment per OSHA guidelines.
❑	5	Washes hands.
❑	5	Documents procedure.
❑	15	Cuts and mounts the tracing, remembering to handle carefully. Labels appropriately and places in patient's record.
❑	5	Completed the tasks within 10 minutes.
❑	15	Results obtained were accurate.
	_______	Earned ADD POINTS OF TASKS CHECKED
	160	Points TOTAL POINTS POSSIBLE
	_______	SCORE DETERMINE SCORE (divide points earned by total points possible, multiply results by 100)

Actual Student Time Needed to Complete Procedure: ____________

Student's Initials: ____________ Instructor's Initials: ____________ Grade: ____________

Suggestions for Improvement: ________________________________

Evaluator's Name (print) ________________________________

Evaluator's Signature ________________________________

Comments ________________________________

DOCUMENTATION

Chart the procedure in the patient's medical record.

Date:____________________

Charting: ________________________________

____

____

Student's Initials:________________

SKILLS COMPETENCY ASSESSMENT

Procedure 14–3: Perform Holter Monitor Application

Student's Name: ______________________________ Date: ____________

Objective: To perform a Holter monitor application.

Conditions: The student demonstrates the ability to perform a Holter monitor application using the following equipment and supplies: Holter monitor, patient activity diary, blank magnetic tape, disposable electrodes, razor, alcohol swabs, gauze, tape, carrying case, belt or shoulder strap.

Time Requirements and Accuracy Standards: 15 minutes. Points assigned reflect importance of step to meeting objective: Important = (5) Essential = (10) Critical = (15). Automatic failure results if any of the **critical** tasks are omitted or performed incorrectly.

STANDARD PRECAUTIONS:

SKILLS ASSESSMENT CHECKLIST

Task Performed	Possible Points	TASKS
❑	5	Washes hands and assembles equipment.
❑	10	Prepares the equipment by removing old (used) battery from the monitor and replacing it with a new battery; inserts a blank magnetic tape into the monitor.
❑	5	*Rationale:* Installing a new battery each 24-hour period will ensure that the monitor will function because it will have sufficient power.
❑	5	Washes hands.
❑	10	Identifies the patient and explains the procedure.
❑	5	*Rationale:* Adherence to patient guidelines helps ensure an accurate tracing.
❑	5	Has patient remove clothing from the waist up.
❑	5	Has patient sit on the examination table or chair.
❑	5	*Rationale:* This allows for patient comfort and relaxation and for the medical assistant to appropriately place the electrodes.
❑	15	Locates the correct electrode placement on the chest wall; prepares the skin in the following way: • Dry shaves the patient's chest at each electrode site, if chest is hairy. • Rubs the shaved area with an alcohol swab; lets area dry. • Abrades the skin slightly with a dry 4 × 4 gauze. Areas should be red.
❑	5	*Rationale:* Shaved site and abraded skin help electrodes adhere better to the skin and facilitate easier removal.

SKILLS COMPETENCY ASSESSMENT — continued

Procedure 14-3: Perform Holter Monitor Application

Task Performed	Possible Points	TASKS
❑	5	Takes the electrodes from the package and peels away the backing from one of them; continues to remove electrodes one by one and attach correctly.
❑	10	Applies adhesive-backed electrodes to the appropriate sites by applying firm pressure at the center of the electrode and moving outward toward the edges; runs fingers along the outer rim to ensure attachment. Avoids moving from one side of electrode to the other to keep gel from being forced out, causing interference.
❑	5	*Rationale:* Firmly attached electrodes ensure a good-quality tracing.
❑	5	Attaches the lead wires to the electrodes; connects them to the patient cable.
❑	5	Secures each electrode with adhesive tape.
❑	5	*Rationale:* The tape secures the electrodes by reducing the tugging and pulling on them.
❑	10	Plugs the monitor into an electrocardiograph with the test cable; runs a baseline tracing.
❑	5	*Rationale:* Running a baseline tracing will validate proper setup of electrodes and confirm that there is no malfunction of the leads or cable.
❑	5	Places the electrode cable so it extends from between the buttons of the patient's shirt or from below the bottom of the shirt.
❑	15	Places the recorder into its carrying case and either attaches it to the patient's belt or over the patient's shoulder; makes sure there is no pulling on the lead wires.
❑	5	*Rationale:* Pulling on electrodes could cause them to become detached.
❑	10	Plugs the electrode cable into the monitor; records the starting time in the patient's activity log.
❑	5	*Rationale:* The beginning time is noted is order to correlate cardiac activity with the patient's activity log.
❑	15	Gives the activity log to the patient, being certain the patient information is completed.
❑	5	*Rationale:* The activity log helps correlate cardiac activity with the patient's symptoms.
❑	5	Informs the patient what time the following day the monitor will be removed; reminds the patient to bring along the activity log.
❑	5	Washes hands.
❑	5	Documents the procedure in the patient's record.
❑	5	Completed the tasks within 15 minutes.

Task Performed	Possible Points	TASKS
☐	15	Results obtained were accurate.

______	Earned	ADD POINTS OF TASKS CHECKED
220	Points	TOTAL POINTS POSSIBLE
______	SCORE	DETERMINE SCORE (divide points earned by total points possible, multiply results by 100)

Actual Student Time Needed to Complete Procedure: ______

Student's Initials: ______ Instructor's Initials: ______ Grade: ______

Suggestions for Improvement: ______

Evaluator's Name (print) ______

Evaluator's Signature ______

Comments ______

DOCUMENTATION

Chart the procedure in the patient's medical record.

Date: ______

Charting: ______

______

______

Student's Initials: ______

EVALUATION OF CHAPTER KNOWLEDGE

How has your instructor evaluated the knowledge you have achieved?

Knowledge	**Instructor Evaluation** *Good*	*Average*	*Poor*
Follows the circulation of blood through the heart, starting at the vena cava	_____	_____	_____
Describes the electrical conduction system of the heart	_____	_____	_____
Identifies reasons a patient requires an electrocardiogram	_____	_____	_____
Identifies the various positive and negative deflections and describes what each represents in the cardiac cycle	_____	_____	_____
Explains the purpose of standardization of the electrocardiograph	_____	_____	_____
Identifies the twelve leads of an ECG and describes what area of the heart each lead represents	_____	_____	_____
States the function of ECG graph paper, electrodes (sensors), and electrolyte	_____	_____	_____
Describes various types of ECGs and describes their capabilities	_____	_____	_____
Explains each type of artifact and how each can be eliminated	_____	_____	_____
Names and describes the purposes of the various cardiac diagnostic tests	_____	_____	_____
Identifies the placement of Holter monitor electrodes	_____	_____	_____
Describes the reason for a patient activity diary during ambulatory cardiography	_____	_____	_____
Identifies common arrhythmias and explains the causes of each	_____	_____	_____
Explains how to calculate heart rates from an ECG tracing	_____	_____	_____
Identifies a common coding system used to code each lead on an ECG tracing	_____	_____	_____
Describes the procedure for mounting an ECG tracing	_____	_____	_____
Documents accurately	_____	_____	_____
Prepares patient for procedures and attends to his or her emotional needs	_____	_____	_____

Student's Initials: ______ Instructor's Initials: ______

Grade: ________

Introduction to the Medical Laboratory

PERFORMANCE OBJECTIVES

Along with clinical laboratory personnel, medical assistants perform a key role in laboratory testing. Medical assistants may be responsible for patient preparation and instruction, obtaining specimens, and testing or sending specimens to a laboratory. It is important that medical assistants have a knowledge of laboratory procedures, perform quality controls, and observe standard precautions for infection control to ensure accurate testing and to safeguard the health of patients and health care personnel. When collecting, processing, or analyzing specimens, medical assistants are aiding in the physician's diagnosis and treatment of conditions and illnesses. Attention to detail and accuracy are essential skills for the medical assistant to possess in performing duties in the medical laboratory.

EXERCISES AND ACTIVITIES

Vocabulary Builder

A. *Insert the proper key vocabulary terms into the sentences below. Each sentence describes a situation you might find in a physician's office laboratory, or in a reference laboratory.*

assay	normal flora	baseline
objective	biopsy	glucose
quantitative tests	condenser	serum
diagnosis	invasive	clinical diagnosis
profile	control test	diaphragm
reagents	qualitative tests	requisition
differential diagnosis	electrolytes	asymptomatic

1. Wanda Slawson, CMA, is examining a specimen in the lab using a compound microscope. The ____________________ is the lense system closest to the specimen she is viewing.

2. Dr. Mark Woo orders laboratory tests for a female emergency patient suffering severe abdominal cramps to make a ______________________ that will distinguish between a diagnoses of appendicitis or an ovarian cyst.
3. Ralph Samson receives a job offer from a construction company that requires all employees to be tested for misuse or abuse of legal or illegal drugs before they can work on the site. Bruce Goldman, CMA, performs Ralph's blood test under the direction of Dr. Whitney; his test comes back clean. The results of Ralph's test can be used in the future as a ______________________ measurement, a record of healthy normal results.
4. Dr. King needs a red blood cell count, a white blood cell count, and a platelet count for Maria Jover. Joe Guerrero, CMA, performs a venipuncture on Maria and sends a tube of her blood to the lab, along with a written ______________________ containing specific information and instructions about what tests to perform on the specimens.
5. Bruce Goldman, CMA, is examining a specimen under a compound microscope. Because he is having difficulty seeing clearly, Bruce opens the microscope's______________________ to increase the amount of light on the specimen.
6. Dr. Lewis asks Audrey Jones, CMA, to send a tube of Herb Fowler's blood to the laboratory for analysis. Dr. Lewis wants to determine the constituents and relative proportion of each of the enzymes in Herb's serum; this type of analysis is called an ______________________.
7. Jim Marshall comes to see Dr. Lewis complaining that he has been constantly tired for the past two or three months. Because Jim's symptoms are so vague, Dr. Lewis orders a blood ______________________ to help narrow the diagnosis possibilities.
8. Bruce Goldman, CMA, always follows standard precautions and washes his hands before touching a patient. Although everyone's body contains many natural microorganisms, called ______________________, aseptic handwashing lessens the potential for exposure to or transmission of pathogens.
9. Hematology laboratories count the white blood cells (WBC) or red blood cells (RBC) in a sample of a patient's blood. In general, these type of counting tests are known as ______________________.
10. As a method of quality control, a ______________________ sample is tested along with a patient's sample as a method of ensuring the accuracy of test results.
11. Joe Guerrero, CMA, asks Abigail Johnson, whom he knows is diagnosed with diabetes mellitus, whether she regularly tests her blood at home to measure her ______________________ level.
12. The hematology laboratory performs tests that measure characteristics of blood such as size, shape, and maturity of cells. These types of tests are known in general as______________________.
13. Histology is the study of tissue samples to determine disease. In most cases, a frozen tissue sample or ______________________ is sliced, stained, and microscopically examined for anomalies.

14. Urinalysis performed on a urine specimen from patient Annette Samuels shows that she has a mild bladder infection. Annette is surprised at this diagnosis; she does not feel sick. Dr. Esposito explains that it is possible to be ______________________ and still have an infection.
15. Most of the patient samples that Audrey Jones, CMA, prepares to send to the laboratory are samples of __________________________, the liquid portion of blood obtained after blood has been allowed to clot or has been separated.
16. If a control sample shows inaccurate results after testing, one possible explanation is that the __________________________ are faulty or have expired.
17. In microscopic analysis of specimens, the light, or image, is reflected by the __________________________ onto the specimen to the ocular lenses for visualization.
18. Fine-needle aspiration is an __________________________ procedure used in a preliminary diagnosis of breast cancer; the test involves inserting a needle into the suspicious breast lump and extracting cells for analysis under a microscope. Because this test is not always reliable, often a mammogram is also performed.
19. A __________________________ of Lyme disease can be confirmed by performing laboratory tests on patient blood specimens.
20. Dr. Rice makes a __________________________ of asthma for patient Rhea Epstein, based on subjective and objective information gathered after obtaining an in-depth patient history and performing a complete physical examination.
21. __________________________ are substances that split into electrically charged particles, or ions, when dissolved or melted. These electricity conductors are important in maintaining fluid and acid-based homeostasis in the body.

B. Match each laboratory facility or department to the statement that best describes it.

A. Reference Laboratories
B Clinical Chemistry
C. Cytology
D. Hematology
E. Histology
F. Immunology/Immunohematology
G. Hospital-Based Laboratories
H. Parasitology
I. Microbiology
J. Mycology
K. Physician's Office Laboratories
L. Procurement Stations
M. Urinalysis

____ 1. This laboratory department performs blood typing procedures, cross matching, and the separation and storage of blood components for transfusion as well as antibody-antigen reactions.

____ 2. This subdivision of the microbiology department detects the presence of disease-producing human parasites or ovas present in patient specimens such as feces and blood. Name three diseases caused by parasites.

1.____________________ 2.____________________ 3.____________________

____ 3. Independent laboratories often have smaller satellite or ______________________ located near isolated medical facilities or in areas convenient to patients.

____ 4. This laboratory department performs qualitative and quantitative tests on blood and blood components. Identify each test named below:

Hgb ______________________ ESR ______________________

Diff ______________________ Hct ______________________

____ 5. This subdivision of the microbiology department is where fungi are grown and identified. ______________________

____ 6. ______________________ are independent, regionally located laboratories used by hospitals and physicians for complex, expensive, or specialized tests.

____ 7. Some procedures performed by this department include assays of enzymes in the serum, serum glucose, or electrolyte levels. Name three electrolytes.

1. ______________ 2. ______________ 3. ______________

____ 8. This laboratory department analyzes patient specimens for the presence of disease-producing microorganisms. Name three infectious diseases.

1. ______________ 2. ______________ 3. ______________

____ 9. ______________________ perform medical laboratory tests easily and inexpensively in the office by the medical assistant.

____ 10. ______________________ perform most of the tests required in patient and hospital clinics.

____ 11. ______________ is the microscopic study of the form and structure of the various tissues making up living organisms. Tissue analysis and biopsy studies are performed in this area of the laboratory.

____ 12. This laboratory department performs microscopic examinations of cells to detect irregularities in growth and development. Name two types of tests performed.

1. ______________________ 2. ______________________

____ 13. ______________________ involves the physical, chemical, and microscopic examination of urine as a diagnostic tool for physicians.

Learning Review

1. Physicians depend on medical laboratories to help them ascertain a patient's state of health or state of disease. There are eight main reasons why a physician might need a laboratory test performed. Identify the proper reason laboratory testing is required for each example given.

A. After feeling the abdomen for bladder distention and performing a rectal examination, Charles Williams's symptoms suggest to Dr. Lewis that Charles may be suffering from an enlarged prostate. Dr. Lewis orders blood tests and a urinalysis to confirm his diagnosis.

____

B. Patient Janet Renquiz, a retired homemaker, complies with the treatment plan for her diagnosed case of chronic lymphocytic leukemia by submitting to a regular testing of her blood for the presence of leukemic cells, which monitors the progress of the disease.

____

C. Anna Ortiz, who is pregnant, has had genital herpes for several years. In the week before her child is to be born, Dr. King takes a culture of Anna's cervical and vaginal mucosa to determine whether her baby is at risk for contracting herpes in the birth canal.

____

D. Dr. Mark Woo has been treating Edith Leonard, who complains of poor vision and fainting spells. Because Edith's symptoms are vague and he cannot make a firm diagnosis, Dr. Woo orders a complete blood profile to give him additional information about Edith's case.

____

E. Louise Kipperly comes to Inner City Health Care for her yearly medical checkup. Dr. Esposito orders a series of blood tests to make sure that Louise's cholesterol level is within a normal, healthy range.

____

F. Fifteen-year-old Corey Boyer comes to Inner City Health Care with what seems to be a severe sore throat. A physical examination reveals the presence of fever, headache, difficulty swallowing, and inflamed tonsils. Dr. Whitney orders a CBC and a heterophil antibodies test to confirm a diagnosis of either tonsillitis or infectious mononucleosis. When the results of Corey's blood tests come back from the laboratory, however, atypical lymphocytes in the blood indicate the early onset of infectious mononucleosis.

____

G. When Jaime Carrera's laboratory tests come back positive for *herpesvirus hominis,* his girlfriend Eleanor is instructed to come into Inner City Health Care for testing. Eleanor, who has no symptoms, is tested for herpes simplex and nonspecific urethritis.

____

H. Maria Jover, diagnosed with HIV, takes protease inhibitors to help her immune system fight the disease. Dr. King orders blood tests to determine how Maria is responding to the treatment.

____

2. A. Name five tests commonly performed in a physician's office laboratory (POL).

1. _______________
2. _______________
3. _______________
4. _______________
5. _______________

B. Name three reasons point-of-care testing might be used to obtain lab results.

1. _______________ 2. _______________ 3. _______________

3. Identify each entry that follows as a way an infectious agent leaves the body of a sick person (L), the way an organism may be transmitted (T), or the way an organism enters the body (E).

_____ A. discharges from infected eyes
_____ B. contaminated needles and syringes
_____ C. milk from an infected cow
_____ D. directly onto mucous membrane
_____ E. breast milk
_____ F. towels
_____ G. health care workers exposed to blood
_____ H. transplacentally to fetus
_____ I. contact with blood and body fluids
_____ J. discharges from respiratory tract
_____ K. feces and urine
_____ L. flies
_____ M. excreta from intestinal tract
_____ N. directly on the conjunctiva

4. The accuracy of any laboratory test result depends on the performance of quality controls by all health care workers who handle a specimen. Medical assistants must have a thorough knowledge of quality controls and standards.

A. List five factors that can compromise the accuracy of laboratory test results.

1. ______________________________
2. ______________________________
3. ______________________________
4. ______________________________
5. ______________________________

B. What is the reason for using a control test sample? Explain in detail.

____
____
____

5. Knowing how to perform tasks safely is critical when working in a medical laboratory. Medical assistants must understand the different types of hazards present in a medical laboratory and know how to protect themselves and other health care professionals from possible harm.

A. It is important to avoid ingestion or exposure to chemicals and pathogens. Name four ways this can be avoided.

1. ______________________________
2. ______________________________
3. ______________________________
4. ______________________________

B. What is the first action to take when a surface becomes contaminated?

____

C. Explain why it is important to avoid wearing loose clothing or accessories in the laboratory.

____
____

D. In terms of safety issues, why is it important to properly maintain laboratory equipment?

____
____

6. For each method of exposure, list one circumstance in which pathogens may be transmitted in the ambulatory care setting and standard precautions that are effective in reducing or preventing the transmission of pathogens under each circumstance.

   A. Direct contact

      Pathogens may be transmitted ____________________

      Standard precautions: ____________________

   B. Ingestion

      Pathogens may be transmitted ____________________

      Standard precautions: ____________________

   C. Mucous membranes

      Pathogens may be transmitted ____________________

      Standard precautions: ____________________

7. A. What is the purpose of a microscope?

   ____

   B. Name the five parts of a microscope.

      1. ____________________
      2. ____________________
      3. ____________________
      4. ____________________
      5. ____________________

   C. The ____________________ microscope is the most commonly used microscope in a medical laboratory.

   D. Name three other types of microscopes and explain what each is designed for viewing.

      1. ____________________
      2. ____________________
      3. ____________________

   E. Name the two adjustments found on a microscope and explain the purpose of each.

      1. ____________________
      2. ____________________

   F. Name six practices that should always be followed to properly care for a microscope.

      1. ____________________
      2. ____________________
      3. ____________________
      4. ____________________
      5. ____________________
      6. ____________________

Investigation Activity

HOW DETAIL-ORIENTED ARE YOU?

Working in a medical laboratory requires spending large amounts of time performing extremely detail-oriented procedures, such as observing specimens through a microscope for signs of disease. Laboratory analysis also involves maintaining high quality controls and safety standards to ensure the accuracy and reliability of results. The way we deal with details in our everyday lives can reveal much about our predisposition for detail-oriented analytical tasks. For each statement, circle the response that best describes you.

1. When walking along a city street, I
   A. notice each person who passes me, remember details from storefronts, and even recognize the make and model of cars as they drive by.
   B. like to listen to other people's conversations and/or enjoy interacting with friends who are accompanying me.
   C. usually spend my time daydreaming.
2. If I think about the way a pine tree looks, I
   A. visualize the rough texture of its bark and see its long, thin leaves perfectly in my head.
   B. think about the great Christmas trees my family always had when I was a kid.
   C. see two blobs of color, green and brown.
3. I prefer working in an atmosphere
   A. that is structured and involves analytical thinking.
   B. where the decision-making process is cut-and-dry and the options are well-defined.
   C. where I don't have to make decisions or interpret anything.
4. When preparing a meal or recipe, I
   A. am very careful to make sure I read the recipe over twice before I start and have each of the ingredients on hand.
   B. read the recipe quickly just to make sure I understand the basics.
   C. just wing it; I cook by intuition.
5. When preparing for a trip or vacation, I
   A. know exactly where my passport and other important papers are located, make a list of all essential items to bring and check off the list as each is packed, and leave detailed written instructions for the housesitter.
   B. know pretty much what I need and where I can find it; but I wait until the day before to get it all together.
   C. let someone else do all the packing and handle all the arrangements; too many details for me.
6. After a conversation with someone I've just met, I
   A. remember the exact color of their eyes.
   B. would be able to make a pretty good guess about what color their eyes are.
   C. have no idea what color their eyes are.
7. When giving people driving directions to a destination, I
   A. make sure to give detailed instructions, using at least two different routes, noting landmarks and the location of gas stations along the way.
   B. say basically what area of town they need to head toward and the street address; I know they can figure out the rest on their own.
   C. usually give people the wrong directions, so I tell them to ask someone else.

8. In regard to friends' birthdays,
   A. I have them all written down in my calendar, and I send cards out four days before the date.
   B. I know what month they fall in, and make sure to wish them a happy birthday somewhere around the middle of the month.
   C. I'm usually embarrassed when I find out a friend's birthday has passed; I can never remember dates.

Scoring: If most of your answers were "A"s, you are an extremely detail-oriented and observant person. You are well-suited to the tasks performed in the medical laboratory. If your answers were mostly "B"s, you can be observant, but you do not always pay close attention to details. If your answers were mostly "C"s, you will need to work on your observation skills.

CASE STUDY

At Abigail Johnson's annual physical examination on June 5, xxxx, at 2 P.M., Dr. Elizabeth King orders several laboratory tests to monitor Abigail's diagnosed conditions of hypertension, diabetes mellitus, and moderate angina pectoris. Dr. Frank Jones, Abigail's cardiologist, will also receive a copy of the final laboratory report. Ellen Armstrong, CMA, prepares the laboratory requisition form. Complete Ellen's laboratory requisition form for Abigail's lab work.

Patient:
Abigail Johnson
225 River Street
Northborough, OH 12336
Phone: 389-2631
Date of Birth: March 1, 1920
Social Security Number: 011-11-1231
Medicare #: 021-45-6712-D

Physicians:
Dr. Elizabeth King
Northborough Family Medical Group
2501 Center Street
Northborough, OH 12345
Phone: 651-8000
Dr. Frank Jones
815 Heart Health Blvd.
Northborough, OH 12339
Phone: 655-7000

Physician's Order for Lab Testing: Blood profile to include BUN, Chloride, Cholesterol, Creatinine, Glucose, LDH, Potassium, SGOT, SGPT, Sodium, Triglycerides.

NORTHBOROUGH REFERENCE LABORATORIES

128 Analysis Way
Northborough, OH 12468

BILL TO: ❑ GROUP ACCOUNT ❑ PATIENT

LAST NAME	FIRST NAME	MI	SEX	DATE OF BIRTH

ADDRESS	CITY	STATE	ZIP

PHONE # Home Work	SOC. SEC. #

COMPLETE SHADED BOX BELOW FOR PATIENT AND THIRD PARTY BILL ONLY

RESPONSIBLE PARTY LAST NAME	FIRST NAME	MI	MEDICARE ❑ MEDICAID ❑ #
ADDRESS	CITY	STATE ZIP	PHONE #
INSURED NAME	INSURANCE CO. NAME/ADDRESS		
INSURED'S EMPLOYER	RELATIONSHIP TO PATIENT ❑ Self ❑ Spouse ❑ Dependent	CONTRACT #	GROUP #

REASON FOR TEST (A DIAGNOSIS IS NECESSARY FOR ALL INSURANCE CLAIMS) *SEE REVERSE FOR CODES*

Ordering Physician Signature

PRIMARY CARE PHYSICIAN

____

SPECIMEN INFORMATION

❑ **STAT**

Date of Collection ____________

Time of Collection ____________

❑ Serum ❑ Plasma

❑ Urine (Volume) ____________

Hours ____________

❑ Other ____________

CALL RESULTS TO:

____

Phone #:( ) ____________

Copy Results to:

____

____

____

SPECIMEN CODES: G - GEL, L - LAVENDER, R - RED, B - BLUE, BK - BLACK, U - URINE

PROFILES (See Reverse for Contents)

Profile	Code	Profile	Code	Profile	Code	Profile	Code
❑ BIOCHEM BASIC	1G	❑ BIOCHEM PROFILE III	2G, 1L	❑ LIPID 12-16 HOUR FAST REQUIRED	1G	❑ THYROID	1G
❑ BIOCHEM PROFILE I	1G, 1L	❑ ARTHRITIS	2G,1BK	❑ LIVER	1G	❑ HYPERTHYROID	1G
❑ BIOCHEM PROFILE II	1G, 1L	❑ HEPATITIS	1G	❑ PRENATAL	1G, 1L, 1R	❑ HYPOTHYROID	1G
						❑ TORCH PROFILE	1G

INDIVIDUAL TESTS

Test	Code	Test	Code	Test	Code
❑ ALBUMIN	G	❑ FSH	G	❑ PROSTATE SPECIFIC ANTIGEN	G
❑ ALK. PHOSPHATASE	G	❑ GC CULTURE, SOURCE ______		❑ PT W/INR	B
❑ AMYLASE	G	❑ GLUCOSE	G	❑ PTT	B
❑ ANA SCREEN	G	❑ GLYCATED HEMOGLOBIN	L	❑ RHEUMATOID FACTOR	G
❑ BILIRUBIN, TOTAL	G	❑ hCG, BETA SUBUNIT QUANT.	G	❑ RPR	G
❑ BILIRUBIN, TOTAL + DIRECT	G	❑ HDL	G	❑ RUBELLA IgG ANTIBODY	G
❑ BILIRUBIN, NEONATAL	G	❑ HEPATITIS B SURF. ANTIBODY	G	❑ SEDIMENTATION RATE	BK
❑ BUN	G	❑ HEPATITIS B SURF. ANTIGEN	G	❑ SGOT	G
❑ CALCIUM, TOTAL	G	❑ HEPATITIS C ANTIBODY	G	❑ SGPT	G
❑ CBC W/AUTOMATED DIFF	L	❑ HIV ANTIBODY (SIGNED CONSENT REQUIRED)	G	❑ SPUTUM CULTURE	
❑ CBC W/MANUAL DIFF	L	❑ LACTIC DEHYDROGENASE	G	❑ STOOL CULTURE	
❑ CHLAMYDIA SCREEN, SOURCE ______		❑ LEAD, PEDIATRIC	L	❑ THROAT, GROUP A STREP CULTURE	
❑ CHOLESTEROL	G	❑ LH	G	❑ TOTAL PROTEIN	G
❑ CREATININE	G	❑ LIPASE	G	❑ TSH	G
❑ CULTURE, SOURCE ______		❑ LITHIUM	G	❑ URIC ACID	G
❑ ELECTROLYTES	G	❑ OVA & PARASITE PREP.		❑ URINALYSIS	U
❑ ESTRADIOL	G	❑ PHOSPHORUS	G	❑ URINE CULTURE	U
❑ FERRITIN	G	❑ PREGNANCY TEST, BLOOD	G	❑ VITAMIN B12	G
❑ FOLIC ACID	G	❑ PROGESTERONE	G		
❑ FREE T4	G	❑ PROLACTIN	G		

REV 12/95

LAB COPY

ICD-9-CM DIAGNOSIS CODES

- ☐ 648.80 ABN GLUC TOL/PREG OR PP
- ☐ 682.9 ABSCESS
- ☐ 042 AIDS
- ☐ 477.9 ALLERGIC RHINITIS
- ☐ 626.0 AMENORRHEA
- ☐ 285.9 ANEMIA
- ☐ 413.9 ANGINA
- ☐ 716.90 ARTHRITIS
- ☐ 414.00 ASHD
- ☐ 493.90 ASTHMA
- ☐ 600 BENIGN PROSTATIC HYPERTROPHY
- ☐ 466.0 BRONCHITIS
- ☐ 199.1 CA SPECIFY SITE:__________
- ☐ 428.0 CHF
- ☐ 496 COPD
- ☐ 436 CVA
- ☐ E934.9 COUMADIN THERAPY
- ☐ 250.00 DIABETES
- ☐ 558.9 DIARRHEA
- ☐ 562.11 DIVERTICULITIS
- ☐ 780.4 DIZZINESS
- ☐ 276.9 ELECTROLYTE IMBALANCE
- ☐ 259.9 ENDOCRINE DISORDERS
- ☐ 530.10 ESOPHAGITIS
- ☐ 780.6 FEVER
- ☐ 558.9 GASTROENTERITIS
- ☐ 784.0 HEADACHE
- ☐ 599.7 HEMATURIA
- ☐ 573.3 HEPATITIS
- ☐ 070.9 HEPATITIS, VIRAL
- ☐ 272.4 HYPERLIPIDEMIA
- ☐ 401.9 HYPERTENSION
- ☐ 244.9 HYPOTHYROID
- ☐ 628.9 INFERTILITY, FEMALE
- ☐ 487.1 INFLUENZA
- ☐ 774.6 JAUNDICE OF NEWBORN
- ☐ 782.4 JAUNDICE NOT NEWBORN
- ☐ V72.6 LAB EXAMINATION
- ☐ 709.8 LESION, SKIN
- ☐ 573.9 LIVER DISEASE
- ☐ 785.6 LYMPHADENOPATHY
- ☐ 780.7 MALAISE & FATIGUE
- ☐ 382.9 OTITIS MEDIA
- ☐ 789.0 PAIN, ABDOMEN
- ☐ 724.5 PAIN, BACK
- ☐ 723.1 PAIN, CERVICAL NECK
- ☐ 786.50 PAIN, CHEST
- ☐ 719.40 PAIN, JOINT
- ☐ V76.2 PAP SMEAR
- ☐ 614.9 PID
- ☐ 462 PHARYNGITIS
- ☐ 486 PNEUMONIA
- ☐ V22.2 PREGNANCY, NORMAL
- ☐ 593.9 RENAL DISEASE
- ☐ 461.9 SINUSITIS
- ☐ 462 SORE THROAT
- ☐ V67.0 SURGICAL FOLLOW UP
- ☐ 780.2 SYNCOPE
- ☐ 465.9 URI
- ☐ 599.0 UTI
- ☐ 616.10 VAGINITIS
- ☐ 079.9 VIRAL SYNDROME
- ☐ 998.5 WOUND INFECTION
- ☐ OTHER: __________
- ☐ __________
- ☐ __________
- ☐ __________

PROFILES / CPT CODES

BIOCHEM BASIC / 80019

Albumin
Alkaline Phosphatase
Anion Gap
Bicarbonate
Bilirubin, Total
BUN
Calcium
Chloride
Cholesterol
Creatinine
GGTP
Glucose
LDH
Phosphorus
Potassium
Protein, Total
SGOT (AST)
SGPT (ALT)
Sodium
Triglycerides
Uric Acid

BIOCHEM PROFILE I / 80019, 85025, 85029

Biochem Basic
CBC w/Automated Diff

BIOCHEM PROFILE II / 80019, 85025, 85029, 83718

Biochem Basic
CBC w/Automated Diff
Lipid Profile

BIOCHEM PROFILE III / 80019, 85025, 85029 83718, 80091

Biochem Basic
CBC w/Automated Diff
Lipid Profile
Thyroid Profile

ARTHRITIS PROFILE / 80072

ANA
Rheumatoid Factor
Sed Rate
Uric Acid

HEPATITIS PROFILE / 80059

Hepatitis A Ab (HAAB)
Hepatitis B Core Ab (HBCAB)
Hepatitis B Surf Ab (HBSAB)
Hepatitis B Surf Ag (HBSAG)
Hepatitis C Ab (HCAB)

LIPID PROFILE / 80061
12-16 Hour Fast Required

Cholesterol
HDL
LDL
Triglycerides

LIVER PROFILE / 80058

Albumin
Alkaline Phosphatase
Bilirubin, Total
SGOT (AST)
SGPT (ALT)

PRENATAL PROFILE / 80055

ABO/Rh type
Antibody Screen
CBC w/Automated Diff
Hepatitis B Surf Antigen
Rubella IgG Antibody
RPR

THYROID PROFILE / 80091

Free Thyroxine Index
T_3 Uptake
T_4

HYPERTHYROID PROFILE / 80091, 84480

Thyroid Profile
T_3 Total

HYPOTHYROID PROFILE / 80092

Thyroid Profile
TSH

TORCH PROFILE / 80090

CMV IgG Ab
Herpes I and II Ab
Rubella IgG Antibody
Toxoplasma IgG Ab

SUPPLEMENTARY RESOURCES

Study Guide Disk: Additional practice exercises for this chapter are available on the study guide disk found in the back of the textbook.

Medical Assisting Videos: Appropriate content is available on Delmar's Medical Assisting Videos, 2nd edition, for the following topics:

Tape 13: Basic Information for Specimen Taking and Laboratory Work
When the Physician Orders a Specimen

Tape 14: Quality Control in Collecting and Processing Specimens
Perform Microscopic Examination of Urine

SKILLS COMPETENCY ASSESSMENT

Procedure 15-1: Using the Microscope

Student's Name: ______________________________ Date: ____________

Objective: To properly use a microscope.

Conditions: The student demonstrates the ability to use a microscope properly to view microscopic organisms using the coarse and fine adjustments as well as the low- and high-power and oil objectives. The student uses the following equipment and supplies: hand disinfectant, microscope (monocular or binocular), lens paper, prepared slides, immersion oil, surface disinfectant. Note: Procedure will vary slightly according to microscope design. Consult the operating procedure in the microscope manual for specific instructions.

Time Requirements and Accuracy Standards: 20 minutes. Points assigned reflect importance of step to meeting objective: Important = (5) Essential = (10) Critical = (15). Automatic failure results if any of the **critical** tasks are omitted or performed incorrectly.

STANDARD PRECAUTIONS:

SKILLS ASSESSMENT CHECKLIST

Task Performed	Possible Points	TASKS
❑	5	Washes hands.
❑	5	Assembles equipment and materials.
❑	5	Cleans the ocular(s) and objectives with lens paper.
❑	10	Uses the coarse adjustment to raise the nosepiece unit.
❑	5	Raises the condenser knob as far as possible by turning the condenser knob.
❑	5	Rotates the 10× objective into position, so it is directly over the opening in the stage.
❑	5	Turns on the microscope light.
❑	5	Opens the diaphragm until maximum light comes up through the condenser.
❑	5	Places the slide on the stage, specimen side up, and secures with clips.
❑	5	Condenser is positioned so it is almost touching the bottom of the slide.
❑	5	Locates the coarse adjustment.
❑	5	Looks directly at the stage and 10× objective and turns the coarse objective until the objective is as close to the slide as it will go.
❑	5	Stops turning when the objective no longer moves.
❑	5	*Rationale:* Understands not to lower any objective toward a slide while looking through the ocular(s).

SKILLS COMPETENCY ASSESSMENT — continued

Procedure 15-1: Using the Microscope

Task Performed	Possible Points	TASKS
❑	15	Looks into the ocular(s) and slowly turns the coarse adjustment in the direction to raise the objective (or lower the stage) until the object on the slide comes into view.
❑	5	Locates the fine adjustment.
❑	10	Turns the fine adjustment to sharpen the image.
		Adjusts oculars for each individual's eyes if a binocular microscope is used:
	❑ 5	• Adjusts the distance between the oculars so one image is seen.
	❑ 5	• Uses the coarse and fine adjustments to bring the object into focus while looking through the right ocular with the right eye.
	❑ 5	• Closes the right eye, looks into the left ocular with the left eye, and uses the knurled collar on the left ocular to bring the object into sharp focus. Does not turn the coarse or fine adjustment at this time.
	❑ 5	• Looks into the oculars with both eyes to observe that the object is in clear focus. If not, repeats procedure.
	20 Points	(subtotal for adjusting oculars with binocular microscope)
❑	10	• Uses the stage knobs the move the slide left and right and backward and forward while looking through the ocular(s), or • Moves the slide with the fingers while looking through the ocular(s) (for a microscope without a movable stage).
❑	10	Rotates the 40× objective into position while observing the objective and slide to see that the objective does not strike the slide.
❑	5	Looks through the ocular(s) to view the object on the slide.
❑	5	Locates the fine adjustment.
❑	15	Looks through the ocular(s) and turns the fine adjustment until the object in focus. Does not use coarse adjustment.
❑	5	Scans the slide, using the fine adjustment to keep the object is in focus if necessary.
❑	5	Rotates the oil-immersion objective to the side slightly (so that no objective is in position).
❑	10	Places one drop of immersion oil on the portion of the slide that is directly over the condenser.
❑	5	Rotates the oil-immersion objective into position and is careful not to rotate the 45× objective through the oil.

Task Performed	Possible Points	TASKS
❑	15	Looks to see that the oil-immersion objective is touching the drop of oil.
❑	5	Looks through the ocular(s) and slowly turns the fine adjustment until the image is clear. Uses only the fine adjustment to focus the oil-immersion objective.
❑	5	Scans the slide.
❑	10	Rotates the 10× objective into position. Does not allow the 45× objective to touch the oil.
❑	15	Removes the slide from the microscope stage and gently cleans the oil from the objective with clean lens paper.
❑	10	Cleans the oculars, 10× objective and 45× objective with clean lens paper.
❑	15	Cleans the 100× objective with lens paper to remove all oil.
❑	15	Cleans any oil from the microscope stage and condenser.
❑	5	Turns off the microscope light and disconnects.
❑	5	Positions the nosepiece in the lowest position, using the coarse adjustment.
❑	5	Centers the stage so it does not project from either side of the microscope.
❑	5	Covers the microscope and returns it to storage.
❑	5	Cleans the work area; returns slides to storage.
❑	5	Washes hands.
❑	5	Completed the tasks within 20 minutes.
❑	15	Results obtained were accurate.

______	Earned	ADD POINTS OF TASKS CHECKED
335	Points	TOTAL POINTS POSSIBLE (Binocular +20)
______	SCORE	DETERMINE SCORE (divide points earned by total points possible, multiply results by 100)

Actual Student Time Needed to Complete Procedure: ____________

Student's Initials: ____________ Instructor's Initials: ____________ Grade: ____________

Suggestions for Improvement: ______________________________

Evaluator's Name (print) ______________________________

Evaluator's Signature ______________________________

Comments ______________________________

EVALUATION OF CHAPTER KNOWLEDGE

Knowledge	Instructor Evaluation *Good*	*Average*	*Poor*
Explains the purposes of laboratory testing	_____	_____	_____
Understands the differences and similarities between independent laboratories and physician's office laboratories	_____	_____	_____
Identifies departments within the medical laboratory and lists the types of testing performed within each department	_____	_____	_____
Knows nine of the most common laboratory profiles and the body system that each covers	_____	_____	_____
Understands quality control programs in the medical laboratory	_____	_____	_____
Knows the general safety rules within the medical laboratory	_____	_____	_____
Knows how to fill out a laboratory requisition form	_____	_____	_____
Understands the information required on a written laboratory requisition form	_____	_____	_____
Can explain the function of and identify the parts of a compound microscope	_____	_____	_____
Understands how to properly use and care for a compound microscope	_____	_____	_____
Follows all standard precautions	_____	_____	_____

Student's Initials: ______ Instructor's Initials: ______

Grade: _______

CHAPTER 16

Venipuncture

PERFORMANCE OBJECTIVES

Venipuncture is the process of collecting patient blood samples for the purpose of diagnostic testing. Although the health care professional responsible for performing this important task varies according to the type and needs of the ambulatory care setting, medical assistants often are required to perform venipuncture. The goal of venipuncture is to obtain blood specimens that are collected and processed in a manner that will provide accurate and reliable diagnostic test results. To achieve this goal, medical assistants will draw on a combination of clinical, social, and administrative skills. Aseptic technique and standard precautions for infection control, including the proper handling and disposal of sharps, must be observed when performing venipuncture.

EXERCISES AND ACTIVITIES

Vocabulary Builder

1. Unscramble the following vocabulary terms.

A. ocyteskeul ____________

B. quotali ____________

C. demaetous ____________

D. cythroerytes ____________

E. nacunal ____________

F. rule ____________

G. milsyohes ____________

H. niqutouret ____________

I. scivostiy ____________

J. aetplpa ____________

K. ialpmei ____________

L. otbelhmoyp ____________

M. ertuicpehta ____________

N. ugaantitanloc ____________

2. Match the vocabulary terms listed below with the correct definitions.

hypoglycemia	diurnal	plasma
additive	thixotropic gel	serum
hematoma	hemoconcentration	thrombocytes
venipuncture		

_______________ A. The fluid portion of blood from an anticoagulated tube.

_______________ B. The state of having a lower-than-normal blood glucose level.

_______________ C. The process of collecting blood.

_______________ D. Any material placed in a tube that maintains or facilitates the integrity and function of the specimen.

_______________ E. The body's daily cycle; levels fluctuate during this cycle.

_______________ F. An accumulation of blood around the venipuncture site during or after venipuncture, caused by the leakage of blood from where the needle punctured the vein.

_______________ G. The fluid portion of the blood after clotting has taken place.

_______________ H. A gel material capable of forming an interface between the cells and fluid portion of the blood as a result of centrifugation.

_______________ I. Platelets.

_______________ J. Leaving a tourniquet on the arm longer than one minute, causing blood to pool at the location of the venipuncture, resulting in inaccurate blood samples.

3. Write a brief definition of the following vocabulary words.

A. Integrity _______________

B. Oxygenated _______________

C. Primary container_______________

D. Dilate _______________

E. Centrifuge _______________

F. Buffy coat_______________

G. Constrict_______________

Learning Review

1. Identify and describe the first, second, and third choices of sites on the human body used to perform venipuncture.

(1) _______________

(2) _______________

(3) _______________

2. Tourniquets play a critical role in venipuncture and must be applied and used properly to obtain a blood specimen for analysis.

A. What is the purpose of a tourniquet? ______________________________

____

B. Where is the tourniquet placed? ______________________________

C. How long should the tourniquet remain on the arm during the procedure? __________

____

D. At what point during the procedure should the tourniquet be removed? Why is the timing of removal so important? ______________________________

____

3. Match the collection tubes containing anticoagulants with their corresponding color stoppers: Green, gray, blue, and lavender.

A. Coagulation "citrate" tube: ______________________________

B. EDTA tube: ______________________________

C. Oxalate/fluoride tube: ______________________________

D. Heparin tube: ______________________________

4. Discuss how the five factors listed below might have an effect on blood test results.

(1) Exercise ______________________________

____

(2) Tourniquet ______________________________

____

(3) Volume of blood drawn ______________________________

____

(4) Heparin ______________________________

____

(5) Temperature of specimen ______________________________

____

5. Vein stimulation refers to techniques used when initial attempts to obtain a blood sample are not successful. What are five techniques used to stimulate veins?

(1) ______________________________

(2) ______________________________

(3) ______________________________

(4) ______________________________

(5) ______________________________

6. What is the purpose of additives? How do they differ from anticoagulants? Give examples of each.

____

____

____

____

7. A. How can medical assistants be sure they have found a vein and not an artery or a tendon when preparing to draw blood from a patient? Describe the characteristics of each.

____

____

____

B. Arteries and veins are crucial elements of the circulatory system. Indicate which of the following are functions or characteristics of arteries (A) and which are functions of veins (V).

____1. normally brighter in color

____2. no pulse

____3. carry blood to heart; carry deoxygenated blood (except pulmonary)

____4. thin wall and less elastic

____5. carry blood from heart, carry oxygenated blood (except pulmonary)

____6. no valves

8. Identify the recommended venipuncture method for each of the situations listed below.

____________________ A. When drawing blood from a seventy-five-year-old patient with thin veins.

____________________ B. For collecting a blood specimen from children, who have small veins and a tendency to move during the venipuncture procedure.

____________________ C. When elimination of any risk of needlestick accident is desired.

____________________ D. When multiple blood samples must be obtained from one venipuncture procedure.

Investigation Activity

For medical assistants to become confident and skilled at performing venipuncture, they must acquire clinical knowledge of, and hands-on experience with, a variety of procedures and techniques. In addition, and equally as important, they must possess the capacity to empathize with and respond to patients' concerns and questions. A medical assistant's own venipuncture experiences, either positive or negative, can play a role in developing these very important therapeutic skills. Answer the following questions honestly. Share your stories, reactions, feelings, and observations with your classmates.

What do you remember most about your last blood test: the room, the needle, the person who took the blood sample, the pain, the wait, etc.?

Overall, have your experiences with having blood drawn been positive or negative? How so?

Describe how you generally feel when you are having your blood drawn (relaxed, tense, annoyed, scared, light-headed, anxious, etc.).

Do you think it is silly for people to be afraid or squeamish about blood and syringes? Have you ever fainted during or after you had your blood drawn? Do you know someone who has?
How does the sight of your blood leaving your body and entering a syringe make you feel? If you feel uncomfortable, how do you cope with your feelings?
In what way, if any, does the demeanor or personality of the person taking your blood affect your experience?
How might your personal experiences influence your ability to perform this procedure?
How might you draw upon your personal experiences to help patients feel comfortable with the procedure and confident in your skills?
Do you feel comfortable with the idea of drawing blood from patients? How would you feel about drawing blood from a patient who is in pain? who cries? who faints? who needs to carry on a conversation with you to feel comfortable? who is not cooperative? who criticizes you during the procedure?

CASE STUDY

Wanda Slawson, CMA, performs a successful venipuncture on Jaime Carrera using the evacuated tube system and a 21-gauge needle. Wanda is now preparing to label the tubes for laboratory analysis. She is careful to label all tubes at the patient's side before leaving the examination room.

Discuss the following:

1. What information must be included on the specimen labels for the specimen to be accepted for analysis?
2. What guidelines must Wanda follow during the venipuncture procedure to ensure that anticoagulated blood specimens are acceptable for analysis?
3. Once Wanda has followed all procedures for the correct labeling and processing of the blood specimens, what standard precautions must she perform?

SUPPLEMENTARY RESOURCES

Study Guide Disk: Additional practice exercises for this chapter are available on the study guide disk found in the back of the textbook.

Medical Assisting Videos: Appropriate content is available on Delmar's Medical Assisting Videos, 2nd ed., Tape 13, for the following topics:

Basic Information for Specimen Taking and Laboratory Work
When the Physician Orders a Specimen
Collect and Label a Blood Specimen
Butterfly Collection From Hand Vein
Collecting Tubes
Capillary Puncture

SKILLS COMPETENCY ASSESSMENT

Procedure 16-1: Finding a Vein in the Upper Arm

Student's Name: ______________________________ Date: ____________

Objective: To correctly administer a subcutaneous injection.

Conditions: The student demonstrates the ability to correctly administer a subcutaneous injection after receiving a physician's order, using the following equipment and supplies: medication ordered by physician, medicine card, appropriately sized needle-syringe unit, antiseptic wipe, disposable gloves, sharps container.

Time Requirements and Accuracy Standards: 10-20 minutes. Points assigned reflect importance of step to meeting objective: Important = (5) Essential = (10) Critical = (15). Automatic failure results if any of the **critical** tasks are omitted or performed incorrectly.

STANDARD PRECAUTIONS:

SKILLS ASSESSMENT CHECKLIST

Task Performed	Possible Points	TASKS
❑	5	Identifies the patient, asking patient's name and verifying it with the computer label or identification number. Verifies compliance with fasting instructions, if appropriate.
❑	5	Washes hands and puts on gloves. Puts on goggles and mask if potential for blood spatter is present.
❑	5	Applies tourniquet three to four inches above the venipuncture site. Applies tightly enough to stop blood flow but not so tight that blood flow in arteries is stopped.
❑	5	Instructs patient to close hand.
❑	10	Places patient's arm in a downward position.
❑	15	Palpates upper region of the patient's arm and feels for the median cubital, basilic, or cephalic vein with the tip of the index finger.
❑	15	Feels for a soft bounce and roundness to the vein and follows direction of the vein.
❑	10	Feels the vein for its center and possibility of rolling.
❑	15	After locating an acceptable vein, mentally maps the locations and visualizes the puncture site.
❑	15	Cleans the venipuncture site with a 70 percent isopropyl alcohol swab and completes the venous blood collection from the site.
❑	5	If the vein cannot be located in the upper arm region, the student follows the same procedure, checking the veins in the hand. Chooses the butterfly system for hand vein collection.

Task Performed	Possible Points	TASKS
❑	5	*Rationale:* Understands that hand veins have a greater tendency to roll.
❑	5	Completed the tasks within 10-20 minutes.
❑	15	Results obtained were accurate.

_________	Earned	ADD POINTS OF TASKS CHECKED
130	Points	TOTAL POINTS POSSIBLE
_________	SCORE	DETERMINE SCORE (divide points earned by total points possible, multiply results by 100)

Actual Student Time Needed to Complete Procedure: ____________

Student's Initials: ____________ Instructor's Initials: ____________ Grade: ____________

Suggestions for Improvement: ____

Evaluator's Name (print) ____

Evaluator's Signature ____

Comments ____

SKILLS COMPETENCY ASSESSMENT

Procedure 16-2: Venipuncture by Syringe Procedure

Student's Name: ______________________ Date: __________

Objective: To obtain venous blood acceptable for laboratory testing, as required by a physician. To aliquot venous blood collected into evacuated tubes and/or special collection containers.

Conditions: Students demonstrate the ability to obtain and aliquot venous blood using the following equipment: gloves, goggles and mask, syringes, disposable needle for syringe (21- or 22-gauge needle), evacuated tubes(s) or special collection tube(s), tourniquet, 70 percent isopropyl alcohol swab, gauze or cotton balls, adhesive bandage or tape, and sharps and biohazard waste containers.

Time Requirements and Accuracy Standards: 15 minutes. Points assigned reflect importance of step to meeting objective: Important = (5) Essential = (10) Critical = (15). Automatic failure results if any of the **critical** tasks are omitted or performed incorrectly.

STANDARD PRECAUTIONS:

SKILLS ASSESSMENT CHECKLIST

Task Performed	Possible Points	TASKS
☐	15	Positions and identifies the patient, asking patient's name and verifying it with the computer label or identification number.
☐	10	Verifies compliance with fasting instructions, if appropriate.
☐	5	Washes hands.
☐	5	Puts on gloves and, if potential for blood spatter is present, puts on goggles and mask.
☐	5	Opens the sterile needle and syringe packages, attaching the needle if necessary.
☐	10	Prevents the plunger from sticking by pulling it halfway out and pushing it all the way in one time.
☐	10	Selects the proper tube(s) to transfer the blood after collection.
☐	10	Finds the vein and applies the tourniquet.
☐	5	Instructs patient to close hand.
☐	5	*Rationale:* Patient should not pump hand, as this action will change the values of the laboratory tests.
☐	10	Places patient's hand in a downward position.
☐	10	Selects a vein, noting location and direction of the vein.
☐	10	Cleans the venipuncture site with a 70 percent isopropyl alcohol swab in a circular motion from the center outward.

Task Performed	Possible Points	TASKS
❑	15	Does not touch venipuncture site.
❑	10	Draws patient's skin taut with thumb, placing thumb one to two inches below the puncture site.
❑	10	Positions the bevel of the needle up and lines up the needle with the vein.
❑	10	Enters the vein approximately ¼ inch below the vein location at the point where the vein was palpated.
❑	5	Pushes needle into the skin.
❑	5	Feels the "pop" (sense of resistance followed by easy penetration), stops, and does not move.
❑	10	Takes the opposite hand and pulls gently on the plunger of syringe. Pulls only as fast as the syringe will fill with blood.
❑	5	*Rationale:* Pulling too hard or too fast will cause the vein to collapse temporarily. If the vein collapses, stops pulling on plunger and lets the vein refill with blood.
❑	5	Pulls plunger back until the desired amount of blood is obtained.
❑	5	Asks patient to open hand.
❑	5	Releases tourniquet.
❑	5	Lightly places sterile gauze or cotton ball above the venipuncture site.
❑	5	Removes needle from the patient's arm.
❑	5	Applies pressure to site for three to five minutes. May ask patient to assist by elevating arm above heart level.
❑	15	Aliquots blood into appropriate tube(s). Punctures the stopper of the evacuated tube with the syringe needle and allows the blood to enter the tube freely until the flow stops. Does not push on plunger. Mixes if any anticoagulant is present.
❑	5	Immediately discards the syringe and needle in the appropriate waste containers.
❑	5	*Rationale:* All sharps must be discarded in a sharps container.
❑	5	Discards the gauze and other waste in biohazard containers.
❑	15	Labels all tubes before leaving the examination room.
❑	5	Applies adhesive bandage.
❑	5	Removes and discards gloves, goggles, and mask in biohazard container.
❑	5	Washes hands.
❑	5	Documents procedure.

SKILLS COMPETENCY ASSESSMENT — continued

Procedure 16-2: Venipuncture by Syringe Procedure

Task Performed	Possible Points	TASKS
❑	5	Completed the tasks within 15 minutes.
❑	15	Results obtained were accurate.

______	Earned	ADD POINTS OF TASKS CHECKED
295	Points	TOTAL POINTS POSSIBLE
______	SCORE	DETERMINE SCORE (divide points earned by total points possible, multiply results by 100)

Actual Student Time Needed to Complete Procedure: ____________

Student's Initials: ____________ Instructor's Initials: ____________ Grade: ____________

Suggestions for Improvement: ____

Evaluator's Name (print) ____

Evaluator's Signature ____

Comments ____

DOCUMENTATION

Chart the procedure in the patient's medical record.

Date: ______________________

Charting: ____

____

____

Student's Initials: ________________

SKILLS COMPETENCY ASSESSMENT

Procedure 16-3: Venipuncture by Evacuated Tube System

Student's Name: ______________________ Date: __________

Objective: To obtain venous blood acceptable for laboratory testing, as required by a physician.

Conditions: Students demonstrate the ability to obtain venous blood using the following equipment: gloves, goggles and mask, evacuated tube holder, disposable needle for evacuated system (20-, 21-, or 22-gauge needle), evacuated tube(s) or special collection tube(s), tourniquet, 70 percent isopropyl alcohol swab, gauze or cotton balls, adhesive bandage or tape, and sharps and biohazard waste containers.

Time Requirements and Accuracy Standards: 15 minutes. Points assigned reflect importance of step to meeting objective: Important = (5) Essential = (10) Critical = (15). Automatic failure results if any of the **critical** tasks are omitted or performed incorrectly.

STANDARD PRECAUTIONS:

SKILLS ASSESSMENT CHECKLIST

Task Performed	Possible Points	TASKS
❑	5	Positions and identifies the patient, asking patient's name and verifying it with the computer label or identification number. Verifies compliance with fasting instructions, if appropriate.
❑	5	Washes hands and puts on gloves. Puts on goggles and mask if potential for blood spatter is present.
❑	5	Assembles equipment. Assembles tubes in correct order of draw and keeps extra tubes on hand.
❑	5	*Rationale:* Access to extra tubes is important in the event of a faulty vacuum.
❑	5	Breaks needle seal. Threads the appropriate needle into the holder using the needle sheath as a wrench.
❑	10	Before using, taps all tubes containing additives to ensure that all additive is dislodged from the stopper and wall of the tube.
❑	5	Inserts the tube into the holder until the needle slightly enters the stopper.
❑	5	*Rationale:* Avoids pushing the needle beyond the recessed guideline, because a loss of vacuum may result.
❑	5	If tube retracts slightly, leaves it in the retracted position to avoid prematurely puncturing the rubber stopper.
❑	5	Applies tourniquet.
❑	5	Instructs patient to close hand.

SKILLS COMPETENCY ASSESSMENT — continued

Procedure 16-3: Venipuncture by Evacuated Tube System

Task Performed	Possible Points	TASKS
❑	5	*Rationale:* Patient must not be allowed to pump the hand, as this action will change the values of the laboratory tests.
❑	10	Places patient's arm in a downward position.
❑	10	Selects a vein, noting its location and direction.
❑	10	Cleans the venipuncture site with a 70 percent isopropyl alcohol swab.
❑	15	Does not touch venipuncture site.
❑	10	Draws patient's skin taut with thumb, placing thumb one to two inches below the puncture site.
❑	15	Positions the bevel of the needle up and lines up the needle with the vein.
❑	10	Punctures the vein. Removes hand from drawing skin taut. Grasps the flange of the evacuated tube holder and pushes the tube forward until the butt end of the needle punctures the stopper.
❑	15	Does not change hands while performing venipuncture. The hand performing the venipuncture is the hand that holds the evacuated tube holder; the other hand manipulates the tubes.
❑	5	Fills the tube until the vacuum is exhausted and blood flow into the tube ceases.
❑	5	*Rationale:* Ensures the proper blood-to-anticoagulant ratio.
❑	10	When blood flow ceases, removes the tube from the holder. Grasps the evacuated tube holder securely with one hand and changes the tubes with the other hand. The shutoff valve recovers the point, stopping the flow of blood until the next tube of blood is inserted.
❑	10	Immediately mixes each tube containing an additive by inverting the tube five to ten times to provide adequate mixing without causing hemolysis.
❑	10	Asks patient to open hand. Releases the tourniquet. Lightly places sterile gauze or cotton ball above the venipuncture site.
❑	15	Removes needle from the arm. Checks to make sure that the last tube drawn was removed from the holder before removing the needle.
❑	5	*Rationale:* This prevents blood from dripping off the tip of the needle.
❑	5	Applies pressure to site for three to five minutes. May ask patient to assist by elevating arm above heart level to reduce blood flow.

Task Performed	Possible Points	TASKS
☐	15	Immediately discards the needle and disposable tube holders in the appropriate waste containers.
☐	5	*Rationale:* All sharps must be discarded in a sharps container.
☐	15	Labels all tubes at the patient's side before leaving the examination room.
☐	5	Applies adhesive bandage.
☐	5	Removes and discards gloves, goggles, and mask in a biohazard container.
☐	5	Washes hands.
☐	5	Documents the procedure.
☐	5	Completed the tasks within 15 minutes.
☐	15	Results obtained were accurate.

______	Earned	ADD POINTS OF TASKS CHECKED
300	Points	TOTAL POINTS POSSIBLE
______	SCORE	DETERMINE SCORE (divide points earned by total points possible, multiply results by 100)

Actual Student Time Needed to Complete Procedure: ____________

Student's Initials: ____________ Instructor's Initials: ____________ Grade: ____________

Suggestions for Improvement: ____________

Evaluator's Name (print) ____________

Evaluator's Signature ____________

Comments ____________

DOCUMENTATION

Chart the procedure in the patient's medical record.

Date: ____________

Charting: ____________

____

____

Student's Initials: ____________

SKILLS COMPETENCY ASSESSMENT

Procedure 16-4: Venipuncture by Butterfly Needle System

Student's Name: ______________________________ Date: ____________

Objective: To obtain venous blood acceptable for laboratory testing, as required by a physician.

Conditions: Students demonstrate the ability to obtain venous blood using the following equipment: gloves, goggles and mask, evacuated tube holder, disposable needle for evacuated system (21-, 23-, or 25-gauge needle with or without leur adapter), evacuated tube(s) or special collection tube(s), tourniquet, 70 percent isopropyl alcohol swab, gauze or cotton balls, adhesive bandage or tape, and sharps and biohazard waste containers.

Time Requirements and Accuracy Standards: 15 minutes. Points assigned reflect importance of step to meeting objective: Important = (5) Essential = (10) Critical = (15). Automatic failure results if any of the **critical** tasks are omitted or performed incorrectly.

STANDARD PRECAUTIONS:

SKILLS ASSESSMENT CHECKLIST

Task Performed	Possible Points	TASKS
With Evacuated Tube Leur Adapter		
❑	10	Positions and identifies the patient, asking the patient's name and verifying it with the computer label or identification number. Verifies compliance with fasting instructions, if appropriate.
❑	5	Washes hands and puts on gloves. Puts on goggles and mask if potential for blood spatter is present.
❑	5	Assembles equipment.
❑	5	Opens the butterfly needle system package with evacuated tube leur adapter. Screws leur into the evacuated tube holder. Threads the leur needle into the holder.
❑	5	Before using, taps all tubes that contain additives to ensure that all additive is dislodged from the stopper and wall of the tube.
❑	10	Inserts the tube into the holder until the needle slightly enters the stopper. Avoids pushing the needle beyond the recessed guideline.
❑	5	*Rationale:* Understands that pushing beyond the recessed guideline may result in a loss of vacuum.
❑	5	If tube retracts slightly, leaves in the retracted position.
❑	5	Applies the tourniquet.
❑	5	Asks patient to close the hand and places the patient's arm in a downward position.
❑	5	*Rationale:* Does not allow patient to pump hand, as pumping the hand will change the values of laboratory tests.
❑	10	Selects a vein, noting its location and direction.
❑	10	Cleans the venipuncture site with a 70 percent isopropyl alcohol swab.
❑	15	Does not touch the venipuncture site.
❑	10	Draws the patient's skin taut with the thumb; places the thumb one to two inches below the puncture site.
❑	10	Holds the wings of the butterfly with the bevel up. Lines up with needle with the vein and performs the venipuncture. Removes hand from drawing the skin taut.
❑	5	Grasps the flange of the evacuated tube holder and pushes the tube forward until the butt end of the needle punctures the stopper.
❑	10	Fills the tube until the vacuum is exhausted and blood flow into the tube ceases.

Task Performed	Possible Points	TASKS
❑	5	*Rationale:* Understands that this will assure the proper blood-to-anticoagulant ratio. Due to air in the tubing, a loss of approximately 0.5 mL will result when collecting the initial evacuated tube.
❑	5	When the blood flow ceases, removes the tube from the holder. While securely grasping the evacuated tube holder with one hand, uses the other hand to change the tubes.
❑	5	*Rationale:* The shutoff valve recovers the point, stopping the flow of blood until the next tube of blood is inserted. Multiple draws require the same order of draw as an evacuated system draw.
❑	10	After drawing, immediately mixes each tube that contains an additive. Gently inverts the tube five to ten times providing adequate mixing without causing hemolysis.
❑	5	Asks the patient to open hand and releases tourniquet.
❑	5	Lightly places a sterile gauze square or cotton ball above the venipuncture site.
❑	5	Removes the needle from the arm. Is certain to remove the last tube drawn before removing the needle.
❑	5	*Rationale:* This prevents blood from dripping off the tip of the needle.
❑	5	Applies pressure to the site for three to five minutes. Asks patient to assist by elevating the arm above heart level to reduce blood flow.
❑	15	Immediately discards the needle and disposable butterfly assembly in the appropriate waste containers.
❑	5	*Rationale:* All sharps must be discarded in a sharps container.
❑	15	Labels all tubes at the patient's side before leaving the examination room.
❑	5	Applies an adhesive bandage.
❑	5	Removes and discards gloves, goggles, and mask in a biohazard container.
❑	5	Washes hands.
❑	5	Documents procedure.
❑	5	Completed the tasks within 15 minutes.
❑	15	Results obtained were accurate.

_______		Earned	ADD POINTS OF TASKS CHECKED
	260	Points	TOTAL POINTS POSSIBLE
_______		SCORE	DETERMINE SCORE (divide points earned by total points possible, multiply results by 100)

By Syringe

Task Performed	Possible Points	TASKS
❑	10	Positions and identifies the patient, asking the patient's name and verifying it with the computer label or identification number. Verifies compliance with fasting instructions, if appropriate.
❑	5	Washes hands and puts on gloves. Puts on goggles and mask if potential for blood spatter is present.
❑	5	Assembles equipment.
❑	5	Opens the butterfly needle system package. Attaches syringe.
❑	5	Before using, taps all tubes that contain additives to ensure that all additive is dislodged from the stopper and wall of the tube.
❑	10	Inserts the tube into the holder until the needle slightly enters the stopper. Avoids pushing the needle beyond the recessed guideline.
❑	5	*Rationale:* Understands that pushing beyond the recessed guideline may result in a loss of vacuum.
❑	5	If tube retracts slightly, leaves in the retracted position.
❑	5	Applies the tourniquet.
❑	5	Asks patient to close the hand and places the patient's arm in a downward position.

SKILLS COMPETENCY ASSESSMENT — continued

Procedure 16-4: Venipuncture by Butterfly Needle System

Task Performed	Possible Points	TASKS
☐	5	*Rationale:* Does not allow patient to pump hand, as pumping the hand will change the values of laboratory tests.
☐	10	Selects a vein, noting its location and direction.
☐	10	Cleans the venipuncture site with a 70 percent isopropyl alcohol swab.
☐	15	Does not touch the venipuncture site.
☐	10	Draws the patient's skin taut with the thumb; places the thumb one to two inches below the puncture site.
☐	10	Holds the wings of the butterfly with the bevel up. Lines up with needle with the vein and performs the venipuncture. Removes hand from drawing the skin taut.
☐	5	Draws blood with a butterfly system
☐	15	Aliquots blood into appropriate tube(s). Punctures the stopper of the evacuated tube with the syringe needle and allows the blood to enter the tube freely until the flow stops. Does not push on plunger. Mixes if any anticoagulant is present.
☐	5	Immediately discards the syringe and needle in the appropriate waste containers.
☐	5	*Rationale:* All sharps must be discarded in a sharps container.
☐	15	Labels all tubes before leaving the examination room.
☐	5	Applies an adhesive bandage.
☐	5	Removes and discards gloves, goggles, and mask in a biohazard container.
☐	5	Washes hands.
☐	5	Documents procedure.
☐	5	Completed the tasks within 15 minutes.
☐	15	Results obtained were accurate.

______	Earned	ADD POINTS OF TASKS CHECKED
210	Points	TOTAL POINTS POSSIBLE
______	SCORE	DETERMINE SCORE (divide points earned by total points possible, multiply results by 100)

Actual Student Time Needed to Complete Procedure: ____________

Student's Initials: ____________ Instructor's Initials: ____________ Grade: ____________

Suggestions for Improvement: ______________________________

Evaluator's Name (print) ______________________________

Evaluator's Signature ______________________________

Comments ______________________________

DOCUMENTATION

Chart the procedure in the patient's medical record.

Date: ____________________

Charting: ______________________________

____

____

Student's Initials: ____________

EVALUATION OF CHAPTER KNOWLEDGE

How has your instructor evaluated the knowledge you have achieved?

Knowledge	Instructor Evaluation *Good*	*Average*	*Poor*
Understands the principles and usage of venipuncture procedures	_____	_____	_____
Identifies and describes venipuncture equipment and techniques	_____	_____	_____
Demonstrates understanding of the physiology of the circulatory system	_____	_____	_____
Differentiates between serum and plasma	_____	_____	_____
Describes purpose of additives and anticoagulants	_____	_____	_____
Demonstrates ability to respond correctly to adverse patient reactions to venipuncture	_____	_____	_____
Recalls vein stimulation techniques	_____	_____	_____
Identifies correct color-coded tubes used with specific anticoagulants	_____	_____	_____
Identifies correct order of draw for blood collection	_____	_____	_____
Facilitates therapeutic communication with patients, putting them at ease during venipuncture	_____	_____	_____
Observes aseptic technique and standard precautions for infection control, including proper disposal of sharps	_____	_____	_____
Understands effects of factors on accurate laboratory test results	_____	_____	_____
Possesses the ability to handle and process acceptable specimens for accurate analysis in the laboratory	_____	_____	_____

Student's Initials: _______ Instructor's Initials: _______

Grade: ________

Hematology

PERFORMANCE OBJECTIVES

Hematology is the study of the blood in both normal and diseased states. As a diagnostic tool hematological tests are invaluable to the physician in determining illness, evaluating a patient's progress, and deciding upon treatment modalities. The most common hematological tests include: hemoglobin, hematocrit, white blood cell count, red blood cell count, platelet count, differential white blood cell count, erythrocyte sedimentation rate, and prothrombin time. Included in the study of hematology is the study of hemopoiesis, the formation of blood cells. It is important for the clinical medical assistant to understand the process of hemopoiesis, normal blood values, and how to perform various blood collection and testing procedures. Following safety and quality control guidelines will protect medical assistants and others and contribute to the accuracy of test results.

EXERCISES AND ACTIVITIES

Vocabulary Builder

A. To test your spelling skills, unscramble the key vocabulary terms below:

1. LETEMCOP ODBOL UNTOC ____________________
2. HEYOSRYTETCR ____________________
3. OCHYTREEMAMET ____________________
4. HOPINLOISE ____________________
5. LOBEHOMYPINHGOAT ____________________
6. RAYMOCPOHCITL ANSITS ____________________
7. MOTHEGLYAO ____________________
8. TIRCCMIOYC ____________________
9. YSNCAITSIOOS ____________________
10. DEEPINCAM LIPRINCEP ____________________
11. TYKULESOCE ____________________

12. MICROTHATE ____________________
13. BLEMONOGHI ____________________
14. PABLOHIS ____________________
15. TYCOREYTREH DENICIS ____________________
16. PHIEMISOOSE ____________________
17. GITALFERNUC LEMOTHGAYO SALISANY ____________________
18. CROMYONCIT ____________________
19. GBEACYMNNHIMOLOET ____________________
20. BYRHOCOTTSEM ____________________
21. HUNTERLIPO ____________________
22. CLYHPTMSOYE ____________________
23. PITROENYHTOIER ____________________
24. TCKISOPILOYSIO ____________________
25. TEMSCONOY ____________________
26. CRCITAMCYO ____________________
27. PYROMOCHCIH ____________________
28. FEFRUB ____________________
29. YETORTERCHY MOSNDETINIETA TEAR ____________________

Learning Review

1. When Dr. Winston Lewis orders CBCs on his patients, what are the six general parameters the physician will study to help him make a diagnosis?

A. ____________________
B. ____________________
C. ____________________
D. ____________________
E. ____________________
F. ____________________

2. While Dr. Elizabeth King is reviewing bloodwork drawn on one of her patients, she notes the hematocrit is normal yet the hemoglobin is low. Which of the following diseases is this indicative of ?

A. Sickle Cell Anemia.
B. Rouleau.
C. Leukemia.
D. Iron Deficiency Anemia.
E. Malaria.

3. Match the appropriate adult parameters with the following blood tests.

1. 36–55%
2. 80–100 fL
3. 4,500–11,000/mm^3
4. 3236 g/dL
5. 4.0–6.0 ' 106/mm3
6. 12–18 g/dL
7. 27–33 pg

A. Hemoglobin
B. White Blood Cell Count
C. Mean Corpuscular Volume
D. Hematocrit
E. Mean Corpuscular Hemoglobin Concentration
F. Red Blood Cell Count
G. Mean Corpuscular Hemoglobin

4. A. Identify the formula for calculating a red blood cell count.

B. Identify the formula for calculating a white blood cell count.

C. What three white blood cell features on a stained differential slide are studied to assist in the identification of the cell?

(1) ______________________ (2) ______________________ (3) ______________________

D. Draw a box identifying the correct area of the slide to be viewed for differential count. Then, within that area, indicate the correct counting pattern.

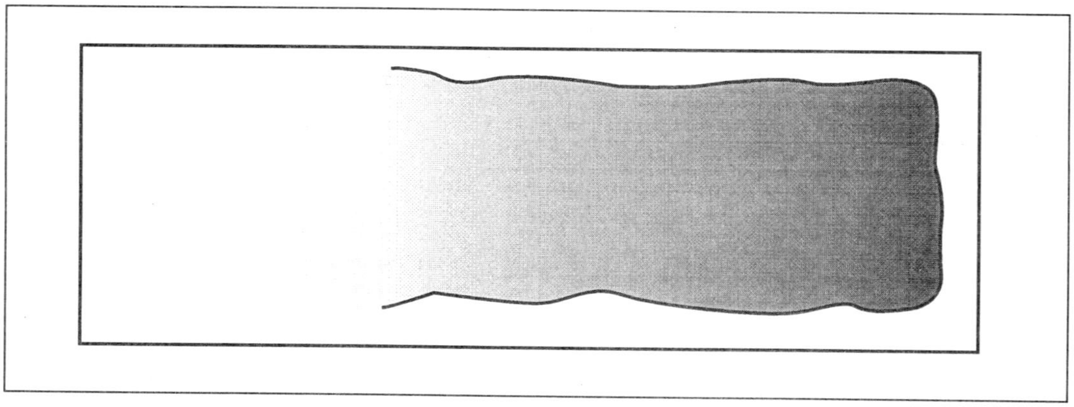

5. Identify the following erythrocyte indices and list the correct formula for determining each.

MCH ____

MCV ____

MCHC ____

6. A. Audrey Jones, CMA, in Dr. Lewis's office, performs an erythrocyte sedimentation rate using the Wintrobe method, while Walter Seals, CMA, at Inner City Health Care, uses the Westergren method. Describe the difference in the two procedures.

____

____

B. Sedimentation rate results vary with different states of health. Name two factors that influence the sedimentation rate. Why is the ESR a more accurate tool in diagnosing the onset of a disease than in checking on the progress of treatment?

____

____

____

7. A. At Inner City Health Care, Karen Ritter, CMA, uses automated hematology instruments. Automated hematology procedures have many advantages over the manual methods. List five of these advantages.

1. ______________________ 4. ______________________

2. ______________________ 5. ______________________

3. ______________________

B. Name three procedures required by CLIA '88 regulations for automated hematology instruments.

(1) ______________________

(2) ______________________

(3) ______________________

Investigation Activity

Hematological tests are the second most common tests performed in the physician's office laboratory (POL) (the most common is urinalysis). The results of hematological tests provide valuable information used by the physician when making a diagnosis, evaluating a patient's progress, and/or regulating further treatment.

A. In the space below, list five diseases or disorders that are monitored through routine analysis of the blood.

(1) ______________________

(2) ______________________

(3) ______________________

(4) ______________________

(5) ______________________

B. Choose one of the diseases or disorders listed above. Using a medical reference or encyclopedia, research the blood testing performed for that disease or disorder. What test result values will the physician be looking for and what do these values indicate about states of health or illness in the patient? Write your findings in the space below.

____

____

____

____

C. How can the medical assistant who is performing routine blood collection procedures on patients who require blood monitoring support and encourage these patients, who may be depressed or very anxious and fearful of the blood testing process and who often grow tired of constantly being stuck like a pincushion?

____

____

CASE STUDY

Case 1

Wayne Elder is a regular patient at Inner City Health Care. Two days ago, he began to feel fatigued, developing a cough, fever, and chills. Dr. Ray Reynolds has examined Mr. Elder and, based on the presented symptoms, makes a clinical diagnosis of influenza.

Discuss the following:

1. What type of blood test will Dr. Reynolds order to confirm his diagnosis?
2. What type of results are to be expected based on a diagnosis confirming clinical data?

Case 2

Maria Jover is complaining of a constant rundown feeling. After examining her, Dr. Elizabeth King has ordered a hemoglobin determination. Also, due to a past history of blood transfusion, she has also ordered an HIV test to be done at an outside reference laboratory. Dr. King asks Ellen Armstrong, CMA, to perform the venipuncture procedure on Maria to obtain the blood specimens for analysis.

Discuss the following:

1. What tube will Ellen use to collect the blood sample to be used for the hemoglobin determination test?
2. What is Dr. King hoping to learn from the hemoglobin determination results?
3. With the fact that HIV infection cannot yet be ruled out, what standard precautions should Ellen follow in performing the venipuncture and the automated hemoglobin determination test?
4. What are your personal feelings about performing venipuncture on individuals who may be infected with HIV?

SUPPLEMENTARY RESOURCES

Study Guide Disk: Additional practice exercises for this chapter are available on the study guide disk found in the back of the textbook.

Medical Assisting Videos: Appropriate content is available on Delmar's Medical Assisting Videos, 2nd ed., Tape 13, on the following topics:

Basic Information for Specimen Taking
and Laboratory Work
Butterfly Collection From Hand Vein
Capillary Puncture
Perform Hematologic Tests and Record the Results
When the Physician Orders a Specimen
Collect and Label a Blood Specimen
Collecting Tubes
Blood Smear

SKILLS COMPETENCY ASSESSMENT

Procedure 17–1: Hemoglobin Determination (Manual Method Using a Spectrophotometer)

Student's Name: ______________________________ Date: ____________

Objective: To properly and safely perform a manual hemoglobin determination.

Conditions: The student demonstrates the ability to properly and safely perform a manual hemoglobin determination using a spectrophotometer to evaluate the oxygen-carrying capacity of the blood, using the following equipment and supplies: gloves, hand disinfectant, EDTA blood sample(s), spectrophotometer, hemoglobin standard solution, cuvettes, laboratory stretch film, 10 percent chlorine bleach solution, UNOHEME® hemoglobin system or supplies for manual hemoglobin, biohazard container. Consult operating manual for specific instructions for spectrophotometer.

Time Requirements and Accuracy Standards: 20 minutes. Points assigned reflect importance of step to meeting objective: Important = (5) Essential = (10) Critical = (15). Automatic failure results if any of the **critical** tasks are omitted or performed incorrectly.

STANDARD PRECAUTIONS:

SKILLS ASSESSMENT CHECKLIST

Task Performed	Possible Points	TASKS		
❑	5	Washes hands and puts on gloves.		
❑	5	Assembles equipment and materials.		
❑	10	Turns on spectrophotometer, sets wavelength at 540 nm.		
		UNOHEME® Method		
		❑	5	Draws 20 μL of well-mixed blood into the UNOHEME capillary.
		❑	15	Inserts capillary into UNOHEME reservoir and draws blood into reagent. Rinses capillary several times, taking care not to overflow pipette.
		❑	5	Mixes contents by swirling; lets sit five minutes.
		❑	10	Transfers contents of reservoir to a cuvette.
		❑	15	Places diluting fluid from an unused UNOHEME reservoir into a cuvette labeled "blank."
		❑	5	Pipettes 5 mL of a hemoglobin standard into cuvette labeled "Std."
			55	(Subtotal for UNOHEME® Method)
		or		
		Manual Method		
		❑	5	Labels test tubes blank, standard, and unknown.

SKILLS COMPETENCY ASSESSMENT — continued

Procedure 17–1: Hemoglobin Determination (Manual Method Using a Spectrophotometer)

Task Performed	Possible Points	TASKS		
		❑	15	Dispenses 5.0 mL of Drabkins reagent into blank and unknown tubes and 5.0 mL of hemoglobin standard into standard tube.
		❑	10	Mixes blood samples for two minutes.
		❑	5	Draws up 0.02 mL of blood with micropipette, wiping off excess blood.
		❑	5	Dispenses blood sample into unknown tube.
		❑	15	Mixes contents thoroughly and lets stand for at least ten minutes.
			55	(Subtotal for Manual Method)
❑	10	Transfers contents of the tubes to cuvettes.		
❑	15	Places "blank" cuvette in spectrophotometer well; sets absorbance to zero following manufacturer's instructions.		
❑	10	Places "standard" cuvette into spectrophotometer well; reads and records absorbance.		
❑	10	Places "sample" cuvette into spectrophotometer well; reads and records absorbance.		
❑	15	Uses proper formula to calculate hemoglobin concentration; records results.		
❑	5	Properly discards specimens and disposes of waste in biohazard container.		
❑	5	Disinfects and cleans equipment and work area. Returns equipment to storage.		
❑	5	Removes gloves; properly disposes of gloves in biohazard container; washes hands with disinfectant soap.		
❑	10	Documents procedure.		
❑	5	Completed the tasks within 20 minutes.		
❑	15	Results obtained were accurate.		

______	Earned	ADD POINTS OF TASKS CHECKED
180	Points	TOTAL POINTS POSSIBLE
______	SCORE	DETERMINE SCORE (divide points earned by total points possible, multiply results by 100)

Actual Student Time Needed to Complete Procedure: ____________

Student's Initials: ____________ Instructor's Initials: ____________ Grade: ____________

Suggestions for Improvement: ____________

Evaluator's Name (print) ____________

Evaluator's Signature ____________

Comments ____________

DOCUMENTATION

Record test results in the patient's medical record.

Date: ____________

Charting: ____________

____

____

Student's Initials: ____________

SKILLS COMPETENCY ASSESSMENT

Procedure 17–2: Hemoglobin Determination (Hemoglobin Analyzer)

Student's Name: ______________________________ Date: ____________

Objective: To properly and safely perform an automated hemoglobin determination.

Conditions: The student demonstrates the ability to properly and safely perform an automated hemoglobin determination to evaluate the oxygen capacity of the blood using the following equipment and supplies: gloves; hand disinfectant; 10 percent chlorine bleach solution; capillary puncture equipment or blood samples collected in EDTA; HbDirect™ System, HemoCue®, or other hemoglobin analyzer with appropriate supplies; biohazard container; sharps container.

Time Requirements and Accuracy Standards: 20 minutes. Points assigned reflect importance of step to meeting objective: Important = (5) Essential = (10) Critical = (15). Automatic failure results if any of the **critical** tasks are omitted or performed incorrectly.

STANDARD PRECAUTIONS:

SKILLS ASSESSMENT CHECKLIST

Task Performed	Possible Points	TASKS		
❑	5	Washes hands and puts on gloves.		
❑	5	Assembles equipment and materials.		
❑	5	Turns on, warms up, and calibrates or standardizes instruments following manufacturer's instructions.		
❑	10	Performs a capillary puncture observing Bloodborne Pathogen Standards. Wipes away the first drop of blood with tissue or sterile cotton ball.		
❑	15	Collects blood from puncture into capillary tube or cuvette appropriate for analyzer being used; avoids trapping air bubbles.		
❑	5	Wipes off excess blood without touching open end of device.		
		HbDirect™		
		❑	5	Inserts filled capillary tube into a cyanmethemoglobin vial and caps tightly.
		❑	15	Inverts five to ten times to empty vial of blood; lets stand for five minutes at room temperature.
		❑	10	Inverts vial slowly, holds horizontally for three seconds, slowly returns to upright position.
		❑	5	Positions vial so capillary tube is at the back of the vial.
		❑	5	Wipes fingerprints from sides of vial.
		❑	5	Checks that the reagent vial is tightly capped.
		❑	10	Properly inserts into Hemoglobin Analyzer.
		❑	5	*Rationale:* Understands that following proper steps for insertion ensures that the analyzer light path is not obstructed.

Task Performed	Possible Points	TASKS		
		❑	5	Waits five seconds, reads the analyzer display; checks that capillary tube remains in upper half of vial.
			65	(Subtotal for Hb Direct™ Method)
		or		
		HemoCue®		
		❑	15	Inserts filled cuvette into HemoCue® photometer within ten minutes of filling.
		❑	10	Reads and records hemoglobin value.
			25	(Subtotal for HemoCue® Method)
❑	5	Properly disposes of contaminated waste in biohazard container.		
❑	5	Returns all equipment to proper storage.		
❑	5	Cleans and disinfects counters.		
❑	5	Removes gloves; properly disposes of gloves in biohazard container; washes hands with disinfectant soap. Documents procedure.		
❑	5	Completed the tasks within 20 minutes.		
❑	15	Results obtained were accurate.		

________	Earned	ADD POINTS OF TASKS CHECKED
150	Points	TOTAL POINTS POSSIBLE FOR HbDIRECT™
110	Points	TOTAL POINTS POSSIBLE FOR HEMOCUE® METHOD
________	SCORE	DETERMINE SCORE (divide points earned by total points possible, multiply results by 100)

Actual Student Time Needed to Complete Procedure: ____________

Student's Initials: ____________ Instructor's Initials: ____________ Grade: ____________

Suggestions for Improvement: ________________________________

Evaluator's Name (print) ________________________________

Evaluator's Signature ________________________________

Comments ________________________________

DOCUMENTATION

Record test results in the patient's medical record.

Date: ____________________

Charting: ________________________________

____

____

Student's Initials: ____________

SKILLS COMPETENCY ASSESSMENT

Procedure 17–3: Microhematocrit

Student's Name: ______________________ Date: __________

Objective: To properly and safely perform the microhematocrit procedure.

Conditions: The student demonstrates the ability to properly and safely perform the microhematocrit procedure using a few microliters of blood in a capillary tube to separate the cellular elements of the blood from the plasma by centrifugation, using the following equipment and supplies: gloves; hand disinfectant; capillary tubes, plain and with heparin; acrylic safety shield; precalibrated capillary tubes (optional); sealing clay or disposable plastic sealing caps; microhematocrit centrifuge and reader; tube of anticoagulated venous blood; paper towels or soft laboratory tissue; 70 percent alcohol or alcohol swabs; sterile, disposable blood lancets; surface disinfectant; biohazard and sharps containers.

Time Requirements and Accuracy Standards: 20 minutes. Points assigned reflect importance of step to meeting objective: Important = (5) Essential = (10) Critical = (15). Automatic failure results if any of the **critical** tasks are omitted or performed incorrectly.

STANDARD PRECAUTIONS:

SKILLS ASSESSMENT CHECKLIST

Task Performed	Possible Points	TASKS		
❑	5	Washes hands and puts on gloves.		
❑	5	Assembles equipment and materials for capillary puncture and microhematocrit.		
❑	5	Fills two capillary tubes from a capillary puncture.		
		❑	5	Performs capillary puncture.
		❑	5	Wipes away first drop of blood.
		❑	10	Touches one end of heparinized capillary tube to the second drop of blood, fills tube ¾ full. For precalibrated tubes, fills to the line.
		❑	5	Fills second tube in same manner.
		❑	5	Wipes excess blood from sides of tubes.
		❑	10	Seals the capillary tubes by placing clean end into tray of sealing clay.
❑	5	Fills two capillary tubes using EDTA anticoagulated blood.		
		❑	10	Mixes blood for two minutes by gently rocking tube from end to end by mechanical mixer or fifty to sixty times by hand.
		❑	5	Uses acrylic safety shield to remove cap from tube.
		❑	5	Tilts tube, inserts tip of plain capillary tube, and fills ¾ full by capillary action. For precalibrated tubes, fills to the line.
		❑	15	Seals the tube. If using self-sealing tubes, checks that plug has expanded.

Task Performed	Possible Points	TASKS
		❑ 5 Fills second tube in same manner.
❑	10	Makes sure interior sealing clay edge appears level in tubes.
❑	10	Places tubes in the microhematocrit centrifuge with sealed ends securely against gasket; fastens both lids securely.
❑	15	Sets timer, centrifuges for prescribed time (varies from two to five minutes, depending upon the equipment used).
❑	5	Unlocks lids after centrifuge comes to complete stop.
❑	15	Determines microhematocrit values using the appropriate method.
❑	10	Averages the values from the two tubes and records results.
❑	5	Discards capillary tubes and used lancets into sharps container.
❑	5	Cleans and returns equipment to proper storage; cleans and disinfects work area.
❑	5	Removes and discards gloves into biohazard container; washes hands with disinfectant soap.
❑	5	Completed the tasks within 20 minutes.
❑	15	Results obtained were accurate.

______	Earned	ADD POINTS OF TASKS CHECKED
200	Points	TOTAL POINTS POSSIBLE
______	SCORE	DETERMINE SCORE (divide points earned by total points possible, multiply results by 100)

Actual Student Time Needed to Complete Procedure: ____________

Student's Initials: ____________ Instructor's Initials: ____________ Grade: ____________

Suggestions for Improvement: ____________

Evaluator's Name (print) ____________

Evaluator's Signature ____________

Comments ____________

DOCUMENTATION

Record test results in the patient's medical record.

Date: ____________

Charting: ____________

____

____

Student's Initials: ____________

SKILLS COMPETENCY ASSESSMENT

Procedure 17–4: White Blood Cell Count (Unopette Method)

Student's Name: ______________________________ Date: __________

Objective: To determine white blood cell count using a self-contained system.

Conditions: The student demonstrates the ability to properly and safely perform the white blood cell count using a self-contained system to determine the total number of white blood cells per cubic millimeter of blood using the following supplies and equipment: gloves, surface disinfectant, tube of EDTA blood or supplies for capillary puncture, hand disinfectant, unopette WBC or WBC/Platelet system, hemacytometer with coverglass, hand tally counter, 70 percent alcohol, microscope, lens paper, acrylic safety shield, biohazard and sharps waste containers. This procedure demonstrates use of the Unopette system; consult manufacturer's package insert for specific instructions.

Time Requirements and Accuracy Standards: 30 minutes. Points assigned reflect importance of step to meeting objective: Important = (5) Essential = (10) Critical = (15). Automatic failure results if any of the **critical** tasks are omitted or performed incorrectly.

STANDARD PRECAUTIONS:

SKILLS ASSESSMENT CHECKLIST

Task Performed	Possible Points	TASKS
☐	5	Assembles equipment and materials.
☐	5	Places clean hemacytometer coverglass on a clean hemacytometer.
☐	5	Pierces the diaphragm of the Unopette reservoir with pipette shield.
☐	5	Sets up acrylic safety shield, washes hands, puts on gloves.
☐	5	Removes shield from pipette assembly. Uses safety shield as barrier from blood or blood solution.
☐	15	Fills capillary tube from capillary puncture or tube of well-mixed EDTA blood.
☐	10	Allows blood to rise in capillary until it automatically stops.
☐	5	Wipes off excess blood from exterior of pipette without touching the tip with the tissue.
☐	15	Squeezes the reservoir slightly, careful not to expel any liquid. Maintains pressure on reservoir and inserts capillary pipette, seating pipette firmly into the neck of the reservoir without expelling any liquid.
☐	5	Releases the pressure on the reservoir, drawing blood out of the capillary into the diluent.
☐	10	Squeezes reservoir gently three to four times to rinse remaining blood from the pipette without allowing blood-diluent mixture to flow out of the top.

Task Performed	Possible Points	TASKS
❑	10	Swirls to gently mix contents of reservoir; lets system sit for ten minutes (but not longer than one hour) to destroy red blood cells.
❑	10	Removes pipette from reservoir and inserts into neck of reservoir so pipette tip extends upward from the reservoir.
❑	5	Thoroughly mixes contents of reservoir, inverts reservoir, and gently squeezes to discard four or five drops onto paper towel.
❑	5	Touches tip of pipette to edge of coverglass and counting chamber. Fills both counting chambers.
❑	15	Places filled hemacytometer into a Petri dish beside a damp cotton ball; lets stand for ten minutes.
❑	5	Carefully places hemacytometer on the microscope stage to secure it; uses low-power objective (10×) to bring ruled area into focus.
❑	15	Counts white blood cells within all nine counting squares using the boundary rule; records results.
❑	10	Repeats count using other side of hemacytometer; records results.
❑	10	Averages results of the two sides.
❑	10	Calculates 10 percent of the average and adds that figure to the average; multiplies total by 100. Documents results.
❑	5	Places hemacytometer and coverglass in bleach solution for ten minutes; rinses with water, dries carefully with lens paper.
❑	5	Discards sharps and Unopette assemble in sharps container. Returns tube of blood to storage or discards appropriately.
❑	5	Returns equipment to storage.
❑	5	Cleans and disinfects work area.
❑	5	Removes and discards gloves in biohazard container.
❑	5	Washes hands with hand disinfectant.
❑	5	Completed the tasks within 30 minutes.
❑	15	Results obtained were accurate.

______	Earned	ADD POINTS OF TASKS CHECKED
230	Points	TOTAL POINTS POSSIBLE
______	SCORE	DETERMINE SCORE (divide points earned by total points possible, multiply results by 100)

SKILLS COMPETENCY ASSESSMENT — continued

Procedure 17–4: White Blood Cell Count (Unopette Method)

Actual Student Time Needed to Complete Procedure: ____________

Student's Initials: ____________ Instructor's Initials: ____________ Grade: ____________

Suggestions for Improvement: ____

Evaluator's Name (print) ____

Evaluator's Signature ____

Comments ____

DOCUMENTATION

Records results in the patient's medical record.

Date: ________________________

Charting: ____

____

____

Student's Initials: ______________

SKILLS COMPETENCY ASSESSMENT

Procedure 17–5: Red Blood Cell Count (Unopette Method)

Student's Name: ______________________________ Date: ____________

Objective: To count red blood cells.

Conditions: The student demonstrates the ability to accurately count red blood cells using the Unopette method and the following equipment and supplies: gloves, hand disinfectant, materials for capillary puncture or blood sample anticoagulated with EDTA, hemacytometer with coverglass, test tube rack or beaker, Unopette for RBC count, microscope, lens paper, 70 percent alcohol, hand tally counter, surface disinfectant, sharps and biohazard containers, acrylic safety shield. Procedure follows use of Unopette system; consult package insert for specific instructions.

Time Requirements and Accuracy Standards: 30 minutes. Points assigned reflect importance of step to meeting objective: Important = (5) Essential = (10) Critical = (15). Automatic failure results if any of the **critical** tasks are omitted or performed incorrectly.

STANDARD PRECAUTIONS:

SKILLS ASSESSMENT CHECKLIST

Task Performed	Possible Points	TASKS
❑	5	Assembles equipment; sets up acrylic safety shield.
❑	5	Places clean hemacytometer coverglass over a clean hemacytometer.
❑	5	Washes hands and puts on gloves.
❑	10	Punctures diaphragm of the Unopette by holding reservoir firmly on flat surface with one hand and using the pipette shields tip to make a puncture large enough to easily accommodate the pipette.
❑	5	Removes shield from pipette assembly.
❑	15	Fills capillary pipette from capillary puncture or a well-mixed tube of EDTA anticoagulated blood. Pipette fills by capillary action and stops automatically.
❑	5	*Rationale:* Understands that pipette must be kept horizontal or at a slight (5°) upward angle to avoid overfilling.
❑	5	Wipes excess blood from exterior without allowing tissue to touch pipette tip.
❑	10	Squeezes reservoir slightly, careful not to expel liquid.
❑	15	Maintains pressure on reservoir and inserts capillary pipette into reservoir, seating pipette firmly into the reservoir neck without expelling any liquid.
❑	15	Releases pressure on reservoir, drawing blood out of capillary pipette into diluent.

SKILLS COMPETENCY ASSESSMENT — continued

Procedure 17–5: Red Blood Cell Count (Unopette Method)

Task Performed	Possible Points	TASKS
❑	10	Squeezes reservoir gently, three to four times, to rinse remaining blood from pipette without allowing blood-diluent mixture to flow out of the top.
❑	5	Gently swirls reservoir to mix contents.
❑	10	Withdraws pipette from the reservoir and inserts it into neck of reservoir in reverse position (pipette tip projects upward from reservoir).
❑	10	Thoroughly mixes reservoir contents. Inverts and gently squeezes to discard four to five drops onto a paper towel.
❑	15	Fills both sides of hemacytometer, places on microscope stage, and secures. Uses low-power (10×) objective to bring the ruled area into focus; locates large central square.
❑	10	Rotates high-power objective (45×) into position; uses fine adjustment knob to focus image.
❑	5	Adjusts light and/or condenser so red blood cells are visible.
❑	15	Counts cells in four corner squares and one center square within the large center square using left-to-right, right-to-left counting pattern; records results for each of the five squares.
❑	15	Repeats count using other side of hemacytometer; calculates RBC count using work-sheet; records.
❑	5	Disinfects hemacytometer and coverglass. Discards specimens and disposable materials appropriately.
❑	5	Returns equipment to proper storage; cleans and disinfects work area.
❑	5	Removes gloves and discards in a biohazard waste container; washes hands with hand disinfectant.
❑	5	Completed the tasks within 30 minutes.
❑	15	Results obtained were accurate.

______	Earned	ADD POINTS OF TASKS CHECKED
225	Points	TOTAL POINTS POSSIBLE
______	SCORE	DETERMINE SCORE (divide points earned by total points possible, multiply results by 100)

Actual Student Time Needed to Complete Procedure: ____________

Student's Initials: ____________ Instructor's Initials: ____________ Grade: ____________

Suggestions for Improvement: ____________

Evaluator's Name (print) ____________

Evaluator's Signature ____________

Comments ____________

DOCUMENTATION

Record results in the patient's medical record.

Date: ____________

Charting: ____________

____

____

____

____

____

Student's Initials: ____________

SKILLS COMPETENCY ASSESSMENT

Procedure 17–6: Preparation of a Differential Blood Smear Slide

Student's Name: ______________________________ Date: ____________

Objective: To properly and safely prepare an anticoagulated blood smear to microscopically view the cellular components.

Conditions: The student demonstrates the ability to properly prepare an anticoagulated blood smear and a capillary blood smear by spreading blood on a microscopic slide, altering the form, structure, and distribution of cells (morphology) as little as possible to microscopically view the cellular components. The student uses the following equipment and supplies: gloves, hand disinfectant, pencil, microscope slides (1″ × 3″), 95 percent ethyl alcohol, laboratory tissue, capillary tubes (plain and heparinized) slide drying rack, hot water, detergent, distilled water, methanol in coplin jar, fresh EDTA anticoagulated blood specimen, materials for capillary puncture, surface disinfectant, sharps and biohazard waste containers.

Time Requirements and Accuracy Standards: 30 minutes. Points assigned reflect importance of step to meeting objective: Important = (5) Essential = (10) Critical = (15). Automatic failure results if any of the **critical** tasks are omitted or performed incorrectly.

STANDARD PRECAUTIONS:

SKILLS ASSESSMENT CHECKLIST

Task Performed	Possible Points	TASKS
❑	5	Assembles equipment and materials.
❑	5	Places clean slide on flat surface, touching only edges with fingers; writes patient's ID on frosted area.
❑	5	Washes hands and puts on gloves.
❑	10	Uses anticoagulated blood sample supplied by instructor; mixes blood well and fills a plain capillary tube.
❑	10	Dispenses a small drop of blood from the capillary tube onto the slide ½″ to ¾″ from right end (if left-handed, reverse instructions).
❑	10	Places end of clean, polished unchipped spreader slide at 30–35° angle in front of the drop of blood, balancing spreader lightly with fingertips.
❑	10	Slides spreader back into the drop of blood until the blood spreads along three-fourths of the width of the spreader.
❑	5	*Rationale:* Spreader slide is held at a 30–35° angle to ensure proper thickness of the smear.
❑	10	Pushes the spreader forward with a quick, steady motion, using the other hand to keep the slide steady. Examines to see if smear is satisfactory.

Task Performed	Possible Points	TASKS
❑	15	Repeats procedure until two satisfactory smears are obtained.
❑	10	Places slide on end in slide drying rack and allows to air dry quickly.
❑	5	Places dried smear in absolute menthol for 30 to 60 seconds to preserve smear; removes and allows to air dry.
❑	5	Stores slide for staining.
❑	15	Performs a capillary puncture, wipes away the first blood drop, fills one or two heparinized capillary tubes, prepares two blood smears from capillary blood. Stores slides for staining.
❑	5	Discards blood specimens appropriately or stores for later use. Places contaminated materials in proper biohazard or sharps containers.
❑	5	Cleans equipment and returns it to proper storage, cleans and disinfects work area.
❑	5	Removes and discards gloves in biohazard waste container, washes hands with hand disinfectant.
❑	5	Completed the tasks within 30 minutes.
❑	15	Results obtained were accurate.

_______	Earned	ADD POINTS OF TASKS CHECKED
155	Points	TOTAL POINTS POSSIBLE
_______	SCORE	DETERMINE SCORE (divide points earned by total points possible, multiply results by 100)

Actual Student Time Needed to Complete Procedure: ____________

Student's Initials: ____________ Instructor's Initials: ____________ Grade: ____________

Suggestions for Improvement: ________________________________

Evaluator's Name (print) ________________________________

Evaluator's Signature ________________________________

Comments ________________________________

SKILLS COMPETENCY ASSESSMENT

Procedure 17–7: Staining a Differential Blood Smear Slide

Student's Name: ______________________________ Date: ____________

Objective: To properly and safely apply a stain to a blood smear.

Conditions: The student demonstrates the ability to properly and safely apply a stain to a blood smear so the cells and structures may be more easily viewed through microscopic examination. The student uses the following equipment and supplies: gloves, hand disinfectant, freshly prepared or preserved blood smears, blood stain reagents, tube of EDTA anticoagulated blood (optional), staining rack, immersion oil, microscope, lens paper, forceps, laboratory tissue, lap apron or coat, staining jars for quick stains, surface disinfectant, sharps and biohazard waste containers, slide storage box. Stain characteristics may vary with stain lot; follow the manufacturer's instructions for best results.

Time Requirements and Accuracy Standards: 30 minutes. Points assigned reflect importance of step to meeting objective: Important = (5) Essential = (10) Critical = (15). Automatic failure results if any of the **critical** tasks are omitted or performed incorrectly.

STANDARD PRECAUTIONS:

SKILLS ASSESSMENT CHECKLIST

Task Performed	Possible Points	TASKS
Two-Step Method		
❑	5	Washes hands, puts on gloves.
❑	5	Assembles equipment and materials.
❑	5	Prepares blood smear (see Procedure 17–6), or obtains a previously prepared, fixed smear.
❑	5	Stains a blood smear by one of the following methods:
❑	5	Places dried smear on staining rack or flat surface, blood side up.
❑	15	Floods smear with Wright's stain without allowing stain to flow over sides of slide; leaves stain on slide for exact time supplied by instructor (one to three minutes; time varies according to manufacturer's instructions).
❑	15	Adds buffer, dropwise, to stain until buffer volume is equal to the stain.
❑	5	Blows gently on fluid surface to mix the solutions. Observes for metallic green sheen.
❑	15	Leaves buffer on slide for exact time supplied by instructor (two to four minutes; time varies according to manufacturer's instructions); does not allow mixture to run off slide.
❑	5	Rinses thoroughly and continuously with gentle stream of tap or distilled water, drains water off.
❑	5	Wipes backs of slides with wet gauze to remove excess stain, stands smears on end to air dry.
❑	5	Completed the tasks within 30 minutes.

Task Performed	Possible Points	TASKS
❑	15	Results obtained were accurate.

________	Earned	ADD POINTS OF TASKS CHECKED
105	Points	TOTAL POINTS POSSIBLE
________	SCORE	DETERMINE SCORE (divide points earned by total points possible, multiply results by 100)

Three-Step Method

Task Performed	Possible Points	TASKS
❑	20	Performs the first four steps of the Two-Step Method.
❑	15	Dips dry smear into solutions following manufacturer's instructions without allowing slide to dry between solutions; rinses slide if necessary.
❑	5	Removes excess stain from back of slide with wet gauze; stands slide on end to air dry.
❑	5	Places dry slide on microscope stage, stain side up; focuses on low power (10×) objective.
❑	10	Scans slide to find area where cells are barely touching each other.
❑	15	Places drop of immersion oil on slide, rotates oil immersion lens carefully into position, focuses with fine adjustment knob only.
❑	15	Observes erythrocytes, leukocytes, nuclei, neutrophil granules, and platelets for proper stain color.
❑	5	Rotates low power (10×) objective into position; removes slide from microscope stage.
❑	5	Cleans oil objective thoroughly with lens paper; gently wipes oil from slide with soft tissue.
❑	5	Cleans equipment and returns to proper storage; cleans work area with disinfectant.
❑	5	Removes and discards gloves in a biohazard waste container; washes hands with hand disinfectant.
❑	5	Completed the tasks within 30 minutes.
❑	15	Results obtained were accurate.

________	Earned	ADD POINTS OF TASKS CHECKED
125	Points	TOTAL POINTS POSSIBLE
________	SCORE	DETERMINE SCORE (divide points earned by total points possible, multiply results by 100)

Actual Student Time Needed to Complete Procedure: ____________

Student's Initials: ____________ Instructor's Initials: ____________ Grade: ____________

Suggestions for Improvement: ________________________________

Evaluator's Name (print) ________________________________

Evaluator's Signature ________________________________

Comments ________________________________

SKILLS COMPETENCY ASSESSMENT

Procedure 17–8: Differential Leukocyte Count

Student's Name: ______________________________ Date: ____________

Objective: To properly and safely examine a stained blood smear for differential leukocyte count.

Conditions: The student demonstrates the ability to properly and safely examine a stained blood smear to observe, identify, and record 100 leukocytes and differentiate the five types of leukocytes by size, nuclear characteristics, and cytoplasmic characteristics. The student uses the following supplies and equipment: gloves, hand disinfectant, stained normal blood smears, microscope with oil immersion objective, immersion oil, lens paper, soft tissue or soft paper towels, blood cell atlas, tally counter or differential counter, worksheet, sharps and biohazard waste containers, surface disinfectant.

Time Requirements and Accuracy Standards: 30 minutes. Points assigned reflect importance of step to meeting objective: Important = (5) Essential = (10) Critical = (15). Automatic failure results if any of the **critical** tasks are omitted or performed incorrectly.

SKILLS ASSESSMENT CHECKLIST

Task Performed	Possible Points	TASKS
❑	5	Washes hands, puts on gloves.
❑	5	Assembles equipment and materials.
❑	5	Places stained smear on microscope stage and secures; uses low power (10×) objective to locate feathered edge of smear.
❑	5	Focuses cells using coarse adjustment.
❑	10	Scans smear to find area where red blood cells are barely touching.
❑	10	Places one drop of immersion oil on smear; rotates oil immersion objective carefully into position; focuses cells using fine adjustment.
❑	15	Allows maximum light into the objective by raising condenser and opening diaphragm; scans the smear to observe leukocytes.
❑	15	Studies smear to identify all five types of leukocytes, platelets, and red cells. Repeats procedural steps until cells can be readily identified.
❑	5	Using the same slide or a different one, restarts procedure, performing each procedural step through identification of cells.
❑	15	Counts 100 consecutive leukocytes using appropriate counting pattern. Moves the slide or movable stage so consecutive microscopic fields are viewed.
❑	10	Observes the red blood cells in at least ten fields, noting hemoglobin content and recording as normochromic or hypochromic.
❑	15	Observes red blood cell size, recording as normocytic, microcytic, or macrocytic. Uses appropriate method to record an approximation of the number of cells affected.

Task Performed	Possible Points	TASKS
❑	15	Observes platelets in at least ten fields, noting morphology and estimating number of platelets per oil immersion field and recording appropriately.
❑	5	Rotates low power (10×) objective into place; removes slide from stage.
❑	5	Cleans the oil immersion objective with lens paper and checks microscope stage and condenser for oil; cleans with soft tissue if necessary.
❑	5	Places slide properly in slide box or disposes of slide as instructed; cleans equipment and returns it to proper storage.
❑	5	Disposes of waste in appropriate sharps or biohazard waste container.
❑	5	Cleans and disinfects work area.
❑	5	Removes gloves and discards in biohazard container; washes hands with hand disinfectant.
❑	5	Completed the tasks within 30 minutes.
❑	15	Results are within acceptable range.

________	Earned	ADD POINTS OF TASKS CHECKED
190	Points	TOTAL POINTS POSSIBLE
________	SCORE	DETERMINE SCORE (divide points earned by total points possible, multiply results by 100)

Actual Student Time Needed to Complete Procedure: ____________

Student's Initials: ____________ Instructor's Initials: ____________ Grade: ____________

Suggestions for Improvement: ______________________________

Evaluator's Name (print) ______________________________

Evaluator's Signature ______________________________

Comments ______________________________

DOCUMENTATION

Record results in the patient's medical record.

Date: ______________________

Charting: ______________________________

____

____

Student's Initials: ______________

SKILLS COMPETENCY ASSESSMENT

Procedure 17–9: Erythrocyte Sedimentation Rate

Student's Name: ______________________________ Date: __________

Objective: To properly and safely examine a blood sample to determine erythrocyte sedimentation rate.

Conditions: The student demonstrates the ability to properly and safely examine a blood sample by using either the Sediplast (Westergren) or Wintrobe method to record the erythrocyte sedimentation rate. The student uses the following equipment and supplies: gloves, hand disinfectant, sample of venous blood collected in EDTA, equipment for Sediplast kit or Wintrobe method, timer, 10 percent chlorine bleach solution, sharps and biohazard waste containers, acrylic safety shield. Consult the manufacturer's package insert for specific instructions for ESR kit use.

Time Requirements and Accuracy Standards: 75 minutes. Points assigned reflect importance of step to meeting objective: Important = (5) Essential = (10) Critical = (15). Automatic failure results if any of the **critical** tasks are omitted or performed incorrectly.

STANDARD PRECAUTIONS:

SKILLS ASSESSMENT CHECKLIST

Task Performed	Possible Points	TASKS
☐	5	Washes hands and puts on gloves.
☐	5	Assembles equipment and materials. Gently mixes blood sample for two minutes.
		Sediplast ESR (modified Westergren)
☐	15	Removes stopper from Sedivial and fills with 0.8 mL blood to indicated mark. Replaces stopper and inverts vial several times to mix.
☐	15	Places vial in Sediplast rack on level surface. Gently inserts disposable Sediblast pipette through pierceable stopper with twisting motion; pushes down until the pipette rests on the bottom of the vial. Pipette autozeros blood and excess flows into sealed reservoir compartment.
☐	10	Sets timer for one hour; returns blood sample to proper storage.
☐	15	Lets pipette stand undisturbed for exactly one hour; records results. Uses scale on the tube to measure the distance from the top of plasma to the top of red blood cells. Records sedimentation rate.
☐	10	Disposes of tube and vial in appropriate biohazard waste container.
☐	5	Completed the tasks within 75 minutes.
☐	15	Results obtained were accurate.

________	Earned	ADD POINTS OF TASKS CHECKED
95	Points	TOTAL POINTS POSSIBLE
________	SCORE	DETERMINE SCORE (divide points earned by total points possible, multiply results by 100)

Task Performed	Possible Points	TASKS
		Wintrobe Method
❑	10	Places tube in Wintrobe sedimentation rack; checks leveling bubble to ensure rack is level.
❑	15	Fills Wintrobe tube to the zero mark with well-mixed blood using Pasteur pipette and being careful not to overfill. Fills tube from bottom to avoid air bubbles.
❑	5	Sets timer for one hour, being certain tube is vertical.
❑	10	Returns blood sample to proper storage.
❑	15	After exactly one hour, correctly measures the distance the erythrocytes have fallen, in mm, and records the sedimentation rate.
❑	5	Disinfects and clean equipment, returning it to proper storage.
❑	5	Disposes of waste in appropriate biohazard or sharps container.
❑	5	Cleans and disinfects work area.
❑	5	Removes gloves and discards in a biohazard waste container; washes hands with hand disinfectant.
❑	5	Completed the tasks within 75 minutes.
❑	15	Results obtained were accurate.

______	Earned	ADD POINTS OF TASKS CHECKED
95	Points	TOTAL POINTS POSSIBLE
______	SCORE	DETERMINE SCORE (divide points earned by total points possible, multiply results by 100)

Actual Student Time Needed to Complete Procedure: ____________

Student's Initials: ____________ Instructor's Initials: ____________ Grade: ____________

Suggestions for Improvement: ____

Evaluator's Name (print) ____

Evaluator's Signature ____

Comments ____

DOCUMENTATION

Record results in the patient's medical record.

Charting: ____

____

____

Student's Initials: ____________

EVALUATION OF CHAPTER KNOWLEDGE

How has your instructor evaluated the knowledge you have achieved?

Knowledge	Instructor Evaluation *Good*	*Average*	*Poor*
Can discuss the role and importance of hematological studies as a diagnostic tool for physicians	_____	_____	_____
Can discuss clinical science of hematology	_____	_____	_____
Compares normal and abnormal values of CBC parameters and understands how CBC is used in diagnosis and treatment of disease	_____	_____	_____
Maintains aseptic technique and follows standard precautions throughout all procedures	_____	_____	_____
Understands the importance of following all quality control guidelines	_____	_____	_____
Displays the appropriate techniques in collecting and processing specimens	_____	_____	_____
Performs tests with competent skill necessary for entry-level employment	_____	_____	_____
Performs calculations accurately	_____	_____	_____
Documents all procedures according to laboratory policy	_____	_____	_____
Describes physiological reasons for different variations of test results in different states of health and disease	_____	_____	_____
Operates and maintains facility and equipment safely	_____	_____	_____
Exhibits empathy for patient and attends to patient's emotional needs during the collection of patient blood samples for analysis	_____	_____	_____

Student's Initials: ______ Instructor's Initials: ______

Grade: _______

CHAPTER 18

Urinalysis

PERFORMANCE OBJECTIVES

Urinalysis refers to the examination of urine as an aid in patient diagnosis or to follow the course of a disease. Urinalysis is a routine procedure in most physical examinations. Physicians often order a variety of tests on urine to help determine or rule out certain aberrations in order to make accurate patient diagnoses. It is essential that medical assistants understand both the importance of urinalysis and their own role in assisting in patient diagnosis and treatment. In this chapter, medical assisting students learn the basics of urinalysis, examination of urine specimens, including proper collection techniques for urine specimens, safety guidelines involved in collecting and handling specimens, and measures to ensure a consistent quality control program. Students learn to properly perform urinalysis testing and become cognizant of factors that may intervene with urinalysis accuracy. Observing standard precautions is mandatory in urinalysis procedures.

EXERCISES AND ACTIVITIES

Vocabulary Builder

A. *Match the following terms listed in Column A with corresponding definitions listed in Column B.*

Column A	Column B
1. Clinitest	A. Urine testing that includes physical, chemical, and microscopic testing of a urine sample.
2. Ketone	B. Crystalline material found in urine sediment; shapeless; possessing no definite form.
3. pH	C. Tiny structures usually formed by deposits of protein (or other substances) on the walls of renal tubes.
4. Urochrome	D. Reagent table test that confirms the presence of reducing sugars in the urine.

5. Sediment	E. Found in normal urine sediment, these structures generally have no particular significance; a few should be noted as they may indicate disease states.
6. Amorphous	F. Microorganisms cultivated in a nutrient medium.
7. Ictotest	G. Transparent, clear casts that are often hard to see in urine; these casts should be examined under subdued lighting.
8. Cultures	H. Confirmatory test for bilirubin.
9. Casts	I. Chemical compound produced during increased metabolism of fat; tested on a reagent strip.
10. Urinalysis	J. Curvature appearing in a liquid's upper surface when the liquid is placed in a container.
11. Acetest	K. Urine sample collected in the middle of the flow of urine.
12. Quality control	L. Test results that indicate a potentially life-threatening or greatly debilitating situation that must be reported to a physician immediately.
13. Specific gravity	M. Scale that indicates the relative alkalinity or acidity of a solution; measurement of hydrogen ion concentration.
14. Hyaline	N. Program that ensures accurate and dependable test results.
15. Crystals	O. Narrow strip of plastic on which pads containing reagents are attached; used in urinalysis to detect a variety of substances and values.
16. Midstream collection	P. Insoluble matter that settles to the bottom of a liquid; material examined in the urinalysis microscopic examination.
17. Panic values	Q. Ratio of weight of a given volume of a substance to the weight of the same volume of distilled water at the same temperature; test often performed during the urinalysis physical examination (can also appear on the reagent strip).
18. Reagent test strip	R. Opaque; lack of clarity.
19. Urea	S. Product used to test for the presence of abnormal amounts of acetone in the urine.
20. Meniscus	T. Principal end product of protein metabolism.
21. Turbid	U. Yellow pigment that provides color to urine.
22. Screening	V. Condition that occurs when the net rate at which the body produces acids or bases is equal to the net rate at which acids or bases are excreted.
23. Acid/base balance	W. Preliminary examination used to detect the most characteristic signs of a disorder that may entail further investigation.

B. Unscramble the following items to create the proper terms relating to urinalysis.

1. INUBBIRIL ______________________________

   Orange-yellow pigment that forms from the breakdown of hemoglobin in broken-down red blood cells. It usually travels in the bloodstream to the liver, where it is converted to a water-soluble form and excreted into the bile.

2. ARUTAHEMI ________________________________

   Abnormal presence of blood in urine, symptomatic of many disorders of the genitourinary system and renal diseases.

3. SLOGCUE ________________________________

   Simple sugar that is a major source of energy in the human body; monitoring of its levels in the urine and blood is a vital diagnostic test in diabetes and other disorders; a test on a reagent strip.

4. TEKYLCOUE SEESATER ________________________________

   Test on a reagent strip that indicates the presence of white blood cells in the urinary tract.

5. GENNUROBILIO ________________________________

   Colorless compound produced in the intestine after the breakdown by bacteria of bilirubin.

6. GEARSTEN ________________________________

   Chemical substances that detect or synthesize other substances in a chemical reaction and are used in laboratory analyses because they are known to react in a specific way.

7. CASISETOOKID ________________________________

   Accumulation of ketones in the body, occurring primarily as a compilation of diabetes mellitus; if left untreated, it could cause coma.

8. NICCARDIA MHYRTH ________________________________

   Pattern based on 24-hour cycle that emphasizes the repetition of certain physiologic phenomena such as eating and sleeping.

9. ERCTIENINA ________________________________

   Waste product formed in muscle that is excreted by the kidneys; elevated in blood and urine when kidney function is abnormal.

10. FAREOTCRETEM ________________________________

    Instrument that measures the refractive index of a substance or solution; used in the urinalysis chemical examination to measure the urine specimen's specific gravity.

11. RETINOMERU ________________________________

    Device used to measure specific gravity; consists of a float with a calibrated stem.

12. STRAPTUNANE ________________________________

    Urine that appears to be above the sediment when centrifuged; poured off before sediment is examined in the urinalysis microscopic examination.

13. MATM-LAFSHORL ________________________________

    Mucoprotein excreted by the epithelial cells of the renal tubules.

Learning Review

Fill in the blanks in the following paragraphs with the appropriate terms.

1. Urea
Filtration
Tubule
Homeostasis
Nephron
Soluble
Glomerulus
Salts
Electrolytes
Milliliters
Excess fluid
Urine
Waste products
Metabolism

The formation and excretion of ________________ is the principal method by which the body excretes water and the ________________ waste products of ________________. The kidneys control this process and also regulate the fluid outside the cells of the body, carefully maintaining the body's balance of fluids eliminated or retained, or ________________ of body fluids. The kidneys are responsible for the ________________ of __________, __________ and ________________ from the blood. Substances filtered out of the body can include water, ammonia, ______________, glucose, amino acids, creatinine, and __________. These wastes leave the body through the eliminated urine. The filtering unit of the kidney is called the ____________________. The ________________ is the part of the kidney that concentrates the filtered material. Together, these elements of the kidney form the ______________. Each minute, more than 1,000 ________________ of blood flows through the kidney to be cleansed.

2. Creatinine | Amino acids | Concentration
Threshold | Glucose | Kidney
Protein | Blood

While passing through the __________, some substances, such as __________ and __________, need to be reabsorbed into the __________. These substances are reabsorbed in relation to their __________ in the blood and are known as __________substances. Some of these substances need only be partially reabsorbed, such as __________ and __________.

3. Urine | Kidney | Sodium
Drugs | Hydrogen | Ammonium
Secreted | Blood

Toward the end of the ________________'s sojourn through the ________________, other substances that have not already been filtered are secreted into the ________________. For instance, substances such as ________________ and ________________ ions may be __________ in the urine in exchange for ________________. In addition, certain ________________ in the blood at this point may also be secreted into the urine.

4. A. After passing through a healthy kidney, urine composition is approximately ____ percent water and _____ percent dissolved substances, which generally come from dietary intake or metabolic waste products.

B. Identify each substance below as a normal (N) or an abnormal (AB) substance found in urine.

____ (1) Urobilinogen | ____ (4) Multiple Leukocytes | ____ (7) Erythrocytes
____ (2) Potassium | ____ (5) Lipids | ____ (8) Creatinine
____ (3) Uric acid | ____ (6) 1+ Protein | ____ (9) Chloride

C. When certain disease processes occur in the human body, changes in urine production can occur. List six possible changes.

(1) ______________________ (4) ______________________
(2) ______________________ (5) ______________________
(3) ______________________ (6) ______________________

5. When handling urine specimens, standard precautions must be followed to ensure that proper infection control standards are observed. In the space provided below, list five precautions used when handling urine specimens.
   (1) ______________________
   (2) ______________________
   (3) ______________________
   (4) ______________________
   (5) ______________________

Circle the correct response for each multiple choice question below.

6. Quality control (QC) programs
   A. provide a random spot-check of accuracy.
   B. ensure accurate and reliable results for the patient.
   C. provide comparisons with patient specimens necessary to interpret urinalysis test results.
7. Equipment and instruments used for urine testing
   A. must be disposed of properly in biohazard containers after each procedure.
   B. are self-calibrating and require no adjustment.
   C. should be checked daily for proper calibration.
8. Quality control procedures should be performed
   A. exactly as procedures are performed on patient specimens.
   B. on every other urine specimen tested.
   C. only by a licensed health care professional trained to interpret the results.
9. Urine control samples
   A. have no special storage requirements.
   B. are purchased commercially from manufacturers.
   C. are used to obtain baseline urinalysis results from healthy patients.
10. Documentation of quality control testing
   A. must be recorded in a daily urinalysis QC log and kept for at least three years.
   B. is not necessary unless the equipment is malfunctioning.
   C. should be recorded in the patient's medical record.
11. List six Clinical Laboratory Improvement Amendments (CLIA) regulations that apply to the clinical medical assistant performing urine testing:
   (1) ______________________
   (2) ______________________
   (3) ______________________
   (4) ______________________
   (5) ______________________
   (6) ______________________

12. A. One of the most important steps in the collection of urine specimens is to correctly identify the specimen through proper labeling. Using your own Social Security number as your ID number and Dr. Mark Woo as your physician, write out complete labeling information for a specimen of your own urine below.

Correct urine specimen label: ______________________________

____

B. What is the proper procedure for testing an unlabeled or incorrectly labeled specimen?

____

C. Name the four types of urine specimens frequently ordered by physicians.

(1) ______________ (3) ______________

(2) ______________ (4) ______________

D. Name the four methods of urine collected ordered by physicians.

(1) ______________ (3) ______________

(2) ______________ (4) ______________

13. A. What are the four steps in a physical examination of a urine specimen?

(1) ______________________________

(2) ______________________________

(3) ______________________________

(4) ______________________________

B. What does the specific gravity of urine indicate? ______________

____

C. Name three methods of measuring the specific gravity of a urine specimen and state the advantages or disadvantages of each. Which method is available in conjunction with chemical testing?

(1) ______________________________

(2) ______________________________

(3) ______________________________

14. Reagent test strips, or dipsticks, are used to test urine for many metabolic processes, including kidney and liver functions, urinary tract infection, and pH balance.

A. Match each test below to the information that best describes it.

______ 1. Glucose
______ 2. pH
______ 3. Urobilinogen
______ 4. Blood
______ 5. Nitrites
______ 6. Leukocyte
______ 7. Specific gravity
______ 8. Ketones
______ 9. Protein
______ 10. Bilirubin

A. These occur during prolonged fasting. They appear when excessive amounts of fatty acids are broken down into simpler compounds and when glucose availability is limited.

B. Increased levels of this substance suggest liver disease or bleeding disorders. It is a degradation product of bilirubin formed by intestinal bacteria.

C. This substance in a urine sample indicates infection, urinary tract trauma, kidney bleeding, and menses.

D. This substance can increase during a high fever and also indicates injury to the kidney, specifically to the glomerular membrane.

E. This test indicates white blood cells in the urinary tract, presumably attracted by invading bacteria.

F. This test detects unsuspected diabetes or is used to check the efficiency of insulin therapy in diabetics.

G. This test changes color, depending on the ion concentration in urine. The highest reading available on the test is 1.030.

H. This test has a range of 4.6 to 8.0 and measures the acidity or alkalinity of the urine. A reading under 7.0 indicates increased acidity; above 7.0 indicates increased alkalinity.

I. The presence of this substance indicates a urinary tract infection, as it is normally absent from urine. It is formed from the conversion of nitrates by certain species of bacteria.

J. This substance, a product of the breakdown of hemoglobin, breaks down in the light; a urine sample should be protected from light during testing.

B. How should reagent test strips be handled and stored?

____

____

____

15. The results of reagent strips are screening results; some positive results must be confirmed by further testing. For each substance below, identify the confirming test used. Then match each entry to the information that best fits each test.

_______________________ (1) Reducing sugars

_______________________ (2) Protein

_______________________ (3) Ketones

_______________________ (4) Bilirubin

___ A. This test includes a tablet and an absorbent mat. A purple color will develop when a urine drop is placed on a moist mat if the substance is present.

___ B. This test is used to detect lactose and galactose and is performed when the glucose test is positive on the reagent test strip.

___ C. In this test, a 2+ result is cloudy and granular.

___ D. A drop of urine added to a tablet will produce a purple color when this substance, produced during an increased metabolism of fat, is present.

16. Microscopic examination of urine sediment is also a valuable diagnostic tool for physicians.

A. Match each type of sediment listed to the statement that best describes it.

A. White blood cells	D. Renal epithelial cells	G. Red blood cells
B. Yeast	E. Bacteria	H. Protozoa
C. Squamous epithelial cells	F. Artifacts	I. Sperm

____ 1. Hair, fiber, air bubbles, and oil are common examples.

____ 2. These skin cells are not medically significant and are sloughed off continuously in urine.

____ 3. *Trichomonas vaginalis* is the most common example.

____ 4. Cocci, bacilli, and spirilla.

____ 5. These cells appear as pale, light-refractive disks. They are counted in a microscopic field and reported as cells per high-power field (HPF).

____ 6. These cells are larger than erythrocytes, have a visible nucleus, and may appear granular. They are reported as cells per high-power field (HPF).

____ 7. These are reported only when seen in male urine, unless specifically requested by the physician.

____ 8. *Candida albicans* is the most common example.

____ 9. These cells can indicate kidney disease if present in large numbers and are easily confused with leukocytes and other skin cells. If suspected, the slide should be reviewed by the physician. They are reported as cells per high-power field (HPF).

B. In the circles below, draw an example of the sediment as seen under a microscope.

1. Fiber, hair, air bubble artifact 2. Yeast 3. Squamous epithelial cells 4. Bacteria

17. Crystals are the most insignificant part of urinary sediment and are not usually an important element of microscopic analysis, though many labs do report them. However, a few crystals may indicate disease states; name three.

(1) ____________ (2) ____________ (3) ____________

18. Identification of casts in urine requires an experienced eye; medical assistants who encounter them should ask for assistance in confirming identification. Casts are formed when protein accumulates and precipitates in the kidney tubules and are then washed into the urine. Identify each cast below and draw an example in the circle provided.

A. **B.** **C.**

_______________ A. These casts contain remnants of disintegrated cells that have a fine or coarse appearance.

_______________ B. These casts contain leukocytes, erythrocytes, or skin cells.

_______________ C. These casts are difficult to see under the microscope without some light adjustment because of their near transparency.

Investigation Activity

Standard precautions are essential when performing urinalysis on patient urine specimens. As responsible health care professionals, medical assistants must be aware of the possible hazards of procedures performed in the ambulatory care setting and the proper techniques for preventing or reducing any potential risk to patients, employees, or visitors. Consider the urine Clinitest, which detects the presence of reducing sugars in specimens (Procedure 18–6). Complete the Office Procedures Safety Form below, which will become part of the medical practice's Office Procedures Manual for employees.

OFFICE PROCEDURES SAFETY FORM

Procedure: _______________ Type of hazard: _______________

Person performing procedure: _______________ PPE required: _______________

Proper techniques for safety: _______________

____

____

What is done with used materials and soiled instruments? _______________

____

____

____

What chemical products are involved? _______________

____

____

____

What are the specific risks of the procedure? _______________

____

____

____

Additional comments: _______________

____

____

Prepared by: _______________ Date: _______________

CASE STUDIES

Case 1

At Inner City Health Care, Wanda Slawson, CMA, gives patient Wendy Janus written directions for a 24-hour urine collection to be performed at home, but Wendy misplaces them. Wanda must give directions to Wendy over the telephone.

1. What directions should be given to the patient to correctly perform the urine collection?
2. What communication techniques should Wendy use to make sure the patient understands the collection procedures? What other potential alternatives for communicating the information, besides the telephone, are available?

Case 2

Wanda Slawson, CMA, is asked to give a male adolescent patient the proper procedure for a clean-catch specimen. The fifteen-year-old boy is visibly embarrassed and will not hold eye contact with Wanda as she relates the instructions for collection to him.

1. What instructions are relevant for a clean-catch specimen for this patient?
2. What communication techniques should Wanda use in working with this patient?

SUPPLEMENTARY RESOURCES

Study Guide Disk: Additional practice exercises for this chapter are available on the study guide disk found in the back of the textbook.

Medical Assisting Videos: Appropriate content is available on Delmar's Medical Assisting Videos, 2nd ed., Tape 14, for the following topics:

Quality Control in Collecting and Processing Specimens
Collect and Label Random Urine Specimens
Perform a Routine Urinalysis and Record Results
Perform Microscopic Examination of Urine

SKILLS COMPETENCY ASSESSMENT

Procedure 18-1: Assessing Urine Volume

Student's Name: ______________________________ Date: ______________

Objective: To accurately determine and document the volume of a urine sample.

Conditions: The student demonstrates the ability to determine and document the volume of a urine specimen using the following supplies: gloves, graduated urine container, graduated cylinder, biohazard container, and laboratory report form.

Time Requirements and Accuracy Standards: 5 minutes. Points assigned reflect importance of step to meeting objective: Important = (5) Essential = (10) Critical = (15). Automatic failure results if any of the **critical** tasks are omitted or performed incorrectly.

STANDARD PRECAUTIONS:

SKILLS ASSESSMENT CHECKLIST

Task Performed	Possible Points	TASKS
❑	5	Washes hands.
❑	5	Puts on gloves.
❑	5	Assembles equipment and materials.
❑	5	Follows all safety guidelines.
❑	5	Is careful not to splash urine. Wipes up any and all spills with antiseptic cleaner.
❑	5	Observes sample for proper labeling.
❑	5	*Rationale:* Understands that unlabeled urine is not tested and can state correct procedure for obtaining a new, properly labeled sample.
❑	15	Checks to see that urine container lid is tightly closed, then mixes the urine by inversion in the sealed container.
❑	5	Pours the urine into a suitable measuring device if the container is not graduated.
❑	15	Records the volume of the urine in milliliters. If urine volume is between 4 and 10 mL (or less), makes the proper documentation.
❑	10	Marks samples of less than 4 mL (except for newborns) with appropriate documentation. Insufficient samples are not tested.
❑	10	After volume is recorded, places an aliquot in a standard urinalysis centrifuge tube for continuation of urinalysis.
❑	5	Completed the tasks within 5 minutes.

SKILLS COMPETENCY ASSESSMENT — continued

Procedure 18-1: Assessing Urine Volume

Task Performed	Possible Points	TASKS
❑	15	Results obtained were accurate.

______	Earned	ADD POINTS OF TASKS CHECKED
110	Points	TOTAL POINTS POSSIBLE
______	SCORE	DETERMINE SCORE (divide points earned by total points possible, multiply results by 100)

Actual Student Time Needed to Complete Procedure: ____________

Student's Initials: ____________ Instructor's Initials: ____________ Grade: ____________

Suggestions for Improvement: ________________________________

Evaluator's Name (print) ________________________________

Evaluator's Signature ________________________________

Comments ________________________________

DOCUMENTATION

Record the volume of the urine sample in milliliters (mL): ____________________

Record the proper documentation for a specimen of 4 to 10 mL ____________________

____

If the urine volume is below 4 mL, the specimen is marked: ____________________

Student's Initials: __________

SKILLS COMPETENCY ASSESSMENT

Procedure 18-2 Observing Urine Color

Student's Name: ______________________________ Date: ____________

Objective: To observe and record the color of a urine specimen.

Conditions: The student demonstrates the ability to observe and document the color of a urine specimen using the following supplies: gloves, urine specimen, centrifuge tube, white card, biohazard container, and laboratory report form.

Time Requirements and Accuracy Standards: 5 minutes. Points assigned reflect importance of step to meeting objective: Important = (5) Essential = (10) Critical = (15). Automatic failure results if any of the **critical** tasks are omitted or performed incorrectly.

STANDARD PRECAUTIONS:

SKILLS ASSESSMENT CHECKLIST

Task Performed	Possible Points	TASKS
❑	5	Washes hands.
❑	5	Puts on gloves.
❑	5	Assembles equipment and materials.
❑	5	Follows all safety guidelines.
❑	5	Is careful not to splash urine. Wipes up any and all spills with antiseptic cleaner.
❑	10	Mixes the urine specimen thoroughly.
❑	15	Observes the color of the urine in a clear centrifuge tube using good light against a white background (white card).
❑	5	Records results on laboratory report form.
❑	5	Completed the tasks within 5 minutes.
❑	15	Results obtained were accurate.

________	Earned	ADD POINTS OF TASKS CHECKED
75	Points	TOTAL POINTS POSSIBLE
________	SCORE	DETERMINE SCORE (divide points earned by total points possible, multiply results by 100)

SKILLS COMPETENCY ASSESSMENT — continued

Procedure 18-2 Observing Urine Color

Actual Student Time Needed to Complete Procedure: ____________

Student's Initials: ____________ Instructor's Initials: ____________ Grade: ____________

Suggestions for Improvement: ____________

Evaluator's Name (print) ____________

Evaluator's Signature ____________

Comments ____________

DOCUMENTATION

Record the labeling of the urine specimen. ____________

____

Record the color of the urine sample. ____________

What is the proper documentation for each abnormally colored urine sample due to the causes listed?

(1) Hematuria: ____________

(2) Bladder infection treated with Pyridium: ____________

(3) Liver disease: ____________

(4) Vitamin intake: ____________

(5) Dehydration: ____________

Student's Initials: ____________

SKILLS COMPETENCY ASSESSMENT

Procedure 18-3: Observing Urine Clarity

Student's Name: ______________________________ Date: __________

Objective: To observe and record the clarity of a urine sample.

Conditions: The student demonstrates the ability to observe and document the clarity of a urine specimen using the following supplies: gloves, urine specimen, centrifuge tube, white sheet of paper with print, biohazard container, and laboratory report form.

Time Requirements and Accuracy Standards: 5 minutes. Points assigned reflect importance of step to meeting objective: Important = (5) Essential = (10) Critical = (15). Automatic failure results if any of the **critical** tasks are omitted or performed incorrectly.

STANDARD PRECAUTIONS:

SKILLS ASSESSMENT CHECKLIST

Task Performed	Possible Points	TASKS
☐	5	Washes hands.
☐	5	Puts on gloves.
☐	5	Assembles equipment and materials.
☐	5	Follows all safety guidelines.
☐	5	Is careful not to splash urine. Wipes up any and all spills with antiseptic cleaner.
☐	15	Holds the centrifuge tube close to a printed piece of white paper.
☐	10	Observes the clarity and records results on laboratory report form.
☐	5	Dispose of all biohazardous wastes in the biohazard container.
☐	5	Completed the tasks within 5 minutes.
☐	15	Results obtained were accurate.

________	Earned	ADD POINTS OF TASKS CHECKED
75	Points	TOTAL POINTS POSSIBLE
________	SCORE	DETERMINE SCORE (divide points earned by total points possible, multiply results by 100)

SKILLS COMPETENCY ASSESSMENT — continued

Procedure 18-3: Observing Urine Clarity

Actual Student Time Needed to Complete Procedure: ____________

Student's Initials: ____________ Instructor's Initials: ____________ Grade: ____________

Suggestions for Improvement: ____

Evaluator's Name (print) ____

Evaluator's Signature ____

Comments ____

DOCUMENTATION

Record the labeling of the urine specimen. ____

____

Record observations regarding the color and clarity of the urine specimen.

____

____

Student's Initials: __________

SKILLS COMPETENCY ASSESSMENT

Procedure 18-4: Using the Refractometer to Measure Specific Gravity

Student's Name: ______________________________ Date: ____________

Objective: To measure and record the specific gravity of a urine specimen.

Conditions: The student demonstrates the ability to observe and document the specific gravity of a urine specimen using the following supplies: gloves, urine specimen, refractometer, pipettes, distilled water, 5 percent saline solution lint-free tissues, quality control urine sample, biohazard container, and laboratory report form.

Time Requirements and Accuracy Standards: 10 minutes. Points assigned reflect importance of step to meeting objective: Important = (5) Essential = (10) Critical = (15). Automatic failure results if any of the **critical** tasks are omitted or performed incorrectly.

STANDARD PRECAUTIONS:

SKILLS ASSESSMENT CHECKLIST

Task Performed	Possible Points	TASKS
❑	5	Washes hands.
❑	5	Puts on gloves.
❑	5	Assembles equipment and materials.
❑	5	Follows all safety guidelines.
❑	5	Is careful not to splash urine. Wipes up any and all spills with antiseptic cleaner.
❑	10	Checks the value of the distilled water at 1.000 as a quality control check for the refractometer.
❑	5	Cleans surface of cover and prism with a lint-free cloth moistened with distilled water. Wipes dry.
❑	10	Closes the cover. Applies a drop of distilled water to the notched portion of the cover so it flows over the prism.
❑	10	Tilts the instrument to allow light to enter and reads specific gravity scale.
❑	5	Wipes the cover and prism.
❑	15	Tests sample of 5 percent saline solution, which should read 1.023 ± 0.001, thereby standardizing the equipment.
❑	15	Tests quality control urine sample and records results on quality control sheet.
❑	5	Wipes cover and prism.

SKILLS COMPETENCY ASSESSMENT — continued

Procedure 18-4: Using the Refractometer to Measure Specific Gravity

Task Performed	Possible Points	TASKS
❑	10	Tests patient urine specimen and records results on patient requisition form.
❑	5	Cleans area after finishing procedure, including wiping up any spills with antiseptic solution, wiping refractometer clean with a lint-free tissue and distilled water, and disposing of all biohazardous waste in the biohazard container.
❑	5	Completed the tasks within 10 minutes.
❑	15	Results obtained were accurate.

______	Earned	ADD POINTS OF TASKS CHECKED
135	Points	TOTAL POINTS POSSIBLE
______	SCORE	DETERMINE SCORE (divide points earned by total points possible, multiply results by 100)

Actual Student Time Needed to Complete Procedure: ____________

Student's Initials: ____________ Instructor's Initials: ____________ Grade: ____________

Suggestions for Improvement: ____

Evaluator's Name (print) ____

Evaluator's Signature ____

Comments ____

DOCUMENTATION

Record the labeling of the urine specimen: ____

____

Record the specific gravity of the quality control urine specimen in the quality control sheet:

____

Record the specific gravity of the patient urine specimen on the patient requisition form:

____

Student's Initials: __________

SKILLS COMPETENCY ASSESSMENT

Procedure 18-5: Performing a Urinalysis Chemical Examination

Student's Name: ______________________ Date: __________

Objective: To detect any abnormal chemical constituents of a urine specimen.

Conditions: The student demonstrates the ability to perform a urinalysis chemical examination using the following supplies: gloves, dipsticks, urine specimen, biohazard container, and laboratory report form.

Time Requirements and Accuracy Standards: 10 minutes. Points assigned reflect importance of step to meeting objective: Important = (5) Essential = (10) Critical = (15). Automatic failure results if any of the **critical** tasks are omitted or performed incorrectly.

STANDARD PRECAUTIONS:

SKILLS ASSESSMENT CHECKLIST

Task Performed	Possible Points	TASKS
❑	5	Washes hands.
❑	5	Puts on gloves.
❑	5	Assembles equipment and materials.
❑	5	Follows all safety guidelines.
❑	5	Is careful not to splash urine. Wipes up any and all spills with antiseptic cleaner.
❑	10	Mixes the urine specimen well by inverting it several times, making sure the cover is on tightly before inverting.
❑	10	Removes test strip from a container, making sure the desiccant packet, which ensures dryness, remains in the container; replaces the cap tightly.
❑	10	Immerses strip completely in the uncentrifuged urine and removes it immediately.
❑	10	While removing the strip from urine, runs its edge against the rim of the container, tapping it lightly on the container to remove any excess urine. Does not allow urine drops to run down the strip from one reagent pad to another after tapping.
❑	5	*Rationale:* Understands that excess urine can bridge the gap between reagent pads, causing inaccurate results.
❑	15	Follows the proper timing listed on the dipstick container.
❑	5	*Rationale:* Understands that precise timing is critical to obtaining accurate results.
❑	15	Holds dipstick close to container. Compares the test areas to the proper area on the container and records results on the laboratory report form. Uses correct manufacturer's chart to determine test results.

SKILLS COMPETENCY ASSESSMENT— continued

Procedure 18-5: Performing a Urinalysis Chemical Examination

Task Performed	Possible Points	TASKS
❑	5	Properly disposes of the used reagent strips and other disposable items in the proper waste receptacles. Properly stores reagent strip container according to manufacturer's instructions. (Reagent strips should never be refrigerated or frozen.)
❑	5	Completed the tasks within 10 minutes.
❑	15	Results obtained were accurate.

________	Earned	ADD POINTS OF TASKS CHECKED
130	Points	TOTAL POINTS POSSIBLE
________	SCORE	DETERMINE SCORE (divide points earned by total points possible, multiply results by 100)

Actual Student Time Needed to Complete Procedure: ____________

Student's Initials: ____________ Instructor's Initials: ____________ Grade: ____________

Suggestions for Improvement: ________________________________

Evaluator's Name (print) ________________________________

Evaluator's Signature ________________________________

Comments ________________________________

DOCUMENTATION

Record the labeling of the urine specimen. ________________________________

____

Record the results of the urinalysis chemical examination. ________________________________

____

____

____

Student's Initials: ____________

SKILLS COMPETENCY ASSESSMENT

Procedure 18-6: Testing for Reducing Sugars

Student's Name: ______________________________ Date: __________

Objective: To perform a Clinitest on a urine specimen to detect reducing sugars.

Conditions: The student demonstrates the ability to perform a Clinitest on a urine specimen using the following supplies: gloves, Clinitest tablets, urine specimen, clean glass test tube, distilled water, disposable pipettes, biohazard container, and laboratory report form.

Time Requirements and Accuracy Standards: 10 minutes. Points assigned reflect importance of step to meeting objective: Important = (5) Essential = (10) Critical = (15). Automatic failure results if any of the **critical** tasks are omitted or performed incorrectly.

STANDARD PRECAUTIONS:

SKILLS ASSESSMENT CHECKLIST

Task Performed	Possible Points	TASKS
☐	5	Washes hands.
☐	5	Puts on gloves.
☐	5	Assembles equipment and materials.
☐	5	Follows all safety guidelines.
☐	5	Is careful not to splash urine. Wipes up any and all spills with antiseptic cleaner.
☐	10	Transfers five drops of urine (0.3 mL) into a clean glass test tube.
☐	10	Adds ten drops of water (0.6 mL) and mixes well. Is careful not to splash contents of tube.
☐	10	Drops one tablet into tube and watches mixture while the complete boiling takes place.
☐	5	*Rationale:* Understands that the bottom of the test tube becomes hot enough to cause severe burns.
☐	10	Does not shake the tube after adding the tablet until at least 15 seconds after the boiling stops.
☐	10	Gently shakes tube after appropriate waiting period to mix, without touching bottom of tube.
☐	15	Compares color of liquid to the proper color chart and documents it in laboratory report. Uses the percentage and/or trace through 4+ reporting methods. Ignores any changes in color that occur after the waiting period.
☐	15	Disposes of all biohazardous waste in the biohazard waste container.

SKILLS COMPETENCY ASSESSMENT — continued

Procedure 18-6: Testing for Reducing Sugars

Task Performed	Possible Points	TASKS
❑	5	Completed the tasks within 15 minutes.
❑	15	Results obtained were accurate.

________	Earned	ADD POINTS OF TASKS CHECKED
130	Points	TOTAL POINTS POSSIBLE
________	SCORE	DETERMINE SCORE (divide points earned by total points possible, multiply results by 100)

Actual Student Time Needed to Complete Procedure: ____________

Student's Initials: ____________ Instructor's Initials: ____________ Grade: ____________

Suggestions for Improvement: ________________________________

Evaluator's Name (print) ________________________________

Evaluator's Signature ________________________________

Comments ________________________________

DOCUMENTATION

Record labeling for the urine specimen: ________________________________

____

Record the Clinitest results for the urine specimen: ________________________________

____

____

____

____

Student's Initials: ________

SKILLS COMPETENCY ASSESSMENT

Procedure 18-7: Microscopic Examination of Urine Sediment

Student's Name: ______________________________ Date: ____________

Objective: To perform a microscopic examination of urine sediment.

Conditions: The student demonstrates the ability to perform a microscopic examination of urine sediment using the following supplies: gloves, microscope, centrifuge, microscope slides, cover slips, disposable pipettes, centrifuge tube, urine sediment, containing casts, urine atlas, biohazard container, and laboratory report form.

Time Requirements and Accuracy Standards: 20 minutes. Points assigned reflect importance of step to meeting objective: Important = (5) Essential = (10) Critical = (15). Automatic failure results if any of the **critical** tasks are omitted or performed incorrectly.

SKILLS ASSESSMENT CHECKLIST

Task Performed	Possible Points	TASKS
❑	5	Washes hands.
❑	5	Puts on gloves.
❑	5	Assembles equipment and materials.
❑	5	Follows all safety guidelines.
❑	5	Is careful not to splash urine. Wipes up any and all spills with antiseptic cleaner.
❑	5	Obtains a urine specimen and examines as quickly as possible thereafter.
❑	10	Mixes specimen well, then centrifuges a 10- to 15-mL aliquot at 1,500 revolutions per minute for five minutes.
❑	15	Pours off supernatant after centrifugation, leaving approximately 1 mL in the bottom of the centrifuge tube.
❑	10	Taps or flicks bottom of tube to resuspend the sediment in the remaining fluid.
❑	10	Places a drop of sediment on a microscope slide; places coverglass over drop of sediment.
❑	10	Places slide on microscope stage and immediately examines.
❑	5	*Rationale:* Understands optimum light and focus adjustments for best examination of specimen.
❑	5	Scans sediment using a 100× (low) magnification.
❑	5	*Rationale:* Understands procedure for achieving a 100× magnification.
❑	5	Views ten to fifteen fields and around the edges of the drop for casts.
❑	10	Records the average number of each type of cast viewed per LPF. Uses 45× objective, if necessary, to identify some of the casts.

SKILLS COMPETENCY ASSESSMENT — continued

Procedure 18-7: Microscopic Examination of Urine Sediment

Task Performed	Possible Points	TASKS
☐	10	Scans drop using a 400× (high) magnification. Counts and averages numbers of other formed elements in ten to fifteen fields.
☐	5	Records results on laboratory report form.
☐	5	Disposes of all biohazardous waste in the biohazard container. Cleans microscopic lenses with lens paper and wipes up all spills with antiseptic cleaner.
☐	5	Completed the tasks within 20 minutes.
☐	15	Results obtained were accurate.

______	Earned	ADD POINTS OF TASKS CHECKED
155	Points	TOTAL POINTS POSSIBLE
______	SCORE	DETERMINE SCORE (divide points earned by total points possible, multiply results by 100)

Actual Student Time Needed to Complete Procedure: ____________

Student's Initials: ____________ Instructor's Initials: ____________ Grade: ____________

Suggestions for Improvement: ____________

Evaluator's Name (print) ____________

Evaluator's Signature ____________

Comments ____________

DOCUMENTATION

Record labeling of urine specimen. ____________

____

Record results of microscopic examination of the urine sediment specimen: ____________

____

____

____

Student's Initials: ________

SKILLS COMPETENCY ASSESSMENT

Procedure 18-8: Performing a Urinalysis

Student's Name: ______________________________ Date: __________

Objective: To perform a complete urinalysis.

Conditions: The student demonstrates the ability to perform a complete urinalysis, including physical, chemical, and microscopic examinations using the following supplies: gloves, urine specimen, measuring cylinder, test tubes, pipettes, centrifuge tube, centrifuge, microscope, microscope slides, coverglasses, reagent strips, control urine sample, urine atlas, refractometer (or urinometer), distilled water, lint-free tissues, biohazard container, and laboratory report form.

Time Requirements and Accuracy Standards: 45 minutes. Points assigned reflect importance of step to meeting objective: Important = (5) Essential = (10) Critical = (15). Automatic failure results if any of the **critical** tasks are omitted or performed incorrectly.

STANDARD PRECAUTIONS:

SKILLS ASSESSMENT CHECKLIST

Task Performed	Possible Points	TASKS
❑	5	Washes hands.
❑	5	Puts on gloves.
❑	5	Assembles equipment and materials.
❑	5	Follows all safety guidelines.
❑	5	Is careful not to splash urine. Wipes up any and all spills with antiseptic cleaner.
		PHYSICAL EXAMINATION
❑	10	Obtains a urine specimen.
❑	10	Measures amount of specimen in measuring cylinder and makes sure there is more than 12 mL of urine in specimen.
❑	5	Gently mixes and pours approximately 5 mL of urine into a test tube.
❑	15	Observes and records the color of the urine (see "Documentation").
❑	15	Observes and records the transparency of the urine (see "Documentation").
❑	10	Notes unusual odors of the urine.
❑	15	Measures specific gravity of urine using a refractometer or urinometer and records the results (see "Documentation").

SKILLS COMPETENCY ASSESSMENT — continued

Procedure 18-8: Performing a Urinalysis

Task Performed	Possible Points	TASKS
		Refractometer
❑	10	Places one drop of distilled water on the glass plate and closes.
❑	10	Looks through the ocular and reads specific gravity from the scale: 1.000.
❑	5	Wipes the water from the glass plate with lint-free tissues.
❑	5	Places one drop of urine on the plate and closes.
❑	10	Looks through the ocular, reads and records the specific gravity.
❑	5	Cleans the glass plate with water and dries with a tissue.
		Urinometer
❑	10	Pours 40 to 50 mL distilled water into the glass cylinder.
❑	5	Inserts urinometer with a spinning motion.
❑	15	Reads the specific gravity from the scale on the stem of the urinometer as it stops spinning: 1.000.
❑	5	Rinses the equipment with distilled water.
❑	5	Repeats the procedure using a urine specimen. Reads and records specific gravity.
❑	5	Cleans the equipment carefully using detergent, rinsing thoroughly with distilled water and drying carefully.
		CHEMICAL EXAMINATION
❑	5	Continues wearing gloves and uses the same specimen used in the physical examination.
❑	10	Tests the urine control sample with a reagent strip. Dips the strip into the sample, moistening all pads.
❑	5	Immediately removes strip, taps to remove excess urine.
❑	10	Observes reagent pads and compares colors to color chart at appropriate intervals.
❑	5	Properly disposes of reagent strip and records results on laboratory report form (see "Documentation").
❑	10	Performs appropriate tests on any positive results that need confirmation, following manufacturer's directions and all necessary safety precautions.
❑	5	Documents results of confirmatory tests on laboratory report form (see "Documentation").

Task Performed	Possible Points	TASKS
❑	5	Disposes of all biohazardous materials in a biohazard container.
❑	5	**MICROSCOPIC EXAMINATION** Continues to wear gloves and uses the same urine sample used in the physical and chemical examinations. Follows all necessary safety precautions.
❑	10	Pours 12 mL urine into a specimen tube and centrifuges the specimen at 1,500 to 2,500 rpm for five minutes.
❑	15	Decants the supernatant and resuspends the sediment.
❑	15	Pipettes one drop of resuspended urine on a clean glass slide.
❑	5	Places coverglass over drop of urine.
❑	5	Carefully places slide under microscope.
❑	10	Scans slide under low power (100×) and reduced light for casts. Refers to urine atlas as necessary.
❑	10	Rotates to high power (40× and 45× objective).
❑	10	Scans slide and identifies any blood cells, bacteria, yeast, protozoa, and epithelial cells.
❑	10	Identifies any crystals or amorphous deposits seen.
❑	5	Records all results on laboratory report form (see "Documentation").
❑	5	Discards all biohazardous materials in biohazard container.
❑	5	Cleans and returns equipment to proper storage.
❑	5	Cleans work area with disinfectant.
❑	5	Discards gloves in biohazard container.
❑	5	Thoroughly washes hands with disinfectant soap.
❑	5	Completed the tasks within 45 minutes.
❑	15	Results obtained were accurate.

______	Earned	ADD POINTS OF TASKS CHECKED
395	Points	TOTAL POINTS POSSIBLE
______	SCORE	DETERMINE SCORE (divide points earned by total points possible, multiply results by 100)

SKILLS COMPETENCY ASSESSMENT — continued

Procedure 18-8: Performing a Urinalysis

Actual Student Time Needed to Complete Procedure: ____________

Student's Initials: ____________ Instructor's Initials: ____________ Grade: ____________

Suggestions for Improvement: ____________

Evaluator's Name (print) ____________

Evaluator's Signature ____________

Comments ____________

DOCUMENTATION

Record labeling of urine specimen. ____________

____

Record all observations pertaining to the physical examination.

Color, Transparency, and Specific Gravity ____________

____

Record all observations pertaining to the chemical examination.

____

____

____

Record all observations pertaining to the microscopic examination.

____

____

____

____

Student's Initials: ________

EVALUATION OF CHAPTER KNOWLEDGE

Evaluate your comprehension of urinalysis, including proper collection and handling techniques; safety guidelines involved; and how to properly perform a complete urinalysis, including physical, chemical, and microscopic examinations. Compare this evaluation with the one provided by your instructor:

	Student Self-Evaluation			**Instructor Evaluation**		
Knowledge	*Good*	*Average*	*Poor*	*Good*	*Average*	*Poor*
Understands the importance of urinalysis as a diagnostic tool	_____	_____	_____	_____	_____	_____
Understands how urine is formed and excreted in the human body	_____	_____	_____	_____	_____	_____
Can define key terms related to urinalysis found in glossary	_____	_____	_____	_____	_____	_____
Understands the crucial role safety procedures and quality control play in performing urinalysis	_____	_____	_____	_____	_____	_____
Can accurately perform a physical examination of urine and explain causes of abnormal physical characteristics in urine specimens	_____	_____	_____	_____	_____	_____
Can accurately perform a chemical examination of urine and explain causes of abnormal chemical characteristics in urine specimens	_____	_____	_____	_____	_____	_____
Can accurately perform a microscopic examination of urine and explain causes of abnormal microscopic characteristics in urine specimens	_____	_____	_____	_____	_____	_____
Able to describe confirmatory tests for ketones, glucose, protein, and bilirubin	_____	_____	_____	_____	_____	_____
Can identify the proper method of preparing urine sediment for microscopic examination	_____	_____	_____	_____	_____	_____
Able to identify both normal and abnormal structures discovered during the microscopic examination of urine sediment	_____	_____	_____	_____	_____	_____
Is aware of and can describe factors that may interfere with urinalysis accuracy	_____	_____	_____	_____	_____	_____
Performs proper documentation of procedures	_____	_____	_____	_____	_____	_____
Follows standard precautions	_____	_____	_____	_____	_____	_____

Student's Initials: ______ Instructor's Initials: ______

Grade: _______

CHAPTER 19

Basic Microbiology

PERFORMANCE OBJECTIVES

Microbiology is an area of enormous importance in health care and one in which medical assistants play a role. Specimens are processed in either the physician's office laboratory (POL) or reference laboratory. The emergence of pathogens increasing in resistance to antibiotics makes this area even more significant to the health professions. Rapid and precise culturing and identification of pathogens allows for appropriate treatment of the patient. The quality of the diagnosis and treatment of an infection is rooted in the quality of the specimen obtained and processed. Although laboratories will vary in size and extent of work, one thing will remain constant—safety precautions and quality control procedures must be carefully followed for the protection of health care professionals and for the integrity of test results.

EXERCISES AND ACTIVITIES

Vocabulary Builder

Find the key vocabulary terms in the word search puzzle.

Aerobic
Aerosols
Anaerobic
Biochemical tests
Broth tubes
Check cell slides
Concentration method
counterstain
culture
decolorizer
dermatophyte
DNA
Enterobacteriaceae
Expectorate
Fastidious bacteria
Genus
Gram stain
Holding media
Immunosuppressed
Inoculate
Kirby Bauer
Lumbar puncture
Microbiology
Mordant
Morphology
Mycobacteria
Mycology
Nematode
Normal flora
Nosocomial
Ova
Parasitology
Pathogen
Petri dish
Protozoa
Quality control

Reagents
Sensitivity
Species
Stab culture
Taxonomy
Tetrads
Virology
Wood's lamp

N	Y	R	S	D	A	R	T	E	T	G	K	A	D	S	E	M	L	B	R	I	X	D	S	K	K	H	Q	C	Q	Z
P	E	Z	E	U	T	P	V	F	Y	R	F	N	C	E	D	Y	B	Z	X	N	A	A	T	Q	B	J	U	I	C	A
E	R	G	W	A	N	V	H	V	T	A	N	A	E	I	O	C	B	Y	O	O	Z	R	C	H	X	K	A	X	W	T
H	T	O	O	N	G	E	M	X	C	M	C	E	S	C	T	O	B	V	F	C	C	O	Y	F	L	D	L	L	P	Q
S	S	A	T	H	L	E	G	R	A	S	F	R	W	E	A	L	J	U	L	U	V	L	U	S	E	I	I	W	E	I
I	D	L	R	O	T	A	N	J	K	T	D	O	Q	P	M	O	M	L	U	L	L	F	H	R	U	B	T	R	Q	B
D	Q	A	O	O	Z	A	I	T	N	A	V	B	P	S	E	G	E	Z	M	A	Q	L	M	O	L	U	Y	X	B	D
I	A	H	E	L	T	O	P	M	S	I	G	I	K	D	N	Y	Y	E	B	T	Q	A	X	K	M	C	C	Q	F	D
R	G	M	X	K	D	C	A	M	O	N	V	C	I	R	F	R	N	A	A	E	T	M	Y	D	C	X	O	L	V	Q
T	P	B	I	O	C	H	E	M	I	C	A	L	T	E	S	T	S	A	R	O	G	R	O	D	Z	F	N	J	O	R
E	Z	R	W	Q	N	E	X	P	C	S	O	A	N	J	E	K	C	P	P	C	A	O	P	M	V	C	T	Y	J	W
P	O	V	Y	Z	T	C	A	P	X	C	E	S	V	R	A	P	M	H	U	T	X	N	Z	I	H	M	R	M	Y	L
E	D	S	Q	O	C	K	Y	I	A	E	L	B	O	E	S	V	Y	Y	N	J	C	R	Y	N	I	J	O	Y	S	P
E	R	U	T	L	U	C	D	A	D	R	P	B	U	N	B	T	O	W	C	D	I	V	W	C	C	Y	L	E	R	T
G	U	H	T	U	C	E	S	A	X	E	A	L	O	T	E	V	Q	T	T	O	R	S	R	N	M	Y	N	W	D	Q
B	I	M	N	W	S	L	R	J	U	C	M	S	V	S	H	J	W	W	U	W	B	O	J	O	P	S	V	V	N	L
Y	X	L	K	A	O	L	Y	W	T	I	U	G	I	A	R	T	B	V	R	A	B	A	N	V	I	Z	I	U	X	L
K	Q	K	O	S	Q	S	Z	E	X	D	Z	R	N	T	E	Y	O	A	E	I	P	O	C	T	V	R	Y	G	E	L
R	Q	D	O	X	N	L	R	D	N	S	P	E	T	I	O	R	C	R	O	B	X	P	I	T	O	J	E	U	Q	J
Z	P	R	R	E	Z	I	R	O	L	O	C	E	D	D	D	L	O	L	B	A	Z	V	V	L	E	W	D	K	B	Q
F	E	D	U	X	A	D	Y	U	M	O	B	T	B	V	R	L	O	B	T	O	I	M	O	Y	W	R	A	K	T	Q
A	N	N	K	C	K	E	W	L	Z	V	K	P	U	O	X	G	O	G	I	T	Q	G	J	T	S	Y	I	J	J	V
A	R	M	E	V	B	S	R	C	N	K	P	J	B	B	Y	Z	I	H	Y	C	Y	A	X	G	D	F	F	A	I	X
J	U	A	B	T	W	G	D	E	D	O	H	T	E	M	N	O	I	T	A	R	T	N	E	C	N	O	C	I	U	W
N	E	O	C	O	U	N	T	E	R	S	T	A	I	N	W	O	O	D	S	L	A	M	P	C	A	C	D	X	W	L
A	I	R	E	T	C	A	B	S	U	O	I	D	I	T	S	A	F	R	E	U	A	B	Y	B	R	I	K	A	K	W
I	M	M	U	N	O	S	U	P	P	R	E	S	S	E	D	U	E	M	F	Z	T	N	A	D	R	O	M	W	Z	E
Y	G	O	L	O	H	P	R	O	M	E	R	U	T	L	U	C	B	A	T	S	N	U	X	T	Z	X	M	K	E	E

Learning Review

1. Infections from parasites have increased as more people travel and public awareness of the symptoms grow.

   A. The most common parasite infections seen in the laboratory are ____________________ ____________________, a nematode that causes pinworm infections and ____________________ ____________________, a flagellate causing a sexually transmitted disease in both men and women.

   B. Specimens collected for parasites need to be checked for ____________________, ____________________, and ____________________.

C. Labeling specimens sent for testing with ________________, ________________, and ________________ collected is important, as well as noting if the patient has been ________________ to a specific place, and what the physician suspects.

D. To diagnose the presence of a parasite, either the ____________ ____________ or ________________ must be located in the specimen.

E. Obtaining the specimen to test for pinworms is performed by using a ____________ ____________ ____________ that is placed sticky side down to the skin around the anal area.

F. ________________ ________________ ________________ should be worn when working with specimens. Assuming that all specimens are ________________ is an important element of following standard precautions for infection control.

G. The practice of proper aseptic ________________ ________________ several times a day, including after glove removal, is essential and should become a ________________.

2. Specimen containers will arrive at the laboratory inside plastic bags to avoid danger to laboratory personnel. What precautions are taken before opening the bags?

____

____

3. A laboratory's success in finding and identifying the pathogenic organism depends on multiple factors. Name nine:

(1) ________________ (6) ________________

(2) ________________ (7) ________________

(3) ________________ (8) ________________

(4) ________________ (9) ________________

(5) ________________

4. Describe how you feel about working with patients who have an infection, which is possibly communicable. What, if anything, concerns you? What resources do you have in addressing your concerns?

____

____

____

5. The medical assistant in a physician's office will most likely frequently assist in the care and treatment of patients with sore throats.

Why is it necessary to rapidly identify the cause? ________________________________

What test would be used? ____

What five rules should be followed?

(1) ____________________

(2) ____________________

(3) ____________________

(4) ____________________

(5) ____________________

6. *Label the parts of the cell and check off "some" for the parts that are sometimes present and "all" for the parts that are always present.*

Basic Bacterial Cell

		Some	All
A.	____________	❑	❑
B.	____________	❑	❑
C.	____________	❑	❑
D.	____________	❑	❑
E.	____________	❑	❑
F.	____________	❑	❑

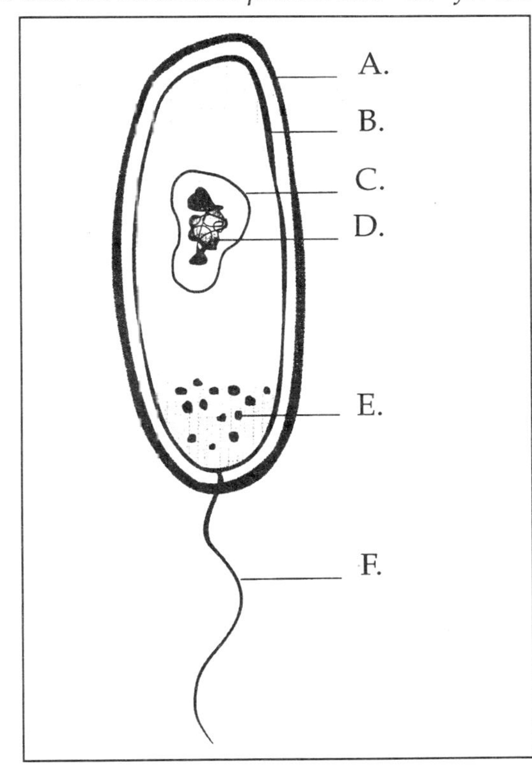

Investigation Activity

Laboratories have many responsibilities in the safety arena. These exist internally, as in the area of employee safety, and externally, as in reporting of the isolation and identification of organisms that are of public health concern. For each example below, research both of these areas at the library, a laboratory, the Public Health Department, or through a regulatory agency.

A. Identify what your course of action might be if you are asked to work without appropriate Personal Protective Equipment (PPE) or to place hazardous waste in the regular waste container.

B. The physician has ordered throat cultures for several patients who are from the same-area school. They are quite ill, with a high fever and sore throat; the physician states that one patient appears to be developing scarlet fever. To whom is this occurrence reported? Is this obligatory for public health? What agency makes the recommendations for public health? Where can you find a list of communicable diseases that laboratories must report? What international agency classifies infectious diseases?

CASE STUDY

Case 1

Winston Lewis, M. D., has ordered a series of three sputum cultures for Herb Fowler, who has been suffering with a productive cough for several months and extreme fatigue. Audrey Jones, CMA, is assigned to obtain the cultures. When each culture is obtained from Mr. Fowler, Audrey brings it to the physician's office laboratory (POL) for culturing.

Discuss the following:

1. What is the procedure for obtaining a sputum specimen? Why are detailed patient instructions critical?
2. Mr. Fowler wishes to give all three specimens in one day to save on the transportation to and from the physician's office. Audrey explains that the specimens must be obtained one each day, upon awakening, for three days. What is the reason for this?
3. What microorganisms might the physician suspect and how should the specimen be treated in the physician's office laboratory (POL)? Under what circumstances should the specimen be sent to an outside reference laboratory for further testing?

Case 2

Mary O'Keefe calls for an emergency appointment for her 3-year-old son Chris because he awakened during the night with a high fever and severe pain in his right ear, which is draining. Dr. King performs the examination, assisted by Ellen Armstrong, CMA. During the examination Dr. King takes a specimen of the fluid ear discharge for laboratory analysis, which the physician suspects will confirm a clinical diagnosis of otitis media. Dr. King asks Ellen to perform a Gram stain on a portion of the patient specimen and to send the remainder of the specimen to an outside reference laboratory for culturing.

Discuss the following:

1. What equipment will Ellen require to perform the Gram staining of the specimen?
2. What standard precautions must Ellen observe while performing the Gram stain procedure?
3. If a strain of *Streptococcus* or *Staphylococcus* bacteria is responsible for the infection producing the patient's condition of otitis media, what Gram staining result will Ellen receive? What will the Gram stained specimen look like under the microscope? *Consult a medical reference or encyclopedia, if necessary.*

SUPPLEMENTARY RESOURCES

Study Guide Disk: Additional practice exercises for this chapter are available on the study guide disk found in the textbook.

Medical Assisting Videos: Appropriate content is available on Delmar's Medical Assisting Videos, 2nd ed., for the following topics:

Tape 5: Perform Medical Aseptic Technique of Hand Washing
- Infections in the Office

Tape 14: Quality Control in Collecting and Processing Specimens
- Collect a Stool Specimen
- Perform a Hemoccult Test
- Collect a Sputum Specimen
- Collect a Throat Culture
- Perform a Strep Screen
- Collect Vaginal Samples
- Streak a Culture Plate
- Make a Gram Stain

SKILLS COMPETENCY ASSESSMENT

Procedure 19-1: Preparing a Bacteriological Smear

Student's Name: ______________________________ Date: ____________

Objective: To prepare a bacteriological smear.

Conditions: The student demonstrates the ability to prepare a bacterial suspension for staining to examine bacteria microscopically using the following equipment: PPE, clean glass slide, distilled water, loop or swab, organism, heat, staining rack, tray, and stains.

Time Requirements and Accuracy Standards: 30 minutes. Points assigned reflect importance of step to meeting objective: Important = (5) Essential = (10) Critical = (15). Automatic failure results if any of the **critical** tasks are omitted or performed incorrectly.

STANDARD PRECAUTIONS:

SKILLS ASSESSMENT CHECKLIST

Task Performed	Possible Points	TASKS
❑	5	Washes hands and puts on PPE.
❑	5	Assembles equipment.
❑	15	Applies thin film of bacteria to slide using a sterile or flamed loop or rolling a swab onto the surface of the slide, making a smear about the size of a nickel.
❑	15	If bacteria is in a liquid suspension, applies directly to the slide; if not, adds a drop of sterile water to the slide first.
❑	10	Allows the bacteria time to air dry.
❑	5	*Rationale:* Can state what will happen if heat is applied before bacteria is completely air dried.
❑	10	Heat fixes slide by passing it through the flame two or three times.
❑	5	*Rationale:* Can state the consequences if heat fixing is omitted or overdone.
❑	10	Allows slide to cool before staining.
❑	5	Follows all safety precautions.
❑	5	Completed the tasks within 30 minutes.
❑	15	Results obtained were accurate.

______	Earned	ADD POINTS OF TASKS CHECKED
105	Points	TOTAL POINTS POSSIBLE
______	SCORE	DETERMINE SCORE (divide points earned by total points possible, multiply results by 100)

Actual Student Time Needed to Complete Procedure: __________

Student's Initials: __________ Instructor's Initials: __________ Grade: __________

Suggestions for Improvement: ______________________________

Evaluator's Name (print) ______________________________

Evaluator's Signature ______________________________

Comments ______________________________

SKILLS COMPETENCY ASSESSMENT

Procedure 19-2: Gram Stain

Student's Name: ______________________________ Date: ____________

Objective: To Gram stain and read a bacteriological slide.

Conditions: The student demonstrates the ability to identify Gram-negative and Gram-positive bacteria microscopically through the staining technique using the following equipment: PPE, distilled water in beaker or plastic squeeze bottle, prepared bacteriological smears, heat, Gram stain reagents or kit, bibulous paper, tray, and paper towels.

Time Requirements and Accuracy Standards: 20 minutes. Points assigned reflect importance of step to meeting objective: Important = (5) Essential = (10) Critical = (15). Automatic failure results if any of the **critical** tasks are omitted or performed incorrectly.

STANDARD PRECAUTIONS:    

SKILLS ASSESSMENT CHECKLIST

Task Performed	Possible Points	TASKS
☐	5	Washes hands and applies PPE.
☐	5	Assembles equipment and supplies.
☐	15	Floods the prepared slide with crystal violet for accurate time, following manufacturer's instructions.
☐	10	Rinses stain off the slide with a gentle stream of distilled water; tilts slide to remove excess water.
☐	15	Floods the slide with Gram's iodine for the recommended time.
☐	5	Rinses slide as before, removing excess water.
☐	15	Holds slide by the short edge using forceps. Adds acetone-alcohol decolorizer by squeeze bottle or pasteur pipette until purple no longer runs off slide.
☐	5	Rinses immediately, as before, removing excess water.
☐	15	Counterstains the smears by flooding the slides with safranin for the recommended time.
☐	10	Rinses slide as before, removing excess water. Wipes back of slide to remove excess stain; stands slide on end or carefully blots between sheets of bibulous paper to dry.
☐	5	Reads and records results according to laboratory policy.
☐	5	Completed the tasks within 20 minutes.

Task Performed	Possible Points	TASKS
☐	15	Results obtained were accurate.

________	Earned	ADD POINTS OF TASKS CHECKED
125	Points	TOTAL POINTS POSSIBLE
________	SCORE	DETERMINE SCORE (divide points earned by total points possible, multiply results by 100)

Actual Student Time Needed to Complete Procedure: ____________

Student's Initials: ____________ Instructor's Initials: ____________ Grade: ____________

Suggestions for Improvement: ____

Evaluator's Name (print) ____

Evaluator's Signature ____

Comments ____

DOCUMENTATION

Record the results according to the laboratory policy.

Date: ________________

Charting: ____

____

Student's Initials:__________

SKILLS COMPETENCY ASSESSMENT

Procedure 19-3: Ziehl-Neelsen Staining

Student's Name: ______________________________ Date: __________

Objective: To perform Ziehl-Neelsen staining.

Conditions: The student demonstrates the ability to use Ziehl-Neelsen staining to identify acid-fast and non-acid-fast organisms using the following equipment: PPE, organism, glass slide, distilled water, heat, Ziehl-Neelsen stain reagents, and staining rack and tray.

Time Requirements and Accuracy Standards: 20 minutes. Points assigned reflect importance of step to meeting objective: Important = (5) Essential = (10) Critical = (15). Automatic failure results if any of the **critical** tasks are omitted or performed incorrectly.

STANDARD PRECAUTIONS:

SKILLS ASSESSMENT CHECKLIST

Task Performed	Possible Points	TASKS
❑	5	Washes hands and puts on PPE.
❑	5	Assembles equipment and materials.
❑	15	Places prepared slide on rack, carefully applies heat, staining with carbolfuchsin. Applies heat under slide until steaming. Does not let stain dry on the slide; applies the carbolfuchsin liberally.
❑	10	Uses distilled water to wash off the stain.
❑	10	Decolorizes with acid alcohol for two minutes, then washes it off with distilled water.
❑	10	Applies counterstain of metheylene blue or malachite green for thirty seconds, then washes off slide with distilled water.
❑	5	Dries slide completely by air or heat block.
❑	5	Caution is shown in following laboratory safety precautions. This type of staining is done under a safety hood.
❑	5	*Rationale:* Knows why this type of slide is prepared under a safety hood.
❑	5	Disposes of hazardous mask appropriately, removes PPE, and washes hands.
❑	5	Documents results.
❑	5	Completed the tasks within 20 minutes.

Task Performed	Possible Points	TASKS
☐	15	Results obtained were accurate.

______	Earned	ADD POINTS OF TASKS CHECKED
100	Points	TOTAL POINTS POSSIBLE
______	SCORE	DETERMINE SCORE (divide points earned by total points possible, multiply results by 100)

Actual Student Time Needed to Complete Procedure: ____________

Student's Initials: ____________ Instructor's Initials: ____________ Grade: ____________

Suggestions for Improvement: ____

Evaluator's Name (print) ____

Evaluator's Signature ____

Comments ____

DOCUMENTATION

Charts the results according to the laboratory policy.

Date: ________________

Charting: ____

____

Student's Initials: ____________

SKILLS COMPETENCY ASSESSMENT

Procedure 19-4: Wet Slide and Hanging Drop Slide Preparation

Student's Name: ______________________________ Date: __________

Objective: To prepare a wet slide and hanging drop slide.

Conditions: The student demonstrates the ability to prepare slides for viewing motility and characteristics of live organisms using the following equipment: Glass slides with concave well, PPE, clean glass slides with coverslips, petroleum jelly, dropper, and bacterial suspension.

Time Requirements and Accuracy Standards: 5 minutes. Points assigned reflect importance of step to meeting objective: Important = (5) Essential = (10) Critical = (15). Automatic failure results if any of the **critical** tasks are omitted or performed incorrectly.

STANDARD PRECAUTIONS:

SKILLS ASSESSMENT CHECKLIST

Task Performed	Possible Points	TASKS
❑	5	Washes hands and puts on PPE.
❑	5	Assembles equipment and supplies.
		Wet Slide Preparation:
❑	10	Places bacterial suspension on clean glass slide.
❑	15	Places petroleum jelly on cover slip and places it appropriately on bacterial slide.
❑	5	*Rationale:* Knows the need to prepare this accurately to prevent drying out and to allow observation microscopically at any power.
		Hanging Drop Slide Preparation:
❑	10	Bacterial suspension placed appropriately on cover slip with petroleum jelly on the edge.
❑	15	Inverts slide with the concave well over the cover slip.
❑	10	Turns slide right side up and examines.
❑	5	Follows all laboratory safety precautions.
❑	5	*Rationale:* Can state why these precautions are so necessary in this procedure.
❑	5	Records results according to laboratory policy.
❑	5	Completed the tasks within 5 minutes each.

Task Performed	Possible Points	TASKS
☐	15	Results obtained were accurate.

_________	Earned	ADD POINTS OF TASKS CHECKED
110	Points	TOTAL POINTS POSSIBLE
_________	SCORE	DETERMINE SCORE (divide points earned by total points possible, multiply results by 100)

Actual Student Time Needed to Complete Procedure: _____________

Student's Initials: _____________ Instructor's Initials: _____________ Grade: _____________

Suggestions for Improvement: ____

Evaluator's Name (print) ____

Evaluator's Signature ____

Comments ____

DOCUMENTATION

Date: _____________

Chart this procedure as laboratory policy indicates. ____

____

____

Student's Initials: _____________

SKILLS COMPETENCY ASSESSMENT

Procedure 19-5: Specimen Inoculation and Dilution Streaking

Student's Name: ______________________________ Date: ____________

Objective: To perform specimen inoculation and dilution streaking.

Conditions: The student demonstrates the ability to inoculate solid media to study bacterial growth on agar using the following equipment: PPE, plates, heat, agar plates, inoculation loop, and bacterial specimens.

Time Requirements and Accuracy Standards: 10 minutes. Points assigned reflect importance of step to meeting objective: Important = (5) Essential = (10) Critical = (15). Automatic failure results if any of the **critical** tasks are omitted or performed incorrectly.

STANDARD PRECAUTIONS:

SKILLS ASSESSMENT CHECKLIST

Task Performed	Possible Points	TASKS
❑	5	Washes hands and puts on PPE.
❑	5	Assembles equipment and materials.
❑	10	Flames the loop (if metal loop is used) and allows to cool. Applies specimen to plate with sterile flamed loop or specimen's swab. Once applied, flames the loop again.
❑	15	Uses loop to streak specimen, being careful not to dig up the agar; remembers to turn plate after each of the three episodes and flames the loop appropriately.
❑	5	Implements all laboratory safety measures, including plating cultures under a safety hood.
❑	5	Records results according to laboratory policy.
❑	5	Completed the tasks within 10 minutes.
❑	15	Results obtained were accurate.

______	Earned	ADD POINTS OF TASKS CHECKED
65	Points	TOTAL POINTS POSSIBLE
______	SCORE	DETERMINE SCORE (divide points earned by total points possible, multiply results by 100)

Actual Student Time Needed to Complete Procedure: ____________

Student's Initials: ____________ Instructor's Initials: ____________ Grade: ____________

Suggestions for Improvement: ____________

Evaluator's Name (print) ____________

Evaluator's Signature ____________

Comments ____________

DOCUMENTATION

Chart the procedure as laboratory policy indicates. ____________

____

____

____

____

Student's Initials: ____________

SKILLS COMPETENCY ASSESSMENT

Procedure 19-6: Broth Tube Inoculation

Student's Name: ______________________________ Date: ____________

Objective: To inoculate a broth tube with bacteria.

Conditions: The student demonstrates the ability to inoculate liquid media to observe bacterial growth using the following equipment: PPE, broth, inoculating loop, liquid specimen, and heat.

Time Requirements and Accuracy Standards: 5 minutes. Points assigned reflect importance of step to meeting objective: Important = (5) Essential = (10) Critical = (15). Automatic failure results if any of the **critical** tasks are omitted or performed incorrectly.

STANDARD PRECAUTIONS:

SKILLS ASSESSMENT CHECKLIST

Task Performed	Possible Points	TASKS
❑	5	Washes hands and puts on PPE.
❑	5	Assembles equipment and materials.
❑	5	Flames the loop, if it is metal.
❑	10	Picks up the specimen with the inoculating loop.
❑	15	Lifts the broth tube with care, slants the tube as required, touches the tube so the inoculation is submerged when upright.
❑	15	Gently mixes the tube to inoculate liquid media for bacterial growth.
❑	5	Follows all laboratory safety measures, particularly using the safety hood when appropriate.
❑	5	Records test results according to laboratory policy.
❑	5	Completed the tasks within 5 minutes.
❑	15	Results obtained were accurate.

________	Earned	ADD POINTS OF TASKS CHECKED
85	Points	TOTAL POINTS POSSIBLE
________	SCORE	DETERMINE SCORE (divide points earned by total points possible, multiply results by 100)

Actual Student Time Needed to Complete Procedure: ____________

Student's Initials: ____________ Instructor's Initials: ____________ Grade: ____________

Suggestions for Improvement: ____________

Evaluator's Name (print) ____________

Evaluator's Signature ____________

Comments ____________

DOCUMENTATION

Chart as required by laboratory policy.

Date: ____________

Charting: ____________

____

____

Student's Initials: ____________

SKILLS COMPETENCY ASSESSMENT

Procedure 19-7: Deep Inoculation/Slant

Student's Name: ______________________________ Date: ____________

Objective: To perform deep inoculation of slant media.

Conditions: The student demonstrates the ability to use deep inoculation of slant media to study motility or biochemical reactions using the following equipment: PPE, inoculating needle, deep agar or slant, heat, and isolated bacteria.

Time Requirements and Accuracy Standards: 5 minutes. Points assigned reflect importance of step to meeting objective: Important = (5) Essential = (10) Critical = (15). Automatic failure results if any of the **critical** tasks are omitted or performed incorrectly.

STANDARD PRECAUTIONS:

SKILLS ASSESSMENT CHECKLIST

Task Performed	Possible Points	TASKS
❑	5	Washes hands and puts on PPE.
❑	5	Assembles equipment and materials.
❑	15	Inoculates slant at 30 to 40 degree angle, stabbing to the bottom, making sure to flame needle before and after procedure.
❑	10	Using a needle, makes an "S" motion to streak up the slanted portion of the agar.
❑	5	Makes a straight deep stab into the upright agar.
❑	5	*Rationale:* Knows the reasoning behind inoculating the agar in these different ways.
❑	5	Follows all laboratory safety procedures.
❑	5	Uses safety hood as required for certain types of plating.
❑	5	Records procedure as laboratory requires.
❑	5	Completed the tasks within 5 minutes.
❑	15	Results obtained were accurate.

________	Earned	ADD POINTS OF TASKS CHECKED
80	Points	TOTAL POINTS POSSIBLE
________	SCORE	DETERMINE SCORE (divide points earned by total points possible, multiply results by 100)

Actual Student Time Needed to Complete Procedure: ____________

Student's Initials: ____________ Instructor's Initials: ____________ Grade: ____________

Suggestions for Improvement: ____________

Evaluator's Name (print) ____________

Evaluator's Signature ____________

Comments ____________

DOCUMENTATION

Chart the procedure as required by laboratory standards.

Date: ____________

Charting: ____________

____

____

Student's Initials: ____________

EVALUATION OF CHAPTER KNOWLEDGE

How has your instructor evaluated the knowledge you have achieved?

Knowledge	**Instructor Evaluation** *Good*	*Average*	*Poor*
Identifies the components of Personal Protective Equipment and important safety procedures	_____	_____	_____
Identifies quality control measures and describes uses	_____	_____	_____
Understands the importance and methods of collecting high-quality specimens	_____	_____	_____
Lists different types of specimens and stains	_____	_____	_____
Describes bacterial cell structure and can discuss identification systems for bacteria	_____	_____	_____
Identifies parasites and fungi	_____	_____	_____
Describes sensitivity testing	_____	_____	_____
Describes the difference between the presence of microorganisms as normal flora and as pathogens	_____	_____	_____
Understands the importance of patient education in obtaining specimens	_____	_____	_____
Can relate what happens when heat is used too long or too little in smear preparation for staining	_____	_____	_____
Understands the importance of the use of quality controls in the laboratory and with equipment	_____	_____	_____
Describes the need to discard media and reagents that have passed the expiration date	_____	_____	_____
Recognizes the role of the CMA in the laboratory	_____	_____	_____
Applies knowledge of microbiological classifications and nomenclature to appropriate use in the laboratory	_____	_____	_____
Follows precisely the procedures in performing tests in the laboratory	_____	_____	_____

Student's Initials: ______ Instructor's Initials: ______

Grade: _______

Specialty Laboratory Tests

PERFORMANCE OBJECTIVES

More tests than ever before are performed in the ambulatory care setting. As a result, the medical assistant's role in laboratory testing is expanding. To meet the challenge, medical assistants must have a solid understanding of medical terminology, laboratory procedures, safety procedures, and standard precautions for infection control. Quality control programs and accuracy in the collection and handling of specimens, including blood specimens obtained by venipuncture, ensure accurate and reliable test results. Therapeutic communication, which helps gain the patient's cooperation in obtaining a good specimen for analysis, is an important skill for medical assistants to develop.

EXERCISES AND ACTIVITIES

Vocabulary Builder

A. *Insert the following key vocabulary terms into the sentences that follow.*

ABO blood group	Epstein-Barr virus	latex beads
agglutination	Guthrie screening test	low-density lipoprotein
antibody	heterophile antibodies	Mantoux test
antigen	high-density lipoprotein	phenylketonuria (PKU)
antiserum	human chorionic gonadotrophin (hCG)	purified protein derivative (PPD)
bilirubin	hydatidiform	Rh factor
blood urea nitrogen	hemolytic anemia	semen
cholesterol	hyperglycemia	tine test
choriocarcinoma	hypoglycemia	triglyceride
Cushing's syndrome	infectious mononucleosis	tuberculosis
diabetes mellitus	immunoassay	wheal
ectopic	insulin	

1. Although the __________ is still used in some areas to test for ________________, most physicians, including Drs. Lewis and King, use the Mantoux test.

2. When a patient's glucose levels test high, Audrey Jones, CMA, knows it could be an indication of diabetes mellitus. She understands, however, that the high glucose levels could also be a sign of ______________ ______________, a hormonal disorder caused by an excess of corticosteriod hormones secreted by the adrenal glands, or a sign of acute stress response. A glucose tolerance test should be performed.

3. When Mary O'Keefe's enzyme __________________ test is positive, Ellen Armstrong, CMA, suspects that this positive reaction indicates a normal pregnancy. However, detection of hCG, ______________________________, can also indicate abnormal conditions such as an __________________ pregnancy; a developing __________________ mole of the uterus; ____________________, a very rare malignant neoplasm, usually of the uterus.

4. When Ellen Armstrong, CMA, performs a test for pregnancy using a slide test, she makes sure that after she adds hCG ________________ (________________ to hCG) to the urine on a microscope slide, she then adds an ________________ reagent containing ________________ coated with hCG to the mixture.

5. Bruce Goldman, CMA, commonly performs tests for blood glucose levels at Inner City Health Care. The results are used to screen for carbohydrate disorders such as ________________, in which a patient has a low blood glucose level.

6. Joe Guerrero, CMA, performs a slide test for pregnancy, remembering that negative ________________ indicates positive pregnancy.

7. When renal disease is suspected, a physician will order, as one of several tests, a BUN or ________________ ________________ ________________ test, which measures the concentration of urea in the blood.

8. Abigail Johnson has been diagnosed with ________________, which is a type of carbohydrate disorder usually characterized by a deficiency of ________________, a hormone secreted by the pancreas.

9. High levels of ________________________, the "bad" cholesterol, are associated with an increased risk of coronary artery disease. Cholesterol bound to ______________________, the "good" cholesterol, is transported to the liver where it is excreted in the form of bile.

10. To determine the severity of ______________________, the quantity of ________________ in the amniotic fluid of pregnant women is evaluated.

11. Serum __________________ concentration will rise moderately after ingesting a meal containing fat, peaking four to five hours later.

12. When a ________________ sample is required of a male patient for analysis, Wanda Slawson, CMA, instructs patients to avoid ejaculation for three days prior to collection of the sample.

13. Liz Corbin performs a ______________ on Lenny Taylor's arm, raising a ______________ where 0.1mL of PPD was administered properly with an intradermal injection.

14. Bruce Goldman, CMA, explains to Corey Boyer that his case of IM, ______________ ______________, is a result of infection of the lymphocytes by the ______________ (EBV). Dr. Whitney confirmed the diagnosis from hematological and clinical findings combined with the detection of ______________ ______________.

15. Nora Fowler was born with ______________, an inherited condition in which the amino acid phenylalanine is not metabolized.

16. To evaluate a newborn for PKU, Audrey Jones, CMA, uses the ______________ to evaluate the baby's blood.

17. The symptoms of ______________ are similar to those of diabetes mellitus: excessive thirst; passing large amounts of urine; glycosuria, high levels of glucose in the urine; and ketosis, the high levels of ketones.

18. Patients exhibiting a positive or questionable ______________ reaction should have a chest Xray to examine for tubercules and a sputum sample should be stained to search for acid-fast rods. The presence of tubercules and acid-fast rods confirms active tuberculosis.

19. Two categories of blood typing are for the ______________ and the ______________.

Learning Review

1. A. Name three reasons for performing a semen analysis on a male patient.

   (1) ______________

   (2) ______________

   (3) ______________

   B. When a semen analysis is performed as part of a fertility workshop, seminal fluid is analyzed to determine what three factors?

   (1) ______________ (2) ______________ (3) ______________

2. A. Name the four blood group categories.

   (1) __________ (2) __________ (3) __________ (4) __________

   B. Fill in the missing information in the chart below.

Blood Group/Type	Antigen on RBC	Serum Antibodies
1. AB	______________	______________
2. ______________	B	______________
3. ______________	______________	No anti-D

C. The Rh type of most North Americans is __________. How can most cases of hemolytic disease of the newborn (HDN) be prevented?

Circle the best answer or answers to the following questions.

3. Which of the following factors can alter the results of semen analysis?
   A. eating foods containing garlic
   B. smoking cigarettes
   C. riding a bicycle on the day of the analysis
   D. drinking milk

4. To ensure an accurate reading, the following precautions should be taken when performing a pregnancy test.
   A. The patient should abstain from having sex within two days of the test.
   B. Refrigerated urine samples and test reagents should be allowed to come to room temperature before testing.
   C. The patient should drink at least eight glasses of water in the six hours preceding the test.
   D. First morning urine or urine with a specific gravity of at least 1.010 should be used.

5. The wheal produced on a patient's arm in response to a Mantoux test is positive for a past or present infection of *Mycobacterium tuberculosis* if it is:
   A. almost invisible.
   B. 15 mm or more of induration.
   C. 10 mm or more of induration.
   D. exactly 2 mm of induration.

6. *Fill in the blanks with the correct term.*
   A. Glucose is the principal carbohydrate found circulating in the ________________.
   B. In glucose analyzers based on ________________, the glucose in the sample reacts with the reagents in the pad, causing a color to develop.
   C. Excess glucose is converted into ________________ for short-term storage in the liver and muscle cells.
   D. The blood glucose level of ________________ patients usually peaks thirty to sixty minutes after consumption of the glucose test solution leading to a level of 160–180 mg/dL and then returns to the fasting level after two to three hours.
   E. A patient should be instructed to eat a diet high in ________________ for three days prior to the glucose tolerance test.
   F. To determine whether diabetic patients are consistently adhering to their diets, physicians can administer the ________________ test.

7. A. Describe the cholesterol molecule.

   ____

   ____

   B. Explain the difference between saturated, monounsaturated, and polyunsaturated fats and give an example of each.

   ____

   ____

C. Look at table 20–6, reference values for total blood cholesterol. What are the levels found in the U. S. population for your age and sex?____________

D. Describe the function of cholesterol.

____

____

Investigation Activity

Learning as much as possible about the characteristics of particular diseases or conditions can help medical assistants provide assistance and support to patients who are undergoing testing.

A. Choose one disease or condition in this chapter and list the tests used to diagnose it.

Disease or Condition: ____

Test(s): ____

B. Contact a national or local health organization, such as the National Institutes of Health or the ODPHP National Health Information Center (Office of Disease Prevention and Health Promotion), to obtain information and resources about the disease or condition you have chosen. Ask for information on topics related to the disease or condition, such as statistics, treatments, diet/exercise programs, patient education, and so on. Use the Internet to conduct a search, or consult your local or school library for other health organizations of interest. National health organizations can be valuable resources for both health care professionals and patients. What organization will you contact?

Organization Name: ____

Address: ____

____

Telephone Number: ____

C. Imagine that you are a patient waiting to hear the test results for this disease or condition. How would you feel? What would you be thinking?

D. What confidentiality issues are involved with the reporting of laboratory test results? Why is patient privacy an important consideration in laboratory analysis?

CASE STUDY

Mary Alexander is an established patient of Dr. Eposito's at Inner City Health Care. Mary, 32 years old, is about 10 pounds overweight for her height. Mary has been diagnosed with Type I insulin-dependent diabetes mellitus since childhood. Dr. Esposito's treatment plan includes administration of 30 units of U-100 NPH insulin by injection every day. Dr. Esposito knows that Mary has trouble complying with the dietary restrictions included in her treatment plan and in observing regular mealtimes. Every now and then, the lifetime rigor of the diet wears Mary down and she begins to eat whatever she likes, whenever she feels like it. To guard against this, Mary must report her average glucose levels to Bruce Goldman, CMA, twice monthly as a safeguard.

At her next regular follow-up examination with Dr. Esposito, the physician orders a glycosated hemoglobin determination and discovers that Mary has been cheating on her diet again and has been reporting inaccurate glucose levels to the physician's office, hoping she would not get caught.

Discuss the following:

1. Why is Dr. Esposito able to tell from the glycosated hemoglobin determination that Mary is not adhering to her diet and health guidelines?
2. What is glycosated hemoglobin?
3. What is the role of the medical assistant in this situation?

SUPPLEMENTARY RESOURCES

Study Guide Disks: Additional practice exercises for this chapter are available on the study guide disks found in the back of the textbook.

Medical Assisting Videos: Appropriate content is available on Delmar's Medical Assisting Videos, 2nd edition, Tape 13, on the following topics:

Basic Information for Specimen Taking and Laboratory Work
When the Physician Orders a Specimen
Collect and Label a Blood Specimen
Perform Blood Chemistry Tests and Record the Results
Perform Immunologic Tests and Record the Results

SKILLS COMPETENCY ASSESSMENT

Procedure 20–1: Pregnancy Tests

Student's Name: ______________________________ Date: ____________

Objective: To accurately perform pregnancy tests.

Conditions: The student demonstrates the ability to perform the enzyme immunoassay and agglutination inhibition tests to detect hCG in urine to determine positive or negative pregnancy results. The student uses the following equipment and supplies: gloves, hand disinfectant, urine specimen, stopwatch, surface disinfectant, biohazard container, hCG negative urine control, hCG positive urine control, pregnancy test kits for enzyme immunoassay and/or the agglutination inhibition pregnancy tests.

Time Requirements and Accuracy Standards: 15 minutes. Points assigned reflect importance of step to meeting objective: Important = (5) Essential = (10) Critical = (15). Automatic failure results if any of the **critical** tasks are omitted or performed incorrectly.

STANDARD PRECAUTIONS:     

SKILLS ASSESSMENT CHECKLIST

Task Performed	Possible Points	TASKS
❑	5	Washes hands and puts on gloves.
❑	5	Assembles all equipment and supplies.
❑	15	*Enzyme Immunoassay Test (EIA)* Performs a modified enzyme immunoassay test for hCG following the manufacturer's instructions.
❑	10	Obtains test kit materials, reagents, and urine specimen.
❑	5	Applies urine to the test unit using dispenser provided.
❑	5	Waits appropriate time interval.
❑	5	Applies first reagent/antibody to test unit using dispenser provided.
❑	5	Rinses unreacted reagent from unit after appropriate time.
❑	10	Applies color reagent/substrate to test unit.
❑	10	Observes color development after appropriate time interval.
❑	5	Stops reaction.
❑	5	Records results; consults manufacturer's package insert to interpret test results.
❑	15	Repeats previous steps for modified enzyme immunoassay test for hCG, using both positive and negative urine controls.

SKILLS COMPETENCY ASSESSMENT — continued

Procedure 20–1: Pregnancy Tests

Task Performed	Possible Points	TASKS	
❑	10	Proceeds with agglutination inhibition pregnancy test.	
❑	5	Completed the tasks within 15 minutes.	
❑	15	Results obtained were accurate.	
	______	Earned	ADD POINTS OF TASKS CHECKED
	130	Points	TOTAL POINTS POSSIBLE
	______	SCORE	DETERMINE SCORE (divide points earned by total points possible, multiply results by 100)

Task Performed	Possible Points	TASKS
		Agglutination Inhibition Pregnancy Test
❑	15	Performs an agglutination inhibition test for hCG following the manufacturer's instructions.
❑	10	Obtains slide test kit, reagents, and urine specimen.
❑	10	Places one drop of antiserum in the center of the circled area of slide.
❑	5	Dispenses one drop of urine beside the drop of antiserum.
❑	5	Mixes urine and antiserum with stirrer provided.
❑	5	Rocks the slide in a figure-eight motion for the appropriate time.
❑	10	Applies one drop of well-mixed indicator particles to mixture on slide.
❑	15	Mixes indicator particles with antiserum-urine mixture and spreads the mixture over the entire circled area of the slide using a stirrer.
❑	5	Rocks slide slowly in a figure-eight motion for the appropriate time.
❑	10	Observes slide for agglutination at the end of the time interval and records the results.
❑	15	Repeats agglutination inhibition test for hCG following the manufacturer's instructions using positive and negative urine controls.
❑	5	Disinfects reusable equipment by soaking in 10 percent chlorine bleach solution a minimum of ten minutes; washes and rinses equipment thoroughly.
❑	5	Discards disposable supplies into biohazard container.
❑	5	Disposes of specimen as instructed.
❑	5	Cleans work area with surface disinfectant.
❑	5	Removes gloves and discards into biohazard container.

Task Performed	Possible Points	TASKS
❑	5	Washes hands with hand disinfectant.
❑	5	Documents procedure.
❑	5	Completed the tasks within 15 minutes.
❑	15	Results obtained were accurate.

_______	Earned	ADD POINTS OF TASKS CHECKED
160	Points	TOTAL POINTS POSSIBLE
_______	SCORE	DETERMINE SCORE (divide points earned by total points possible, multiply results by 100)

Actual Student Time Needed to Complete Procedure: ____________

Student's Initials: ____________ Instructor's Initials: ____________ Grade: ____________

Suggestions for Improvement: ____

Evaluator's Name (print) ____

Evaluator's Signature ____

Comments ____

DOCUMENTATION

Chart the procedure as laboratory policy indicates.

Date: ______________

Charting: ____

____

____

Student's Initials: ______________

SKILLS COMPETENCY ASSESSMENT

Procedure 20–2: Slide Test for Infectious Mononucleosis

Student's Name: ______________________________ Date: ____________

Objective: To perform a slide test for infectious mononucleosis.

Conditions: The student demonstrates the ability to perform an accurate test of serum or plasma sample to detect the presence or absence of heterophile antibodies of infectious mononucleosis. The student uses the following equipment and supplies: gloves, hand disinfectant, sample serum or plasma, stopwatch, surface disinfectant, test kit for infectious mononucleosis, biohazard container.

Time Requirements and Accuracy Standards: 15 minutes. Points assigned reflect importance of step to meeting objective: Important = (5) Essential = (10) Critical = (15). Automatic failure results if any of the **critical** tasks are omitted or performed incorrectly.

STANDARD PRECAUTIONS:

SKILLS ASSESSMENT CHECKLIST

Task Performed	Possible Points	TASKS
❑	5	Washes hands and puts on gloves.
❑	5	Assembles all equipment and supplies.
❑	5	Places the Monospot slide on a flat work surface.
❑	10	Mixes the reagent vials several times by inversion.
❑	15	Fills the capillary pipette to the top mark: • Places the rubber bulb on the end of the capillary pipette with the heavy black line. • Inserts the pipette into the vial of indicator cells. • Allows the pipette to fill by capillary action to the top mark.
❑	10	Places the index finger over the hole in the bulb and squeezes gently to dispense one-half the cells on a corner of square I of the slide.
❑	10	Delivers the remaining cells to a corner of square II.
❑	15	Places one drop of thoroughly mixed reagent I in the center of square I.
❑	15	Places one drop of thoroughly mixed reagent II in the center of square II.
❑	15	Adds one drop of serum to the center of each square using the disposable plastic pipette provided.
❑	10	Uses a clean applicator stick to mix Reagent I with the serum; uses at least ten stirring motions and avoids touching the indicator cells.
❑	15	Blends in the indicator cells in square I with the applicator stick, using no more than ten stirring motions and spreading the mixture over the entire surface of the square.
❑	15	Repeats previous two steps using reagent II in square II, using a clean applicator stick.
❑	10	Starts the stopwatch upon completion of the mixing of both squares.

Task Performed	Possible Points	TASKS
❑	5	Does not pick up or move the slide.
❑	10	Observes for agglutination at the end of one minute without moving the slide or picking it up.
❑	15	Records the agglutination in each square and interprets the results.
❑	5	Records test results as positive or negative.
❑	10	Repeats the test procedure using positive and negative control sera.
❑	5	Discards contaminated materials into biohazard container.
❑	10	Disposes of specimen appropriately and disinfects reusable materials by soaking in 10 percent chlorine bleach solution for at least ten minutes; washes and rinses materials thoroughly.
❑	5	Cleans work area with surface disinfectant.
❑	5	Removes gloves and discards into biohazard container.
❑	5	Washes hands with hand disinfectant.
❑	5	Documents results.
❑	5	Completed the tasks within 15 minutes.
❑	15	Results obtained were accurate.

________	Earned	ADD POINTS OF TASKS CHECKED
225	Points	TOTAL POINTS POSSIBLE
________	SCORE	DETERMINE SCORE (divide points earned by total points possible, multiply results by 100)

Actual Student Time Needed to Complete Procedure: ____________

Student's Initials: ____________ Instructor's Initials: ____________ Grade: ____________

Suggestions for Improvement: ____

Evaluator's Name (print) ____

Evaluator's Signature ____

Comments ____

DOCUMENTATION

Chart the procedure as laboratory policy indicates.

Date:__________

Charting: ____

____

____

Student's Initials:________

SKILLS COMPETENCY ASSESSMENT

Procedure 20–3: Analyzing Semen

Student's Name: ______________________________ Date: ____________

Objective: To properly analyze semen.

Conditions: The student demonstrates the ability to analyze semen to determine the total sperm count, percent of motility, and percent of normally formed sperm cells using the following equipment and supplies: gloves, 10 mL graduated cylinder, pH test paper, automatic pipette, hemacytometer, diluting fluid, sodium bicarbonate, distilled water, slides and coverslips, Petri dishes, microscope, and coplin jar.

Time Requirements and Accuracy Standards: 10 minutes. Points assigned reflect importance of step to meeting objective: Important = (5) Essential = (10) Critical = (15). Automatic failure results if any of the **critical** tasks are omitted or performed incorrectly.

STANDARD PRECAUTIONS:

SKILLS ASSESSMENT CHECKLIST

Task Performed	Possible Points	TASKS
		Macroscopic Examination
☐	5	Washes hands and applies gloves.
☐	5	Assembles all equipment and supplies.
☐	15	Rates viscosity while pouring specimen into a graduated cylinder (rates viscosity within 30 minutes of the time the specimen is taken).
☐	15	Measures volume of specimen.
☐	15	Measures the pH using pH test paper.
☐	5	Removes gloves and washes hands.
☐	5	Documents results.
☐	5	Completed the tasks within 10 minutes.
☐	15	Results are within acceptable range.
	______	Earned ADD POINTS OF TASKS CHECKED
	85	Points TOTAL POINTS POSSIBLE
	______	SCORE DETERMINE SCORE (divide points earned by total points possible, multiply results by 100)
		Microscopic Examination
☐	5	Washes hands and applies gloves.
☐	5	Assembles all equipment and supplies.
☐	10	Mixes semen sample.

Task Performed	Possible Points	TASKS
☐	10	Places one drop of liquified sample and covers with a coverslip; examines for motility.
☐	15	Determines sperm count. • Uses automatic pipettes to make a 1:20 dilution of sample with sodium bicarbonate solution and mixes well. • Fills both sides of the hemocytometer and allows the sperm to settle for five to ten minutes. • Counts the sperm in two large WBC squares or 5 RBC squares and calculates sperm per milliliter.
☐	15	Prepares sperm sample for morphology evaluation by a pathologist or trained technologist. • Prepares two slides using the technique to make a blood smear; does not allow the slides to air dry; immediately immerses both slides into a coplin jar containing 95 percent alcohol. • Delivers the slides to the pathologist to view for morphology.
☐	5	Removes gloves and washes hands.
☐	5	Documents results.
☐	5	Completed the tasks within 10 minutes.
☐	15	Results obtained were accurate.

______	Earned	ADD POINTS OF TASKS CHECKED
90	Points	TOTAL POINTS POSSIBLE
______	SCORE	DETERMINE SCORE (divide points earned by total points possible, multiply results by 100)

Actual Student Time Needed to Complete Procedure: ____________

Student's Initials: ____________ Instructor's Initials: ____________ Grade: ____________

Suggestions for Improvement: ____________

Evaluator's Name (print) ____________

Evaluator's Signature ____________

Comments ____________

DOCUMENTATION

Chart the procedure as laboratory policy indicates.

Date:__________

Charting: ____________

____

____

Student's Initials:________

SKILLS COMPETENCY ASSESSMENT

Procedure 20–4: Obtaining Blood Sample for Phenylketonuria (PKU) Test

Student's Name: ______________________________ Date: __________

Objective: To obtain a blood sample for a phenylketonuria (PKU) test.

Conditions: The student demonstrates the ability to obtain a blood sample using a PKU test card or "filter paper" to determine phenylalanine levels in newborns who are at least three to four days old. The student uses the following equipment and supplies: gloves, PKU filter paper test card and mailing envelope, alcohol swabs, cotton balls, sterile pediatric-sized lancet, biohazard waste container.

Time Requirements and Accuracy Standards: 15 minutes. Points assigned reflect importance of step to meeting objective: Important = (5) Essential = (10) Critical = (15). Automatic failure results if any of the **critical** tasks are omitted or performed incorrectly.

STANDARD PRECAUTIONS:

SKILLS ASSESSMENT CHECKLIST

Task Performed	Possible Points	TASKS
❑	5	Washes hands and puts on gloves.
❑	10	Identifies the infant; explains the purpose of the test and the procedure to the parents.
❑	5	Discusses the feeding pattern of the infant prior to beginning the procedure.
❑	5	*Rationale:* Understands that certain antibiotics, aspirin, or vomiting problems may cause false results.
❑	10	Selects and cleans an appropriate puncture site.
❑	15	Grasps the infant's foot, taking care not to touch the cleansed area; makes a puncture approximately 2-3 mm deep in the infant's heel, making sure the lateral portion of the infant's heel pad is used.
❑	5	Wipes away the first drop of blood with a cotton ball.
❑	5	*Rationale:* The first drop is diluted with alcohol and should not be collected for the test.
❑	15	Collects blood for the test by pressing the back side of the filter paper test card against the infant's heel while exerting gentle pressure on the heel.
❑	10	Makes sure the blood completely soaks through the paper and fills all of the circles on the test card completely.
❑	5	Holds a cotton ball over the puncture and applies gentle pressure until the bleeding stops.
❑	5	Properly disposes of all waste in biohazard container.

Task Performed	Possible Points	TASKS
❑	5	Removes gloves and washes hands.
❑	15	Allows the PKU test card to completely dry on a nonabsorbent surface at room temperature.
❑	5	After the test card is dry, puts on gloves and completes the PKU test card with all patient and physician information.
❑	10	Places the test card in the mailer envelope and sends it to the laboratory within two days.
❑	5	Removes gloves and washes hands.
❑	5	Documents the procedure in the patient's medical record.
❑	5	Documents test results when they are returned in the patient's medical record.
❑	5	Completed the tasks within 15 minutes.
❑	15	Results obtained were accurate.
	_______ Earned	ADD POINTS OF TASKS CHECKED
	165 Points	TOTAL POINTS POSSIBLE
	_______ SCORE	DETERMINE SCORE (divide points earned by total points possible, multiply results by 100)

Actual Student Time Needed to Complete Procedure: ____________

Student's Initials: ____________ Instructor's Initials: ____________ Grade: ____________

Suggestions for Improvement: ____________

Evaluator's Name (print) ____________

Evaluator's Signature ____________

Comments ____________

DOCUMENTATION

Chart the procedure in the patient's medical record.

Date: ____________

Charting: ____________

____

____

Student's Initials: ________

SKILLS COMPETENCY ASSESSMENT

Procedure 20–5: Obtaining Urine Sample for Phenylketonuria (PKU) Test

Student's Name: ______________________________ Date: ____________

Objective: To obtain a urine sample for a phenylketonuria (PKU) test.

Conditions: The student demonstrates the ability to obtain a urine sample using the diaper test or the Phenistik® test to determine phenylalanine levels in newborns who are at least six weeks old. The student uses the following equipment and supplies: gloves, 10 percent ferric acid for the diaper test or Phenistik for the Phenistik Method Test, biohazard waste container.

Time Requirements and Accuracy Standards: 10 minutes. Points assigned reflect importance of step to meeting objective: Important = (5) Essential = (10) Critical = (15). Automatic failure results if any of the **critical** tasks are omitted or performed incorrectly.

STANDARD PRECAUTIONS:

SKILLS ASSESSMENT CHECKLIST

Task Performed	Possible Points	TASKS
❑	15	Identifies the infant; verifies that the infant is at least six weeks old; explains the purpose of the test and the procedure to the parents.
❑	5	Washes hands and applies gloves.
❑	15	Follows one of the two following procedures: • *Diaper Test:* Applies several drops of 10 percent ferric chloride to a diaper that contains fresh urine. • *Phenistik Test:* Dips the Phenistik test strip into fresh urine or presses it against a diaper containing fresh urine.
❑	15	Follows up a positive urine test with a blood test.
❑	5	Properly disposes of waste in a biohazard container.
❑	5	Removes gloves and washes hands.
❑	10	Documents the procedure and results in the patient's medical record.
❑	5	Completed the tasks within 10 minutes.
❑	15	Results obtained were accurate.

________	Earned	ADD POINTS OF TASKS CHECKED
90	Points	TOTAL POINTS POSSIBLE
________	SCORE	DETERMINE SCORE (divide points earned by total points possible, multiply results by 100)

Actual Student Time Needed to Complete Procedure: ____________

Student's Initials: ____________ Instructor's Initials: ____________ Grade: ____________

Suggestions for Improvement: ____________

Evaluator's Name (print) ____________

Evaluator's Signature ____________

Comments ____________

DOCUMENTATION

Chart the procedure in the patient's medical record.

Date: ____________

Charting: ____________

____

____

Student's Initials: ____________

SKILLS COMPETENCY ASSESSMENT

Procedure 20–6: Mantoux Test

Student's Name: ______________________________ Date: ____________

Objective: To properly perform a Mantoux test.

Conditions: The student demonstrates the ability to safely and accurately inject 0.1 mL of intermediate strength (5 TU) purified protein derivative (PPD) intradermally to develop an indurated wheal to determine if an active or inactive tuberculous infection is present. The student uses the following equipment and supplies: gloves, goggles, tuberculin syringe, short (3/8–1/2 inches) 26- or 27-gauge needle, PPD (5 TU strength), alcohol, cotton balls or gauze, sharps container, biohazard waste container.

Time Requirements and Accuracy Standards: 15 minutes. Points assigned reflect importance of step to meeting objective: Important = (5) Essential = (10) Critical = (15). Automatic failure results if any of the **critical** tasks are omitted or performed incorrectly.

STANDARD PRECAUTIONS:

SKILLS ASSESSMENT CHECKLIST

Task Performed	Possible Points	TASKS
❑	5	Washes hands and puts on gloves and goggles.
❑	5	Identifies the patient and explains the procedure.
❑	10	Selects a site approximately three to four inches from the bend of the arm on the anterior side.
❑	10	Cleans the site with alcohol and allows the surface to dry; does not touch the site after cleaning.
❑	5	Uses a 1.0 mL tuberculin syringe fitted with a 3/8 – 1/2 inches, 26- or 27-gauge needle.
❑	10	Draws 0.1 mL of 5 TU strength PPD into the syringe, being careful to draw the exact amount of PPD into the syringe.
❑	5	*Rationale:* Too much or too little PPD will cause erroneous results.
❑	5	Holds the patient's forearm just under the chosen site to prevent movement during the injection.
❑	15	Slowly injects the PPD intradermally into the skin of the anterior portion of the arm to produce a wheal approximately 6–10 mm. Does not rub the injection site. (See Procedure 29–7: Administering an Intradermal Injection.)
❑	5	Disposes of the syringe and needle in a sharps container.
❑	15	Watches the patient carefully and notifies the physician immediately of any adverse reactions to the medication.
❑	10	Instructs the patient to return within 48–72 hours of the injection for test interpretation.

Task Performed	Possible Points	TASKS
☐	5	Removes gloves and washes hands.
☐	5	Documents procedure in the patient's medical record.
☐	5	Completed the tasks within 5 minutes.
☐	15	Results obtained were accurate.
________		Earned ADD POINTS OF TASKS CHECKED
	130	Points TOTAL POINTS POSSIBLE
________		SCORE DETERMINE SCORE (divide points earned by total points possible, multiply results by 100)
		When patient returns for test interpretation
☐	5	Washes hands.
☐	10	Bends the patient's arm at the elbow; inspects the injection site. Gently rubs a finger across the induration to evaluate its size, then measures in millimeters.
☐	15	Reads the test results; retests if site produces questionable results; documents the test results in the patient's medical record.
☐	5	Completed the tasks within 5 minutes.
☐	15	Results obtained were accurate.
________		Earned ADD POINTS OF TASKS CHECKED
	50	Points TOTAL POINTS POSSIBLE
________		SCORE DETERMINE SCORE (divide points earned by total points possible, multiply results by 100)

Actual Student Time Needed to Complete Procedure: ____________

Student's Initials: ____________ Instructor's Initials: ____________ Grade: ____________

Suggestions for Improvement: ____________

Evaluator's Name (print) ____________

Evaluator's Signature ____________

Comments ____________

DOCUMENTATION

Chart the procedure in the patient's medical record.

Date:__________

Charting: ____________

____

____

Student's Initials:________

SKILLS COMPETENCY ASSESSMENT

Procedure 20–7: Measurement of Blood Glucose Using an Automated Analyzer

Student's Name: ______________________________ Date: ____________

Objective: To measure a patient's blood glucose using an automated analyzer.

Conditions: The student demonstrates the ability to analyze blood glucose at timed intervals following the patient's ingestion of a standard glucose dose to aid in the diagnosis and management of diabetes or in the management of hypoglycemia. The student uses the following equipment and supplies: gloves, goggles, sterile lancet, alcohol swabs or 70 percent alcohol and cotton swabs, glucose analyzer, control solutions for glucose analyzer, test strips for glucose analyzer, laboratory tissue.

Time Requirements and Accuracy Standards: 15 minutes. Points assigned reflect importance of step to meeting objective: Important = (5) Essential = (10) Critical = (15). Automatic failure results if any of the **critical** tasks are omitted or performed incorrectly.

STANDARD PRECAUTIONS:

SKILLS ASSESSMENT CHECKLIST

Task Performed	Possible Points	TASKS
❑	5	Reviews the manufacturer's manual for the specific glucose analyzer being used; turns on the analyzer.
❑	5	Cleans the work area and assembles all materials and supplies.
❑	5	Washes hands.
❑	5	Puts on gloves and goggles.
❑	10	Records the control ranges, control lot number, and test strip lot number.
❑	10	Performs the check test and the control test according to the manufacturer's instructions; proceeds to the glucose test if both tests are within range; repeats both tests if either is out of acceptable range.
		To perform the glucose test
❑	5	Removes a test strip from the bottle and replaces the lid.
❑	15	Performs a capillary puncture.
❑	10	Applies a large drop of blood to the test strip.
❑	5	Blots the test strip with tissue after the time interval recommended by the manufacturer.
❑	5	Inserts the test strip into the test chamber.
❑	15	Reads the glucose concentration after the appropriate time interval has passed.

Task Performed	Possible Points	TASKS
☐	5	Documents the results.
☐	5	Removes gloves and washes hands.
☐	5	Disposes of all waste in a biohazard container.
☐	5	Completed the tasks within 15 minutes.
☐	15	Results obtained were accurate.

______	Earned	ADD POINTS OF TASKS CHECKED
135	Points	TOTAL POINTS POSSIBLE
______	SCORE	DETERMINE SCORE (divide points earned by total points possible, multiply results by 100)

Actual Student Time Needed to Complete Procedure: ____________

Student's Initials: ____________ Instructor's Initials: ____________ Grade: ____________

Suggestions for Improvement: ____________

Evaluator's Name (print) ____________

Evaluator's Signature ____________

Comments ____________

DOCUMENTATION

Chart the procedure in the patient's medical record.

Date: ____________

Charting: ____________

____

____

Student's Initials:______

SKILLS COMPETENCY ASSESSMENT

Procedure 20–8: Cholesterol Testing

Student's Name: ______________________________ Date: ____________

Objective: To test a patient's total cholesterol level.

Conditions: The student demonstrates the ability to determine a patient's total cholesterol level to aid in the diagnosis of coronary artery disease using the following equipment and supplies: gloves, blood-collecting equipment, pipettes with disposable tips, chlorine bleach, commercial kit for manual determination of cholesterol, controls and standards, marking pen, biohazard container.

Time Requirements and Accuracy Standards: 15 minutes. Points assigned reflect importance of step to meeting objective: Important = (5) Essential = (10) Critical = (15). Automatic failure results if any of the **critical** tasks are omitted or performed incorrectly.

STANDARD PRECAUTIONS:     

SKILLS ASSESSMENT CHECKLIST

Task Performed	Possible Points	TASKS
☐	5	Assembles all necessary equipment and materials.
☐	10	Washes hands, applies gloves and goggles.
☐	10	Obtains a blood sample from the patient, either by fingerstick or venipuncture (see Procedures 16–1 through 16–4), depending on the manufacturer's instructions.
☐	15	Follows the manufacturer's instructions to perform the cholesterol test.
☐	10	Properly disposes of all waste in a biohazard container.
☐	5	Documents results.
☐	5	Completed the tasks within 15 minutes.
☐	15	Results obtained were accurate.

________	Earned	ADD POINTS OF TASKS CHECKED
75	Points	TOTAL POINTS POSSIBLE
________	SCORE	DETERMINE SCORE (divide points earned by total points possible, multiply results by 100)

Actual Student Time Needed to Complete Procedure: ____________

Student's Initials: ____________ Instructor's Initials: ____________ Grade: ____________

Suggestions for Improvement: ____

Evaluator's Name (print) ____

Evaluator's Signature ____

Comments ____

DOCUMENTATION

Chart the procedure in the patient's medical record.

Date:______________

Charting: ____

____

____

Student's Initials:____________

EVALUATION OF CHAPTER KNOWLEDGE

How has your instructor evaluated the knowledge you have achieved?

Knowledge	**Instructor Evaluation** *Good*	*Average*	*Poor*
Identifies the three main precautions to be observed during all tests and the collection of samples	____	____	____
Knows how to collect samples and perform and interpret test results	____	____	____
Can discuss factors to be considered when evaluating test results	____	____	____
Can discuss transmission, incubation period, and symptoms of EBV infectious mononucleosis	____	____	____
Knows the blood group antigens and antibodies found in each of the four ABO groups and the Rh factor	____	____	____
Identifies the cause of PKU and the symptoms caused by untreated PKU	____	____	____
Recognizes normal and elevated levels of phenylalanine and the dietary restrictions to be observed by PKU patients	____	____	____
Understands the cause of tuberculosis and some major characteristics of *Mycobacterium tuberculosis*	____	____	____
Recognizes the role of insulin in the regulation of blood glucose levels	____	____	____
Knows the differences between the normal values for fasting blood glucose, two-hour postprandial glucose, and the glucose tolerance test	____	____	____
Can explain the importance of cholesterol and triglyceride testing to identify patients at high risk for coronary heart disease	____	____	____
Knows the average values of cholesterol for adults, children, infants, and newborns	____	____	____
Knows the acceptable level of LDL in persons with or without coronary heart disease and the role of HDL and LDL in coronary heart disease	____	____	____
Identifies the normal values of urea nitrogen for adults, children, infants, and newborns and the significance of elevated blood urea levels	____	____	____
Recognizes the importance of quality control programs, including instrument maintenance, reagent shelf life, and test controls	____	____	____
Documents results accurately	____	____	____
Is respectful of the patient's emotional needs	____	____	____

Student's Initials: ______ Instructor's Initials: ______

Grade: ______

Study Guide Software Instructions

MINIMUM SYSTEM REQUIREMENTS

486 or better
8 Mb RAM
Windows 3.1 or Windows 95
Graphics adapter sVGA, 640 × 480, 256 colors, small fonts mode

INSTALLING THE CMA PROGRAM

Before you use the *Comprehensive Medical Assisting Software* (CMA), you must install it on your hard disk. The installer decompresses and copies files from the *Comprehensive Medical Assisting* floppy disks onto your hard disk and creates a Comprehensive Medical Assisting program group. Before installing the program, make a back-up copy of the *Comprehensive Medical Assisting* disks. Then install the program using your back-up copies:

1. Insert the *Comprehensive Medical Assisting* Program Disk 1 into your floppy drive.
2. At the Windows Program Manager, choose **Run** from the File menu.
   Note: Although CMA is designed to run on Windows 3.1, it also runs on Windows 95. If you are installing CMA on a Windows 95 system, open the Start menu and choose **Run** to begin the installation.
3. In the Command Line blank, type **a:\install** (where "a:" represents your floppy drive). Click on **OK.**
4. In the Select Installation Drive dialog box, select the hard disk where you want to install the software and click **OK.**
5. On the command line in the Installation Directory dialog box, type the name of the directory where you want to install the software. The default location is **C:\CMA**. After you type a location, click on **OK.** If you specify a new directory (that is, one that does not yet exist), the installer creates the new directory.
6. The installer now copies files onto your hard disk. When all files from Program Disk 1 are copied, the installer prompts you to switch disks. Insert the next program disk into your floppy drive and click on **OK.**

7. A dialog box asks you to select the location for saving your data. Choose one of the following options and click on **OK:**
   - **Save data in CMA directory:** Choose this option if you are going to store your work in the directory where you are installing CMA.
   - **Save data on A:\:** Choose this option if you are going to store your work on a floppy disk.
   - **Save data to other location:** Choose this option if you are going to store you work in a different location. If you choose Other, the next dialog box asks you to specify a location for your data: type the full path to where you want to store your work, then click on **OK.**

   Note: The installer adds the full path to your data location at the end of the Command Line for the CMA program icon. For example, if you specify the **A:** drive for data storage and you view the properties of the CMA program icon, you will see **C:\CMA\CMA.EXE -C A:** in the Command Line (where **C:** is your hard disk and **\CMA** the directory where you installed CMA). The only time you would need to change the Command Line is if you decide, after installing CMA, that you want to store files in a different location.
8. An information dialog box tells you that installation is complete. Click on **OK.** You are now back at the Program Manager, with your new Delmar's CMA program group open on your desktop.

Note: If CMA is installed on a network drive, the system administrator will need to create a program icon at each workstation on the network that will be using the CMA software. Follow the instructions in your Windows User's Manual for creating an icon.

NETWORK INSTALLATION AND OPERATION

Installing *Comprehensive Medical Assisting Software* (CMA) on a network is the same as installing the program on a local hard disk. Follow the procedures outlined in "Installing the CMA Program" specifying a network drive instead of a stand-alone hard drive. To log on and run CMA on a network, the student follows the same procedures outlined in "Starting the Program" and "Working on CMA Exercises."

STARTING THE PROGRAM

1. Start Windows and open the *Delmar's CMA* program group.
2. Double-click on the *Delmar's CMA* icon.
3. The title screen displays. The log-on procedure varies according to whether or not you have logged on previously.

Initial Log-On:

If this is your first time using CMA, you need to register yourself as follows:

a In the Students dialog box, click on **New Student.**

b. In the New Student dialog box, type your first name, last name, class name (optional), and a password (up to 8 characters, with no spaces). Use the mouse or the **Tab** key to move from one field to the next.

c. When your information is complete and correct, click on **OK** or press **Enter.** In the Verify Password dialog box, retype your password and click on **OK** or press **Enter.**

d. The Main Menu displays.
   - Choose a unit by clicking on the unit's name in the list to the left. When you select a unit, its chapters appear in a list to the right.
   - Choose a chapter by clicking on the chapter's name. When you select a chapter, its exercises appear as buttons at the bottom of the screen.
   - Choose an exercise by clicking on its button.

Subsequent Log On

When you return to CMA after your initial log-on:

a. Double-click on your name in the Students dialog box or highlight your name and click on **Select.**

b. Enter your password in the Password dialog box and click on **OK** or press **Enter.**

c. If you have forgotten your password, click on the **Exit** button to close the program and use another variation of your name with a new password *that you won't forget* or inform your instructor so he or she can contact Delmar Customer Support.

If you were working on an exercise that you did not complete when you exited the program previously, a Bookmark dialog box tells you where you left off and allows you to go to the beginning of that exercise, to the particular question you last worked with, or to the Main Menu. If you were not in the middle of an exercise when you exited the program previously, CMA takes you to the Main Menu.

WORKING ON CMA EXERCISES

1. Start CMA and log on.
2. Select an exercise to work on.
   - If you were in the middle of an exercise the last time you logged off CMA, a Bookmark dialog box gives you several options. Click on **Continue where you left off** to resume working where you left off, **Return to beginning of the exercise** to go back to the beginning of the exercise you were working on, or **Cancel** to go to the Main Menu (where you can select a different exercise).
   - If you were not in the middle of an exercise the last time you logged off CMA, the program takes you to the Main Menu. Select a unit and chapter, then select an exercise.
3. Answer the questions for the exercise. Use the buttons at the top and bottom of the screen to move around within the program:
   - To return to the Main Menu (to work on a different exercise), click on the **Menu** button at the top of the screen.
   - To get directions for completing the exercise, click on the **Help** button at the top of the screen.
   - To go to the previous or next screen in a multiple choice or short answer exercise, click on the left arrow or right arrow button in the bottom right corner of the screen. In other exercise types, all of the questions will appear on one screen. If you are reviewing a previously

completed exercise, you can click on the buttons displaying the correct answers to review the feedback information.

Note: You will only be able to go to the next screen in an exercise by clicking on the right arrow button if you are reviewing a previously completed exercise. If you are working on a Matching, Graphical Matching, or Graphical Short Answer exercise, the right arrow button will not display since all of the questions appear on a single screen. In these cases you can review previously answered questions by clicking on the question button.

- To exit the program at any time, click on the **Exit** button at the top of the screen.

4. After you have gone through all questions in the exercise, the program scores your work and returns you to the Main Menu. To view a Report of your work on any CMA exercise, use the Report option on the File menu.

REPORT OPTIONS

1. To view a Summary Report of your work in CMA, select the Report option in the File menu.
2. The Summary Report lists, for each exercise worked on, the work date, chapter number, exercise, score, and whether or not the exercise was completed. The Summary Report stores up to 500 records and can be printed by clicking on the **Print** button.
3. You can view a Detailed Report for any line item in the Summary Report by highlighting a Summary Report entry and clicking the **Details** button. The Detailed Report lists the chapter number, exercise, work date, each question number, and your performance on each question. Each question is scored on a three-level scale. You get full credit for the question if you answer it correctly on the first attempt. You get half credit for the question if you answer it on the second try. If you answer it incorrectly on the second attempt, you do not receive any points for the question.

ON-LINE HELP

Context-sensitive Help is available by clicking on the Help button on any screen or window. Clicking on the Help button in an activity screen displays directions on how to complete the activity. The *General Help* option of the Help menu lists all of the topics for which Help is available. You can also select items from this list to view detailed Help text on a particular topic.